Work Psychology

Work Psychology

An Introduction to Human Behaviour in the Workplace

Edited by

Lisa Matthewman

Amanda Rose

Angela Hetherington

OXFORD

UNIVERSITY PRESS

OXFORD
UNIVERSITY PRESS

Great Clarendon Street, Oxford OX2 6DP

Oxford University Press is a department of the University of Oxford.
It furthers the University's objective of excellence in research, scholarship,
and education by publishing worldwide in

Oxford New York

Auckland Cape Town Dar es Salaam Hong Kong Karachi
Kuala Lumpur Madrid Melbourne Mexico City Nairobi
New Delhi Shanghai Taipei Toronto
With offices in
Argentina Austria Brazil Chile Czech Republic France Greece
Guatemala Hungary Italy Japan Poland Portugal Singapore
South Korea Switzerland Thailand Turkey Ukraine Vietnam

Oxford is a registered trade mark of Oxford University Press
in the UK and in certain other countries

Published in the United States
by Oxford University Press Inc., New York

British Library Cataloguing in Publication Data
Data available

Library of Congress Cataloging-in-Publication Data

Work Psychology : An Introduction to Human Behaviour in the Workplace/
edited by Lisa Matthewman, Amanda Rose, Angela Hetherington.
      p. cm.
Includes index.
ISBN 978-0-19-922751-8
1. Work environment--Psychological aspects. 2. Personnel management.
I. Matthewman, Lisa. II. Rose, Amanda. III. Hetherington, Angela.
HF5548.8.W65 2009
158.7--dc22

                                              2008046387

Typeset by Macmillan Publishing Solutions
Printed in Italy by
L. E. G. O S. p. A

ISBN 978-0-19-922751-8

1 3 5 7 9 10 8 6 4 2

Editor acknowledgements

The editors and authors would like to thank Angela Adams, Helen Adams, and Gina Policelli of the editorial team at Oxford University Press for their advice, guidance, and direction throughout the production of this text.

In addition, Lisa Matthewman would like to say a special thank you to Gary Corby for support and encouragement and other family and friends for their ideas regarding the case studies.

Amanda Rose would like to thank Harriet Lambert for her tremendous support, insights, and energy, and to Becky and Nick, for everything.

Angela Hetherington would like to thank Imogen Maddock for her assistance in the research and editing of the text and Tamarind Hetherington for her professional opinion on the text.

Oxford University Press acknowledgements

In listing those whom OUP would like to thank, we include the many reviewers who made a direct contribution to the way this book was put together. We express our gratitude to all who helped us, but especially:

Neil Anderson, Amsterdam Business School
David Biggs, University of Gloucestershire
Lee Crofts, University of Wolverhampton
John Duggan, University of Sunderland
Dr George Erdos, University of Newcastle
Doris Fay, Aston University
Peter Foss, Birmingham City University
Christeen George, University of Hertfordshire
Julie Gore, University of Surrey
Dave Griffiths, London Metropolitan University
Astrid Homan, Leiden University
Matthew Jellis, University of Worcester
Stefan Jern, Lund University
Melrona Kirrane, Dublin City University
Abigail Marks, Heriot-Watt University
David McHugh, University of Central Lancashire
Kathryn Mearns, University of Aberdeen
Dr Sarah Nadin, University of Sheffield
Janneke Oostrom, Erasmus University
Frank Preen, Birmingham City University
Peter Robertson, Napier University
Lawrence Smith, University of Leeds
Eva Trokelson, Lund University
Dr Pamela Yeow, University of Kent
Nigel Marlow, London Metropolitan University

Brief contents

Detailed contents

Part I Perspectives

Part II People at work

Part V Management issues

Part VI New directions

List of tables

List of figures

List of activities

List of work psychology in practice

List of case illustrations

A guide to the book

Over the past fifty years, psychologists have systematically applied their skills and knowledge to understanding and enhancing the experience of work. Through both research and its application, work psychologists have contributed significantly to improving performance, productivity, employee satisfaction, and well-being in the workplace. They have become central to assessing, evaluating, and monitoring current working practices and work environments.

However, work psychology is no longer confined to occupational psychologists. Many related professionals for example, in Human Resource Management, Occupational Health, and Business Studies benefit from access to increased intelligence on and the application of work psychology. This knowledge base is authenticated by undergraduate and postgraduate study in work psychology.

This book is designed to provide those students, professionals, and paraprofessionals with a concise and focused survey of psychological theory and research relevant to the effective management of organizations.

Who the book has been written by and why

The editors of the book have extensive experience in academia, research, and consultancy in a broad variety of fields. Their expertise is evidenced in their publications, media presentations, contributions to professional bodies, and board and committee activities at national and international levels. They have contributed to the strategic development of organizations, actively informing and influencing current working practice.

The contributors to the book have varied and diverse backgrounds, combining a background in academia with experience as teachers, consultants, researchers, clinicians, and practitioners. Their combined experience in academia of module development and delivery at undergraduate and postgraduate level has provided the foundation for this text. This is reflected in the valuable teaching and learning aids and resources intended to meet the needs of a diverse and time-pressured readership.

Why use this book?

This book is aimed at undergraduate students studying work psychology as part of a Business and Management or Psychology degree. It also offers an essential knowledge base for postgraduate students in Business and Management, especially those specializing in HRM and on a variety of clinical courses. In addition, it provides a sound reference text for HR and management professionals, covering core issues of central importance to effective management.

The text provides a comprehensive coverage of the core topics that are central to the workplace. Each topic is presented with a balance of theory, case studies, and exercises aimed to develop the reader's ability to critically evaluate the wealth of research and practice available on work psychology and its application.

The book presents the topics essential to effective Business and Management practice including: recruitment and selection; training and development; leadership, health, and safety; organizational change; the experience of working; psychological well-being at work; interpersonal relationships; unemployment and occupational counselling.

The case studies, drawn from the authors' industrial experiences in a wide spectrum of work environments, serve to demonstrate the impact on the organization of the absence of informed management practice and the often reparative effects of the application of work psychology. Detailed case studies, highlighting key concepts and issues from the chapter, are provided at the start and the end of the chapter. Readers are encouraged to draw on their own experiences to create similar illustrations of poor and effective workplace practices.

The book has been designed to encourage active participation in the survey of work psychology through the use of review questions, activities, and assignments, requiring readers to critically evaluate the core concepts of work psychology from their own perspective and that of stakeholders.

To extend learning and to develop skills, the book has an online resource centre which includes a number of additional features to aid study. See: **http://www.oxfordtextbooks.co.uk/orc/matthewman**

What is 'work psychology'?

It is said that 'Psychology is about people. . . . it is about why people do the things they do.' (Davey 2004: 1). Work psychology applies psychological knowledge to the workplace. It focuses on ways people respond to working in the vast and ever changing organizational environments that operate today: from being self-employed to working part time in a small team, to negotiating careers within vast multinational organizations or to managing the complex edifices that deliver our public services.

Work psychology is of considerable value to the organization in contributing to the performance and productivity of the workplace. This is often achieved through applications such as reducing sickness and absence in the workplace, developing employee appraisal programmes, providing occupational counselling and coaching, delivering training and development, and improving selection methods.

An advantage to the employee of the application of work psychology is the extent to which working experience is enhanced by improved management practices that enhance job satisfaction, reduce sickness, provide psychological support, and improve the working culture.

Professionals applying work psychology to enhance individual and organizational functioning would be interested in a range of workplace practices such as:

- Job analysis, person-job fit, psychometrics, assessment, and selection methods.
- Qualifications, experience, and motivations of prospective employees to predict patterns of behaviour, competencies, and individual differences.
- Deficits in employee backgrounds to assess training and development needs and the cost implications to the organization.
- Assessment of strengths and weaknesses in the personality of the employee to predict level of job satisfaction, stress resilience, team functioning, leadership strength, and to inform the management of the employee.
- Monitoring the employee through the probation period by appraisals and performance targets and benchmarks.
- Assessment of the employee for promotion and contingency planning to ensure maximum deployment of skills and resources.
- Appropriate management of incidental workplace events involving the employee such as the development of intimate relationships, occupational accidents, trauma, redundancy.
- Impact of sickness, absence, staff turnover, organizational environment, change, and restructuring on performance and productivity.

Work psychology has developed theories and methods to understand how people might respond to all these circumstances, and the myriad others that are thrown up in our current complex and turbulent work environments. It investigates the individual, the group, and the organization.

Psychology is a wide and varied discipline, characterized by a range of perspectives, theoretical positions, and approaches to research. There is no current orthodoxy within mainstream psychology, nor within work psychology, about what methods are best, nor which theoretical perspectives are paramount. This book acknowledges the debates and diversity of the discipline of psychology and presents impressions from a range of perspectives.

Why is it important to study work psychology?

Psychology, with a history of research, theory development, and application that spans over 150 years, is uniquely placed to throw light both on human behaviour in the workplace and the working environment, providing an understanding of individual, group, and organizational functioning.

In the current rapidly changing world economies, the experience of work is changing dramatically. Students of work, employment, and business will find the perspective of work psychology enlightening in understanding this process. Work psychologists are uniquely placed to comment upon, research, assess, and monitor the impact of current working practices, and to develop work environments that are sensitive to the vast array of human capabilities, skills, preferences, and needs. Perhaps most importantly they are well placed to increase the efficiency and effectiveness of the business organization.

Studying work psychology can also have the added advantage of improving the reader's own personal performance, achievements, and rewards at work as an employee, manager, or employer.

Structure of the book

The chapters in this book have been organized into six parts.

Part I: Perspectives (Chapter 1 and 2)

This part focuses on the theoretical and historical underpinnings of work psychology, and the methods of investigation and analysis the discipline has developed.

Chapter 1 sets out the chronology for the historical development that has made work psychology what it is, introducing key themes and issues which have helped to shape the focus of research and practice. The chapter lays out the differing theoretical perspectives and core concepts of the discipline. It explores the professional status of occupational psychologists, and the relation between Human Resource Management and work psychology.

Chapter 2 looks at research methods in work psychology, exploring a range of methods typically employed by work psychologists to plan, collect, and analyse information.

Part II: People at work

This section looks at the individual at work, examining core psychological processes and how these affect relationships and behaviour in the workplace.

Chapter 3 examines personality and individual differences, and suggests how these may fashion approaches to and styles of working.

Chapter 4 focuses on perception and attitudes, and suggests how these may affect relationships at work.

Chapter 5 looks at motivation, both from the view of the individual at work, and of management understanding and policy in this area.

Part III: The group at work

These three chapters explore the behaviour of small groups and teams, in the work context.

Chapter 6 explores relationships at work, identifying issues of conflict and attraction between individuals and the impact these may have in the workplace.

Chapter 7 looks at group dynamics and teamworking, and explores how the process of group decision-making can impact on organizational effectiveness.

Chapter 8 looks at leadership and critically examines the various ideas put forward to understand who and why people become leaders, and what 'effective' leadership is.

Part IV: The organization at work

This section is concerned with examining the ways individuals may be affected by, and respond to, the organizations in which they work.

Chapter 9 looks at careers and career management; searching for key principles in the myriad different experiences of people interleaving the jobs they do with the rest of their lives.

Chapter 10 explores human performance and the work environment, including an examination of human/machine/systems interfaces, and health and safety at work, identifying for example, how accidents arise and how they might be avoided.

Chapter 11 examines how people respond to change in the workplace, and the different strategies they may follow to manage change in ways that best suit their needs.

Part V: Management issues

This section considers the application of work psychology to the operation of core organizational and management processes and systems.

Chapter 12 looks at recruitment and selection, exploring the pitfalls and good practice in the application of a range of methods for selecting candidates, including psychometric testing, handwriting analysis, and team games. This chapter also takes a detailed look at current practice in graduate recruitment.

Chapter 13 explores at learning, training and development, and examines how psychological theories of how people learn can be applied to enhance training at work.

Chapter 14 looks at psychological health in the workplace, exploring sources of stress and trauma at work, and discusses interventions to promote health in the workplace.

Chapter 15 examines the impact of unemployment, and explores how we respond to this. The chapter also considers how this may throw light on the role work plays in our lives.

Part VI: New directions

Chapter 16 traces trends and predictions about how work may change in the near future as technological innovations are rolled out, and new experiments with working patterns are developed. How will people respond to these changes? What kinds of issues and effects will become paramount? What outcomes might work psychologists predict would affect people at work in the organizations of the future?

How to use this book

There are many key features included in the chapters of *Work Psychology* that are designed to help you both to learn and organize information. Many of these features emphasize how theory is applied in real organizations and others help you to gain a deeper understanding of how this links to practice in order to ground your theoretical understanding of psychology in the workplace.

Chapter objectives

As a result of reading this chapter and using the additional we

- Identify the key aims of research in work psychology.
- Recognize the relationship between theory and research pr
- Appreciate how research in work psychology is designed, p
- Identify a range of methods available for collecting informa strengths and weaknesses.
- Identify key differences between qualitative and quantitati
- Appreciate debates about the appropriateness of different

Chapter objectives

Each chapter opens with a bulleted outline of the main concepts and ideas. These serve as helpful signposts to what you can expect to learn from each chapter.

 KEY LEARNING POINTS

- The assessment and selection process involves a num effective candidates.
- Successful and fair selection requires a detailed knowl is achieved by job analysis.
- The Competency Approach is commonly used to spe incumbents.
- A variety of assessment methods are employed either process.
- The reliability and validity of measures should be estab

Key learning points

Each main section of every chapter ends with a bulleted list to summarize the main points. These are intended to jog your memory about what has been covered and help you recap when revising.

Informal theories of persona

We all use informal or '**impli** ions about the people we me embedded into us and them **constructs** and incorporate see Chapter 4: Perceptions a

Informal theories affect th form some sort of stereotypi behave; for example: an urba behave differently in some r Furthermore, many of us for

Pause for thought
Consider the influence of the culture you grew up in on your personality.

Pause for thought

These are short reflective questions that give you the opportunity to stop and think about what you have learnt and relate the topic to your own experience.

Stereotypes

Stereotyping is one of several examples of distortion in are beliefs about the characteristics, attributes, and beha (Hilton and Von Hippel 1996). The term 'stereotype' was saw stereotypes as 'pictures in the head', simple mental i People use stereotypes in general as **heuristics** or short arrive at quick inferences and judgements, and to save e almost always developed for out-groups. We rarely label beliefs. The explicit and implicit teachings of social age prevalence of stereotyping in the media ensure that ster

Key terms

Key terms, concepts, and theorists are highlighted in red where they first appear. They are also defined in the glossary at the end of the book.

Case illustration
Intelligence tests

The first intelligence tests were developed by Alfred Binet (1912–1...
being established in France, Binet was hired by the French governn...
dren who needed special educational support. For this, it was imp...
cal child could be expected to achieve at different ages. Binet expe...
measures, including phrenology (measuring the skull and explorin...
Through trial and error he developed a set of standardized measure...
children at different ages. He developed the concept of **mental ag...**
tual performance at a specified age, which might not correspond...

Case illustration

The book is packed with examples that link the topics to real-life organizations to help you gain an understanding of psychology in the workplace.

Activity

These are short questions and examples that give you the opportunity to relate the topic to your own experience.

Activity Performance appraisal

Have you or anyone you know ever had a performance appra...
outcome? Did you/they feel it was fair? Did you feel that it he...
it feel only like an assessment?

9.5 Gender and careers

The past few decades has seen an ever increasing nun...

Chapter summary

- The importance of studying perception in the workplaces w...
  be influenced by a various factors it explains why people m...
- Person perception is an important aspect of perception an...
  Perceptual distortions affect our perception of others.
- The Attribution theory explains the ways in which we judge...
  attribute to their behaviour. The chapter examined various...
  theory and addressed how the theory can explain aspects o...
- Various perceptual short cuts were examined in particula...

Chapter summary

Each chapter ends with a list of key points that summarize the most important arguments developed within that chapter.

Review questions and assignments

Review questions have been included at the end of every chapter to check you have grasped the key concepts and provide you with an opportunity for discussion. Assignments are designed to test what you have learnt in the chapter and extend your understanding.

Assess your learning

Review questions

1 What are the main elements of the scientific method?
2 What is a field study? What are the strengths and weaknesses o...
3 What are 'demand characteristics' in psychological research? Ho...
  the impact of this effect?
4 What is participant observation, and what are the main positive...
  technique?
5 Describe one qualitative research method. State how data gene...

Hothersall, D. (2004) *History of Psychology* (4th edn.). New Y...
A history of the development of different focuses in psychology fr...

Jones, D., and Elcock, J. (2001) *History and Theories of Psych...*
Arnold.
A critical evaluation of aspects and approaches in psychology and...
retical positions within psychology.

Shimmin, S., and Wallis, D. (1994) *50 Years of Occupational P...*
The history of the development of occupational psychology in Brit...

Schultz, D. P., and Schultz, S. E. (2004) *A History of Modern P...*
Wadsworth. Thompson Learning.
The historical development of different schools of psychological...

Further reading

An annotated list of recommended reading on each subject will help guide you further into the literature on a particular subject area.

Work psychology in practice

These are more detailed case studies, with questions, at the beginning and end of each chapter. The opening case study provides an introduction to the topic area and the closing case study gives you an opportunity to apply what you have learnt and analyse a real-life example.

Work psychology in practice
Perception—the eye of the be...

Mr Jones sat in a waiting room before his interview. He browsed th...
potential employers and was aware that he must project a professi...
sure that the receptionist saw his best side and to create a positive i...
and David, the two managers, took another glance at Mr Jones's CV...
summary and immediately considered him to be a strong candidat...
sales management, consultative selling, and major account manage...
attributes. David also considered the CV and noted that it provided...
work experience and accomplishments. He noted that Mr Jones wa...

How to use the online resource centre

FOR STUDENTS

Study skills

This section covers the core skills applicable to work psychology and is invaluable for revising or recapping. All you will encounter throughout your course is covered, from what to expect from lectures and seminars to how to tackle research projects, and prepare for exams. Key topics also include personal development planning and reflective learning. A final section details what to expect after completing your degree and guidance is given on searching for jobs.

Flashcards

Learning the jargon associated with the range of topics in *Work Psychology* can be a challenge, so these flashcards have been designed to help you memorize the key terms used in the book. Click through the randomized definitions and see if you can identify which key terms they are describing. You can even download them to your iPod for revision on the go!

Web links

A series of annotated web links to key research and organizations provide a useful guide to helpful material and a stepping stone for further study!

 www.oxfordtextbooks.co.uk/orc/matthewman/

FOR LECTURERS

PowerPoint lecture slides

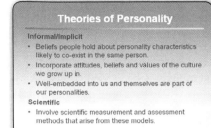

A suite of PowerPoint slides has been designed by the authors for use in your lecture presentations which highlight the main points from each chapter. These can easily be customized to match your own lecture style.

Video library

A bank of links, organized by theme, to online work psychology video clips, providing you with stimulating illustrative examples.

Lecturer's guide

Finding stimulating ways of reinforcing students' understanding of psychology in the workplace can be difficult. A helpful chapter-by-chapter lecturer's guide has been provided by the authors to assist instructors in their teaching of work psychology modules. This includes the rationale for each chapter, how it links to other chapters within the book, suggestions for seminar activities, and exam questions.

Figures and tables from the text

All figures and tables from the text have been provided to download for inclusion in your lecture presentations or handouts.

Test bank

For each chapter a set of questions has been devised by the authors. The test bank is customisable, and fully automated for quick and convenient use online: automated grading allows you to access your students' progress via your university's Virtual Learning Environment, and instant feedback shows your students what they need to work on for revision purposes.

About the editors

Dr Lisa Matthewman is a Principal Lecturer in Occupational and Organizational Psychology at the Westminster Business School, University of Westminster. She is a Chartered Occupational Psychologist and Associate Fellow of the British Psychological Society. Lisa has been involved with the teaching of work psychology for over eight years and is currently responsible for teaching and facilitating group work in all aspects of personal and professional development to both undergraduates and postgraduates. Lisa's current remit involves the design and development of a Postgraduate Certificate in Coaching and Mentoring. Lisa is an experienced psychologist and runs her own consultancy called Life Management Consulting. Lisa has worked extensively with individuals and groups in a variety of psychological consultancy and coaching roles. She is currently Chair of the Division of Occupational Psychology Training Committee.

Amanda Rose studied social psychology at the London School of Economics, and at the University of British Columbia in Canada. Amanda is a Principal Lecturer in occupational and organizational psychology at the University of Westminster, where she has developed and taught a number of modules in work psychology at both undergraduate and postgraduate level. Amanda's research interests are in the areas of women and work and the ethical aspects of business practice. She has worked as a consultant in the public sector in the field of equal opportunities and assessment at work.

Dr Angela Hetherington is a Chartered Psychologist, a BPS registered 'Psychologist, Specialising in Psychotherapy', and a BPS accredited Psychometric Test User. Angela has extensive experience in industry in both the private and public sector. She has served as a full Board Director, Clinical Director, and Operations Director of an international Employee Assistance Provider, delivering 24/7, global, psychological, counselling, coaching, and consultancy services to private and public sector organizations, their staff, and families. She has worked in senior management in public- and private-sector healthcare. Angela lectures in organizational behaviour at the University of Westminster. Her research areas include occupational stress, work-related traumatic stress, organizational dynamics, occupational counselling, and coaching. She has publications, radio and television interviews on the subject of occupational trauma, clinical governance, and occupational health and welfare. She is Trustee of two clinical charities and has served on the Board of two private healthcare organizations and numerous Department of Health committees on medical education.

About the contributors

Kamala Balu is a lecturer is Occupational and Organizational Psychology at the University of Westminster. Kamala teaches on a range of undergraduate modules and leads modules on Work Psychology, Assessment at Work and People and Organizations and coordinates the eMentoring scheme at Harrow Business School. She has led several consultancy and research projects focusing on areas such as Assessment Centres, Management Development, Learning teams, Voluntary employment and motivation and Training and Development. Kamala's past research interests have included the assessment of competence through the use of simulation exercises.

Peter Foss currently works as a visiting lecturer at the University of Birmingham and associate tutor with Oxford Brookes University. He also carries out consultancy and training in the area of developing people. His areas of specialization are in personal, management, and organizational development, change management, leadership, HRM, social psychology, and psychometrics. Peter utilizes action learning, group facilitation, and input-based approaches to learning and development. His research interests are in the areas of intimacy, rumour and gossip, and group development. His work experience has been in the UK, USA, Europe, and China and is he very interested in cross-cultural awareness.

Xanthy Kallis is an Occupational Psychologist and a Visiting Lecturer in the Business School at the University of Westminster. She lectures in areas of Occupational Psychology and Organizational Behaviour. She has over fifteen years' experience working with groups. As a practising consultant Xanthy is involved in designing and implementing bespoke workshops, coaching, and career management. Xanthy is a member of the Division of Occupational Psychology of the BPS and Chair of the Training Practitioners Support Group. She is also on the Training and Development subcommittee of the DOP and is Marketing Director for the Psychometrics User Forum, a voluntary support networking group.

Natasha Marinković Grba is an occupational and organizational psychologist with a background in clinical occupational counselling, treating eating disorders via group therapeutic interventions, and specialist experience in promoting innovation and creativity in the workplace through facilitating tailor-made training and teambuilding exercises. Natasha has balanced her practical consultancy with academic research and lecturing in Psychology, Organizational Behaviour, and HR.

Jenni Nowlan is an Occupational Psychologist and a full-time Senior Lecturer in the Business School at the University of Westminster. As well as teaching in the areas of Postgraduate Coaching and Mentoring, Undergraduate Occupational Psychology and Organisational Behaviour, Jenni also leads a large team on a core mega-module for all first-year undergraduate business students. In addition to her teaching she also works as an independent Business Consultant. Jenni belongs to the British Psychological Society and is a fellow of the Higher Education Academy. Her PhD research is in the area of Occupational Health Psychology looking at the effectiveness of Rational Emotive Behaviour Therapy as a Stress Management Intervention technique.

Nuala OSullivan is an organizational and occupational psychologist specializing in change management, team building, leadership, and communication skills; for groups and on a one-to-one coaching basis. Nuala's work as a corporate counsellor, workshop leader, and change management consultant builds on a background as a cognitive-behavioural counsellor with extensive experience in the field of managing behavioural change. Her work on personal influencing strategies has been effective across organization and cultural boundaries. Consultancy forms a working basis for lecturing in HR and Psychology at both UG and PG levels. Nuala is currently researching her PhD in Communication and Knowledge Management.

Karen Powell-Williams is a Senior Principal Lecturer at Westminster Business School, an Associate Fellow of the British Psychological Society, and a Fellow of the Chartered Institute of Personnel and Development. She first studied social psychology under Cary Cooper, and later Industrial Psychology under David Guest. Her research on students seeking placement or guidance was supervised by Professor Sylvia Shimmin, the first Chair of the Division of Occupational Psychology. In 1998 she set up the National Centre for Work Experience and is currently responsible for developing employability in the Business School students. In 2007–8 she chaired the London branch of the British Psychological Society.

Lauren Thomas has held academic appointments as Deputy Head of the Psychology Department at the University of Chester and Head of the Passenger Safety Group at Cranfield University. She has extensive commercial research and consultancy experience in occupational psychology and ergonomics across a range of safety critical industries, including the aviation, rail, and energy sectors. She is currently working in human factors in air traffic control on projects ranging from selection and training, through to incident investigation and safety culture.

Angela Wright is a Senior Lecturer in Human Resource Management at Westminster University Business School. She has research interests in several aspects of pay and reward including employee benefits, as well as in diversity and equal opportunities. She teaches HRM, reward management, resourcing and diversity; and supervises Masters' dissertations in these fields. During her career in the pay/remuneration field, she worked for the public-sector pay review bodies, as their Remuneration Specialist/Adviser; and she led the pay research team at Industrial Relations Services, following a research role at Incomes Data Services. She is the author of a CIPD (2004) text *Reward Management in Context*.

Studying work psychology

This section briefly introduces the main areas associated with studying and applying work psychology. You may already be familiar with some of these areas; however, the purpose of this section is for you to revise or recap. For those people returning to academic study after a gap of some years, you may find all of these sections helpful before starting your course.

The sections introduce the core skills applicable to work psychology in a question and answer format; additional and more in-depth information on each of these sections can be found on the textbook's supporting online resource centre:

http://www.oxfordtextbooks.co.uk/orc/matthewman/

What skills will I develop whilst studying work psychology?

You will have the opportunity to develop and demonstrate many key skills as you study work psychology. Communication is integral to interpersonal skills, but, because it is such an important set of skills, it is often identified separately. Communication skills, both oral and written, and the ability to listen, are necessary to enable you to communicate concepts efficiently and effectively to colleagues and customers.

Generally, work psychology modules focus on four areas of learning including: development of knowledge and understanding, intellectual skill development, practical skill development, and transferable skill development. The philosophy of learning during the module is based upon group working, utilization of learning resources, self-evaluation, information management, independent study, communication, and problem solving.

Core skills are those developed throughout the course of study in work psychology. Transferable skills are a term used to refer to certain skills that are deemed desirable for all graduates to develop by the time they leave college or university.

All college and university institutes will have developed guides or a model of how such skills should be developed on their courses.

Many of the core skills developed throughout a work psychology module will become transferable skills that you will use beyond the module and in future careers. So, although a distinction can be made, they form part of the same group of skills utilized on a work psychology module as well as being transferable beyond the degree into prospective careers.

 For more information on the core and transferable skills you will develop whilst studying work psychology, go to the online resource centre at

http://www.oxfordtextbooks.co.uk/orc/matthewman/

How do I learn more from lectures?

During a lecture you will be presented with a wide range of material and you are responsible for taking concise notes that you can later elaborate on. Lectures are designed to be a valuable starting point for research, providing an overview of the subject, its central concepts and theories, and evidence of recent research. Combined with seminars, lectures will direct your own reading and research. In addition, a number of transferable skills can be gained from lectures including listening skills, identifying and selecting relevant points, written communication, and information management.

Lectures are seen as a very important part of the work psychology course because it is here that you will be presented with a concise and coherent overview of the topics on the course. Information presented in lectures often contains the central concepts of the course and the relevant theory and research most likely to be included in exams.

Remember the main aim of lectures is to provide you with a skeleton of the topic under consideration from which to work. This means that you must spend some time outside the lecture researching your subject. As you progress through your degree you will be encouraged to look at sources beyond those you are provided with during lectures. If you do this as an ongoing task you will find that it makes revision much more manageable, rather than leaving it all until nearer the deadline for the assessment or examination.

 For more information on learning more in lectures including preparing for your lecture and effective note taking go to the online resource centre at

http://www.oxfordtextbooks.co.uk/orc/matthewman/

How can I be more effective in seminars?

Seminars are more interactive than lectures and give you an opportunity for group discussion and learning from your peers. Seminars usually involve group discussion of material presented either in the lecture or in set reading. There are different types of seminars for example, seminars which follow up discussions to the lecture are usually linked to a piece of writing or a case study, giving you the opportunity to check your understanding, develop, and test your own ideas and consider examples of applications of theories.

Seminars:

- Offer opportunities to think about and discuss theories and issues in more detail than lectures allow.

- Encourage you to provide your own informed opinions about the topic under discussion and gain points of view, which you might not have considered.

- Help to clarify your own thinking through providing an environment in which you can ask questions and discuss parts of the course/subject you find difficult.

- Enable you to develop skills in giving and receiving constructive criticism.

Whatever the educational purpose for which seminars are being used, they have one common feature: to be effective they require active participation by students. This means you must prepare to contribute to seminar discussion.

 For more information on being more effective in seminars, how to prepare, how to participate in discussions and present an argument, go to the online resource centre at

http://www.oxfordtextbooks.co.uk/orc/matthewman/

How can I develop my empirical report writing skills?

Reports are used in organizations to demonstrate current progress and to benchmark the beginning or end of a stage or the project as a whole. They are also used as information documents to circulate within and between departments as well to provide information for clients. Reports are concise and factual allowing the reader to access the information found rapidly.

Reports are structured with headings, subheadings, and numbers to assist navigation of the document. Unlike essays, reports often include bullet points and graphics to illustrate findings as clearly as possible. Their clarity, directness, and accessibility make them a valuable tool.

Report writing will develop your ability to scrutinize information and present it succinctly.

 For more information on developing your empirical report writing skills including structuring your reports, undertaking research, and presenting your findings, go to the online resource centre at

http://www.oxfordtextbooks.co.uk/orc/matthewman/

How can I approach and complete case studies?

Case studies can range from simple paragraphs with one or two key areas to complex studies encompassing numerous issues and areas. They can be based on real situations (or created to illustrate salient learning points).

Cases are used in organizations to illustrate learning and to model successful solutions for others who may encounter similar problems. Counsellors and consultants use case-based reasoning exercises to refine their professional skills and to encourage creative solutions.

At universities cases are used in seminars, exams, and assignments materials to encourage you to transfer learnt theory to practice. You will find that you view research and theoretical concepts in a different way when you recognize the practical applications. This will help with both research and learning as the pragmatic approach is more memorable than a two-dimensional page of notes on a topic.

Case studies have also been shown to develop problem-solving, analytical, decision-making, and prioritizing skills.

 For more information on how to approach and work with case studies including making assumptions, brainstorming and analysing your data, go to the online resource centre at

http://www.oxfordtextbooks.co.uk/orc/matthewman/

How can I prepare for examinations?

Examinations are a means of objectively assessing knowledge or skills by a process of completing set questions in timed papers. You will know at the start of your module whether you will be expected to sit an exam, and this date will be set well in advance.

Protect time for studying and take this commitment seriously. Have a study timetable, outlining what you hope to achieve in each study slot. Use your lecture and seminar notes and other additional material to revise your topics.

On the day:

- Ensure that you wake up in good time and have a breakfast as the brain runs on glucose and fainting is not a useful exam technique!

- Arrive in good time, late arrivals get no extra time and may not be admitted to the exam.

- Rooms are often allocated on the day so give yourself time to find unfamiliar rooms.

Exam questions are generally essay questions; it is therefore important to present your answer in a way that the marker can clearly see logical structure and progression in your response.

During your exam, read the question twice. Draw a quick spider diagram with the topic in the centre and the 3–5 points you plan to make around it. Add models and references to each point (name, date). Try to find a work psychology illustration for the point you are making.

Work out the most logical sequence for your points, and make sure that you link them. Ensure that you plan your time efficiently for all of the questions you are expected to complete, and give yourself equal amounts of time for each question.

 For more information on how to prepare and revise for exams, and what to expect on the day, go to the online resource centre at

http://www.oxfordtextbooks.co.uk/orc/matthewman/

What can I do after studying work psychology?

After completing studies in work psychology, the next step is to decide what to do afterwards. Some students go on to do further training in psychology or a related area. Some students decide to specialize in occupational psychology while others utilize their work psychology skills in a related area such as personnel work or a managerial role.

The types of skills developed by students of work psychology are all attractive to prospective employers. Once they have completed their studies in psychology or undertaken a conversion course, many students go on to obtain graduate status with the British Psychological Society. **The British Psychological Society** is the representative body for psychology and psychologists in the UK.

Chartered Occupational Psychologists are concerned with the performance of people at work and in training, with developing an understanding of how organizations function and how individuals and groups behave at work. Their aim is to increase effectiveness, efficiency, and satisfaction at work.

The services of occupational psychologists are in increasing demand. Organizations are deeply concerned about the need to recruit, retain, and realize the potential of their human resources on which success depends. Occupational psychologists are the best-qualified group to advise on human resource strategies and solutions.

 For more information on your options once you have completed your course, including web links to professional organizations and career guidance, go to the online resource centre at

http://www.oxfordtextbooks.co.uk/orc/matthewman/

Part I
Perspectives

Chapter 1
Introduction and overview of work psychology

Karen Powell-Williams

Chapter objectives

As a result of reading this chapter and using the additional web-based material you should be able to:

- Define work psychology.
- Discuss the role of work psychology in business and management.
- Review the scope of work psychology and the eight areas for chartered status.
- Debate the pure scientist and applied practitioner approaches.
- Identify different theoretical approaches in psychology.
- Explain the development of work psychology in its historical context.
- Show an understanding of the changing nature of work and organizations.
- Reflect on the relationship between work psychology and human resource management.

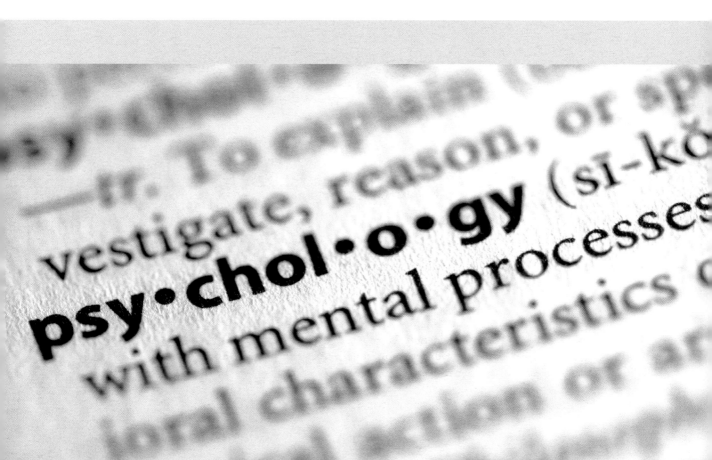

Work psychology in practice
Having it all?

The following case study provides an overview of many aspects of occupational psychology from the individual employee's point of view.

Kate took a deep breath as she put her mobile phone away, took out her planner and settled back into the train seat. She would be home in three-quarters of an hour and she felt that things were under control. Her partner, William, was getting supper ready and their two young children were in bed. On the face of it everything seemed to be well organized and running smoothly. But was it? Kate put the planner away and reflected.

Kate worked for a leading management consultancy, Argylle's, in the West End of London. She had graduated in history and gained an Executive MBA at a London business school, climbing her way up in **fmcg** companies. She had delayed starting a family after she had landed this position at Argylle's a few years ago. Her work in strategy was interesting and highly paid, with the prospects of becoming a partner with greater financial rewards.

Kate worked in a team and knew she had to put in a consistent top performance on each assignment. There were plenty more graduates with similar experience who were waiting to jump into her shoes if she slowed down for a second. She liked the work and the contact with clients and she was beginning to rise up in the consultancy and be given responsibility over younger staff.

But Kate wondered if it was really worth it. On the one hand she had a good income and was able to afford quality care for the children, family breaks abroad together, and a nice house. William was supportive, knowing she really loved the work and was making progress in her career. On the other hand, Kate found it difficult adjusting to the demands of the children when she came home after work.

William was working from home, having left his job at a firm of chartered accountants, to set up on his own and be around more while Kate was out at work. But he was finding it difficult and was thinking of taking another job. He would be earning more money, something which had not yet become an issue between them, but both wondered if it might be later on. Also, if William worked away from home, Kate would have to be more certain about the reliability of the additional childcare she used.

There were other things troubling Kate too. She found the work interesting but it was challenging and she needed to make insightful analyses and bring **bottom line** improvements. This could be hard going if one of the children was unwell and she found travelling away from home on assignments a wrench. Then there was the young male consultant who kept trying to upstage her with quick, witty comments, particularly about her time off work when she had maternity leave. He regularly had a drink with the others after work when she wanted to get home. She felt he was challenging her seniority with his assertive manner.

Kate knew that if she escaped into a career break she would probably never make the same grade again and she didn't feel it would be wise to consult her own manager about the out of London assignments and the younger man in the team.

Questions
- What are the issues facing Kate?
- To what extent do you think Kate's situation is typical of working people today?
- What would you advise Kate to do and why?

1.1 Introduction

For most of us, the world of work is a defining feature of our lives. We not only earn our living from our occupation, we also gain an identity for ourselves both in our own estimation and in other people's eyes; and we may have the opportunity to develop and exercise work-related skills and achieve a range of personal goals.

From the employer's perspective, people are integral to the functioning of an organization. It is people who set the organization's goals and targets, design work to achieve those goals, ensure it is carried out to a standard by managing other people to do this, and develop and use systems and equipment to do it better.

Work psychology brings together these three aspects of people, work, and organizations. It investigates the relationship between employee and employer, between personal goals and organizational goals, between **individual needs** and capabilities and organizational demands and rewards, between the nature and type of work and the type of organization structure required to undertake work and manage it.

This chapter starts by exploring the nature of work psychology, what work psychologists do, and the different terminologies used. It describes the development of psychology as a profession and the basis for chartered status. It explores the scientific basis of psychology, how work psychology relates to psychology as a whole, and how applied areas of psychology have grown from it. It sets out the different approaches or methodologies that have developed in psychology and describes how work psychology has developed in a historical context. It then looks at the relationship between occupational psychology and human resource management. At the end of the chapter some emerging issues are identified for the future of work psychology.

1.2 The nature of work psychology

1.2.1 What do occupational/work psychologists do?

Occupational psychologists are concerned with the performance of people at work and in training, with understanding how organizations function and how individuals and small **groups** behave at work. They aim to improve the job satisfaction of the individual and to increase the effectiveness of the organization. Occupational psychology is much broader in scope than most other areas of psychology, and it touches on a wide range of fields including ergonomics and personnel management. Work is mainly in advisory, teaching, and research roles. The majority of occupational psychologists work as general problem solvers or facilitators across broad areas—such as organizational consultancy; or assessment and training; or ergonomics, health, and safety.

1.2.2 What is work/occupational psychology?

According to Drenth (Drenth et al. 1998) there are three domains within work psychology:

- The behaviour of people at work concerns the feelings, intentions, and activities of people in the workplace, their abilities and aspirations. This includes selection, training, appraisal, management development, career planning, and counselling.
- The work itself concerns the individual's activities, thoughts and feelings and its design, meaning and challenges. This includes **job analysis**, task characteristics, **ergonomics**, fatigue, design of work, and performance measurement.
- The organization is the context in which the work is to be done and concerns its structure, functions, and culture and its internal organization. This includes leadership, decision making, participation, industrial democracy, **conflict**, **power**, quality, organizational design, **culture**, and change.

1.2.3 Where do occupational psychologists work?

Occupational psychologists may work for large companies in the private or public sectors, in government and public services, in management training centres, and in private consultancies either on their own or within a team. They usually work alongside other professionals such as managers, trade union representatives, training officers, and specialist staff from the firm or industry concerned. In the UK the Civil Service is one of the largest single employers of occupational psychologists. The Prison Service, the Home Office, the Employment Department Group (including the Employment Service), the Ministry of Defence, and the Civil Service Commission all employ occupational psychologists. (Division of Occupational Psychology website http://www.bps.org.uk/dop)

1.2.4 Terminology: work psychology or occupational psychology?

Work psychology has been called by different names in the past. Until the 1970s 'industrial psychology' was the term used in both the UK and the USA.

With changes in the economy from the manufacturing to service sector, the term moved to 'organizational psychology' in the USA, and 'occupational psychology' in the UK. Europe, however, preferred the terms 'psychology of work and organizations', or 'work and organizational psychology'. The spectrum of coverage is from occupational psychology, where the focus is on the individual, to organizational psychology, where the focus is on the organization. Work psychology embraces both ends of the spectrum.

1.2.5 Development of the profession of psychology

In most Western countries, national associations of psychologists were established at the turn of the century. The American Psychological Association was founded in 1892, the Société Française de Psychologie in 1901, the British Psychological Society (BPS) in 1901, and the Deutsche Gesellschaft für experimentelle Psychologie in 1904. By 1930 most European countries had a national association. Journals in basic psychology and experimental psychology were founded early on to disseminate the results of their enquiries and by 1930 there were also journals devoted to applied psychology.

Psychology had been studied at university as a branch of philosophy, but after the First World War it developed as a vocational area of training for professional practice. The Industrial Fatigue Board of 1918 was important in this transition in the UK. University Chairs in psychology were established from the 1920s onwards. In addition to experimental psychology, applied psychology became a subject of study at university. The founding of the National Institute of Industrial Psychology (NIIP) in Britain in 1921 by C. S. Myers was important in identifying psychology as a separate profession.

Not only did psychologists use the application of psychological concepts. Other professionals, such as engineers and teachers, applied what they found useful, for example using tests in the selection of workers for jobs. This led to differences of opinion about who was competent to administer such tests. The national associations sought to distinguish trained psychologists from those with no qualifications. They wanted to legally protect their work through registration, restrictions on the use of their title, and closed status for practice. Ethical codes of practice were established with procedures for dealing with misconduct.

The BPS is the professional body which regulates the training of psychologists and their registration and licence to practise in the UK. It has recommended statutory, rather than voluntary, regulation and restrictions on the use of the title 'psychologist', to protect the public.

1.2.6 The division of occupational psychology

The Division of Occupational Psychology (DOP) is the second biggest division in the BPS after Clinical Psychology. It was set up in 1971 with Professor Sylvia Shimmin as its first Chair. Table 1.1 shows some milestones in the parallel professionalization of psychology, occupational psychology, and human resource management in the UK.

The DOP states on its website that its purpose is to 'promote, develop and regulate the work of occupational psychologists in corporate, academic, voluntary, public and private sector settings, to enhance the well-being and work-effectiveness of organisations and individuals within Society'.

1.2.7 Chartered occupational psychologists

Using the title 'chartered' means the public can have confidence that psychologists are fit to practise not only because of their knowledge and skills, but also because they abide by a code of ethics to protect the public.

In order to become a Chartered (Occupational) Psychologist the person must have an approved degree in psychology which leads to the graduate basis for registration (not all psychology degrees have this) plus appropriate postgraduate training and work experience. They must be eligible for membership of the Division of Occupational Psychology of the British

Table 1.1. History of Professionalization

Date	Psychology	Occupational psychology	Human Resource Management
1896			First woman welfare worker at Rowntree's
1901	The Psychological Society founded at UCL (renamed 1906 British Psychological Society (BPS))		
1913			First conference of 60 welfare workers; founded Association of Welfare Workers with 34 members
1916			Welfare workers (female) compulsory in Ministry-controlled establishments. Labour officers (male) appointed for recruitment and industrial relations duties
1918	Myers widens membership of BPS		Industrial Welfare Society formed (1966 called Industrial Society)
1920	BPS membership at 600		*Welfare Work* journal published
1921		National Institute of Industrial Psychology (NIIP) founded	
1924			Association of Welfare Workers became Institute of Industrial Welfare Workers 370 members
1930	Register of professional psychologists	NIIP has 30 staff and 1,600 members	
1931			Institute of Industrial Welfare Workers became the Institute of Labour Management (ILM)
			Estimated 1,800 practitioners; 800 ILM members
1941	BPS incorporated		
1945			Estimated 6,000 practitioners; 2,881 ILM members
1946			The Institute of Labour Management became the Institute of Personnel Management (IPM)
1948	*Quarterly Bulletin* of the BPS launched		Post-war expansion of industrial relations work, industrial training work, and payment systems
1950	Membership of BPS 1,897		
1951		First Diploma in Occupational Psychology at Birkbeck College	1950s membership examinations introduced and publications started
1955			Education scheme introduced via external colleges
1960	Membership of BPS 2,655		
1961		First Department of Occupational Psychology at Birkbeck College	
1965	BPS gets Royal Charter	Journal of Occupational Psychology taken over by BPS from NIIP	
		First textbooks with titles Organizational Psychology (Bass, Schein)	

Date	Psychology	Occupational psychology	Human Resource Management
1966		1960s and 70s The Aston (university) Group undertake applied psychology research into organizations	IPM forms committees to influence government: Committee on Industrial Relations and Education and Training Committee
1968		MRC Unit at Sheffield University set up to undertake applied research. Now the Institute of Work Psychology	
	By now 36 university departments of psychology in UK		
1971		Division of Occupational Psychology founded	Committee on Organization and Manpower and National Committee on Pay and Employment Conditions
1977		NIIP closes due to loss of funding	
1982	Membership of BPS over 10,000		
1987	Register of chartered members of BPS		
1994			IPM (55,000 members) merges with Institute of Training and Development becomes Institute of Personnel and Development
1995			Membership of IPD at 75,000. The largest body of personnel and development specialists in the world.
2000			IPD becomes the Chartered IPD with 105,000 members
2005	Membership of BPS 35,800. 12,800 Chartered Psychologists	Membership of Division of Occupational Psychology 3,259	Membership of CIPD 125,000

Psychological Society demonstrating practical experience, as well as knowledge in several of the eight areas of competence for occupational psychology as defined by the BPS.

The eight areas of competence for occupational psychology are set out in Figure 1.3 and subsequent chapters of the book explore the knowledge in these areas in detail. Each can form the basis of a career specialism: Selection and Assessment, Performance Appraisal and Career Development, Counselling and **Personal Development**, Training, Employee Relations and Motivation, Organization Development and Change, Human-Machine Interaction, Design of the Environment and of Work/Job.

Work psychologists are expected to know about all these areas and be able to diagnose problems, carry out research, provide advice, consultancy, assessment, and training. There is more information on becoming a chartered occupational psychologist at http://www.bps.org.uk/membership/grades/how-to-become-chartered.

KEY LEARNING POINTS

- Occupational psychologists aim to increase the effectiveness of the organization, and improve the job satisfaction of the individual.
- Professional bodies have been set up to define, distinguish, and protect the work of their members and to protect the public that they serve.
- Statutory regulation of psychologists is being introduced.

• In order to become chartered, eight areas of specialization must be studied and appropriate work experience and practitioner competence shown.

1.3 The science of psychology and work psychology

1.3.1 The scientific approach of psychology

The science of psychology sprang predominantly from philosophy and biology, using the methods of physics. **Empiricism, positivism**, and **critical realism** are philosophical influences on its development. Empiricists believe that only objectively observable data should be measured. Positivists believe **scientific method** should be used to study human behaviour. Critical realists, on the other hand, query the extent to which the social sciences can use the methods of the natural/physical sciences. They draw a distinction between reality and our knowledge of reality. This has been influential in the development of cognitive psychology.

Table 1.2 charts when philosophers started writing on their enquiries about the mind. The word 'psychology' first occurred around 1750 with Hartley's 'Observations'. Psychology was very close to philosophy as a discipline.

Biology also has been influential in the emergence of psychology with Darwin's theory of evolution, linking human behaviour to animal behaviour. Genetic discoveries, and medicine, particularly physiology, continue to shape our understanding of behaviour with knowledge about the structure and functioning of the brain, nervous system, and chemistry of the body. Gradually, however, psychology emerged as a separate subject with the work of **Wundt's** Founding Laboratory in Germany in 1879, which undertook physiological experiments to understand behaviour better.

Table 1.2. Chart of the Historical Development of Psychology

Date	History and industry	Philosophy and psychology
1637		Descartes publishes *Discours de la methode*
1690		Locke publishes *On Human Understanding*
1701		
1709	Abraham Darby: coke to smelt iron ore. Start of the Industrial Revolution	
1739		Hume publishes *Treatise on Human Nature*
c.1750		Hartley's Observations. First English work using the term 'psychology'
1782	James Watt's steam engine	
1813		Robert Owen publishes *New View of Society*
1814	George Stephenson's steam locomotive	
1816	Robert Owen opens school at New Lanark Mills	
1819	Peel and Owen Factory Act for children in cotton mills	
1820s		Gall publishes *On the Functions of the Brain*
1830		A. Comte starts publishing *Philosphie positive*
1833	Factories Act sets up the Factories Inspectorate	
1833–4	Abolition of slavery in UK and territories	
1834	Tolpuddle Martyrs deported to Australia for trying to form a union	
1860	Darwin's *Origin of the Species* published	Fechner's *Elements of Psychophysics*
1863	Abolition of slavery USA	
1867	Marx publishes *Das Kapital*	
1868	First Trades Union Congress	

Date	History and industry	Philosophy and psychology
1870s		*Mind*, the first psychology journal in England, published Wundt's Founding Laboratory
1871	Trade Union Act gives full legal recognition	
1876	Bell's telephone	
1879	Edison's light bulb	
1882		American Psychological Association founded
1885	11 unionists elected to House of Commons demanding better pay, hours, and shift system F. W. Taylor starts experimenting with work study. Benz builds the first car.	
		James's *Principles of Psychology*
1900		Freud publishes *Interpretation of Dreams*
1901	Factory and Workshop Act	The Psychological Society founded (renamed British Psychological Society 1906)
1903	Ford Motor Company founded. First aeroplane flight by Wright	
1910		Watson publishes *Psychology as the Behaviourist sees it*
1913		Munsterberg publishes "Psychology of Industrial Efficiency"
1914	Start of First World War	
1915	Einstein publishes *General Theory of Relativity*	
1917–18	Report of the Whitley Committee laid foundations for Joint Industrial Councils Russian Revolution	
1918	End of First World War First votes for women	Industrial Health Research Board established
		Ministry of Reconstruction issued pamphlet on the importance of human element in production
1921		
1929	Great Depression	The Hawthorne Experiments 1927–32
1930		
1936	Turing publishes theory of electronic computing machines	
		American Association for Applied Psychology founded
1939	Start of Second World War	
1945	End of Second World War	
1962		T. Kuhn publishes *The Structure of Scientific Revolutions*
1963	Martin Luther King: beginning of civil rights campaign, USA	
1964	Industrial Training Act	
1965	First Race Relations Act UK	
1967	Abortion Act UK	
1969	Moon landing	
1971	Equal Pay Act UK	
		American Psychological Society founded for academic psychologists
1994		
2000		
2001	World Trade Centre destroyed	

Psychology, then, is a discipline which uses the principles of scientific method to try to understand behavioural aspects of the world. This method has been viewed as the most successful way to produce reliable and valid results (or results which can be repeated and therefore have some lasting value). Consequently, it has been popular and persuasive as an approach. Some of the earliest psychologists came from the natural sciences, like Fechner, who was a physicist. Indeed, so powerful is scientific method as an acceptable tool that the social sciences have tried to analyse the study of behaviour using experiments and measure the results with numbers, as in the physical sciences. This has led to the development of the applied field of study, statistics, which was developed by psychologists utilizing mathematical probability theories.

1.3.2 The relationship of work psychology to psychology as a whole

Pause for thought
Why do you think psychologists are keen to present their subject as a scientific one? Do you think psychology is a science?

Psychology as a discipline covers a large field of interest in individual behaviour. Clinical psychology, which studies problematic and **dysfunctional behaviour**, applies findings of physiological psychology by focusing on the brain, nervous system, and physiology. Similarly, educational psychology applies findings of developmental psychology to the educational development of the individual, particularly children.

Work psychology applies the findings and concepts of physiological psychology (e.g. in examining stress at work), cognitive psychology (e.g. in examining motivation and perception) and social psychology (e.g. in understanding group dynamics) to the study of people in a work context.

1.3.3 Pure scientific and applied practitioner psychologist

In the early days, psychologists aimed to develop a body of knowledge that would explain the mind. They were not concerned with individual differences or applying their findings to solve problems. However, many of Wundt's students such as Hall and Cattell (1890) returned home to apply their knowledge of individual differences to the USA. **Munsterberg**, who was also German, eventually went to the USA where he contributed greatly to the development of applied psychology.

Applied psychologists believe in putting their findings to practical use. Right from the early days of the development of psychology as a discipline, there was a difference of opinion between those who saw psychology as a pure science detached from practical application and those who wanted to apply the principles to practical matters and find solutions to problems (Allport 1940).

Pause for thought
Do you think this debate between pure and applied science in psychology has any relevance today? Why?

These tensions have continued and the history of the professionalization of psychology in the USA shows how psychologists have been divided into two groups each with their own professional association. The first body, the American Psychological Association eventually gave rise to the American Association for Applied Psychology for applied practitioners as well as the American Psychological Society for pure scientific academics.

In the UK, the university departments of psychology that developed in the new universities set up during the 1960s looked more favourably on applied psychology as a legitimate area of study and were instrumental in developing applied psychology in the UK. This also favoured the emergence of occupational psychology as a separate division in British psychology.

Psychologists today may be academic researchers who see themselves as scientists, or practitioners who focus on problem solving for a client (Dunnette 1990).

1.3.4 Theoretical approaches to studying psychology

There are many different ways in which to approach the study of individual behaviour and these have developed over time as psychology has developed as a discipline. Table 1.3 shows the historical timeline of these schools of thought and their major exponents.

Structuralism was the first approach and came from the work of Wundt. He thought that analysis of the conscious mind through introspection could break down the structure of the mind into its component parts, like chemists had done with elements.

Functionalism, advocated by **James**, was influenced by Darwin's theory of evolution and how people adapt their behaviour to the environment. He believed there was a survival function to the mind and that the object of psychology should be the purpose of thoughts and behaviour.

Table 1.3. Schools of thought

	Major exponents	Schools of management thought	Major exponents	Personnel/HR practitioner focus
Structuralism 1875 – 1920s	Wundt, Stumpf, Titchener, Ebbinghaus	Classical School 1900s – 1930s	Henri Fayol, Henry Gantt, Frank and Lillian Gilbreth, F. W. Taylor, Max Weber	1800s – 1920s Social reform Welfare workers Scientific techniques
Psychoanalysis 1900 onwards	Freud, Jung, Adler, Horney	Human Relations School 1930s – 1950s	Elton Mayo, Mary Parker Follett, Rensis Likert, A. Maslow, D. McClelland, D. McGregor	1920s – 1950s Human Relations
Functionalism 1900 – 1950s	James, Dewey, Munsterberg, Hall, Cattell, Woodworth	Socio-technical Systems 1950 – 1960s	Trist and Bamforth (1951), Talcott Parsons, Joan Woodward	1950s – 1960s Birkbeck approach (FMJ/FJM)
Behaviourism 1910 onwards	Thorndike, Pavlov, Watson, Hull, Bekhterev, Tolman, Skinner, Bandura	Contingency Theory 1960s – 1970s	Burns and Stalker (1961), Victor Vroom, Fred Fiedler, Lawrence and Lorsch (1967), Henry Mintzberg	1960s and 1970s Negotiation/ industrial relations
Gestalt psychology 1910 – 1960s	Wertheimer, Koffka, Kohler, Lewin	Total Quality Management 1980s	Deming, Taguchi	1970s and 1980s Organizational integration Manpower analysis
Humanistic psychology 1950s – 1990s	Maslow, Roger	Strategic approaches 1990s	Johnson and Scholes (1989)	1990s Quality performance Diversity Quality of working life Management of unemployment Consultancy Organization Development
Cognitive psychology 1960s onwards	Miller, Neisser	Action research methodologies for reflective learning? Theories of entrepreneurship? 2000s?		2000s Professionalization Strategic HR Portfolio careers Intrapreneurship
Positive psychology 1990s onwards	Seligman			

Psychoanalysis grew into a theoretical approach out of the therapy techniques developed by **Freud**. Freud, who was a medical doctor, argued the unconscious mind was the proper subject of psychological investigation and developed a theory of motivation and personality based on this. Psychoanalysis has been very influential in psychology and has exponents within work psychology in organizational analysis and team and leader behaviour.

Behaviourism, or learning theory, with its basis of experiments in behaviour, has also been very influential on psychology. **Watson** believed that psychology should focus only on observable behaviour and not be concerned with subjective interpretations of the mind. This approach was eventually superseded by the emergence of cognitive and humanistic psychology which viewed the mind as a proper, interesting, and important subject for psychology.

Cognitive psychology focuses on investigation of the mind, the process of knowing, and how the brain works. Based on the information processing work of **Miller**, it used computer models to study the process of knowing and how the mind organizes experiences. **Neisser** built on this, focusing on sensation, perception, memory, and problem solving.

Humanistic psychologists like **Maslow** and **Rogers**, attempted to provide an alternative to the psychoanalytic and functionalist approaches and emphasized the study of conscious experience and the wholeness of human nature. This theoretical approach has been used in the study of motivation at work and in counselling. Gestalt psychologists like **Wertheimer** and **Kohler** focused on the learning and perception derived from combining sensory experiences.

These different approaches led psychologists to focus on different areas of investigation and interpretation. Two approaches to psychology which have made a substantial impact in occupational areas are physiological and social psychology. Physiological findings have emphasized the biological origins and effects on behaviour and have been used in studies of fatigue and stress. Social psychology has emphasized the group context for behaviour and studies of leadership, management selection, and group productivity.

1.4 Two different approaches to investigation in modern psychology: positivism and postmodernism

Positivism and Postmodernism are two contrasting approaches to investigation in psychology. **Positivism** is based on the idea that there is an objective truth or reality that can be identified, and is reflected in the findings of research. This approach stems from the work of **Comte** (1896) in the early nineteenth century. He felt the natural sciences had reached a positivist stage recognizing only those facts or events that are observable, whereas the social sciences were still engaged in metaphysical questions and explanations. At this stage only knowledge derived from observable objective facts was considered to be scientific. Positivists believe there is a universal truth if only we can find it.

Postmodernism is based on the idea that reality is bounded by the perspective of the researcher. It is sometimes also called deconstructionism, a word originating from the philosophical writings of Jacques **Derrida**, or social constructionism. Postmodernism is an approach followed by practitioners in a number of different disciplines as well as psychology. It purports that there is no absolute truth; we cannot be truly objective and there is at least an element of relativeness in everything we do, perceive, and believe. Postmodernists believe behaviour can only be understood in the context in which it occurs and that people view the world from their own particular perspective which colours what they see and their interpretation of it. Postmodern psychologists include Gergen (1985, 1991) whose writing has made psychologists confront a series of problems about the nature of human consciousness, personal integrity, and language.

Writers like James (1888), **Kuhn** (1996) and C. P. Snow (1964) have commented on this continuum of 'tough', scientific, quantitative science at one end and the 'tender', humanistic and qualitative at the other end. Psychologists can be found all the way along this continuum. Postmodernists can be found amongst qualitative researchers who construct theoretical ideas as a result of data they gather through observation or questionnaires and then test it. Positivists would more likely look at large-scale numerical data and look for universal truths based on their analysis.

Figure 1.1. Positive psychology

> **Positive psychology** has had a significant influence on developments in work psychology, particularly as a result of the work of Seligman. After the Second World War much psychological investigation on the individual's well-being at work focused on mental ill health. In the area of occupational psychology, this can be seen in the work of Maslow and Herzberg and to some extent McGregor and McClelland. Herzberg's use of the term 'hygiene' factors is indicative of this orientation and his view of the way people 'ought' to be in order to be healthy. Positive psychology focuses on well-being, happiness, personal development, creativity and wisdom. 'Positive psychology is a scientific study of optimal functioning [that] aims to discover and promote the factors that allow individuals and communities to thrive' (Seligman 1999). It emphasizes the well-being of people rather than the dysfunctional aspects of behaviour.

Positivism should not be confused with Positive Psychology, a more recent approach to studying behaviour. This emerged as a reaction to the emphasis on negative human attributes which was the focus of the humanistic psychologists and earlier psychoanalysts.

 Activity Investigations of motivation at work

Taking the perspective of a positivist psychologist, plan and conduct an investigation of motivation at work. You might choose your lecturers as your subjects. Think about the concepts and methods you would use and whether your findings are likely to be quantitative or qualitative.

Now take the perspective of the postmodern psychologist and undertake another investigation of motivation at work. What sorts of concepts and methods would you use this time and what sorts of findings will you have?

Compare and contrast the two perspectives and sets of results and comment.

Pause for thought
How can psychologists remain independent, objective, and impartial when, for example, advising management about the employment of people? In whose interests do they work: the individual's or the organizations?

Some writers such as Hollway (1991) have shown how the perspective of the psychologist in analysing the employment of people at work is substantially affected by their context, by the questions which management want answered and by contemporary norms and issues of the time. These problems affect all scientists, pure and applied, in their methodological approach, their choice of area of research and the variables they identify.

 KEY LEARNING POINTS

- Psychology is the scientific study of individual behaviour.
- Applied psychology developed as psychologists sought solutions to specific problems.
- Positivism is a belief that only those phenomena that can be objectively observed should be the subject of scientific enquiry.
- Postmodernism believes cultural context is important in explanations and denies that there is a universal abstract truth.
- Definition of work psychology: work psychology is an area of applied psychology concerned with the study of human behaviour and experience in organized work settings (Shimmin and Wallis 1994).

1.5 The world of work and organizations

1.5.1 What is work?

Our subjective understanding of what work means to us is important in our **attitude** towards it. Wikipedia is an online dictionary which is constructed by users and gives some definitions of 'work'. Since these definitions spring from people's understanding of what work is to them, they have relevance in defining what work means to us personally, although Wikipedia would not be considered as a reliable nor academic source.

WORK:
When used in a sentence as an action, work means doing something that requires labor.

A worker is any person that does work, often in exchange for money or helpful services (these workers that receive money or helpful services are said to be holding a job).

So work is what we do when we have a job or employment; it is a trade or profession or other means of livelihood. It is something people do, make, or perform, especially as an occupation, a duty, or task. It frequently involves the notion of physical effort or mental labour. It is also an abstract concept which is bound up with time since work is often used in the context of the period of time given over to employment (e.g. 'I'll meet you after I have finished work'), and with place (e.g. 'I must take this book into work'). Furthermore, work may contain the notion of output or creation.

1.5.2 Historical meaning in the concept of work

Work is often talked about in terms of being a burden; something rather unpleasant and wearisome, which nevertheless has to be done. Argyle (1989) traced the origins of the concept of work through history. He showed how the concept has multiple layers of significance which can be traced historically.

These concepts include the sense of work as an undesirable necessity held by the Ancient Greeks; a means to an end, not in itself satisfying. Over time, Argyle says, it has picked up meanings such as having a moral purpose in keeping us out of trouble and of absolving us from sin.

By the Middle Ages work was a means of structuring society and integrating individuals within it. In the sixteenth century Calvin's Protestant Ethic added a moral dimension as wealth, earned and invested, confirmed one's predestination to heaven. Writers from disciplines outside psychology, such as **Weber** and **Marx**, have furthered our understanding of the position of work in people's lives. Weber (1905) thought that the Protestant Ethic was a cause of the rise of Capitalism in the West. Work thereby, had an added dimension of potential wealth.

Marx (1867) argued that work provided workers with a personal and social identity. Marx thought work in a capitalist society **alienated** people from their true nature and was merely an economic activity. Hence employees would have to find their real existence outside work.

Other writers like F. W. Taylor (1911), McGregor (1960), and sociologists Goldthorpe and Lockwood (1968), have looked at the role of instrumentality in work, where work is seen only as a means to an economic end and where behaviour at work can largely be determined by financial rewards. Writers on motivation such as Herzberg in his **Two Factor Theory of Motivation** (Herzberg et al. 1959), however, have placed greater emphasis on the non-economic rewards of work showing a more positive evaluation of the role of work for people compared to the other more negative approaches.

These multiple layers of meaning and feelings about work, both positive and negative, add to the complexity of individuals' attitudes towards it.

Psychologists have not generally looked at the wider context in which individual behaviour is forged. Factors such as class, status, economic circumstances, and gender are also relevant to the individual's experience of work and need to be understood. For example, Jahoda's (1979) study shows how unemployment may be experienced differently in different sectors of society, and lead to wide social consequences.

Today we can see attitudes emerging in the generation entering the workforce that indicate changes in the way that work is valued by the individual. For example, young people may be less keen to allow long working hours to dominate their lives, less concerned about saving and debt, and more dependent on their families for housing for a longer period of time. These attitudes may partly be the result of the economic climate which has seen great rises in house prices, the availability of credit and rising standards of living, and also a result of the legal environment which has given people greater awareness of human rights.

> **Pause for thought**
> How important is money to you as a reward at work? How important are other factors? To what extent do employers cater for these?

 Activity Survey the concept of work

Using the dimensions of work described in the section on the changing nature of work and organizations, construct questions to identify what the concept of work means to people. Ask these questions of people just about to start full-time work (for example full-time undergraduates) and of people who have been at work for twenty or so years. Then compare and contrast the answers from the two groups. What can you conclude from this and what relevance does it have to the management of people at work today?

1.5.3 What is an organization?

Those organizations that are studied in work psychology are employing organizations, industrial, commercial, or in the not-for-profit sector. Schein (1965) produced a useful definition of organizations:

> An organization is the rational coordination of the activities of a number of people for the achievement of some common explicit purpose or goal, through the division of labour and function, and through a hierarchy of authority and responsibility.

Simply, we can take an organization to mean the structured environment in which work is coordinated to achieve organizational goals.

1.5.4 The changing world of work and of organizations

The world of work has been changing rapidly. The sorts of jobs people do have changed in the past hundred years. For example, there were many women employed in domestic service before the First World War. More recently, new jobs have emerged, for example in the computer and telecommunications industry. The way jobs are done, where they are done, and the nature of the organization in which they are carried out, has also changed.

Figure 1.2 shows some of these changes. Occupational psychologists are interested in the effects these changes have on career patterns, people's preparation and selection for jobs, their expectations about and difficulties experienced at work, and how work and organizations should be designed and management trained.

One significant change is the increased participation in the workforce of women with school-age children. This may be due to the introduction of employment legislation over the past thirty years protecting women's rights at work alongside expectations of higher standards of living.

Issues such as retraining for new jobs, **Continuing Professional Development** (CPD), **portfolio careers**, the development of working day patterns to suit employees, including the introduction of **flexitime**, and different approaches to management such as **total quality management**, have all changed the way people work. Organizations have been forced to **re-engineer** and become smaller in the face of economic pressure. The growth of small businesses and the number of people employed in them suggests an important trend in **entrepreneurship**. Demands for greater consultation in decisions affecting work, partly as a result of increased rights at work from employment legislation, have led to studies on work-life balance, well-being at work, and **locus of control**. Consequently much management literature and training focuses on leadership skills. Psychologists like Bass (1990) have focused on the transformational effects of leadership.

1.5.5 The development of occupational psychology applications and management techniques

In the early 1900s, psychologists, along with engineers, were developing knowledge based on experiments and applying it for specific needs. F. W. Taylor (1911) and the Gilbreths (1911) in the USA were trying to improve efficiency in manual workers by looking at the organization of work. Taylor's studies formed the basis of **'Scientific' management**. He investigated production at the Bethlem Steel Works in the USA and focused on rationalizing the movements of manual workers to increase speed and reduce fatigue along with improved organization and more rest breaks, and appropriate selection, training, diet, and financial reward. At about the same time, the Gilbreths, who were a husband and wife team of engineer and psychologist, developed what we now call **time and motion study**.

Table 1.3 sets out the main Schools of Management Thought based on applied psychology studies. Taylor and Gilbreth belong to the **Classical School** of Management.

The First World War (1914–18) accelerated developments in applied psychology, particularly in selecting the right people for jobs in the armed forces and in improving productivity in the factories. The war also led to the employment of women in new areas such as armaments.

Pause for thought
Are there other aspects of working in organizations that aren't mentioned by Schein? What else do you think is important? What might Kate in the opening case study have to add?

Figure 1.2. UK National statistics on the labour market

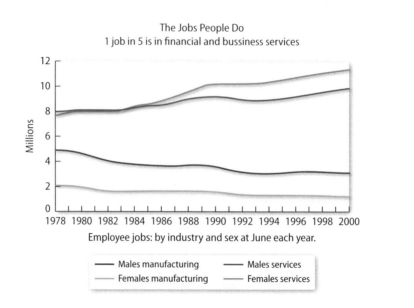

The Jobs People Do
1 job in 5 is in financial and bussiness services

Employee jobs: by industry and sex at June each year.

— Males manufacturing   — Males services
— Females manufacturing   — Females services

Financial and business services now account for about one in five jobs in the UK, compared with about one in ten in 1981.

This sector saw the largest increase in jobs between 1981 and 2001, part of the post-war growth in the service industries and the decline in manufacturing.

Twenty years ago one in three jobs held by men was in manufacturing. By 2001 this had fallen to about one in five. The proportion of female workers in this sector dropped from nearly one in five to under one in ten.

Other changes in Britain's labour force over the last two decades include a marked increase in the number of jobs performed by women. In 1981, men filled 3.2 million more jobs than women. Now the numbers are almost equal, with men performing 12.8 million jobs and women 12.7 million, although almost half of these are part time.

But men and women still follow very different career paths. About a quarter of female employees do administrative or secretarial work, while men are most likely to be managers, senior officials, or in skilled trades.

Similar proportions of men and women work in 'associate professional and technical' occupations—computer programmers, technicians and nurses, for example—while one in eight performs low-skilled jobs, such as those in farming, construction, hotels, and restaurants.

Men are more likely than women to be self-employed—73% of the 3 million self-employed people in spring 2001 were male. Around a fifth of all self-employed people worked in construction, with similar proportions in sales and distribution, hotels and restaurants; and in banking, finance, and insurance.

People from certain ethnic groups are more likely to be self-employed than others. Around one-fifth of working Pakistanis and Bangladeshis are self-employed, compared with only one in ten white people and fewer then one in ten black people. Chinese and Indian people are also more likely than white or black people to be self-employed. Sales and distribution, hotel and restaurant work account for two-thirds of the Chinese, over half of the Indians, and two-fifths of the Pakistanis and Bangladeshis who are self-employed.

Source: Office for National Statistics, 31 July 2002.

Information is collected from employers on the number of men and women they have on their payrolls (filled jobs), and published as 'workforce jobs'. This is the source of the information given on jobs by industry.

The information on occupations and self-employment comes from the Labour Force Survey (LFS). This is a survey of individuals which asks about their work and personal circumstances. If people have more than one job (including self-employment) information about their main job is used.

Psychologists studied their efficiency at work (The Health of Munitions Workers Committee, 1915–20), and the effects of hours of work and of the work environment. They discovered that productivity fell with increased hours of work, rather than rising, due to fatigue and other health problems. When the USA entered the war after 1917, Yerkes, the President of the American Psychological Association, led the development of recruitment tests to select recruits for military service based on their test scores. Tests of mental performance, notably intelligence tests, were developed. These were first devised by **Binet** (Binet and Simon 1905) using his concept of the **intelligence quotient** or IQ and developed by others like **Spearman** (1904) and **Thurstone** (1938) who refined the concept and measurement. These tests became important in the development and application of occupational psychology.

Case illustration
Cowardice or shell shock?

The following case study illustrates a time-bound approach to dealing with an occupational illness.

'Shell shock' is a term used to describe the psychological trauma suffered by men serving on the front line during the First World War, particularly in France, Flanders, and at Gallipoli.

The fierceness of the battles along the front line often caused soldiers to 'crack up'. Symptoms included mutism, limping, mental, or physical paralysis or panic attacks. Some broke down under the pressure and refused to obey orders. In some cases men committed suicide.

Shell shock victims were thought to be suffering from the physical effects of shell blasts, or from a form of monoxide poisoning. Doctors thought that a bursting shell creates a vacuum, and when the air rushes into this vacuum it disturbs the cerebro-spinal fluid and this can upset the working of the brain. However, shell shock began to occur in men who had never come under fire, or been within hearing range of exploding shells.

Some blamed shell shock on a hereditary defect and poor recruitment procedures. A British General said 'there can be no doubt that, other things being equal, the frequency of shell shock in any unit is an index of its lack of discipline and loyalty'.

Sometimes soldiers who disobeyed orders were shot on the spot. Others deserted. This was regarded as cowardice and resulted in a court martial. Official figures state that 304 British soldiers were court-martialled and executed. Between 1914 and 1918 some 80,000 men were identified as suffering from shell shock.

Treatment for shell shock was often harsh and included solitary confinement, disciplinary treatment, electric shock treatment, shaming, and emotional deprivation. Psychological theories governing the treatment of shell shock were slow to develop. At Craiglockhart Hospital, the psychiatrist W. H. R. Rivers began to use psychotherapy on shell shock victims and it became one of the few hospitals to practice this in the UK at the time.

Questions
- What term might we use today to describe the condition of 'shell shock'?
- Would better recruitment methods, training, leadership, or equipment have lessened the incidence of shell shock?
- Why do you think the treatment of shell shock was so punitive?
- What can occupational psychologists learn from this?

Activity Changing public opinion

You have been asked in 2006, by the families of these soldiers, to prepare a publicity campaign explaining what shell shock is and why the court martials were wrong. Draw a diagram of the processes involved and write a list of things that need to be done which you think would help to change public opinion.

After the First World War, the concept of the Labour Exchange (modern equivalent is the Job Shop) was exported from Germany and psychological factors such as individual differences in ability, attitudes, and preferences, were gradually introduced when considering school leavers for employment. Testing children in school had been carried out by Spearman (1904) and this was soon followed by vocational guidance.

In the effort to rebuild society after the war, investigations into industrial efficiency in the armaments factory were extended to industrial output from factories. This was famously investigated at the Hawthorne site of the Western Electric Company near Chicago in the USA in the 1920s. Starting with the effect of illumination on productivity, the studies identified what has come to be known as the **'Hawthorne Effect'** (Mayo 1933). The Hawthorne studies led to the realization that social and group factors and the role of the supervisor were important in understanding peoples' attitudes and performance at work. The Human Relations School of thought developed from these studies.

The Human Relations School has been influential on management techniques. As well as Mayo's focus on supervision and group norms, **Likert's scale** for use in questionnaire design, Maslow's (1970) **Hierarchy of needs**, McClelland's (1961) identification of **Need for Achievement**, Power and Affiliation and McGregor's (1960) **Theory X or Y** Managers are still in use today. (See Chapter 5 on Motivation and Work Satisfaction.)

The Second World War (1939–45) provided another impetus for applied psychology. There was demand for more reliable and valid selection tests and more studies of man-machine interaction to help the design of control displays in aircraft and other equipment, to increase accuracy and reduce fatigue. Motivation, leadership, morale, and group cooperation were all areas of psychological study, as well as propaganda and 'psychological warfare'. The War Office Selection Boards set up in 1942 were based on the German model of holistic assessment. In these, applicants completed individual and group tasks which were the precursor of the modern day **Assessment Centre**. (See Chapter 12 Assessing People at Work.)

The need for designing equipment appropriately led to the growth of Human Engineering (USA) or Ergonomics (UK and Europe). This focused on layout of instruments and dials and the understanding of perception and cognition in their use. (See Chapter 11 on Human Performance and the Work Environment.) The importance of group dynamics emerged based on **Lewin's** field theory (1947) which had been used by the US War Department to foster morale.

The Nazi regime in Germany led to many psychologists leaving for the USA, Kurt Lewin amongst them. This fostered the development of applied psychology in the USA.

Before the Second World War, the work of occupational psychologists in selecting people for employment focused on techniques used by clinical psychologists including psychodiagnostic interviews, observation tests, and projective techniques in attempting to understand the whole personality. This was time consuming and expensive. After the Second World War personnel selection in the UK used test batteries based on those used in the War Selection Boards. These focused on factor-analytic models of individual differences and theories of personality such as those developed by Cattell and Eysenck. (See Chapter 3 on Personality and Individual Differences.)

Europe had to be rebuilt again after the Second World War. There was a need for trade, financial aid, and defence, and the USA provided money and expertise in systems and processes. By the 1950s and 60s industrial psychology was expanding considerably with research from both American and European psychologists. Key areas of interest were motivation, leadership, participation, and job design. As people's expectations rose, the quality of life and, later, the **quality of working life**, were studied.

In the 1960s there was focus on the structure and functioning of organizations and on organizational change and management style. This was mainly studied in the newly established university business schools which were teaching management education. The areas encompassed by this branch of applied psychology grew. Before 1961, there was one chapter in the Annual Review of Psychology called 'Industrial psychology' (Dunnette 1990). But from 1961 onwards there were chapters on personnel management, industrial social psychology,

Pause for thought
What impact do you think wartime developments in selection and testing and ergonomics have had on peacetime employment?

Pause for thought
Why do you think that the study of organization change and development became a focus in the 1960s?

consumer psychology, personnel selection, engineering psychology, and, in 1967, organizational psychology appeared.

In the post-war boom, psychologists were interested in learning, skills acquisition, and job analysis (Blum and Naylor 1968). Programmed instruction developed using the theories of Behaviourism. This did not become widely popular, but has been influential in understanding how learning takes place and methods used in training. (See Chapter 13 on Learning, Training, and Development.)

In the 1970s management training expanded, mainly based on principles of small group dynamics from social psychology to bring about change. T-group training or **sensitivity training** emerged from the National Training Laboratories in Maine, USA, in 1947. This was underpinned by psychoanalytic processes and was used in management training. **Organization development** (OD) became a strong theoretical approach to bring about organizational change, based on the principles of group dynamics and sensitivity training. (See Chapter 10 on Organizational Change and Development.)

Another influential approach to organizational analysis and change, based on the psychoanalytic approach, was that of the Tavistock Institute of Human Relations. Trist and Bamforth's (1951) study identified the interaction of social systems and technology impacting on work performance. This came to be known as the Socio-Technical Systems approach and was influential beyond the UK, particularly in the Netherlands and Norway with experiments in industrial democracy (Emery and Thorsrud 1969). From the 1960s, the Glacier Metal Company practised Elliot Jaques's (1951) **time span of responsibility** and **felt fair pay** as a basis for financial reward. Jaques's work developed into the action-research model favoured by the Tavistock Institute. The impact of modern technology means that the socio-technical systems approach is an important consideration for management when dealing with changes in the workplace.

The social, economic, and political trends taking place in the 1960s and early 70s led to questioning of authority, management, and government. The role of psychologists as instruments of management came under question (Baritz 1960). Intelligence testing was criticized for being culturally bound and potentially racially discriminatory. An awareness of civil and human rights in the USA led to demands for more human rights at work in the UK. Equal opportunities legislation from 1965 onwards may also have encouraged demands for more participation in decision making.

In the 1970s there was a worsening of industrial relations in England and membership of trade unions was high. Bargaining and negotiation skills were important areas of psychological contribution. Interest grew in **Japanese styles of management**, as a result of the growth of the Japanese economy. German models of industrial democracy, or co-determinism, also became popular as a way of seeking a solution to poor labour relations and there was a growing sympathy with the needs of individuals at work amongst psychologists. In Scandinavia there were experiments in **humanizing** work, particularly at the Volvo plant in Sweden. By the 1980s there was much legislation protecting employees' rights at work.

The emphasis in work psychology moved to organization structure and its effect on individuals. Psychologists in the UK investigated organizational variables and the interaction with the environment (Pugh and Hickson 1976). **Contingency theory** was developing. Lawrence and Lorsch (1967) found that the effectiveness of organization structure depended on the context in which it operated. Fiedler (1967) proposed the characteristics appropriate for leadership also depended on the context. Consequently, there might be different styles of leadership and organization structure dependent on whether, for example, the environment is dynamic or stable. (See Chapter 8 on Leadership at Work)

Over the past thirty years certain areas have emerged as important themes in occupational and organizational psychology. These include the writings of Peter Herriot on the employment relationship, Peter Warr on attitudes and well-being at work, Cary Cooper on occupational stress, Marilyn Davidson on women in management, and Ivan Robertson on age, participation in employment, and quality of life. More recently, the area of counselling psychology has grown within the field of work psychology. Subsequent chapters of the book will look at these in more detail.

Pause for thought
Areas of expertise within applied psychology have tended to follow the needs of society and management. Why do you think that is? Are there any alternatives?

Case illustration
Private Henry Farr

The following case study relates to the earlier one on shell shock. It shows how interpretation of behaviour can change over time. Psychology contributed substantially towards that change by providing an understanding of the processes which caused shell shock.

In August 2006, the families of Private Henry Farr and a further 305 soldiers who were shot for cowardice and military offences in the First World War were told by the government that the Armed Forces Bill would be amended so the soldiers could be granted a group posthumous pardon. The families of these men had had to endure a stigma for nearly ninety years. The Minister of Defence said 'That makes this a moral issue too, having reviewed it, I believe it is appropriate to seek a statutory pardon.' Pte Henry Farr was 25 years old when he was executed for refusing to fight and had shell shock. His family had fought for fourteen years to clear his name.

Pte Farr, from the 1st Battalion, the West Yorkshire Regiment, had served in France for two years fighting at Neuve-Chappelle where he was repeatedly shelled until he collapsed with 'the shakes' in May 1915. He was treated several times for being 'sick with nerves' and suffering 'shell shock'. His family argued that his refusal to return to the front line was because of the mental stress he had suffered. He was executed on 16 October 1916.

An Army chaplain sent the following message to his widow, Gertie Batstone, after Pte Farr's execution: 'A finer soldier never lived'. He told the family Pte Farr refused a blindfold when he was shot. Because of his supposed cowardice, his military pension was stopped and Ms Batstone was forced out of their house.

Questions

- Why do you think government opinion about this case has changed; and why has it taken so long to change?
- What role is there for occupational psychologists in shaping legislation?

1.5.6 The relationship between occupational psychology and human resource management

Human Resource Management is the domain of practitioners who manage the people within organizations. They recruit and select people, train and develop them, pay them, and ensure that legislation affecting employment is adhered to such as Health and Safety, anti-discrimination, and other aspects of the terms and conditions of work. They also plan the numbers of people required to do the work and manage the relationships between management and employees through appropriate structures and processes. These activities are embraced by the Chartered Institute of Personnel and Development and increasingly membership of this body is required for employment in this function in organizations.

This chapter has shown how Work Psychology has developed as an applied academic discipline using methods of psychological enquiry to solve problems in the working world. It may be viewed as the academic discipline underpinning the practices developed in Human Resource Management.

Figure 1.3 shows how occupational psychology is placed at the hub of the study of people, work, and organizations. It starts from theoretical bases and uses empirical findings to underpin advisory and implementing roles both internally and externally to management.

Human resource management places emphasis on the business (profit and sustainability) aspect of the organization. It focuses on developing practitioner skills in the operation and delivery of a service within the organization. It emphasizes the 'how to . . .' aspects and the legislation surrounding the employment of people at work and is based on the body of knowledge developed by occupational psychologists.

Pause for thought

What do you observe about the areas of study for Occupational Psychology and for Human Resource Management as represented in Figure 1.3?

Figure 1.3. The founding hub of occupational psychology and the human resource management fit

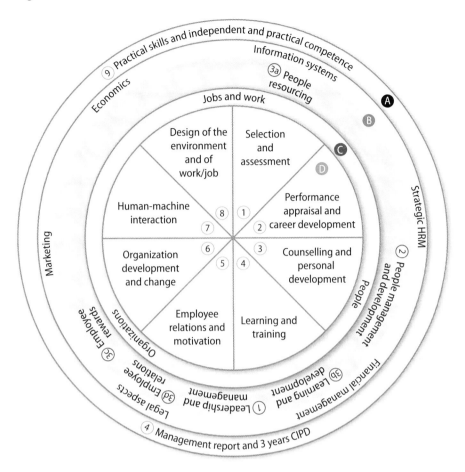

Ring A: The business orientation of HRM.
          Practitioner requirements for chartered status of Occupational Psychology.
          The 4th field of study for membership of CIPD

Ring B: Fields 1–3 of the 4 fields of study in HRM (CIPD)

Ring C: The three underlying dimensions of occupational psychology

Ring D: The 8 areas of occupational psychology underpinning chartered status

 Activity **Researching the profession of psychology**

Using the internet, professional journals and other sources, identify job vacancies available to occupational psychologists in a one-month period. In what areas of occupational psychology are most of these jobs? What is the business reason for this do you think? (Hint: The BPS publishes an Appointments Memorandum which is one source of jobs for occupational psychologists)

 KEY LEARNING POINTS

- Work is a multidimensional concept.

- Organizations are structured work environments with social dimensions.

- The nature of work people do has changed substantially in the last thirty years with the advent of modern technology.

- Scientific Management focused on efficiency to improve productivity.

- The Human Relations School identified that social relationships at work and supervision were more important than management incentives in affecting productivity.
- The socio-technical systems approach identified that technology impacted on social relations at work.
- The Contingency approach identified that the context needs to be taken into account in planning or explaining work behaviour.
- Human Resource Management and Occupational Psychology have overlapping fields of interest.

1.6 Emerging issues in occupational psychology

The pace of change in society means that there are many areas of change affecting people at work and it is likely that new areas of focus will emerge in Occupational Psychology as special areas of investigation (Patterson 2001). Some of these are suggested below:

- Working mothers: roles and stresses and effect on children.
- The younger generations' attitude toward work, employers, and work-life balance.
- Role of entrepreneurs and work psychology.
- The effect of immigration and migration on the workforce.
- E-workforce community.
- The impact of European psychologists on theory and practice.

The careers of psychologists are also likely to change. Issues affecting them include:

- Portfolio careers for psychologists.
- Fragmentation of Occupational Psychology into separate applied areas.
- Differentiation from human resource management practitioners and other professional bodies.
- Development of undergraduate degrees in Occupational Psychology with postgraduate level specialization in one of the eight areas.

Regulation of psychologists:

- The impact of statutory regulation through the Health Professionals' Council on the diverse body of psychologists which includes occupational psychologists as well as healthcare professionals.

Chapter summary

- Psychology is the study of individual behaviour using scientific method to undertake its enquiries.
- Positivism and Postmodernism are two different approaches to investigation. Positivism states that only those things that can be objectively observed are appropriate for scientific enquiry, whereas postmodernism believes that there are no absolute truths and everything needs to be explained in a cultural context.
- Work psychology studies the interaction of people, work, and organizations and is an applied area of psychology seeking to solve problems at work.
- Work is a multidimensional concept having layers of meaning for the individual.
- The world of work and organizations has been changing rapidly in the past thirty years mainly due to advances in technology.
- Many Schools of Thought have developed focusing on different aspects of work and organizations including Scientific Management, the Human Relations School, Socio-Technical Systems, the Contingency approach. These have all given rise to management techniques to improve performance at work.

- Psychology, and work psychology, have professionalized over the past 100 years with the founding of learned societies and associations in Europe and America. These have developed educational programmes. In the UK a Royal Charter was granted and a register of members set up to restrict the practice of psychology to those appropriately qualified in order to protect the public.

- To become a Chartered Occupational Psychologist eight areas of competence must be demonstrated along with relevant work experience and practical competence.

- Human Resource Management, which grew out of welfare work, has overlapping areas of interest and expertise with occupational psychology but is more business and practitioner focused.

- There are many areas of interest emerging for occupational psychologists to study.

- There is a system for the statutory regulation of occupational psychologists.

Assess your learning

Review questions

1 What is scientific method?

2 What are Positivism and Postmodernism?

3 Define work psychology.

4 Describe the differences between the approaches of pure and applied science.

5 What dimensions of change to work and organizations have there been in the last thirty years?

6 Describe Scientific Management, the Human Relations approach, the Socio-technical approach, and the Contingency approach.

7 What management techniques have developed from work psychology?

8 What are the areas of competence that an occupational psychologist must have?

9 In what ways are Occupational Psychology and Human Resource Management similar? How do they differ?

10 What new areas of potential study for occupational psychologists are emerging?

Assignments

Summarize the developments in work psychology since the First World War.

To what extent have historical events shaped the interest areas in the discipline?

Evaluate the impact of three schools of thought in the development of management techniques.

Construct arguments for and against the development of undergraduate degrees in Occupational Psychology.

Further reading

Brennan, J. F. (2003) *History and Systems of Psychology* (6th edn.). Upper Saddle River, NJ: Prentice Hall.
 A history of psychological thought.

Drenth, P. J. D., Thierry, H., de Wolff, C. J., eds. (1998) **Introduction to work and organizational psychology** in *Handbook of Work and Organizational Psychology* (2nd edn.). Hove: Psychology Press Ltd.
An introduction to the scope of occupational psychology in Europe.

Hergenhahn, B. R. (2005) *An Introduction to the History of Psychology* (5th edn.). Belmont, CA: Wadsworth.
A history of the development of philosophical and psychological thought.

Hothersall, D. (2004) *History of Psychology* (4th edn.). New York: McGraw-Hill.
A history of the development of different focuses in psychology from the classical world to Neobehaviourism.

Jones, D., and Elcock, J. (2001) *History and Theories of Psychology: A Critical Perspective*. London: Arnold.
A critical evaluation of aspects and approaches in psychology and the influences on the development of theoretical positions within psychology.

Shimmin, S., and Wallis, D. (1994) *50 Years of Occupational Psychology in Britain*. Leicester: BPS.
The history of the development of occupational psychology in Britain from 1939 to 1994.

Schultz, D. P., and Schultz, S. E. (2004) *A History of Modern Psychology* (8th edn.). Belmont, CA: Wadsworth. Thompson Learning.
The historical development of different schools of psychological thought.

Work psychology in practice
Explorers Holidays Ltd

The following case study focuses on areas of organizational behaviour from the employer's point of view.

Explorers is a medium-sized independent travel agency specializing in historical holidays. They focus on guided tours to European capitals, the Far East, South Africa, and South America, catering largely to an educated middle-class, middle-aged UK market interested in art, history, and archaeology.

The company is based in the west end of London. It gets most of its bookings through mailing its extensive database and from its website. It employs seventy-five people, mostly sales staff, who deal with clients on the telephone and through booking forms. Explorers also has an extensive network of local representatives abroad who organize the local aspects of the holidays and provide trained guides.

The organization structure is quite flat. There are four departments of unequal size: sales (the largest), marketing, finance, and business development. The sales department is product based and divided into five regional areas along with Bespoke and After Sales. The majority of employees are graduates. Pay is in the low to median quartile for the sector and benefits include discounts on company holidays. In addition, the sales department have the opportunity for occasional travel to their specialist area. Senior management consists of an MD and a Director of Finance who also looks after HR matters, supported by the heads of departments.

The age structure of the employees is relatively young. The MD is 43 and has been with the company for thirteen years, having been promoted internally; similarly the Director of Finance is 45 and has been in post for five years. The five Heads of Sales are in their early thirties and have also been internally promoted. They get paid an annual bonus depending on the results of their department. Most of the sales staff are recruited with a couple of years' experience after graduation.

The company has a fair trade and environmental policy which it applies both to its holidays (except for flights) and to its head office. They have been thinking about opening an Active Holiday department covering more rigorous exploration holidays in the jungle and Antarctica and treasure diving holidays.

Lately Explorers has been experiencing difficulties. Their sales have been declining, despite an overall increase in UK per capita spend on holidays. The Board of Directors decided to undertake a study of the market, of the competition, and of the problems facing tours to parts of the world experiencing difficulties in tourism. As a result of this they made certain adjustments. However, the problems in sales, although slightly improved, was not rectified and turnover of staff has been rising.

The Board now thinks that the difficulties may lie internally to the company in the organization itself, rather than externally with the market or the products (holidays) themselves.

Questions

- What would you recommend the senior management team of Explorers International Holidays Ltd do to sort out the problems?
- What aspects of the organization should they look at?
- Who should do this, how, and why?
- What likely findings do you expect?

Online Resource Centre

Visit the supporting online resource centre for additional material which will help you with your research, essays, and assignments, or you may find these additional resources helpful when revising for exams. **http://www.oxfordtextbooks.co.uk/orc/matthewman/**

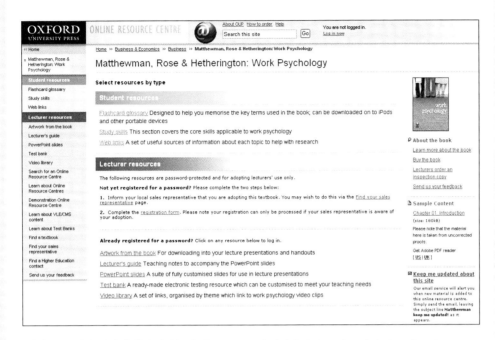

References

Allport, G. W. (1940) The Psychologist's Frame of Reference. *Psychological Bulletin*, 371: 1–28.

Argyle, M. (1989) *The Social Psychology of Work* (2nd edn.). Harmondsworth: Penguin.

Baritz, L. (1960) *The Servants of Power: A History of the Uses of the Social Sciences in American Industry*. Middletown, CN: Wesleyan University Press.

Bass, B. M. (1990) From transactional to transformational leadership: Learning to share the vision. *Organizational Dynamics* (Winter): 19–31.

Binet, A., and Simon, T. (1905) Méthodes nouvelles pour le diagnostic du niveau intellectuel des anormaux. *L'Année psychologique*, 11: 191–244.

Blum, M. L. , and Naylor, J. C. (1968) *Industrial Psychology*. New York: Harper Row.

Burns, T., and Stalker, M. (1961) *The Management of Innovation*. London: Tavistock.

Cattell, J. M. (1890) Mental tests and measurements. *Mind* 15: 373–80.

Comte, A. (1896, original work published 1830) *The Positive Philosophy of Comte*. London: Bell.

Drenth, P. J. D., Thierry, H., and de Wolff, C. J. (eds.) (1998) *Handbook of Work and Organizational Psychology* (2nd edn.), vol. i: *Introduction to Work and Organizational Psychology*. Hove: Psychology Press Ltd.

Dunnette, M. D. (1990) Blending the science and practice of industrial and organizational psychology: where we are and where

we are going. In M. D. Dunnette and L. M. Hough (eds.) (1994) *Handbook of Industrial and Organizational Psychology*. Palo Alto, CA: Consulting Psychologists Press, 127–30.

Emery, F. E., and Thorsrud, E. (1969) *Form and Content in Industrial Democracy*. London: Tavistock Publications.

Fiedler, F. E. (1967) *A Theory of Leadership Effectivenes*. New York: McGraw-Hill.

Gergen, K. J. (1985) The social constructionist movement in modern psychology. *The American Psychologist*, 40/332: 66–275, American Psychological Association.

Gergen, K. J. (1991) *The Saturated Self: Dilemmas of Identity in Contemporary Life*. New York: Basic Books.

Gilbreth, F. B. (1911) *Motion Study*. New York: Van Nostrand.

Herzberg, F., Mausner, B., and Snyderman, B. (1959) *The Motivation to Work*. New York: Wiley.

Hollway, W. (1991) *Work Psychology and Organizational Behaviour*, London: Sage.

Jahoda, M. (1979) The impact of unemployment in the 1930s and the 1970s. *Bull Br Psychol Soc*, 32: 309–14.

Jaques, E. (1951) *The Changing Culture of a Factory*. London: Tavistock Publications.

Johnson, G., and Scholes, K. (1989) *Exploring Corporate Strategy*. Hemel Hempstead: Gower.

Kuhn, T. S. (1996) *The Structure of Scientific Revolutions* (3rd edn.). Chicago: University of Chicago Press.

Lawrence, P., and Lorsch, J. (1967) *Organization and Environment*. Cambridge, MA: Harvard University Press.

Lewin, K. (1947) Frontiers in group dynamics. *Human Relations*, 15/411: 43–153.

Marx, K. (trans. B. Fowkes) (1981) *Capital* (first published 1867). London: Penguin Classics.

Maslow, A. (1970) *Motivation and Personality* (2nd edn.). New York: Harper Row.

Mayo, E. (1933) The Human Problems of an Industrial Civilisation. New York: Viking.

McClelland, D. C. (1961) *The Achieving Society*, Princeton, NJ: Van Norstrand.

McGregor, D. (1960) *The Human Side of the Enterprise*. New York: McGraw-Hill.

Patterson, F (2001) Developments in work psychology: emerging issues and future trends. *Journal of Occupational and Organizational Psychology*, 743: 81–390.

Pugh, D. S., and Hickson, D. J. (1976) *Organizational Structure in its Context: The Aston Programme*. Westmead: Saxton House.

Schein, E. (1965) *Organizational Psychology*. Englewood Cliffs, NJ: Prentice-Hall Inc.

Seligman, M. E. P. (1999) *Mission Statement and Conclusions of Akumal 1*, http://www.ppc.sas.upenn.edu/index.html

Shimmin, S., and Wallis, D. (1994) *50 Years of Industrial Psychology in Britain*. Leicester: British Psychological Society.

Snow, C. P. (1964) *The Two Cultures and a Second Look*. London: Cambridge University Press.

Spearman, C. (1904) General Intelligence objectively measured and determined. *American Journal of Psychology*, 152: 1–293.

Taylor, F. W. (1911) *The Principles of Scientific Management*. New York: Harper.

Thurstone, L. L. (1938) *Primary Mental Abilities*. Chicago: University of Chicago Press.

Trist, E. L. , and Bamforth, K. W. (1951) Social and psychological consequences of the long wall method of coal-getting. *Human Relations*, 4: 1–38.

Weber, M. (2001; first published 1905) *The Protestant Ethic and the Spirit of Capitalism*. London: Routledge (originally published in translation 1930).

Chapter 2
Research methods in work psychology

Amanda Rose

Chapter objectives

As a result of reading this chapter and using the additional web-based material you should be able to:

- Identify the key aims of research in work psychology.
- Recognize the relationship between theory and research practice in work psychology.
- Appreciate how research in work psychology is designed, planned, and executed.
- Identify a range of methods available for collecting information to explore research questions, and identify their strengths and weaknesses.
- Identify key differences between qualitative and quantitative methods and designs.
- Appreciate debates about the appropriateness of different research strategies and methods.
- Recognize and describe ethical issues in the conduct of research in work psychology.
- Appreciate the social nature of research activity in work psychology, and the impact of cultural factors on the research process.

Work psychology in practice
Accident proneness at work

Accidents at work are costly to organizations in terms of lost productivity, and absenteeism. They may lead to serious consequences for individuals such as long- term disability and unemployment. During the period 2006–7, there were a total of 141,350 accidents at work reported to the Heath and Safety Executive, 241 of them fatal (HSE 2008). What are the causes of accidents at work? Could these numbers be reduced?

One issue that has interested psychologists is the possibility that some people may be more prone to accidents than others.

Charles Lardent (1991) explored this idea in a military context. Using a personality questionnaire, he compared the personalities of forty-seven fighter pilots who had been involved in serious accidents with forty-four who had not. His results revealed differences between the typical personalities of the two groups: crash pilots were more tense and anxious and less conscientious than non-crash pilots.

What are the implications of studies such as this?

Questions

- Do you think this study can offer an insight into accident proneness in non-military contexts?
- Are there factors other than the personality of the pilots that might explain these accident figures?
- What are the implications of these findings for management practice in accident reduction?
- Are there ethical implications in the conduct of this research?

2.1 Introduction

Research is the core generative force within work psychology. The exercise of observing people at work and reflecting upon what is observed is the very life blood of the psychologist's enterprise. This chapter will explore various approaches to research design, data gathering, and analysis. It will reflect upon the diversity of approaches that are employed, and will explore some core debates within work psychology about the conduct of research.

Although diverse in approach, work psychologists share a desire to explore and understand how people respond to work environments and how they interact with others in work organizations. From the early experiments of Lippitt and White (1947) which showed that different management styles can have a differerential impact on group performance and productivity, to the findings of surveys of dual career families (Cooper and Lewis 1993), and to recent examinations of types and causes of burnout in managers (Schaufeli et al. 2008) work psychologists have explored problems thrown up by changing working practices, and have tried to examine the human impact of government policy and organizational practice. In doing so, they use a variety of research designs and techniques to gather information about people's experience and behaviour.

This chapter will consider a variety of ways in which work psychologists have conducted research. It will explore how the aims and objectives of research may condition the way researchers design their work and collect and analyse their data. It will discuss a variety of examples of research studies in work psychology. It will also consider research in its social and cultural context, and explore the ethical issues faced by work psychologists in the course of their activites.

2.2 The nature and aims of research in work psychology: the positivist tradition and its critics

From its inception, psychology has been a scientific endeavour. By the term 'scientific' is meant that certain principles are applied in the generation and development of psychological knowledge.

What counts as science in the researching of human experience and action has been the subject of much debate. Johnson and Cassell (2001) have suggested that the dominant approach to both research and the development of theory in work psychology is **positivist** in its approach and epistemology. Positivism, as discussed in Chapter 1, is an approach within the human and physical sciences which stresses the primacy of data that is amenable to sensory perception; which is objective, verifiable, and, in general, quantifiable. It is an approach associated with **empiricism** and the application of the **scientific method**.

The scientific method is characterized by procedures which strive to ensure that the information and data generated though research is: reliable (consistent and repeatable), and valid (represents what it aims and purports to). This leads to an approach that includes:

- Hypothesis testing.
- Systematic control of variables.
- Data analysis.
- Replication.

    (McKenna 2000)

Hypothesis testing

Hypothesis testing involves the process of systematically observing phenomena, and generating tentative ideas about how variables are related. For example, a training manager might observe that new management trainees sent on accountancy training programmes on day release did not perform so well as trainees sent on courses in the evening. She hypothesizes that learning in the evening is superior to daytime learning, and designs a study to test her idea.

Control of variables

The manager identifies two groups of trainees, and establishes that they are similar in age, educational qualifications, and experience on the job.

She sends one group to follow a day release course in accountancy, and send the other group to an evening version of the same course.

Data analysis

The manager records the achievements of each group. She observes that the evening group has gained higher marks in exams and assessed work than the day study group, and concludes that night time learning provides the best experience for adult learners.

Replication

It might be argued that the results achieved by the training manager are due to the specific sample she has employed, or the specific lecturers who taught the evening and day classes. It would be necessary therefore to repeat the study with a variety of management trainees, courses, and lecturers. Would the results hold for other types of subjects, such as engineering or human resource management?

In order to replicate the research, a researcher must have access to full details of how the original study was carried out. The clear and full dissemination of research methodology and details of analysis of results enables an accurate replication to take place, and this is therefore a key component of the scientific method.

As David Duncan suggests: 'Being a scientist in occupational psychology . . . demands systematic collection of relevant data, objective observation of people, and a care for validation of one's techniques' (Duncan 2005: 77).

Pause for thought
What factors might affect the performance of adult learners on vocational courses?

2.2.1 Alternative approaches

Some researchers in work psychology (for example, Burr 1995) have suggested that the positivist approach to research is not applicable to the study of human and social phenomena. They reject the absolutist epistemological stance of the positivists, and suggest a more relativist account of reality. Proponents of such views include **social constructionists** who emphasize that research takes place within a social and cultural context which conditions the experience of researchers and their participants.

Figure 2.1. Model of the research process

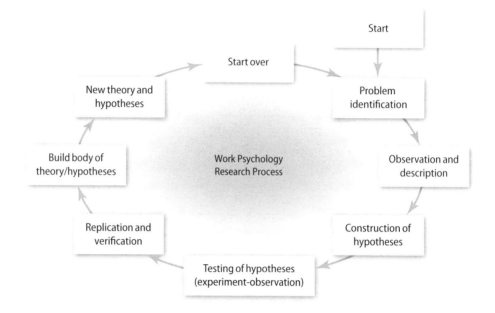

Social constructionists are critical of positivist methods, and suggest that as these were developed to explore the physical world, they are not necessarily applicable to the world of human, social, and cultural phenomena (Richardson and Fowers 1997).

From this perspective the goal of objectivity is seen as unachievable and illusionary, as external reality is not something that is independent of the observer. What the researcher observes is always a function of their specific psychological, social, and cultural history.

Researchers in work psychology deal with sentient beings who have their own values, beliefs, and cultural heritage. With the best will in the world they cannot be 'controlled' like plants in a fertilizer trial.

Social constructionism leads to the endorsement of very different research methods from those employed by positivists.

Social constructionists tend to employ **qualitative** research methods, for example **depth interviewing** or participant observation, which aim to capture and explore the unique, subjective experience of individuals and groups.

2.2.2 Theory and research in work psychology

A **theory** is a set of propositions about relationships amongst phenomena. A theory may comprise a specific model of how things work or develop. Theories aim to predict future events, and generate testable propositions.

Theory in work psychology may emerge developmentally from the accumulation of evidence. For example, Holland (1973) developed a theory of vocational choice based on his long experience as a psychologist working in career counselling. Meredith Belbin (1981) developed his theory of team roles, from the observation of work teams in action over a number of years.

Theory may be used to generate additional hypotheses, which may then be tested through research. This may lead to support for the original theory, or to its rejection or modification. In practice, as Thomas Kuhn (1962) has noted, much of the general work of researchers consists of doing research within a small number of theoretical frameworks, and exploring, confirming, or refuting, the work of others.

In the area of psychology, a historical appreciation of the development of patterns of research would suggest that there are in fact a number of distinct theoretical traditions existing side by side simultaneously, as discussed in Chapter 1.

Because of their employment in live organizations, researchers in the area of work psychology tend to be concerned with the exploration of practical problems. Often working to strict

Case illustration
Experiments in bystander intervention

Laboratory experiments may increase the researcher's ability to control events, but the environment they create can seem highly artificial to participants. This may compromise the validity of the results.

For example, in the 1960s, two American researchers conducted a series of experiments on the important issue of bystander intervention in emergency situations (Darley and Latane 1968). In one study for example, they invited volunteer participants into their psychology department to take part in what they were informed was an attitude survey.

While waiting alone or in small groups for the study to start, filling in their personal details on a questionnaire, the experimenters arranged for smoke to be pumped into the room. This was the real experiment. How would the volunteers react? The researchers were interested to see how group size affected the latency of responses to seek help and report the emergency. The results of their studies suggested that people waiting alone were more likely to report the 'accident' than those waiting with one or more other participants. Some participants were still quietly filling in forms while smoke completely filled the room, and they could hardly see to write.

However, critics have pointed out that in real fires people in groups may panic in trying to exit buildings. Many case studies of real fires testify to such effects. Interestingly, in the Psychology Department of a Canadian University in the early 1970s, a fire started in the basement of a building which housed the psychology labs. As fire stewards tried to clear the building, many people refused to go—convinced that that a professor was performing some sort of experiment!

So, the behaviour of these people who have come to a psychology department to take part in an experiment may not be very typical. As Rosenthal and Rosnow (1969) pointed out, experiments generate 'demand characteristics'. When people know they are taking part in a scientific experiment they develop their own hypotheses about what the study is about, and adapt their responses accordingly. They may decide to be helpful and demonstrate what they think the experimenter is looking for. Also, in the prestigious confines of a university department, it may be that people think no harm can come to them, and abrogate all responsibility for their own welfare to the professors.

deadlines with limited resources, they tend, as Adrian Furnham (2005) suggests, to be eclectic in their employment of theory and in their use of procedures and techniques.

 KEY LEARNING POINTS

- Research in work psychology is a scientific endeavour.
- There are a variety of conceptions of what is meant by scientific. These vary in terms of their **epistemology** and this leads to an acceptance of different goals for research and different research methods.
- Positivism is an approach characterized by the pursuit of objective knowledge, through the application of specific scientific principles embodied in the scientific method.
- Social constructionists are critical of the validity of this approach, and suggest an alternative agenda for research in work psychology using qualitative approaches.
- A key goal of research in work psychology is the generation of theory, which can offer a synthesizing explanation about observed phenomena.
- Research can challenge or support theory, and lead to its modification or rejection.

2.3 Research designs

The inspiration and impetus for research may arise from a number of sources: the desire to develop an understanding of some core aspect of human experience, such as learning a new skill, or the desire to understand and offer solutions to social problems and issues, for example, the impact of bullying at work or the reduction of conflict between work groups. Sometimes, researchers may want to replicate findings from earlier research, or explore whether a research finding is applicable in a different context or culture from that where it was originally established.

Case illustration
Grandey et al.

Alicia Grandey and her associates (2005) were interested in exploring the relationship between work-family conflict and job satisfaction. Do people who experience conflict between the demands of home and family and those of their careers tend to also experience low job satisfaction? They might have surveyed a group of people at one point in time (a cross-sectional approach) but decided instead to monitor levels of job satisfaction over a period of twelve months. They argued that as both conflicts between work and home, and job satisfaction are likely to be highly variable over short periods of time, a long-term perspective was essential to explore their hypothesis.

Questions

- What other aspects of working might usefully be explored using longitudinal approaches?
- What might be some of the problems and difficulties with this approach?

A *research strategy* is an overall plan of action developed in order to achieve the specific aims of an investigation.

A *research design* is the embodiment and operationalization of the strategy and includes the choice of specific methods and techniques.

Researchers may choose to structure their work in a variety of ways, depending on their aims and other practical considerations, for example, the availability of resources and the nature of support for projects from both management and employees within organizations.

2.3.1 Research designs

Depending on the aims of a project, a researcher may utilize a number of different approaches.

- Cross-sectional versus longitudinal.
- Experimental versus naturalistic.

Cross-sectional research attempts to gain a picture or impression of psychological phenomena at one particular point in time; whereas **longitudinal designs** follow human action over a period of time. Research interests concerned with development, for example with career paths and **career choice**, might follow this approach.

2.3.2 Experimental designs

Experimental designs examine phenomena by manipulating an **independent variable** and observing its impact on a **dependent variable**. For example, a researcher may be interested in determining what type of payment systems are most effective at improving worker output. They might decide to manipulate the way that workers are paid, comparing individual bonuses with group bonuses in a sales department. The independent variable will be the various payment methods, and the dependent variable will be sales over time. Researchers may choose to create an experimental situation within highly controlled laboratory settings, or in real settings (field studies), or they may prefer to observe natural situations unfolding, watching and questioning participants about their social actions.

In a **naturalistic design** the researcher would aim to gather information from being in or observing an ongoing real situation. For example, in order to understand how the design of work stations might affect the experience of work, Peter Vink (1997) compared different designs and layouts in a real office environment. Kevin Kniffin and David Wilson (2005) worked with sports teams over an eighteen-month period to explore the role of gossip in organizational life. Erving Goffman (1961) worked in a mental hospital as an orderly and recorded his observations of management practice and patient's responses.

Each design has its strengths and weaknesses, and the researcher will make choices, searching for the best vehicle with which to achieve their research aims.

Figure 2.2. Mind map: planning research

Stimulus for research: Reading details of a study that finds continuing pay gap between male and female workers—30 years on from Equal Pay Act. Why? Many reasons—Social attitudes? Family responsibilities? Is it that women are not promoted at work? Or they don't apply for better-paid jobs? Can we talk about sex differences in attitudes? Or are cultural and economic factors more important? Narrow down focus to look at the decision to seek promotion at work. Are there sex differences?

↓

Plan research: Better to design a cross-sectional or a longitudinal study—what are the problems with each?

↓

What are the independent variables here? Gender? Are there moderating and mediating variables here? What about personality? What about culture and social beliefs? What groups do I need to sample?

↓

What are the dependent variables? Promotion successes? Or what about attitudes, values, and beliefs?

↓

Qualitative or a quantitative approach? What would be the advantages of each? Shall I use both? Do I want to see the extent of the issues? Or understand people's beliefs and feelings?

↓

What would be an appropriate sample?

↓

Could I compare male and female students in a role play?

↓

Or observe managers in real work situations?

↓

How will I analyse my results?

↓

Are there any ethical issues arising from the approach I have chosen?

↓

What are my resources? How long will the study take? Do I have appropriate contacts?

 Activity **Choosing research designs**

There is much debate about the relative effectiveness of different training methods. List the factors you would take into account when exploring the relative effectiveness of online learning versus classroom training for acquiring knowledge of spreadsheet packages. Ask someone you know to complete the same activity. Compare your list with that of your partner.

2.3.3 Qualitative and quantitative methods and designs

One key choice for researchers is whether to employ qualitative or **quantitative** approaches to data collection, or some combination of both these types (Burt and Oaksford 1999).

Quantitative methods are data-gathering techniques that generate quantitative data. This will include a whole range of information, for example the results of **psychometric tests** of various sorts, details of the time taken to produce some result under different conditions at work, output and productivity over time.

However, many experiences and aspects of human action cannot be quantified and counted, for example feelings, beliefs, or fears, and much psychological investigation is concerned with exploring just these aspects. Also, researchers may not aspire to making comparisons or testing hypotheses that require quantification of information. Thus, qualitative methods for example, depth interviews, are frequently used in work psychology.

The distinction between qualitative and quantitative methods is often a very fine line, and qualitative data can be collected and categorized in ways that are amenable to quantitative statistical analysis.

In practice, researchers may used both approaches within a single research project; generating ideas through qualitative data that are then tested with more quantitative methods.

2.3.4 Evaluating design

A key aim of the work psychology researcher is to produce information that is reliable, valid, and generalizable.

- **Reliability**. This refers to the consistency of the measures taken. Measures taken again in similar circumstances should produce similar results.

- **Validity**. By this is meant that the data collected are in accordance with the core aims and strategy of the research, that they are a true measure of the variables under consideration in the project. This may apply to any particular tests that are used, or manipulations made.

- **Generalizability**. Do the findings transfer beyond the time and space of the particular study? This may or may not be the concern of researchers, but where a researcher makes claims about the transferability of their findings to other groups and other contexts, for example that research into motivation at work in the USA is applicable to workers in other cultures, or that accident proneness of one set of workers tells us something about all workers, this may be an important consideration.

Work psychologists are sometimes constrained in their choice of design by cultural and political factors. For example, in reviewing the interest of work psychologists in the area of employee relations, Jean Harley and John Kelly (1986) suggest that both management and trade unions are unwilling to talk to researchers about issues concerned with bargaining and negotiation situations. This may be because each party seeks to keep hold of information about tactics and strategies. Research into this area therefore might need to adopt approaches that do not require direct engagement with union and management representatives in real bargaining situations. The research approaches adopted by psychologists must acknowledge the impact of power and politics within work organizations and how these issues may mediate their access to information.

KEY LEARNING POINTS

- The design of a research project develops from the strategy and aims of researchers.
- Designs may be cross-sectional or longitudinal, experimental or naturalistic.
- Researchers may employ a qualitative or quantitative approach to the generation of data.
- Choice of design will depend of the theoretical preferences of the researcher, and also upon practical considerations.

2.4 Research methods and techniques

Having decided on an overall design, there are many ways of actually collecting data. The choice of technique will be determined by the aims of the researcher, and also by their theoretical perspectives and preferences. Many researchers will use multiple techniques within a single study.

Methods include:

- Observation
- Experimentation (laboratory or quasi-experiments)
- Questionnaires
- Interviews
- Diary studies
- Group discussion and focus groups
- Analysis of archival information
- Discourse analysis.

The nature of the research question will condition the method chosen. However, in practice, work psychologists will also make research decisions in terms of pragmatic, resource constraints as well as ethical concerns.

2.4.1 Observation

Perhaps the most straightforward way of gathering psychological data is just to observe or watch people. Researchers can position themselves within a group, or they may film behaviour and rate the material, or watch unobtrusively behind a one-way mirror.

In some cases, researchers may participate in the work of some group in order to observe behaviour. This is *participant observation*. For example, in a study of violence in the workplace, Vicky Bishop, Marek Korczynski, and Laurie Cohen (2005) used participant observation to try and gather information about the experience of violence in job centres in the UK. Admitting to experiences of violence at work might be difficult for some people, so it was important for the researchers to choose a method which didn't put pressure on people to disclose their own experiences.

Another study which demonstrates the specific usefulness of these approaches explored reactions to unemployment in a group of American managers and professionals. Raymond Garrett-Peters (2005) was interested in examining how such occupational groups cope with the negative impact of unemployment. As well as conducting interviews, this researcher also joined a self-help group of out of work managers in order to observe their transitions and adjustments to their new status.

To collect data from observation sessions, researchers will use predetermined categories in line with their research aims and objectives. For example, if observing leadership behaviour, a set of behaviours and attributes relevant to leadership would be devised and applied.

Advantages and disadvantages

Observation allows researchers to follow sequences of live action as they unfold, and a vast amount of rich data can be collected, including non-verbal cues, which other methods may miss. Action can be filmed, and this allows for fine and detailed analysis by more than one observer, thus aiding reliability of impressions. However, the richness of data that presents itself is not always easy to record, and much may be lost. In observing, the researcher has to decide what to focus on, and this may bias results. The use of rating categories may help, but the data will also be constrained by these categories, and much may be missed.

As David Waddington (1994) points out, a main problem with this approach is that the presence of researchers may have an impact on the very processes they are observing. David Waddington suggests the longer the observation continues, the less this effect will operate.

2.4.2 Experimentation: laboratory versus quasi-experiments

In an experiment, the researcher *creates* a situation by placing people into specific contexts, and sometimes into specific roles. The researcher will endeavour to control the environment of their participants, and record the impact. This is very analogous to the work of physical scientists.

This technique has many diverse applications in the area of work psychology. For example, a researcher interested in the effects of different types of payment schemes, might select groups of workers, and arrange that their efforts were differently rewarded in terms of time rate or piece rate for example, and observe the impact on their productivity over time.

Case illustration
An experiment on the impact of threatening emails

A growing number of people use email as the main form of communication at both work and home. Email is sometimes considered an impersonal mode of communication, which lacks the informational cues of face-to-face meetings. Howard Taylor and George Fieldman (2005) wanted to investigate the effect of aggressive emails on recipients. They carried out the following experiment to gauge changes in blood pressure following receipt of threatening messages.

Groups of students were recruited to fill in questionnaires for research online at their university. During completion sessions different groups of students were sent emails which were either threatening or non-threatening, from a person who was either of the same or higher status than them. Throughout the sessions their blood pressure was monitored. Taylor and Fieldman found that students receiving threatening emails from a high-status source showed significant increases in blood pressure.

Questions

- What variables might the researchers have controlled for in this experiment?
- What other features of email communication might a researcher investigate using the experimental method?

Advantages and disadvantages

The advantage of this approach is that it offers the researcher a degree of control over the process. However, the method may create artificial and unreal situations, and people may respond atypically so that the manipulations become invalid. (See Case illustration: Experiments in bystander intervention, above.)

Quasi-experiments are designed to offer a more naturalistic setting for experimental manipulations. In such cases, the researcher will attempt to introduce controlled manipulations into real-life situations (Fife-Schaw 2006). For example, in order to examine the effects of different payment systems on productivity, an appraisal system might be experimentally introduced at one site within an organization, and the impact on output observed over a period of time.

These types of manipulations may get over the unreality of the pure laboratory settings, but they may provide less control, and make it harder for the researcher to attribute their results to the impact of their manipulations (Muchinsky 2006). Will Evers, Andre Brouwers, and Welco Tomic (2006) used quasi-experimental methods to assess the impact of coaching on managerial effectiveness. They randomly assigned a group of sixty managers working in the federal government in the Netherlands into two groups, one of which participated in a management coaching programme. They gave pre- and post-experimental questionnaires to both groups, and found that the coaching group displayed significant increases in measures of **self-efficacy** beliefs, and setting their own goals on completion of the course and four months after the course.

2.4.3 Questionnaires and surveys

Questionnaires and surveys are extensively used in management practice, as well as in the research process in work psychology. They consist of a set of written questions, which are presented to people for completion. They may be emailed, posted, distributed by hand, or personally administered. The format of the question list may vary. Common formats include the **Likert Scale**.

The scales are constructed by **piloting** questions on groups of people who are representative of the populations that will be used in the final study. Items are selected which maximally distinguish between high and low total scorers. So, for example if an item is equally likely to be checked by both low and high total scorers, it is dropped from the pool.

Figure 2.3. Questionnaire format: a Likert scale

	Strongly agree	Agree	Neutral	Disagree	Strongly disagree
Trade unions can improve employee's working conditions					
Without trade unions, employers would not feel obliged to review pay					
Employee should be given time off to attend trade union meetings					
Trade unions do little for their members					

Question wording

The wording of questions, for example the use of superlatives such as 'extremely', has been shown to have an effect upon the way that respondents respond (Wood and Williams 2007). Care is required therefore in the formulation of questions.

Questions need to be clear and unambiguous in their meaning, and free from complex sentence construction, and double negatives. They should avoid rhetoric and bias. The language used should be recognizable and familiar to respondents, thus it is often considered good practice to base statements on pilot interviews with members of the target research group.

Advantages and disadvantages

The advantage of questionnaire methods is that they are easy to administer to large samples. If this is a requirement of the research strategy, they are invaluable in providing a forum for reaching large groups. The method can be used to explore complex issues, using careful **sampling**.

Figure 2.4. Questionnaire techniques: examples of question wording

Good questions
- Are clearly worded and unambiguous in meaning.
- Use language that is familiar to respondents.
- Are short—usually consisting of just one sentence.

Examples:
- How many times each year do you meet with your line manager to discuss your work performance?
- Did you contribute to the Vice-Chancellor's suggestion scheme?
- How many people work in your department?

Poor questions
- Are leading and/or rhetorical.
- Contain more than one issue.
- Use technical jargon.
- Use language that is unfamiliar to the respondent.
- Are long winded, and complex in structure.

Examples:
- Is partnership the only approach for the trade unions?
- Would you agree that managers should never join a trade union?
- Are accidents at work always the fault of management?
- Do you prefer methods of pay that challenge you or which are regular or easy to achieve?
- Would you characterize your current management style as transformational?
- Would you describe yourself as a good manager?

Figure 2.5. What is sampling?

> All research is concerned with some aspect of the experience or behaviour of a target group of people. This may be **the whole human race**, but more likely it is some sub-sample, for example: all female managers in the UK, all trainee nurses, all people with a specific visual disability.
>
> As it is not possible for a researcher to survey an entire population in their research, they have to utilize a group of people from their target population who will represent the group of interest. This is a sample.
>
> In selecting a sample, the aim is to strive to make that sample representative of the population as a whole.
>
> The selection of a sample begins with a **sampling frame**—a list of the total population.
>
> **Methods of selection:** A sample may be chosen **randomly** (for example selected by computer) or **systematically** (for example, every seventh person listed on the sampling frame). Samples may also use a **Quota method** where a researcher attempts to fashion a sample that mirrors the composition of the population under review, for example 50% male and 50% female, 20% aged 20–45 and so on.
>
> The representativeness of a sample may affect the reliability, generalizability, and validity of results.

Questionnaires offer a direct way of ascertaining people's views and may circumvent some ethical problems concerning informed consent, and deception, that other methods, including experimentation and observation, might fall foul of. Questionnaires can be administered online, and this is a fast and simple method of contacting, and such surveys are easy to reply to. Reminders may be sent electronically to people to try to stimulate higher response rates.

The disadvantages of such methods is that response rates can be low. It is not uncommon in studies employing postal questionnaire to achieve less than 25 per cent response rates. The representativeness of views discovered is therefore called into question. It may well be that only those who feel strongly about an issue, who may be highly untypical, will bother to respond.

Also, researchers have little control over the way that people approach the task of answering a questionnaire. People may fill in answers randomly, or may deliberately try to give a certain impression, or get their friends to answer for them. Studies have demonstrated that the way a questionnaire is administered, for example, by telephone, face to face, or self-administered, can affect the nature of responses (Schwarz et al. 1991).

Christiane Spitzmuller (Spitzmuller et al. 2006) explored non-respondents to an organizational survey at an American university. Students who decided not to participate in the survey were shown to have negative perceptions of the university, and to see the organization as less procedurally just and supportive than students who did participate. This demonstrates how the questionnaire method might produce a false picture of the attitudes of a group.

2.4.4 Interviews

Kahn and Cannell (1957) famously defined an interview as a 'conversation with a purpose'. Like questionnaires, interviews are devices for gaining information that can be used in many contexts other than that of research.

There are many different types of interviewing situation and format. They are used in many stages of the research process, in fact it is likely that all research in work psychology will involve an interview at some stage. Many people might believe that there's not much skill in conducting an interview, because they mirror typical interaction. However, interviews involve complex social processes, and researchers may find that the interaction sometimes qualifies and alters their research objectives.

Interviews can be **structured** where a researcher devises a set of questions akin to the format of a questionnaire. Respondents are presented with set questions and their responses are largely constrained, possibly just a 'yes' or 'no' being required. Responses can be directly recorded onto questionnaire answer sheets. Interviews may also be unstructured. Respondents may be presented with themes and asked to talk freely about their views and experiences. These types of conversations can be recorded, or filmed, and transcribed.

The role that the interviewer takes within the research conversation has been critically explored by a number of researchers. For example, in her research on women managers career patterns, Judy Marshall (1995) reflects on how her participants appraised her, and what impact she may have had on the responses she elicited in her interviews.

 Activity Interviewer characteristics

Design a study to investigate the impact of interviewer characteristics on participants' behaviour. What variables would you focus on and why?

Advantages and disadvantages

Data collected via interviews is highly various and flexible, and both qualitative and quantitative information can be gathered. However, as a method of data collection it relies on direct interaction between people, and can therefore be liable to bias and distortion. All research involves some form of social interaction between researcher and participant, but this is most clearly evident in the case of interviews.

The participants may form judgements about the interviewer and will develop emotional responses to them. Also, researchers may respond emotionally to their participants. One way of positively acknowledging this aspect of the interaction within the research process comes from the idea of **reflexivity**. This has been explored by feminist researcher such as Sue Wilkinson (1996). Here researchers try to become aware of their own biases, and to reflect on their own social and cultural history and how this might appear to and impact on the people they are researching. This development of personal awareness may help to mitigate the impact of bias, but it is by no means an easy stance to achieve. Interviewers can check on whether they have accurately recorded and represented the views of respondents by presenting their impressions back to the respondent and asking for comments, and clarifications.

2.4.5 Group discussions and focus groups

When researching some topics and issues in work psychology, isolating people from their usual social context may be unrealistic (for example, in exploring the impact of teamworking). In such cases, it may be more useful to gather data from people in group settings. Groups may be directly observed, or their activity may form the basis of an experiment. Where people are questioned about their attitudes in groups, this is generally termed a **focus group**.

Pause for thought
Questionnaire and interviews are both methods that involve posing questions to research participants. Think of a research topic, where it might be preferable to use: Depth Interviews? Structured questionnaires?

 Case illustration
Focus groups

Terence Lee (1998) used focus groups to elicit beliefs about safety at work with groups of managers and workers at the Sellafield Nuclear power plant in Cumbria. Results were then used to design a questionnaire on safety which was distributed to a large group of respondents.

Gillespie et al. (2001) used focus groups to examine the impact of wide organizational change in the Australian university sector. In the late 1990s, Australian universities underwent a great deal of change, including downsizing, restructuring, and government funding cuts. Gillespie and his colleagues sampled a total of 178 academics and general staff at 15 universities, and explored their experience through 22 focus groups. Their results showed common sources of stress which included poor management practice, work overload, and insufficient recognition and reward.

Case illustration
Diary studies

Adam Butler, Joseph Grzywacz, Brenda Bass, and Kirsten Linney (2005) used the diary study method to explore aspects of work-family conflict, and work-family facilitation in a sample of non-professional working couples with children, in the Midwest of the USA. They asked their 91 participants to complete diaries every day for fourteen consecutive days, just before sleep every night.

Their results showed clear variations in both work-family conflict and work-family facilitation over time, and indicated that high demands at work were associated with reported work-family conflict, suggesting that for this sample at least, work demands often do carry over into life outside of work. This is a complex effect that other methods which sample experience at just one point in time, might have failed to capture. Diary studies explore events as they happen, and can thus avoid problems of distortion through memory failure.

Advantages and disadvantages

The benefit of this approach is that people are viewed in context. Groups can be filmed, and the interaction can be finely analysed.

New technology has allowed the development of *e-focus groups*. Many people now experience discussion boards at work, in education or in their leisure pursuits, and have developed skill in communicating electronically. This approach can increase sample sizes, and can be used to look at areas where anonymity is appropriate.

However, problems with focus groups include issues around generalizability and the operation of group dynamics. In general the responses of people will be conditioned by the composition of their group, which may contain dominating individuals, or members who rarely speak. Focus groups involve some input from the researcher in terms of briefing and possibly some observation of the discussion. Thus they may be subject to all the problems arising from the observation of people, including **demand characteristics** and the **Hawthorne effect**. Groups which have been artifically created for research purposes may fall foul of the phenomenon of **group think** (discussed in Chapter 7 on Groups, Teams, and Decision Making**)** where social pressures to present the work of the group in a positive light, and overidentification with a team, may lead members to take inappropriate decisions.

Social and cultural effects may surface in group discussions. Studies suggest that women speak less in mixed groups (Sheridan 2007) and that ethnic minorities may also speak less in culturally mixed groups (Labov 1969). Researchers need to be sensitive to such effects, and make allowances in controlling the composition of groups.

2.4.6 Diary studies

The use of diary studies in work psychology has increased over the years. This method can be used to investigate change over time or to explore the complex interaction between issues in a live context. Asking people to keep a track of actions, experiences, feelings, etc. over time may give an insight into the dynamic processes of change. Results may suggest interesting interrelationships that may be subsequently investigated through other methods. Diaries can also be used to map unusual and rare events (Bolger et al. 2003).

The specific nature of the diary kept will depends on the purpose of the research. People may be required to keep a journal covering certain key questions and issues, or they may be asked to reflect upon a set of questions on a daily or other periodic basis.

Advantages and disadvantages

There are however a number of drawbacks and problems with the technique.

- They may require detailed training sessions to make sure that participants understand the full requirements of the method of data collection.
- They may place substantial demands on participants in terms of time.

- The method may lead to 'reactance' in the participants who may find their pre-study behaviour and attitudes and values challenged and even altered by the impact of actually recording and reflection on their lives.
- Participants may become habituated to the process (participant fatigue) and record their experience in stereotypical ways, missing variations and nuances.

Activity Keeping a diary

Keep a diary yourself for one week (seven days). You might choose from the following activities:

- Record the amount of time you spend travelling, and the activities you engage in during travelling. Record your information every day when you arrive at university or at work.
- Record each day, rate how positively you feel about your current job, or your current course of study on a scale of 1–10. List activities you have enjoyed each day, and activities you have not enjoyed.
- List each day the number of people you talked to in doing your job, or following your course. List their roles; and record how long the interaction was.

At the end of the week, review your entries. How much variation is there from day to day?
    Reflect on your experience of keeping a diary.

2.4.7 Discourse analysis

This technique is derived from the social constructionist approach, which emphasizes the role of language in the creation and sustaining of social action. The definition of **discourse** includes all human production and uses of language, in oral and written/symbolic forms, as well as complex levels of motivated language such as propaganda and rhetoric. Techniques for analysing discourse include the micro-analysis of talk, and content analysis, a method for uncovering and exploring recurring themes.

Advantages and disadvantages

The technique is useful in many research contexts that require the analysis of subjective meaning and the technique requires skill in teasing out themes and issues. It is generally considered good practice to feed back details of the analysis to participants in order to ensure that their position has been accurately represented.

    Researchers however, are often seen as authority figures, and ironically, though such methods are often used to explore power relationships, participants may be constrained by the social position of work psychologists from challenging research accounts.

Case illustration
Discourse analysis

Gill Kirton (2006) used discourse analysis to explore the responses of trade unions to the switch by management from initiatives involving 'equal opportunities', to those focused on 'celebrating diversity'. She analysed the talk of National Trade Union equality officers in exploring differences between the two concepts. Her results demonstrated a complex pattern of appraisal by the trade unionists. They were concerned about the primacy of the 'business case' in the diversity rhetoric, and felt that the new terminology shifted practice away from a focus on disadvantage and discrimination, leaving these issues unacknowledged.

2.4.8 Archival material

Much information about aspects of working in organizations may be gleaned from the examination of records, and other sources of printed and recorded information. This would include, for example, annual reports, departmental reports, communications to employees and shareholders. Also, organizations may hold interesting data on labour turnover, payment and reward system, appraisal, and so on. This is rich data about the life of work organizations. Archival material may be used to answer primary research questions or may be used to supplement views obtained through other methods, for example interviews or diary studies.

The information can be can be subjected to content analysis to search for common themes. For example, Carole Michaels (1995) collected performance appraisal data for pregnant women from a four-year period, from a range of companies. She found that ratings for pregnant women increased compared to before pregnancy ratings.

Advantages and disadvantages

This method allows facilitates a long-term view of organizations, and the activities of people who work within them. However, a problem with the method is that the records that are retained may be saved in order to create a certain impression of the organization. The records will generally be those of management. However, given that management perspectives and ideologies may be the focus of study, these methods can prove very fruitful.

 Activity Looking at archival material

Get hold of the annual report of your own organization, or look at any annual company report from the net.

- What kinds of issues are reported here? What does this say about the image the company is trying to portray?
- Look at the photographs in the report. How are employees and customers/clients portrayed? What does this say about the culture of the company?
- Look at the language that is employed in the report. List all the adjectives in the introduction. What kind of image are they trying to portray about the company?
- Is there anything negative here in tone, language, or image? What is it and what does it imply about the company?

2.4.9 Conclusions

There are a variety of methods that work psychologist may use to gather information in order to explore research questions. Each method has its distinct uses and applications, its advantages over other methods, and its problems and difficulties.

In many research studies, it is appropriate to use multiple methods, and to balance the specific impression of experience offered by different techniques. This is termed **triangulation**, where different views of the research area are gained by using different methods, including feeding back results to participants for comment.

 KEY LEARNING POINTS

- Researchers in work psychology may choose from a range of data collection methods.
- Selection of a method will be determined by the aims of the study, the nature of the participants, and also on practical and resource considerations.
- Each method is suited to different circumstances and situations, and the researcher must carefully judge the appropriateness of the methods they choose, in line with their research aims.
- Research is an interactive process, and researchers must gauge how demand characteristics will affect the validity of the methods employed.
- Researchers may use a combination of methods in a single investigation and capitalize on the key advantages of each technique.

Method	Principal uses	Positive features	Negative features
Observation	Analysing groups and social interaction.	Focuses on spontaneous and ongoing action	Hawthorne effect. Bias and perceptual error.
Laboratory experiments	Exploring differential effect of variables and conditions	Researcher/ experimenter control	Artificial; Hawthorne effect. Demand characteristics. Experimenter effects.
Quasi-experiments	Exploring differential effect of variables and conditions	Vibrant, real life unfolding	Lack of experimental control. Experimenter effects. Observer error.
Interviews	Pilot work. Exploring experience of work.	Allows exploration of subjective experience	Faking. Demand characteristics. Memory effects.
Surveys and questionnaires	Exploration of attitudes and opinions. Research work with large samples	Allows standardized questioning of large samples	Faking. Memory distortions. Low response rates, therefore unrepresentativeness of responses
Focus groups	Pilot work	Allows observation of interaction	Group dynamics may contaminate effects.
Diary studies	Examination of social and psychological processes over time	Less reliant on memory	Participant fatigue. Contamination of spontaneous process. Self-consciousness of participants.
Archival data	Historical change	Objective, allows long-term analysis	Bias of records. Partiality of keeper of records. Issues of access.
Discourse analysis	Exploring subjective meaning	Allows exploration of varieties of levels of meaning	Is the account a true one? Power relations between researcher and participant may mitigate against honesty and openness.

2.5 Analysing data

The generation of data by these diverse methods is only the start of the research process. Data must be analysed in relation to the original research aims and objectives, to explore how far the research questions have been answered. This chapter will explore some common approaches to the analysis of results, but further information can be found in the section on recommended reading, and in the recommended websites, listed at the end of the chapter.

2.5.1 Types of data

Different methods produce different types of data. A distinction is generally made between **primary** and **secondary** data.

Primary data is generated afresh by the researcher; secondary data is that which has been collected by some other agent, and subsequently used by the researcher. Archival data would fall into this category.

As discussed earlier, data may be quantitative, in which case numerical information will be generated, or qualitative, in which case data that include un-quantifiable information will be produced. The nature of the analysis will depend on the sort of data that has been produced.

2.5.2 Correlation

Correlation allows exploration of the relationship between two or more variables. In many of the studies in this chapter, correlation has been the main tool of analysis. For example, the diary study by Butler et al. (2005) used correlation to explore measures of job satisfaction, work-life balance, and conflict at work.

Correlation establishes the co-variation between variables. The statistic produced from the analysis is termed the **correlation coefficient**. This varies from unity (1.00: a positive correlation) through zero (no correlation) to minus one (-1.00: a negative correlation).

Two variables are positively correlated when one variable increases, the other increases correspondingly. They are negatively correlated when increases in one variable are associated with corresponding decreases in the other variable. In Butler's (2005) study of work-life balance, a correlation of -0.44 (negative) was observed between perceptions of demands at work, and the perceived amount of personal control with life: the higher the demands at work, the lower the sense of being in control of one's life. A statistical correlation between variables does not necessarily imply causality, and work psychologists must explore their data carefully in order to establish why a certain pattern of results has occurred.

 Activity Correlation

Predict whether the correlation between each of these pairs of variables might be positive or negative:

- Number of emails received per day and physiological measure of stress.
- Bonus payments and employee turnover.
- Hours of overtime worked and romantic affairs at work.
- Number of changes of manager per year and departmental absenteeism.
- Redundancies and absenteeism.

2.5.3 Searching for causality in data: moderation and mediation

Research in work psychology often seeks to understand or establish causes in observed patterns of results. In the psychological realm, behaviour and experience are more usually the result of the complex interplay or interaction of multiple variables. Reuben Baron and David Kenny (1986) have attempted to highlight the importance of such complex interactions in the area of psychology in their focus upon **moderator** and **mediator** variables. A moderator is a variable that affects the direction and/or strength of a relationship between an independent and dependent variable. For example, many studies have found that stressful life events (for example death of a spouse or loss of employment) are associated with physical illness. However, studies have demonstrated that the nature of the events differentially affects the impact on health. For example, it matters greatly if the events are perceived as within or beyond the control of the person, for example death of a partner, as opposed to divorce (Stern et al. 1982).

A mediator is a variable which directly affects the impact of an independent variable on a dependent variable; for example, studies of training may find that managerial competence increases with age; however the increase is *caused* by a third variable: wisdom or **tacit knowledge**.

Analysing qualitative data: content analysis

The analysis of qualitative data can take many forms, and will depend on the aims of the researcher, and upon their own epistemological approach. A common technique is termed **content analysis**. This allows the researcher to classify responses to interviews or open-ended questions into specific categories or groups.

The nature of the categories may be determined and decided by the original research questions, or may emerge from careful analysis of the data itself. For example, in a Finnish study of ward sisters' attitudes towards the training and development of nurses in their team, Koivula and Paunonen-Ilmonen (2002) used open-ended questions to elicit perceptions. One question was: 'What problems do you identify in developing nurses on your ward?'

Responses were classified into three categories: 'resources' (lack of time); 'the work organization' (access to information and the constraints of working times); and 'the working community' (relations with doctors and the hospital administration. Using these categories the responses of the sisters were coded and classified, and the results demonstrated a commonality of experience and perceptions.

Pause for thought
Think of a mediator that might affect the correlation between reactions to unemployment and job level.

Activity **Analysing field observation data**

Try out some field observation methods, working in small groups. Allocate specific tasks to team members for observation and recording of specific events.

- Observe people negotiating a major road crossing which is controlled by traffic lights. How many people 'jaywalk'—or cross when the lights are against them? Record the demographic characteristics of the jay walkers. Are they male/female? How old are they?
- Observe people in canteen at work or in a university at lunchtime. What size of groups can you see? How many people are on their own? In pairs? In larger groups? Are they male or female?
- Do women behave differently in public spaces to men?

  Observe men and women working in a university library. Make a note of any gestures that are used when people are working alone.

  Classify your data, and record it in table form. What trends do you observe?

2.6 Critical issues

2.6.1 Cultural context of research

Research in work psychology is part of broader social processes concerned with government, education, and the management of work organizations. These institutions are characterized by social divisions in terms of class, ethnicity, culture and religion, gender, age, sexual orientation, and disability.

Work psychology has been criticized for its focus on the experience of white, middle-class males in the development of theory about work behaviour (Hollway 1991) This bias comes from the nature of samples used in research, and from the assumptions of researchers, who tend to emanate from certain social groups themselves. However, by becoming aware of the narrowness of its focus, work psychologists can strive to become more inclusive in their studies.

2.6.2 Gender bias

One example of cultural contamination of psychological research is that of gender bias.

The study of sex differences has always been a research interest in psychology, but work psychology has tended to ignore women and women's experience in the generation of theory and research. For example, theories of career development are generally silent about the impact of family life upon career choices, and have used male experience as the 'norm' (Arnold et al. 2005).

2.6.3 Ethnicity and research

Etlyn Kenny and Rob Briner (2007) have suggested that the employment experiences of different ethnic groups have been under-researched by British psychologists. In a survey of research published between 1952 and 2005 they found only 2 per cent of studies focused upon ethnicity in the workplace, despite the growth of employees from ethnic minorities during the same period. Most of this work was concerned with recruitment and selection issues, leaving many aspects of working life experience relatively unexplored. Kenny and Briner point out that current theory in work psychology is impoverished by its lack of focus on issues of ethnicity.

2.6.4 Ethics

Psychology in general has had to counter many ethical issues about the conduct of research. In asking people to become research participants, the researcher in work psychology is almost always asking people to disclose personal information, which may sometimes lead to distress. Researchers must adhere to ethical principles in order to ensure that participation in their studies does not lead to any negative outcomes. For example, the assurance of anonymity and confidentiality is one essential requirement.

Pause for thought
Do religious beliefs mediate attitudes to being unemployed? Suggest a method for exploring this.

Deception

The experimental method often requires that participants are naive about the purpose of research, in order to ensure that responses are spontaneous. This raises the concern about whether it is ever justified to deceive people in order to research some area.

Participants in work psychology studies are in a special position in this respect, as frequently they are not volunteers in the research project, but are participating by virtue of the fact that they are employed by a company that has commissioned, or been selected for research. Researchers have a responsibility to ensure that freedom of choice is protected for their research participants.

Non-maleficence

Pause for thought
How might a researcher ensure that employees taking part in a research project in the workplace had freedom to choose whether to participate or not?

Medical research ethics requires researchers to ensure that procedures do not cause harm to participants. Although psychologists are unlikely to use techniques that cause physical pain or injury, it is possible that participants may feel stress, threats to self-esteem, or some other psychological impact from research interventions.

Procedures for briefing research participants before they agree to take part in studies, and for debriefing them and discussing their results after participation should be part of the research design.

Privacy and data protection

Participants in work psychology research are often asked to give personal details information. Researchers therefore have an obligation to respect the privacy of their participants, and to ensure that any information they hold is kept securely. This is required by both UK and EU law (Data Protection Act 1999).

Ethical codes

In order to ensure that the design and conduct of research does not lead to negative effects for participants, professional codes of conduct have been developed by national associations of psychologists and health professionals, for example the Americal Psychologcial Association and the British Psychological Society, and the Société Française de Psychologie. Individual universities and colleges also have research ethics committees which scrutinize and approve proposals.

2.6.5 The role of the researcher in the practice of work psychology

Researchers in work psychology will operate in a variety of contexts, under different contracts and conditions. They may be employed as academics in university departments, and their research may be funded by that university, or by government bodies. Work psychologists may be also be directly employed by organizations in the public or private sector on a consultancy or full-time basis. This highlights the issue that there are multiple stakeholders in any research process, including the researcher and their team, professional bodies, the owners and management of the commissioning organization, and the research participants.

This working context may create ethical dilemmas for researchers. These might include a consideration of the impact of the research process on the working lives of participants. Who 'owns' the findings of such research?

Research is not just an intellectual activity; it takes place within a social, cultural, and economic context. The impact on this context upon the work of researchers in work psychology must be taken into account to appreciate the process as a whole.

 KEY LEARNING POINTS

- Research takes place in a social and cultural context which conditions and affects the process.
- Research activity will reflect the surrounding culture that generates it, thus divisions of gender, class, and ethnicity may permeate research processes.
- Research with people generates ethical concerns and dilemmas, and researchers must be guided by the codes of practice of their professional organizations.
- Research takes place within communities, and researchers can gain support from discussion with colleagues and peers.

Case illustration
Codes of conduct: the British Psychological Society

The British Psychology Society Code of Ethics and Conduct (2006) is founded on the ethical principles of respect, competence, responsibility, and integrity. It contains sections applicable to psychologists working in different contexts.

It contains a section dedicated to ethics and research (section 3.3) which includes the following items: Psychologists should:

- Consider all research from the standpoint of research participants, for the purpose of eliminating potential risks to psychological well-being, physical health, personal values, or dignity.
- Inform research participants from the first contact that their right to withdraw at any time is not affected by the receipt or offer of any financial compensation or other inducements for participation.
- Debrief research participants at the conclusion of their participations, in order to inform them of the outcomes and nature of the research, to identify an unforeseen harm, discomfort, or misconceptions, and in order to arrange for assistance as needed.

Questions
- Comment on this list of ethical guidelines. Are there any ethical aspects that it misses?
- How can work organizations ensure that researchers adhere to ethical guidelines?

Chapter summary

- Work psychology is a scientific discipline characterized by research activity, which is the bedrock of the generation of knowledge, concepts, and understanding.

- There are a variety of approaches to the research enterprise and selection will depend on the theoretical perspective of the researcher, as well as their specific aims in conducting the research.

- There are a variety of research designs, and researchers choose approaches that best fit their aims and objectives.

- Researchers may choose from a variety of data-gathering methods, and in practice a plurality of methods may be employed in a single investigation.

- There are different techniques for the analysis of quantitative and qualitative data. Care must be taken that statistical tests employed are appropriate to the research data.

- Research is a social activity, and must be viewed in its historical and cultural context, in order to appreciate debates and controversies.

- Researchers in work psychology are employed in a variety of public and private sector contexts. Business strategy and resource considerations may affect the conduct of their role. This may result in professional dilemmas and conflict.

- The conduct of research may generate ethical concerns and dilemmas. Codes of conduct have been devised and are applied by professional bodies in work psychology.

Part I

Assess your learning

Review questions

1 What are the main elements of the scientific method?

2 What is a field study? What are the strengths and weaknesses of this method?

3 What are 'demand characteristics' in psychological research? How can the researcher reduce the impact of this effect?

4 What is participant observation, and what are the main positive and negative features of this research technique?

5 Describe one qualitative research method. State how data generated by this method could be analysed.

6 Describe two critical points that have been made against the use of experiments in work psychology.

7 How can interviewer bias be reduced and controlled?

8 In the context of the study or stress at work, think of an example of a moderator variable and a mediator variable.

9 Describe two different types of diary study technique. When would it be appropriate to use diary techniques in work psychology research?

10 List three ethical problems that may arise from the conduct of work psychology research. How might such problems be ameliorated?

Assignments

ASSIGNMENT 1: WRITE AN ESSAY ON THE FOLLOWING QUESTION:
A researcher wishes to examine the impact of redundancy on psychological well-being. What quantitative and qualitative methods might be appropriate for such a study? What would be the relative advantages and disadvantages of each approach?

ASSIGNMENT 2: RESEARCH INTO ABSENTEEISM
The HR manager of an **SME** in Leeds, which produces and markets computer games, observes from figures prepared by his department that labour turnover of the last twelve months is up 25 per cent, over the last annual analysis. Examining the figures, he observes that the highest turnover is in the sales department, where a high proportion of the staff are female.

He wants to understand why the figures have increased.

- Design a study to explore reasons for the observed increase.

- State what your research hypothesis would be.

What methods of data collection would be appropriate? Give full reasons for your choice.

Further reading

Bryman, A., and Bell, E. (2003) *Business Research Methods.* **Oxford: Oxford University Press.**
A highly comprehensive survey of techniques for researchers in business organizations.

Breakwell, G., Hammond, S., Fife-Schaw, C., and Smith, J. A. (eds.) (2006) *Research Methods in Psychology* **(3rd edn.). London: Sage.**
A thorough and critical discussion of key research designs and methods in general psychology, with a strong emphasis on qualitative methods and techniques. This volume contains good coverage of methods of analysis for psychological research data.

Work psychology in practice
Education versus on-the-job learning

How is expertise and competence on the job best achieved? A debate rages about the value of experience over education. In the world of business, it is often argued that on-the-job training is superior to classroom learning.

Barbara Summers, Trevor Williamson, and Daniel Read (2005) conducted a study to investigate the relative effectiveness of education and experience in making credit decisions. They compared the accuracy of credit ratings made by four groups of participants who varied in their experience of credit management.

Group 1 were experienced credit managers, who had gained an average of eleven years' on-the-job experience. These managers were actively involved in professional updating in their field.

Group 2 and 3 were lecturers (who had little practical experience in the area, an average of twelve months only) and students in finance and accounting, who were familiar with the literature on this area.

Group 4 was a control group who had neither relevant experience nor education. They were all graduate students or administrative staff in the psychology department. There were twenty people in each group.

All groups were given the same information about a set of six companies, and were asked to make the following judgements. Firstly, did they think the company would fail? If they thought it would fail, they were asked to estimate the length of time before failure. Secondly, they were asked to assess the likelihood of late payments. Finally, participants were asked if they would grant credit to the company. The companies used were real, and information about their performance was therefore known.

Results showed that lecturers had the highest mean number of correct corporate failure predictions, followed by the students. The credit managers and lay people scored less well. There were no differences between the groups in accuracy of predicted time to failure.

Similarly, there were no significant differences in the accuracy of predictions about late payment by companies.

The authors conclude that their results suggest that education can be a more effective route to expertise than experience. 'Credit managers never did any better, and often did worse than students and lecturers who had no experience, but at least some book learning' (p. 256).

(Adapted from Summers, Williamson, and Read (2005).

Questions

- Do you feel that these results would hold for areas other than credit rating?
- Comment of the way they have operationalized the qualities of 'education' and 'experience'.
- What is the role of the control group in this study?
- What other methods of data collection might the researchers have used to explore their hypothesis?
- If you were replicating this study, what changes would you make to the design?
- What ethical issues are raised by this study?

 **Online Resource Centre**

Visit the supporting online resource centre for additional material which will help you with your research, essays, and assignments, or you may find these additional resources helpful when revising for exams.

http://www.oxfordtextbooks.co.uk/orc/matthewman/

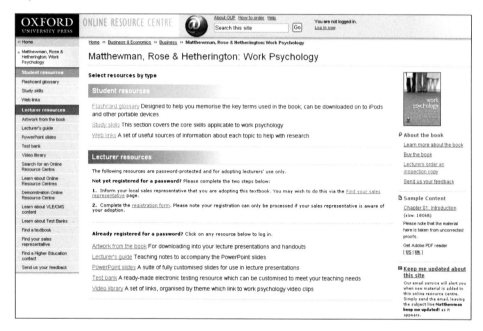

References

Arnold, J., Silvester, J., Patterson, F., Robertson, I., Cooper, C., and Burnes, B. (2005) *Work Psychology: Understanding Human Behaviour in the Workplace* (4th edn.). Harlow: Prentice Hall.

Baron, R. M., and Kenny, D. A. (1986) The mediator-moderator variable distinction in social psychological research: conceptual, strategic, and statistical considerations. *Journal of Personality and Social Psychology*, 51/6: 1173–82.

Belbin, M. (1981) *Management Teams*. London: Heinemann.

Bishop, V., Korczynski, M., and Cohen, L. (2005) The invisibility of violence: constructing violence out of the job centre workplace in the UK. *Work, Employment and Society*, 19/3: 583–602.

Bolger, N., Davis, A., and Rafaeli, E. (2003) Diary methods: capturing life as it is lived. *Annual Review of Psychology*, 54: 579–616.

Burr, V. (1995) *Introduction to Social Constructionism*. London: Routledge.

Burt, K., and Oaksford, M. (1999) Qualitative methods: beyond beliefs and desires. *The Psychologist*, 12/7: 323–35.

Butler, A. B., Grzywacz, J. G., Bass, B. L. and Linney, K. D. (2005) Extending the demands-control model: a daily diary study of job characteristics, work-family conflict and work-family facilitation. *Journal of Occupational and Organizational Psychology*, 78: 155–69.

Cooper, C. L., and Lewis, S. (1993) *The Workplace Revolution: Managing Today's Dual-Career Families*. London: Kogan Page.

Darley, J., and Latane, B. (1968) Bystander interventions in emergencies. *Journal of Personality & Social Psychology*, 8: 377–83.

Duncan, D. (2005) Scientific occupational psychology: a personal Odyssey. *History and Philosophy of Psychology*, 7/1: 70–8.

Evers, W. J. G., Brouwers, A., Tomic, W. (2006) A quasi-experimental study on management coaching effectiveness. *Consulting Psychology Journal: Practice and Research*, 58/3: 174–82.

Fife-Schaw, C. (2006) Quasi-experimental designs. In Breakwell et al. (see above).

Furnham, A. (2005) *The Psychology of Behaviour at Work* (2nd edn.) Hove: Psychology Press.

Garrett-Peters, R. D. (2005) *Coping with Unemployment: Strategies of Self-Concept Repair among Displaced Managers and Professionals.* Philadelphia: Society for the Study of Social Problems.

Gillespie, N. A., Walsh, M., Winefield, A. H., Dua, J., and Stough, C. (2001) Occupational stress in universities: staff perceptions of the causes, consequences and moderators of stress. *Work & Stress*, 15/1: 53–72.

Goffman, E. (1961) *Asylums*. New York: Doubleday Anchor.

Grandey, A. A., Cordeiro, B. L., and Crouter, A. C. (2005) A longitudinal and multi-source test of the work-family conflict and job satisfaction relationship. *Journal of Occupational and Organizational Psychology*, 78: 305–23.

HSE (Health and Safety Executive) (2008) http://www.hse.gov.uk/statistics/overall/fatl/0607.pdf

Holland, J. (1973) *Making Vocational Choices: A Theory of Careers.* Englewood Cliffs, NJ: Prentice-Hall.

Hollway, W. (1991) *Work Psychology and Organizational Behaviour.* London: Sage.

Johnson, P., and Cassell, C. (2001) Epistemology and work psychology: new agendas. *Journal of Occupational and Organizational Psychology*, 74: 125–43.

Kahn, R. L., and Cannell, C. F. (1957) *The Dynamics of Interviewing.* John Wiley.

Kenny, E. J., and Briner, R. B. (2007) Ethnicity and behaviour in organisations: a review of British research. *Journal of Occupational and Organizational Psychology*, 80: 437–57.

Kirton, G. (2006) The discourse of diversity in unionised contexts: views from trade union equality officers. *Personnel Review*, 35/4: 431–42.

Kniffin, K. M., and Wilson, D. S. (2005) Utilities of gossip across organizational levels: multilevel selection, free-riders and teams. *Human Nature*, 16/3: 278–92.

Koivula, M., and Paunonen-Ilmonen, M. (2002) Ward sisters' objectives in developing nursing and problems with development. *Journal of Nursing Management* 9/5: 287–94.

Kuhn, T. S. (1962) *The Structure of Scientific Revolutions*. Chicago: University of Chicago Press.

Labov, W. (1969) The logic of non-standard English. In N. Kelly (ed.), *'Tinker, Taylor.'* Harmondsworth: Penguin Books.

Lardent, G. L. (1991) Pilots who crash: personality constructs underlying accident prone behaviour of fighter pilots. *Multivariate Experimental Clinical Research*, 10: 1–25.

Lee, T. (1998) Assessment of safety culture at a nuclear processing plant. *Work & Stress*, 12/3: 217–37.

Lippitt, R., and White, R. K. (1947) An experimental study of leadership and group life. In T. M. Newcomb and E. L. Hartley (eds.), *Readings in Social Psychology*. New York: Holt, Rinehart and Winston.

McKenna, E. (2000) *Business Psychology and Organisational Behaviour* (3rd edn.). East Sussex: The Psychology Press.

Marshall, J. (1995) *Women Managers Moving on: Exploring Career and Life Choices*. London: Routledge.

Michaels, C. A. (1995) Pregnancy in the workplace: does pregnancy affect performance appraisal ratings? *Journal of Business & Psychology*, 10/2: 155–67.

Muchinsky, P. M. (2006) *Psychology Applied to Work*. Belmont, CA: Wadsworth Thomson.

Richardson, F. C., and Fowers, B. J. (1997) Critical theory, postmodernism, and hermeneutics: insights for critical psychology. In D. Fox and I. Prilleltensky (eds.), *Critical Psychology: An Introduction*. London: Sage.

Rosenthal, R., and Rosnow, R. L. (eds.) (1969) *Artefacts in Behavioural Research*. New York: Academic Press.

Schaufeli, W. B., Taris, T. W., and van Rhenen, W. (2008) Workaholism, burnout and work engagement: three of a kind or three different kinds of employee well-being? *Applied Psychology: An International Review*, 57/2: 173–203.

Schwarz, N., Strack, F., Hippler., H., and Bishop, G. (1991) The impact of administrative mode on response effects in survey measurement. *Applied Cognitive Psychology*, 5/3: 193–212.

Sheridan, F. (2007) Gender, language and the workplace: an exploratory study. *Women in Management Review*, 22/4: 319–36.

Spitzmuller, C., Glenn, D., Barr, C. D., Rogelberg, S. G., and Daniel, P. (2006) 'If you treat me right, I reciprocate': examining the role of exchange in organisational survey response. *Journal of Organizational Behaviour*, 27/1: 19–35.

Stern, G. S., McCants, T. R., and Pettine, P. W. (1982) The relative contribution of controllable and uncontrollable life events to stress and illness. *Personality and Social Psychology Bulletin*, 8: 140–5.

Summers, B., Williamson, T., and Read, D. (2005) Does method of acquisition affect the quality of expert judgement? A comparison of education with on-the-job learning. *Journal of Occupational and Organizational Psychology*, 77: 237–58.

Taylor, H., and Fieldman, G. (2005) The impact of a threatening e-mail reprimand on the recipient's blood pressure. *Journal of Managerial Psychology*, 20/1: 43–50.

Vink, P. (1997) Improving office work: a participatory ergonomic experiment in a naturalistic setting. *Ergonomics*, 40/4: 435–49.

Waddington, D. (1994) Participant observation. In C. Cassell and G. Symon (eds.), *Qualitative Methods in Organisational Research: A Practical Guide*. Thousand Oaks, CA: Sage.

Wilkinson, S., and Kitzinger, C. (eds.) (1996) *Representing the Other*. London: Sage.

Wood, T. R., and Williams, R. J. (2007) How much money do you spend on gambling? The comparative validity of question wordings used to assess gambling expenditure. *International Journal of Social Research Methodology*, 10/1: 63–77.

Part II
People at work

Chapter 3
Personality and individual differences

Natasha Marinković Grba

Chapter objectives

As a result of reading this chapter and using the additional web-based material you should be able to:

- Describe the elements that comprise personality.
- Distinguish between implicit and scientific theories of personality.
- Understand main personality models and in what way are they significant to work psychology.
- Recognize the areas of work where personality assessment is commonly used.
- Be aware of the significant role intelligence plays in the workplace.
- Critically evaluate emotional intelligence and its application to modern business.
- Identify what is meant by creative individual at work.

Work psychology in practice
People watching—episode 1

University of East London: Campus cafeteria

Have you ever caught yourself lingering over your table or a spot in a busy public place and watching/ listening to other people with immense interest? Have you ever become consumed with the characters of complete strangers, trying to guess who they are and what do they do for living? Here is a snapshot of a busy morning in the campus cafeteria of one eminent university in London, about ten years ago. Take a look at the three young hopefuls sitting at a table in the left corner. They each arrived that day to put their names down for a new optional module in work psychology.

Ingolf is loud as always, so even if you were minding your business thus far, you could not but stop and listen to him as his words seem to be intended for a wider audience. 'I love the coffee here—they have most amazing cups. I must get those for my office in Harley Street when I open it one day . . . Can't wait to start milking those celebrities . . . They'll all be coming to me for life coaching—remember what I said! Or why not become one of them myself?! West End, Hollywood—here I come! . . . Milla, how do you enrol for this module? Oh dear, I hope I'm not late for it—psychology always fascinated me . . . '

Milla says little, nods often and you can tell she's a bit embarrassed by being at the table that attracts so much attention. She's wondering how she can cope with yet another year at University. She heard that assessment for this module might include public presentations—that's the last thing she needs: complete embarrassment in front of other students. Also the professor is known for being strict—'I'll never get this degree!' Milla sighs. 'The statistics aren't encouraging either; apparently, 1 in 3 students had to take a resit last semester.'

Orlagh doesn't seem to be listening to either of her friends. She's got a killer headache. As a matter of fact she looks as if she's fed up with both or just fed up. 'I'm not sure what I'm doing here? I should've chosen something more profitable than studying psychology.' . . . 'What's the point, when everything revolves around money and power in this world!?' she exclaims angrily.

Questions

- From your brief encounter with these three students, try to analyse what makes them different from each other.
- Then, take a brave step further and make a guess about the details that are not included in the text: such as their likes and dislikes, the kind of clothes they might be wearing, their social life?
- What do you think made Ingolf, Milla, and Orlagh behave in this cafeteria the way they did? Who does seem more oriented to the outer world of things and events (extrovert) and who to the inner world of ideas and concepts (introvert)?
- According to your analysis and conclusions so far, could you suggest what line of profession would suit each one of them?
- If you're still in that cafeteria, lingering on to hear more about our three different characters and have even become curious about what became of them in the past ten years—then you have an affinity for the psychology of individual differences and personality. Find out what they are doing today, ten years on, at the end of this chapter.

3.1 Introduction

Individual differences are important in the work environment as potential predictors of training effectiveness, individual responses to stress, and overall productivity. People's personality, abilities, intelligence, background, attitudes, perceptions, motivation, culture, roles they play, gender, race, and disability are amongst those fundamental factors that make us into individuals. This chapter takes a close look at some of these characteristics linking them with organizational behaviour, while other factors are examined elsewhere in the book (Chapter 4 on Perceptions and Attitudes at Work, Chapter 5 on Motivation at Work, and Chapter 8 on Leadership at Work).

The chapter starts by defining **personality** and goes on to investigate some major theoretical perspectives of personality: humanistic, behavioural, cognitive-behavioural, type, and trait. This is followed by the definition of **intelligence** and its application at workplace.

One of the newer concepts, a personality component: **emotional intelligence**, which seems to have caught the particular interest of organizational psychologists and management training programmers, is also explored in some detail.

Finally, the chapter looks at another individual quality that is highly sought by business today: **creativity** at work.

3.2 Definition of personality

There are many definitions of **personality** and as many theoretical approaches. Major theories of personality are outlined in this chapter in more or less depth according to their relevance to workplace. Generally, there is an agreement between most of the theorists that personality is a complex phenomenon built on a wide range of the physical, mental, ethical, and social qualities specific for each individual (McKenna 2006).

This specific content and composition of various natural and acquired impulses, habits, interests, ideals, mannerisms, opinions, and beliefs is projected out to the world and is how we present ourselves to others. However, the special mix that makes our personality is also what makes us, individuals unique and distinguishable from each other. All the aspects that form personality are relatively stable and enduring; therefore, at least theoretically, it should be possible to form predictions about people's behaviour based on our knowledge and understanding of their personalities (Wright et al. 1970; Bettencourt et al. 2006). This is why business has always flirted with the theory of personality and has especially shown an interest in personality assessments. Wouldn't it be wonderful if business could simply pick future employees in the sure knowledge that they would be productive under pressure, loyal to the company, creative and enthusiastic workers? To what extent that is possible and how reliable predictors of behaviour at work are will be amongst the topics discussed in this chapter.

3.2.1 Theoretical approaches to personality

This section looks at informal and everyday theories of personality, that all of us use to make assessments of the people we meet; followed by more detailed examination of major scientific theories of personality.

Informal theories of personality

We all use informal or **'implicit' theories of personality** to make assessments or form opinions about the people we meet in our everyday life. The implicit personality theories are well embedded into us and themselves are part of our personalities. They stem from **personal constructs** and incorporate attitudes, beliefs, and **values** of the culture we grow up in. (Also see Chapter 4: Perceptions and Attitudes at Work.)

Informal theories affect the judgements we make about people's personalities. Most of us form some sort of stereotypical expectations of gender differences or how other cultures will behave; for example: an urban child raised by series of different foster parents is expected to behave differently in some respects from a child raised by a family in middle-class suburbs. Furthermore, many of us form occupational **stereotypes**. (See Activity).

Pause for thought
Consider the influence of the culture you grew up in on your personality.

 Activity **Occupational stereotypes**

Fill in the right column of the table below, writing down the first things that spring to your mind when thinking about the indicated occupation on the left.

An occupation	The description of the person
A professor in quantum physics	
A geriatric nurse	
A fireman	

Our implicit shortcuts are useful to us, as they help us make sense of the complex world around us. We use our everyday theories of personality and make quick references to them to sort out people in groups and to pigeon-hole numerous stimuli that come our way. However, sometimes these theories can bias our opinions of other people and influence poor decision making. Examples of this are the Halo and Horns effect (see Figure 3.1) and interviewers are regularly warned of this most common human mistake (see Chapter 12 on Assessing People at Work).

Scientific theories of personality

In order to take a scientific approach to personality it is necessary to take a step back from ourselves. The psychologists sometimes refer to this 'purification' of all implicit, everyday theories and stereotypes as putting all previous knowledge (explicit and implicit) into brackets, in order to start examining the research topic with a clear, fresh mind (Allport 1937; Fontana 2000). Furthermore, unlike informal theories, scientific personality models involve scientific measurement and assessment methods that arise from these models.

Different theorists have emphasized different aspects. Though, not all personality theories are relevant to psychology at work. For example, although psychoanalytic theory has important uses in certain clinical situations and it has influenced some of our own implicit theories of personality (how often do we say: 'He's in denial of his drinking' or connect hate with love), the psychoanalytic techniques are seldom used in selection or training and development. Some other theoretical approaches to personality have more applications to business and therefore are examined next.

The humanistic approach

The humanistic theories differ widely in the concepts on which they focus, but they share following views:

1 Each of us is largely responsible for what happens to us, or the cards are in our hands and we are not merely driven and controlled by dark forces within our personalities.

Figure 3.1. Horns and halo effect

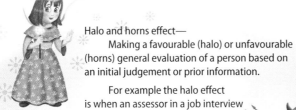

Halo and horns effect—
Making a favourable (halo) or unfavourable (horns) general evaluation of a person based on an initial judgement or prior information.

For example the halo effect is when an assessor in a job interview decides that a candidate is best for the job based on the first impressions and the fact that the candidate attended the same university as the assessor.

The horns effect would be when a candidate is late for an interview and the assessor decides they have poor time management and no respect and are therefore not serious enough to be considered for the job, despite the information derived in the interview itself.

2 The focus of personality development is on the present and traumatic experiences from our childhood do not have to have an overwhelming effect on our personalities.

3 Humanistic approach stresses the importance of 'personal growth' stating that people are not content with simply meeting their current needs but wish to progress toward bigger goals such as becoming the best they can be: or achieving self-actualization (Rogers 1980; Maslow 1970).

Self-actualized people are those who accept themselves as they are, recognizing their strengths as well as their weaknesses. Such people are in touch with their own personalities and as result less inhibited and less likely to conform than most of us. Self-actualized people would retain their childhood curiosity and fascination with the world. For them boredom is a rare state of mind as they see each day as an exciting adventure. Finally, self-actualized people at times have 'peak experiences' or instances in which they have powerful feelings of unity with the universe with waves of great power and wonder. Such experiences are linked to further personal growth as, following them, they report feeling more spontaneous and more appreciative of life (Maslow 1970).

 KEY LEARNING POINTS

- Implicit theories of personality are beliefs people hold about personality characteristics likely to coexist in the same person.
- Scientific theories of personality involve scientific measurement and assessment methods that arise from these theories.

The behaviourist and cognitive-behaviourist approaches

The behaviourist approach   The behaviourist approach in psychology understands us as a consequence of conditioning. We become conditioned to respond to our environment as a result of learning by association or operant conditioning. Learning by association is attributed to Ivan Pavlov in the 1920s and his theory of **classical conditioning**, while **operant conditioning**, or learning by way of reward and unpleasant consequence, is credited to B. F. Skinner in 1950s.

Early behaviourists argued that most human behaviour is conditioned or driven by **reinforcers** such as money and social praise (Skinner 1974). For example, people work for money because they know that it will result in food and other direct comforts. Over the course of a lifetime, people accumulate innumerable associations between stimuli they encounter, their behavioural responses to them, and the **reinforcement** or **punishment** that results. Since each person's history of exposure to such environmental contingencies varies, each person's behaviour will also differ. Thus a person who had a frightening experience with an in-class presentation as a student might avoid presentations in the future; if the experience was particularly punishing, they may develop a phobia that has an overly strong influence on their behaviour. At the same time, a person who had had mostly positive experiences with presentations would behave differently when speaking publicly.

Furthermore, the behaviourist approach emphasized the central role of learning in forming personality. The **reinforcement theory** underpins training programmes concerned with developing skills through instruction and **feedback** (Armstrong 2003; B. Wilson 2005; K. C. Wilson 2005). Employees going through such programmes are conditioned to respond and receive immediate feedback, making step-by-step progress, which takes them to a positive outcome.

The cognitive-behaviourist approach   As opposed to early advocates of behaviourist approach who considered external conditions the only determinants of human behaviour and personality development, most modern psychologists take into account internal factors, such as: motives, intentions, goals, or traits and especially aspects of cognition. The cognitive-behaviourist approach sees people as active learners who acquire knowledge and understanding by being exposed to different situations and by solving problems. This approach is utilized when developing learning and training programmes that include: self-directed learning, **personal development planning** activities, and discovery learning processes with the help of facilitators, coaches, or mentors. Armstrong (2003) notes the

Pause for thought
Think about famous writers, artists, revolutionaries, politicians, scientists, or just people who surround you. Who would you identify as a fully self-actualized person as described by Maslow, and why?

practical implication that these techniques have had on modern learning, such as e-learning. Learners go on to internalize and enrich their knowledge by examining case studies, taking on projects, and solving problems in given activities (Cannon 2004). Similarly, today's textbooks aim not only to present the learning material but also to get the reader to actively participate in learning process.

Most personality theorists now believe that behaviours are acquired and modified through learning (Plomin et al. 2001). Furthermore, there is general consensus that cognitive factors play an important role in human behaviour (Cooke and Sheeran 2004). This approach has been successfully used in clinical settings to modify maladaptive forms of behaviour. Cognitive Behaviour Therapy (CBT) has also proved a particularly popular and effective means of counselling and coaching in organizational stress management programmes (van den Bossche and Houtman 2004; also see Chapter 14 on Psychological Health in the Workplace).

Finally, this approach is significant for work psychology as the techniques based on it are commonly used in selection process and involve: situational tests and work simulations such as: in-tray exercises, presentations, leaderless group discussions, and role plays.

Pause for thought
Identify a learning technique utilized by the authors of this book that works well for you.

KEY LEARNING POINTS

- In the behaviourist approach, behaviour patterns are seen in relation to the external conditions that evoke, maintain, or modify them.

- In the cognitive-behaviourist approach the greater acknowledgement is given to variables within the person.

The type approach

Personality type theory aims to classify people into distinct categories, i.e. this type or that. Personality types are synonymous with 'personality styles'.

Types refer to categories that are distinct and discontinuous. A person is either one or the other. In order to clearly recognize the difference between types and traits, the example of the personality dimension of 'introversion' is considered next. Thus, introversion can be viewed differently depending on the theoretical approach in use:

The personality type approach states a person is either an introvert or an extrovert; while personality **trait approach** emphasizes that a person can be anywhere on a continuum ranging from introversion to extroversion, with most people clustering in the middle, and fewer people towards the extremes.

Extroversion–introversion typology   Devised by Carl Gustav Jung (1875–1961) this is probably the most widely used and amongst the best known in everyday life. As with personality types, according to Jung people are either extrovert or introvert. The two orientations are seen as distinct categories, each having its own value. The extrovert is oriented to the outer world of things and events, while the introvert is oriented to the inner world of thoughts and ideas (Jung 1933).

BIG4 personality functions   Further development of Jung's personality typology is found in the work of Isabel Myers and Katherine Briggs. They developed the **Myers-Briggs Type Indicator** (MBTI), a questionnaire which is widely used in business and training, and which provides information and exercises for better understanding one's own personality type and others with whom the individual interacts and works (Myers and Briggs 1962). There are four basic personality traits (functions) or what is known in the literature as 'BIG4':

1 *Extroversion (E) or Introversion (I)* Does the person recharge their energy via external contact and activity (Extroversion) or spending time in their inner space (Introversion)? Is the person orientated to the outer world of things and events (E) or inner world of ideas and concepts (I)?

2 *Intuition (N) or Sensing (S)* Does the person rely on their inner voice (Intuition) or observation (Sensing)? Do they perceive means of the five senses (S) or go beyond what is concretely present and focus on associations between what is perceived via senses (N)?

3 *Thinking (T) or Feeling (F)* When making decisions, what do they rely most on? Thoughts (T) or feelings (F)? Are the person's decisions made objectively (T) or subjectively (F)?

4 *Judgement (J) or Perception (P)* Do they tend to set schedules and organize life (Judgement), or do they tend to leave the options open and see what happens (Perception)? Does the person close their mind once decision is made (J) or remain open to further information (P)?

Case illustration
Personality differences at work

All Go Consultancy's consultants took personality tests prior to being placed in consulting teams. Tatijana as an ENTP got on well with Una (ENFP) but both struggled to relate to Samira (ISTJ). When sent out on observations both Tatijana and Una brainstormed and were quick to pick up on the personality and behavioural traits of those observed. They were keen to formulate plans for the way ahead. Every single time Samira listened with a pained expression before refusing to cooperate with these 'ad hoc' arrangements. Samira was keen to run some tests and to monitor before planning. When Tatijana voiced her approval of Samira's thoroughness Samira found her condescending and difficult.

Samira confided to their manager that she found her colleagues brash, loud, and unprofessional while Una and Tatijana both concurred that Samira was uncooperative, difficult, and managed to pour cold water on even the brightest plans.

Dr Doyle, who is managing them, has a challenge ahead of her and calls all three in to inform them of her decision.

We can use all aspects of our personality; however, we feel more comfortable with some than others, i.e. being more iNtuitive than Sensing. Our preference is the one we use at work, with others and in our relationships socially.

Using the letters above, it is possible to have a unique four-letter code to indicate each of the sixteen personality types. The sixteen types represent 'pure' types and Myers (1987) acknowledges that it is unlikely that people will be purely one type or another. A person may be in the middle of any categorization; extroverted at times and introverted at others, they may be capable of both objective and subjective decision making.

Pittenger (1993) argued that the Myers-Briggs type approach may be too general to make fine discriminations between the people and its value as a job performance predictor may be overrated. Nevertheless, the MBTI remains immensely popular, particularly in business and in careers and personal counselling (Huszczo 2007).

Type A and B personalities Friedman, an American cardiologist, noticed in the 1940s that the chairs in his waiting room got worn out from the edges. He then hypothesized that his patients were driven, impatient people, who sat on the edge of their seats when waiting and labelled these people 'Type A' personalities (Friedman and Ulmer 1984). Furthermore, **Type A** personalities are workaholics, always busy, somewhat impatient, extremely competitive, often irritable and aggressive (Williams 1993). Type B personalities, on the other hand are laid back and easy going as they are not highly competitive nor do they always fight the clock (Bortner 1969; Strube 1989). Fontana (2000) points out that this typology has also an emotional component, namely the emotional reaction to pressure which is linked to self-esteem; with Type A personalities driven by a desire for success in order to prove themselves, and Type B personalities able to take a more objective view of the issues in front of them and of themselves.

Described here are the extreme ends of the A-B dimension. Most people will show some Type A characteristics, at least on occasion. Certainly, the successful managers are able to balance the objective view of the task ahead with their drive for success (Fontana 2000).

It is worth noting that the concept of 'Type A personality' has found its way into general jargon.

The trait approach   In some ways, the trait approach is an extension and development of the type approach. But, instead of placing people in different categories, trait theorists consider each personality characteristic as a continuum and describe personality in terms of where a person comes on these continua.

In our informal assessment of other people's personalities in our everyday lives, we come closest to trait approach. We make the following comments: 'He is quite bossy' or 'she is very shy'. There are thousands of words in the English language and equally many in other languages that could be considered as traits: warmth, liveliness, sensitivity, perfectionism, to name a few. Allport and Odbert (1936) found around 18,000 words that described personality in the English dictionary. So what is a trait?

Trait is any persisting characteristic, whether emotional, cognitive, or behavioural, which influences the way personality is manifested in a relatively permanent and consistent way. Trait theorists (Allport 1937; Murray 1976; Eysenck 1967; Cattell 1971 and 1978) usually try to describe the basic traits that can all come under a meaningful description of personality, then they try to measure them. This is done by shortlisting the most important traits from which can be drawn a comprehensive profile of the individual's personality.

The trait approach can be enhanced by the use of psychometric techniques. The main statistical tool used to refine personality models is called factor analysis. By using factor analysis, R. B. Cattell (1978) identified sixteen important factors which are underlying influences on the way we are seen to behave. Each factor is the source of a range of observable behaviours. Each is referred to as a source trait while associated observable behaviours are referred to as surface traits. His sixteen factors form the basis of the 16PF questionnaire, also used as a reputable tool in business.

The 5 factor model represents the most basic dimensions underlying the personality traits identified in both the language and the extensive psychological research built up on the trait approach models such as Eysenck's and Cattell's (Fiske 1977; Costa and McCrae 1985). The BIG5 embody a general agreement about five factors that provide most of what can be said about personality (Wiggins 1996). The BIG5 personality factors (dimensions) with their descriptions are (McCrae and Costa 1990; Deary and Matthews 1993):

- *Extroversion*: warmth, **assertiveness**, activity, seeking excitement, enthusiasm, and sociability on one side and caution, reserve, silence, and sobriety on the other side.

- *Emotional stability*: anxiety, self-consciousness, vulnerability, hostility, depression on one side and emotional stability on the other side.

- *Openness to experience*: flexibility with openness to change and new ideas at one end to down-to-earth, simple, and narrow interests on the other end.

- *Agreeableness*: honest, straightforward, altruistic, modest, tender-minded, obedient, conformist on one side and irritable, suspicious, and uncooperative on the other.

- *Conscientiousness*: competent, duty driven, self-disciplined, thoughtful on one end of the dimension to disorganized, impulsive, careless, and undependable on the other end.

These five factors can be assessed by two personality assessment instruments: NEO Inventories: NEO-FFI and NEO-PI (Costa and McCrae 1985 and 1992). Comparing the results collected by the NEO Inventories on different nations: American, Chinese, German, Hebrew, Japanese, Korean, and Portuguese; Costa and McCrae (1993) also found that these five basic factors are consistent across different cultures. Using the NEO-PI, the two psychologist carried out a longitudinal study in which they followed hundreds of men and women for six years. Results found that the factors all show a high degree of stability (Costa and McCrae 1993).

....

 Activity BIG5

Estimate your rating on each of the BIG5 dimensions as described previously. Use a 5-point scale (ranging from: 1—don't like that at all to 5—totally like that).

Then ask someone who knows you well to rate you too.

Compare the two ratings.

....

Self and peer ratings on BIG5 dimensions (see Activity) tend to agree reasonably well (Berkenan and Liebler 1993). The closer the agreement, the greater one's self-insight appears to be. On the other hand, if the disagreement is high, the peer report seems to be more accurate of the two (Funder 1995).

Many psychologists view BIG5 as providing important insights into key dimensions of personality. Where people stand on BIG5 dimensions is closely linked to their success in performing many jobs (Hogan and Roberts 1996). An individual's success in starting and running a business also seems to be associated with BIG5 (Ciavarella et al. 2004) as well as whether they will make good leaders and what leadership style will they will adopt (Judge and Bono 2001). All these findings suggest that the BIG5 are related to many important aspects of behaviour and they are big indeed, especially for work psychology.

Evaluation of type and trait approaches   The main appeal of type and trait approaches is not only that they provide frameworks for describing personality, but also that based on these frameworks the inventories can be, and have been, constructed and used for personality assessment (Bayne 1994). However, their predictive value is limited to typical behaviours (Hough 1992; Pervin 1994). Individuals do not always behave in a typical way (Armstrong 2003; Block 1995; Goldberg 1993) and human behaviour is influenced by various situational factors (Bandura 1999). A mainly reserved, introverted scientist can give an inspired and enthusiastic speech to a wide audience, which both the scientist and the audience will enjoy. On this particular occasion, this person is behaving in an extroverted way.

Furthermore, the key dimensions of personality, such as BIG5, are described in great detail, but there is little attempt to determine how they develop, and how and why they influence human behaviour, which essentially is of main interest to work psychology. In addition Makin et al. (1996) observed that studies using types and traits to predict work-related behaviours are difficult to interpret and their level of predictability is not very high.

KEY LEARNING POINTS

- The type approach places people in discrete categories.
- The trait approach considers each personality characteristic as a continuum.

3.2.2 Personality assessment at work

The personality assessment topic is closely linked to Chapter 12 on Assessing People at Work; therefore, it is strongly suggested that the student follows up the study of this topic by further reading of Chapter 12.

A wide variety of techniques exist for assessing personality characteristics. They range from more objective methods with high **validity** (**assessment centres**, ability tests, and certain **personality questionnaires and inventories**) to the low validity, more subjective (unstructured interviews), and unorthodox techniques (graphology, palm reading, etc.). For example, Smart (1983) reported that only 10 per cent of interviewees respond honestly in conventional interview. Similarly, the meta-analysis of validity coefficients does not show personality questionnaires and inventories to have such high empirical validities to match their popularity (Schmitt et al. 1984; Flint-Taylor et al. 1999; Robertson and Callinan 1999).

Still, when used well, psychometric tests can provide valuable information about job applicants that is free from the bias that commonly occurs in face-to-face interviews (Fletcher 1991; Ones et al. 2005). There is some supporting evidence for these techniques too (Bartram 1995). In their meta-analysis Barrick and Mount (1991) found that conscientiousness was linked to performance across all job types (with 0.22 criterion validity), while there was a strong link between extroversion and performance in sales and managerial jobs (0.17 criterion validity).

Ones et al. (2005) list the areas of work where personality assessment is commonly used:

- selection (hiring and promotion);
- counselling;
- identifying training and development needs;
- career guidance.

Finally, the widespread use of personality assessment in work psychology today is to evaluate individuals' management potential (Joiner 2002). In a study of 205 senior managers—high-flyer versus non-high-flyer managers—promotability (likelihood of being promoted) showed a statistically negative relationship with the agreeableness (Flint-Taylor et al. 1999), while it was positively related to extroversion and low conscientiousness (Robertson et al. 2000).

Extroversion was also found to be associated with higher levels of job satisfaction, while neuroticism is associated with lower job satisfaction (Cropanzano et al. 1993). These results require psychologists to rethink the status and determinants of job satisfaction. If personality predicts job satisfaction then the potential to influence satisfaction through job and work design is limited (Robertson and Callinan 1999).

As well as with performance and job satisfaction, personality is also linked with **organizational citizenship** (i.e. aspects of non-task specific behaviour which reinforce relationships between people and help the organization to function well), group performance training success, and leadership (Robertson and Callinan 1999).

The personality assessment techniques based on behaviour approach often used in selection for employment and job promotion are situational tests and **simulations**, where for example a job candidate is subjected to performing typical work tasks while being observed and assessed on performance. Simulations such as group activities and presentation exercises have been extensively used, particularly at management level, to assess personality characteristics such as leadership, **interpersonal skills**, and sensitivity. The disadvantage of these methods is that less experienced candidates due to maybe anxiety may underperform and therefore not demonstrate their real potential. The other problem with situational tests is their artificiality.

 Activity **Simulation exercises**

In small groups or individually, design simulation exercises to help in selection of suitable candidates for trainee police officers. To start with, write a list of personality characteristics that are desirable for the post, followed by the design of half-day exercises aiming to assess the characteristics from your list.

 KEY LEARNING POINTS

- The various theoretical approaches focus on different aspects of personality, and the assessment techniques that arise from them show the same variety of focus.
- Self-report questionnaires that arise from type or trait approach are a way of providing empirically based information on personality relatively simply and quickly.

Situational tests that arise from behaviourist approach are commonly used during selection events to observe job candidates in situations other than interview.

3.3 Intelligence

Intelligence can be broadly defined as a facility for solving problems. It is a cognitive capability that involves abilities such as: reasoning, planning, abstract thinking, understanding of complex ideas, 'making sense' of our surroundings, and 'figuring out' what to do. Intelligence is also a person's capacity for goal-directed, adaptive behaviour.

Therefore, intelligence is very much a part of the general reaction to life that we call personality. Cattell (1978) made this point when he included intelligence or reasoning, as one of the factors measured by his personality tests. Intelligence, like personality, or as a factor of personality, is an aspect of the way individuals think, feel, and act in the world. Those two concepts closely interact. There is a particularly strong connection between intelligence and the level of the life goals that individuals set themselves, and between intelligence and the kind of interpretations that are put on life experiences (Fontana 2000).

3.3.1 Different approaches to intelligence

Sternberg (1996), an eminent intelligence theorist himself is also known for dividing intelligence theorists into two groups: lumpers and splitters. Lumpers are advocates of general intelligence 'g' and they argue that the IQ score could be a highly predictive of a range of future life achievements, including education, finances, social status, and work performance (Jensen 1993). The more 'g' a person has, the more successful in various aspects of work and general life they will be (Jensen 1997). Furthermore, 'g' cannot be acquired, as it is inherited. Splitters are more focused on different types of intelligences, and they remind us that some people are great artists or even physicists but poor mathematicians or some are fantastic orators but struggle to park their car in reverse (Cattell 1978; Gardner 1983; Eysenck and Eysenck 1985; Sternberg 1985).

Most modern theories of intelligence recognize that intelligence may involve a general ability to handle a wide range of cognitive tasks and problems, as Spearman suggested, but also that intelligence is expressed in many different ways and that persons can be high on some aspects of intelligence but low on others. An example is Cattell's theory of intelligence outlined next.

Cattell (1971) made a distinction between **fluid** and **crystallized intelligence**, where fluid intelligence is our ability to reason and process information. We rely on our fluid intelligence when faced up with new situations, having to solve unfamiliar problems or when we have to learn something new. On the other hand, crystallized intelligence consists of acquired skills and specific knowledge in our unique experience. Crystallized intelligence continues to increase as long as we stay mentally and physically active—the more experience we have the more skills we acquire—while fluid intelligence peaks sometime before our twenties and remains constant until more mature age, when it starts declining. An experienced surgeon uses his crystallized intelligence to operate on the appendix for the 76th time in his career, but he will use his fluid intelligence when he is left with his twin grandchildren for the first time to look after them for a day.

Most intelligence tests use and measure both types of intelligence, however, the preference is to identify and measure fluid intelligence.

3.3.2 Nature/nurture debate

There has been an ongoing nature/nurture debate amongst scholars, which is often politically charged: is intelligence inherited or could it be improved by education?

More moderate scientific voices have found evidence for a compromise between nurture and nature. This is the view accepted by most modern psychologists. However, controversy remains concerning the relative contribution of each of the factors. Do environmental or genetic factors play a stronger role in shaping intelligence? Existing evidence seems to support the view that genetic factors may account for more of the variance in IQ scores within a given population than environmental factors (Plomin et al. 2001; Neisser 1996). Perhaps we can shift our IQ by a few points if we were lucky enough to have been born to good parents, have had a good education, and have developed a positive attitude towards learning and self-development. However, we cannot go beyond the mental capability potential that we inherited.

3.3.3 Intelligence in the workplace

There is a large and convincing literature and research showing that intelligence, especially general intelligence, is a good predictor of both job performance and work training proficiency (Dragsow 2003; Furnham 2005). Research by Tenopyr (1981) concludes that no other employee selection method is as good as intelligence tests, in comparison to more subjective selection methods. It appears further that 'g' is a particularly good predictor of performance in complex jobs, but it also predicts lifetime productivity (Ree and Carretta 1999). Raven's Progressive Matrices is a well-known test that measures 'g'.

Generally, brief intelligence screening tests that can be distributed to a group of applicants are most popular in personnel selection. For example, the Wonderlic Personnel Test takes only twelve minutes to complete and consists of items that measure verbal, numerical, and spatial abilities. The most successful use of this test has been in predicting success in low-level jobs, especially clerical ones (Krumm 2001).

For further reading on use of intelligence testing at workplace refer to Chapter 12 on Assessing People at Work.

 KEY LEARNING POINT

- A measure of intelligence is found to be a good job performance predictor.

3.4 Emotional intelligence

The concept of emotional intelligence (EI) originates from two published articles by psychologists John Mayer and Peter Salovey in 1990 and 1993 (Mayer and Salovey 1990, 1993); furthermore it entered the pop-psychology arena with a help of Daniel Goleman (1995, 1998) and his best-selling books on the topic. Since then it has stirred up a lot of discussion amongst scholars, while the business largely bought into the idea of getting and developing more competencies that stem from EI. Here three models of EI are presented:

- The *Mayer-Salovey model* defines EI as the ability to perceive, understand, manage, and use emotions to facilitate thinking. They postulated the following thesis: though frequently conceived as opposites, emotions and intellect often work in concert, each enhancing the other. 'Our ability to engage in the highest levels of thought isn't limited to intellectual pursuits like calculus,' Mayer contends (Mayer and Salovey 1997). 'It also includes reasoning and abstracting about feelings. That means that among those people that we refer to as warm-hearted or romantic or fuzzy—or whatever sometimes demeaning expressions we use—there are some who are engaging in very, very sophisticated information processing. This type of reasoning is every bit as formal as that used in solving syllogisms.' Authors further argued that emotions sometimes enrich thought and that the experience of strong feeling may help individuals perceive fresh alternatives, make better choices, and, paradoxically, maintain an even emotional keel.

Therefore, certain interactions between feelings and intellect that authors term emotional intelligence could make the difference between a conventional decision and an enterprising one, between a stilted speech and an inspiring one.

McCrea (2000) points to a subtle distinction between the mental abilities of the Mayer and Salovey model of EI as opposed to personality traits: 'People can be optimistic simply because they have a cheerful disposition (which requires no intelligence of any kind); or they may understand that they can create an optimistic assessment by deliberately calling to mind the chances of success or by summoning social support from others. This process of manipulating one's own emotional state requires a certain degree of psychological mindedness that Mayer and his colleagues deem a form of intelligence.'

Goleman's model views EI as an array of emotional and social competencies that contribute to managerial performance. He defined emotional intelligence as 'The capacity for recognizing our own feelings and that of others, for motivating ourselves, for managing emotions well in ourselves as well as others' (Goleman 1995). According to Goleman (1995) EI consists of following major components:

- self-awareness—the ability to understand personal moods, emotions, and drives as well as their effect on others;
- managing emotions—ability to control or redirect disruptive impulses and moods, and regulate one's behaviour;
- self-motivation—the ability to motivate oneself and pursue goals with energy and persistence;
- recognizing the emotions of others—the ability to understand the emotional make-up of others and skilfully treating other people according to their emotional reactions;
- handling relationships—ability of building relationships, finding common ground, and building rapport. Also ability to manage conflict efficiently.

Goleman portrayed the emotionally intelligent person as one possessing all the qualities of a 'nice person': kind, warm, and friendly, while the original researchers focused more on the fluid interplay between emotions and intelligence (Hein 2006). Goleman also expanded the boundaries of EI, including in it a range of qualities, like zeal and persistence, not usually associated with emotion. He equated high EI with 'maturity' and 'character', an association that Salovey and Mayer denied (Mayer et al. 1998). Finally, there is a test for measuring Goleman's concept of EI: ECI-360, which is widely used (Boyatzis et al. 2000).

Finally, the Bar-On model describes EI as a cross-section of interrelated emotional and social competencies, skills, and facilitators that impact intelligent behaviour. According to Bar-On (1997) being emotionally and socially intelligent involves effective management of following elements:

- personal: self-awareness and effective self-expression;
- social: understanding and successfully relating to others;
- environmental: coping with daily demands, challenges, and pressures.

To do this, Bar-On argues (2006), we need to manage emotions so that they work for us and not against us, and we need to be sufficiently optimistic, positive, and self-motivated. He went on to develop measures of EI: EQ-i (Emotional Quotient Inventory, Bar-On 1997) and EQ-360 (Emotional Quotient-360, Bar-On and Handley 2003), which are both widely used EI measures to date.

Some researchers question weather EI is truly distinct from related aspects such as social intelligence or even aspects of personality such as empathy (Davies et al. 1998; Roberts et al. 2002). However, there is a general agreement that emotional abilities do exist and do indeed affect social competence and there has been some evidence supporting the argument that emotional abilities cluster together as a single, universal factor (Mayer et al. 1998).

Furthermore, many argue that by itself EI probably is not a strong predictor of job performance (Goleman 1998; Mayer et al. 1998). Rather, it provides the foundation for competencies that are. In this context **competency** refers to the personal and social skills that lead to superior performance at work. For instance, the ability to recognize accurately what another person is feeling enables one to develop a specific competency such as **Influence**. Similarly, people who are better able to regulate their emotions will find it easier to develop a competency such as Initiative or Achievement drive. Ultimately it is this social and emotional **competency framework** that business needs to identify and measure in order to predict performance (see Table 3.1).

Miller et al. (2001) found that 30 per cent of surveyed organizations include EI-type factors such as interpersonal skills at work in their frameworks. In addition, 25 per cent of companies have had training that is based on EI. The most common skills targeted are: leadership skills, effective management skills, and skills required when working in successful teams (Miller et al. 2001).

Qualities that come under the EI umbrella are regularly rated as highly important in good leaders: self-awareness, emotional security, and ability to handle relationships (Bar-On 1997). However, good leadership, even an individual's survival in a harsh office culture of competition and battle for dominance, sometimes may require qualities not related to high EI, such as competitive spirit, and certain ruthlessness when dealing with rivals. In such work climates the key to success would be the low EI of a 'ruthless person' as opposed to Goleman's 'nice person'. Equally, displaying high EI may be a disadvantage in jobs requiring a task-centred rather than a people-centred approach, leading those who score highly on it to suppress their ability.

Nevertheless, the idea of emotional intelligence is an appealing one with important implications not only in the workplace but generally in a person's life and happiness. Importantly, business remains interested. The study of 108 managers and white-collar workers found that inappropriate criticism, followed by mistrust, personality conflicts, and disputes over power were the main reason for conflict at work (Baron 1990). The unresolved conflict is very costly for both an organization and individual's well-being. Therefore, introducing EI-based training programmes in the workplace while nurturing the culture where employees are motivated by praise and constructive criticism; where their issues and emotions are accepted, acknowledged, and dealt with where appropriate—all seem like a good business investment.

Pause for thought

Optimism is one of the EI components measured by the ECI-360 test. Think of someone who puts too much money in a stock feeling optimistic that it will double in value. Instead, the company goes bankrupt. High optimism scores you a high EQ, but it seems that you can get too much of it.

Table 3.1. Link between components of emotional intelligence (EI) and competencies at work

EI component	Work competencies
Self-awareness	Self-confidence Realistic picture of self Emotional self-awareness
Managing emotions	Self-control Integrity Adaptability—comfort with ambiguity
Self-motivation	Initiative Openness to change Strong desire to achieve Self-drive
Recognizing the emotions of others	Empathy Conflict management
Handling relationships	Trustworthiness Influencing skills Communication skills Leadership Expertise in building and retaining talent Expertise in building and leading teams

Source: Armstrong (2003).

KEY LEARNING POINT

- Emotional intelligence has been linked to competencies that are strong predictors of job performance.

3.5 Creativity and innovation at work

Psychology's enduring interest in the creative act has been fuelled by the hope that a sound understanding of the phenomenon would lead to a more effective use of this precious social resource (Taylor and Getzels 1975). Recently, this mission has become even more relevant to psychology at work, owing to a high value placed on creative performance and innovative behaviour in the context of the rapidly changing world of work (see Chapter 10 on Organizational Change and Development and Chapter 16 on The Future of Work). Creativity and innovation have become not only buzzwords of the twenty-first century's global work market, but also an integral part of every employee's job description.

3.5.1 Definition of creativity and innovation

The terms of 'creativity' and 'innovation' are often used interchangeably in research studies, and the distinction between the two concepts may be more one of emphasis than substance (West and Farr 1990). Nonetheless, some agreement about terms of definition has emerged recently; creativity has to do with the production of novel and useful ideas, it involves an ability to come up with new and different viewpoints on a subject, it implies breaking down and restructuring our knowledge about the subject in order to gain new insights into its nature. While **innovation** has to do with production or adoption of useful ideas and idea implementation, it is about using information from a variety of different sources to create unique solutions to a problem. Although creativity is often framed as 'doing something for the first time

Figure 3.2. Stages of innovation process

1. problem recognition →
2. generation of ideas or solutions →
3. seeking support from others →
4. production of a prototype or model of innovation

anywhere or creating new knowledge' (Woodman et al. 1993), innovation also encompasses the adaptation of products or process from outside an organization.

Furthermore, researchers exploring innovation have recognized that this is a multistage process (see Figure 3.2) on which many social factors impinge (Kanter 1988).

From this perspective, individual innovation begins with problem recognition and the generation of ideas or solutions, either novel or adopted. Generating ideas is not just a chance process. Ideas appear to arise by chance only when people are actually looking for them. It happens to people who are curious or who are engaged in a hard search for challenges, opportunities, possibilities, new questions, and answers. During the next stage of the process, an innovative individual seeks sponsorship for an idea and attempts to build a coalition of supporters for it. Here, motivation seems to play an important role in our ability to pursue innovative behaviour.

3.5.2 Innovative behaviour in the workplace

A large body of literature has focused on determining a set of personal characteristics and attributes associated with creative performance and innovative behaviour (Barron and Harrington 1981; Martindale 1989). This research has examined personal characteristics ranging from biographical factors to measures of cognitive styles and intelligence.

There are some suggestions that there are the BIG5 creativity components (Sternberg and Lubart 1992; Amabile 1983):

1 *expertise*—relevant knowledge upon which to draw;

2 *imaginative thinking*—the ability to see things from a different angle and make connections between them;

3 *a venturesome approach*—a readiness to take risks with material and to tolerate ambiguity;

4 *intrinsic motivation*—personal interest, enjoyment, with ability to work hard and perseverance.

5 *a creative environment*—a stimulating and supportive culture in creative endeavour.

Case illustration
Stifling climates and lack of innovation at work

Dizzily is a well-established animation company employing hundreds of writers, animators, and creative staff. Dido was delighted when she managed to get a job with them straight from Art college. Her excitement was quickly muted during the induction when it became apparent that Dizzily was target driven and her boss, Evan Evans, was a business manager and not a creative graduate. He disliked Dido's habit of wandering around looking for inspiration and found her habit of looking out the window or listening to music on her i-pod deeply irritating. Dido tried to conform, telling herself that this was the best vehicle for her talent and how jealous her college peers had been.

At the end of the first six months Dido's work was hailed as the best of the graduates and she was pleased with the accolade until she saw Evan's disgusted face. Now she is looking to the company's competitor for work as she has heard that the environment is less stressful.

Studies, at both the organizational and subunit level, offer empirical support for the effect of a creative environment (Abbey and Dickinson 1983; Siegel and Kaemmerer 1978). People's perception of supportive environment was also positively related to innovative behaviour at work (Scott and Bruce 1994; West et al. 2000). In other words, a highly creative individual working in a non-supportive environment is not likely to sustain his or her high level of creativity at work.

BIG5 creativity components offer a general idea of the things that work best for creative people. However, not all of them are necessary in every creative act and at any circumstances (consider the next Activity).

 Activity The creative act

Think of notable works of genius created in the highly 'non-creative' environment. Discuss in class.

A number of studies have pointed to a stable set of core personal characteristics that relate positively and consistently to measures of creative performance across a variety of domains (Barron and Harrington 1981; Gough 1979; Oldham and Cummings 1996). They include:

- broad interest;
- attraction to complexity;
- intuition;
- aesthetic sensitivity;
- tolerance of ambiguity and;
- self-confidence.

Like intelligence and emotional intelligence, creativity and innovation should be seen as integrated parts of personality. People who come up with innovations at work are likely to be creative in their general approach to life (Fontana 2000).

Chapter summary

- Personality is a complex phenomenon built on a wide range of the physical, mental, ethical, and social qualities specific to each individual. Psychology of personality and individual differences is a popular branch of psychology and consists of a large body of research and theory.

- Alongside everyday or implicit personality theories that every individual creates for themselves, there are many theoretical perspectives of personality that include humanistic, behaviourist, cognitive, type, and trait.

- Personality assessment is used in psychology at work to match individuals to certain jobs/career choices and particular organizations. It is also widely used in training development.

- Intelligence is an important part of an individual's personality. It is a cognitive capability that involves abilities such as: reasoning, planning, abstract thinking, understanding of complex ideas, 'making sense' of our surroundings, and 'figuring out' what to do.

- The measure of intelligence or intelligence quotient (IQ) plays an important role in the workplace because it is considered to be a strong predictor of job performance.

- The advocates of the importance of emotional intelligence argue that it is crucial to performance. The important distinction between IQ and EQ is that the former is largely believed to be a capability an individual is born with, while EQ can be improved with learning and practice. Others argue that EI is not a separate entity but only a type of intelligence and therefore is measured by standard IQ tests.

- Creativity is a highly sought-out personality trait in the modern workplace. However it is only in organizations that have a supportive atmosphere that individuals can and will express their creativity.

Assess your learning

Review questions

1 What are implicit theories of personality? How do people form and develop these theories?
2 What is the major application of the behaviourist approach in personality assessment often used at work?
3 What is the difference between the type and trait approach to personality?
4 What are the BIG5 personality factors and what do they mean? Which one of them is linked to good leadership?
5 Summarize the major differences between fluid and crystallized intelligence.
6 How is the measure of intelligence linked to psychology at work?
7 What are the five components of emotional intelligence and what are the work competencies associated with them?
8 What are the Big5 creativity components?

Assignments

ASSIGNMENT 1: TYPE DESCRIPTION
Using the Myers-Briggs BIG4 type description, try to guess your own personality profile.

ASSIGNMENT 2: BOOSTING INNOVATION
Assume thea role of an HR assistant. You were assigned the task of unleashing the creative potential of the design team in your middle-size company, working on the new product. Prepare a five-minute presentation on proposed strategies for boosting innovation in the workplace.

Further reading

Barrick, M., and Ryan, A. M. (2003) *Personality and Work: Reconsidering the Role of Personality in Organizations.* New York: Wiley.
This book offers an in-depth examination of the role of personality in work behaviour.

Ciarrochi, J., Forgas, J. P., and Mayer, J. D. (2001) *Emotional Intelligence in Everyday Life: A Scientific Inquiry.* New York: Psychology Press.
An interesting read that provides a comprehensive review of the field and the ways in which EI is important to everyday life.

Fonseca, J. (2002) *Complexity and Innovations in Organisations.* London: Routledge.
The book is bursting with innovation process case illustrations that bring to life this important topic.

Furnham, A. (2003) *Personality at Work.* E-books. http://www.ebookmal.com.
This is a critical and comprehensive review of the role that personality testing plays in the management of the workplace.

Hall, C. S., and Lindzey, G. (1978) *Theories of Personality.* New York: John Wiley and Sons.
An excellent overview of primary sources and research from which the most prominent personality theories arise.

Work psychology in practice
People watching—episode 2

Ten years on

Milla is working in a public institution that oversees and controls national occupational health and safety issues. She has the responsible role of running psychology health assessments and personality profiling. Recently she's taken on a postgraduate degree and still stresses over her exams and wonders if she is equal to it. Sometimes, when she gets very anxious, she tends to turn to compulsive internet shopping. Her wardrobe is full of high-heeled shoes that she hardly ever wears.

Ingolf hasn't made it to Hollywood yet but has been on TV on a number of occasions. He is planning to climb Mount Everest next year. He only needs to sort out this high blood pressure . . . He has been working on a variety of projects and has launched his own line of designer ties that is yet to become a commercial success. Most notably for Ingolf, he's sure to be seen at every important party in town and mingles with celebrities as he always wanted to.

Orlagh is still fighting her migraines, runs her own training and development centre, and continues to look for what's out there that is more lucrative, or satisfying . . . She seems to have found two different ways of combating stress and feelings of disappointment. One is destructive, and there are times when she reaches for the bottle and tends to drink too much; and the other way is more constructive: when she reaches for the paint brush and channels her vast energy creatively on the canvas. Unfortunately, Orlagh's paintings have not been seen by the public yet.

Questions

- Analyse these three characters in light of their individual differences by choosing one or two personality dimensions (i.e. extroversion–introversion) for comparison reference.
- Establish relationships between their unique personalities and career choices.
- Establish links between their unique personalities and their health.
- How do you think improving their EQ could benefit each of them?

Online Resource Centre

Visit the supporting online resource centre for additional material which will help you with your research, essays, and assignments, or you may find these additional resources helpful when revising for exams.
http://www.oxfordtextbooks.co.uk/orc/matthewman/

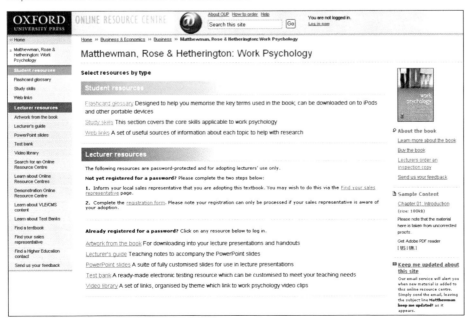

References

Abbey, A., and Dickinson, J. (1983) R&D work climate and innovation in semiconductors. *Academy of Management Journal*, 26: 362–8.

Allport, G. W. (1937) *Personality: A Psychological Interpretation*. New York: Holt, Rinehart and Winston.

Allport, G. W., and Odbert, H. S. (1936) Trait names: a psycho-lexical study. *Psychological Monographs*, 47: 211.

Amabile, T. M. (1983) *The Social Psychology of Creativity*. New York: Springer-Verlag.

Armstrong, M. (2003) *Human Resource Management Practise* (9th edn.). London: Kogan Page.

Bandura, A. (1999) A social cognitive theory of personality. In L. Pervin and O. P. John (ed.), *Handbook of Personality: Theory and Research* (2nd edn.), New York: Guilford Publications, 154–96.

Baron, R. A. (1990) Environmentally induced positive affect: its impact on self-efficacy, task performance, negotiation and conflict. *Journal of Applied Social Psychology*, 20/5: 368–84.

Bar-On, R. (1997) *Bar-On Emotional Quotient Inventory: User's Manual*. Toronto: Multi-Health Systems.

Bar-On, R. (2006) The Bar-On model of emotional-social intelligence (ESI). *Psicothema*, 18, suppl.: 13–25.

Bar-On, R., and Handley, R. (2003) *The Bar-On EQ-360: Technical Manual*. Toronto: Multi-Health Systems.

Barrick, M. R., and Mount, M. K. (1991) The big five personality dimensions and job performance: a meta analysis. *Personnel Psychology*, 44: 1–26.

Barron, F., and Harrington, D. M. (1981) Creativity, intelligence and personality. *Annual Review of Psychology*, 32: 439–76.

Bartram, D. (1995) *Review of Personality Assessment instruments (Level B) for Use in Occupational Settings*. Leicester: The British Psychological Society.

Bayne, R. (1994) The Big Five versus the Myers-Briggs. *The Psychologists*, Jan.

Berkenan, P., and Liebler, A. (1993) Convergence of stranger ratings of personality and intelligence with self ratings, partner ratings and measured intelligence. *Journal of Personality and Social Psychology*, 65: 546–53.

Bettencourt, B. A., Talley, A., Benjamin, A. J., and Valentine, J. (2006) Personality and aggressive behaviour under provoking and neutral conditions: a meta-analytic review, *Psychological Bulletin*, 132/5.

Block, J. (1995) A contrarian view of the five-factor approach to personality description. *Psychological Bulletin*, 117: 7–215.

Bortner, R. W. (1969) A short rating scale as a potential measure of pattern A behaviour. *Journal of Chronic Diseases*, 22: 87–91.

van den Bossche, S., and Houtman, I. L. D. (2004) *Work Stress Interventions and Their Effectiveness: A Review*. Report for stress impact. Hoofddorp: TNO Work and Employment

Boyatzis, R. E., Goleman, D., and Rhee, K. (2000) Clustering competence in emotional intelligence: insights from the emotional competence inventory (ECI)s. In R. Bar-On and J. D. A. Parker (eds.), *Handbook of Emotional Intelligence*. San Francisco: Jossey-Bass, 343–62.

Cannon, R. J. (2004) *Organisation and Assessment in the E-learning Environment*. Cardiff: Cardiff University.

Cattell, R. B. (1971) *Abilities: Their Structure, Growth and Action*. New York: Houghton-Mifflin.

Cattell, R. B. (1978) *Sixteen Personality Factor Questionnaire*. Champaign, IL: IPAT.

Ciavarella, M. A., Bucholtz, A. K., Riordan, C. M., Gatewood, R. D. and Stakes, G. S. (2004) The BIG five and venture survival: is there any linkage? *Journal of Business Venture*, 4/19: 465–83.

Cooke, R., and Sheeran, P. (2004) Moderation of cognition–intention and cognition–behaviour relations: a meta-analysis of properties of variables from the theory of planned behaviour. *British Journal of Social Psychology*, 43/2:159–86.

Costa, P. T., and McCrae, R. R. (1985) *The NEO Personality Inventory Manual*. Odessa, FL: Psychological Assessment Resources, Inc.

Costa, P. T., and McCrae, R. R. (1992) *The NEO PI-R Professional Manual*. Odessa, FL: Psychological Assessment Resources, Inc.

Costa, P. T., and McCrae, R. R. (1993) Ego development and trait models of personality. *Psychological Inquiry*, 4: 20–3.

Cropanzano, R., James, K., and Konovsky, M. A. (1993) Dispositional affectivity as a predictor of work attitudes and job performance. *Journal of Organisational Behaviour*, 14: 595–600.

Davies, M., Stankov, L., and Roberts, R. D. (1998) Emotional intelligence: in search of an elusive construct. *Journal of Personality and Social Psychology*, 4/75: 989–1015.

Deary, I. J., and Matthews, G. (1993) Personality traits are alive and well. *Psychologist*, 6: 299–311.

Drasgow, F. (2003) Intelligence and the workplace. In W. C. Borman, D. R. Ilgen, and R. J. Klimoski (eds.), *Handbook of Psychology*, 12: 107–30.

Eysenck, H. J. (1967) *The Biological Basis of Personality*. Springfield, IL: Thomas.

Eysenck, H. J., and Eysenck, M. (1985) *Personality and Individual Differences: A Natural Science Approach*. London: Plenum Press.

Fiske, A. P. (1977) An issue that won't go away. *The New York Times Magazine*, 27 March, 58.

Fletcher, C. (1991) Study shows personality tests are useless for predicting performance, *Personnel Management Plus*, 3.

Flint-Taylor, J., Graymja, J., and Robertson, I. T. (1999) *The Five-Factor Model of Personality: Levels of Measurement and the Prediction of Managerial Performance and Attitudes*. Paper presented at Occupational Psychology conference of the British Psychological Society; Blackpool, UK.

Fontana, D. (2000) *Personality in the Workplace*. (3rd edn.) London: Macmillan Press Ltd.

Friedman, M., and Ulmer, D. (1984) *Treating Type A Behaviour and Your Heart*. New York: Knopf.

Funder, D. C. (1995) On the accuracy of personality judgment: a realistic approach. *Psychology Review*, 102: 652–70.

Furnham, A. (2005) *The Psychology of Behaviour at Work: The Individual in the Organisation* (2nd edn). Hove: Psychology Press.

Gardner, H. (1983) *Frames of Mind: The Theory of Multiple Intelligences*. New York: Basic Books.

Goldberg, L. R. (1993) The structure of phenotypic personality traits. *American Psychologist*, 8: 26–34.

Goleman, D. (1995) *Emotional Intelligence*. New York: Bantam Books.

Goleman, D. (1998) *Working with Emotional Intelligence*. New York: Bantam Books.

Gough, H. G. (1979) A creative personality scale for the adjective check list. *Journal of Personality and Social Psychology*, 37: 1398–405.

Hein, S. (2006) *Emotional Intelligence Tests* http://eqi.org/eitests.htm.

Hogan, J., and Roberts, B. (1996) Issues and non-issues in the fidelity-bandwidth trade-off. *Journal of Organisational Behaviour*, 17: 627–37.

Hough, L. M. (1992) The BIG5 variables—construct confusion: description versus prediction. *Human Performance*, 5: 139–55.

Huszczo, G. E. (2007) The business of getting into the MBTI business. *Bulletin of Psychological Type*, 30/2:14–15.

Jensen, A. R. (1993) Why is reaction time correlated with psychometric *g*? *Current Directions in Psychological Science*, 2: 53–6.

Jensen, A. R. (1997) The psychometrics of intelligence. In H. Nyborg (ed.), *The Scientific Study of Human Nature: Tribute to Hans J. Eysenck at Eighty*. New York: Elsevier, 221–39.

Joiner, D. A. (2002): Assessment centers: what's new? *Public Personnel Management* 31/2: 179–85.

Judge, T. A., and Bono, J .E. (2001) Relationship of core self-evaluations traits—self-esteem, generalized self-efficacy, locus of control, and emotional stability—with job satisfaction and job performance: a meta-analysis. *Journal of Applied Psychology*, 86: 80–92.

Jung, C. G. (1933) *Psychological Types*. New York: Harcourt, Brace and World.

Kanter, R. M. (1988) When a thousand flowers bloom: structural, collective and social conditions for innovation in organisation. *Research in Organisational Behaviour*, 10: 169–211.

Krumm, D. (2001) *Psychology at Work*. New York: Worth Publishers.

McCrae, R. B. and Costa, P. T. (1990) *Personality in Adulthood*. New York: Guilford.

McKenna, E. (2006) *Business Psychology and Organisational Behaviour: A Student's Handbook* (4th edn.) Hove and New York: Psychology Press; Taylor and Frances Group.

Makin, P., Cooper, C., and Cox, C. (1996) *Organisations and Psychological Contract*. Leicester: BPS books.

Martindale, C. (1989) Personality, situation, and creativity. In J. A. Glover, R. R. Ronning, and C. R. Reynolds (eds.), *Handbook of Creativity*. New York: Plenum Press.

Maslow, A. H. (1970) *Motivation and Personality* (2nd edn.). Reading, MA: Addison-Wesley.

Mayer, J. D., and Salovey, P. (1993) The intelligence of emotional intelligence. *Intelligence*, 17: 433–42.

Mayer, J. D., and Salovey, P. (1997) 'What is emotional intelligence?' In P. Salovey and D. Sluyter (eds.), *Emotional Development and Emotional Intelligence: Implications for Educators*. New York: Basic Books, 3–31.

Mayer, J. D., Salovey, P., and Caruso, D. (1998) Competing models of emotional intelligence. In R. J. Sternberg (ed.), *Handbook of Human Intelligence* (2nd edn.). New York: Cambridge University Press.

Miller, L., Rankin, N., and Neathey, F. (2001) *Competency Frameworks in UK Organisations*. London: CIPD.

Murray, H. A. (1976) *Thematic Apperception Test*. Pretoria: Human Science Research Council.

Myers, I. B. (1987) Introduction to the Type: A Description of the Theory and Application of the Myers-Briggs Type Indicator. Palo Alto, CA: Consulting Psychologist Press.

Myers, I. B., and Briggs, K. C. (1962) *The Myers-Briggs Type Indicator*. Princeton: Princeton Educational Services.

Neisser, U. (1996) Intelligence: knowns and unknowns. *American Psychologist*, 51: 77–101.

Oldham, G. R., and Cummings, A. (1996) Employee creativity: personal and contextual factors at work. *Academy of Management Journal*, 39: 607–34.

Ones, D. S., Viswesvaran, C., and Dilchert, S. (2005) Personality at work: raising awareness and correcting misconceptions. *Human Performance*, 18/4: 389–404.

Pervin, L. A. (1994) A critical analysis of current trait theory. *Psychological Inquiry*, 5/2: 103–13.

Pittenger, D. J. (1993) The utility of the Myers-Briggs Type Indicator. *Review of Educational Research*, 63: 467–88.

Plomin, R., Asbury, K., and Dunn, J. (2001) Why are children in the same family so different? Nonshared environment a decade later. *Canadian Journal of Psychiatry*, 46: 225–33.

Ree, M. J., and Carretta, T. R. (1999). Lack of ability is not always the problem. *Journal of Business and Psychology*, 14: 165–78.

Roberts, R. D., Zeidner, M., and Mathews, G. (2002) Does emotional intelligence meet traditional standards for intelligence? Some new data and conclusions. *Emotion*, 1: 196–231.

Robertson, I. T., Baron, H., Gibbons, P., MacIver, R., and Nyfield, G. (2000) Conscientiousness and managerial performance. *Journal of Occupational and Organisational Psychology*, 73: 171–80.

Robertson, I. T., and Callinan, M. (1999) Personality and work behaviour. *European Journal of Work and Organisational Psychology*.

Rogers, C. (1980) *A Way of Being*. Boston: Houghton Mifflin.

Schmitt, N., Gooding, R. Z., Noe, R. A., and Kirsch, M. (1984) Meta-analysis of validity Studies published between 1964 and 1982 and the investigation of study characteristics. *Personnel Psychology*, 37: 407–22.

Scott, S. G., and Bruce, R. A. (1994) Determinants of innovative behaviour: a path model of individual innovation in the workplace. *Academy of Management Journal*, 37: 580–607.

Siegel, S., and Kaemmerer, W. (1978) Measuring the perceived support for innovation in organisations. *Journal of Applied Psychology*, 63: 553–62.

Skinner, B. F. (1974) *About Behaviourism*. London: Cape.

Smart, D. (1983) *Selection Interviewing*. New York: Wiley.

Sternberg, R. J. (1985) *Beyond IQ: A Triarchic Theory of Human Intelligence*. Cambridge: Cambridge University Press.

Sternberg, R. (1996) *Successful Intelligence*. New York: Simon & Schuster.

Sternberg, R. J., and Lubart, T. I. (1992) Investing in creativity. *American Psychologist*, 51: 677–88.

Strube, M. J. (1989). Evidence for the 'type' in Type A behaviour: a taxometric analysis. *Journal of Personality and Social Psychology*, 56: 972–87.

Taylor, I. A., and Getzels, J. W. (1975) *Perceptiveness in Creativity*. Chicago: Aldine.

Tenopyr, M. L. (1981) The realities of employment testing. *American Psychologist*, 36: 1120–7.

West, M., and Farr, J. (1990) *Innovation and Creativity at Work: Psychological and Organisational Strategies*. New York: Wiley.

West, M. A., Patterson, M., Pillinger, T., and Nickell, S. (2000) *Innovation and Change in Manufacturing*. Birmingham: Aston Business School, Aston University.

Wiggins, J. S. (1996) *The Five-Factor Model of Personality: Theoretical Perspectives*. New York: Guilford Press.

Williams, R. (1993) *Anger Kills*. New York: Times Books.

Wilson, B. (2005) Unlocking potential. Paper presented at the 2005 ANZSOG conference. University of Sydney.

Wilson, K. C. (2005) Learning reinforcement. *Management Consulting*. Proceedings of the sixth conference on IASTED International Conference Web-Based Education, Chamonix, France.

Woodman, R., Sawyer J., and Griffin, R. (1993) Toward a theory of organisational creativity. *Academy of Management Review*, 18: 293–321.

Wright, D. S., Taylor, A., Davies, D. R., Sluckin, W., Lee, S. G. M., and Reason, J. T. (1970) *Introducing Psychology: An Experimental Approach*. London: Penguin.

Chapter 4
Perceptions and attitudes at work

Kamala Balu

Chapter objectives

As a result of reading this chapter and using the additional web-based material you should be able to:

- Understand the importance of perception in the workplace.
- Understand how instinctive perceptual short cuts can lead to perceptual errors.
- Describe examples of person perception in the workplace.
- Describe how person perception can be managed and the accuracy of person perception.
- Describe how attitudes are formed.
- Explain how attitudes can be changed.
- Explain why attitudes and behaviour are not always consistent.
- Explain the causes of job satisfaction and how it can be measured.
- Describe the components of organizational commitment, its influence on other work place outcomes, its relationship with organizational citizenship behaviour, and how it can be measured.

Work psychology in practice
Perception—the eye of the beholder

Mr Jones sat in a waiting room before his interview. He browsed through a company newsletter from his potential employers and was aware that he must project a professional demeanour. He wanted to make sure that the receptionist saw his best side and to create a positive impression. In the interview room Simon and David, the two managers, took another glance at Mr Jones's CV. Simon looked at Mr Jones's professional summary and immediately considered him to be a strong candidate. He noted Mr Jones's strongest skills, sales management, consultative selling, and major account management and was impressed by his personal attributes. David also considered the CV and noted that it provided a professional description of Mr Jones's work experience and accomplishments. He noted that Mr Jones was an advertising director of a city firm and then spent four years working as a consultant. After a short career break and now in his mid-50s Mr Jones was currently working in another managerial role.

As Mr Jones entered the interview room he greeted both interviewers with a warm smile and an extended hand. Simon saw that Mr Jones was confident, friendly, and enthusiastic. At the end of the interview Mr Jones shook hands with both interviewers and walked away confidently head up and shoulders squared. Simon was happy to put Mr Jones's CV in the definitely pile whereas David was not. In further discussion David commented that Mr Jones would only be marking his time before he packed up for a life of golf.

After the interview Simon shared with David how much he enjoyed interviewing and how talking and getting to know someone for him was an enjoyable aspect of management. David replied that he thought it was a chance for a little diversion from the routine and just another management obligation.

Questions

- What were the first impressions formed about Mr Jones by each of the interviewers?
- How did the two interviewers end up with such diverse impressions?
- How may have the interviewer's attitudes effected their perceptions?
- How can person perception be improved?

4.1 Introduction

The purpose of this chapter is to examine how perception and attitudes shape and direct behaviour in the workplace. It examines an important aspect of perception in the workplace: **person perception**. The chapter explores **attribution** theory and examines how it helps us to understand our internal and external environment and considers the short cuts we use to make judgements about others. The chapter moves on to describe examples of person perception in the workplace and examines the actions that can be taken to minimize perceptual errors. Attention then turns to attitudes. The chapter explores issues associated with the formation and function of attitudes and attitude change. Finally, the chapter addresses the question of whether attitudes influence behaviour. Two key job-related attitudes, job satisfaction and organizational commitment, are considered. Their relationship with other workplace outcomes is examined as well as their measurement.

4.2 Perception

The study of perception in the workplace is important simply because it is our perception of reality and not reality itself that shapes and directs our behaviour. Perception can be defined as a subjective process by which we select, organize, and interpret the incoming stimuli in our environment to make it meaningful to ourselves. Subjective processes, including the phenomena of **selective attention**, personal judgement, and interpretation affect meaning we give to our environment.

Figure 4.1. Perceptual process stages and influencing factors

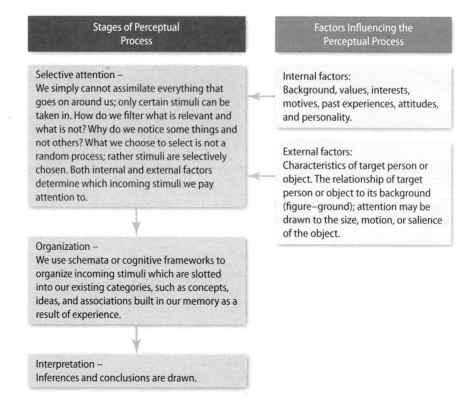

The perceptual process follows a number of stages and is influenced by a number of factors (see Figure 4.1).

Perception acts as a filter to simplify and order our experiences so that we are not overwhelmed by the constant bombardment of sensory information. It explains how people may look at the same thing yet perceive it differently. Figure 4.1 shows both internal and external factors influence perception. Another factor that can influence the perception is the context in which we see the target person or object; for example the social, physical, or organizational context can influence our perception.

KEY LEARNING POINTS

- Perception shapes and directs our behaviour.
- Perception is influenced by internal and external factors as well as the context.

4.2.1 Person perception

Person perception is the process by which individuals attribute characteristics or traits to other people. Macrae and Bodenhausen (2000) note that in person perception, rather than viewing individuals on their unique attributions, the perceiver's evaluations, impressions, memories are shaped and guided by their knowledge and pre-existing beliefs. As our behaviour is based on the world as we perceive it and not reality itself we often experience distortions in our perception. Although the process of perception is equally applicable in the perception of objects and people, there is more scope for subjectivity, bias, errors, and distortions when we perceive others. In the workplace person perception plays a major role in areas such as hiring and firing, appraisals, and promotion in an organization.

4.2.2 Attribution theory

Attribution theory has been proposed to develop explanations of the ways in which we judge people differently, depending on what meaning we attribute to a given behaviour (Kelly 1971). According to this theory, when people observe behaviour they want to attribute causes to behaviours they see rather than assuming that these behaviours are random. By making such inferences people are assumed 'to achieve greater understanding of, and hence greater control over, their environment' (Harvey and Weary 1984). They attempt to determine whether the behaviour was internally or externally caused. Internally caused behaviours are those that are believed to be under the personal control of the individual; whereas, externally caused behaviour is seen as resulting from an outside factor or force. However, the determination of whether the behaviour is attributable to internal rather than external (situational) causes is largely dependent on three factors:

1 **Distinctiveness**—How different is the behaviour being observed from other related behaviour? Is it distinctive or not?

2 **Consensus**—Does everyone who is faced with a similar situation behave in the same way? If so we can assume the behaviour shows consensus.

3 **Consistency**—Is the behaviour repeated over time and in different situations? If so we can assume the behaviour is consistent.

The attribution theory provides a useful conceptual framework for understanding how attributions are made. However, research into attributions shows that the attributions that people make are subject to a range of irrational biases and people are poor in their attribution of causation (Nisbett and Ross 1980).

Research has revealed patterns in our attributions particularly with respect to biases that distort our attributions about success and failure (Weiner 1979). There is a tendency for individuals to attribute their own success to internal factors such as their capabilities, but when they are explaining their failures they blame them on external causes that are beyond their control. This is known as **self-serving bias**. Thus, a common attribution of a person's success might be

Case illustration
The Entertainment Guide

Fiona is a general manager for an arts charity which organizes arts courses and performances. As part of their publicity, the charity produces *The Entertainment Guide* three times a year. The A5 guide includes information about forthcoming events, courses run by the charity, and advertisements from other arts organizations. The organization has produced this publication since it started in the 1970s. The publication costs £5 to post out to customers and is also available for free from the arts charity or local libraries in the borough.

In order to make the publication more cost effective Fiona decided to redesign the publication. During a meeting to discuss its new design, the marketing manager noticed Fiona was overruling about its new look, dismissive of his suggestions, and dictated what the final publication should look like, including its new name.

The marketing manager complained to his manager, Helen. Helen observed Fiona for several days and found that Fiona continued to overrule the marketing manager in other meetings, which indicates an internal cause and consistency in behaviour. Secondly, Helen discovered that Fiona was currently involved in an industrial tribunal case with a colleague of hers who claimed that she was fired because she refused to stand for Fiona's overruling manner; this is distinctiveness, and again points to an internal cause. Finally, Helen observed that when other managers had worked with Fiona on the new publication they too had experienced problems indicating that Fiona was opposed to their ideas and had usually made decisions prior to attending meetings. This is consensus, and it also points to an internal cause. Based on these observations, Helen can attribute Fiona's poor relationship with colleagues to an internal cause, or namely Fiona's own lack of skill or effort.

'I was promoted because of the effort I've put into my job.' A common attribution of a person's failure might be 'I didn't get the promotion because personnel lost my application.' Research from a meta-analysis published in 2004 by Mezulis et al. examined more than 500 published research studies and generally found there to be no difference between men and women in their self-serving biases; men were just as likely as women to make self-serving attributions.

When we make judgement of other people we are generally more inclined to make internal attributions to explain their behaviour and underestimate the influence of external factors (Miller and Lawson 1989). This is called the **fundamental attribution error**: for example, if a manager assumes that an employee's poor performance is due to a lack of effort rather than attributing the behaviour to external contributors such as lack of support or problems with equipment. This is likely to be negative for that employee. Conversely, if a manager perceives that an employee's poor performance is due to lack of support or faulty technology, the manager may assign the employee to further training or provide support. Inaccurate attributions about the causes of poor performance can have negative repercussions for the organization.

Attribution theory can explain aspects of **discrimination** in organizational settings. Discrimination arises as a result of unequal treatment based on arbitrary characteristics such as race, gender, ethnicity, or age and is demonstrated through behaviours. Discrimination differs from **prejudice** in that prejudice occurs as a result of prejudging others and perceiving others based on stereotypes (positive or negative); it usually has negative connotations. Prejudice is shown through attitudes.

Discrimination against particular groups and individuals, on the basis of gender, sexual orientation, disability, age, or ethnic background, is widely recognized. However, legislation seeks to address discrimination against these groups and consequently social attitudes towards them in organizational settings do appear to be changing. For example, the Employment Equality (Age) Regulations 2006 came into force in October 2006 in the UK. These regulations mean that age discrimination in employment is unlawful. Countries such as the USA have had age discrimination legislation for many years.

One of the limitations of the attribution theory is that it disregards the social context and the culture in which the behaviour occurs (Semin 1980). These provide us with 'rules or reference points' of meaningful behaviour and are explanations in themselves. Semin (1980) argues everyday explanations are contained within the meaningful social context of the behaviour and only when something unexpected happens do we go through the process of casual attribution. Another criticism of the attribution theory is that it is a limited investigation of potential cause and effect of behaviour and it disregards moral considerations such as right or wrong behaviour and responsibility (Billig 1987; Howitt et al. 1989).

KEY LEARNING POINT

- Attribution theory is the process of attaching causes and reasons to the actions and events we see.

4.2.3 Frequently used short cuts in judging others/ perceptual distortions

In trying to understand others, we instinctively use short cuts when we judge them. An understanding of these short cuts can be helpful in understanding significant distortions.

Stereotypes

Stereotyping is one of several examples of distortion in the perceptual process. Stereotypes are beliefs about the characteristics, attributes, and behaviours of members of certain groups (Hilton and Von Hippel 1996). The term 'stereotype' was popularized by Lippman (1922). He saw stereotypes as 'pictures in the head', simple mental images of groups and their behaviour. People use stereotypes in general as **heuristics** or short cuts to fill in information they lack, to arrive at quick inferences and judgements, and to save effort (Lippman 1922). Stereotypes are almost always developed for out-groups. We rarely label people who share our attributes or beliefs. The explicit and implicit teachings of social agents such as parents, peers, or subtle prevalence of stereotyping in the media ensure that stereotypes are transmitted at a young age, often before we have had opportunities to develop our own personal beliefs based on our own personal experiences (Allport 1954) A or B?? And only one referred to in the chapter anyway. Stereotypes serve to minimize information processing and serve as a social function.

Stereotypes can help people to quickly form impressions, in circumstances where experience is limited or absent. Macrae et al. (1994) concluded 'stereotypes, accordingly, serve to simplify perception, judgement and action. As energy-saving devices, they spare perceivers the ordeal of responding to an almost incomprehensibly complex social world.'

Rather than see stereotypes as irrational and invalid, social identity theorists argue that stereotyping is inevitable in that by categorizing both **in-groups** and **out-groups** we establish our own social identity. Social identity theory suggests that stereotyping 'reflects, and functions in the context of, changing inter-group relations' (Haslam et al. 1992).

An individual's social identity may be derived not only from the organization but also from his/her work group, department, union, and other business units. Stereotypes evolve for members of these different business units and influence person perception and group interaction within the organization (Ashforth and Mael 1989; Northcraft et al. 1995; Levy 2001).

Fein and Spencer (1997) indicate such stereotyping is likely to occur when people experience a threat to their self-esteem as it serves to bolster their own self-esteem. Ashforth and Mael (1989) suggest negative stereotypical perceptions are usually stronger when groups are similar because people feel the need to reinforce their own distinctiveness. Fiske (1993) suggests that stereotyping subordinates could fulfil motivational pressures that accompany power holders' position of control and unique authority to judge. People in power are less motivated to go beyond their stereotypes. Such stereotyping is seen as a deliberate control device rather than an inevitable consequence of individual cognition or group relations.

The **self-fulfilling prophecy** is one way in which stereotypes can be harmful. Self-fulfilling prophecies emerge when people hold expectations that lead them to alter their behaviour, which in turn causes the expected behaviour to be exhibited by people who are targets of the expectations. Rosenthal and Jacobson (1968) were the first to demonstrate experimentally that a simple manipulation of teacher expectancy could improve pupil achievement and they dubbed this special case of self-fulfilling prophecy as the Pygmalion effect.

A survey of 584 blue-collar workers and 158 white-collar workers found that employees will come to believe they have creative capability when their supervisors build their confidence through verbal persuasion and serve as models. This demonstrates how supervisors can create a self-fulfilling prophecy and influence the creativity ability of the workers by their expectations (Tierney and Farmer 2002).

Falkenberg (1990) states that a relatively long period of time is required to accumulate enough information of non-stereotypic behaviours to warrant revising a stereotype, recognize individuals rather than groups, and identify other categories of stereotypes. Devine (1989) argues that we cannot avoid starting out with stereotypes. The difference between prejudiced and non-prejudiced individuals is that the latter try to deliberately suppress stereotypical thoughts with more open-minded thoughts. However, efforts to suppress stereotypical thoughts can backfire and produce a rebound effect, such that stereotypical thinking increases to a level that is even greater than if no attempt at stereotype control was initially exercised (Macrae et al. 1994). Devine suggests personal commitment to changing one's perception or behaviour is required to change stereotypes.

Implicit personality theory

The **implicit personality theory** is the general assumptions we build up about a person's personality after we know something about their central traits. The logical error occurs when we form assumptions about what traits go together in a person. When we are faced with incomplete information we almost intuitively use this information to form an extensive and consistent view of other people. The **horns and halo effect** takes place when we draw a general impression about an individual on the basis of a single good or bad characteristic or piece of information and it carries disproportionate weight. For example, in an interview situation, if the interviewer perceives in the interviewee desirable characteristics such as, intelligence, sociability, or appearance, a **halo effect** is operating. We place an imaginary halo around their head. The entire evaluation is tainted by one trait. On the other hand if the reverse were true then the deficiency is identified at the outset. This is referred to as the horns effect. The employment interview situation is one of the most common examples in organizations of where the halo and horns effect is applied. The halo and horns effect acts as an early screen that filters out later information that is not consistent with our earlier judgements.

Projection is where there is a tendency to attribute one's own characteristics to other people. For example, if I want challenge and responsibility in a job, I assume that others want the same. Alternatively, a person may project their own feelings of inferiority onto other groups. This tendency to project one's own shortcomings or feelings to another person can relieve one's own sense of guilt or failure and enhance self-esteem.

KEY LEARNING POINTS

- We instinctively use short cuts to judge others which can lead to perceptual errors.
- Stereotypes are beliefs held by one group of people about the personal attributes of another group.
- Stereotypes are resistant to change.

4.2.4 Examples of the application of person perception in organizations

The selection interview and employee performance appraisals are two common examples used to demonstrate person perception in organizations.

Perception in the employment interview

The employment interview is an important source for information and remains by far the most frequently used technique for selecting employees (Eder and Harris 1999; Posthuma et al. 2002). Given its popularity it is important to understand the persistence of bias that surrounds the interview process. There is evidence that the interviewer makes implicit decisions to accept or reject a candidate remarkably early on in the interview. Springbett (1958) noted that the outcome of the great majority of interviews was typically settled within the first four minutes. More recent research by Otting (2004) suggests as many as four out of five hiring decisions are made in the first ten minutes of an interview. Since the whole hiring process can be driven by the interviewer's first impressions this could have an adverse effect on the outcome of the interview if the initial opinion is unfavourable. Such a quick decision precludes a full evaluation of the candidate and can be very misleading.

Impressions are also based on non-verbal cues such as **body language**, vocal tone, and appearance all these are non-verbal clues for impression formation (Posthuma et al. 2002).

Subtle cues may play a role in triggering implicit discriminatory responses such as the applicant's accent. Research has shown that in the USA the French accent is associated with sophistication and Asian accents are associated with high economic and educational attainment (Cargile 2000; Lippi-Green 1997).

Stereotypes may affect the interviewer's perceptions of applicants. Research has suggested that prejudice tends to evoke negative stereotypes these could be elicited through the use of a cue or a category label (Kawakami et al. 1998).

Dipoboye (1982, 1992) presented a model of self-fulfilling prophecy in the employment interview. The model specifies that both cognitive and behavioural biases mediate the effects of pre-interview impressions on applicants' evaluations. These 'expectancy confirmation' behaviours which the interviewers engage in are thought to confirm first impressions of applicants. Cognitive bias occurs if interviews distort information to support first impressions, using selective attention and recall of information. Dipoboye's (1982, 1992) model suggested that applicants may respond in a manner that is consistent with interviewers' behaviour, for example positive interviewer behaviour results in higher levels of rapport and more positive interactions between the interviewer and applicant.

In the employment interview it is important that candidates are evaluated against objective criteria related to job performance (predictors). **Contrast error** is a term used when interviewers evaluate candidates against the prior candidate rather than the objective criteria. This can cause errors in the evaluation. For example, an average candidate interviewed after a poor candidate might be evaluated higher than average.

Performance evaluation or appraisal

The overall objective of performance appraisal is to provide an accurate and objective measure of how well a person is performing a job. It involves making judgements and an assessment of performance of another person. An employee's appraisal is very much dependent on the perceptual process and can affect judgement (Bretz et al. 1992). Some common errors include the halo effect, systematic bias, most recent-performance error, and inadequate information error.

The systematic bias is a source of error in performance appraisal, based on different standards used by appraisers, for example the top rating given by one manager may not equate to a top rating given by another manager. The most-recent-performance error is a source of error that occurs in performance appraisals in which the managers rate an employee on the most recent behaviour rather than throughout the period since the last appraisal. The inadequate error occurs when appraisers rate their employees even though they may not know enough about them to rate them accurately. One of the most common rating errors is **central tendency**. This occurs where appraisers assign average ratings to performance dimensions. Krystofiak et al. (1988) suggest that busy appraisers, or those wary of confrontation and repercussions, may be tempted to assign middle-of the-ratings such as 'satisfactory' or 'adequate' regardless of the actual performance of the subordinate.

KEY LEARNING POINT

- The employment interview and performance appraisal are susceptible to perceptual errors.

4.2.5 Managing the perceptual process—impression management

Impression management plays an important role in person perception. It refers to the process by which people seek control or influence the impressions that others form (Schlenker 2000). Therefore, to some extent the perceiver only sees what the target person wants him or her to perceive. Impression management can be discreet or direct; however, in evaluative contexts such as the employment interview it can be heightened (Gilmore et al. 1999). In employee and appraisal interviews the target person is the candidate and the appraisee respectively, seek to SENSE?? influence events in a way that they believe will create a favourable impression of them (Stevens and Kristof 1995; Wayne and Kacmar 1991). The interviewer has to make sense of the information that is accumulated about the target person and this information processing is inherently subjective.

Assertive impression management tactics are used to acquire and promote favourable impressions and consist of both ingratiation and self-promotion tactics. Ingratiation tactics are behaviours designed to evoke interpersonal attraction or liking. Self-promotion tactics are somewhat different from ingratiation tactics in that they are behaviours intended to evoke attributions of competence or respect rather than attractiveness. Rosenfeld et al. (2002) highlight a number of forms of ingratiation such as opinion conformity, favour-doing, flattery and compliments, and self-enhancement (Table 4.1).

Although self-promotion has not been investigated as extensively as ingratiation (Stevens and Kristof 1995), theorists have identified several specific tactics that maybe used effectively to promote one self, such as entitlements, enhancements, and overcoming obstacles.

Impression management tactics can also be used to protect or repair one's self-image when it has been damaged either by one's behaviour or by information that surfaces during the interaction. These are called defensive impression management tactics and may include tactics such as excuses, justifications, and apologies (Gardner and Martinko 1988).

In the employee interview, while it might be obvious to appreciate that the target person is engaging in impression management tactics (supported by research: Fletcher 1990; Stevens and Kristof 1995), it is also the case that the interviewer is simultaneously attempting to 'create an impression' because he or she wants to attract or retain the 'best' candidates. Researchers have suggested that structured interviews are able to reduce the potential of impression management tactics (Campion et al. 1994).

Table 4.1. Descriptions of impression management tactics

Ingratiation tactics	Descriptions
Opinion conformity	Expressing opinions or acts in ways which are consistent with the person one is trying to impress in order to increase liking.
Favour-doing	Putting ourselves out or appearing to do so in order to receive a positive evaluation.
Flattery and compliments	Using forms of strategic praise that are effective in winning liking and respect of others.
Self-enhancement	Directly using acquisitive impression management to make oneself be seen as more attractive.
Self-promotion tactics	
Entitlements	Tactics which involve taking credit for positive outcomes or events, even if personal credit for such outcomes is unmerited.
Enhancements	Claims that the value of a positive event, for which the individual was responsible, was greater than most people might think.
Overcoming obstacles	Revealing obstacles that have been overcome in order to gain credit for success.
Defensive tactics	
Excuses	Claims that one is not responsible for the negative behaviour or outcome
Justifications	Claims that the behaviour for which one is responsible is not as bad as it appears.
Apologies	Accepting responsibility for a negative outcome or behaviour with acknowledgment that certain actions were unacceptable and should be punished.

4.2.6 Accuracy in person perception

Misjudgement in person perception can have far-reaching consequences in the workplace. A number of studies have focused on determining the reliability and accuracy with which people perceive others (Funder 1999; Kenny 1994). Cook (1984) argued that accurate perception cannot be achieved as there may not be a 'real' personality to compare judgements with. The implicit personality theory emphasizes that we perceive the world differently and when we agree with others it corresponds to common implicit ideas rather than accuracy. Other researchers argue that there is more than one type of accuracy and the social context in which we perceive others has a bearing on our judgemental accuracy (Cronbach 1955; Swann 1984; Kenny and Albright 1987).

Funder (1987) supports the idea that the accuracy of person perception should be studied in real world situations rather than in a laboratory and has carried out various studies. His research indicates that people tend to be reasonably accurate in their perceptions about others when meeting them. Funder and Colvin (1988) and Funder et al. (1995) found during face-to-face interactions judges tended to obtain moderate agreement with each other in their impressions of a common target person.

However, most of us have experienced instances where our perceptions have been clearly erroneous and the people and events around us were not what they appeared to be. To avoid the many problems associated with perceptual distortions Buchanan and Huczynski (2004) provide a number of remedies for improving person perception. These include:

1 Allowing more time and avoiding 'snap' judgements of others.

2 Collecting and consciously using more information about others.

3 Self-awareness and understanding of how our own biases and preferences affect our perceptions.

4 Checking our attributions.

A popular framework for understanding and knowing ourselves is the **Johari Window**. The basic concept of the Johari Window is that we can learn more about our hidden selves as we disclose more of our selves to others and receive feedback from others about our blind areas (see Chapter 6 on Relationships at Work).

4.3 Perception and attitudes

Attitudes can have an implicit effect on perception. Greenwald and Banaji (1995) noted that an attitude can have implicit effects on social judgement, for example the halo effect. Attitudes can also bias judgements. These biases are likely to be stronger when judgements are made under time pressure (Klauer and Stern 1992). The next part of the chapter focuses on attitudes and their impact on perception and behaviour. Attitudes at work are important for a number of reasons. They affect job satisfaction, cooperation with others, the image of how the organization is presented to clients or customers, work motivation, and the employee's psychological or physical well-being. We all hold attitudes not least because we usually attach an evaluation to our perception of people and things around us (Ajzen and Fishbein 2000).

Pause for thought
What can we do to improve our ability to perceive others more accurately?

4.3.1 Attitudes

Attitudes have been defined in a variety of ways, and central to most definitions is the notion of evaluation. Krech et al. (1962) define attitudes as enduring systems of positive or negative evaluations, emotional feelings, and action tendencies with respect to an individual's social world. A simple definition of attitudes is proposed by Makin et al. (1996): 'An attitude contains an assessment of whether the object to which it refers is liked or disliked.'

Attitudes act as an initial screen; people select information that is consistent with their attitudes and ignore that which is opposed to them. They are developed through experience but they are less stable than traits and change as new experiences are gained or influences absorbed.

Within organizations attitudes are affected by cultural factors, for example the values and norms in the organization, management style, policies such as those concerned with pay, recognition, promotion, and the quality of working life and the influence of the 'reference group' (the group with whom people identify).

Attitudes are often described as having three evaluative components:

- An Affective component—feelings or emotions that the object evokes.
- A Behavioural component—tendency or disposition to act in a particular way towards the object.
- A Cognitive component—our perception, thoughts, beliefs, and ideas about the object.

The affective or feeling component is of prime importance and it can have a significant impact on the other two components.

 Activity Work attitudes

If you are currently working, identify which work attitudes are important to you personally and whether or not these attitudes are supported at your workplace. Describe your feelings, thoughts, and behaviours towards work. If you are not working currently, this is a good time to reassess what attitudes are important to you so that you can incorporate these into your job search.

4.3.2 Attitude formation

Attitude formation can occur by simple associative processes of classical conditioning or direct reinforcement of behaviours consistent with attitudinal position. Attitudes can also be formed through observation of others. Thus most of our attitude formation can be traced back to our early socialization, the groups that we belong to, and our own experience of the world. Attitudes can also be formed consciously or unconsciously. Research shows that mere exposure to a stimulus or conditioning can influence attitude formation at below-conscious level (Olson and Fazio 2001, 2002; Lee 2001).

4.3.3 Functions of attitudes

Attitudes are thought to have various functions: mainly they are thought to provide order to our social world. They provide stability to the world we live in and help us cope with our environment so that we know our place in it (Kelman 1969).

Katz (1960) proposed a functionalist theory of attitudes which suggest attitudes are determined by the functions that they serve for us. People hold given attitudes to help them to achieve their basic goals. Katz distinguishes four types of psychological functions that attitudes fulfil; however these have not been experimentally tested to any great extent:

- Instrumental function—favourable attitudes are developed towards things that aid or reward us, for example the groups that we belong to.
- Knowledge function (mainly the belief component) —attitudes provide a meaningful, structured environment. This function helps us to organize our social world, making it more familiar and predictable.
- Value-expressive function—attitudes help in the expression of our own self-concept and are a central part of our self-concept.
- Ego-defensive/expressive function—attitudes serve to protect us from acknowledging basic truths about ourselves or the harsh realities of life. They can help us to protect our image of ourselves.

The basic idea behind the functional approach is that attitudes help a person to mediate between their own inner needs (expression, defence) and the outside world (social information).

4.3.4 Changing attitudes—theories of attitude change

According to the Yale Attitude Change Approach (Hovland et al. 1953) attitude change or persuasion is influenced by three factors: the message source (the originator of communication), the message itself (features of communication), and the audience (characteristics of those receiving the message).

The source

The major source characteristics are credibility and attractiveness. McGuire (1985) suggested communicator credibility is perceived by the target in terms of expertise and trustworthiness. Fluent communicators are associated with perceptions of higher credibility and found to be more expert than slow hesitant ones (Smith and Shaffer 1995).

When considering the credibility of the source, the **sleeper effect** should be noted. The sleeper effect is thought to develop after a lapse of time after which a person is thought to be more influenced by the content of the message rather than the credibility of the source.

Source attractiveness/likeability can also influence attitude change, the degree to which attitudes change positively is directly proportioned to the degree of attractiveness of the communicator (Tannenbaum 1956). Attractiveness is also thought to be useful if the message is unpopular although its power can diminish if the communicator intentionally exploits his or her attractiveness (Eagly and Chaiken 1975).

The message

A message can appeal to an individual's cognitive evaluation to help change an attitude. The nature of the message plays a key role in the persuasion process. When a two-sided message is presented it is generally more persuasive compared to a one-sided one (Hovland et al. 1949). The advantage to the receiver in a two-sided message is that they have a right of reply; also it allows the receiver more time to think about the issues raised in the message.

The message is likely to be influential when emotion is aroused in people. For example, people are more likely to be influenced by a message when fear is aroused, provided they are given clear practical guidance on how to deal with the fear that has been aroused. Das et al. (2003) examined attitude change in response to fear appeals and found vulnerability to treat results in attitude change.

The audience

There are characteristics of the audience that can make them more susceptible to the message. People with low self-esteem are likely to be relatively easily persuaded. Related to the issue of self-esteem, research shows that people who seek social approval are affected more by social influences than other people.

4.3.5 Central route versus peripheral route

Another explanation for attitude change includes the dual-process theory (Petty and Cacioppo (1985). This approach focuses on the message used to create attitude change and the thoughts that are processed by an individual during the persuasion attempt. The dual-process theory argues that attitude change occurs utilizing one of two routes. The first route is taken when a receiver carefully evaluates the most important factors in the persuasive situation. This is referred to as the 'central route'. Attitude changes induced via the central route are thought to be relatively enduring and predictive of behaviour.

The second route is called the 'peripheral route' persuasion. It is based on factors unrelated to the quality of the message. In the peripheral route to attitude change, the individual is encouraged to not look at the content but at the source. The peripheral route requires little effort or attention from the receiver who instead focuses upon variables that are not directly central to the attitude object for example, signing a petition based on the attractiveness of the requester.

 KEY LEARNING POINTS

- The three components of an attitude can be classified as affective, behavioural, and cognitive.
- Attitudes are thought to provide order to our social world.
- Attitudes can be changed.

4.4 Attitudes to work

The next part of the chapter will discuss attitudes and behaviour and consider the importance of two key job-related attitudes: job satisfaction and organizational commitment.

4.4.1 Attitudes and behaviour

The relationship between how much attitudes predict behaviour is not simple. Early research evidence suggested a weak to moderate link between attitudes and behaviour and that attitudes were fairly poor predictors of subsequent behaviour (Wicker 1969). However, Pratkanis and Turner (1994) propose there are some factors that can strengthen the relationship between attitudes and behaviour, these are:

- when attitudes are based on a solid foundation of knowledge;
- when attitudes can be easily identified and retrieved from the mind;
- when attitudes are protective and support important aspects of the self and the object they relate to.

Another area that has received attention is the relationship between intention and behaviour. The reasoned action theory (Ajzen and Fishbein 1980) suggests that a person's attitudes are best predicted by their intentions and intentions are determined by a person's attitudes and expectations others hold of them. The theory of planned behaviour (Ajzen and Madden 1986) is an extension of the theory of reasoned behaviour. The key element in the theory of planned

behaviour is the person's intention to perform a given behaviour. The theory suggests that intentions capture motivational factors that influence behaviour, so the stronger the intention to engage in behaviour, the more likely it is it will be performed by the person. The intention is only of value in predicting a person's behaviour if he or she can control whether to engage in the behaviour or not. Consequently, behavioural achievement depends jointly on motivation (intention) and ability (behavioural control).

4.4.2 Attitudes and job satisfaction

Job satisfaction is an affective or emotional reaction to the experience of work. It is concerned with feeling about the job rather than perceptions of it. However, it may be heavily influenced by perceptions. The set of feelings or attitudes we hold about the job can be positive or negative. There are many factors of the job that influence a person's job satisfaction these include attitudes towards pay and benefits, promotion, working conditions, colleagues, and characteristics of the job itself such as skill variety and interest and challenge. It is usually assumed that if workers are satisfied that they should be motivated to perform better and as a result performance will improve. However, research shows that the relationship between job performance and worker behaviour does not always occur as there are many contaminating factors which cloud the relationship (Iaffaldano and Muchinsky 1985).

Locke (1976) proposed a widely accepted definition of job satisfaction as 'a pleasurable positive emotional state resulting from the appraisal of one's job or job experiences'. The definition highlights the importance of the emotional aspect of job satisfaction. The idea that job satisfaction is some kind of emotional disposition has also been supported by other researchers Briner (1999) suggest that emotion to be a fundamental aspect of much of what we do at work.

There are numerous theories that have tried to explain the causes and sources of job satisfaction. The next part of this chapter will look at some of the literature and theory related to job satisfaction.

4.4.3 Job satisfaction and job design

Hackman and Oldham (1976) proposed a model of job satisfaction and job design. The model adopts a straightforward approach of looking for causes of job satisfaction in the characteristics of the job. According to Hackman and Oldham there are five core job characteristics that increase job satisfaction. These include:

1 skill variety—the perceived range of competencies required to perform the job;
2 task identity—the extent the job is seen as involving a whole, identifiable task;
3 task significance—the extent that the job affects the well-being of others;
4 autonomy—the extent the job is seen as allowing for personal initiative in performing the work;
5 job feedback—the extent that the job, itself, provides information about job performance.

These five characteristics give meaning to work, responsibility to the job holder, and provide knowledge on how they are doing. The worker in this awareness is then in a position to produce outcomes of the work with satisfaction. Hackman (1987) suggests that good results can be achieved on the five characteristics by:

- Forming natural work units—so work to be done has logic and makes sense to the job holder.
- Combing tasks—natural work units are combined to make a bigger and more coherent job.
- Establishing links with clients—the job holder has contact with people using the service or products supplied.
- Vertical loading—job holders take on more of the management of their jobs.
- Opening feedback **channels**—so job holders can discover more about how they are doing.

Job satisfaction can be improved by redesigning the job taking into consideration the above. Job design may include job rotation, enlargement or enrichment, autonomous work teams, and flexibility.

The approach most frequently used to measure employee attitudes is questionnaires with rating scales. The most popular of these are the Job Descriptive Index (JDI), Minnesota Satisfaction Questionnaire (MSQ), and Job Satisfaction Scales. The Job Descriptive Index contains five job factors: pay, promotion, supervision, nature of work, characteristics of one's co-workers. The Minnesota Satisfaction Questionnaire covers twenty job facets and requires the respondent to rate these from various levels of satisfaction. The MSQ poses each item as follows: 'In my present job, this is how I feel about . . . ' (for example, being able to keep busy all the time, the chance to do different things from time to time). The Job Satisfaction Scale requires the respondent to rate how they think or feel about various aspects of their job on a number of statements using a Likert scale. The individual scores are added up to create an overall job satisfaction score. Likert scale approaches are commonly used to measure attitudes providing the respondent with a range of responses to a given question or statement (Likert 1932). Typically there are five categories of responses, from strongly agree to strongly disagree. Likert scales are designed to measures the strength of a person's agreement with a clear set of statements.

The use of questionnaires to measure job satisfaction has not gone without criticism. Researchers have suggested that the simple summation of job facets scores does not capture all aspects of job satisfaction (Scarpello and Campbell 1983).

Other techniques for measuring job satisfaction are interviews. These are sometimes used in conjunction to questionnaires. Another method used is the Critical Incident technique—basically, the technique requires employees to recall job situation/incidents that occurred at times when they felt very good or very bad about their jobs. The advantages of using both interviews and the Critical Incident technique is that they provide respondents greater freedom to express themselves. However, they can be time consuming and open to bias.

Theories of job satisfaction have also looked at the relationship of job satisfaction and performance, turnover, and absenteeism. There is some evidence to show that performance is related to job satisfaction although findings have shown the relationship to be weak (Iaffaldano and Muchinsky 1985). Performance is thought to be good where it differentially rewarded, that is if people see performers get a bonus or more pay then it seems to reinforce and their positive feelings and enhance job performance.

Research on the relationship with turnover generally shows lower levels of job satisfaction are linked with an individual's propensity to leave (Mowday et al. 1984; Lee and Mowday 1987). However, leaving a job is a huge decision and there are many factors which play a part in it, such as the condition of the labour market, tenure within organization, and also the prospect of finding an alternative job. As with turnover there are many factors which could lead to absenteeism. The relationship between low job satisfaction leading to high levels of absenteeism is not a strong one (Clegg 1983).

4.4.4 Attitudes and organizational commitment

Another important work-related attitude is organizational commitment. Organizational commitment has been defined as the relative strength of an individual's identification with and involvement in an organization (Mowday et al. 1982). Meyer (1997) argues that organizational commitment comprises three distinct components:

- An employee's acceptance of the values and goals of the organization.
- A willingness to exert effort on behalf of the organization.
- A desire to remain affiliated with the organization.

Organizations however are complex and made up of a number of divisions each with their own agendas and goals. Commitment can therefore be directed at specific aspects of a person's job, for example the department, the location, trade unions. Cohen (1993) suggests that employees are more likely to develop their strongest attachment to subgroups or teams rather than the organization itself since these are more significant to their day-to-day meaning.

Researchers have identified three types of organizational commitment: affective commitment, continuance commitment, and normative commitment (Allen and Meyer 1990; Meyer 1997).

- Affective commitment—the employee's emotional attachment to the organization. The employee identifies with the organization and absorbs its values and complies with its demands.

- Continuance commitment—the employee's perception of the cost and risks associated with leaving their current organization. For example, an employee may be bound to the organization by peripheral factors such as pension plans which would not continue if he/she left.

- Normative commitment—denotes a moral dimension based on an employee's obligation and responsibility to remain with the organization. For example, such a feeling could be developed through receiving benefits such as specific skills training.

Employees can exhibit varying degrees of all three components. A number of studies have looked more closely at these components of commitment and their influence on outcomes such as performance and turnover. Research relating to the affective component shows that intrinsic factors related to the job such as challenge and autonomy are more important in fostering this component than extrinsic factors such as pay and work conditions (Dunham et al. 1994). Similarly Mathieu and Zajac (1990) found the strongest correlates of affective organizational commitment were 'job characteristics' (**job enrichment**) and group-leader relations (for example, communication, participative leadership, task interdependence). With relation to performance Meyer et al. (1989) found that workers high on affective commitment to their organization tended to be better performers that those rating low affective commitment. The findings also show that continuance commitment is negatively related to job performance. A study by Meyer (1997) suggests low affective commitment relates to a desire to leave the organization. Research related to the normative commitment shows that commitment is influenced to some extent by a person's personality or disposition and that commitment is more natural to some than others (Bateman and Strasser 1984).

4.4.5 Organizational citizenship behaviour

Despite the intuitive appeal of a strong relationship between commitment and performance empirical evidence to support this theory appears to be lacking. One explanation for this is performance is influenced by too many other variables such as, individual skills and behaviour of co-workers to show a strong link to an attitudinal construct like commitment (Biggs and Swailes 2005).

In order to understand the relationship between commitment and performance the concept of organizational citizenship behaviour was introduced. Organizational citizenship behaviour (OCB) refers to 'individual contributions in the workplace that go beyond the role requirements and contractually rewarded job achievements' (Organ and Ryan 1995). This includes behaviour such as staying late to finish work when not specifically asked to do so, or helping a co-worker who is having difficulty when that is not part of the role requirement of the job. Such behaviours are helpful to the organization but may not be directly or explicitly recognized in the organization's formal reward system (for a recent review see Podsakoff et al. 2000).

Organizational citizenship behaviour can exist at an individual, group, or organizational level and has a number of aspects. Several types or dimensions of OCB have been identified (Podsakoff et al. 2000); however, Schnake and Dumler (2003) highlight five dimensions that are frequently examined by researchers. These include:

- Altruism—helping behaviours directed at individuals in the organization; for example, helping a co-worker who has fallen behind in his or her work.

- Conscientiousness—behaviours which benefit the organization and not specific individuals or groups; for example, performing one's role in a manner which is beyond the norm.

- Civic virtue—responsible participation in the political process of an organization; for example, keeping abreast of organizational decisions or issues.

- Sportsmanship—tolerating the inconveniences and annoyances of organizational life without complaining.

- Courtesy—preventing problems by keeping others informed of your decisions which may affect them and passing information on to those who find it useful.

Research shows that organizational citizenship behaviours are a 'robust' correlate of job satisfaction (Organ and Konovsky 1989) and commitment (Feather and Rauter 2004). Organ and Ryan (1995) found that organizational commitment has a stronger relationship with organizational citizenship behaviours than with performance.

4.4.6 Measuring organizational commitment

A number of instruments are available to measure organizational commitment. Some specifically measure the affective component such as the Organizational Commitment Questionnaire (OCQ) developed by Mowday et al. (1979) and an instrument developed by Warr et al. (1979). The OCQ is a fifteen-item scale inviting employees to respond to questions such as 'I am proud to tell others that I am part of this organization.' Researchers have reported good reliability and validity data for the OCQ across various studies (Meyer and Allen 1997). More recent instruments such as the one developed by Allen and Meyer (1990) measure all three: affective, continuance, and normative components.

KEY LEARNING POINTS

- The relationship between how much attitudes predict behaviour is not clear-cut.
- Job satisfaction and organizational commitment are two key job-related attitudes.
- Job satisfaction and organizational commitment attitudes are usually measured with questionnaires with rating scales.

Chapter summary

- The importance of studying perception in the workplaces was examined. Our perceptual process can be influenced by a various factors it explains why people may perceive the same thing differently.

- Person perception is an important aspect of perception and plays a vital role in the workplace. Perceptual distortions affect our perception of others.

- The Attribution theory explains the ways in which we judge people differently by the meaning we attribute to their behaviour. The chapter examined various research studies related to the attribution theory and addressed how the theory can explain aspects of discrimination and prejudice.

- Various perceptual short cuts were examined in particular stereotypes. The process of stereotyping is often judged to be dysfunctional leading to errors, problems, and prejudices. Yet the process underpinning stereotyping can be seen as inevitable and useful, stereotypes serve to as a social function and simplify perception. Dependency on these processes makes stereotypes resistant to change.

- The employment interview and performance appraisal were used as examples to demonstrate perceptual distortion in organizations.

- The role that impression management plays in the perceptual process was examined in addition the tactics used to form impressions were also explored. Although research suggests that our perception of others is generally accurate it can be improved by using remedies such as checking our attributions and developing self-awareness.

- The chapter turned attention to attitudes, what they are, how they are formed, and the functions of attitudes were described with reference to Katz's functionalist theory. Attitude change with respect to persuasion was examined and various theories of attitude change were examined.

- The relationship between attitudes and behaviour was introduced.

- Two key job attitudes—job satisfaction and organizational commitment—were examined. The research shows that the relationship these two attitudes have with other work outcomes such as performance, turnover, and absenteeism is not a strong one. However, a stronger relationship exists between organizational commitment and Organizational Citizenship Behaviour. Finally, the chapter examined the measurement of job satisfaction and organization commitment and noted that the two attitudes are frequently measured using rating scales.

Assess your learning

Review questions

1 Define perception.

2 What is attribution theory? What are its implications for explaining behaviour in organizations?

3 What are stereotypes?

4 What are the problems associated with stereotyping at work? Give examples in the workplace of how stereotyping can create perceptual distortion.

5 How can person perception be improved?

6 What are attitudes? What is meant by the components of an attitude?

Assignments

ASSIGNMENT 1: Person perception
Describe the common errors that occur in person perception and explain the Implications of these for work situations.

ASSIGNMENT 2: Job satisfaction
The relationship between job satisfaction and outcomes (e.g. performance and absenteeism) may not be as strong as many people think. Discuss.

Further reading

Rosenfeld, P., Giacalone, R., and Riordan, C. (2002) *Impression Management: Building and Enhancing Relationships at Work* (2nd edn.). London: Thomas Learning.
An accessible text which describes how people use impression management tactic in the workplace.

Posthuma, R. A., Morgeson, F. P., and Campion, M. A. (2002) Beyond employment interview validity: a comprehensive narrative review of recent research and trends over time. *Personnel Psychology*, 55: 1–81.

Work psychology in practice
The Box Office

Lara worked for an arts centre which promoted arts throughout the local borough and programmes to schools and community groups. The centre recognized the unique contribution that the arts made to the development of a more inclusive society and promoted this in its programmes. The local city council that supported the centre also recognized this and encouraged the centre to continue to present a programme that reflected the cultural diversity of its borough.

Lara had been working at the centre for two years, starting as a Box Office Assistant. This role involved serving customers, answering queries about courses, and dealing with course bookings. Lara enjoyed this job—after all, all she had to do was serve customers and when there were no customers she had time to surf the internet. The only frustration was the low salary and sometimes customers were difficult. Her relationship with the Box Office Supervisor was great, in fact her supervisor was like a good friend rather than a boss. As Lara worked full-time and her supervisor only worked part-time Lara felt competent running the department in her supervisor's absence. Lara felt confident working with her supervisor and sometimes felt that she should be employed as a Supervisor's Assistant rather than a Box Office Assistant and also be paid more.

After two years Lara's supervisor decided to apply for another position internally and was offered the job which meant that there was an opening for the Box Officer Supervisor position.

The Director of the organization, Sarah, had a close working relationship with Peter, an Arts Councillor. Peter was keen that the centre should represent a more ethnically mixed workforce and so recommended someone he had in mind for the supervisor job. This potential candidate had worked with him on another project, but had little supervisory experience.

On learning that the supervisor's job was being offered to a minority member so that the organization was perceived to employ a 'token representative' Lara and her colleagues were furious, and felt that the position should have been advertised. In a meeting with Sarah, Lara and her colleagues expressed their frustration and were opposed to the unfair recruitment decision. Sarah realized this decision was unfair and reviewed it; however, she was also aware the current Box Office Supervisor would soon be moving into her new position and the centre would need to fill this vacancy rapidly. She was aware external recruitment would be a lengthy process so she advertised the position internally and to her surprise nobody applied.

So Sarah approached Lara about taking on the Box Office Supervisor position. Lara was aware that the position needed to be filled immediately and felt pressured to accept it. However, Lara disapproved of Sarah's management style and felt the work atmosphere had changed since Sarah had joined the centre—it was no longer a pleasant work environment. Lara reminisced about the harmonious and pleasant work atmosphere of the centre when it was run by their previous director. She toyed with the decision: the supervisor job would be good experience and she could do with the extra money. It would make her CV stronger and doing the job would not be a huge transition from the job she was already doing, so she decided to take the job.

Lara enjoyed her new role, she had less to do with difficult customers and felt confident managing the department, although what she didn't like was Sarah's management style. Their attitudes and values differed so much that it was causing friction. Sarah's approach involved firing anyone that did not behave the way she wanted, whereas Lara's approach was to try to work things through. Lara didn't appreciate the way Sarah spoke down to her and was beginning to feel less confident. Her workload had increased as Sarah often delegated extra jobs to her. Lara would do these jobs but never felt that she got any gratitude for the extra work. Lara feared if she refused to do the extra work she would get fired. The increased workload sometimes meant that Lara had less time for her own duties. Sarah had also cut staff from Lara's department, which soon began to reflect on customer service. Lara feared complaints made by customers would point towards her management of the department and she would be blamed.

Six months into the job Lara was frustrated and felt less committed to the arts centre. Lara was desperate to find a new job, she had lost motivation to go to work, and while she was at work she feared that one simple mistake could get her fired.

Questions

- Consider how the research on organizational commitment and behaviour relates to the case study.
- Consider how the research on job satisfaction and behaviour relate to the case study.
- What does the case study tell you about organizational commitment and how managers in organizations should take care about how committed their staff are?

Online Resource Centre

Visit the supporting online resource centre for additional material which will help you with your research, essays, and assignments, or you may find these additional resources helpful when revising for exams.
http://www.oxfordtextbooks.co.uk/orc/matthewman/

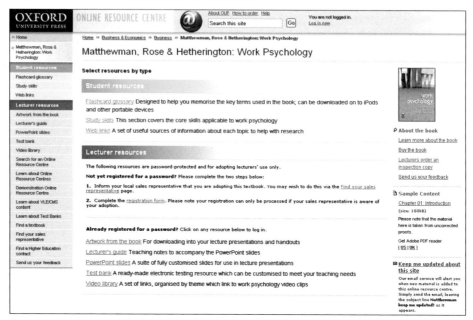

References

Ajzen, I., and Fishbein, M. (1980) *Understanding Attitudes and Predicting Social Behavior*. Englewood Cliffs, NJ: Prentice Hall.

Ajzen, I., and Fishbein, M. (2000) Attitudes and the attitude–behaviour relation: reasoned automatic process. In W. Stroebe and M. Hewstone, *European Review of Social Psychology*. Chichester: John Wiley.

Ajzen, I., and Madden, J. T. (1986) Prediction of goal-directed behavior: attitudes, intentions, and perceived behavioral control. *Journal of Experimental Social Psychology*, 22: 453–74.

Allen, N. J., and Meyer, J. P. (1990) The measurement and antecedents of affective, continuance and normative commitment to the organization. *Journal of Occupational Psychology*, 63: 11–18.

Allport, G. W. (1954) *The Nature of Prejudice*. Reading, MA: Addison-Wesley.

Ashforth, B. E., and Mael, F. (1989) Social identity theory and the organization. *Academy of Management Review*, 14: 20–39.

Bateman, T., and Strasser, S. (1984) A longitudinal analysis of the antecedents of organizational commitment. *Academy of Management Journal*, 27: 95–112.

Biggs, D., and Swailes, S. (2005) Relations, commitment and satisfaction in agency workers and permanent workers. *Employee Relations*. 28/2: 130–43.

Billig, M. (1987) *Arguing and Thinking: A Rhetorical Approach to Social Psychology*. Cambridge: Cambridge University Press.

Bretz, R. D., Milkovich, G. T., and Read, W. (1992) The current state of performance-appraisal research and practice: concerns, directions, and implications. *Journal of Management*, 18: 321–52.

Briner, R. (1999) Emotion at work: feeling and smiling. *The Psychologist*, Jan.: 16–19.

Buchanan, D., and Huczynski, A. (2004) *Organisational Behaviour: An Introductory Text* (5th edn.). Harlow: Prentice Hall.

Campion, M. A., Campion, J. E., and Hudson, J. P. (1994) Structured interviewing: a note on incremental validity and alternative question types. *Journal of Applied Psychology*, 79: 998–1002.

Cargile, A. C. (2000) Evaluations of employment suitability: does accent always matter? *Journal of Employment Counselling*, 37: 165.

Clegg, C. W. (1983) Psychology of employee lateness, absence and turnover: a methodological critique and an empirical study. *Journal of Applied Psychology*, Feb.: 88–101.

Cohen, A. (1993) Organizational commitment and turnover: a meta-analysis. *Academy of Management Journal*, 36: 1140–7.

Cook, M. (1984) The good judge of others' personality: methodological problems and their resolution. In M. Cook (ed.), *Issues in Person Perception*. London: Methuen.

Cronbach, L. J. (1955) Processes affecting scores on 'understanding of others' and 'assumed similarity'. *Psychological Bulletin*, 52: 177–93.

Das, E. H. H., de Wit, J. B. F, and Stroebe, W. (2003) Fear appeals motivate acceptance of action recommendations: evidence for a positive bias in the processing of persuasive messages. *Personality and Social Psychology Bulletin*, 29: 650–64.

Devine, P. G. (1989) Stereotypes and prejudice: their automatic and controlled components. *Journal of Personality and Social Psychology*, 56: 5–18.

Dipoboye, R. L. (1982) Self-fulfilling prophecies in the selection-recruitment interview. *Academy of Management Review*, 7: 579–86.

Dipoboye, R. L. (1992) *Selection Interviews: Process Perspectives*. Cincinnati: South-Western.

Dunham, R., Grube, J. A., and Castaneda, M. B. (1994) Organizational commitment: the utility of an integrative definition. *Journal of Applied Psychology*, 79: 370–80.

Eagly, A. H., and Chaiken, S. (1975) An attribution analysis of the effect of communicator characteristics on opinion change: the case of communicator attractiveness. *Journal of Personality and Social Psychology*, 33: 136–44.

Eder, R. W., and Harris, M. M (1999) Employment interview research: historical update and introduction. In R. W. Eder and M. M. Harris (eds.), *The Employment Interview Handbook*. Thousand Oaks, CA: Sage Publications, 1–27.

Falkenberg, L. (1990) Improving the accuracy of stereotypes in the workplace. *Journal of Management*, 16: 107–18.

Feather, N. T., and Rauter, K. A. (2004) Organisation citizenship behaviour in relation to job status, job security, organisational commitment, job satisfaction. *Journal of Occupational and Organisational Psychology*, 77: 81–94.

Fein, S., and Spencer S. J (1997) Prejudice as self-image mainte-nance: affirming the self through derogating others. *Journal of Personality and Social Psychology*, 73: 31–44.

Fiske, S. T. (1993) Controlling other people: the impact of power on stereotyping. *American Psychologist*, 48: 621–8.

Fletcher, C. (1990) The relationship between candidate personal-ity, self presentation strategies, and interviewer assessments in selection interviews: an empirical study. *Human Relations*, 43: 739–49.

Funder, D. C. (1987) Errors and mistakes: evaluating the accuracy of social judgement. *Psychological Review*, 101: 75–90.

Funder, D. C. (1999) Prospects for improving accuracy. Ch. 8 in *Personality Judgement: A Realistic Approach to Person Perception*. San Diego: Academic Press.

Funder, D. C., and Colvin, C. R. (1988) Friends and strangers: acquaintanceship, agreement, and the accuracy of personality judgement. *Journal of Personality and Social Psychology*, 55: 149–58.

Funder, D. C., Kolar, D. C., and Blackman, M. C. (1995) Agreement among judges in personality: interpersonal relations, similarity and acquaintanceship. *Journal of Personality and Social Psychol-ogy*, 69: 656–72.

Gardner, W. L., and Martinko, M. J. (1988) Impression management in organizations. *Journal of Management*, 14: 32–138.

Gilmore, D. C., Stevens, C. K., Harrell-Cook., G., and Ferris, G. R. (1999) Impression management tactics. In R. W. Eder and M. M. Harris (eds.), *The Employment Interview Handbook*. London: Sage, 321–36.

Greenwald, A. G., and Banaji, M. R. (1995) Implicit social cognition: attitudes, self-esteem, and stereotypes. *Psychology Review*, 102: 4–7.

Hackman, J. R. (1987) Work design. In R. M. Steers and L. W. Porter (eds.), *Motivation and Work Behaviour* (4th edn.). London: McGraw-Hill.

Hackman, J. R., and Oldham, G. R. (1976) Motivation through the design of work: test of a theory. *Organizational Behavior and Human Performance*, 16/2: 250–79.

Harvey, J. H., and Weary, G. (1984) Current issues in attribution theory and research. *Annual Review of Psychology*, 35: 427–59.

Haslam, S. A., Turner, J. C., Oakes, P. J., McGarty, C., and Hayes, B. K. (1992) Context-dependent variation in social stereotyping: the effects of intergroup relations as mediated by social change and frame of reference. *European Journal of Social Psychology*, 22: 3–20.

Hilton, J. L., and Von Hippel, W. (1996) Stereotypes. *Annual Review of Psychology*, 47: 237–71.

Howitt, D., Billig, M., Cramer, D., Edwards, D., Kniveton, B., Potter, J., Pearson and Radley, A. (1989) *Social Psychology: Conflicts and Controversies*. Milton Keynes: Open University Press.

Hovland, C. I., Janis, I. L., and Kelley, H. H. (1953) *Communications and Persuasion: Psychological Studies in Opinion Change*. New Haven: Yale University Press.

Hovland, C. I., Lumsdaine, A., and Sheffield, F. (1949) *Experiments on Mass Communication*. Princeton: Princeton University Press.

Iaffaldano, M. T., and Muchinsky, P. M. (1985) Job satisfaction and job performance: a meta-analysis. *Psychological Bulletin*, 97: 251–73.

Katz, D. (1960) The functional approach to the study of attitudes. *Public Opinion Quarterly*, 24: 163–204.

Kawakami, K., Dion, K. L., and Dovindio, J. F. (1998) Racial prejudice and stereotype activation. *Personality and Social Psychology Bulletin*, 24: 407–16.

Kelly, H. H. (1971) *Attribution in Social Interaction*. Morristown, NJ: General Learning Press.

Kelman, H. C. (1969) Patterns of personal involvement in the national system: a social psychological analysis of political legiti-macy. In J. N. Rosenau (ed.), *International Politics and Foreign Policy*. New York: Free Press.

Kenny, D. A. (1994) *Interpersonal Perception: A Social Relations Analysis*. New York: Guilford.

Kenny, D. A., and Albright, L. (1987) Accuracy in interpersonal perception: a social relations analysis. *Psychological Bulletin*, 102: 309–402.

Klauer, K. C., and Stern, E. (1992) How attitudes guide memory-based judgements: a two process model. *Journal of Experimental Social Psychology*, 28: 186–206.

Krech, D., Crutchfield, R. S., and Ballachey, E. (1962) *Individual in Society*. New York: McGraw-Hill.

Krystofiak, F., Cardy, R., and Newman, J. (1988) Implicit personality and performance appraisal: the influence of trait inferences on evaluation of behaviour. *Journal of Applied Psychology*, 73/3: 515–21.

Lee, A. Y. (2001) The mere exposure effect: an uncertainty reduction explanation revisited. *Personality and Social Psychology Bulletin*, 27: 1255–66.

Lee, T. W., and Mowday, R. T. (1987) Voluntarily leaving an organisa-tion: an empirical investigation of Steers and Mowday's model of turnover. *Academy of Management Journal*, Dec.: 721–43.

Levy, P. F. (2001) The Nut Island effect: when good teams go wrong. *Harvard Business Review*, 79/5: 51–9.

Likert, R. (1932) A technique for the measurement of attitudes. *Archives of Psychology*, 140: 52.

Lippi-Green, R. (1997) *English with an Accent: Language, Ideology, and Discrimination in the United States*. London: Routledge.

Lippman, W. (1922) *Public Opinion*. New York: Harcourt Brace.

Locke, E. A. (1976) The nature and causes of job satisfaction. In M. D. Dunnette (ed.), *Handbook of Industrial and Organisational psychology*. Chicago: Rand McNally.

Macrae, C. N., and Bodenhausen, G. V. (2000) Social cognition: thinking categorically about others. *Annual Review of Psychology*, 51: 93–120.

Macrae, C. N., Milne, A. B., and Bodenhausen, G. V. (1994) Stereotypes as energy-saving devices: a peak inside the cognitive toolbox. *Journal of Personality and Social Psychology*, 66: 37–47.

Makin, P., Cooper, C., and Cox, C. (1996) *Organizations and the Psychological Contract*. Leicester: BPS Books.

Mathieu, J. E., and Zajac, D. M. (1990) A review and meta-analysis of the antecedents, correlates and consequences of organiza-tional commitment. *Psychological Bulletin*, 108: 171–94.

Meyer, J. P. (1997) Organizational commitment. In C. L. Cooper and I. T. Robertson (eds.), *International Review of Industrial and Organisational Psychology*, vol. xii. Chichester: John Wiley.

Meyer, J. P., and Allen, N. J. (1997) *Commitment in the Workplace: Theory, Research and Application*. Thousand Oaks, CA: Sage.

Meyer, J. P., Paunonen, S. V., Gellatly, I. R., Goffin, R. D., and Jackson, D. N. (1989) Organizational commitment and job performance: it's the nature of the commitment that counts. *Journal of Applied Psychology*, 74: 152–6.

Mezulis, A. H., Abramson, L. Y., Hyde, J. S., and Hankin, B. L. (2004) Is there a universal positivity bias in attributions? A meta-analytic review of individual, developmental, and cultural differences in self-serving attributional bias. *Psychological Bulletin*, 130/5: 711–47.

Miller, A. G., and Lawson, T. (1989) The effect of an informational option on the fundamental attribution error. *Personality and Social Psychology Bulletin*, June: 194–204.

Mowday, R. T., Koberg, C. S., and McArthur, A. W. (1984) The psychology of the withdrawal process: a cross-validation test of Mowday's intermediate linkages model of turnover in two samples. *Academy of Management Journal*, 27: 79–94.

Mowday, R. T., Porter, L. W., and Steers, R. M. (1982) *Employee-Orientation Linkages: The Psychology of Commitment, Absenteeism, and Turnover.* New York: Academic Press.

Mowday, R. T., Steers, R. M., and Porter, L. W. (1979) The measurement of organizational commitment. *Journal of Vocational Behaviour,* 14: 224–7.

Nisbett, R. E., and Ross, L. (1980) *Human Inference: Strategies and Shortcomings of Social Judgement,* Englewood Cliffs, NJ: Prentice-Hall.

Northcraft, G. B., Polzer, J. T., Neale, M. A., and Kramer, R. M. (1995) Diversity, social identity, and performance: emergent social dynamics in cross functional teams. In S. E. Jackson and M. N. Ruderman (eds.), *Diversity in Work Teams: Research Paradigms for a Changing Workplace.* Washington, DC: American Psychological Association, 69–96.

Olson, M. A., and Fazio, R. H. (2001) Implicit attitude formation through classical conditioning. *Psychological Science,* 12: 413–17.

Olson, M. A., and Fazio, R. H. (2002) Implicit acquisition and manifestation of classically conditioned attitudes. *Social Cognition,* 20: 89–104.

Organ, D. W., and Konovsky, M. (1989) Cognitive versus affective determinants of organisational citizenship behaviour. *Journal of Applied Psychology,* 74/1: 157–64.

Organ, D. W., and Ryan, K. (1995) A meta-analytical review of attitudinal and dispositional predictors of organizational citizenship behaviour. *Personnel Psychology,* 48: 775–802.

Otting, L. G. (2004) Don't rush to judgements. *HR Magazine,* 49/1: 95–8.

Petty, R. E., and Cacioppo, J. T. (1985) The elaboration likelihood model of persuasion. In L. Berkowitwz (ed.), *Advances in Experimental Psychology,* vol. xix. New York: Academic Press.

Podsakoff, P. M., MacKenzie, S. B., Paine, J. B., and Bachrach, D. G. (2000) Organisational citizenship behaviours: a critical review of the theoretical and empirical literature and suggestions for future research. *Journal of Management,* 26: 513–63.

Posthuma, R. A., Morgeson, F. P., and Campion, M. A. (2002) Beyond employment interview validity: a comprehensive narrative review of recent research and trends over time. *Personnel Psychology,* 55: 1–81.

Pratkanis, A. R., and Turner, M. E. (1994) Of what value is a job attitude? A socio-cognitive analysis. *Human Relations,* 47: 1545–76.

Rosenfeld, P., Giacalone, R., and Riordan, C. (2002) *Impression Management: Building and Enhancing Relationships at Work* (2nd edn.). London: Thomas Learning.

Rosenthal, R., and Jacobson, L. (1968) *Pygmalion in the Classroom.* New York: Holt, Rinehart & Winston.

Scarpello, V., and Campbell, J. P. (1983) Job satisfaction: are all the parts there? *Personnel Psychology,* 36: 577–600.

Schlenker, B. R. (2000) Impression management. In A. F. Kazdin (ed. in chief), *Encyclopedia of Psychology.* Washington, DC: American Psychological Association of Books.

Schnake, M. E., and Dumler, M. P. (2003) Levels of measurement and analysis issues in organizational citizenship behaviour and research. *Journal of Occupational and Organisational Psychology,* 76: 283–301.

Semin, G. R. (1980) A gloss on attribution theory. *British Journal of Social and Clinical Psychology,* 19: 291–300.

Smith, S. M., and Shaffer, D. R. (1995) Speed of speech and persuasion: evidence for multiple effects. *Personality and Social Psychology Bulletin,* 21: 1051–60.

Springbett, B. M. (1958) Factors affecting the final decision in the employment interview. *Canadian Journal of Psychology,* 12: 13–22.

Stevens, C. K., and Kristof, A. L. (1995) Making the right impression: a field study of applicant impression management during job interviews. *Journal of Applied Psychology,* Oct.: 587–606.

Swann, W. B., Jr. (1984) Quest for accuracy in person perception: a matter of pragmatics. *Psychological Review,* 91: 457–77.

Tannenbaum, P. (1956) Initial attitude toward source and concept as factors in attitude change through communication. *Public Opinion Quarterly,* 20: 413–26.

Tierney, P., and Farmer, S. (2002) Creative self-efficacy: its potential antecedents and relationship to creative performance. *Academy of Management Journal,* 45: 1137–48.

Warr, P., Cook, J., and Wall, T. (1979) Scales for the measurement of some work attitudes and aspects of psychological well-being. *Journal of Occupational Psychology,* 52: 129–48.

Wayne, S. J., and Kacmar, K. M. (1991) The effects of impression management on the performance appraisal process. *Organisational Behaviour and Human Decision Processes,* Feb.: 70–88.

Weiner, B. (1979) A theory of motivation for some classroom experiments. *Journal of Educational Psychology,* 71: 3–25.

Wicker, A. W. (1969) Attitudes versus actions: the relationship of overt and behavioural responses to attitude objects. *Journal of Social Issues,* 25: 41–78.

Chapter 5
Motivation and work satisfaction

Jenni Nowlan and Angela Wright

Chapter objectives

As a result of reading this chapter and using the additional web-based material you should be able to:

- Understand content theories of motivation.
- Understand process theories of motivation.
- Explore the concept of goal-setting theory.
- Discuss the power of pay to motivate people in the workplace.
- Identify some of the factors, which influence job satisfaction.
- Discuss the relevance of motivation theory to the optimizing of employee performance.
- List some of the influences of motivation on employment areas such as training and employee retention.

Work psychology in practice
On the high street

A large chain of fashion retail outlets recently contracted an occupational psychologist in an initiative to try to improve profits as sales had been falling. It was thought this was not only because of the general high street trend but that there were other issues underlying this as when benchmarking it was clear to see that sales were down considerably more than in other similar retail stores.

After conducting surveys, interviews, and analysing the data the consultant found several areas that required further exploration. One of these was the general attitude to some of the changes that had occurred previously and this applied to employees across various departments. In the warehouse, Jim, a supervisor, who was only ten years off from retirement and who had worked his way up from the age of 16, had seen many changes throughout the years and not only in technology. He had tried hard to keep up with how his job had changed, availing himself of all training courses offered to him by the organization. However, he now felt, although a latest initiative (before the consultant had been called in) had been to try to simplify his job some-what because others carrying out similar roles had suffered from long-term sickness due to stress from the long hours and responsibilities that had grown throughout the years, that he had little control over his job. Yes, it was easier to get through the day and he even finished work at a reasonable time but the challenge was gone for him. His agenda for the week was set by his line manager (instead of doing this important role him-self) and he felt that he had become more of a 'form-filler'. In fact, he even felt rather overpaid for what he was doing. He wondered to himself why he couldn't be happy about this, after all there were many of the staff there (or so he thought) that would jump at the chance of getting reasonable money for little input. He real-ized, of course, that the company had changed things to try to save money, clearly because it was very expen-sive to pay people on long-term sick leave and they also had a duty of care so he could see that they would not want more staff going off sick.

Jim, though, was a hardy man and he knew that he hadn't been stressed and that he had thrived on the challenge of each day, logistically making everything come together. He felt a sense of pride that he was able to be so successful at achieving this. Now, it seemed that anyone could take over his job, and, he thought, he might as well take early retirement. Perhaps he could find more challenges in the world outside work now.

Questions

- In your opinion, why do you think it was important to Jim to be able to make his own goals each day?
- Do you think the organization in the case study was 'right' to move the responsibilities to the line manager?
- Do you think it highly unlikely that Jim would feel tension at being paid for more than he felt he was actually doing each day?
- What do you think the occupational psychologist could recommend to the organization in regards to employees feeling as Jim did?

5.1 Introduction

Motivation is one of the oldest and important concepts in psychology but remains difficult to define and in addition there is not even a universally accepted generalized theory. Therefore, possibly the best way to view the theories is to look at them collectively and to use them as a framework for guidance.

Of the many theories that have been put forward over the years, there are four basic areas that an understanding of motivation needs to cover. These areas are: arousal, or inducement of effort; how to get that effort directed in the right place (and clearly in an organizational con-text that would mean organizational goals); degree of effort or how to obtain the maximum effort; and finally maintenance and how to sustain a high level of effort.

This chapter will analyse the main theories of motivation developed over the years, look at job satisfaction and dissatisfaction, consider how a realistic modification of work behaviour might be achieved, cover various ways to measure job satisfaction, and finally look at possible ways forward for researchers and practitioners alike.

5.2 Theories of work motivation

From the early Scientific Management work of F. W. Taylor (1911) with his time and motion studies with monetary incentives, to Mayo (1933) and the Hawthorne Effect in Western Electric in Chicago (1927, 1932), whereby output increased when employees were paid attention, the development of many theories of work motivation have continued to evolve that largely compete with each other. However, when criticizing these theories we should consider that many of the theories put forward were not intended to be applied to the workplace and many of them were originally proposed as general theories of motivation.

5.2.1 McGregor (1960)—Theory X and Theory Y

Following on from Taylor and Mayo another early approach to motivation was that of McGregor (1960) with his Theory X and Theory Y. In Theory X, people are thought to be inherently lazy, unreliable, and not to be trusted. These people need to be motivated possibly by rewards and/or punishments in order to control them. This is in stark contrast to Theory Y people who are creative, independent, and who will strive for their true potential and their personal best.

In the preceding case study, we can clearly see that Jim fell under the category of Theory Y. He suffered when he had less to do and was clearly not lazy, he was very reliable and was most certainly not motivated by rewards but more by a sense of achievement.

However, it is probably true to argue that McGregor's ideas were little more than common sense and although written about as if it were a theory there is no data to back up the claims. It is now to the content theories and to a slightly stronger research base that this chapter turns.

Theories of motivation can be categorized in different ways, and classically are divided into **content theories** (also known as need theories) or into **process theories**. Content theories of motivation look at what actually motivates people, so peoples' needs are considered, the strengths of those needs, and the goals they follow in order to pursue them. Process theories, on the other hand, consider how motivation actually works through the relationship between the various variables that motivate someone in order for it to be initiated in the first place, where the motivation is directed and then maintained.

5.2.2 Maslow's hierarchy of needs

No doubt **Maslow's hierarchy of needs** (1943, 1954) is one of the better-known and one of the older theories that are still widely quoted today. It should be borne in mind however that his work was one of the theories mentioned above whereby it was not originally intended to be used in a work setting but more as a general theory of psychology, coming from the Humanistic school. This does have strong influences on interpreting how valid this theory might be because if someone does not obtain all their needs from work it may be that they can find them elsewhere.

According to Maslow, a person will move up the hierarchy or levels of needs, depicted in a triangle, and as each need is satisfied will then be motivated to move up to the next level. If a need or level is not satisfied, it will create desire and therefore the motivation to achieve fulfilment of that need. According to this theory, it is only possible to move in one direction and that is upwards.

So, according to Maslow, physiological needs are the most basic that need to be met first and until these are satisfied with, for example, food, water, air, and shelter it is not feasible to move onto the next level. The second level is safety needs—being in a safe environment with neither physical nor psychological threats. Once safety needs are met social needs are triggered and the need for affiliation with others, to be accepted, to be liked, becomes strong.

Pause for thought
Do you recognize yourself, or someone that you know in one of these categories, i.e. are you more X or Y?

Likewise, once social needs are met, then esteem needs are activated whereby someone needs to have feelings of self-respect, of success, and to feel significant to self and others. Finally, when all the previous levels have been accomplished the need to become self-actualized will develop, whereby all that one is capable of becoming and achieving will become ever stronger.

However, Maslow's final level has never been clear in the literature and different writers have different interpretations as to what self-actualization really means. In addition in the literature after the 1970s there have appeared some adaptations of Maslow's original five levels. These are: cognitive needs, such as knowledge, meaning, etc; aesthetic needs, which is a search and appreciation for beauty, balance, form, style; and transcendence needs, which in some interpretations give connotations of a spiritual feel to the meaning of the word and could be related to having mystical experiences and a detachment from the world as most Westerners experience it. It must be borne in mind that these latter, some 'unofficial' adaptations, largely appear in 'pop' psychology; and, in addition, it could be argued that in any case Maslow's final level, self-actualization, does actually include the added levels anyway. Furthermore, in Maslow's later work he did refer to a distinction in self-actualization between an expression of real self and a more mystical existence with a closeness to humanity or to God (Cleary and Shapiro 1996).

Whatever the strength of the case for the number of levels in the hierarchy it is clear that organizations could do much either to support or to hold back individuals' transition along the hierarchy. For example, they can provide sufficient salaries, which in turn provide the employee with the funds to purchase their basic needs of food and shelter. They can ensure that the environment in which their employees work is safe both physically, through health and safety checks, and mentally, for example, by following policies on bullying. Organizations can arrange working conditions so that there is plenty of opportunity for social needs to be met. For example, through the use of teamwork; self-esteem needs can be met by celebrating successes, awarding of prizes, etc.; and they can allow their employees to fulfil their true potential perhaps by creative working or by good **career management** support. In the opening case study, it would seem that Jim had reached a creative level on Maslow's hierarchy in his working conditions but the organization, through attempting to stop stress in the workplace, had actually taken this away. This, as we saw, did not have the desired affect and had resulted in de-motivation.

....

 Activity Maslow's hierarchy of needs

Consider Maslow's hierarchy of needs and try to place yourself on the triangle. Where are you? At what level?

Assuming this level is not fully fulfilled think about whether you feel motivated to strive to the next level.

According to your answer, did this agree with Maslow's theory or not?

Do you agree with his theory? Whether yes or no, think of reasons for your answer.

....

With the changing nature of work and the downsizing, de-layering, re-engineering, and new psychological contracts apparent in many organizations today, it can reasonably be argued that most organizations would struggle to provide all of the above. With a tendency towards a reactional psychological contract these days and an increased threat of redundancy compared to when Maslow devised this theory, people's safety needs are not being fully met.

Even if organizations are in a position to provide some or most of the above then the problem of evaluating whether it is motivational or not is still very difficult to research either way, so perhaps it should come as no surprise that there is little evidence to support this theory (Wahba and Bridwell 1976). In addition, not much direct research has been conducted, especially recently, hence the older references here. But, intuitively we only have to look at the classic view of the true artist who gives up everything in order to create to tell us that there are examples of where this theory does not seem adequate. Clearly there are some people that do seek to satisfy higher-order levels without meeting the lower ones first (Williams and Page 1989).

Despite this and the fact that evidence is lacking for the tier system (Mitchell and Mowdgill 1976) it still seems that this theory is as popular today as it ever was.

Berry (1998) suggests that this popularity may be because of the incorporation of such terms as 'self-actualization' into our everyday language, so it tends to make sense to us, especially in a humanistic way. The theory might be used to explain why money does not always motivate some employees, which is obviously very useful to Managers and to Human Resource Managers, who are trying to find ways to motivate their staff. Finally Cooper (2001) reminds us that Maslow's hierarchy of needs and McGregor's Theory X and Y have both been very significant contributions to work motivation, especially in light of the changing nature of work with short-term contracts, insecurity, and the need for workers to maintain sufficient motivation just to find work.

5.2.3 Alderfer ERG (1972)

Likewise, **Alderfer's theory** concentrates on peoples' needs. Specifically they are:

Existence,

Relatedness

Growth.

Existence is similar to Maslow's physiological and safety needs, whereas Relatedness is equivalent to Maslow's social needs, and finally Growth needs relate to Maslow's esteem and self-actualization needs.

Because of the fewer categories and because the levels are not necessarily activated in any particular order, this theory is classified as being simpler. In addition, more than one level can be activated at the same time, even all three but at different degrees. Alderfer's theory was written for the workplace, and although there is still disagreement as to how many levels there should be, this could be a reason why some researchers feel that Alderfer's ERG fits better with research evidence. However, the fact remains that Maslow remains the most cited and popular of the two.

5.2.4 Need for achievement

In 1938, Murray put forward an interesting theory, whereby he saw motivation as being the main focus in personality theory and based on twenty needs. These needs underlie motivation, with need for achievement being one of them. However, not all the twenty needs are as easy to observe as needs may be expressed as a combinations of needs; and some needs might be in conflict with one another.

It must also be borne in mind that like other need theories already mentioned, they are only labelling tools rather than diagnostic tools, because they cannot tell us how or even why a particular need will be triggered.

Although, these criticisms can be directed at Murray's theory, it remains that his influence has been strong on other researchers. For example, McClelland (1961, 1962) put forward the idea that the extent for the need for achievement (N.Ach) and need for power (N.Pow) could predict work motivation. His theory also encompassed Need for Competence and Need for Affiliation.

McClelland believed that if need for achievement is generally high in a population, then that country will prosper economically. He also stated that parental conditioning would affect a person's need for achievement but also considered that training was possible to increase this. Achievement motivation, termed N.Ach, can be measured, according to McClelland, by analysing people's principal needs through their unconscious projections, making analysis possible. Need for power is measured in a similar way.

Perhaps the occupational psychologist consultant in the opening case study at the fashion retail outlet could measure its employees' Need for Achievement and use the results in the recommendations to the organization. This could potentially help employees like Jim, who were de-motivated by lack of responsibility.

Other researchers influenced by Murray were Cassidy and Lynn (1989) and they proposed six components to a standard of excellence in achievement motivation. These are, firstly, work ethic, whereby the need to work is just good in itself. Then comes excellence and the pursuit of it, where a person will perform to their absolute potential; followed by a desire for status and moving up the organizational hierarchy. A further construct is that of mastery of their tasks; they also saw competitiveness against others as important; and finally the desire for wealth or acquisitiveness.

Sagie et al. (1996) have also advanced the literature with their emphasis on the importance of analysing factors relating to tasks rather than power and status. For Sagie et al. there are six task preferences that indicate a high need for achievement. These task preferences involve uncertainty as opposed to definite outcomes; tasks being more difficult rather than too easy; having personal ownership on a task; having calculated risks; allowing creativity rather than following set rules; and finally a sense that the task will allow success rather than just failure avoidance.

Task analysis is usually tested by using projective tests and results have shown, at least for need for achievement, that they can be surprisingly more valid than using questionnaires (Spangler 1992). This is rather an unusual finding as projective tests, of any kind, do not normally predict behaviour higher than that of questionnaires or other measures.

Miner (1964) looked at motivation through the concept of 'motivation to manage' and the measurement of someone's level to manage through the Miner Sentence Completion Scale (MSCS). In this measurement, incomplete sentences are presented on motivation to manage, and the manager then completes these sentences, which are then interpreted by an expert. Motivation to manage seems to be underpinned mostly by need for power and self-control with low need for affiliation. The need for power is best explained by considering that a manager does not operate alone in an organization and by necessity needs to influence others.

Carson and Gilliard (1993), across various studies, have shown findings that demonstrate that the higher a manager's motivation to manage, the higher someone's salary, status, and work performance. In addition, most researchers agree with Miner and McClelland in that the higher the degree of motivation to manage in any one country the higher the economic prospects of that country.

In summary, content theories concentrate on how organizations can motivate their employees by helping them to fulfil their needs and they do this by considering *what* it is that actually motivates them. This chapter now turns to a consideration of the process theories of motivation whereby the emphasis is on *how* something might motivate an employee to work harder.

KEY LEARNING POINTS

- Content theories of motivation look at *what* motivates an individual.
- In Maslow's hierarchy of needs it is not possible to be motivated to move up the levels until the current or lower level need has been satisfied.
- Alderfer's levels are more flexible—it is possible to move up and down and even for more than one to be activated at the same time.
- Not all the content theories of motivation were originally intended to be used in a work setting.

5.2.5 Expectancy theories

Expectancy theory (VIE), also known as instrumentality theory, from a cognitive perspective of motivation, considers the process from the point of view that people will be motivated when they expect that they will be able to achieve what they want from the effort that they put in. Therefore someone needs to firstly sufficiently value the outcome (valence) and to feel that there is a causal relationship between effort and outcome (instrumentality) and finally to feel capable of actually achieving or performing (expectancy). If someone feels that despite effort they will not be able to achieve the reward or goal, or that the reward or goal is not desired sufficiently, then little motivation will ensue. After a cognitive evaluation, the person will make their choice of action or inaction according to whether all three conditions are met or not. The higher the levels of expectancy, instrumentality, and valence the higher the motivation. However, even if only one of these is zero then motivation will not ensue.

Vroom (1964) developed the theory by stating that both expectancy and instrumentality can be expressed as a probability and valence can be expressed subjectively. Therefore, $E \times I \times V$ will give the probability of how motivated someone is.

Most research on this theory, was carried out before 1990 but Van Eerde and Thierry (1996) have found some general evidence in support of the theory.

However in more recent studies Thompson and McHugh (2002) state that although the rather simplistic nature of the theory in predicting behaviour is powerful and appealing there are problems with measurement. In addition, they question whether people always make rational cognitive decisions when making their choices and there has been a lack of attention to the context of the situation. In replicating the methodology, difficulties have been found.

Porter and Lawler (1968) adapted Vroom's theory and expanded job performance to being a mixture of multiple skills and abilities, of perceptions of effort and role. Therefore, if someone has the necessary skills and abilities, their role perception is clear and there is sufficient motivation to exert necessary effort then that individual should perform well. Performance can produce either extrinsic or intrinsic outcomes. Extrinsic being possibly monetary reward whereas intrinsic, for example, might invoke internal feelings of achievement or accomplishment. In our opening case study Jim was not so interested in **extrinsic rewards** and for him the feelings of intrinsic values were totally important to him. The application of expectancy theory in relation to pay and reward systems is further explored below.

5.2.6 Equity Theory (Adams 1963, 1965)

Originating from Social Psychology, Equity Theory, when considered in the world of work psychology, is credited to Adams (1963, 1965). Equity theory, as the name implies, is all about a judgement whereby one considers if they are treated fairly in comparison with another person or another group. If a feeling of fairness is apparent then we can say that the person feels that there is equity but if not, and their outcomes do not equal their inputs, then a feeling of inequity will follow.

The desire for equity in inputs and outcomes through social comparison causes people to be motivated to obtain what they consider to be fair reward in return for their efforts. This is in contrast to the, perhaps, more instinctual view that people will try to get as much as they can. However, the former seems to be true, to the extent that some people, if they are being paid more than they consider they should be for the effort that they are putting in, they will then put in more effort in order to return to a state of equity. The reverse is noted whereby someone who feels they are being underpaid for their outputs is likely to decrease their efforts. Consider the case of Jim in our opening case study, he clearly felt that he was being overpaid for his efforts and this made him feel uneasy.

Adams states that people do this because when feelings of inequity ensue, this causes an unpleasant state of tension and the natural tendency is to alleviate it. Adams has suggested various other ways in addition to the above that people will try to alleviate this tension.

One such way is that someone might attempt to change the outcomes through a pay rise perhaps or title but to keep the outputs the same. Another way to relieve inequity might be through cognitive distortion of inputs and/or outcomes rather than real changes, for example through distorting how important it is to get a required qualification or promotion. Someone could actually leave and find another job, or just be absent from work. In addition, some people might even try to influence others and try to make them decrease their outputs. Finally, someone might change the comparison group in order to have feelings of equity again.

However, Greenberg (2001) criticizes the theory and says that it is rather vague and that people may adopt any of the above strategies and it is not possible to be precise which one will be chosen. In addition, Mowday (1991) tells us that although some people will feel uncomfortable if they consider they are being paid too much by way of reward, research tells us that these feelings occur less often in this group than to those who are being underpaid. In other words more people will feel tension and want to relieve their feelings of inequity if they feel they are being underpaid compared to those being overpaid. Perhaps this does not sound so surprising?

Pause for thought
Think about an example of a task you need to complete and consider if you scored zero on either *E*, *I*, or *V* would you feel little or no motivation to complete it?

Activity   Inequity in pay

If you found yourself in a position of inequity over pay and you felt that you were being underpaid, what would you do about it? What strategies would you use?

If you found yourself in a position of inequity over pay and you felt that you were being overpaid, what would you do about it? Again, as above, what strategies would you use in order to regain equity and would they differ much to those above?

Of course, both equity theory and expectancy theory have huge implications for using pay as a motivator and much of the remainder of this chapter will be dedicated to this extremely important issue. But, before we turn to the arguments concerning money as a motivator we still need to look at Goal-Setting Theory.

5.2.7 Goal-Setting Theory (Locke et al., 1960s onwards)

A popular way forward to look at motivation these days, Goal-Setting Theory is continually being refined, but its basic premise is that by the setting of goals which stretch someone, but that are not impossible to attain, motivation to reach those goals will be strengthened. However, this only occurs provided that sufficient feedback is also given. Mento et al. (1987) tell us that this implies that both knowledge and motivation are necessary to achieve successful work performances.

Goal commitment is an important concept in Goal-Setting Theory and means that if someone is committed to a specified goal it is much less likely that that person will abandon the goal. Latham et al. (1988) also tell us that if people are allowed to participate in setting their own goals they will be much more committed to them than if someone else sets the goals for them.

Although, there is more consensus on Goal-Setting Theory than any other form of motivation of course there are still criticisms of this method. Austin and Bobko (1985) put forward the following areas for concern: quality versus quantity issues, jobs having conflicting goals, assessing individuals as not being an appropriate measure. Many jobs rely on quality issues rather than a quantitative output, but it could be argued that this probably depends on the type of job so it may be appropriate to argue this as a criticism for some roles but not all, for example someone in a creative industry as opposed to someone turning out components in a factory setting. Again, as the research stated, many jobs do actually have conflicting roles and neglecting one aspect of a job may be to the detriment of another part of it. In addition, as teamwork is prevalent these days how appropriate is it to measure the individual? The relevance of goal theory to the organizational practices of performance management are further considered on p. 102 below.

Case illustration
Goal commitment

Jill had a new line manager. At first, she thought it a little strange how this person was so democratic in their style compared to the previous one who had insisted on setting all her goals for her. Jill did not mind her job, after all she knew where she stood, the pay was reasonable, but she felt little commitment to the organization—she often thought to herself along the lines of 'it was only a job'. However, something strange had occurred with the arrival of the new line manager. Jill suddenly enjoyed the prospect of going in to work, even arriving early on some days. She experienced a new kind of energy and commitment to the organization, that she had not felt before with her old line manager. Jill felt that she could make a difference, that she now managed to feel a part of the company and that she had much more control over her job. The new line manager worked from the premise of goal commitment and allowed Jill to participate highly when setting organizational goals.

KEY LEARNING POINTS

- Process theories of motivation look at *how* motivation works, i.e. what the underling processes are.
- According to expectancy theory if a reward is not valued highly enough then someone is unlikely to be motivated.
- People will suffer tension if a feeling of inequity ensues.
- There is more consensus amongst researchers on Goal-Setting Theory than any other of the motivational theories that have been forward over the decades

5.3 Job satisfaction, job dissatisfaction, and causes

5.3.1 Job satisfaction and motivation identifying the links

Defining what constitutes 'job satisfaction' can be problematic, as can relating job satisfaction to motivation and work performance. These concepts may be linked but exactly how is not clear. Latham (2007) shows how early work, drawing on the Hawthorn studies and the developing Human Relations School, tended to assume more clear-cut and perhaps simplistic relationships than more recent work. In the 1960s, the work of Frederick Herzberg stressed the nature of the work itself in leading to employee satisfaction and motivation. To improve performance and job satisfaction he stressed the importance of enriching job content, workers' responsibilities, and possibilities for achievement and advancement. He thought that what he termed the 'hygiene factors'—pay, working conditions, managerial supervision—could only increase or decrease dissatisfaction, not positively affect satisfaction. These ideas proved controversial and more recently Clark et al. (1996) provide evidence that job satisfaction may be more a complex cluster of attitudes than the sort of rather simple relationships suggested by Herzberg. Clark et al.'s study gives evidence that job satisfaction is affected, for example, by non-job factors such as life stage and personal circumstances, as well as job-related factors. It also shows the importance of changing expectations that occur with increasing age. Measures of job satisfaction therefore need to take account of these complexities.

Kay (1996) points to a survey, which reveals that British employees are second only to the Hungarians in their level of dissatisfaction with work. Employee lack of satisfaction is also worse in the public sector than the private sector.

In the 2004 Workplace Employee Relations Survey (WERS), Kersley et al. (2005) asked employees how satisfied or dissatisfied they were with eight aspects of their job. The results are summarized in Table 5.1. The survey found that employee job satisfaction varied markedly across the eight items covered by the survey, being highest with respect to 'the work itself', 'scope for using own initiative', and 'sense of achievement'. It was lowest in respect of 'involvement in decision-making' and in relation to pay. Responses from individual employees on each of the eight items were positively correlated, but employees were not equally satisfied across the various items. The mean score on this overall job satisfaction measure differed across workplaces in a statistically significant way, giving some confirmation that employees' job satisfaction is partly determined by workplace factors. Employees have become somewhat more positive in their view since the previous survey, particular in relation to the positive sense of achievement they get from work (which rose from 64 per cent in 1998 to 70 per cent in 2004). In contrast, satisfaction with pay has remained very low.

Given the low scores on some aspects of job satisfaction shown by such empirical research, we can question whether the generality of employees are provided by employers with work which meets employees' needs, desires, and values. An important concept in this context is Value Theory (Locke 1976). In this theory job satisfaction is related to the extent to which jobs are viewed by individuals as fulfilling values, which they hold. The degree of satisfaction is related to the difference between their preferences in relation to certain job factors—such as pay or autonomy of work—and their perceptions of the actual state.

Table 5.1. How satisfied are UK employees? (% of employees)

	Very satisfied	Satisfied	Neither	Dissatisfied	Very dissatisfied
Sense of achievement	18	52	19	8	3
Scope for using initiative	20	52	18	8	3
Influence over job	12	45	28	11	3
Training	11	40	26	16	7
Pay	4	31	24	28	13
Job security	13	50	22	11	5
Work itself	17	55	19	7	3
Involvement in decision-making	8	30	39	17	6

Source: Adapted from Kersley et al. (2005).

5.3.2 Causes of job satisfaction

Pay and benefits is often cited by employees as a cause of, or reason for, dissatisfaction, and indeed the WERS survey data tends to bear this out as Table 5.1 above shows. However, in any particular organization context, it may be questioned whether the root cause of dissatisfaction is really pay and benefits—or if this becomes a focus for dissatisfaction

Job enrichment and job redesign have been experimented with since the 1970s as ways of tackling the tendency of managements to design jobs narrowly in Taylorist styles (Payne and Keep 2003). It is argued that many UK employers are locked into a business strategy that focuses on defining jobs narrowly and treating employees as costs rather than a broader approach to job design. While such narrow job design remains extant in many organizations—we have only to consider the modern-day call centre—employers also consider other ways of building employee satisfaction.

Hackman and Oldham (1975) developed a method of analysing jobs, the Job Diagnostic instrument. This can help us to decide what constitutes a narrowly defined job and a broader one. This (Figure 5.1) consists of five key dimensions—skill variety, task identity, task significance, autonomy, and feedback—and links these to the critical psychological states. Although, the model can be critiqued, it is, as Rollinson and Broadfield (2002) suggest, still useful in analysis and in showing that people who hold jobs that are designed with more thought are more highly motivated.

Figure 5.1. Job diagnostic model

Job dimensions	Psychological states	Individual and organizational outcomes
Skill variety – the degree to which a job includes a variety of different activities	Meaningfulness of work as experienced by the individual	Intrinsic motivation
Task identify – the degree to which a is doing the work as a whole - ie from start to finish		Performance quality
Task significance – the perceived impact of the job on the lives or work of others		Job satisfaction
Autonomy – perceived amount of freedom to act, independence and discretionary ability within the job	Individuals' perceptions of their own responsibility in relation to work outcomes	Performance quality
Feedback – the degree to which individuals receives feedback on their performance	What individuals know about the results of their work	Employee absence and staff turnover rates

Source: Adapted from Hackman and Oldham (1975).

Activity Job satisfaction

Interview two people, one who has a professional-level job and one who has a more routine, probably lower-paid job. Ask them questions about the respective levels of skill variety, task identity, task significance, autonomy, and feedback in their jobs, and the degree to which they feel motivated to work.

What conclusions can you draw about the two jobs? To what extent does the job diagnostic model help in understanding job satisfaction and in remedying job dissatisfaction?

In tackling job dissatisfaction in practice in the modern organizational setting, companies are beginning to address this problem by paying attention to employee communication and management style. While not drawing specifically on motivation theory, Messmer's (2005) ideas on how employers might build employee job satisfaction may be interpreted in relation to such theory. He says that employers should:

- Offer work-life balance so that employees can balance the needs of their work with other aspects of life.
- Provide intellectual challenge and training opportunities for all, regardless of whether this is directly related to the immediate job. Avoid micromanaging and provide some autonomy of work.
- Provide ongoing feedback on how well employees are doing.

On the specific links between performance and job satisfaction, Latham (2007) suggests his work as a practitioner would argue that performance and performance goals should be the focus for improving both job satisfaction and performance. He points to a recent study (among professional and managerial staff), which suggests that opportunities for 'self actualization' (Latham 2007: 37) are the essential requirements for both job satisfaction and job performance. He further emphasizes the importance of goal setting (p. 102) in relation to both because people who achieve their goals tend to be more satisfied with their jobs as well as performing better.

KEY LEARNING POINTS

- Job satisfaction and motivation are linked in complex ways.
- Pay may become the focus for employee expressions of dissatisfaction, but may not be the root cause.
- Analysing job content entails the consideration of skill variety, task identity, task significance, autonomy, and feedback.

To increase job satisfaction, modern employers are examing their communication with employees, their management styles, and issues such as work-life balance.

5.3.3 Pay as a motivator in practice

The pervasiveness of the notion that 'money motivates' tends to be counterpointed by both theoretical deficiencies underpinning the concept and the preponderance of studies showing mediocre effectiveness in practice. Sisson and Storey (2000) claim that only if people ignore a substantial body of evidence which casts doubt on the links between pay and performance does the case for prp (**performance-related pay**) become plausible. But is this just an example of an aspect of organizational life where quite obviously the academic view is remote from the real world, which managers know best? Certainly many studies show the value that managers place on the facility to reward performance and there is little doubt that they are themselves perhaps strongly motivated to achieve by the prospect of enhanced rewards. Although there is a quantity of research on this topic, there remains a polarization of views—between managers, HR specialists, and consultants who 'believe' in what they may regard as the self-evident and practitioner-led case for prp; and most of the academic writers who are sceptical of the value of the practice. Some of the scepticism relates back to motivation theory. Thompson's (1993) study reveals that employees did not perceive their prp scheme as motivational—even for those with high performance ratings. Moreover, the study shows that the scheme had the capacity to de-motivate some employees.

Kohn (1993 and 1998) expresses fundamental concerns about the conceptual underpinning of prp. Prominent among the critics of prp, he forcefully argues that any form of performance pay can have a detrimental impact on intrinsic motivation. He emphasizes that higher-quality jobs, which offer challenging work tasks and opportunities to exercise creativity, are more motivational than level of pay. He says that extrinsic motivators, such as pay, are less effective as motivators than when individuals experience a sense of self-determination, as opposed to feeling controlled by praise or reward.

Kohn further argues that prp is counterproductive to building long-term performance. He suggests that extrinsic rewards only succeed at securing the temporary compliance of employees with the employers' work demands. Pay is not conducive, he argues, in producing lasting changes in attitudes and behaviour.

In some contrast to the views of Kohn, Latham (2007) suggests that the sort of polarization between *extrinsic* rewards (related to tangible rewards such as pay and benefits) and **intrinsic rewards** (meaningful work, achievement, recognition) assumed by writers such as Kohn is debatable. Moreover, he criticizes research which shows that offering extrinsic rewards can in certain circumstances undermine intrinsic motivation, quoting the words of Bandura (Latham 2007: 103), who illustrates this argument by saying that it is unlikely that concert pianists would lose interest in playing the piano, simply because they are offered high recital fees.

However, Pfeffer (1998) agrees with Kohn that even at its best performance pay may gain only employee compliance, not their long-term commitment, because of the broader nature of employee motivation than a restricted view related principally to extrinsic rewards would suggest. Hence, if we accept that money does have some power to motivate, we need to be aware that the degree of motivational value of a reward or proposed reward may be constrained by a number of factors. Both expectancy theory and equity theory can help us to understand these situational factors. Under *expectancy* theory, it may be assumed that prp could work if employees:

- Believe they are able to achieve the objectives set for them.
- Perceive their effort will result in improved performance.
- Believe good performance will be recognized and rewarded by managers.
- Put a value on the reward—and the reward is seen as large enough to justify the effort expended.

Some common failings with prp such as lack of transparency, problems in measuring outcomes, or setting objectives and/or isolated incidences of favouritism in application of the scheme could—if expectancy theory were to work in practice—be enough to undermine the whole scheme. More broadly, expectancy theory—as in the Porter and Lawler (1968) model—implies a complex web of individual and organizational relationships. This makes it complex to rely on in practice.

Newman and Milkovich (1990) point to accumulating research on the importance of procedural justice in the reward field: the concepts of **distributive justice**—or the perceived fairness of the outcome; and **procedural justice**—fairness of how the rewards are allocated or decisions made can be deployed to evaluate the working of any prp scheme. The work of Folger (1989) shows that although perceptions of *distributive* justice are associated with employee levels of pay satisfaction, it is *procedural* justice that is more strongly associated with employee commitment.

In the author's experience of conducting reviews of performance pay schemes in organizations, it tends to be fears that managers will not act procedurally fairly which can critically undermine the confidence of employees in prp schemes. Managers may have a variety of reasons for the decisions they reach, but even a minor 'breaking of the rules' can have fatal consequences for employee trust and confidence. Two people with the same pay outcome in an organization may view fairness differently, because they are comparing their experience with different other people.

The impact of fairness of employers' decisions on pay for employees on the 'bottom line' of the business has been addressed by a few studies. West's study (2005) on rewarding customer service demonstrates a strong relationship between employee commitment and reward and a relationship between employee satisfaction and commitment and reward. The perceived fairness of the organizational processes used to determine rewards is shown by

Bowen et al. (1999) to have significance for business outcomes. Fairness in reward decisions (or lack of it!), is seen as translating directly into the quality of service provided by employees to the organization's customers.

Marsden and French (1998) show that there is a particular problem in using prp in the public services, prompting the question as to whether there are different factors at work in the motivation of employees in private and public sectors. There is somewhat mixed evidence on the question as to whether public-sector employees are as motivated by financial rewards as their counterparts in the private sector (Brown 2001; Dowling and Richardson 1997). In summarizing some of the special characteristics of public service organizational contexts for performance pay Brown (2001) shows there is a generally high level of employee support for the principle of pay for performance but this is contrasted with concerns about inadequacies of the practice of performance pay by the organizations, in particular concerns about both distributive and procedural justice.

Of course, many of the studies which have examined the links between the use of performance pay and employee motivation have relied, at least to some extent, on individuals reporting whether or not they considered themselves to have been motivated by performance pay. Rynes et al. (2004) point out that there are differences in this area between what individuals say and what they do. They conclude that pay might be used as a general motivator but that it is not equally important in all organizational situations or for all individuals. For example, high performers tend to expect to be well paid.

Consider the following two organizations and assess the power of pay to motivate.

Case illustration
Commerzbank

Commerzbank is an international German bank providing retail and corporate banking worldwide. Its UK operation employs around 700 staff in London, roughly split half and half between traders and middle- and back-office support. Commerzbank competes for front-office staff such as sales and traders against larger investment banks by offering individuals the chance to specialize in niche products. While lucrative, the life cycle of investment products can be very short, three or four years. Staff, including traders, then have to acquire a new expertise, or stay with it but accept that their earnings potential is unlikely to increase. Commerzbank also attracts traders by offering to be a stepping stone to the larger investment banks, or by developing a career within the bank. While the rewards for traders can be high, so too are the expectations. The bank typically offers traders a £100,000 base annual salary, and a discretionary bonus with a linked share plan. The annual base salary, which is market linked, is not perceived as the major part of the package. Staff are eligible for the firm's annual discretionary bonus plan. Important factors in deciding the bonus level include the performance of the business area in which the employee is working, the performance of the bank overall, and individual performance. Employees can earn bonuses worth between zero and many multiples of salary. As well as the bonus scheme there is a share plan, which is a conditional scheme with stock options restricted for between one- and two-year periods. The amount awarded depends on bonus level, market, and economic conditions. Initially, while the plan was good at tying in staff, over time this has reduced, as many banks are now prepared to buy out talented individuals. While few traders leave because of the money, most that leave do so because they want a different challenge or to go to a bigger bank. The reward specialists at the bank believe that the bonus scheme motivates staff.
(Adapted from CIPD 2007)

Questions
- Identify the motivating factors that are reflected in the bank's performance pay scheme.
- What do you see as the main advantages and disadvantages of the scheme described?
- What further information would you like to have to make a more informed judgement?
- Consider the possible effects of the 2008 'credit crunch' in limiting the effectiveness of performance pay in a finance sector company.

Case illustration
Citibank

Citibank is a global bank employing over 300,000 people across 100 countries. The consumer business in the UK has an annual turnover of £350 million and has 850 employees across three divisions—retail, cards, and consumer finance. The vast majority of employees are full time (90 per cent). Employees are split into two main groups, referred to as officers (managerial and professionals) and non-officers (operational and support staff, mostly employed in retail and consumer finance). The majority of the UK officer population is covered by the Citibank global performance-based bonus plan, awarded each January. Typically, staff receive the bonus in cash, though senior employees receive a proportion either as restricted or deferred stock. The global business allocates a bonus pool to each of the regions, based on their performance. This pool is then cascaded down through regions into the various business units. From this pool, individual awards are based on assessment of performance, taking into account the rating on a five-point scale. Those with scores one to three qualify for a discretionary bonus payment. Performance is assessed on a judgement of outputs, such as how much new business they have brought in or how much efficiency they have achieved, as well as inputs and how they have achieved these results. The 'how' element is important given that Citibank operates in a highly regulated environment. In addition to performance, the size of the bonus may be influenced by market data and review by the general managers of the business and the regional chief financial officer. Reward and general managers will also focus on the large payments to ensure that they are justified. Different jobs and skill sets are treated differently, for instance fee earners can receive a bonus typically worth between 30 and 40 per cent, while those in professional roles can expect between 10 and 20 per cent of base pay for good performance. Typically, the non-officer population will participate in a formula-driven incentive plan which comprises five elements: financial results, other results, customer acquisitions, cross-sell, and a discretionary element worth up to 10 per cent. All elements have different weightings. Within these elements there are a number of key factors that are assessed. There is sufficient flexibility for line managers to adjust the criteria to meet local business needs. The aim is that the bonus makes up 40 per cent of total pay of those employees who hit their targets. Depending on the 'line of sight', these awards can be made quarterly, bi-annually, or annually. Bonus schemes are seen by the company as a powerful way of telling employees: 'this is what we need from you and this is how we will reward you'. (Adapted from CIPD 2007)

Questions

- Looking at expectancy theory (p. 100), what do you think is meant by the term 'line of sight'? Why is it important in performance pay?

- Which other motivation theories do you think are being relied on specifically by this organization?

- Consider the effect on teamwork when people in the same team receive very different, individualized rewards, based on managerial assessments of their own individual performance.

5.3.4 Recognition in practice

Perhaps because of the limited success of performance pay schemes human resource professionals have become interested in developing recognition schemes. Such schemes may offer (Suff 2004) small symbolic gifts as a recognition of good service or performance in the organization, or they may be 'employee of the month' or similar awards. Reward and recognition are, argue Hansen et al. (2002), fundamentally different. They suggest reward or pay for performance schemes are essentially instrumental in nature, and perceived as such by employees. They further say (p. 65) that recognition is about 'honoring and noticing' and lacks the instrumentality of a cash reward. The example quoted is that of the award of a gallantry medal to a soldier—a recognition in a situation in which the offer of a cash reward might be seen as wholly inappropriate.

5.3.5 Managing performance in practice

Performance-related pay is often linked to performance management systems in which individual performance in the organization is reviewed on a regular, say six-monthly or annual,

Case Illustration
Something for nothing?

A survey conducted by centre right thinktank the Bow Group found that about one in ten firms will still pay bonuses to chief executives and other senior directors, even when their company performance and profits fail to beat inflation. The study shows that 33 companies in the FTSE 100 use such performance shares, which are handed out to chief executives if profits rise by a certain amount, but some companies will award the shares even if performance is low.

   Christopher Mahon, author of the report, said: 'Boardroom bonuses should reward exceptional performance and should not be paid by default.'
Adapted from *Personnel Today* (2008).

Question

• Imagine you are the lowest-paid worker in a company which has awarded its Chief Executive and Directors performance shares, when you and all the other employees have been told that you will not be getting a pay rise this year because of the poor financial position of the company. You do not know how you are going to make ends meet and are thinking about what you are going to do, when the newspapers publish this story about your bosses. Using motivation theories, including organizational justice theory (Greenberg 1987), explain what effect this decision of the company will be likely to have on you, and why.

basis. There are debates as to how effective systems can be, based on the setting of targets at the start of the year and assessment of performance against these targets at the year's end. Locke and Latham's Goal Setting Theory suggests that individuals are more likely to achieve agreed goals, which they believe are achievable. This led to the development of the SMART concept in setting performance goals in organizations as part of schemes designed to manage employee performance. SMART goals are those which are given to or agreed by employees at the start of a performance year, on which their individual performance, is judged, at the end of the year. They are SMART because they are Specific, Measurable, Achievable, Realistic, and Time-bound.

Activity   Drawing on Dilbertisms

Does Dilbert give support to goal theory? How do you view the comments attributed to Dilbert below in relation to goal theory and other motivation theories?

   'I love deadlines. I especially like the whooshing sound they make as they fly past.'

   'If it weren't for the last minute, nothing would ever get done.'

Adapted from CIPD (2006).

   Arnolds and Boshoff (2002) suggest that self-esteem is an important mediating factor in understanding employee job performance in relation to motivation. Specifically, if the employees' needs are not being satisfied then this may affect their self-esteem, which will in turn affect their job performance. Arnolds and Boshoff (2002) look at Alderfer's ERG theory in respect to job performance. The study assesses the influence of need satisfaction on self-esteem and the influence of self-esteem on job performance. They conclude, that self-esteem has a significant influence on the job performance of both managers and other employees. The context and environmental factors are vital as Amin's (2003) study reveals. A supportive and working environment increases motivation and will in consequence increase the chances of performance improvements being made. Figure 5.2 summarizes the 'psychological climate' factors which McHenry (1997) suggests have the most significance for employee performance.

Figure 5.2. The psychological climate for motivation of employee performance

Psychological safety	
Support	Employees are given authority and their decisions are backed by their boss
Role clarity	Employees know what is expected of them and what standards their work is measured against
Recognition	Employees are given praise for what they do
Meaningfulness	
Self-expression	Employees are encouraged to express their personality at work and to be a person in their own right
Contribution	Employees can see that their individual effort makes a difference
Challenge	Employees are often stretched by doing their job

Source: Adapted from McHenry (1997).

Chapter summary

- Motivation theories have a rich history from the early content theories through to later process theories.

- Even though some concepts were developed half a century ago they remain hotly debated and are also relied on in practice in organizations seeking to manage and improve the performance of their employees by various means, including the controversial topic of pay as a motivator.

- Debates will continue but are likely increasingly to recognize that both modern organizations and the jobs within them are becoming more complex and that the usefulness of simplistic concepts will be open to question.

Assess your learning

Review questions

1 Explain what we mean by a needs or content theory of motivation.

2 Explain what we mean by a process theory of motivation.

3 List the levels of Maslow's theory.

4 List the levels of Alderfer's theory.

5 According to McClelland which needs could predict work motivation?

6 Describe expectancy theory.

7 If someone feels that they are receiving too many rewards what might they do about it?

8 What does SMART stand for and what do you think it means in practice?

9 To what extent is pay a motivator? Review the evidence for and against this proposition?

Assignments

ASSIGNMENT 1: Comparing the theories of motivation
Reread the opening section of this chapter and consider carefully the theories on motivation.

Draw up a table with the theories down the side of the page and key factors across the top. Now tick all those factors common to each theory. This will give you an overview of the similarities and the differences between the theories.

ASSIGNMENT 2: Motivation interview
Interview a manager or anyone who supervises or manages staff. Ask them what they feel they can do positively to motivate unmotivated staff.

Write up your findings, drawing on motivation theory as a framework for analysis.

Further reading

Latham, G. (2007) *Work Motivation: History, Theory Research and Practice*. Thousand Oaks, CA: Sage Publications.

Latham gives a very useful history of motivation theory and some balanced arguments on the theories from other writers, as well as providing strong justifications for his own theoretical stances.

Porter, L. W., Bigley, G. A., and Steers, R. M. (eds.) (2002) *Motivation and Work Behavior.* New York: McGraw-Hill.

This is a comprehensive text on motivation and work behaviour which includes classic and contemporary theories, case studies, and encourages critical thinking.

Work psychology in practice
Glossy Goods Ltd

Glossy Goods Ltd is a company specializing in top of the range clothes, bags, and other accessories, which are high-priced and associated with the sort of consumers, who have a lot of money to spend. The company's retail outlets are in the major cities of the world, with a headquarters in central London. Traditionally the company has employed well-educated, well-spoken older people to work in their prime retail outlet in London's Bond Street. However, recent cutbacks in company expenditure on staffing and problems in recruitment, combined with the retirement of many of the longer-serving staff have changed the profile of the staff. They are now younger, less consciously 'upper class' in demeanour, and do not react as well to the rather old-fashioned 'command and control' style of management of the company's managers. The company is facing a downturn in demand from consumers for its products and some unfavourable criticism in the consumer pages of the magazine *Country Life*, which has never previously criticized the company. A recent article commented on the lack of education and 'couldn't care less' attitude of some of the retail staff.

Amongst other decisions the company's senior managers have decided to commission a survey of the employees in the company and have brought in some consultants and psychologists to advise them. When the senior managers begin to look at the results of the survey they become increasingly alarmed about the attitudes of their employees. The following is an extract from the results:

Attitude survey results

I am kept well informed by the company:

Strongly agree	Agree	Disagree	Strongly disagree	No opinion on this
10%	15%	35%	20%	20%

At work my opinions seem to count:

Strongly agree	Agree	Disagree	Strongly disagree	No opinion on this
7%	23%	54%	14%	2%

I have good friends at work:

Strongly agree	Agree	Disagree	Strongly disagree	No opinion on this
35%	41%	9%	6%	9%

At work I have the opportunity to learn and grow:

Strongly agree	Agree	Disagree	Strongly disagree	No opinion on this
2%	13%	38%	25%	22%

My supervisor seems to care for me as a person:

Strongly agree	Agree	Disagree	Strongly disagree	No opinion on this
15%	32%	33%	18%	2%

My manager has told me what my job is and what I need to do to do it well:

Strongly agree	Agree	Disagree	Strongly disagree	No opinion on this
51%	26%	5%	4%	14%

I trust my manager/supervisor:

Strongly agree	Agree	Disagree	Strongly disagree	No opinion on this
12%	36%	17%	11%	23%

I think customers are satisfied with the level of customer service they receive from me:

Strongly agree	Agree	Disagree	Strongly disagree	No opinion on this
7%	48%	5%	1%	40%

I think action will be taken after this survey:

Strongly agree	Agree	Disagree	Strongly disagree	No opinion on this
11%	39%	7%	6%	37%

Questions

- You are one of the psychologists advising the company. Draft a note suggesting which of the motivation theories described on pages 000–00 would be appropriate to use as a basis for analysing the responses to the survey, and why.
- Which motivation theory or theory is most important in analysing the responses to the survey?
- Suggest further research questions you would like to ask in a follow-up employee survey, giving your reasons for asking them.

Online Resource Centre

Visit the supporting online resource centre for additional material which will help you with your research, essays, and assignments, or you may find these additional resources helpful when revising for exams.
http://www.oxfordtextbooks.co.uk/orc/matthewman/

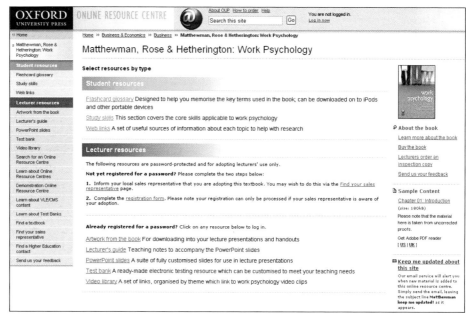

References

Adams, J. S. (1963) Towards an understanding of inequity. *Journal of Abnormal and Social Psychology*, 67: 422–36.

Adams, J. S. (1965) Inequity in social exchange. In L. Berkowitz (ed.), *Advances in Experimental Social Psychology*, vol. ii. New York: Academic Press.

Alderfer, C. P. (1972) *Existence, Relatedness and Growth: Human Needs in Organisational Settings*. New York: Free Press.

Amin, R. (2003) Towards a Deterministic Theory of selective individual performance. *Journal of Management Research*, 3/2: 61–72.

Arnolds, C., and Boshoff, C. (2002) Compensation, esteem valence and job performance: an empirical assessment of Alderfer's ERG theory. *International Journal of Human Resource Management*, 13/4: 697–719.

Austin, J. T., and Bobko, P. (1985) Goal-setting theory: unexplored areas and future research needs. *Journal of Occupational Psychology*, 58: 289–309.

Berry, L. (1998) *Psychology at Work*. New York: McGraw-Hill.

Bowen, D., et al. (1999) How being fair with employees spills over to customers. *Organisational Dynamics*, 27/3: 7–23.

Brown, M. (2001) Merit pay preferences among public sector employees. *Human Resource Management Journal*, 11/4: 38–54.

Carson, K. P., and Gilliard, D. J. (1993) Construct validity of the Minor sentence completion scale. *Journal of Occupational and Organizational Psychology*, 66: 171–5.

Cassidy, T., and Lynn, R. (1989) A multifactorial approach to achievement motivation: the development of a comprehensive measure. *Journal of Occupational Psychology*, 62: 301–12.

CIPD (2006) Northants Branch Newsletter. CIPD Northants Branch.

CIPD (2007) *Reward Management Survey 2007*. London: Chartered Institute of Personnel and Development.

Clark, A., Oswald, A., and Warr, P. (1996) Is job satisfaction U-shaped? *Journal of Occupational and Organizational Psychology*, 69/1: 57–81.

Cleary, I. S., and Shapiro, S. I. (1996) Abraham Maslow and Asian psychology. *Psychologia*, 39: 213–22.

Cooper, C. L. (2001) Great motivators at work. *The Psychologist*, 14: 94.

Dowling, F., and Richardson, R. (1997) Evaluating performance-related pay for managers in the NHS. *International Journal of Human Resource Management*, 8/3: 348–66.

Folger, R., and Konovsky, M. A. (1989) Effects of procedural and distributive justice on reactions to pay raise decisions. *Academy of Management Journal*, 32/1: 115–30.

Greenberg, J. (1987) A taxonomy of organisational justice theories. *Academy of Management Review*, 12: 9–22.

Greenberg, J. (2001) Setting the justice agenda: seven unanswered questions about 'what, why and how'. *Journal of Vocational Behavior*, 58: 210–19.

Hackman, R., and Oldham, G. (1975) Development of the Job Diagnostic survey. *Journal of Applied Psychology*, 60/2: 159–70.

Hansen, F., Smith, M., and Hansen, R. (2002) Rewards and recognition in employee motivation. *Compensation and Benefits Review*, Sept./Oct.: 64–72.

Kay, H. (1996) Motivation blues. *Human Resources*, 26: 39, 41–2.

Kersley, B., Alpin, C., Forth, J., Bryson, A., Bewley, H., Dix, G., and Oxenbridge, S. (2005) *Inside the Workplace: Findings from the 2004 Workplace Employment Relations Survey* (WERS 2004). Abingdon: Routledge.

Kohn, A. (1993) Why incentive plans cannot work. *Harvard Business Review*, 71/5: 54–63.

Kohn, A. (1998) Challenging behaviorist dogma: myths about money and motivation. *Compensation and Benefits Review*, 30: 27–37.

Latham, G. (2007) *Work Motivation: History, Theory Research and Practice*. Thousand Oaks, CA: Sage Publications.

Latham, G. P., Erez, M., and Locke, E. A. (1988) Resolving scientific disputes by the joint design of crucial experiments by the antagonists: application to the Erez–Latham dispute regarding participation in goal setting. *Journal of Applied Psychology*, 73: 753–72.

Locke, E. A. (1976) The nature and causes of job satisfaction. In M. D. Dunnett (ed.), *Handbook of Industrial and Organizational Psychology*. Chicago: Rand McNally, 1297–349.

McClelland, D. C. (1961) *The Achieving Society*. Princeton: Van Nostrand.

McClelland, D .C., (1962) Business drive and national achievement. *Harvard Business Review*, 40: 99–112.

McGregor, D. (1960) *The Human Side of Enterprise*. New York: McGraw-Hill.

McHenry, R. (1997) Spurring stuff. *People Management*, 3 (24 July).

Marsden, D., and French, S. (1998) *What a Performance: Performance-Related Pay in the Public Services*. London School of Economics, Centre for Economic Performance Working paper.

Maslow, A. H. (1943) A theory of motivation. *Psychological Review*, 50: 370–96.

Maslow, A. H. (1954) *Motivation and Personality* (3rd edn.). New York: Harper and Row.

Mayo, E. (1933) *The Human Problems of an Industrial Civilization*. New York: Macmillan.

Mento, A. J., Steel, R. P., and Karren, R. J. (1987) A meta-analytic study of the effects of goal setting on task performance: 1966–1984. *Organizational Behavior and Human Decision Processess*, 39: 52–83.

Messmer, M. (2005) Building employee job satisfaction. *Employment Relations Today*, Summer: 53–9.

Miner, J. B. (1964) *Scoring Guide for the Minor Sentence Completion Scale*. Atlanta, GA: Organizational Measurement Systems Press.

Mitchell, V., and Mowdgill, P. (1976) Measurement of Maslow's need hierarchy. *Organizational Behaviour and Human Performance*, 16: 334–49.

Mowday, R. T. (1991) Equity theory predictions of behaviour in organisations. In R. M. Steers, and L. W. Porter (eds.) *Motivation and Work Behaviour* (5th edn.). New York: McGraw-Hill, 111–31.

Murray, H. (1938) *Explorations in Personality*. New York: Oxford University Press.

Newman, J., and Milkovich, G. (1990) Procedural justice challenges in compensation: eliminating the fairness gap. *Labor Law Journal*, Aug.: 575–80.

Payne, J., and Keep, E. (2003) Re-visiting the nordic approaches to work re-organization and job redesign: lessons for uk skills policy. *Policy Studies*, 24/4: 206–25.

Personnel Today (2008) More than a quarter of UK's largest company chief executives get 'bonuses for nothing. *Personnel Today*, 4 February 2008, available at http://www.personneltoday.com, accessed 11 May 2008.

Pfeffer, J. (1998) *The Human Equation: Building Profits by Putting People First*. Cambridge, MA: Harvard Business School Press.

Porter, L. W., and Lawler, E. E. (1968) *Managerial Attitudes and Performance*. Homewood, IL: R. D. Irwin.

Rollinson, D., and Broadfield, A. (2002) *Organisational Behaviour and Analysis: An Integrated Approach* (2nd edn.),. Harlow: Pearson Educational, FT/Prentice Hall.

Rynes, S., Gerhart, B., and Minette, K. (2004) The importance of pay in employee motivation: discrepancies between what people say and what they do. *Human Resource Management*, 43/4: 381–94.

Sagie, A., Elizur, D., and Yamauchi, A. (1996) The structure and strength of achievement motivation: a cross-cultural comparison. *Journal of Organizational Behavior*, 17: 431–44.

Sisson, K., and Storey, J. (2000) *The Realities of Human Resource Management*. Buckingham: Open University Press.

Spangler, W. D. (1992) Validity of questionnaire and TAT measures of need for achievement: two meta-analyses. *Psychological Bulletin*, 112: 140–54.

Suff, R. (2004) Thank you goes a long way. *IRS Employment Review*, 792/23: 32–6.

Taylor, F. W. (1911) *Principles of Scientific Management*. New York: Harper & Brothers.

Thompson, M. (1993) *Pay and Performance: The Employee Experience*. Institute for Employment Studies, report 258.

Thompson, P., and McHugh, D. (2002) *Work Organisations* (3rd edn.). Basingstoke: Palgrave.

Van Eerde, W., and Thierry, H. (1996) Vroom's expectancy models and work-related criteria: a meta-analysis. *Journal of Applied Psychology*, 81: 575–86.

Vroom, V. H. (1964) *Work and Motivation*. New York: Wiley.

Wahba, M. A., and Bridwell, L. B. (1976) Maslow reconsidered: a review of research on the need hierarchy theory. *Organizational Behaviour and Human Performance*, 15: 212–40.

West, M., et al. (2005) *Rewarding Customer Service? Using Reward and Recognition to Deliver your Customer Service Strategy*. CIPD Research Report.

Williams, D. E., and Page, M. M. (1989) A multi-dimensional measure of Maslow's hierarchy of needs. *Journal of Research in Personality*, 23: 192–213.

Part III
The group at work

Chapter 6
Relationships at work

Lisa Matthewman and Peter Foss

Chapter objectives

As a result of reading this chapter you should be able to:

- Define different types of relationships in the workplace.
- Explain interpersonal attraction in terms of cognitive dissonance theory and balance theory.
- Explain style differences in the context of personality, values, and style preferences.
- Outline the theory underpinning dysfunctional behaviour at work.
- Illustrate the development of dark side traits.
- Understand the role of dark side management on power and conflict.
- Explore research on sexual and romantic relationships in the workplace.
- Understand how harassment and bullying can lead to the breakdown of work relationships.
- Illustrate coaching psychology as an intervention to aid the development of effective work relationships.
- Discuss change in a wider context.

Work psychology in practice
Bad day at work

Elizabeth Green, aged 42, had worked at Green and Black Legal Services for three years. Initially she had enjoyed her work within the Secretarial Division. However, in recent months, she had come to endure a campaign of harassment at the hands of her co-workers including mocking and offensive remarks. Having raspberries blown at her had become a regular part of her day. It had reached a point where Elizabeth had come to feel that she was on the edge of a mental breakdown and could not endure the constant bullying any longer.

'It was not playful, it was malicious and vicious constant teasing,' said Elizabeth as she told the High Court Judge. She reported how she had suffered psychiatric injury because of 'offensive, abusive, degrading and humiliating comments and behaviour from her work colleagues'. Elisabeth went on to tell the court hearing that from her initial joining of the Firm in 2005, five women grouped together to make her work life unbearable. There were constant silly schoolgirl taunts, childish pranks, and bullying type behaviour. Elisabeth began to feel more and more isolated in the workplace and would spend many hours crying quietly in the toilets. Gradually she began to be absent more and more from work until it got to the point when she went to see the HR department for support. It was decided that she would go on sick leave but Elizabeth by this time was suffering serious mental problems and never did return to work before the court hearing.

What surfaced at the hearing was that the secretariat Division had a long-standing problem in the department but the Legal Services management had been weak and ineffective in curtailing it.

Mrs Green was finally awarded £820,000 and Green and Black Legal Services was ordered to pay her legal costs. Still, Green and Black denied that Mrs Green had been bullied or that it had breached its statutory duty and insisted that Mrs Green had a vulnerability to mental illness. Green and Black were considering an appeal and to this day no disciplinary action has been taken against anyone. Though they did not dispute the facts, they did dispute the judge's interpretation of them.

Mrs Green has since started retraining for an academic career and concludes that bullying is certainly a big issue in the city and that her case is not an isolated one.

Adapted from *The Times* (Wednesday, 2 August 2006)

Questions

- How do you think Mrs Green might have felt during her bullying at Green and Black?
- How could HR have intervened to help develop better working relationships within Green and Black?
- What 'duty of care' do employers have in relation to their employees?
- What could Green and Black do to help other staff who might be experiencing bullying?

6.1 Introduction

This chapter is concerned with relationships in the workplace. The chapter starts by placing working relationships in the context of the changing work environment and indicates that relationships at work meet specific needs for **intimacy**, social support, personal growth, and security. The next section of the chapter explores how social psychology has explained interpersonal attraction in the workplace. In particular, **cognitive dissonance** (Baron and Byrne 2002) and **balance theory** are noted. The chapter then explores **self-disclosure** and feedback in relation to the Johari Window Model. The popular model of **Transactional Analysis** is indicated as a vehicle for exploring how individuals in the workplace may relate to each other and develop rapport.

The middle section of the chapter highlights different areas of research that have explored relationships at work. The first of these is an area of research entitled 'The Dark Side of Management'. Many high-flying executives have personality characteristics that make them successful; however these characteristics may be poorly emotionally managed and lead to destructive work relationships in the form of neurotic, **narcissistic**, and obsessive behaviours. Research on sexual and romantic relationships in the workplace is highlighted along with the problems that can result and the implications for management indicated. Harassment and bullying at work explore why people become bullies and how their destructive relations with others can lead to stress and trauma for their victims. Suggestions are given as to how to tackle bullying in the form of organizational policy.

The chapter concludes with sections detailing practical applications that can be employed to facilitate better working relationships. Conflict resolution is noted in relation to personality clashes, emotional intelligence acknowledged in view of developing emotional competence, communication enhancement is noted as a useful tool, and the place of Coaching Psychology in the workplace to reduce dysfunctional relationships is explored.

6.2 Relationships in the workplace

In the world of work, having good relationships with superiors, colleagues, and subordinates is important for achieving career success. Dealing with customers requires good interpersonal relations too. Negotiating salary increases or promotions or dealing with difficult situations requires good, workable relationships and the ability to communicate and act professionally. Good working relationships lead to **cooperation** in order to get tasks done and decisions made. The opinion of others is essential in the world of work. There are numerous behaviours that contribute to good working relationships that are valuable for working at many different levels within the organizational hierarchy, such as being courteous.

6.2.1 Work relationships in context

In the modern workplace, writers such as Senge (1990) and Handy (1995) have observed a rise in organizational restructuring resulting in a downsizing of employee numbers and flatter hierarchies. This has created a need for greater collaboration and mutually beneficial approaches to organizational behaviour. Castells (1996) has looked at the effect of globalization which includes such factors as technological changes, economic shifts, organizational restructuring and networking. Globalization has also required a greater cross-cultural understanding of the norms and values considered appropriate in doing business. Stewart and Powell (2004) looked at the influence of multicultural teams and recognized the importance for managers to act within a framework where people of other nationalities will see things differently.

Even though there is more than adequate technology for individuals to stay in their home office locations and communicate with people in any location throughout the world, there is still a need for people to meet face to face. A conversation with a bank executive working in Sierra Leone (interview, 3 October 2007) revealed that he travels at least once a month, usually to other countries for meetings. This underlines the increased need for workplace relationships to be handled with an efficient and personal tone.

The emphasis on effective workplace relationships highlights the need for workplace learning. Boud and Garrick (1999) stated that workplace learning needs to be focused on future work competencies as well as current work competencies. Complexity and uncertainty surround the way people do business as well as our workplace relationships. Marquardt (2000: 238) commented on action learning when he said that 'it stresses the importance of learning about self and the influence that our attitudes and assumptions have on how we lead and make decisions'. One implication is that we need to be aware of our personal preferences and attitudes and their influence on communication whenever we interact with others. It also points to the need for intimacy in relationships as Boyd and Foss (1997) outlined the delicate balance between trust and risk within the construction industry which is often perceived as machismo.

When workplace relationships are handled effectively, one outcome of this would be an increase in production, motivation, and job satisfaction. Looking at the needs of people in the workplace, Hersey et al. (2001) made some general observations:

1 People need security.

2 People seek social systems.

3 People want personal growth.

The next section of the chapter explores how social psychology has explained interpersonal attraction in the workplace. Cognitive dissonance, self-disclosure, communication styles, and rapport will be explored.

6.2.2 Attraction in the workplace

Before exploring how working relationships can be enhanced or consequently break down, it is important to explore the psychology of interpersonal attraction. Cognitive dissonance theory provides a systematic explanation of why some people get along with each other. Generally it is assumed that people of similar interests and backgrounds flock together, and research supports this contention. People with similar attitudes and values are more attracted to each other than those of dissimilar attitudes and values.

This notion can be explained by the idea of cognitive consistency. The concept of cognitive dissonance attempts to explain how people reduce internal conflicts when they experience a clash between information they receive and their actions. The same process is used when a person has to resolve two different sets of data or information. In both cases, the discrepancy between belief and action creates anxiety within a person and so the person strives to reduce the anxiety. Thus cognitive dissonance theory explains the mental process by which people try to reduce or eliminate inconsistency in the information they receive.

The principle of cognitive dissonance has been applied to interpersonal relationships in the form of balance theory. According to balance theory, people tend to prefer relationships that are consistent or balanced. If a person is very similar to another person, it makes sense to like that person as there is balance in the relationship. Seeking out relationships with others is focused on finding people who are similar to us and therefore able to validate and reinforce our self-image. Having relationships with similar people can be rewarding and reassuring.

Critique

Balance theory can have its limitations as a comprehensive explanation of why people are attracted to each other. Although individuals generally like people who are similar to them, the belief that opposites attract also has merit as people generally get along best with those people who are similar to themselves but are also complementary in certain characteristics too. For example, a talkative and domineering manager may prefer a group member who enjoys listening and is more submissive.

6.2.3 Self-disclosure and feedback

When individuals work within a team and organization, it is useful to be aware of how they come across to others. Self-awareness is associated with personal work values in the practice of self-disclosure and feedback through communication and decision making. Jourard (1971) proposed that openness and accessibility of the self to others is related to positive psychological and physical health and adjustment. Luft (1969) proposed a model of self-awareness known as the Johari Window (Figure 6.1).

In this model, the metaphor of a window is used to describe the degree of self-awareness a person possesses. Individuals will have varying preferences around how much they know about themselves and how much they divulge to others. These differences could potentially result in conflict. However, the underlying belief is the more people know themselves and share appropriate work preferences with others, the better is their self-image and effectiveness at work. People can increase their self-awareness through appropriate self-disclosure and requesting feedback,

Figure 6.1. Johari window

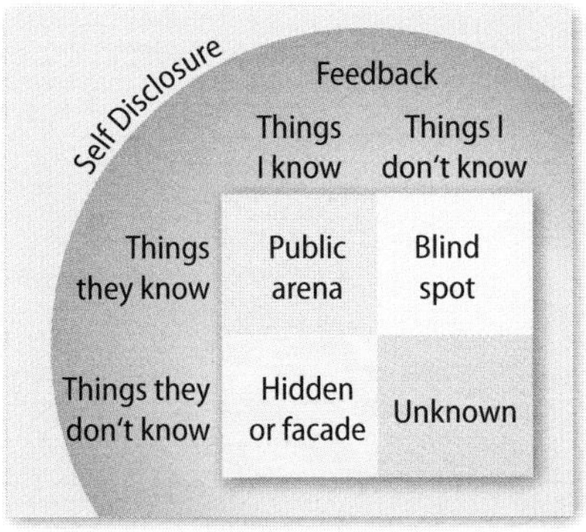

Source: Riley (2006).

which develops a sense of self. This means increasing our public arena, and decreasing the other three elements in the window. The process of self-awareness involves the following:

Some behaviours are obvious to you and others and are called 'public'.

Other behaviours are things known only to you, and are called 'hidden'.

Managing hidden behaviours through self-disclosure.

Reducing blind spots by requesting feedback from others.

Increasing your awareness of unknown behaviours.

As individuals increase their self-awareness, they become more aware of strengths and development needs, thus increasing their effectiveness in working relationships. There are three elements that can assist this process:

1 Who am I? (Personality: such as the Myers-Briggs Type Indicator. See Chapter 3 for more on personality)

2 How do I interact with others? (Communication: Transactional Analysis)

3 How might I change? (Change: Neurolinguistic Programming)

Critique

While self-disclosure has many advantages, such as increasing awareness of one's working preferences within a team to increase effectiveness of communication and decisions, it also has limitations. These include variations of self-awareness, differing preferences for self-disclosure, and existing levels of trust. If conditions such as trust and openness are not present, then individuals will not be inclined to share their working preferences with others. In addition, feedback needs to be given in a sensitive and appropriate way.

6.2.4 Internal and external communication

Transactional analysis (TA) (Berne 1972; Harris 2004) is a rational approach to analysing our internal and external communication. It enables us to diagnose and change our approach if necessary. Here, the three TA concepts of **Life Positions**, **Ego States**, and **Working Styles** will be discussed.

One concept was initially described as life positions, though reframed by Hay (1993) as 'Windows on the world'. This assists us in labelling attitudes. The four key window frames are beliefs and attitudes that people have about themselves and others. Depending on people's choice of frame and focus they may look at the world and see what they expect to see, which reinforces their attitudes. Individuals' choice of frame is the degree to which individuals perceive themselves and others to be OK or not OK. There are four evaluative positions noted in Figure 6.2 that people can adopt depending on their attitude and perception:

Figure 6.2. Windows on the world

I'm not OK, You're OK

I'm OK, You're OK

I'm not OK, You're not OK

I'm OK, You're not OK

Source: Adapted from Hay (1993).

On a typical day, people usually spend the majority of their time in one of these four positions or windows. The 'I'm OK, you're OK' position is a clear and undistorted assertive view. Individuals want to be around others who adopt this position, as it assists people to work well together. This would be our preferred choice. The 'I'm OK, you're not OK' is one of blaming others and non-cooperation where people can come across as superior, and often blame others. Frequently, this position results in short-term relationships as people are pushed away by criticism. The 'I'm not OK, you're OK' position is one where people feel inferior to others. The perception that individuals cannot do things as well as others is natural when they are younger, though not so useful as they mature. Feelings of being helpless, clumsy, incompetent, or a nuisance are common and can sometimes lead to a stance of hero worship. The 'I'm not OK, you're not OK' is a position of hopelessness and despair. People expect the worst to happen and feel out of control. Individuals expect themselves and others to fail, and project a negative view of the world. People who share this position will often pair up in a 'misery loves company' orientation. Becoming aware of our preferred position can in itself give people options for behaving differently.

Life Position	Non-verbal Behaviour
I'm Ok, you're OK	
I'm OK, you're not OK	
I'm not OK, you're OK	
I'm not OK, you're not OK	

Pause for thought
In each of the above life positions people can adopt specific non verbal behaviours. Some examples are: smiling, frowning, open posture, slumped shoulders, etc. Using the life position chart, which specific non-verbal behaviours would be associate d with each of the four positions?

A second concept in transactional analysis (TA) is that of ego states or personal styles (Hay 1993). An ego state is a person's system of thinking and feeling. As can be seen from Figure 6.3 below, the main ego states are Parent, **Adult**, and Child. These reflect our roles in life, with Parent and Child containing subdivisions. Ego states can be seen as our 'frame of reference' or 'where individuals are coming from'. Each person will 'choose' the amount of time or energy that they will put into a particular state. If a person has a good self-awareness of their ego state preferences, then they can more easily choose appropriate alternative behaviours for a specific situation. For example, a **controlling parent** is firm, directs others, and uses the words 'should and ought'. Individuals who want to shift from a Controlling to **Nurturing Parent** will need to become more caring and encouraging toward others. The Adult state gathers, exchanges, and evaluates information. The **Natural Child** does what it wants when it wants, whereas the **Adapted Child** responds to the expectations of others by

Figure 6.3. Personal styles

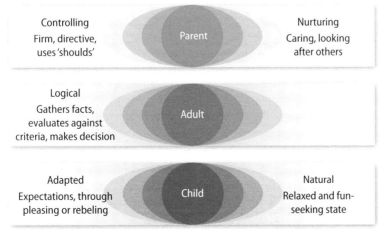

Source: Adapted from Hay (1993).

Figure 6.4. Egogram

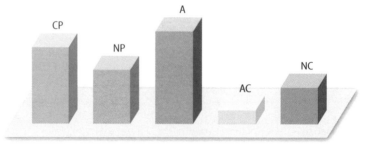

CP – Controlling parent; NP – Nurturing parent; A – Adult;
AC – Adaptive child; NC – Natural child

Source: Adapted from Dusay (1977).

either pleasing (complying) or rebelling. The personal styles that individuals can choose to activate are shown in Figure 6.3.

As an example, a colleague may typically act like a rebellious child (adapted). Managers would find him easy to work with, as all they need to do is ask him to do the opposite of what they really want—since he would rebel and then do precisely what managers want! Not all employees are that easy to manage. Rodrigues (1997) states cross-cultural managers may need to develop a 'my culture OK', 'your culture OK' attitude.

Wagner (1981) believes the Natural Child, Adult, and Nurturing Parent are more effective in communication and getting your needs and wants met. However, Hay (1993) sees the Controlling Parent as having a valuable function in providing structure and guidance. This can be useful in leading people who prefer to be directed, although employees with this preference may not be sufficiently mature or OK with themselves. To determine where a person puts their prioritised energy an egogram could be constructed. This is a histogram that shows the relative sizes of our personal styles, Figure 6.4 as described by Dusay (1977). Then consider whether this egogram helps a person achieve their goals. If so, that is great! If not, then an individual could consider what are the ego state behaviours they want to do more of and which ego state behaviours they want to do less.

Another TA concept is that of drivers, which have also been called working styles. These are typified by behaviours that often feel driven and can result in conflict when people encounter someone with another style. There are five styles, and you will probably see yourself falling more in one or two styles than in others. Unlike the MBTI (Myers 1976) and Belbin (1981, 1996) roles that encourage a mix of styles, this approach suggests that you recognize working style preference(s) and how these might potentially cause conflict or stress within a workplace. Figure 6.5 summarizes these five styles.

Figure 6.5. Working styles

Working style	Typical behaviours
Hurry up	Motivated by doing things in the shortest possible time, looking for efficiency. The problem is when we are in a hurry, mistakes can happen due to lack of preparation.
Be perfect	This style is opposite of hurry up's, and want to do things precise and right the first time. They may not get things done on time due to misjudgement of time and detail required.
Please people	This style wants to please other people without having to ask. They value harmony, and make good team members. The downside is that they are reluctant to upset anyone and often avoid challenging others' ideas. They often smile and nod.
Try hard	This style is focused on enthusiastically putting effort into a task, and is less concerned about succeeding. They may volunteer for more tasks before completing current ones.
Be strong	Be strong people are able to handle tasks with a sense of calm. They are able to juggle many tasks with skill. Their difficulty is not wanting to show or admit a weakness.

Source: Adapted from Hay (1998).

Case illustration
Conflict at work

John had worked at Abyworks pet supplies for ten years and had always received satisfactory or above ratings on his performance reviews. He had a good working relationship with his work colleagues, especially Andrea. He describes himself as a hard-working employee, who is always willing to put extra effort into doing things, and frequently volunteers for new projects as he likes new challenges. His working style could be described as a 'try hard'. Andrea's evaluation supported John's view of his work, and her working style was a 'please people'.

Within the last three months, Andrea was promoted and transferred to another location. John's new line manager is Eva, whose approach is one of getting things right first time. She enjoys perfection in herself, and expects others to do the same. If her employees do not get things right, she will tell them right away. Since her first day on the job, she made it clear to all employees that she has high expectations of everyone, including herself. Her working style can be described as 'be perfect'.

Since Eva first came, John has felt under a lot of pressure. It seems that his best efforts are not recognized, and frequently criticized for not achieving agreed targets. He is very confused and upset by this, as his previous manager praised his work. He cannot understand how his work is now seen as below standard.

Yesterday, Eva met with John for his annual performance review with the following observations:

- He does put a lot of effort into his work.
- His effort is often directed into what he thinks is important rather than toward meeting agreed targets.
- He frequently does not finish one task before volunteering for another one, thus requiring other people to finish off the first task.
- He has recently shown a lack of interest in his work, and his dress has not been up to standard.

For these reasons, John was given an unsatisfactory evaluation and will have a progress review in three months. Following that evaluation, John went to his doctor and was given a note allowing him to be off work for two weeks due to stress.

Questions

- What is the role that working styles have played in the conflict between John and his new line manager, Eva?
- With a knowledge of working styles, what might Eva do to help John come back to work and have a better understanding of the change in expectations between herself and Andrea?
- What suggestions might you have for Abyworks so that managers and employees can develop a better understanding and work relationship?

Critique

Transactional Analysis provides us with a rational and methodological approach for making sense of our communication. However, it is dependent upon accurate assessment of locating or positioning of individuals in relation to a concept such as ego states. It is also dependent on a degree of self-awareness, which varies across individuals.

6.2.5 Foundations of rapport and change

The final element of approaches to working relationships is known as **Neurolinguistic Programming** (NLP). Admittedly, it is a mouthful and can be seen as a series of techniques to help us understand how our brain works and how people can change. It is aimed at helping you to do what you already do well better, acquire skills you do not currently possess, and communicate more effectively with others. More than anything else, it is a strategy for success. This section will look at a few aspects of NLP.

'Neuro' refers to how the mind and body interact.

'Linguistic' refers to the insights into a person's thinking that can be obtained by careful attention to how they use language.

'Programming' refers to the study of thinking and behavioural patterns or programmes which people use regularly.

O'Connor and McDermott (1996) discuss four pillars of wisdom:

1 Rapport with yourself and with others. This can be called being 'in tune'.

2 Know what you want. This way people can set their goal or outcome.

3 Sensory acuity—using your senses to notice what is happening in relation to your goal. Then, use this feedback to make any necessary adjustments.

4 Developing behavioural flexibility so that individuals have many choices for action that can lead to success.

First, rapport can be established at the following levels:

Body language including body, face, and voice that can reinforce or discount what our words say. It is common to notice when people's body language conflicts with their words. At these times, individuals tend to pay more attention to language of the body.

Voice covers such things as matching someone's tone, volume, and speed to create a climate of harmony.

Words can become more significant if we understand their vocabulary and literal meaning. The five senses of Visual, Auditory, Kinaesthetic, Olfactory, and Gustatory are used in learning, language, and acting. Each person will have a sensory preference which is reflected in their speech and can be used to establish rapport by matching others' preferences (Figure 6.6).

Second, it is important for people to understand what they want through the setting of sensory specific outcomes. This ties into sensory awareness and acuity with the use of feedback in learning. The final point is to develop a number of behavioural options that people can draw on rather than relying on just a few.

Critique

Neurolinguistic Programming has recently enjoyed a peak of interest within the management context. The strength of NLP is providing a range of techniques that help individuals achieve success. Its drawbacks are that it can be seen primarily as a buffet of techniques rather than a unified approach to personal development. Furthermore, an individual may use a certain technique that does not achieve the desired outcome. Rather than seeing this as a learning experience, and either adapting or trying another approach, the individual may discount the entire field of NLP.

Pause for thought
Think of ways individuals could develop their assertiveness.

KEY LEARNING POINTS

- The social psychologists offer valuable theory as a way of understanding attraction in the workplace.
- Self-disclosure and feedback lead to more effective communication and decision making.
- Clash of personalities is one key cause of conflict.
- Being aware of our and others' personal style (TA) can greatly improve our communication.
- Rapport is a key factor in improving work relationships.

Figure 6.6. Sensory preference key words

Visual	Auditory	Kinaesthetic	Olfactory	Gustatory
See	Hear	Touch	Smell	Taste
Look	Listen	Feel	Nose	Bitter
View	Tone	Hold	Fragrant	Sweet
Picture	Clear	Warm	Stink	Swallow

6.3 Relationship issues

The chapter will now look at key relationship issues. These include the '**dark side of management**', sexual harassment, bullying at work, and sex and romance in the workplace.

6.3.1 The dark side of management

Not all managers act in a benevolent manner. The 'dark side' or as Jung (1953) called it, 'the shadow side' is the part of personality that people are less aware of or generally hide from others. Most people have a dark side and find it unacceptable to show this to others and so it remains very much part of their hidden world. Usually, it is childhood experience that contributes to how people respond to stress and anxiety, developing defence mechanisms in order to manage perceived threats from our environment and others. Horney (1937) believes that these defence behaviours lead to the development of neurotic needs. She classified these neurotic needs under three headings relating to how an individual might react when stressed. Often these styles of coping may be displayed inappropriately in adult relationships, and people may over-react to perceived threats. A person may transfer these childhood reactions to the world of work, affecting working relationships with others.

The three styles are:

The Neurotic Personality—may move away from people and show a need for independence and solitude. Characteristics include volatile, mistrustful, cautious, detached, passive-aggressive. These people may lack a control of their emotions and thus socially withdraw from stressful situations. They may be viewed as isolated and aloof by their colleagues.

The Narcissistic Personality—may move against other people to dominate them and regain control. Characteristics include arrogance, manipulation, drama, and eccentric behaviour. The narcissistic style characterizes people who might be loud, energetic, active, extrovert, and like social contact. These people like attention and like to be perceived as charming and charismatic and competent. However, under pressure their behaviour may change to impulsive, overbearing, delusional confidence, and intimidation. They can be manipulative and dramatic too. The narcissistic personality disorder (NPD) is a specific form of **toxic leadership**. It is based on the mythical boy Narcissus whose qualities were applauded by Echo. This psychological disorder is characterized by a pattern of self-importance and overestimation of their own abilities, a need for being admired, boastful, lacking empathy, and devaluing achievements of others. Other features of this disorder include the use of charm to generate compliments and the need to surround themselves with others who echo their strengths, which can result in the formation of a cult with anti-organizational norms such as bullying. They may mislead others in their achievements, often lacking competence, yet overworking those around them and squandering resources. Their self-esteem can be fragile, showing an emotional coldness. Explosive anger is often close to the surface, and can appear with the least provocation. They can form romantic relationships in order to advance their career.

These type of leaders can emerge in organizations that do not challenge this type of behaviour. Therefore, it is imperative that dark side managers are challenged. Toxic leaders can only exist through the approval of others. As Asch (1956) discovered in researching **conformity**, if one person broke with the majority opinion, conformity was greatly reduced.

The Obsessive Personality—may move towards others in order to please and placate them. Behaviours include being overly eager to please, compliant, over-conscientious, stubborn, fussy, indecisive, and perfection seeking. A person may appear as conservative and conforming and might under pressure be viewed as being over-compliant and eager to please. They might **avoid** standing up to managers and thus remain subservient. Anxiety and stress may lead the manager who has obsessive characteristics to avoid trusting others, not delegate well and generally obsessively attempt to create an ordered environment around them.

These behaviours arise out of childhood development and so in the world of work, personality may be assessed by specially designed psychometrics. Dysfunctional work relationships may result from incompetent managers and toxic work environments polluted by dark side management characteristics and erode trust building as well as increase the potential for power abuse.

There are many leaders who consistently abuse their power. Pascale (1990) stated that it is necessary to study both healthy and sick organizations in order to have insight into this process. Vaughan (1999) found that routine nonconformity, mistake, misconduct, and disaster are given birth by the links between environment, organization, cognition, and choice. This can identify some of the symptoms that help diagnose the dark side condition.

Cupach and Spitzberg (2007) cite six characteristics of the dark side:

1 It focuses on the dysfunctional, distorted, and destructive aspects of behaviour.

2 It links with deviance and violation which include being awkward, rude, and disruptive.

3 It goes into the overt and covert implications of human exploitation.

4 It uncovers unfulfilled, underestimated, and unappreciated domains of behaviour.

5 It is attracted to the unattractive, unwanted, distasteful, and repulsive.

6 It seeks to understand the process of objectification.

Dark side management practice can initially reside within individual managers who have unfulfilled power and status needs. Lipman-Blumen (2005: 18) define toxic leadership as 'leaders who engage in numerous destructive behaviours and who exhibit certain dysfunctional characteristics . . . which inflict some reasonably serious and enduring harm on their followers and their organizations'. This can turn into an addictive process where the manager is never fulfilled, no matter how much power they may gain. Research has indicated that those under the subordination of a 'derailed manager' will be most effected as the manager's integrity gradually diminishes. Certainly, work-related stress is one by-product of the 'darker side of management'. Managerial pressure can manifest itself through workplace bullying which can lead to long-term sickness absence for the victims.

It appears that senior management have a need to be nurtured so that they learn to manage their dark side characteristics effectively. Developing emotional maturity and emotional integrity can be enhanced with the use of psychometric testing. Developing emotional stability and emotional intelligence is referred to later in the chapter. Emotional intelligence refers to the ability of an individual to be able to deal with their emotional states in a mature constructive manner. How people feel emotion and then consequently display it to others appears to be an area that needs to be addressed so that it does not add to the manifestation of the dark side of personality at work. The 'derailed' manager will view others actions towards them as hostile and malicious and thus react accordingly. This attribution bias can further contribute the breakdown of relationships at work.

 Activity **The dark side**

Try this self-assessment exercise to identify your 'dark side' characteristics:

- Pick your strengths from the following list—enthusiastic, shrewd, perfectionism, independent, confident, sociable, gregarious and entertaining, creative, conscientious, harmonious.

- Now list each of your strengths and describe how you might act when stressed or under pressure.

- What potential 'dark side' characteristics might you be showing to others?

- How can the following dark side characteristics be managed—volatile, mistrustful, cautious, detached, passive-aggressive, arrogant, manipulative, dramatic, eccentric, perfectionist, dependent?

6.3.2 Sexual harassment

Bullying and harassment can occur in the workplace, leading to relationship breakdown. This section will now explore bullying in particular as harassment has received much attention in the literature but bullying is a newer field of work, specifically resulting from toxic management as noted in the previous section.

Sexual harassment is defined as any sexually-based behaviour that is generally unwanted. It can have an adverse effect on a person's status, affects job performance, and can create a hostile working environment. Many organizations have been guided by laws and now have policy to guard against sexual harassment at work. Sexual harassment consists of three components, namely: gender harassment, unwanted sexual attention, and sexual coercion. Thus, insulting attitudes, and job outcomes linked to sex both constitute sexual harassment (Gelfand et al. 1995).

Both men and women have been found to report sexual harassment but harassment is more likely to be perceived when: (a) the victim is female and the perpetrator is male; (b) the victim has less power than the perpetrator; (c) the behaviour is repeated; (d) the victim has requested that the perpetrator stop; (e) negative outcomes follow; (f) the victim suffers emotional symptoms; and (g) the organization has been lenient on perpetrators in the past.

In comparison to ten years ago, there are now more lawsuits as people's perception of harassment have changed. Public awareness and understanding has increased. There is much more self-reporting, especially regarding the psychological impact of harassment. The role of occupational psychologists is to help organizations to develop effective polices and procedures on sexual harassment. They should also be instrumental in designing training initiatives to promote:

1 an awareness of sexual harassment;

2 communication skills so that harassment situations can be avoided before they happen;

3 conflict resolution skills to address harassment events as they occur.

6.3.3 Bullying at work

Billions of pounds every year are lost through absences caused by work stress that is now believed to be the result of bullying. Hoel et al. (1999) note that bullying at work is quite common. It can be reflected in actions designed to humiliate, ridicule, and socially isolate a person. It can manifest in various behaviours and might include giving a subordinate difficult work tasks or withholding important information from a colleague, thus permitting ridicule and criticism over performance. Bullying may take the form of insulting comments or practical jokes. It can be a traumatic and demoralizing experience for the victim and can produce symptoms of post-traumatic stress disorder, irrational rage, weeping, humiliation, feelings of failure, and nightmares which can last for years. Victims of bullying are often encouraged to keep a record of the bullying incidents in the form of a diary so as to illustrate the extent of the abuse.

Bullying is defined as persistent behaviour against an individual which is intimidating, offensive or malicious and undermines the confidence and self esteem of the recipient. (Charted Institute for Personnel Development)

Hoel et al. (1999) undertook research on bullying and found that survey data revealed that men and women were guilty of bullying in fairly equal numbers. The top three negative behaviours by bullies were ignoring opinions, withholding information, exposing the victim to high workloads, and personal derogation.

Often bullying starts due to stress and feelings of inadequacy, jealousy, or envy over a pay rise, promotion, or the victim drawing attention through good performance. It is important for victims of bullying not to put up with it, or stay off work. They are encouraged to get an ally and work with a psychologist to overcome psychological issues.

Many organizations have attempted to tackle bullying in the workplace by introducing initiatives that enhance physical and psychological health, safety, and employee welfare. The

Pause for thought
What factors might discourage workers from reporting incidents of bullying?

Mr Horkulak was a senior director in the UK of cantor Fitzerald, the US-based broker. Foul language and bullying were part of the dealing room culture. Generally, top managers were allowed to behave aggressively towards those reporting to them. During the court case Mr Horkulak claimed that Lee Amaitis, the firm's president, regularly screamed obscenities at him and once threatened to break him in two. The firm claimed that Mr Horkulak, who admitted to using cocaine and heavy drinking while at work also had a long history of stress and anxiety at work and was said to walk away from difficult situations.

director of human resources at Chelsea and Westminster Healthcare NHS Trust introduced a 'Dignity at Work Policy' which specified the different forms harassment can take. Employees are advised to discuss incidences of bullying with someone who is impartial, empathetic, and trained in issues of equality. Harassment Advisers have been trained in this role and provide a professional and friendly service, which staff can use with confidence and which is independent of line management systems. The advisers work with victims and bullies to find resolutions.

6.3.4 Sex and romance in the workplace

Many individuals often meet their partners in the workplace. As a result of longer working hours and a blurring of the home-work interface, this is a very common occurrence. Social-sexual behaviour at work is a widespread occurrence. Gutek (1985) was one of the first to research this phenomena.

Key definitions on the subject can be noted.

- Workplace relationships are defined as some form of intimate relationship between two employees who have expressed their romantic feelings in the form of dating or other intimate association (Mainiero 1986).

Workplace relationships are defined as mutually desired relationships between two people at work, in which some element of sexuality or physical intimacy exists (Powell and Foley 1998).

Due to the increased participation of women in the workforce, sexual harassment policy has developed in recent years. However, no such policy really exists for many organizations in relation to sexual and romantic relationships at work. Many organizations take a punitive approach and condemn all such types of behaviour while others have more open and liberal cultures sanctioning the development of romantic relationships in the workplace.

Human Legal Resources (HLR) reported in 2004 that romantic attachments in the workplace are common with 93 per cent of their 1,072 respondents indicating that they had a romantic relationship at work and that 3 in 10 people had sexual relations in the workplace. Interestingly, more than a third commented that they were unclear on their workplace policy regarding intimate relationships.

Quinn (1977) undertook observations of workplace relationships, using a survey instrument in an airport waiting room. The author looked at motives and deviant behaviour in order to produce a model or organizational romance. Later, Mainiero (1986) indicated that research in the area had explored antecedents in terms of proximity, intimacy, intensity of work, and mutual arousal. Outcomes of such relationships have further been noted as leading to conflicts of interests, poor team dynamics, and conflicts of loyalty.

Gutek (1985) conducted a random telephone survey of 399 adult workers in Los Angeles exploring social-sexual behaviours and sexual harassment at work. In addition, Lobel et al. (1994) reviewed published theoretical and empirical literature on sexuality in organizations, with the objective of evaluating whether sexuality should or can be eradicated from the workplace as an effective antidote to sexual harassment. The author suggests that sexuality cannot be eradicated from the workplace and that future researchers need to explore and define appropriate sexuality at work and identifying situations of conflict of interest. Sexuality in the workplace is viewed as a taboo subject.

Pierce et al. (1996) looked at interpersonal attraction and romantic attraction and how it led to workplace romance (wpr) and how it was dependent on attitudes. First feelings of interpersonal attraction arise towards another organizational member; second feelings of romantic attraction arise towards the same person; and third, the decision is made to participate in a wpr. Powell and Foley (1998) reviewed the management and organizational literature on romantic relationships in organizational settings. They suggested that this was a topic where much further research was needed. Kakabadse and Kakabadse (2004) concluded that workplace wpr occurs due to the blurred home-work distinction. They looked at intimacy in relationships, and concluded that relationships were positive and not a problem if they were well managed.

Finally, Riach and Wilson (2007) conducted interviews with 48 managers and workers in the pub industry in Glasgow. Romance was conceptualized as natural and something that could not be legislated for, where unwritten rules were defined but ignored. Outcomes were dependent on gender, hierarchical position, and sexual identity.

However, emotionally intimate relationships at work (whether romantic or sexual) can have serious consequences. Certainly sexual and romantic relationships at work may affect worker conduct and lead to negative synergy within relationships (Mainiero 1986). However, there is research that suggests that the office romance can increase synergy/productivity and improve work climate and culture (Quinn 1977); and add excitement, enhance communication, stimulate creativity, and lead to higher job satisfaction (Pierce et al. 1996).

Whatever the motives for engaging in sexual and romantic relationships, whether it be for a quick lustful sexual fling or longer-term love and intimacy, the vast majority of workers are very unlikely to tell managers or the HR department about their relationship or a colleague's relationship until it leads to negative outcomes. These negative outcomes can include jealousy and gossip, an abuse of power, poor team dynamics, reductions in productivity, or breaches of confidentiality. In today's workplace, employers need to ensure that they have a clear policy to guard against the potential impact of sexual and romantic relationships at work and to ward off sexual harassment claims. Kakabadse and Kakabadse (2004) comment on how organizations are found wanting in not having institutional policies and practices to equitably address this emerging phenomenon. But how far are employers prepared to take action so as to prevent claims of favouritism, sexual harassment, injury to feelings, damage to reputations, and in some cases forced career changes or dismissal.

In the USA, many organizations have generally chosen to condemn such activity and have introduced 'Love Contracts' which are clauses that either discourage inter-office relationships or prohibit them entirely. Extensive policies have also been introduced to regulate or suppress sexual and romantic relationships. It is questionable as to whether expressions of sexuality in the workplace can be regulated and suppressed through moral legislation and such policies may be counter-productive as individuals are forced into a secrecy culture. It might be viewed that sexual and romantic relationships at work are the norm and so people should not discriminate against staff in such relationships just because they (the relationships) might create difficulties or unless the consequences of such relationships are positive or negative.

In contrast, a more positive approach has been taken in the UK. Depending on the specific industry, condoning policy is implemented which is fair and accepts that workplace relationships will happen and encourages employees to be open about them. Issues that arise as a result of sexual and romantic relationships can be dealt with professionally and legally, perhaps by allocating the individuals engaged in such relationships to different teams or departments. Often open and well-communicated 'Conflicts of Interests' policies are utilized by organizations. But as employees may be secretive about their behaviour or work in a culture of secrecy, it is difficult for such policies to be implemented effectively. Few organizations have formal codes of behaviour concerning such matters and so perhaps organizations need to continue to think about the implications and likely impact of sexual and romantic relationships in the workplace by undertaking risk assessment that aims to identify what areas of the business might need protecting.

Risk assessment of the likely impact of relationships on the workplace

- Identify what aspects of the business need protecting: financial exposure, breach of confidence, conflict of interest, team issues, professional distance.
- Policy for displays of affection, acting professionally, safe communication channels, thinking ahead in case of break-up.
- Is the climate pro-interactive?
- What policy already exists?
- Is the couple in a superior/subordinate relationship?
- Do any other conflict of interests exist?
- Does one of the parties need to transfer or leave?

Activity Workplace romance

Imagine you are an HR manager, how might you manage a team when there has been a breakdown of communication due to the breakdown of a romantic relationship of two of the team members.

- What policies might you introduce?
- Would you enlist the help of a psychologist, and how might they help?
- How could you get the team back on track?

KEY LEARNING POINTS

- Understand that not all managers are benevolent, and can act in devious ways.
- Understand and share awareness of toxic leaders with others.
- Sexual harassment is increasing and management must intervene to reduce its psychological impact.
- Bullying can result from stress and can lead to the psychological harm of others.
- Sexual and romantic relationships at work can lead to positive outcomes such as increased productivity, happier workers, more creativity but they can also lead to negative outcomes such as jealousy, favouritism, poor team dynamics, office gossip, distraction from work, reputation damage, and job loss.

6.4 Developing effective relationships

The next section of the chapter will explore how it is possible to develop better working relationships. Previously, the chapter discussed a number of factors that impact on work relationships. The chapter will now look at some interventions. There can be difficulties or conflict due to such factors as: communication, style preferences, values, organizational structure, personality clashes, power struggles, stress, and time pressure, among others. This section will be divided into:

Personality conflict

Emotional intelligence

Communication

Recognizing others and drama

Change strategies

Coaching psychology.

6.4.1 Personality conflict

Personality clashes can be destructive and obstruct task effectiveness. During personality clashes, people frequently focus on the person rather than the behaviour, and may assume their particular style is the correct one. It is important to remember that no one personality is better than another, and personality is a preference for behaviour patterns, rather than a rationale for our actions. In dealing with personality clashes, it can be approached by:

- acknowledging that conflict exists in the form of personality differences;
- beginning to understand differences by using language such as the MBTI or a similar tool that will allow individuals to openly discuss their differences;
- looking at the behaviours that are creating problems rather than the people;
- looking at the benefits of personality differences as well as the drawbacks (i.e. intuitives need sensing types to point out the details);
- exploring the options available to the parties involved, including organizational barriers such as structures, systems, and role conflict;
- choosing an option which is acceptable to both persons and give the option time to be a success;
- reflecting and reviewing relationships.

The issue of conflict has been discussed in relation to personality and values. Huczynski and Buchanan (2007) reported that Thomas (1976) differentiated five approaches to conflict resolution based on the opposing dimensions of assertiveness vs. unassertiveness and cooperation vs. uncooperation. These are important distinctions, as Flannes and Levin (2005) state that one goal for project managers is knowing which approach will be best in a given situation. As it is common for project managers to get into conflict, this is a key skill. If two people both have **competing** as a preferred conflict style, then the potential for resolution is low. Therefore, people need to develop comfort zones in a range of different conflict styles to look for a win-win situation. For further discussions on the subject of personality, see Chapter 3.

Conflict can easily occur in organizations if individuals have different values. Unless individuals are aware of these underlying influences the roots of the conflict may never be acknowledged. Alignment of values between the individual and organization contributes to satisfaction and effectiveness.

The technology company Apple has a reputation for innovative products (imac, ipod, iphone). From this, it can be assumed that one of their organizational values is creativity, which implies they recruit and select creative individuals who then behave creatively if they want to remain and progress within the organization. The job title of 'creative' is applied to Apple employees who teach customers how to use their products. These 'creatives' come from such industries as art, music, and photography.

Figure 6.7. Conflict resolution styles

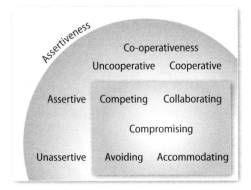

Source: Huczynski and Buchanan (2007).

Figure 6.8. Values to behaviour link

6.4.2 Emotional intelligence

A further issue within personality is emotional intelligence, sometimes called EQ or EI. It 'refers to the capacity for recognizing our own feelings and those of others, for motivating ourselves, and for managing emotions well in ourselves and in our relationships' (Goleman 1999: 317). This same author presented an emotional competence framework which includes Personal Competencies (self-awareness, self-regulation, and motivation) and Social Competencies (empathy and social skills). Goleman (1995) believes EQ is more important than high IQ. Whetten and Cameron (2002) stated that when companies hire new employees, emotional competences make up the majority of desirable attributes.

People live in a world where emotions boil over, which dilutes our quality of life. Morand (2001) suggests using emotional intelligence as a guide to success in leadership, human relations skills, and communication with Moriarty and Buckley (2003) adding teamworking. Jordan et al. (2002) found that coaching can be used to elevate people's emotional intelligence and moderates concerns for job insecurity. Goleman believes EQ should be raised to a higher place in the value hierarchy of organizations that can be learned. Simple techniques, such as counting to ten when angry before responding, are useful.

6.4.3 Communication

Pause for thought
Why do you think EQ is argued to be more important than IQ? Do you agree with this notion?

Communication is often grouped under the heading 'interpersonal skills'. The foundations of interpersonal communication are: observing, listening, questioning, giving and receiving feedback, and non-verbal behaviour. These support such second-order interpersonal skills as: assertiveness, influencing, persuading, negotiating, leading, managing conflict, and teamworking (Oxford Institute of International Finance 2004). Empowerment is also a key issue for individuals and teams as Greasley et al. (2005) feel it is important for employees to be heard. Communication always has a purpose and is directed towards meeting some objective. It can be face to face, or at a distance, using multiple sources of technology. There is the well-known saying that you cannot not communicate. Looking at the outcome of your communication compared to your objective will determines its effectiveness. A good starting point is to look at the communication process outlined by Huczynski and Buchanan (2007) with potential errors (Oxford Institute of International Finance (2004) (Figure 6.9).

There is also a group of potential errors under the headings of **encoding**, transmission, and **decoding**.

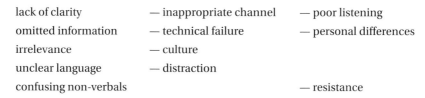

lack of clarity	— inappropriate channel	— poor listening
omitted information	— technical failure	— personal differences
irrelevance	— culture	
unclear language	— distraction	
confusing non-verbals		— resistance

In this model, encoding relates to how the transmitter (communicator) chooses to express a message, decoding is how it is interpreted by someone else (receiver), and the channel is the method, such as face to face, telephone, electronic, etc. Perceptual filters can get in the way of accurate decoding such as predispositions to hear or not, and our emotional state, so people need to recognize the validity of others' perceptions as well as their own. Due to the complexity of this process when considering such aspects as experience and culture, it is important to check out whether our message has been received as sent (feedback), as Kelly (2000) observed that breakdowns can occur at any point in the process. You may want to refer back to the Johari Window, where feedback can be used to open up our public arena.

Figure 6.9. Communications process

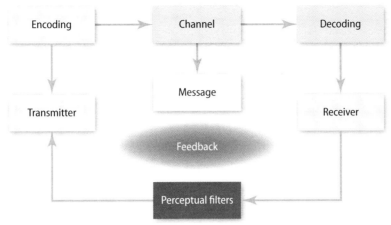

Source: Huczynski and Buchanan (2007).

Non-verbal behaviour is a key factor in any communication. In earlier research, Mehrabian (1970) identified that when individuals engage in face-to-face communication, 55 per cent of the message is relayed by body language, 38 per cent by voice tone, and only 7 per cent by verbal content. Pivcevic (1999) claims there to be common agreement that 80 per cent of communication is non-verbal. Non-verbal communication can include such factors as facial expression, eye behaviour, posture, limb, and arm movements, distance, and voice quality. Guirdham (2002) has described non-verbal behaviour as a relationship language which could include such notions as trust, submission, and dislike. However, the role of verbal communication is highly significant in our relationships, as Mullins (2008) stated that language reflects and shapes our experience, which includes both verbal and non-verbal factors. It is important to focus on both verbal and non-verbal elements, and to look for the degree of congruence between these two aspects. This was previously addressed under neurolinguistic programming.

Giving and receiving feedback is a vital part of many organizational processes and can be a vital aid to increasing interpersonal competence. Feedback is more effective when it is requested rather than being forced, and it is important to adopt an 'I'm OK, you're OK' position even if the feedback is unpleasant. Avoiding attribution error with feedback is important, as it is easy to wrongly attribute others' behaviour to internal rather than external causes. Looking for evidence to support our attributions can help prevent this error. Furthermore, people are often nervous at performance appraisals since they may not have received regular feedback prior to that meeting. Some behaviours to keep in mind with feedback are:

Giving:	Receiving:
be sensitive to others	be receptive to feedback
focus on behaviours, not the person	avoid defensive behaviours
check that meaning is understood	clarify what is said
use neutral non-verbal behaviours	use open non-verbals

There is no shortage of research and models in the field of communication. Perhaps one of the issues is an over-reliance on models that can give the impression of communication as being a linear and rational process. On the contrary, it is a very complex process that is moderated by our perception, mood, experience, and context. It is highly important that individuals

Figure 6.10. Non-verbal and verbal communication

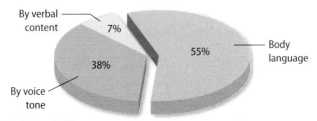

Source: Statistics from Mehrabian (1970).

Figure 6.11. Drama triangle

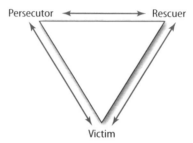

Source: Karpman (2007).

remain sensitive to the effect that one's communication style has on others, and not jump to conclusions about a person's intention too quickly.

6.4.4 Recognizing others and drama

Feedback is an opportunity to motivate others, and the transactional analysis notion of **stroking** is a useful skill. Stroking is a unit of recognition (Hay 1993) which can be done by speaking, looking, or touching someone. People who do not have sufficient strokes in their lives will respond disproportionally to a minor stroke such as a smile or head nod. Strokes can be positive or negative, conditional or unconditional, and vary in intensity. The labelling of positive or negative strokes can often be confused with the use of sarcasm. You may receive a stroke that has positive content, but negative tones.

A person's communication improves greatly if they omit the disguise of sarcasm and say what they want. In the UK, shaking hands is the most common form of non-verbal stroking.

While assertiveness is mentioned above as one of the second-order skills, it is quite important as a style in meeting our needs while allowing others to do the same. By being assertive, people can maintain an 'I'm OK, you're OK' position that blocks bullying, prejudice, and discrimination. An approach that will assist our understanding of games and roles is Karpman's (2007) **drama triangle** where people may prefer the **persecutor**, **rescuer**, or **victim** role. A willing victim is the basis for a game. TV dramas such as *The Bill* and *CSI* focus their stories around this concept.

People will sometimes move between the three positions at a rapid pace, which is where the drama comes in. The switch of drama positions can occur from one sentence to the next. People can end up in the victim role due to their life position ('I'm not OK, you're OK'), payoff associated with role, and excessive need for attention no matter how this is achieved. A variation known as the compassion triangle occurs when each person is secretly stuck in all three roles at once. According to Karpman this can occur through socially identified or denied roles and assists in understanding the person. Every player in the game is motivated and experiences all roles in some way. It helps to notice the links between our life position (**OKness**), ego state (P-A-C), working styles, stroking, and the drama triangle. All of these open up ways for improving our communication patterns.

When communication does not go as desired, individuals can respond by adopting one of four **stress styles** described by Satir (1988) originating from our families, though also relevant in work settings. It is important to recognize these as responses to stress, and measure our responses accordingly. Therefore, if a person's coping style is blaming, then they need to consider the usefulness of this style and its effect on others. The stress styles are:

1 **Blamer**—takes the position of it's not my fault, somebody else caused this to happen. This person perceives that they have no role in the problem. They are quite willing to blame anyone.

2 **Placator**—takes the position of smoothing things over, accepting blame even when they had nothing to do with the problem. Here, the placator hopes to please others and imagines they will be grateful for their acceptance of responsibility. Blamers and Placators often cooperate to form an alliance.

3 **Super-reasonable**—this response adopts the ultra logical-position even when it is clear that logic is not working. One of the motives here is the avoidance of emotions.

Figure 6.12. Levels of change

Purpose
Identity
Beliefs and values
Capabilities and skills
Behaviours
Environment

Source: Knight (1999).

4 **Super-irrelevant**—this style attempts to avoid confrontation by confusion. If they are asked when the **CEO** can expect their report, they might respond by asking what everyone is planning to do for the upcoming weekend.

6.4.5 Change strategies

Changing behaviour can be a challenging process, and previous discussion has highlighted some of the ways this can be done. However, Knight (1999: 88) takes a strategic view in describing the **levels of change** model as one of 'alignment'. The basic premise is that whenever an individual, group, or organization wants to change, they need to consider all levels.

If you want to change from being passive to assertive, then you need to consider not only the behavioural change related to assertiveness, but also how this change will impact on your purpose, identity, beliefs and values, capabilities and skills, and environment as noted in Figure 6.12.

There are questions you can ask yourself about each element of this model to see if your change is aligned into a unified whole:

Purpose: Am I fulfilling my sense of purpose?

Identity: Am I living out my mission?

Beliefs and values: Am I being true to my beliefs and values?

Capabilities and skills: Am I realizing my potential?

Behaviours: Am I acting in ways true to who I am?

Environment: Am I influencing my environment the way I want?

6.4.6 Coaching psychology

Coaching psychology is an applied positive psychology, drawing on and developing established psychological approaches, and can be understood as being the systematic application of behavioural science to the enhancement of life experience, work performance and well-being for individuals, groups, and organizations who do not have clinically significant mental heath issues or abnormal levels of distress.

The term 'coaching' has become one of the popular names now used for the application of psychologically focused techniques for both life and business improvement. The Special Group in Coaching Psychology (SGCP) has now been established to provide psychologists who are members of the British Psychological Society with an easy and effective means of sharing research as well as practical experiences that relate to the psychology of coaching.

A key driver in creating the SGCP was that coaching psychologists are drawn from a diverse range of BPS divisions including, but not restricted to, occupational, counselling, and sports psychology. Coaching sessions have been utilized with derailed managers and is a productive intervention method that can change long-held dysfunctional behaviours and lead to more effective work relationships. The coach can help individuals to develop more effective work relationships by enhancing emotional awareness, effective communication, stress management, and managing personality clashes.

KEY LEARNING POINTS

- Exploring conflict resolution strategies is fundamental to reducing personality conflict.
- Developing emotional resilience in the form of Emotional Intelligence is a useful tool in developing effective relationships.
- Acknowledging the communication process and checking messages have been received can aid relationship effectiveness.
- People all have different preferences and dislikes around work relationships and task performance; acknowledging these is important.
- Appreciate the impact that our styles have on others' perceptions and behaviours.
- Utilizing coaching psychologists in the workplace can help to alleviate dysfunction relationship behaviours.

Chapter summary

- Relationships at work meet specific needs for intimacy, social support, personal growth, and security.
- It is important to be aware of our personal preferences and attitudes and their influence on communication whenever we interact with others.
- Social psychology can help us to understand the factors that lead to individuals developing relationships at work.
- The Johari Window is a useful tool for reviewing the extent of our self-disclosure in relationships.
- It is useful to be aware of the style preferences that a person and others display, and use this language (such as TA and MBTI) as a guide to exploring behavioural preferences.
- Managers have many characteristics that make them successful; however, poor emotional intelligence can lead to management derailment in the form of neurotic, narcissistic, and obsessive personality types. These styles of coping with anxiety and stress in the workplace can lead to dysfunctional relationships at work.
- Sexual and romantic relationships in the workplace are on the increase and organizations have a responsibility to manage them accordingly.
- Bullying in the workplace is a serious phenomenon and needs the intervention of a mediator to help resolve the problems between perpetrators and victims.
- Conflict resolution styles can be employed by managers to minimize conflict in working relationships.
- Emotional intelligence can be used as a guide to success in leadership, human relations skills, and communication.
- The development of interpersonal skills can lead to enhanced communication.
- Coaching psychology is one way of offering support to managers as a way of raising awareness of their style of management under pressure.

Assess your learning

Review questions

1 Review the factors that contribute to the context of work relationships.

2 How are people attracted to each other in the workplace? And what are the criticisms of balance theory and cognitive dissonance theory?

3 Discuss the role that personality and **value conflict** has on work relationships.

4 Choose one of the models from transactional analysis. Describe the model, and how it could be applied in a work setting.

5 Describe what is meant by 'the dark side of personality' and what is meant by 'management derailment'.

6 What are some of the characteristics of dark side management and why is it important to recognize these?

7 How can managers help to alleviate bullying in the workplace?

8 How can managers manage the increasing rise of sexual and romantic relationships in the workplace?

9 What is the role of emotional intelligence in workplace relationships?

10 What is 'coaching psychology' and how can it be used as an intervention for building more effective work relationships?

11 What is one approach you would recommend to a manager for improving relationships?

Assignments

ASSIGNMENT 1: Team conflict

Your manager has been frustrated recently due to the increase in unproductive conflict within the team. The manager has asked you for advice on some of the causes of conflict, and what might be done about it. What would you say?

ASSIGNMENT 2: Developing effective work relationships

Design a training event that will help employees to build effective relationships in the workplace.

- What topics will you cover?
- What activities will be utilized to enhance communication?
- What type of role-play scenarios might be useful?

Further reading

Baron, R. A. and Byrne, D. (2002) *Social Psychology* (10th edn.). Boston: Allyn and Bacon.
A comprehensive treatment of key topics in the field of social psychology.

Brandt, R. (2005) *Effective Human Relations: Personal and Organizational Applications* (9th edn.).
Houghton Mifflin.
A more in-depth book on human relationships and associated aspects of relationship dynamics including self-disclosure, emotional balance, building strong relationships, and resolving conflict.

Clark, I. (2001) *The Post-Cold War Order: The Spoils of Peace*. Oxford: Oxford University Press.
The most recent guide to the debates about the post-cold war period, viewing it as a kind of peace settlement.

Cooper, C. L. (2001) Great motivators at work. *The Psychologist*, 14: 95.
A useful article on general motivation factors

DuBrin, A. J. (2000) *Applying Psychology and Individual Organizational Effectiveness*. (5th edn.) New York: Prentice-Hall.
A valuable book based on years of research and experience in business psychology; it has an excellent chapter on building strong work relationships and developing communication in the workplace.

Handy, C. (1995) *Gods of Management: The Changing Work of Organisations*. New York: Oxford University Press.

Hay, J. (1993) *Working it out at Work*. Watford: Sherwood.
A useful and well-grounded guide to transactional analysis with practical personal and organizational examples.

Knight, S. (1999) *NLP Solutions*. London: Nicholas Brealey.
A clear and practical guide to the field of neurolinguistic programming and change.

Work psychology in practice
The Devil Wears Prada

The film *The Devil Wears Prada* is about the fashion industry. Miranda, the Runway CEO, projects an air of superiority. This is coupled with excessive demands and expectations. When Miranda came in each morning, she arrogantly threw her coat and purse onto Andrea's (PA) desk to be put away. When she joined Runway, Andrea was not particularly interested in fashion until Nigel and Miranda pressured her into conforming to fashion industry dress standards. By changing her dress style and attitude, Andrea began to abandon her previous values. In doing so, she became more distant from her friends, who could not understand the change. Andrea became more calculative and willing to do whatever it took to please Miranda, who seemed to enjoy challenging her. Miranda once asked Andrea to come up with a copy of a book that had not yet been published for her children to read. Miranda projected personal, expert, and **reward power** as part of her influencing tactics. There was a pivotal quote that Andrea's lover in Paris made about her moving closer to Miranda's way of thinking:

'You, my friend are crossing over to the dark side.'

Andrea was only able to regain her core values and friends and escape the tyranny of Miranda (even though Miranda respected her privately) by resigning her position.

Questions

- What are some of the attitudes and behaviours that Miranda used to create the image of 'the dark side manager'?
- What role does abandoning our core values play in conforming to dark side management?
- What personal skills or attributes do you believe Andrea possessed which enabled her to break free of Miranda's spell?

Online Resource Centre

Visit the supporting online resource centre for additional material which will help you with your research, essays, and assignments, or you may find these additional resources helpful when revising for exams.
http://www.oxfordtextbooks.co.uk/orc/matthewman/

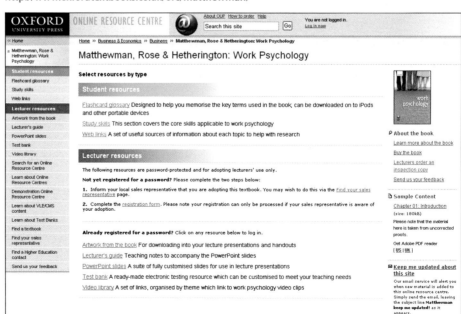

References

Asch, S. (1956) Studies of independence and conformity: a minority of one against unanimous majority. *Psychological Monographs*, 70/416.

Baron, R. A., and Byrne, D. (2002) *Social Psychology* (10th edn.). Boston: Allyn and Bacon.

Belbin, R. M. (1981) *Management Teams: Why they Succeed or Fail*. London: Butterworth Heinemann.

Belbin, R. M. (1996) *The Coming Shape of Organizations*. London: Butterworth Heinemann.

Berne, E. (1972) *What do you Say after you Say Hello?* New York: Grove Press.

Boud, D., and Garrick, J. (1999) *Understanding Learning at Work*. London: Routledge.

Boyd, D., and Foss, P. (1997) *Developing Intimacy in Construction Industry Groups*. 13th Annual Conference of the Association of Researchers in Construction Management (ARCOM), Cambridge, Sept., ed. P. Stephenson.

Castels, M. (1996) *The Rise of the Network Society*, vol. i. Oxford: Blackwell.

Cupach, W. R., and Spitzberg, B. H. (2007) *The Dark Side of Interpersonal Communication*. New York: Routledge.

Dusay, J. (1977). *Egograms: How I See You and You See Me*. New York: Harper and Row.

Flannes, S., and Levin, G. (eds.) (2005) *Essential People Skills for Project Managers*. New York: Management Concepts.

Gelfand, M. J., Fitzgerald, L. F., and Drasgow, F. (1995) The structure of sexual harassment: a confirmatory analysis across cultures and settings. *Journal of Vocational Behaviour*, 47: 164–77.

Goleman, D. (1995) *Emotional Intelligence*. London: Bloomsbury.

Goleman, D. (1999) *Working with Emotional Intelligence*. London: Bloomsbury.

Greasley, K., Bryman, A., Dainty, A., Price, A., Soetanto, R., and King, N. (2005) Employee perceptions of empowerment. *Employee Relations*, 27/4: 354–68.

Guirdham, M. (2002) *Interactive Behaviour at Work* (3rd edn.). Harlow: Financial Times Prentice Hall.

Gutek, B. A. (1985) *Sex and the Workplace: The Impact of Sexual Behaviour and Harassment on Women, Men and the Organisation*. San Francisco: Jossey-Bass.

Handy, C. (1995) *Gods of Management: The Changing Work of Organisations*. New York: Oxford University Press.

Harris, T. (2004) *I'm OK, You're OK*. New York: Harper Paperbacks.

Hay, J. (1988) *Dealing with Difficult People: The Workbook*. Watford: Sherwood.

Hay, J. (1993) *Working it out at Work*. Watford: Sherwood.

Hersey, P., Blanchard K., and Johnson D. (eds.) (2001) *Management of Organisation and Behaviour Leading Human Resources*. Upper Saddle River, NJ: Prentice Hall.

Hoel, H., Raynor, C., and Cooper, C. L. (1999) Workplace bullying. In C. L. Cooper and I. T. Robinson (eds.), *International Review of Industrial and Organizational Psychology*, xiv. Chichester: J. Wiley.

Horney, K. (1937) *The Neurotic Personality of Our Time*. London: Norton and Co.

Huczynski, A. A., and Buchanan, D. A. (2007) *Organizational Behaviour* (6th edn.). Harlow: Financial Times Prentice Hall.

Jordan, P. J., Ashkanasy, N. M., Härtel, C. E. J. and Hooper, G. S. (2002) Workgroup emotional intelligence: scale development and relationship to team process effectiveness and goal focus. *Human Resource Management Review*, 12: 195–214.

Jourard, S. (1971) *Self-disclosure: An Experimental Analysis of the Transparent Self*. Toronto: John Wiley and Sons, Inc.

Jung, C. G. (1953) *Collected Works*. New York: Bollingen Series/Panthenon.

Kakabadse, A., and Kakabadse, N. (2004) *Intimacy: An International Survey of the Sex Lives of People at Work*. Basingstoke: Palgrave Macmillan.

Karpman, S. B. (2007) The new drama triangles. USATAA/ITAA conference lecture.

Kelly, D. (2000) Using vision to improve organisational communication. *Leadership and Organization Development Journal*, 21/2.

Knight, S. (1999) *NLP Solutions*. London: Nicholas Brealey.

Lipman-Blumen, J. (2005) *The Allure of Toxic Leaders*. Oxford: Oxford University Press.

Lobel, S. A., Quinn, R. E., St Claire, L., and Warfield, A. (1994) Love without sex: the impact of psychological intimacy between men and women at work. *Organizational Dynamics*, 23: 5–16.

Luft, J. (1969) *Of Human Interaction*. Palo Alto, CA: National Press.

Mainiero, L. (1986) A review and analysis of power dynamics in organizational romances. *Academy of Management Review*, 11: 750–62.

Mansi, A. (2008) The dark side of management: the consequences for organizations. In Porter, C., Bingham, C., and Simmonds, D. (eds.) (2008) *Exploring Human Resource Management*. McGraw Hill Higher Education.

Marquardt, M. J. (2000) Action learning and leadership. *The Learning Organization*, 7/5.

Mehrabian, A. (1970) *Tactics of Social Influence*. Princeton, NJ: Prentice Hall.

Morand, D. (2001) The emotional intelligence of managers: assessing the construct validity of a nonverbal measure of 'people skills'. *Journal of Business and Psychology*, 16/1. 21–33.

Moriarty P., and Buckley, F. (2003) Increasing team emotional intelligence through process. *Journal of European Industrial Training*, 27/2–4.

Mullins, L. J. (2008) *Essentials of Organisational Behaviour* (2nd edn.). Harlow: Financial Times Prentice Hall.

Myers, I. B. (1976) *Introduction to Type* (2nd edn.). Gainesville, FL: Center for Applications of Psychological Type.

O'Connor, J., and McDermott, I. (1996) *Principles of NLP*. San Francisco: Thorsons.

Oxford Institute of International Finance (2004) *Managing Self Development*. London: BPP Professional Education.

Pascale, R. (1990) *Managing on the Edge: How Successful Companies Use Conflict to Stay Ahead*. Harmondsworth: Penguin.

Pierce, C. A., Byrne, D., and Aguinis, H. (1996) Attraction in organisations: a model of workplace romance. *Journal of Organizational Behaviour*, 17: 5–32.

Pivcevic, P. (1999) Taming the boss. *Management Today*, Mar: 70.

Powell, G. N., and Foley, S. (1998) Something to talk about: romantic relationships in organisational setting. *Journal of Management*, 24: 421–48.

Quinn, R. (1977) Coping with Cupid: the formation, impact and management of romantic relationships in organisations. *Administrative Science Quarterly*, 22: 30–45.

Riach, K., and Wilson, F. (2007) Don't screw the crew: exploring the rules of engagement in organizational romance. *British Journal of Management*, 18: 79–92.

Rodrigues, C. A. (1997) Developing expatriates' cross-cultural sensitivity: cultures where 'your culture's OK' is really not OK. *Journal of Management Development*, 16/9: 690–702.

Satir, V. (1988) *The New Peoplemaking*. Mountain View, CA: Science and Behavior Books.

Senge, P. (1990) *The Fifth Discipline*. New York: Doubleday.

Stewart, B., and Powell, S., (2004) Team building and team working. *Team Performance Management*, 10/1–2.

Thomas, K. W. (1976) Conflict and conflict management. In M. D. Dunette (ed.), *Handbook of Industrial and Organizational Psychology*. Chicago: Rand McNally, 889–935.

Vaughan, D. (1999) The dark side of organizations: mistake, misconduct, and disaster. *Annual Review of Sociology*, 25: 271–305.

Wagner, A. (1981) *The Transactional Manager*. Denver, CO: TA Publications.

Whetten, D., and Cameron, K. (2002) *Developing Management Skills* (5th edn.). Princeton: Prentice Hall.

Chapter 7
Group, teams, and decision making

Xanthy Kallis

Chapter objectives

As a result of reading this chapter and using the additional web-based material you should be able to:

- Understand the importance of groups in general and teams in organizations in particular.
- Define the term 'group' and how 'team' is a distinct class of group.
- Describe the meaning of the terms 'formal' and 'informal' groups.
- Appreciate the social aspect of group existence especially to individuals' self-identities.
- Understand the influence group membership has on individuals' performance, especially in making them conform.
- Discuss group development using Tuckman's stage model.
- Critically evaluate the importance of group composition and how it impacts on team effectiveness.
- Critically evaluate group decision making and dangers of 'dysfunctional' behaviour.
- Discuss group conflict and how it can be managed.

Work psychology in practice
Local estate agent

Molly Brown began to work part time for a small local estate agent's after working many years in larger companies within different types of work groups. It was a small office owned by a woman in her mid-fifties, Jennifer Carter, and managed by another woman, Jane Turner, who had been working there for thirteen years. Molly's role as she understood it was to job share with another employee, Ann Johnson, who wanted to work part time and who had been working for the company for eight years, since she left school in fact. On entering the office on her first day Molly noticed all the desks except the manager's were facing the wall with people busy at their telephones or their computers. The manager's desk was in the middle of the office facing the door so she was the only one who had visibility of who came in or went out. The owner had an office cut off from the rest of the workforce. Molly walked in on her first day and noticed that no one looked up or said good morning to her. She walked up to the manager, Jane (who had interviewed her for the job) to report for duty. 'Ah,' she said and got up, 'this is who you will be working with' and walked over to Ann, who had her back to them. Ann gave a quick nod of acknowledgement to her manager and carried on working. Jane left Molly in Ann's hands so that she could 'show her the ropes'. Molly stood by Ann's desk waiting and feeling awkward while Ann continued to busily get on with her work. Molly was not sure what she ought to do, she found it difficult to ask Ann anything, as she was not really given the opportunity to. She was not offered a chair, but neither was there room for two people to sit and work at the same time, as the idea was to job share. Jane came over to Molly with a book of rules, regulations, and procedures that she was told to read through as this would inform her all about the company's policies and procedures. Molly sat quietly reading for most of the morning and hardly said a word to anyone. The office was quiet; hardly anyone spoke except the odd word here or there. There were three other people in the office all busy making calls.

In the afternoon, after Ann had left for the day, Molly picked up some calls, one of which was a message for Jane, so she went over to give it to her. She was stopped in mid-sentence and told to 'write it in the book' and was shown a message book. She was informed all messages were written in the book addressed to the person who it was relevant to, with the date and time the message was received. It would be read by the relevant person. Apparently everyone had to read the message book once in the morning and once in the afternoon, as this ensured messages were not missed or forgotten. No one actually told Molly she ought to read this book—she learnt it through trial and error.

Questions

- How much teamwork is going on in this office?
- How motivating is this environment?
- What effects does management style have on this group?

7.1 Introduction

This chapter begins by defining a group, which is an interesting concept because although a very familiar word, 'group' is very difficult to define. The definition of group this chapter uses is that of Schein's (1980) psychological approach to a group. Following this it looks at the different groups people are members of and critically looks at the function of formal and informal groups in organizations and in particular the psychological impact of membership on its members. The chapter uses classical studies of group conformity in order to show the influence groups have on individuals within them.

The chapter then moves on to give a possible way groups might develop into effective teams and uses Tuckman's stage model to do this, which suggests that people pass through a series of stages to become a cohesive group, which then develops its own unique characteristics. The chapter discusses the benefits of teamwork and the importance of information sharing that leads to better decision making within teams and the importance of diversity in the workforce especially with the changing composition of working life.

Whether a group forms into an effective team will in part depend on the groups' dynamics, and in the fast changing workplace of modern times it is essential that effective teams form quickly. One approach that is used to illustrate how this might be possible is Belbin's team roles, which proposes that for a team to be effective it needs to consist of nine roles. These approaches are by no means the only approaches to the study of group development and group dynamics, as there are many different models and perspectives on group processes.

Group **cohesion** is an important characteristic of effective teams and one that is considered in depth together with group decision making and dysfunctional behaviour that can arise within highly cohesive teams. It is by no means suggesting that highly cohesive teams will inevitably fall foul to dysfunctional behaviour such as group polarization and groupthink, simply that as far as the research is concerned these types of teams are seen to be prone to it. We also discuss social loafing and social facilitation in an effort to give a better understanding of group processes.

The literature sings the praise of teamwork and talks as if it is prevalent around the world. However, a recent survey that looks at European differences in group participation in decision making shows that this is the exception rather than the norm! This section moves onto cultural differences that impact on group work and colour people's views of their place within groups and ends by looking at group conflict and how it can be managed. Finally, leadership in groups is briefly touched, as there is a whole chapter on leadership, but is considered here because of the importance of leadership in groups and the need for leadership awareness and the need for change if the situation called for it.

7.2 Defining a group

Group, is a very familiar word but a difficult concept to define. It is a word that is used so often but there is no universally accepted meaning of what a group is (Rollinson 2002). In an effort to define a group, Cartwright and Zander (1968) cited many different definitions of group, each of which describe a group depending on its most important characteristics.

Social psychologists have been studying groups for many years. In everyday life any collection of people can be termed a group. However, for the purposes of this chapter a group will not simply be any collection of people that happen to be in the same place at the same time, for example students waiting to enter an exam room or hanging around for their exam results. Their goals may be the same, they may also share the same frustration or anxieties, but to qualify as a group they need to meet certain criteria. Hence, in the example of the students waiting to enter an exam room, these individuals need to perceive themselves as a group, and experience a sense of belongingness and a common sense of identity. They also have to have regular face-to-face interactions with each other and work towards the same aims. In the words of Schein (1980) who takes a psychological approach to a group, it is:

> any number of people who interact with each other and perceive themselves to be a group.

7.2.1 Types of groups

Formal groups

How does this definition of groups help us and how does it differ from teams? Groups tend to fall into two main categories, formal and informal. **Formal** groups are those that are purposely put together within organizations and serve a specific function. Organizations divide their overall goals into smaller tasks and create sub-structures, which can be large departments within an organization that are further divided into smaller groups in order to achieve these tasks. Groups within an organization can be command groups or task groups (Rollinson 2002). **Command groups** are the permanent formal groups that arise as a result of relatively fixed structures within an organization and are usually under a single manager. Likert (1961) argues that organizations are an elaborate set of overlapping groups and that at each level of the hierarchy as well as being a manager, a manager would also inevitably be a subordinate too as he or she would have a superior above them (Rollinson 2002).

Task groups are temporarily put together to tackle specific problems but are then dismantled once their task is completed. Tasks groups can be various types of teams too, which Cohen and Bailey (1997) identify as coming under four broad areas within organizations and term them 'work teams', 'parallel teams', 'project teams', and 'management teams'. The term **team** is much used in organizational literature and the virtues of teamworking praised throughout the literature (Johnson and Johnson 1987; Katzenbach and Smith 1993; Sundstrum et al. 1990). The differences between a team and a group is that a team is specifically put together, one might think of it in terms of the formal group but where a group can be just a crowd of people with no particular shared goals or aims, a team will always be put together for an aim. For example, students at university are put together in teams in order to work on a particular project and their life as a team will last as long as the project lasts, perhaps two months, and then they are dismantled.

According to Adair (1986) it is best to think of the concept of team as a distinct class of group which is highly task orientated, which can be either permanent or temporary. Within an organizational context the term 'team' is used to refer to a collection of people purposely organized around an interdependent set of tasks and who share particular outcomes (Guzzo and Dickson 1996). In this sense a definition that fits the team is one from Baron and Greenberg (1990), who define it as:

> a group whose members have complementary skills, and are committed to a common purpose for which they hold themselves mutually accountable.

Informal groups

Informal groups emerge from these formal groups especially if the formal group does not meet the needs of its members. Formal and **informal groups** are never totally separate; the composition, structure, and operation of informal groups will in part be determined by the formal arrangement (Rollinson 2002). Organizations are seen as social entities which serve a dual purpose. As well as people earning a living within them, they also serve a social role for individuals. A role that some argue (Likert 1961) is an important source of social need satisfaction and one that management has a duty to ensure it creates the right environment to allow people to develop supportive relationships (Furnham 2001).

These relationships have a significant effect on the way people work together and hence have an impact on both the quality and quantity of that work. There are powerful psychological benefits deriving from group membership and these informal groups have a stronger influence on their members, more so than the formal ones. It is well documented that group membership either inhibits or enhances individual performance (a topic we discuss later on in this chapter). Hence by understanding how group membership do this, organizations can create the right environment to enhance rather than inhibit performance at work.

 Activity Groups

In pairs summarize the following:

- What two categories do all groups fall into?
- What type of group is a team?
- How many different groups can individuals belong to?
- What does informal group membership offer individuals?

7.2.2 Influence of group membership on individuals

A step back to classic conformity studies

Before moving on to discuss group development it is well worth looking at some of the early research into the influences of group membership and the effects they can have on individuals within them. Psychologists researching group processes have gone to great lengths and have developed quite complex experiments in order to capture human nature in groups. Humans, being very complex creatures, are not easy to predict and some of these studies show how individuals can succumb to group pressure to conform even when they are relative strangers.

In a very early study Sherif's (1936) '**autokinetic effect**', an optical illusion, demonstrates how people coordinate their behaviour in social situations. In this study people were asked to make a decision first on their own about where they could see a moving light and they made their decisions fairly quickly. However, when making decisions with others, individuals were more hesitant and ended up coordinating their decisions with others. This piece of research gave some insight into how norms might start to develop and be accepted by members within a group.

Asch's (1951) study was another classic experiment aimed at finding out what conditions make people either resist or yield to group pressures. His research study was unambiguous and straightforward. The participants were given a card with three different lengths of lines drawn on them that they had to match with one line on another card. In the experiment there was only 'one' real participant and all others were in on the experiment and were told to agree unanimously to a wrong response each time. Most 'real' participants did go along with the majority response even knowing the reply was wrong. In later interviews with some of these participants it was found that, of those who yielded, some had unconsciously distorted their own perceptions to believe they too were seeing the same thing; while others who resisted experienced tension, doubt, and conflict under the pressure of the situation. Again this demonstrates how people can be affected by the pressure of a group, which may in the long term lead to illhealth (see Chapter 14 on Psychological Health in the Workplace).

Asch's studies were replicated in the 1970s (Larsen 1974) and, interestingly, the results demonstrated significantly lower rates of conformity in American students than those found by Asch in the 1950s. Larsen attributes this difference in the outcomes to the changing social attitudes in the 1970s, which encouraged independent thought. We need to remember that all knowledge, including scientific knowledge, is embedded in a particular culture and history (Brown 1990). Social values of the time will no doubt have an effect on how people respond within certain situations. Even in Milgram's famous studies of the 1960s, 'obedience to authority', most people did obey. However, in a variation of his studies, where Milgram allowed people to mix during the break, he found that where there was support even by one other person, people did resist obedience to authority.

Pause for thought
Think of a group you are a member of, that you want to belong to, and consider how many times you actually yield to the pressure of your group's members and requests.

KEY LEARNING POINTS

- There is no universally accepted definition of a group and a team is a distinct class of group.
- People are members of both formal and informal groups. The latter is usually voluntary, the former purposely put together, hence a team.
- Groups serve a formal function but more importantly they serve a less formal psychological function.
- There are many studies on conformity within groups. Some go back and are classical studies of conformity.

7.3 Stages of group development

The chapter so far has looked at types of groups and how individuals might conform to group norms. But how do a collection of individuals develop into a cohesive group in the first place? Why is it that some groups evolve and change continuously while others collapse? If organizations are able to understand the underlying processes of group dynamics then more effective teams can be develop. There are several different stage models of group formation, but the best known and one we are going to use here is Tuckman (1965). According to Tuckman (1965), before a group can function effectively, it passes through a number of stages, **forming**, **storming**, **norming**, **performing**, and later **adjourning** (Tuckman and Jensen 1977) which was added later to reflect the fact that many teams in today's workplace temporarily form for specific tasks and then dismantle (see Figure 7.1).

Figure 7.1. Stage model of group development

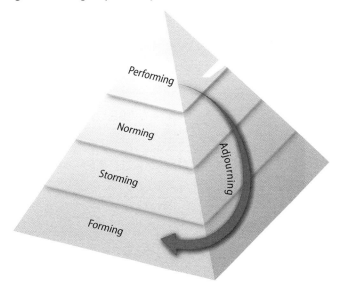

Tuckman's model has been popular partly because it offers a set of guidelines which suggests reasons why some groups or teams fail to gel while others become successful. Regardless of this, there are a number of limitations of Tuckman's theory which raise a series of questions about the stages. For example, he suggests that it is important to have sufficient time for each stage to develop but does not give any indication of how long each stage needs to be and at what point a particular stage is accomplished. There is also the importance of all members of a group being present at the initial meeting of a collection of people, because bonding could actually take place very quickly and anyone arriving late may have problems integrating, being accepted, or even resented (see the closing case study on the project team, below).

Furthermore, the model also implies a linear process where one stage has to complete before the next stage commences but in some groups the stages may occur simultaneously or not at all. It seems some groups bond very quickly and do not necessary go through all the stages. It may be that these stages are also cultural concepts. Considering Japanese quality circles we could ask whether they go through such stages. It would seem that national culture too has an impact on the way individuals see their roles within groups.

There is strong empirical evidence that teams who perceive themselves as well developed and cohesive are far more effective in terms of task performance (Neck et al. 1999). Group dynamics are the psychological processes going on in groups which determine a group's effectiveness, but are not the only factors to consider when determining the effectiveness of a group and work output. Other factors are seen to influence effectiveness such as the group's ability, training of employees, or their personal motivation (Cordery 2002 cited in Warr 2002), which all play a role in determining productivity of a group along with group dynamics. Put simply, group dynamics plus all these factors determine the productivity of a group.

7.3.1 Group characteristics

Once a group successfully completes its developmental process and reaches maturity, it will have developed certain characteristics that are unique to that group, the group's own unique personality. Characteristics which distinguish one group from another are factors such as their own set of norms, role and communication structures, and the cohesiveness of the group.

Norms

Norms are the unspoken and unwritten standards or rules of expected behaviour that apply to a team's members (Feldman 1984). **Norms** prescribe the type of behaviour that is acceptable to the group and also dictates the behaviours that are not acceptable. They are the group's code of conduct which evolves through the group's existence and regulates its members. Norms make behaviour consistent, stable, and predictable to its members. They are the shared beliefs and values of a group that lead to shared attitudes. Interestingly Xie and Johns (2000) found that where norms are strong; absenteeism is higher for the high cohesive group.

Roles

The **roles** within a group are the sets of expected patterns of behaviours for particular positions that each member holds. In organizational settings these are prescribed by a job description and make life predictable and hence easier. There are three aspects of a role that are noted (McKenna 2002); the first already mentioned above deals with expected behaviour and also forms part of the **psychological contract** (see also Chapter 16 on The Future of Work). The 'perceived role' includes all the activities the occupant of the role sees as necessary in order to fulfil the expected role and the 'enacted role' emerges from the perceived role. This particular aspect of the role refers to the way the person actually behaves in the role, all of which make life predictable.

Size

There is also something about the group size which is important in the formation of a group and is highly relevant to how it operates and ultimately performs. Some literature mentions the optimal size of a group is anything from 6 to 12 people (Hall 1976); any more and can make communication and also face-to-face interaction difficult.

The characteristics of the group make life predictable for its members and it is these group norms and expected behaviours that members conform to. The section on classic conformity studies demonstrates how individuals can be pressurized to conform when in a gathering of strangers. These examples just demonstrate the power group membership has on its individual members and the pressure to conform to the group's norms if one wants to remain a member.

....

 Activity Group formation

Consider a group you are a part of. Were you formally put together to work on a project? Were all individuals present at the forming stage of the group?

What happened to any late members, what were other members' feelings towards them or if you were a late member, how did you feel?

What were your experiences in these forming stages of the group? How do they fit in with the stage model?

Were there people within the group who knew each other? How did that affect the group bonding?

....

7.3.2 Communication structure

Another important characteristic that determines a group's success is how it communicates with its members and how reliable that communication system is. Research into the types of structures that groups use found five different patterns of communication (Bavelas 1950, cited in Rollinson 2002) which were investigated further by Leavitt (1951), who found advantages and disadvantages in each structure (see Figure 7.2).

The Y structure has a vocal point in the middle, through which messages pass to a main person who tends to be the leader of the group and ensures all members receive these messages. The wheel structure also has a vocal point in the middle and is similar in structure to the Y approach in that there is a single person responsible for receiving all the information and passing it on. Leavitt argues (1951) that these two communication structures are the fastest and give rise to fewer distortions of messages because there is a main person responsible for communicating the incoming information. However, there is a problem of information overload for that one person receiving and passing on all the messages and potentially other issues that could arise from this as a result such as health problems associated from stress or burnout (see Chapter 15 on The Loss of Work).

The Circle and all channel structures of communication involves all members of the group in the communicating system, which is useful for highly complex tasks that require a greater amount of interaction between the members. These types of communication also yield a greater degree of member satisfaction but are less effective if fast decisions are needed.

Figure 7.2. Communication structures

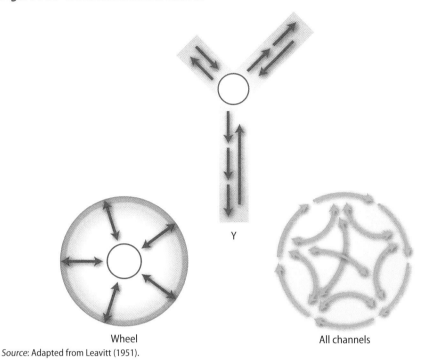

Y

Wheel   All channels

Source: Adapted from Leavitt (1951).

The chain structure of communication is very much like 'Chinese whispers' and is very prone to distorting messages, as the message passes along from one member to another. It is also the slowest form of communication and the one most likely to be seen in traditional hierarchical types of structures in an organization where each level of seniority passes the message to the one below him or her.

 KEY LEARNING POINTS

- A collection of individuals becomes an effective team through a series of stages. Here we use Tuckman's stage model to demonstrate this development.

- According to Tuckman, groups go through a linear series of stages, forming, storming, norming, performing, and adjourning.

- Groups that successfully develop through the stages have a number of characteristics that make them unique. These are their norms, roles, size, and communication structure.

7.4 Why people conform to group membership

Much of the research from the early classic studies on conformity demonstrates how membership of a group makes people conform to a group's norms even when the individuals are fairly unknown to each other. It is true to say that whether formal or informal, group membership has a very strong psychological impact on most people. However, why people conform is an entirely different issue. What is it about membership that makes people want to conform?

7.4.1 Social Identity Theory

In order to understand group processes we need to understand what meaning group membership gives to the individuals within the group or groups. **Social Identity Theory** (Tajfel and Turner 1979) is about the value individuals place on their social identity within groups, which becomes the basis of their self-definitions (Wetherell 1997) and one that gives way to their personal identity. Psychologically what happens is that people begin to categorize themselves in terms of their group—for example 'I am a student', 'I am a Catholic or Muslim', 'I am a woman', and so on. A person's self-esteem is very much tied into their group membership.

Group members will display in-group favouritism even when individuals are put together 'as a group' for the most trivial of criteria. For example, splitting people into two groups, 'the red group and the blue group', immediately sets off a need for members within each group to be different and better than the other team. Thus categorizing oneself as a member of a group gives the person's behaviour distinct meaning and creates a positive valued social identity. This group identity then becomes an aspect of the member's sense of who they are (Tajfel and Turner 1979)—it enhances their self-esteem. However, this does not imply that the theory does not acknowledge the impact of individual differences, but that in some circumstances and contexts our social identity is more salient than our personal identity (Bellanca 2006).

7.4.2 Social Exchange Theory

Another way of looking at ways to make sense of why people conform to group norms and why individuals set aside their own preferences in order to do what the group prefers is by using the framework of the **Social Exchange Theory** (Homans 1961). The basic assumption of this approach is that all human relationships are based on a subjective cost-benefit analysis which determines whether a group is worth belonging to or not. For example, if an individual perceives the costs of being involved in the group outweighs the benefits then he or she will leave the group. However, if the benefits outweigh the costs then it is worth continuing the involvement with the group and abiding by the group's norms, an issue that is discussed further down in more detail.

Hence, this theory views relationships as a series of social performances and exchanges and acknowledges that the basic motivation to enter into any relationship (whether dyad or a group) is the expectation of obtaining something from that relationship, some kind of reward. In looking at highly cohesive teams within this framework, we can better understand how members of such groups may enjoy membership of such groups. Thus one reason why a group is able to exert influence over the behaviour of individuals within the group context is the implication that the benefits are worth it and they will be withdrawn if individuals do not comply. Hence the group has attraction for its members and because they want to remain a part of it, they conform.

7.4.3 Cohesiveness

As mentioned above members conform to group norms because there is something about being a group member that outweighs the costs. And highly cohesive groups are also very successful ones and ones that individuals want to remain members of. Cohesion is another important characteristic found in groups and one that is immediately evident if one observes a group. It is also a characteristic that has been extensively researched because of its strong influence on group performance. We can define cohesiveness as:

> The attractiveness of a group to its members, together with their motivation to remain as part of the group and resist leaving it. (Piper et al. 1983)

In general there are three sets of factors that influence cohesiveness. Those we associate with the group level, those associated with the group's environment, and those associated with the organization within which the group operates.

At the group level, members are seen to have similarities, the group has past successes, it frequently interacts with its members, and the size of the group is small enough to allow face-to-face interaction. At the environmental level there are factors such as how isolated the group is, the external threats to the group, favourable self-evaluation of the group, and rewards the group receives. Finally, at the organizational level there are factors such as physical conditions, technology, job design, all of which influence how cohesive a group would be (Cordery 2002).

Factors such as job design have a huge impact on the motivational state of people within groups. There are certain features of job design that are known to have a positive impact on team effectiveness. The most widely cited classification system is proposed by Hackman and Oldham (1980), who identify five motivating task characteristics of job design that are autonomy, variety of the task, the significance of the task, identification, and feedback. If a job design has all these features then an individual's job satisfaction and motivation is high.

Autonomy, a feature within the job design is one that the literature refers to a great deal in regards to team effectiveness. People like to be trusted and respected (McGregor's Theory Y, 1960). Hence allowing them to make their own decisions or be a part of the decision-making process gives them a sense of trust and respect which itself increases self-esteem, has motivating factors, and gives job satisfaction. It is worth pointing out that as the team becomes more cohesive and gains experience and as it deals with different problems over time (McGrath 1991; Weldon 2000) its group processes (norms, routines, etc.) change too (Gersick 1988). This also means that its leadership style (see also Chapter 8 on Leadership at Work) should adapt to such changes (Cordery 2002) if it is to continue to be effective and not fall foul of dysfunctional behaviour.

Generally speaking cohesiveness is associated positively with performance and member satisfaction. For example, Xie and Johns (2000) found that cohesiveness has the potential to interact and impact with other aspects of team functioning (Cordery 2002). There is evidence to support this as there are lower degrees of problem behaviour such as absenteeism and quitting (Hodgetts 1991) within cohesive groups than groups that do not have it. Such groups offer a degree of predictability to its members which increases their willingness to conform to the group's norms. They also meet objectives better (Keller 1986) and have a high degree of job satisfaction which shows in the energy they devote to accomplishing their goals rather than squabbles.

Pause for thought
Consider a group you are a member of with the above information about cohesiveness. Consider the factors that influence your group's cohesiveness.

 KEY LEARNING POINTS

- Social Identity Theory discusses reasons why personal identity gives way to social identity.
- Group identity is the way people categorize themselves and identify with their groups, this in turn enhances self-esteem.
- Social exchange theory is another framework for understanding why individuals conform to group norms.
- Cohesion has a strong influence on group performance, influenced at the group level, the group's environment, and the organization within which it operates.

7.5 Functional behaviour

7.5.1 Benefits of group life

There are many benefits to the organization for bringing people together to work in teams. According to Schein (1980) there are many formal functions for doing this. For example, teams can more easily accomplish complex tasks. They can act as mechanisms which integrate different parts of an organization. In addition they implement decisions so that common objectives can be set for a number of people. The literature from early studies by Lewin et al. (1939) demonstrates how beneficial group participation in decision making can be especially when change is needed or **resistance to change** avoided.

Information exchange

Organizations create teams in order to improve productivity and efficiency. One way of doing this is to pool together people with a range of knowledge, skills, and experiences so that teams have wider access to a rich source of information. In harnessing this managers can develop teams that are effective and that work well together and share this information and experience. On the basis of this, groups of people sharing their knowledge means there is more information accessible to the team as a whole on which to make better decisions (Vathanophas and Liang 2007). Teams can achieve goals more efficiently than one person alone because people pool together specialists' skills, knowledge, and experience in order to achieve more complex tasks.

Diversity in the workforce

Over the last decade and into the twenty-first century, we have seen a change in the composition of the workforce which also mirrors the changes in our society (Church 1995). Diversity issues have become a major component of work-life experience (Ginzberg 1992) which needs

Figure 7.3. Key team roles

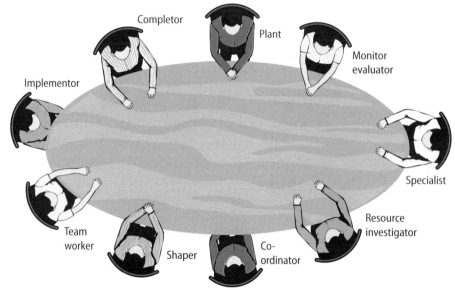

Completor
Plant
Monitor
evaluator
Implementor
Specialist
Team
worker
Shaper
Co-
ordinator
Resource
investigator

Source: Adapted from Belbin (1981).

to be managed. Diversity is defined in terms of a group of individuals who differ on one or any of a number of dimensions which includes culture, education, values, gender, marital status, and so forth (Church 2005). Seen in this way it is clear that diversity is an important issue in the workplace that needs to be acknowledged, understood, and addressed. When there are differences between people this can create conflict and managers have to manage this diversity in order to pool together this rich source of knowledge and experiences from their workforce and aid the exchange of information.

Composition of groups

The composition of a group or the group dynamics—the make-up of the group—are vital to a group's effectiveness. The interest in the composition of the group brings about several theories and questionnaires in an effort to make up groups that have the right characteristics, skills, and experiences. The best known is Belbin's (1981, 1993) **Team Role Types**, where he identifies nine key roles (see Figure 7.3) that he deems necessary for a team to consist of if it is to have the right composition that makes a team effective. There is some strong empirical support for Belbin's suggestion that a well-balanced team with different roles is more effective (Senior 1997). However, there is also some debate as to whether the number of roles he suggests are necessary with some arguing (Fisher et al. 1998) that perhaps it may not be as many as Belbin suggests. There is ongoing debate about this, but it remains true that Belbin's roles are of interest to some.

Pause for thought
List the benefits of groups and describe, with illustrations, how these apply to groups to which you belong.

7.5.2 Decision making in groups

Early research into the advantages of group participation in decision making demonstrates well the benefits of this to organizations, which we briefly touched on earlier. Group decision making is more accurate and workable than an individual making the decisions alone. The research suggests that employees who participate in the decision-making process have greater satisfaction, are more committed to and take ownership of the decisions they make, and hence are more likely to ensure that those decisions are implemented.

However, the downside of group decision making is that it can take longer to make a decision as more voices and ideas need to be heard and whether this is always practical is really down to how much time a team or group has at their disposal to make its decisions (see Vroom's decision-making tree in Chapter 8 on Leadership at Work). In their decision making theory Vroom and Yetton (1973) suggest that a manager or supervisor needs to answer two criteria before deciding whether to involve a team or make the decision alone. Limitations such as time can be an issue if an urgent or an immediate response has to be made (Rollinson 2002).

- Information exchange within the work group allows potential for innovation and creation of new ideas.
- Diversity issues in the workplace need to be harnessed.
- The composition of the group is vital and using Belbin's Team Role Types is one way of getting the right mix.
- There are advantages of group participation in the decision-making process.

7.6 Dysfunctional behaviour

Groups that are perceived as effective are also associated with high cohesiveness and effective decision-making processes. However, it is also known that highly cohesive groups are particularly prone to making 'impaired' decisions too, of which two are discussed here. These are group polarization (risky shift) (Stoner 1961) which is well documented in a series of studies (Clark 1971; Stoner 1968) and the other is groupthink (Janis 1972).

7.6.1 Group polarization

Group **polarization** (risky shift) (Stoner 1961) is the behaviour groups use to make riskier decisions for a number of reasons. For example diffusion of responsibility, which simply means that no one person takes full responsibility for making the decision as it is a group decision hence it is more acceptable to take risks. Another is that the group values risk as one of its 'norms', which may be seen as macho or advantageous to do so by members of the group. There is also the danger that the more a group discusses a problem the more familiar it becomes and hence the less risky it seems. Moreover, in such groups it may be that the leader can exert more influence over other members towards a riskier decision and hence a decision is made because of prominence of leadership effects. A good example of this is the Blair government and the weapons of mass destruction that never were. Tony Blair, as leader, managed to convince his party that there was a legitimate reason for going to war.

Although there is a lot of debate about circumstances within which these decisions occur, there is much consensus that it is more likely to occur within a highly 'cohesive group' because the group can exert strong pressure on its members to go along with the decisions it promotes and abandons any caution they may have and agree with the riskier decision put forward.

7.6.2 Groupthink

Groupthink is another type of dysfunctional behaviour again seen in highly cohesive teams which are said to be prone to such behaviour. **Groupthink** (Janis 1972) describes impaired decision making at very high levels of management and describes a desire for unanimity which overrides examining alternatives and consequences of a decision that have been made. It is a process that can stand in the way of effective group decision making and seems to be associated particularly with highly cohesive groups that have a record of success. Janis's interest in decision making in higher positions of the hierarchy of an organization came about as a result of a number of very bad decisions such senior people make which have had disastrous outcomes, such as the famous '*Challenger* disaster'.

In cases where a team suffers from groupthink, there are certain symptoms that can be observed that give them away(see Figure 7.4).

These symptoms have several potential consequences. The group curtails discussions in order to go with the dominant decision made. It limits its search for information which can inform the decision they make. It fails to import expert opinion, for example, in the case of the *Challenger* disaster; engineers knew that it was dangerous for the rocket to take off because of certain elements that were not right. However, this expert advice was kept from reaching the right ears, a symptom Janis termed 'mindguarding' so that the take-off would go as planned. Such highly cohesive groups fail to audit any decisions they make or their potential outcomes.

The interesting point about groupthink is that it does not appear to be a universal dysfunction of teams. This behaviour is not found in Chinese teams and seems be dysfunctional behaviour found amongst USA and UK teams, which suggests that national cultures have an impact on

Figure 7.4. Some symptoms of groupthink

- Illusion of Invulnerability
- Assumption of Morality
- Realisation
- Stereotyping
- Self Censorship
- Illusion of unanimity

how individuals view their membership within groups (culture is discussed further down). The UK and USA have very individualist type cultures in comparison to the Chinese collectivist one.

7.6.3 Social processes that affect performance

What happens to people within group situations has been the subject matter for many social psychologists for many years. The first controlled experiment dates back to 1897 (Triplett) where cyclists were studied either against the clock or in the presence of other people and it was discovered that the presence of others enhances performance. This prompted a series of experiments which identified a number of processes that are directly relevant to people's performance when working in groups, two of which we discuss here. These are social facilitation and social loafing.

Social facilitation

Social facilitation refers to the influence of the presence of others when doing a task or activity that has positive effects on performance. Studies such as Triplett's (1897) and following studies thereafter investigating these effects support these findings, which suggests that the presence of others is motivational and does indeed enhance performance. However, other researchers within the same field of study found quite opposite results, that in fact the presence of others can inhibit behaviour. It appeared that something more was going on.

Does the presence of others enhance or inhibit performance? This it transpires is something that can potentially happen depending on the situation. According to Zajonc (1965) social facilitation is caused by heightened arousal, which leads people to perform their dominant response more quickly and accurately. Zajonc argues that this depends on what people are doing while they are being watched. If they are watched while they are doing something they are good at then it enhances their performance. However, if they are watched while they are doing something they are not particularly good at or confident doing then it inhibits their performance. This may also shed some light on how well some people do in many situations such as examinations or going for a driving test. If someone does not feel confident then they are likely to do much worse than if they are not watched at all.

Social loafing

The other social process that affects performance is **social loafing** (Latane et al. 1979), which indicates how people exert less effort in a group setting because they can get away with it. According to Ringlemann (fifty years ago) people work less efficiently when working on **additive tasks** (tasks which involve many people, such as the tug of war). The larger the group the less effort individual's within it will put into the task because responsibility for its outcome is diffused, so that each member feels less responsible for pulling his/her weight (Furnham 2001). The motivational processes (see Chapter 5 on Motivation and Work Satisfaction) going on here are that individuals use less effort in performing tasks if their contribution is hard to measure or detect.

Furthermore, Erez and Somech (1996) found that social loafing only occurs when the respondents are given a 'do your best' type of approach. In other words when the goal is not very challenging or specific, what does 'do your best' look like? So people's efforts are not motivated enough to increase effort.

However, it has been suggested that there are ways to overcome social loafing, such as to make workers identifiable and to get them more involved in the task (by participation) and by rewarding individuals for contribution to the group (Baron and Greenberg 1990). Although it seems that such incentives are more likely to encourage individuals to work for themselves rather than the greater good of the team which so much of the literature seems to extol.

Interestingly, it would seem that social loafing is culture specific as it is not found in Chinese workgroups.

7.6.4 Conflict and conflict management

Conflict defines the behaviour of an individual or group that purposely blocks another individual or group from achieving some goal. Schmidt and Kochan (1972) argue that much of what is described as competitive behaviour is actually conflict as defined above. Taking the example of sports such as football, cricket, and squash, one party purposely sets out to block another from achieving their goals, which can be seen as conflict. However, in cases such as gymnastics, mountaineering, or even students working on project work in groups, each person or group attempts to do their best in order to achieve their goal rather than block one another from doing so. In this sense, they are competing rather than in conflict with each other (Schmidt and Kochan 1972).

Rollinson (2002) argues that there is a fine line between competition and conflict and the boundaries are sometimes blurred. There are many perspectives of conflict, such as the unitarist approach which sees conflict as negative and something that should be avoided. The pluralist approach, like the unitarist, recognizes that cooperation and harmony can exist, but it does not view this as the natural state of affairs, rather it sees conflict as natural and something that needs to be handled. However, the interactionist approach (McKenna 1994) to conflict sees it as inevitable and that it is neither good nor bad. It also acknowledges that too much conflict will hold back progress because people may spend too much of their energy on it rather than pursuing more constructive activities. But also where there is not enough conflict, ideas will not be challenged, reducing the impetus for change.

Within an organization a group rarely exists alone or in isolation but is dependent on other groups and people in order to achieve their task or objectives. Sometimes they compete for resources which may lead to conflict, where they depend on the same resources, which is where a blurring of the boundaries between conflict and competition may occur.

At the group's boundary level it is how the group differentiates itself from and how it integrates with other groups. The interactions of group members both within and between groups are seen as strong predictors of group effectiveness. These interaction predict team performance and membership satisfaction (Guzzo and Dickson 1996). Sometimes this brings up the issue of in-group out-group conflict.

7.6.5 How prevalent is teamworking?

The virtue of working in teams is one that is widely extolled in the literature and implies that enthusiasm towards working in teams is something that is seen across the world. The Japanese work groups in particular demonstrate quite well how productive and efficient people working in teams can be, so the idea that it is a concept accepted worldwide seems an obvious one. However, a more recent study (Benders et al. 2001) found that teamwork seems to be the exception rather than the norm in many countries across Europe.

The study investigates senior managers in ten countries across Europe, involving 6,000 workplaces. Managers were asked to indicate the extent to which teamworking is evident in their workplaces (Benders et al. 2001) according to two criteria. Benders et al. (2001) quote eight decision areas: work allocation, scheduling work, quality of the work, time keeping, attendance and absence control, job rotation, coordination, and improving work processes.

The first criterion measures the extent to which teams have responsibility for making decisions on at least four of the above areas. The second criterion is that at least 70 per cent of employees should be involved in these decision-making teams. However, only 4 per cent of the 6,000 workplaces met both criteria. Perhaps not surprisingly Sweden, with its tradition of participative democracy and socio-technical work design, is at the top of the table. There seems to be low teamworking in Southern Europe, in countries such as Spain and Portugal, which is consistent with evidence of their cultures, which tend to emphasize status and hierarchy quite highly (see Figure 7.5).

Pause for thought
Social loafing is experienced by some members of a group; however it can be overcome by ensuring members within are identified

Figure 7.5. Participation of teams in the decision making across 10 European countries

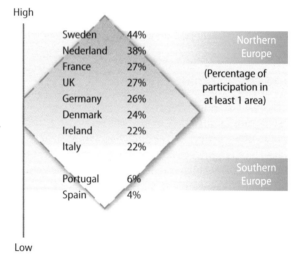

High

Sweden	44%
Nederland	38%
France	27%
UK	27%
Germany	26%
Denmark	24%
Ireland	22%
Italy	22%
Portugal	6%
Spain	4%

Northern Europe

(Percentage of participation in at least 1 area)

Southern Europe

Low

Source: Adapted from Benders et al. (2001)

7.6.6 Culture and groups

Culture, and more to the point national culture, seems to be linked to corporate culture. According to Hofstede (1980) culture is the mental programming which predisposes individuals to particular ways of thinking, perceiving, and believing. In a study that extended over thirteen years, Hofstede developed four dimensions of culture. He considers power distance and uncertainty avoidance as the decisive dimensions of organizational culture (Hofstede 1991) that link national and corporate cultures. This implies that the preferred way of doing things within organizations is based on national tendencies (Martin 2005). One can argue that this is very plausible when a phenomenon such as groupthink is found in individualistic cultures such as America and United Kingdom but not within Chinese teams that have a collectivist national culture. This example implies something about their national culture which tends to influence individual's experience within the group context.

Hofstede suggests that cultures can be divided in terms of individualism versus collectivism, which refers to the degree to which people define themselves as individuals or group members in their societies (Hofstede 1980). The Chinese culture is very much a collectivist one in comparison to the individualist culture of the USA and the UK. If groupthink is an impaired decision-making behaviour that is not found in Chinese culture, then it can be argued that group work and working towards the greater good of all was embedded in one's national culture. Furthermore, even though much of the research praises teamworking and extolls its benefits, when it comes down to it, the individual within the team is rewarded in individualist type cultures. This because it reduces the effects of social loafing, again a concept that is not found among team members in more collectivist cultures such as Hong Kong.

The Japanese too have a collectivist culture and demonstrate how successful their teams work together and how effective they are. There have been many examples of effective teamwork from them, such as quality circles, which other nations (including the UK) have tried to imitate. Within these nations it is easy to form teams that share responsibility and work for the greater good of all rather than individual expectations because they have the collectivist attitudes from the start. Motivation is linked to cultural differences in self-concept and in particular to the degree to which individual's within groups possess individualistic or collectivist values.

It also questions whether development within these teams would strictly go through Tuckman's (1965) stages and particularly whether there would necessarily be any 'storming' going on as they would all be working together for the good of all and hence particular roles may not be as important to individuals as they would be to any one working in the USA or UK, where much of the research stems from. What is happening in Europe?

A study that focused on psychological well-being at work and specifically looked at the effects of job demands on such issues as stress, anxiety, depression, and absenteeism (Schaubroeck et al. 2000) found that where there are strong collective beliefs and values the impact of job demands and stress are lower than individualist cultures such as America and Britain. Moreover, research shows that motivation is linked to cultural differences to the sel-concept and where individuals possess individualist values they resist teamworking (Kirkman et al. 2000).

7.6.7 Leadership in groups

Leadership in groups is also an important topic. Where there is a group, a leader will inevitable emerge. However, in most formal groups within organizations an authority figure is appointed to a group. This can be a manager or a supervisor who is granted a degree of power over his or her subordinates. Research shows that the leader has a very important impact on a team, a department, etc. (Eden 1990; George and Bettenhausen 1990) and that the better the leader's moods are the fewer employees quit (George and Bettenhausen 1990). Leadership is covered more extensively in Chapter 8.

KEY LEARNING POINTS

- Group polarization is dysfunctional behaviour used by groups to make risky decisions.
- Groupthink is dysfunctional behaviour which describes impaired decision making.
- Social facilitation and social loafing our two processes that effect performance in groups.
- Conflict defines behaviour that aims to block another's goals but some conflict is necessary in organizational settings.

Pause for thought
What was the initial problem with this group that prevented them from developing into a team? How could this situation have been avoided?

Case illustration
The consultant team

Sally, Michael, Peter, Jamie, and Pauline were brought together to work on a group project. Their aim was to be a consultant group who were going to see a client about certain issues in his organization. The group's task was to outline these issues and discuss recommendations which aimed at helping the client solve some of the problems he was having within his organization. The team were to write a report and present their findings and conclusions three months hence.

On the first official day of the group meeting formally, two of its members, Jamie and Pauline, were genuinely unable to attend. The meeting went ahead as scheduled and decisions about future plans were made by the three members who did attend. At this point in time their client was unable to see them for at least two weeks from this first group meeting.

On the second meeting a week later, Jamie and Pauline were informed of the decisions taken by Sally, who had nominated herself as the leader of the group. Sally told them that the three original members—herself, Peter, and Michael—would be the main ones to have contact with the client. However, as the client was unable to see them for at least two weeks their plans were suspended (as the next step of the project depended on the outcomes of the first meeting with the client). Jamie was not happy with the arrangement made in her absence especially as she too wanted the opportunity and experience of visiting the client and made the suggestion that as all the members of the team were now present they should re-discuss the issues and make a more democratic decision that all would be happy with. Sally, the self-appointed leader, brushed this suggestion off, saying the decisions had been made and that there was nothing to discuss. Jamie did not respond but kept quite during the rest of the meeting and did not participate further.

In subsequent meetings the group could be seen to have split into two subgroups, one between Sally, Peter, and Michael and the other between Jamie and Pauline. The group began to slacken in its tasks and not all the members turned up to the meetings thereafter. Jamie did not particularly feel a part of this group and was reluctant to attend as she felt she was not heard anyway and that Sally did exactly as she pleased. The rest of the group would turn up late to meetings, if they attended at all. Some members made excuses why they could not make meetings, while others were hard to find either via email or their mobile phones as they did not respond to either, so no one really knew what was happening. The whole thing felt like a disaster.

Chapter summary

- Defining a group is not easy as there is no universal definition of what a group is. However, rather than term any collection of people as a group, to qualify as a group people need to perceive themselves as a group, interact face to face, and aim for the same goals.

- Groups fall into two main categories, formal and informal. Formal groups are those that are purposely put together by organizations and serve a specific function. Some formal groups were permanent, others temporary task groups.

- Informal groups emerge from formal groups and could be more powerful. They serve a very important psychological function for people at work, which helps in all aspects of organizational life.

- Classical studies into conformity are used to illustrate the power of a group even when the individuals within are strangers. Sherif's Autokinetic effect and Asch's line matching study are used to do this but any research should be considered in the context, culture, and time within which it is done as social values change over time.

- Tuckman's stages theory of group formation was used as a guideline to demonstrate the possible stages groups may go through before they become an effective team, which are forming, storming, norming, and performing. A last stage of adjourning was added as more and more groups are temporarily formed for specific tasks and then dismantled.

- Groups that successfully emerge from their developmental stages evolve unique characteristics, such as norms, roles, communication structures, and cohesiveness.

- The social identity theory and the social exchange theory discuss why individuals conform to group norms and accepted behaviour. The basic assumption of the social exchange theory is that the benefits of being in the relationship outweigh the costs, and hence it is worth it.

- Effective teams are considered in terms of functional behaviour such as information sharing and the benefits of working in teams for the organization. Also the diversity of the workforce is touched on and the importance of team composition and compiling effective teams immediately. Belbin's team roles were used as an example of this.

- Dysfunctional behaviour, such as group polarization and groupthink were discussed and how it is mainly highly cohesive teams that suffer from these.

- Social psychologists working in this area found many group processes that effect performance, of which two were mentioned: social facilitation, which refers to performance being enhanced or inhibited, and social loafing which refers to individuals within a group context exerting less effort than when working alone.

- Teamwork is praised in the literature for all the benefits it offers but it is not happening on a universal level.

- It would seem that workplaces that use teams and teamworking especially for decision making are the exception rather than the norm.

- Conflict and conflict management is discussed and the need to differentiate between conflict and competition.

- Finally, the impact of national culture and group membership is also considered, which looks especially at differences between individualistic and collectivist cultures and their approaches to group membership.

Assess your learning

Review questions

1 What is a group? What criteria does a group of people need to have to qualify as a group?

2 What are the two main categories groups fall into? What is the difference between them?

3 What is the difference between a group and a team?

4 What is a possible theory of why groups are able to make their members conform to their norms and the acceptable behaviour?

5 Name three characteristics that groups have that make them unique?

6 What are the stages of development that groups are said to go through before they become effective teams?

7 What are the nine roles that Belbin suggested are needed within every team in order for it to be effective?

8 What does group cohesiveness mean?

9 Name the two dysfunctional behaviours found in highly cohesive groups.

10 Why might such behaviours develop? List a couple of examples of both.

Assignments

ASSIGNMENT 1: Cohesive teams

Highly cohesive teams are always prone to dysfunctional behaviour such as groupthink. Discuss.

- The question aims at getting you to think about both the advantages and disadvantages of cohesive teams.

Consider dysfunctional behaviour, describe it, and discuss whether cohesive teams are 'always' prone to such behaviour. Give reasons either way.

ASSIGNMENT 2: Types of groups

What are the two types of groups people are usually found in? What are the advantages to an organization of bringing people together to work in groups?

- Describe what a formal group means and what the advantages of such groups are to the organization.

- Discuss the differences between a group and a team.

- Describe what is meant by informal groups and what functions these have for people within organizations.

Further reading

Furnham, A. (2001) *The Psychology of Behaviour at Work: The Individual in the Organisation* (Hove: Psychology Press).
This book is excellent for in-depth information on group dynamics.

Rollinson, D. (2002) *Organisational Behaviour and Analysis: An Integrated Approach*. Englewood Cliffs, NJ: FT Prentice Hall.
This is an excellent book which gives a good coverage of groups and teamworking.

Work psychology in practice
The project team

The Virtual View advertising company had just swept the boards at the industry awards ceremonies and Greg Rice was in several newspapers receiving awards on behalf of his team. The Creative Director Alison Hopkins took them all to dinner to celebrate and made clear that, as project manager, Greg would be in line for a large bonus this year. Greg thanked the team for their professionalism and dedication and hoped that they would continue to win him awards in the future.

When Alison and Greg had left the rest of the team stayed on to finish the evening, except Mara Kendle, who was having trouble with her babysitter. She had just asked Greg if she could work part time again but he had refused as Mara's child was in nursery now and he didn't see the need. He explained that legally she could but he couldn't be sure she would still have a job in the next reshuffle.

Conor Rafferty had asked to go on a cutting-edge training course but what with all the work coming in it would be 'all hands on deck' as Greg put it. Kitt Joseph and Amy Blass were annoyed that they had not been mentioned in any press releases; especially as it had fallen to them to put in the extra hours to meet the deadlines and two of the winning innovation ideas were Kitt's. Still they were in a top agency doing the interesting work that they both loved so why should they mind?

On Monday morning Greg held a meeting to discuss the new projects and announced that Amy was to join a new matrix team while Kitt stayed to oversee the new project. He introduced them to the latest addition to the team: Philip Weaver, the CEO's nephew and a recent graduate with a 2:2 in his BA in Marketing. Philip asked Mara, who was late for the meeting, to get him a coffee and went to sit by Conor, who was busily circling adverts in the industry paper for job vacancies. Kitt was discouraged about losing Amy but decided that, perhaps, if Greg wanted to take all the credit and the rewards, he could pick up the slack this time. Kitt resolved to keep a low profile on the next job. Each time that Greg asked for a volunteer there was a stony silence until Philip offered. As he'd been on many teams at university he felt sure that he could deliver in this one especially as they all seemed so jaded and unenthusiastic.

Questions

- Identify the key problems in Greg's team.
- What could be the potential outcome if he allows them to continue?
- What steps should he take to rebuild the morale and motivation of the team?

 # Online Resource Centre

Visit the supporting online resource centre for additional material which will help you with your research, essays, and assignments, or you may find these additional resources helpful when revising for exams.
http://www.oxfordtextbooks.co.uk/orc/matthewman/

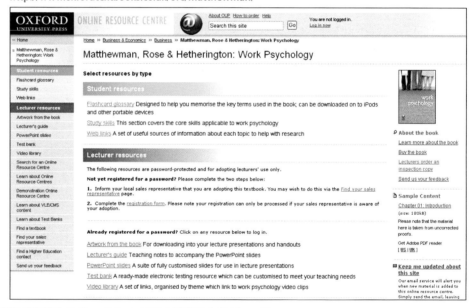

References

Adair, J. (1986) *Effective Team Building*. London: Pan.

Asch, S. E. (1951) Effects of groups pressure upon the modification and distortion of judgements. In H. Guetzkow (ed.), *Groups, Leadership and Men*. Pittsburgh: Carnegie Press.

Baron, R. A., and Greenberg, J. (1990) *Behaviour in Organisations*. London: Allyn and Bacon.

Belbin, R. M. (1981) *Management Teams: Why They Succeed or Fail*. Oxford: Heinemann Professional Publishing

Belbin, R. M. (1993) *Team Roles at Work*. Oxford: Butterworth-Heinemann.

Benders, J., Huijgen, F., and Ulricj, P. (2001) Measuring group work: findings and lessons from a European survey. *New Technology, Work and Employment*, 16/3: 204–17.

Brown, R. H. (1990) Rhetoric, textuality and the postmodern turn in sociological theory. *Sociological Theory*, 8: 188–97.

Cartwright, D., and Zander, A. (1968) *Group Dynamics: Research and Theory* (3rd edn.). Evanston, Ill.: Tavistock.

Church, A. H. (1995) Diversity in workgroup setting: a case study. *Leadership and Organisation Development Journal*, 16/6: 3–9.

Clark, R. D. (1971) Group-induced shifts towards risk: a critical appraisal. *Psychological Bulletin*, 76: 251–70.

Cohen, S. G., and Bailey, D. E. (1997) What makes teams work: group effectiveness research from the shop floor to the executive suite. *Journal of Management*, 23: 239–90.

Cordery, J. (2002) *Team Working*. Department of Organisational and Labour Studies, University of Australia, cited in Warr (2002).

Eden, D. (1990) Pygmalion without interpersonal contrast effects: whole groups gain from raising manager expectations. *Journal of Applied Psychology*, 75: 394–8.

Erez, M., and Somech, A. (1996) Is group productivity loss the rule or the exception? Effects of culture and group-based motivation. *Academy of Management Journal*, 39/6: 1531–7.

Feldman, D. C. (1984) The development and enforcement of group norms. *Academy of Management Review*, 9/1: 47–53.

Fisher, S. G., Hunter, T. A., and Macrosson, W. D. K. (1998) The structure of Belbin's team roles. *Journal of Occupational and Organisational Psychology*, 71/3: 283–8.

Furnham, A. (2001) *The Psychology of Behaviour at Work: The Individual in the Organisation*. Hove: Psychology Press.

George, J. M., and Bettenhausen, K. (1990) Understanding prosocial behaviour, sales performance and turnover: a group-level analysis in a service context. *Journal of Applied Psychology*, 75: 698–70.

Gersick, C. J. G. (1988) Time and transition in work teams: toward a new model of group development. *Academy of Management Journal*, 31: 9–41.

Guzzo, R. A., and Dickson, M. W. (1996) Teams in organisations: recent research on performance and effectiveness. *Annual Review of Psychology*, 47: 307–38.

Hackman, J. R., and Oldham, G. R. (1980) *Work Redesign*. Boston: Addison-Wesley.

Hall. J. F. (1976) *Classical Conditioning and Instrumental Learning*. Philadelphia: Lippincott.

Hodgetts, R. M. (1991) *Organisational Behaviour: Theory and Practice*. London: Macmillan.

Hofstede, G. (1980) *Culture's Consequences: International Differences in Work-related Values*. Beverly Hills, CA: Sage.

Hofstede, G. (1991) *Cultures and Organisations: Softwares of the Mind*. New York: McGraw-Hill.

Homans, G. C. (1961) *Social Behaviour*. New York: Harcourt Brace and World.

Janis, I. L. (1972) *Victims of Groupthink*. Boston: Houghton Mifflin.

Johnson, E. W., and Johnson, F. P. (1987) *Joining Together: Group Theory and Group Skills*. Englewood Cliffs, NJ: Prentice-Hall.

Katzenbach, J. R., and Smith, D. K. (1993) *The Wisdom of Teams: Creating the High Performance Organisation*. Cambridge, MA: Harvard Business School Press.

Keller, R. T. (1986) Predictors of the performance of project groups in research and development organisations. *Academy of Management Review*, 11/4: 715–26.

Kirkman, B. L., Jones, R. G., and Shapiro, D. L. (2000) Why do employees resist teams? Examining the 'resistance barrier' to work team effectiveness. *International Journal of Conflict Management*, 11: 74–92.

Larsen, K. (1974) Conformity in the Asch experiments. *Journal of Social Psychology*, 94: 303–4.

Latane, B., Williams, K., and Harkins, S. (1979) Many hands make light work: the causes and consequences of social loafing. *Journal of Personality and Social Psychology*, 37: 822–32.

Leavitt, H. J. (1951) Some effects of certain patterns on group performance. *Journal of Abnormal and Social Psychology*, 46/1: 38–50.

Lewin, K., Lippit, R., and White, R. K. (1939) Patterns of aggressive behaviour in experimentally created social climates. *Journal of Social Psychology*, 10/2: 271–99.

Likert, R. (1961) *New Patterns in Management*. New York: McGraw-Hill.

McGrath, J. E. (1991) Time, Interaction and Performance (TIP): a theory of groups. *Small Group Research*, 22: 147–74.

McGregor, D. M. (1960) *The Human Side of Enterprise*. New York: McGraw-Hill.

McKenna, E. (1994) *Business Psychology and Organisational Behaviour*. Hove: LEA.

McKenna, E. (2002) *Business Psychology and Organisational Behaviour* (4th edn.). Hove: Psychology Press.

Martin, J. (2005) *Organisational Behaviour and Management* (3rd edn.). London: Thomson Publishers.

Neck, C. P., Connerley, M. L., Zuniga, C. A., and Goel, S. (1999) Family therapy meets self-managing teams: explaining self managing team performance through team member perception. *Journal of Applied Behavioural Science*, 35: 2245–59.

Piper, W. E., Marrache, M., Lacroix, R., Richardson, A. M., and Jones, B. D. (1983) Cohesion as a basic bond in groups. *Human Relations*, 36: 93–108.

Rollinson, D. (2002) *Organisational Behaviour and Analysis* (2nd edn.). Englewood Cliffs, NJ: FT Prentice Hall.

Schaubroeck, J., Lam, S., and Xie, J. L. (2000) Collective efficacy verses self efficacy in coping responses to stressors and control: a cross cultural study. *Journal of Applied Psychology*, 85: 512–25.

Schein, E. H. (1980) *Organisational Psychology* (3rd edn.). Englewood Cliffs, NJ: Prentice-Hall.

Schmidt, S. M., and Kochan, T. (1972) Conflict: towards conceptual clarity. *Administrative Science Quarterly*, 17/3: 359–70.

Senior, B. (1997) Team roles and performance: is there really a link? *Journal of Occupational and Organisational Psychology*, 70/3: 241–58.

Sherif, M. (1936) *The Social Psychology of Group Norms*. San Francisco: Harper and Row.

Stoner, J. A. F. (1961) A comparison of individual and group decisions involving risk. In R Brown (ed.), *Social Psychology*. New York: Free Press.

Stoner, J. A. F. (1968) Risky and cautious shifts in group decisions: the influence of widely-held values. *Journal of Experimental Social Psychology*, 4/2: 442–39.

Sundstrum, E., DeMeuse, K. P., and Futrell, D. (1990) Work teams: applications and effectiveness. *American Psychologist*, 45: 120–33.

Tajfel, H., and Turner, J. (1979) An integrative theory of intergroup conflict. In W. G. Austin and S. Worchel (eds.), *The Social Psychology of Intergroup Relations*. Monterey, CA: Brooks/Cole, 33–47.

Triplett, N. (1897) The dynamogenic factor in pace making and competition. *American Journal of Psychology*, 507–33.

Tuckman, B. W. (1965) Developmental sequences in small groups. *Psychological Bulletin*, 63: 384–99.

Tuckman, B. W., and Jensen, N. (1977) Stages of group development revisited. *Group and Organisation Studies*.

Vathanophas, V., and Liang, S. Y. (2007) Enhancing information sharing in group support systems (GSS). *Computers in Human Behaviour*. 23/3: 1675–91.

Vroom, V. H., and Yetton, P. W. (1973) *Leadership and Decision-Making*. Pittsburgh: University of Pittsburg Press.

Warr, P. (2002) *Psychology at Work* (5th edn.). Harmondsworth: Penguin.

Weldon, E. (2000) The development of product and process improvements in work groups. *Group and Organization Management*, 25/3: 244–68.

Wetherell, M. (1997) *Identities, Groups and Social Issues*. Berverley Hills, CA: Sage Publications.

Xie, J. L., and Johns, G. (2000) Interactive effects of absence culture salience and group cohesiveness: a multi-level and cross-level analysis of work absenteeism in the Chinese context. *Journal of Occupational and Organisational Psychology*, 73: 31–52.

Zajonc, R. B. (1965) Social facilitation. *Science* 149: 269–74.

Chapter 8
Leadership at work

Xanthy Kallis

Chapter objectives

As a result of reading this chapter and using the additional web-based material you should be able to:

- Understand the complexities surrounding an accepted definition of leadership.
- Critically evaluate the different approaches to leadership.
- Identify early theoretical approaches to leadership (i.e. trait, behavioural).
- Understand the impact situational factors have on leadership style.
- Critically examine the importance of 'Follower-ship' to leaders.
- Understand current theories of leadership (i.e. transformational).
- Critically evaluate the differences between leadership and management.
- Discuss whether transformational style of leadership has a gender.

Work psychology in practice
Leading from the front

Frontline Services is a thriving Brighton-based service which offers to arrange, organize, or manage events or day-to-day hassles so that clients have more time to spend as they would choose. They have a range of diverse requests from picking up laundry to wedding planning, researching best prices to private detective work, and they boast that they will take any work as long as it is not illegal.

Maisie and John Blake started up the business in 1982 and it has been family owned ever since. Maisie died in 1998 and John rarely involves himself with the day-to-day running anymore. Their two children Verity (36) and James (32) run a Frontline staff of 34. A recent trade article on them described their contrasting management styles as complementary.

Verity is a qualified accountant and has always had a keen eye for figures and making the most of resources. She cannot abide waste and regularly tours the offices switching off idling computers or unwanted lights. Overtime is unheard of but if things are quiet staff are encouraged to go and leaflet local offices. Verity sets clear deadlines and is known for her inability to 'suffer fools gladly'. All hiring and firing goes through Verity as she believes she has an eye for a good candidate. Turnover is currently running at 28 per cent, almost 12 per cent higher than average. Verity has recently decided to run the training workshops herself as the visiting consultants were too expensive and did not seem to motivate the workforce. Verity believes that if only she can keep the pace up for staff they will enjoy seeing the results of their hard work in renewed and new business.

James took a BSc in Psychology followed by an MA in HRM. He is keen to bring change management practices to Frontline and suggested a reward menu to Verity, who promised she would look at it. When he went to her desk to collect some documents he noticed that his planned outlines were in the bin. Upset by this he asked Verity about it. 'Oh dear, James, you have so much to learn about business,' was her response. James has been conducting a staff satisfaction survey and has found that only 20 per cent of staff are satisfied or extremely satisfied with their job at the moment. He has identified some rather worrying patterns, including the staff tendency to use the 'leafleting' euphemism for taking an afternoon off, since Verity won't sanction time off for dental or medical appointments. James is keen to branch out into more specialized service industries and would like to offer the option of training to current staff first before employing from outside. Verity believes that this would be a waste of funds as it would be cheaper to try to get student beauticians to sign up with Frontline.

James is worried and now Emily, who has been with Frontline since she was a school leaver in 1984, has come to complain that once again she has lost an afternoon's work as someone shut down her computer. Yesterday when she asked Verity about organizing the training rota she was told to leave everyone over 40 off the list. James is upset that Emily is so unhappy but is more anxious about upsetting Verity.

Questions

- Highlight the main dysfunctional areas in the case.
- How well is Verity running the organization?
- What should James do now with his dilemma?

8.1 Introduction

In the case study we see two contrasting approaches to managing an organization or a department. One is very traditional, the other takes on a more contemporary approach to running an organization and how it values people they employ by, for example, developing their staff. What we will discuss in this chapter are some of the influential approaches to leadership that have helped advance our understanding of the topic and how beneficial leadership is in the workplace.

Interest in leadership is not new, it has been around since the times of Alexander the Great, Sun Tzu, Julius Caesar, and Genghis Khan, to name but a few. Most of this earlier interest in leadership and empirical investigation was directed at great generals or statesmen in history.

However, in the fast changing world of work, there has been a great surge of interest in leadership within organizational settings too and the type of style a leader needs in order to take a company forward into success.

We start the chapter by looking at the trait theories that focused attention on particular characteristics people had that could predict their future performance as effective leaders. We then turn our attention to theorists researching leaders' behaviour and the style theories that paved the way for training programmes into leadership skills.

Leadership is a very complex concept and what early approaches ignored was the important role contextual factors play on who will emerge as a leader. The impact of contextual factors is addressed by some of the most influential contingency or situational theories, in particular Fiedler's contingency theory (1967), Path-goal theory, and Vroom's decision-making model.

We move the discussion on to the important role followers play in the leadership process, and question whether it is right to call subordinates 'followers' in organizations at all, as they do not have a 'choice' of who leads them. We follow this by tackling the question of whether managers are leaders and leaders managers. Which brings the discussion onto defining transformational leadership versus transactional and the emerging fact that managers seem to be equated with a transactional approach and leaders with a transformational style of leadership. Furthermore, research indicates that it seems to be a style that is used by women in high positions rather than men and some have questioned whether transformational leadership has a gender (Doyle 2002).

8.2 Definitions of leadership

Definitions into leadership are very complex and there are as many definitions of leadership as there are theorists trying to define it (Rollinson 2002), with little agreement between them! It seems that attempts to define it inevitably give a different perspective on what leadership is. What most theorists agree on is that leadership consists of certain themes that are typically emphasized in all theories (Alimo-Metcalfe and Alban-Metcalfe 2000). These themes are that leadership is a *process*, that it involves the *influencing* of others, takes place within a *group context*, and involves *achieving goals* (Northouse 2001).

In considering the above themes, a definition that is often quoted in the leadership literature sees it as a:

> process whereby one individual influences other group members towards the attainment of defined group or organizational goals. (Barron and Greenberg 1990)

Another slightly different perspective on leadership perceives it as:

> a process of creating a vision for others and having the power to translate this vision into a reality and then to sustain it. (Kotter 1988)

What these definitions actually demonstrate to us is that leadership is a challenging concept to define! Moreover, there also seems to be some confusion in the literature between defining or differentiating between what a leader is and what a manager is (a subject discussed later in the chapter).

However, what these definitions give rise to is a somewhat oversimplified process based on the assumption that the nature of leadership is a one-sided affair, which tends to ignore the interactive relationship between a leader and his or her followers. This assumption sees followers as passively following. Furthermore, leadership is seen as a non-coercive process in which influence is used to direct the activities of a group. It also expresses the notion that followers perceive the person who is leading them to have certain attributes that enable him or her to exert this influence over them (Jago 1982).

Hence, a working definition of leadership that actually projects the importance of a two-way process between followers and leaders is one put forward by Rollinson (2002) as:

> A process in which a leader and followers interact in a way that enables the leader to influence the actions of followers in a non-coercive way towards the achievement of certain aims or objectives.

The difference with this definition is that it perceives the interactive nature of the relationship in the leadership process between leader and follower; it is no better or worse than any other. However, it does give an interactive flavour which is more closely associated with the relationship between leaders and followers, which we will discuss in more detail later in the chapter.

8.3 Early theories of leadership

8.3.1 Trait theory

This section begins by looking at some of the earliest research in this area. According to Rollinson (2002) all theories of leadership adopt one of two distinctive approaches. They either fall into the category of the descriptive approach of leadership or the functional approach of leadership. Furnham (2001) on the other hand suggests that it is possible to categorize the major theories of leadership into three groups, the trait theory, the behavioural theory, and the contingency or situational theory.

Starting then with the first of these categories, this section evaluates the **trait approach**, which is a descriptive approach to leadership and one that focuses on the innate characteristics of great leaders. The trait theories are the oldest systematic studies of leadership which go back to the beginning of the twentieth century. Most of these early investigations mainly involve great military leaders, such as Alexander the Great and Julius Caesar and great statesmen such as George Washington and Abraham Lincoln. These early theories are also known as the 'Great Man approach' because of the unquestioned assumption that successful leaders are born to be great (Statt 1994).

On the basis of this assumption, theorists analysed great people throughout history trying to capture the characteristics they shared which could predict future greatness in people (if they possessed them). Furthermore, and interestingly, their investigations looked at great people at a point in their lives when they were successful and assumes they are always successful no matter what they do. However, there are many examples of great people not so great in a different situation, for example Churchill, who was great in wartime but not so great in times of peace. These investigations were based on people's biographies and similar documents that were one step removed from the subject (Statt 1994).

Trait theorists argue that leadership is something people are born with or characteristics they develop early on in life. As such these traits differentiate them from non-leaders who could not possess them. However, this assumption is far from being correct as there are many cases of non-leaders possessing the same traits, for example local heroes such as William Wallace, a great Scottish hero, and Joan of Arc, a great French heroine. Both these people were made famous as a result of their achievements and determination.

Traits theorists identified dozens of seemingly important traits, so many that it is impossible to find any that are common to all people identified as effective leaders (Byrd 1940). One of the most penetrating reviews of the literature is one undertaken by Stogdill (1948), who argues that most of the research points to five key traits that differentiate leaders from followers and these are:

- Intelligence
- Dominance
- Self-confidence
- High level of energy
- Task-related knowledge.

However, Stogdill (1948) also argues that the qualities, characteristics, and skills that a leader needs are to a large extent determined by the demands of the context within which these take place and emphasizes the importance of the situation in making a leader effective. For example, if we take one of our heroes from above, would William Wallace have been an effective 'leader', if leader we can call him, had it not been for Scottish history at the time and a need to fight for freedom? If he were to return, would he be as successful in today's Scotland? The evidence suggests that traits are, at least on their own, poor predictors of who emerges as a leader.

But what has this to do with leadership in the organization, you ask yourself? The search for which traits will predict great leaders extended to an interest beyond the military and political arena to whether they can also be applied in the workplace to predict who could be an effective head of an organization. Moreover, as already mentioned some traits that we see as being important characteristics of leaders are also found in non-leaders, a finding that is confirmed by Mann (1959). Furthermore, Stodgill suggests that people successful in one situation would not necessarily be successful or effective in another and the reason for this is that whatever else leadership might be it is always about a relationship between people (Statt 1994).

There is however, strong criticism of the trait approach mainly because there is no agreement on which traits are the most important for effective leaders. Even though Stogdill (1948) suggested five particular traits as key, more recent research identifies other relevant characteristics, such as 'need for achievement', 'need for power', and 'goal-directedness' as important characteristics in leaders too (Stogdill 1974; House and Baetz 1979; Bass 1985). Theorists' conclusions about the usefulness of the trait theory remains the same (Statt 1994), that it is a subjective matter and very much in the 'in the eyes of the beholder'. Furthermore some psychologists such as Yetton (1984) remain unconvinced that there is a link between any specific characteristic and leadership.

Nevertheless, in spite of all the important shortcomings of this approach, it is unwise to dismiss traits as unimportant all together, as there does seem to be evidence of a combination of characteristics that leaders must have (Zaleznik 1993). A review of the literature (Kirkpatrick and Locke 1991) reveals that effective leaders are different from others and even Stogdill (1974) revised his stance and cautions against the assumption that leadership is totally situational and devoid of any personal effects (Stogdill 1974).

The current thinking regarding the trait approach is that while there is no universal agreement on which traits are important, some traits are likely to be crucial to leadership, such as intelligence and determination (Northouse 2001). Moreover, a strength of the trait approach is that it focuses on the leader (rather than management) component of leadership (Alimo-Metcalfe and Alban-Metcalfe 2002, cited in Warr 2002).

....

 Activity **Great leaders at work**

Think of your own work experiences and in particular a line manager or boss you most admired.

- How would you characterize them? What traits did they have?
- What made them different from other people you worked with?

....

8.3.2 Behavioural approach

The behavioural approach to leadership came about as a result of dissatisfaction with the trait approach: thus theorists turned their attention to towards the behavioural styles of leaders (Statt 1994). This interest coincided with the rise in popularity of Behavioural Psychology and, hence, they turned their attention from who the person was to what the person did. The behavioural or style approach involves three steps: to observe leader behaviour, to categorize it, and then determine which behaviour will be the most effective for successful leadership. However, like the trait approach before it, the behavioural theories were also in search of a 'one best style' fits all situations. It was like the search for the Holy Grail.

Much of the work in this area is influenced by **human relations theory** and an early piece of research by Lewin and his colleagues (1939) triggered much of the work that followed (Statt 1994). The study involved children at hobby clubs who were divided into three groups, each of which was led by an adult with a different style, **autocratic**, **democratic**, or **laissez-faire**. What this research identified was the effects each behavioural style had on its followers. For example, although both autocratic and democratic approaches produced very similar results in productivity, they differed enormously where follower satisfaction was concerned. Those working under a democratic leader tended to participate in decision making, were given more responsibility, and were more satisfied compared to the autocratic or laissez-faire styles.

We can illustrate the autocratic approach in the person of Alan Sugar, who is very authoritarian and very much in control of everything that goes on in his company, giving little to no responsibility to his workforce, compared to Richard Branson who takes a democratic approach to his employees, giving them responsibilities, empowering them, and involving them in the decision-making process. Looking back at the opening case study, see if you can identify which styles the two managers had. Both the approaches are effective in the sense that both produce similar results, but who would you be happier working for? Needless to say the researchers in Lewin's day were very much in favour of the democratic style. However, we must note that this may also reflect the social values of the day.

The style approach to leadership concerns itself with identifying what successful leaders do in order that people can learn to be successful leaders. The research that is seen as the milestone development of style theories (Rollinson 2002) are two independent studies that took place in the late 1940s to investigate the behaviour that we associate with effective leadership. These are the Ohio State Leadership Studies and the Michigan Leadership Studies.

The Ohio studies

Data from the Ohio study was collected using questionnaires from people actually at work, which resulted in what is known as the two-factory theory of leadership (Fleishman 1953; Fleishman et al. 1953), and is based on two independent dimensions of leader behaviour:

- Initiating structure
- Consideration.

The first behaviour indicates a leader's concern for the task, whereas the other indicates a leader's concern for people and involves interpersonal behaviour. Because the two dimensions are independent it implies that a supervisor will pay attention to one or the other of the two dimensions. Thus, leader effectiveness is assessed on whether the task is complete or members are satisfied. For example, a supervisor who is high on initiating structure will ensure that the task is clear and unambiguous and will be high on productivity, but he or she might also find high levels of grievance and staff turnover because too much attention is given to doing the task and not enough to the people side of work. Conversely, a supervisor who is more concerned with people might be low on productivity but high on staff morale and satisfaction.

The Michigan studies

The Michigan studies found similar findings to the Ohio team, but they came to different conclusions. Rather than the two dimensions being independent they conclude that these are different behavioural styles that lie on opposite sides of a continuum, with production-centred leadership at one end and employee-centred leadership at the other.

Some have argued that what these findings suggest is that an effective leader is one who is concerned with people or creating a pleasant atmosphere and high morale and raise questions as to whether an effective leader can be both a people person and task orientated too (Shackleton and Wale, cited in Chmiel 2000). It also raises questions as to whether a manager's superior will not see an employee-centred type style or the consideration approach as less effective because these types of managers are more reluctant to reprimand subordinates and hence productivity would suffer (Shackleton and Wale, cited in Chmiel 2000).

8.3.3 Managerial grid

The conclusions drawn from the Ohio and Michigan studies found widespread application in leadership training programmes for supervisors and managers. Many questionnaires have since been developed but the best known and probably less complicated is Blake and Mouton's (1964) **Managerial grid** (see Figure 8.1). This grid is intended only as a diagnostic tool aiming to explore a manager's leadership styles to the extent to which they have either

Pause for thought
Looking back at the case study, which of the two managerial styles do you think might motivate the staff to work more effectively?

Figure 8.1. Managerial grid

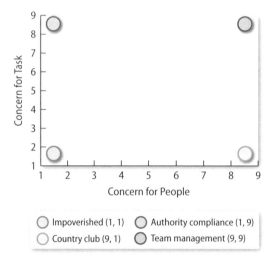

Source: Blake and Mouton (1964).

'concern for people' or 'concern for task'. It also aimed to answer the question of whether an effective leader can be both person centred and task orientated. There have been various versions of this grid, the most up-to-date version being the '**Leadership grid**' (Blake and McCanse 1991), which indicates a combination of concern for people and tasks.

The managerial grid describes a person's style in relation to two independent dimensions:

Concern for people

Concern for task.

On the basis of the score which is a scale ranging from 1 (low) to 9 (high): there are four possible styles that a person can score (see Figure 8.1).

However, like the trait theory before it, it suggests that there is one universal style that suits all situations. For example, having a score of 9.9—hence high on consideration and high on concern for the task—indicates that 'Team Management' is the best style and one that the authors of the grid favoured as the best approach. However, this too ignores situational differences which may demand different types of leadership approaches and that perhaps there are situations when high-high will not be the most effective style to use.

Although style theories moved thinking about leadership on from the rigidness of the trait approach, they nevertheless also give a universalist view of leadership (Rollinson 2002) which assumes that there is a superior style that would fit all situations. Despite this fact the behavioural approach has helped to broaden the focus of research to include leader behaviour and does offer the possibility of training people to develop effective leadership skills.

Furthermore, the style approach suggests people can learn how to be effective leaders in contrast to the trait approach. This approach opened the doors for training programmes paving the way for development of questionnaires to identify people's approaches to leadership and hence to designing training programmes to develop further skills necessary for effective leadership (Shackleton and Wale, cited in Chmiel 2000). However, as situational factors too are important in determining which effective style will emerge, research again turned its attention to consider how the situation might impact on the leadership style that would emerge.

KEY LEARNING POINTS

- Trait theory assumed that great leaders are born or develop the characteristics early in life.
- Behaviour approaches moved theory away from the rigidity of trait.
- Behavioural or style theories were concerned with what behaviour leaders used that made them effective.
- Style theories were based on observable behaviour that could be categorized.
- Style theories opened the opportunity for people to train in effective behaviours.

8.3.4 Situational-contingency

The **contingency** or **situational theories** address the omission made by earlier theories and emphasize the important role contextual factors play in determining which appropriate leadership style will emerge. The realization that there is no universal style to fit all situations prompted research into a new direction that included the situation and the need for managers or supervisors to adapt their style to fit the situation. An effective leader according to the underlying assumptions of contingency theories is one who could match his or her style to the particular demands of the specific situation.

Leadership continuum indicator

One of the earliest pieces of work by Tannenbaum and Schmit (1958) first appeared in this area at a time when style approaches were still in fashion, and so they did not develop these ideas beyond their initial model of the **leadership continuum**, which is still used as an indicator of leadership type (see Figure 8.2). However, they did pave the way for other theorists to expand and develop leadership research. Their ideas were influenced by the basic distinctions between job-centred and employee-centred behaviour or boss centred and follower centred respectively. Between the two extremes a variety of styles are shown, each corresponding to a different pattern of interactions between followers and managers; the appropriateness of these styles depends on a number of factors such as the manager's value system, personal wants, confidence in employees, and willingness of the subordinates to accept responsibility.

Using the continuum we can place two business women on this almost at either end of each other. Gabrielle Channel is considered a very authoritarian type of manager who was in complete control of her company, giving no responsibility to her staff and even having special mirrors fitted into her shop so that she could spy on them from her upstairs flat, indicating no confidence in her staff at all. To be fair the Channel of today is a different place from its founder. But it does raise questions of staff morale and motivation when they know they are not trusted. On the other hand we have Dame Anita Roddick of Body Shop fame, who was more participative in her approach and demonstrated concern for her environment and how people are being treated for their labour, being very much in favour of 'fair trade'.

Fiedler's contingency theory

Probably the best-known contingency approach is **Fiedler's contingency theory** (1967) of leadership, which advocates that leadership is a function of both the person and the situation (Spector 2006). It appeared some thirty years ago and is sometimes referred to as **LPC** (Least Preferred Co-Worker). Fiedler's theory attempts to match leaders and situations in order to find the optimal leadership style suited to that situation and to do this Fiedler attempts to combine both trait theory and style theory (Statt 1994). It is dependent on three contextual variables which determine the favourability of the situation for a particular leadership style.

These three variables are the *group atmosphere*, which is the extent to which the group trusts and accepts their manager; the extent to which *task structure* is clear and unambiguous; and finally the *position of power* that the leader possesses and how much control he or she has to reward or punish subordinates. Fiedler measures these traits by asking managers to assess their least preferred person to work with along sixteen bipolar dimensions.

These are scored on a scale from 1 to 8, 8 being the highest mark, and they reflect the manager's underlying disposition towards others (Furnham 2001). They reveal managers' relationships with subordinates; hence, those high on LPC are relationship orientated and tend to evaluate people they least like to work with more favourably while those low on LPC are very much task oriented. The suggestion is that some situations favour certain managerial approaches or styles more than others.

Figure 8.2. Leadership style continuum

Autocratic/
little follower
involvement

Democratic
high follower
empowerment

Figure 8.3. Fiedler's bipolar examples

Source: Fiedler (1967).

However, Fiedler argues that a leader's style is part of a person's personality and thus is relatively fixed and unchanging, which means that if the person's style does not fit the situation, there are two alternatives open to him or her: either to leave the leadership position or change the situation. Although this may sound difficult, Fiedler suggests a range of actions that can bring about changes to the contextual factors and developed a programme to teach managers to do just that (Fiedler and Mahon 1976). This is because Fiedler felt circumstances can change whereas relatively stable and unchanging traits could not.

Studies testing the validity of Fiedler's theory have come up with mixed evidence to support its accuracy (Graen et al. 1971). There is some evidence that other variables and not just the three Fiedler suggests could influence leader effectiveness (Peters et al. 1985). Moreover, Fiedler's sole criterion for evaluating the effectiveness of leaders is task performance. He neglected the equally important factor of follower satisfaction, which we will look at shortly.

The interesting point of Fiedler's model and that which makes it unique compared to other contingency models is that it is the only one that believes that style is relatively permanent and reflects deep-rooted psychological characteristics. However, for all its criticism Fiedler's work has made a significant contribution to leadership theory by recognizing the importance of contextual circumstances and the impact they can have on leadership style.

KEY LEARNING POINTS

- The leadership continuum indicator is a useful tool indicating patterns of interaction between leaders and followers.
- Fiedler's theory attempts to match leaders and situations for optimal leadership style.
- Fiedler argued that a person's style of leadership was part of their personality and hence relatively stable and unchanging.

Path-goal theory

Another contingency theory is the **path-goal theory** which was developed by House and Mitchell (1974) and concerns itself with issues of what motivates employees in given circumstances. According to this theory different types of leadership styles are appropriate for different situations and it implies that an effective leader in one situation will not necessarily be as effective in another. The theory is based on the **Expectancy theory of motivation** (see also Chapter 5 on Motivation and Work Satisfaction) which suggests that it is dependent on 'expectancy', 'instrumentality', and 'valence':

- 'expectancy' in the belief that effort will result in performance;
- 'instrumentality' in that the individual's performance will be rewarded;
- 'valence' in that the reward or outcome is valued by the individual who is putting in the effort.

Thus, a supervisor's role is to enhance motivation and job satisfaction by providing rewards and making it easier for subordinates to achieve their goals (Spector 2006). To do this, they have to ensure all three factors are at the right level (something which is calculated). The basic principle of this theory is that subordinates act favourably to a leader who will help them achieve their goals (which they value) and that the leader will do this by adopting one of four types of leader behaviour:

- directive
- supportive
- participative
- achievement oriented.

The basic assumption is that leaders will have the ability to analyse the situation and the capabilities of their subordinates and in so doing adjust their style of leadership to match people's capabilities. For example if a subordinate has a need for a clarity type characteristic then the leader will adopt a more directive approach in order to help the subordinate by setting out the task so that it will be clear and unambiguous—telling them what he or she wants them to do which then allows subordinates to go away and get on with the task. Conversely if a subordinate has been in the job for a while and is experienced in doing it they need a more participative type leadership style, which will allow them the freedom of working independently and being allowed to make some decisions.

Unlike Fiedler's model, House and Mitchell's (1974) path-goal theory assumes the 'same' leader possesses these four styles and can adapt the style to suit the different situations. What the leader aims to do according to the path-goal approach is to help subordinates find the best path or way to accomplish their goal, by making the path challenging and stress free. Thus, depending on the situation and the subordinates themselves, the leader will adopt one of the four styles that he or she perceives as the most appropriate for the particular subordinate and situation.

One of the criticisms of this approach is the authors' assumption that a manager is able to analyse the situation and know which style will be the most appropriate to use and will have developed the flexibility to change style when necessary.

The criterion House (1974) uses to assess the effectiveness of leadership style is subordinate satisfaction, which was a huge omission in Fiedler's work, who did not consider the important role subordinates play in the relationship between a manager and his or her subordinates. Hence it made a significant step forward in contingency theory.

Case illustration
Sally's work experience at Typecast Plc

'At my most recent job, at Typecast, I really enjoyed going into work every morning as the atmosphere was really great and so different from other places I worked in, especially as a temp last Christmas. At Typecast Plc, it was an office setting and everyone worked as part of a team. There was good communication between colleagues and the supervisors. Our hard work was valued more than the other places I worked in. I felt more like a member of a team. Appreciation for our work was shown by the supervisors and the manager by letting us leave early on a Friday if all the tasks were completed early and all staff were allowed to dress down on Fridays. Occasionally the supervisor used to bring in cakes that she baked for the staff to have. The office atmosphere was so pleasant everyone got on well and worked hard. The supervisors were easy to talk to and were clear on what jobs had to be done and when. The relationship between colleagues was good, I could ask for help whenever I needed it and good training was given if ever I needed to do a new task. In general the manager was strict in her approach to making sure all the deadlines were met and at the same time she would tell jokes and entertain the staff in the office. I feel this was a good quality for a manager to have as it will gain the respect from the colleagues, hard work, motivation and enthusiasm as well as a good pleasant workplace.'

Questions
- What management approach can you identify in this case study?
- What kind of behaviour does this approach encourage?
- How important is the manager's leadership behaviour to subordinates?

8.3.5 Vroom–Yetton–Jago

We now turn to **Vroom's decision-making theory**, which is very narrow in focus and only concentrates on the decision-making aspect of leadership. It was first developed by Vroom and Yetton (1973) and then revised by Vroom and Jago (1988). It focuses on situations that are more or less preferable for a leader to involve subordinates in decision making.

Like House, Vroom (1983) argued that most leaders can change their patterns of behaviour and identified five styles of decision making that are placed on a continuum from autocratic at one end to highly participative at the other, known as:

- AI (Autocratic)
- AII (Information seeking)
- CI (Consulting)
- CII (Negotiating)
- G (Group).

They argue that the choice as to which style a manager or supervisor uses will depend on the situation, such as whether the manager has the information he or she needs to make a decision alone and how quickly that decision has to be made. In order for a manager to decide which style to adopt, two criteria are used which give rise to four basic situations. These criteria are:

- Does the decision affect the whole group or one individual?
- Does the leader place priority on speed in decision making?

Managers select the appropriate style on the basis of responses they give and each combination is covered by a separate tree. So, for example, the 'participative' style involves considerable participation by their subordinates whereas 'authoritarian' not at all. These styles range from decisions the leader makes alone to leaders chairing meetings which involve the whole group to find solutions. Although this theory is one that is supported by empirical results more than any other theory of leadership (Yukl 1994) it is seen as too complex to be useful (House and Baetz 1979).

KEY LEARNING POINTS

- Path-goal theory is based on the expectancy theory of motivation and dependent on: 'expectancy', 'instrumentality', and 'valence'.
- Four styles arise within this approach: directive, supportive, participative, and achievement orientated.
- Managers help subordinates to find the best way to accomplish goals by adopting one of the above styles
- Vroom's decision-making theory focuses on situations that are favourable for participative decision making and those that need a faster decision-making style.

8.3.6 Hersey and Blanchard

A model devised by Hersey and Blanchard (1982) sought to specify which leadership style is most appropriate to a specific development level of subordinates. The behaviour-situation Situational Leadership model (SL11), also known as **Situational Leadership**, is very appealing and is the theory managers and trainers like the most, probably because it lends itself easily to training leadership skills and gives a developmental approach to managers, who want to build their leadership skills. However, it is worth noting that it is not supported very well empirically, so the validity of the instrument to actually train people to be effective leaders is questionable as the research does not support its claims to do so.

The assumption of this approach is that an effective leader is one who takes account or considers his or her subordinates needs and adapts their behavioural style to the demands of the different situations. Leadership is defined with reference to two dimensions, directive behaviour and supportive behaviour, and combinations of high and low are used to identify four styles, which are:

- directing (H-L)
- coaching (H-H)
- supporting (L-H)
- delegating (L-L).

Hersey and Blanchard (1982) argue that a manager must adjust his or her style according to the readiness of his or her subordinates to take on responsibility. This, however, means that a manager must be able to recognize and analyse the level of readiness in his or her subordinates. Managers would do this using two facets of their subordinates' behaviour, their task-related readiness and their psychological readiness. Like the path-goal model (House and Mitchell 1974), this too assumes managers have the ability to diagnose the readiness of their subordinates accurately and are able to adapt their styles accordingly.

Overall, contingency theory is well supported by research and has broadened our understanding of leadership and the impact of both the situation and the style of leadership. It recognizes that not all leaders are effective in all situations and it has some predictive value (Alimo-Metcalfe and Alban-Metcalfe 2002, cited in Warr 2002). However, it fails to explain why some styles are more effective than others and the validity of measures such as Fiedler's LPC scale are questionable (Rollinson 2002). Current trends of leadership seem to be moving towards a contingency model (Statt 1994), although after nearly a century of research into leadership what we can conclude with a degree of confidence is that effective leadership is dependent on a number of things (which are still a contentious subject) and that it is a good idea for leaders to be interested in people (Statt 1994).

 Activity Identifying leadership styles

Think of three or four leaders you consider effective or successful.

- Describe these leaders and write down what type of leadership approach they had.
- Be aware of the type of words you have used to describe them. What approach are you using?
- What theoretical approach best describes you?

8.4 Leader–follower relationship

Although the theories we have been discussing thus far deal with slightly different contingencies and circumstances, they are seen as complementary rather than contradictory. However, a common feature that puts limitation on the application of these contingency theories is that in every case the leader is selected from higher up in the organization (Rollinson 2002). As a result they are given authority from above, so if all else fails they can resort to using their authority over subordinates in order to get the tasks done, for example by the use of punishment.

In this sense, using 'leaders' to refer to managers or supervisors is an overstatement because a leader uses influence that is non-coercive and is given the authority to exert this influence from below, from his or her followers. Another limitation of these approaches is the assumption that the leader–follower relationship is a passive one. Much of the literature on leadership has until recently treated the relationship between followers and leaders as a one-sided process. It assumes that followers passively accept the influence of the person leading them. But it is a two-way process where leaders and followers interact in ways that achieve their goals. Furthermore, a leader cannot be a leader without followers and followers are a very important part of the leadership process (Statt 1994). Followers are the ones who give consent to a leader to influence them and this power from below can be more powerful than formal authority given from above.

8.4.1 Leadership and power

The power that a 'leader' exerts on his or her followers is the type that followers have given consent to. DuBrin (2000) argues that leaders need to use power in order to influence others to achieve objectives and goals and that leaders cannot do it without the use of power (DuBrin 2000). The type of power that a leader uses stems from his or her personal characteristics and skills and is known as **personal power** (French and Raven 1959). This includes **referent power**, which enables a leader to have control over others based on their loyalty to him or her and the desire to please that person (DuBrin 2000). It also includes **expert power** (French and Raven 1959) which refers to the degree to which subordinates believe the person has the necessary skills to achieve a group's goals (Schultz and Schultz 2002). In contrast managers and supervisors are given authority to exert power from above, **legitimate power** (French and Raven 1959), which is a different kind of power and includes **coercive power** and the ability to reward or punish subordinates through the use of power in order to achieve tasks or goals.

Moreover, a new wave of interest in the approaches to leadership is that they emphasize the importance of follower attitudes and feelings which have largely been ignored in most studies of leadership. Since leadership is ultimately a social process (Bass 1998; Conger 1989) follower perceptions of leadership might be a better measure of evaluating what makes a good leader rather than researchers' observations of distant leaders.

8.4.2 Reciprocal causality

There are a number of different ways to consider the functions a person needs to perform in order to be perceived as a leader by others. Some approach this from an operant conditioning perspective (Scott and Podsakoff 1982) and consider 'leadership as the behaviour that results in a difference in the behaviour of others' (Bowers and Seashore 1966). The reasoning behind this approach is that leaders receive psychological satisfaction or reward when they succeed in getting people to do things and that this follower behaviour prompts them to behave in ways to get this reward. This idea is known as '**reciprocal causality**' within the follower–leader relationship, which means that one is the cause of the other. Early theories of leadership fail to acknowledge that while a leader has an effect on his or her followers, their followers too have an effect on them (Green 1975). It is more useful to see leadership from the social exchange theory perspective.

Action-centred leadership

Adair bases his action-centred approach (1979, 1984) on the social exchange perspective, which argues that for a leader to be effective he or she needs to meet three sets of interrelated needs that give rise to three functions that the leader must perform in order to be effective. These are to:

- ensure the group has clarity of task and the resources to perform the task;
- hold the team together and ensure team cohesiveness;
- ensure that individual needs of members within the group are met.

An effective manager will be aware of ensuring all three needs are met and that a balance is kept between them. Managers that focus too much on the task may find they ignore individual needs. This means that they need to:

- have an awareness of the group's processes and know people within the group;
- be able to spot which of the three functions needs attention;
- have interpersonal skills to bring about any changes that are needed to achieve this.

What is crucially important according to the action-centred approach is that a leader needs to serve the interest of the group and as such leadership is essentially a social function and a process of facilitating social exchange. Adair's model (1979, 1984) has also been developed in a successful method of leadership training by the Industrial Society (Smith 1983).

Figure 8.4. Adair's action-centred theory

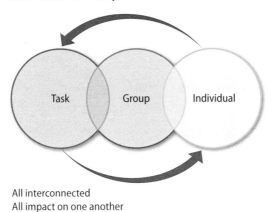

All interconnected
All impact on one another

Source: Adair (1979).

Leader–member exchange theory

The leader–member exchange (LMX) theory (Danserau et al. 1975) recognizes the importance of individual differences and the importance of the dyadic relationships between the leader and each of his or her subordinates. Dansereau et al. argue that a major limitation of most leadership research is the assumption that supervisors use the same approach with all individuals within a group (Spector 2006). Danserau et al. (1975) propose two types of relationships develop between supervisors and subordinates. The in-group, which consists of trusted and influential subordinates, and the out-group. Members of in-groups demonstrate more job satisfaction and have better relations with their supervisors (Spector 2006).

The argument is that supervisors exercise leadership with in-group members rather than supervision, and assign such subordinates more responsible tasks (Schultz and Schultz 2002) compared to out-group members, with whom they use a more directive approach. A study of salespeople in a large retail organization found that employees who have strong relationships with their supervisor (high LMX) are more committed to achieving objectives than those with low LMX (Klein and Kim 1998, cited in Schultz and Schultz 2002). These early studies focus on the quality of leader–subordinate interaction, which leads to the distinction between 'in-group' and 'out-group' communication, and favoured or disapproved followers (Alimo-Metcalfe and Alban-Metcalfe 2002, cited in Warr 2002).

8.4.3 Managers and leaders, are they the same thing?

Turning our discussion now to managers and leaders, the question really is are they indeed the same thing or are there distinct differences between them? The interest in the **transformational** leader in the workplace is fairly recent and was prompted by an analysis by Peters and Waterman (1982) which emphasizes how such people were able to 'transform' an organization, turning it right round into success. This came after the recession of the 1990s which prompted research into what is fast becoming known as the new **paradigm models** as coined by Bryman (1996). Bryman argues (along with other writers) that early situational models of leadership are more to do with management of organizations during relatively stable times than with leadership, which is about handling change (Alimo-Metcalfe and Alban-Metcalfe 2002, cited in Warr 2002) in a tubulant fast-moving environment.

The distinction between transformational and transactional leadership was first made by Burns (1978) when he distinguished between different types of politicians. He argues that transformational politicians are those who are able to move their followers away from self-interest and work for the greater good of all. Some examples in history are charismatic figures such as John F. Kennedy, Mahatma Gandhi, and Martin Luther King., in contrast to the transactional politicians who trade promises for votes. These types of leaders influence followers by transactions of exchange. Both approaches can be successful but it is the effect they have on their followers that makes the difference. What makes people go the extra mile is a point of interest in organizations, where motivating people to do this is important (see Chapter 5 on Motivation and Work Satisfaction).

Pause for thought
The terms 'leader' and 'follower' are used in an organizational context. How far do you think this is justified? Can a person be a leader just because he or she is in a managerial position? If so, why?

The functions then of **transactional managers** are to ensure the smooth running of the organization based on exchanges between themselves and their subordinates, because as managers they are given power to exercise authority from above, which authority may be from a 'transformational leader'! Managers will use different styles of approach to achieve goals and objectives based on exchanges with subordinates, but if all else fails they do have the authority to exercise power over their subordinates to get the tasks done.

In contrast transformational leaders are given power from below and this is what makes the difference between followers and subordinates. A leader is such because he or she has been given power from the people themselves and as such the relationship between followers and their leaders can also be a fragile state of affairs (Rollinson 2002) because the needs of both can change at any time. This means that either the leader has to change his or her style to suit the new circumstances or be replaced. We can see this clearly in our political history, especially when we change political leaders whenever we are unhappy with the state of affairs. In the London Mayor elections of May (2008) Boris Johnson took over office from Ken Livingstone: a cry of the people's discontent perhaps, either towards Ken or the Labour party, but change was brought about nevertheless. As our focus is on leaders in organizations, do people have the same power within organizations to change their managers?

Bass bases his model on this distinction made by Burns (1978) which he translates to apply to managers within organizations and argues (1998) that an essentially distinguishing feature of leaders is their 'ability to transform' followers to perform beyond expectations. For example, would Richard Branson's employees go that extra mile for him compared to Alan Sugar's? Bass (1998) also argues that transformational leaders are not sufficient on their own in organizations and that transactional managers are also necessary, that the two roles are complimentary rather than contradictory, and both are essential to an organization if it is to function effectively.

What this means is that if we consider Richard Branson as a transformational leader, he is very creative, innovative, and willing to take risks and go for new ventures. However in order to run a successful business, he also needs to rely on managers to ensure the smooth running of the place and achieve his organizational goals through transactional exchange. Richard Branson may be inspiring but he cannot do it alone and that is when managers need to be employed in order to ensure that organizational goals are met.

What this demonstrates is that there are distinct differences between the roles of leaders and managers which the literature very often fails to draw attention to (Alimo-Metcalfe and Alban-Metcalfe 2001). Some of the reasons for this confusion in the literature has been because most theories (Rollinson 2002) originate in America and focus exclusively on leadership in organizational setting. While none of the theories actually state that being a leader or a manager are the same thing, neither do any theories really differentiate between the two. They focus on the manager and treat that person as someone who occupies a position of leadership.

However, in considering the functions of both management and leadership, Kotter (1990) argues that management is concerned with planning, organizing, staffing, and so forth, whereas leadership deals with taking the organization forward, with leaders with a vision and the ability to communicate that vision and inspire people beyond their potential.

In fact, some writers argue that not only do they have different functions but that leaders and managers are different kinds of people altogether, indeed are of different psychological types and have different orientations to work (Zaleznik 1993). Moreover, the emerging issue in leadership is perhaps that **transformational style** is fast becoming equated with leadership itself and transactional with closed-ended, relatively static management (Alimo-Metcalfe and Alban-Metcalfe 2001).

It is not all rosy for transformational leadership, as it has been criticized for having poorly defined parameters (Northouse 2001). Although Bass's model is undoubtedly well respected (Alimo-Metcalfe and Alban-Metcalfe 2001) and his contribution to the leadership literature has been great, his work has also been criticized because most of the research in this area has come from American companies and is based on a very white male sample (Hunt 1996). Furthermore, Gronn (1995) agues that the transformational leader is a current obsession and that the notion of the heroic leader has long since been discredited.

Figure 8.5. Differences between leadership roles and managerial duties

Leadership roles	Managerial duties
Having a vision	Planning
Translating that vision	Organizing
Establish direction	Achieve results
Motivating	Dealing with human resources
Inspiring	Controlling
Energizing	Ensuring smooth running of
Power given from below	Power given from above
Ideal in fast changing workplace	Ideal in predictable, stable workplace
People follow willingly	People do as they have to

Source: Adapted from Kotter (1990), cited in Chmiel (2000).

Pause for thought
In considering the above information, how far do you feel managers can call themselves leaders just because they are given the authority to lead in an organization?

Moreover, Alimo-Metcalfe and Alban Metcalfe (2001) argue that the model having been derived from the USA is based on what they call '**distant leaders**', people such as chief executives, religious leaders, and so forth, rather than '**close or nearby leaders**' who might be one's immediate boss and that this makes a difference to the type of leaders being discussed.

8.5 Gender and leadership

Another interesting take on leadership is that, historically, studies of leadership have tended to concentrate on men from the beginning of research into this topic. As such the literature portrays men's perceptions of leadership that are then superimposed on women (Alimo-Metcalfe and Alban-Metcalfe 2002, cited in Warr 2002). This is based on the assumption that there are no differences between male and female leadership styles. However, a review of the literature by some writers concludes that there has been a distinct male bias in the construction of leadership (Alimo-Metcalfe 1995; Bass 1990).

8.5.1 Differences in leadership approaches

Prior to the 1970s there was little interest in gender differences in leadership but with the introduction of equal opportunities legislation in the UK and the USA the interest in this area has increased with a series of studies into differences. Some argue that there are few if any differences found (such as Powell 1993) and where they are found they are minor. Whereas, others believe these differences are very real and should be researched as differences—neither better nor worse than each other, just different.

These differences emerged in the 1990s with findings from a US survey that asked executives from both groups to describe their leadership approaches (Rosener 1990). This revealed that women use more transformational behaviour compared to their male counterparts in their style of approach. These findings are further supported by two independent British studies which investigated constructs of leadership style held by senior female and male managers (Alimo-Metcalfe 1995; Sparrow and Rigg 1993).

8.5.2 Does transformational leadership have a gender?

The differences found suggest women are developing behaviours more in line with transformational leadership, being more participative and democratic in their decision-making styles (Eagly and Johnson 1990) and also more team orientated (Ferrario 1994) compared to men. Many studies have found that women consistently use clusters of behaviours associated with transformational styles in leadership (Bass et al. 1996) that prompts the question of whether transformational leadership has a gender (Doyle 2002). Although Bass et al. (1996) found that women are higher on transformational leadership, unfortunately their study did not allow conclusions to be made about effectiveness (Spector 2006).

Furthermore, although there is evidence that women work harder (Lyness and Thompson 2000) and face more barriers than men, it does seem to depend on the organization (Spector 2006) and they do seem to be breaking through the **glass ceiling**. That women can achieve higher management roles is evident from the various women in high positions across the world—current trends indicate many female heads of state, such as Germany's Angela Merkel, who is the Chancellor, after what some have called a 'remarkable' political career. In Latvia Vaire Vike-Freiberga is the first female president of that country and joins Mary McAleese of Eire and Ruth Dreifuss of Switzerland as the female elected heads of state in Europe. These are not the first women to hold such positions: in the United Kingdom Margaret Thatcher was the first woman Prime Minister and Golda Meir was Prime Minister of Israel.

There are various explanations why women have difficulties achieving high positions. Some explanations focus on the differences between male and female attitudes and preparations of careers (see Chapter 9 on Career Management and Development). A Dutch study found women are less ambitious, care less about salary and status, and are more concerned about work-family conflict than men (van Vianen and Fischer 2002).

Chapter summary

- Leadership is a very complex concept which is hard to define. However, most theorists agree that it inevitably consists of three components. It is a process that involves influencing others, it occurs within a group context, and is aimed at achieving goals.

- Early approaches to leadership such as trait theory go back to the beginning of the twentieth century. The trait approach or 'great man' theories were interested in discovering what traits make people successful leaders. They argue that great people are born with the characteristics that make them successful or they develop these traits early in life.

- In an effort to pin down the most important traits five key characteristics were found, but there is no consistent agreement about these traits, especially as some of these can also be found in non-leaders too.

- The behavioural style approach followed the trait and focuses attention on what effective leaders do that makes them successful. Their interest is on observable behaviour that can be categorized in order to identify the most successful behaviour for leadership.

- Much of the work in the style approach is influenced by human relations theory and in particular the work of Lewin and his colleagues, which identified how different leadership styles can affect the performance of followers.

- Two dimensions of leadership style were found, initiating structure and consideration, or production or employee centred, that influence much of the work in the style approach and found widespread application in leadership training programmes, the best known being the Managerial Grid, which explores the extent to which managers can have concern for both the task and the people.

- However, like the trait theories before it the behavioural approach too assumes that there is a 'one best style' to fit all situations and ignores the contextual factors that determine which style will emerge.

- The contingency or situational approaches to leadership emphasize the importance of contextual factors on which leadership style will emerge and argue that managers need to adopt their style to suit the situation.

- The best known of these contingency theories is Fiedler's, which is based on three contextual factors which determine the favourability of the situation for a particular style: the group atmosphere, task structure, and position of power the leader possesses.

- Other contingency theories such as path-goal theory and Vroom's decision-making theory assume leaders can change their style according to the situation, which is a different assumption from Fiedler's, who saw style as part of a leader's personality and hence relatively fixed and unchanging.

- Although contingency theory broaden the focus of research into the leadership topic, it nevertheless ignored the equally important relationship between followers and their leaders. The research turned to what functions a leader needed to perform in order to be given consent to lead by his or her followers.

- Theories that investigated the leader–follower relationship began to look at the influence both parties have on each other and with a social exchange perspective that suggests that there is mutual influence and interrelatedness, such as Adair's action-centred approach.

- In considering the relationship between followers and leaders the question of whether managers could lay claim to being leaders is posed, as managers are generally people who are appointed by the organization in order to manage subordinates.

- The difference between transformational leaders and transactional managers indicates that the roles are separate and someone is a leader because people from below give him or her power to lead them, as opposed to power given from the top.

- Considering gender and leadership, the chapter briefly looked at women in senior positions and how they differ from men. Research suggests that women are more likely to have transformational leadership behaviour and males transactional.

- This posed the question of whether transformational leadership has a gender.

Assess your learning

Review questions

1 Leadership is a process that involves three themes, what are they?

2 What is trait theory based on?

3 How different from trait theory is the behavioural approach?

4 What are the five key traits identified as differentiating leaders from non-leaders?

5 What does the Managerial Grid assess? What are the four styles it proposes? (There are five in the Leadership Grid, can you name the fifth?)

6 What was significantly different with the contingency theory that earlier theories did not consider?

7 Name three contingency theories.

8 What function do leaders need to perform to be perceived as leaders?

9 Why are followers as significant in the leadership relationship as leaders themselves?

10 Are managers and leaders the same thing? Give reasons for your reply

Assignments

ASSIGNMENT 1: Leadership and management

The terms leadership and management are used interchangeably in the literature. Discuss whether this is justified and give evidence for your answer.

- What is a transformational leadership and how does it differ from transactional managers? How far do you agree with this? Discuss.

- Using the case studies, what theories and leadership approaches would you give them. Give reasons for your answers.

ASSIGNMENT 2: Core of leadership

The topic of leadership has become of interest in the workplace. In what ways does leadership style affect outcomes within the workplace?

- Consider the different approaches and styles of leadership. How do they impact on the workforce?
- Is there one particular approach that would be more effective than others? If so, which one and why? Give reasons for your response.

Further reading

Furnham, A. (2001) *The Psychology of Behaviour at Work: The Individual in the Organisation.* **Hove: Psychology Press.**
This is an excellent book which gives a good coverage of leadership theories and cross-cultural perspectives.

Warr, P. (2002) *Psychology at Work.* **Harmondsworth: Penguin.**
The chapter on leadership by Alimo-Metcalfe and Alban-Metcalfe gives a very detailed account of the most current thinking in the field of leadership and is one of the few that considers gender and leadership.

Work psychology in practice
Whitefields

Margaret Palmer was a manager of a small local business where she had been working for eighteen years. The owner, Sarah Mills had very recently taken over the whole company when the partnership was up for sale. The layout of the office was such that Sarah had a separate office cut off from the rest of the office that usually had the door closed when Sarah was in. When she was out of the office the door was seen to be open, which signalled that she was away. When she was out Margaret ran the office pretty much as Sarah would like. She kept an eye on the staff and made sure they were all working hard on their tasks. She regularly checked up on them to ensure that things ran the way they ought to. Any new member of staff was given a rule and procedure book to read through in order to familiarize themselves with the way the company operated. Margaret ensured her team followed her instructions and did what they were told. People did not tend to talk to each other apart from asking the odd question here and there. She avoided 'chit chatting' to her subordinates about issues that were not work related in case they became too familiar and began to slack in their work. The design of the room was such that it did not give such opportunities anyway. All the desks around the office were set in such a way that people could not see each other, in fact mainly people faced the wall; if you wanted to say something to a colleague you needed to turn round and Margaret would then know, having her desk in the middle of the office and straight in front of the door. She was the only one who had full visibility of who came in and who left the office. Margaret worked from 9.30 a.m. to exactly 6.00 p.m., she never left before the clock struck 6.00 p.m. unless she had an appointment and Sarah knew she would be gone at a specific time. She would often be seen dressed and ready to go home with her eye on the clock. Sarah had been known to ring the office at 5.55 p.m. when she was out with clients to ask for something.

Questions

- What is the owner's style of management?
- What kind of behaviour was she encouraging from her subordinates?
- What style of management did the manager adopt?
- Would employees go the extra mile for either the owner or the manager in this case study? Give reasons for your answer.

Online Resource Centre

Visit the supporting online resource centre for additional material which will help you with your research, essays, and assignments, or you may find these additional resources helpful when revising for exams.
http://www.oxfordtextbooks.co.uk/orc/matthewman/

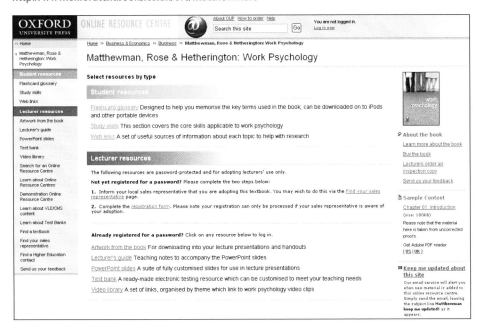

References

Adair, J. (1979) *Action-Centred Leadership*. Aldershot: Gower.

Adair, J. (1984) *The Skills of Leadership*. Aldershot: Gower.

Alimo-Metcalfe, B. (1995) An Investigation of female and male constructs of leadership and empowerment. *Women in Management Review*, 10: 3–8.

Alimo-Metcalfe, B., and Alban-Metcalfe, R. J. (2000) An analysis of the convergent and discriminant validity of the Transformational Leader Questionnaire. *International Journal of Selection and Assessment*, 8: 158–75.

Alimo-Metcalfe, B., and Alban-Metcalfe, R. J. (2001) The development of a new transformational leadership questionnaire. *Journal of Occupational and Organisational Psychology*, 74: 1–27.

Barron, R. A., and Greenberg, J. (1990) *Behaviour in Organisations*. Needham Heights, MA: Allyn and Bacon.

Bass, B. M. (1985) *Leadership and Performance beyond Expectations*. New York: Free Press.

Bass, B. M. (1990) *Bass and Stodgill's Handbook of Leadership: Theory, Research and Application* (3rd edn.). New York: Free Press.

Bass, B. M. (1998) *Transformational Leadership: Industrial, Military and Educational Impact*. Hillsdale, NJ: Erlbaum.

Bass, B. M., Avolio, B. J., and Atwater, L. (1996) The transformational and transactional leadership of men and women. *International Review of Applied Psychology*, 45: 5–34.

Blake, R. R., and McCanse, A. A. (1991) *Leadership Dilemmas: Grid Solutions*. Houston: Gulf.

Blake, R. R., and Mouton, J. (1964) *The Managerial Grid*. Houston: Gulf.

Bowers, D. G., and Seashore, S. E. (1966) Predicting organisational effectiveness with a four-factor theory of leadership. *Administrative Science Quarterly*, 11/2: 238–63.

Bryman, A. (1996) *Leadership in Organisations*. London: Sage.

Burns, J. M. (1978) *Leadership*. San Francisco: Harper and Row.

Byrd, C. (1940) *Social Psychology*. New York: Appleton Century Crofts.

Chmiel, N. (2000) *Work and Organisational Psychology: A European Perspective*. Oxford: Blackwell Publishers.

Conger, J. A. (1989) *The Charismatic Leader: Behind the Mystique of Exceptional Leadership*. San Francisco: Jossey-Bass.

Danserau, F. D., Graen, G., and Haga, W. J. (1975) A vertical dyad linkage approach to leadership within formal organizations: a longitudinal investigation of the role of making process. *Organisational Behaviour and Human Performance*, 13/1: 46–78.

Doyle, C. E. (2002) *Work and Organisational Psychology: An Introduction with attitude*. Hove: Psychology Press.

Dubrin, A. J. (2000) *Applying Psychology: Individual and Organisational Effectiveness* (5th edn.). Englewood Cliffs, NJ: Prentice Hall Publishers.

Eagly, A. H., and Johnson, B. T. (1990) Gender and leadership style: a meta-analysis. *Psychological Bulletin*, 108: 233–56.

Ferrario, M. (1994) Women as managerial leaders. In M. J. Davidson and R. J. Burke (eds.), *Women in Management: Current Research Issues*. London: Paul Chapman.

Fiedler, F. E. (1967) *A Theory of Leadership Effectiveness*. New York: McGraw-Hill.

Fiedler, F. E., and Mahon, L. (1976) A field experiment validating contingency paradox: prospect theory explanations. *Journal of Applied Psychology*, 64/2: 247–54.

Fleishman, E. A. (1953) The measurement of leadership attitudes in industry. *Journal of Applied Psychology*, 38/1: 153–8.

Fleishman, E. A., Harris, E. F., and Burtt, H. E. (1953) *Leadership and Supervision in Industry*. Columbus, OH: Bureau of Educational Research, Ohio State University.

French, J., and Raven, B. (1959) The bases of social power. In D. Cartwright (ed.) *Studies in Social Power*. Ann Arbor: Institute for Social Research.

Furnham, A. (2001) *The Psychology of Behaviour at Work: The Individual in the Organisation*. Hove: Psychology Press.

Graen, G. J., Orris, J. B., and Alvares, K. (1971) The contingency model of leadership effectiveness: some experimental results. *Journal of Applied Psychology*, 55/1: 196–201.

Green, C. (1975) The reciprocal nature of influence between leader and subordinate. *Journal of Applied Psychology*, 60/2: 187–93.

Gronn, P. (1995) Greatness re-visited: the current obsession with transformational leadership. *Leading and Managing*, 1: 14–27.

Hersey, P., and Blanchard, K. H. (1982) *The Management of Organisational Behaviour: Utilizing Human Resources* (4th edn.). Englewood Cliffs, NJ: Prentice-Hall.

House, R. J., and Baetz, M. L. (1979) Leadership: some empirical generalisations and new research directions. *Research in Organisational Behaviour*, vol. i. Greenwich, CT: JAI Press.

House, R. J., and Mitchell, T. (1974) Path-goal theory of leadership. *Journal of Contemporary Business*, 3: 81–99.

Jago, A. G. (1982) Leadership: perspectives in theory and research. *Management Science*, 28/3: 315–36.

Kirkpatrick, S. A., and Locke, E. A. (1991) Leadership: Do traits matter? *Academy of Management Executive*, May: 48–60.

Kotter, J. P. (1988) *The Leadership Process*. New York: Free Press.

Kotter, J. P. (1990) *A Force for Change*. New York: Free Press.

Lewin, K., Lippit, R., and White, R. K. (1939) Patterns of aggressive behaviour in experimentally created social climates. *Journal of Social Psychology*, 10: 271–99.

Lyness, K. S., and Thompson, D. E. (2000) Climbing the corporate ladder: do female and male executives follow the same route? *Journal of Applied Psychology*, 85: 86–101.

Mann, R. D. (1959) A review of the relationships between personality and performance in small groups. *Psychological Bulletin*, 64: 241–70.

Northouse, P. (2001) *Leadership: Theory and Practice* (2nd edn.). Beverly Hills, CA: Sage.

Peters, L. H., Hartke, D. H., and Pohlman, J. T. (1985) Fiedler's contingency theory of leadership: an application of the meta-analytic procedures of Schmidt and Hunter. *Psychological Bulletin*, 97/2: 274–85.

Peters, T. J., and Waterman, R. H. (1982) *In Search of Excellence: Lessons from America's Best-Run Companies*. San Francisco: Harper and Row.

Powell, G. N. (1993) *Women and Men in Management* (2nd edn.). Beverly Hills, CA: Sage.

Powell, G. N., Butterfield, D. A., and Parent, J. D. (2002) Gender and managerial stereotypes: have the times changed? *Journal of Management*, 28: 177–93.

Rollinson, D. (2002) *Organisational Behaviour and Analysis* (2nd edn.). Englewood Cliffs, NJ: FT Prentice Hall.

Rosener, J. (1990) Ways women lead. *Harvard Business Review*, Nov./Dec.: 119–25.

Schultz, D. P., and Schultz, E. (2002) *Psychology and Work Today: An Introduction to Industrial and Organisational Psychology* (8th edn.). Englewood Cliffs, NJ: Prentice Hall Publishers.

Scott, W. E., and Podsakoff, P. M. (1982) Leadership supervision and behavioural control: perspectives from an experimental analysis. In L. W. Fredericksen (ed.), *Handbook of Organisational Behaviour Management*. New York: Wiley.

Smith, E. P. (1983) *The Manager as a Leader*. London: The Industrial Society.

Sparrow, J., and Rigg, C. (1993) Job analysis: selecting for the masculine approach to management. *Selection and Development Review*, 9: 2, 5–8.

Spector, P. E. (2006) *Industrial and Organisational Psychology: Research and Practice* (4th edn.). New York: John Wiley and Sons, Inc.

Statt, D. A. (1994) *Psychology and the World of Work*. New York: Palgrave Publishers.

Stodgill, R. M. (1948) Personal factors associated with leadership: a survey of the literature. *Journal of Psychology*, 25/1: 35–71.

Stodgill, R. M. (1974) *Handbook of Leadership: A Survey of Theory and Research*. New York: Free Press.

Tannenbaum, R., and Schmit, W. H. (1958) How to choose a leadership pattern. *Harvard Business Review*, Mar./Apr.: 95–102.

Van Vianen, A. E. M., and Fischer, A. H. (2002) Illuminating the glass ceiling: the role of organisational culture preferences. *Journal of Occupational and Organisational Psychology*, 75: 315–37.

Vroom, V. H. (1983) Leadership re-visited. In B. Staw (ed.), *Psychological Foundations of Organisational Behaviour*. Glenview, IL: Scott Foresman.

Vroom, V. H., and Jago, A. G. (1988) *The New Leadership*. Englewood Cliffs, NJ: Prentice-Hall.

Vroom, V. H., and Yetton, P. W. (1973) *Leadership and Decision Making*. Pittsburgh: University of Pittsburgh Press.

Warr, P. (2002) *Psychology at Work* (5th edn.). Harmondsworth: Penguin.

Yetton, P. W. (1984) Leadership and supervision. In M. Gruneberg and T. Wall (eds.), *Social Psychology and Organisational Behaviour*. New York: Wiley.

Yukl, G. (1994) *Leadership in Organisations* (3rd edn.). Englewood Cliffs, NJ: Prentice-Hall.

Zaleznik, A. (1993) Managers and leaders: are they different? In W. E. Rosenback and R. L. Taylor (eds.), *Contemporary Issues in Leadership*. Boulder, CO: Westview Press.

Part IV
The organization at work

Chapter 9

Career management and development

Jenni Nowlan

Chapter objectives

As a result of reading this chapter and using the additional web-based material you should be able to:

- Develop awareness of careers within the context of the changing nature of work.
- Critically evaluate different career theories.
- Realize the necessity for career management for all.
- Appreciate how the changing nature of work has disadvantaged some people's careers.
- Appreciate how the changing nature of work has advantaged some people's careers.
- Understand the concept of a portfolio career.
- Understand the concept of a boundaryless career.
- Reflect on the necessity for career management for everyone.
- Discuss the role of emotion in career management.
- Evaluate the changes that need to take place in order to redress the balance between men's and women's careers.

Work psychology in practice
Career management

Davina wondered just which path to take. She wondered how she had managed to end up in her situation as she felt that she had made careful choices when she was younger. However, through a cascade of unforeseen events she now found herself unemployed, in temporary rented accommodation, and her children had left home to live their own lives. Now in her mid-forties, she had some tough decisions to make.

At the age of 18 it had been Davina's choice to go to university to study business, as she had felt that that was a 'safe' choice. This was mainly because really she had no idea of what world she wanted to be in, but she reasoned to herself that all organizations, and work in general, would appreciate someone with knowledge of how the business world operates.

After graduating she went to work for a small charity, mainly promoting and fund raising, in which she excelled. After one year of this work she had pretty much proven herself and was given the opportunity to work overseas for the same charity and travelled to various counties, mainly off the beaten track and places not seen by holiday makers. Every day that passed Davina never failed to appreciate the wonderful opening she had been given and worked extremely hard.

It was in South America that she had met her husband and they had a fairy-tale wedding in Argentina. Two years later she gave birth to her daughter and shortly afterwards her son. These early days were very happy ones, she recalled, still working for an organization whose values and beliefs she held dear to herself and being married to a man with similar ideals.

When the children became of school age Davina and her husband made the decision to return to England, mainly because the part of the world that they were living in, at that time, did not have good schools. Also, part of her job needed her to be available to travel around freely, which wasn't a problem when the children were little, but wasn't appropriate any longer. Fortunately she was able to return to the English-based charity headquarters but at the time there wasn't anything for her husband. He managed to retrain and got himself a good job in IT. This enabled Davina to leave her job and become a full-time mum as his pay was good and she enjoyed being able to be a full-time mum and wife, at least while the children were small. She also felt that her job had reached a natural end, in a way, because she had felt for a while that she had reached her full potential. She didn't have the enthusiasm that she once had as there was nothing really to strive for anymore.

Later on, when the children were a little older she had a series of jobs, mostly fixed-term, temporary, and even buying and selling on ebay! It hadn't worried her at the time that she hadn't managed to obtain another full-time career job, after all they weren't too short of money as her husband was now earning a very good salary.

However, as the years passed it transpired that her husband missed South America too much and made the decision that it was necessary for his own happiness to return 'home'. Davina was shocked, but also knew South America was not her 'home' anymore and decided she had to stay in England. They eventually divorced and their teenagers occasionally went to see their father when Davina or her ex-husband could afford the air fares.

Davina had bought her husband out of the joint mortgage and had to find ever higher repayments with the credit crunch. When she wasn't able to find temporary work she put her increasing debts on her credit cards. Eventually, though, this had to stop as she reached the limits of the cards. Sadly she lost the house as she couldn't afford to make the repayments on her own and subsequently found herself in temporary rented accommodation (unable to obtain another mortgage). She had ended up with a whole lifestyle and situation that she would never have thought possible. After all, she had been so careful to choose a degree that could get her into most worlds, or so she thought. Now, though, no one wanted to employ her with her lack of current professional skills in the workplace. She was also highly intimidated by the competition she found at every stage of the selection process. Things had changed. Perhaps if she had been able to add to her skills, or to retrain like her ex-husband had, she thought to herself, but she never had sufficient money to be able to do that after the divorce. Even so, she thought negatively to herself, who would want me now at 46, with no prospects, little current experience, and even verging on depression. She felt a failure.

Questions

- Do you consider that Davina made naive decisions when she was younger?
- Do you think that if Davina had been more careful over career planning she would have had a different story to tell?
- Do you believe it is never too late to study or do you think learning is only for the young?
- What do you think Davina should do now to get herself out of her current situation?

9.1 Introduction

The changing nature of work has meant that within the workplace there have been many varying and shifting patterns of work and practices. Organizations have downsized, de-layered, and re-engineered themselves. This chapter aims to put some of these changes that have taken place and indeed are still taking place into some kind of context with regard to people's careers.

Firstly, a consideration of some of the changes that have taken place will be discussed in light of the effects that this has had for people's careers. One of these changes is the way in which people view the psychological contract (e.g. Argyris 1960; Levinson et al. 1962; Schein 1978; Herriot and Pemberton 1995; Guest and Conway 2002) and this will be discussed along with concepts of the **boundaryless** and portfolio career. As well as different ways of working there are of course many ways to look at people's careers and the second aim of this chapter will be to consider the main theories and models by looking at developmental stages, personality and self-concept categories, transitions, and vocational choice. As a number of these were written several decades ago, it will be necessary to consider whether they still stand up well in light of the changing nature of work.

This chapter will then move on to discuss career management and what this really means for workers today. Career guidance and counselling will be covered along with other techniques used in career management. Performance appraisal and emotion in careers will also be included in this section.

Finally the last part of the chapter will be dedicated to gender and careers. There are still vast differences for men and women in the workplace and issues such as socialization, prejudice, barriers, unequal pay, and the glass ceiling will be examined in order to try to determine what this actually means to female workers. In some cases this can have a knock-on effect for men too and this will also be discussed.

9.2 Careers in context: the changing nature of work

Technological advances have helped to enable many people to work away from the office and to work from home or on the road. These advances have also assisted in opening up global markets. Many organizations have sold off unneeded office space and have outsourced a lot of their departments such as Human Resource and Payroll. Most readers will also be familiar with the call centres that might be based far away from the country of the original caller. There has also been much relocation of manufacturing to developing countries because the wages are much lower.

Other changes in the workforce have come about because of demographic changes whereby the average age of the working population is increasing, and because of people having smaller families there are fewer young people entering the workplace. This of course has grave implications for pensions (i.e. not enough money being paid in to cover the growing numbers of pensioners that there will be drawing the money out). This has been much documented in the media in recent times. People are also living longer than ever before, so this too puts a heavy burden on pensions.

With the passing of much legislation there have definitely been some improvements in equal opportunities and diversity in the workplace. However, there is still a long way to go, especially demonstrated by the increased numbers of women in the workplace but the relatively few percentage of them that are in managerial roles. However, even for those women who are in managerial positions inequality of pay often still exists.

Other changes that have taken place in the economic climate of **globalization** and increased competitiveness are the growing number of short-term, part-time contracts which have replaced the 'job for life'. Many people now work in a more mobile and boundaryless way, moving from organization to organization. Indeed workers need to have a 'portfolio' of skills that they can take with them to any new contract.

These days there are also more educational opportunities than there once were, which is fortunate for the 'portfolio' worker who is always having to update his/her skills.

The flatter hierarchies, downsizing, and de-layering of organizations have brought fewer opportunities for promotion, and workers are often forced to make a sideways move rather than an upwards one. When promotion does come it is likely to be a bigger jump than once was the case.

9.2.1 Effects of changes

But have things changed that much? Some writers feel that they haven't and just one example of this is that bounded careers are still being pursued in some industries (e.g. Gunz et al. 2000).

Clearly there are both negative impacts of changes and some positive effects for some people. For example some people will feel empowered, more fulfilled, and enthusiastic about the concept of being able to have a boundaryless career. Some people will also feel that it is a positive move for them to be able to work further into old age. However, for others some of these changes will make them feel that the lack of security that a boundaryless career gives them does not outweigh any potential benefits. Again, some people will feel cheated that they have worked for a large part of their lives and think that it is their 'right' to have retirement at a certain age with a pension. Individual differences are very clear here.

Although personality differences will always exist with different people having different needs and opinions one thing is for certain and that is that there is still a need for a change in the unequal conditions that still exist for women at work.

9.2.2 The psychological contract

Another area that has changed due to the changing nature of work is what is known as the psychological contract (e.g. Argyris 1960; Levinson et al., 1962; Schein 1978; Herriot and Pemberton 1995; Guest and Conway 2002). The legal contract of employment is explicit and formal and makes clear the agreement between the employer and the employee. However, the psychological contract, although not explicit either in words or writing, still exists. The old deal was loyalty in exchange for security and could be described as more of a relationship whereby trust existed between the two parties. With the new ways of working there exists a new psychological contract. The new deal is now transactional in nature rather than relational and so it needs to be thought about it in a very different way. Both parties give each other something specifically in exchange for something. Herriot and Pemberton (1995) also state that neither the employee nor the employer will go beyond the psychological contract; both sides check that the terms are fulfilled, any changes to the psychological contract are negotiated, and that commitment is calculated.

Broken promises or violations to the psychological contract have caused many people, according to Herriot and Pemberton (1995), to respond either by getting out (to leave and find another job), getting safe (to keep one's head down), or getting even (to get revenge). In order to 'get even' cases have been reported, for example, whereby an employee has left and taken all passwords with him/her, thereby locking important databases.

Broken psychological contracts could be another reason for the increase in 'portfolio workers', whereby there are no psychological contracts to contend with and a self-employed status becomes desirable.

Rousseau (1995) blurred the distinction between the psychological contract and the economic contract and Guest et al. (1996) also put forward a more comprehensive model. However, this has been dealt with in other chapters so it is the intention here only to remind the reader rather than to give a detailed explanation. So, the psychological contract does seem to prove useful in understanding perhaps why people have reacted the way they have in terms of their careers. These days employees do not stay as long in a job as they did in the past and for a lot of people there is a lot of calculation going on about what they can gain from a particular position (for example training, experience, etc.). When whatever it was that they wanted has

Pause for thought
The changing nature of work has caused huge changes in the way people work nowadays. Discuss in groups whether you believe there really have been great shifts in the way people work and think of examples where these changes have occurred.

been fulfilled they are more than ready to move on in their careers without thinking of the loyalty issues that the old psychological contract used to induce in people, i.e. their loyalty is to themselves now and not the organization.

Activity The psychological contract

Consider the followng questions to help you think about how the psychological contract may or may not have changed.

- Think about a few of the people you know who have full or part-time jobs and also yourself if you are working. Think about each person in turn and consider if they appear to work in a way that seems in keeping with the old or the new psychological contract, as described above.
- Are there differences in the kind of organization that they work for?
- Is there a vast difference in their ages?
- Does the way they work seem to fit with what you might think of as their 'personality'?

Although the psychological contract has been criticized by some as being overcomplicated and overlapping with organizational commitment and job satisfaction, Guest (1998) maintains that is still a useful concept.

9.2.3 Boundaryless careers

Along with changes to the psychological contract there have also been many changes in the way that people are employed. These days there are many more workers on part-time and fixed-term contracts than there used to be before the 1980s and this in turn has perhaps helped to lead to the notion of a 'boundaryless career' whereby people are no longer bounded or organizationally constrained (Arthur 1994; Arthur et al. 1999). Many of the traditional boundaries appear to be disappearing in any case, which further assists with the ability to be able to work in this way.

This might have advantages for some and disadvantages for others. This way of working brings with it a sense of freedom and empowerment for some people but for others it can be threatening and even confusing. Some writers, e.g. Hirsch and Shanley (1996), believe that those people who already have good jobs will do better and those with lower-paid jobs will become worse off making the divide between the two even greater.

Increasingly, too, people need a 'portfolio' of skills and activities and careers which might include some voluntary work, some study work, and some training (Handy 1989).

Case illustration
Loyalty

Tom had been with his current organization in the Human Resources Department for almost eighteen months. During that time he had received specific job-role training which had lasted for several months. He had also been sent on various short one- and two-day workshops in order to help improve his counselling skills in the workplace. He was now at the point where no more training was planned, he did not seem due for any more salary increases, and therefore he knew that it was time for him to move on. He had taken all he could from the situation and the next promotion he could see would be a number of years away. Before the psychological contract changed it was more of a relational contract and under those circumstances Tom would have most probably felt some kind of loyalty to his organization, after all they had spent quite a lot of money on his training so far. So as things stood he was ready to move on, adding to the statistics that people don't stay in jobs for as long these days as they used to.

KEY LEARNING POINTS

- Careers have changed because of the downsizing, de-layering, and re-engineering of organizations.
- The psychological contract has changed from a relational contract to a transactional contract.
- Many people increasingly work in a boundaryless way, moving between departments and organizations.
- Many people have a portfolio of skills.

9.3 Career theories

There are many ways to approach looking at people's careers and over the decades numerous theories have been presented in attempts to analyse the differences between people and their choices. The different theories that have been proposed throughout the decades can be considered as being either organizational models or individual models of career development and they can also be put into different categories such as: developmental, personality, and self-concept approaches, transitions, and vocational choice. However, changes in the ways of working have meant that careers are much more difficult than they once were to describe and to predict. This chapter will now take a more detailed look at some of the most influential of these ways of looking at career development, including a consideration of whether or not these theories might fit with the new ways of working.

9.3.1 Super (1953, 1957, 1980, 1985, 1990): lifespan approach

Donald Super applied ideas from developmental and humanistic psychology to career management. This was largely in response to the then dominant approach of differential psychology whereby people were measured on ability, personality, and interests and subsequently matched to an occupation.

Super's **lifespan approach** (1957) was an influential theory for many years with four age-linked stages of development linked to employment. These are: exploration, establishment, maintenance, and disengagement. See Table 9.1 for an explanation of these stages.

Super's stages might be considered as being altogether very pessimistic (e.g. Arnold et al. 2005; Doyle 2003). For example Super's emphasis on 'hanging on' in middle age could be viewed alternatively as a time for 'growth', which of course would be a much more positive way of viewing this stage.

However, Super acknowledged that his stages might not represent the careers of everyone and the acknowledgement of someone entering a career later in life, together with the changing nature of work, did lead Super to adapt his theory to become more flexible. In later years he included six roles which are better viewed as a framework for not only a person's career but their life too. The six roles that Super identified and that people perform in Western societies

Table 9.1. Super's (1957) lifespan approach

Stages	Ages	
Exploration	15–24	A search for occupations that fit with the increasing awareness of the self-concept
Establishment	25–44	Success is strived for in the chosen occupation
Maintenance	45–65	With enforced competition from younger people and technology people will strive to maintain their position
Disengagement	65+	People gradually become observers rather than participants as they distance themselves from the world of work

Source: Adapted from Super (1957).

are: homemaker, worker, citizen, leisurite, student, and child. These roles represent differing priorities for many people and at different times in their lives. However, it must be noted that within these different roles people still go through the four stages, i.e. exploration, establishment, maintenance, and disengagement.

There is a questionnaire associated with this approach, the Adult Concerns Inventory (ACCI) (Super et al. 1985). It has been criticized because the outcome of it is probably obvious to most people. However, a better use of this questionnaire might be to conduct a survey in an organization, using the questionnaire, to discover employee career concerns (Arnold 1997).

 Activity **Super's stages**

- Do you think that Super's stages are pessimistic?
- Do you think that Super's theory can fit in with today's changed working conditions?
- Do you think there is still some value in his theory or do you think it is of no use any longer?

9.3.2 Erikson (1968): life stages and development

Erik Erikson came from the psychoanalytic school of psychology and proposed what might be considered a slightly more optimistic way of viewing stage theories of career development when compared to Super's ideas. The main reason why Erikson's theory can be viewed as being more optimistic is because all of adult life can be considered as a period for growth and creative striving unlike the 'hanging on' written about by Super. This idea would seem to fit well with the changing nature of work whereby we all need to constantly update our skills and to focus on our professional development plans. In addition and to his credit, Erikson's views also do not appear gender biased, unlike much other research.

Erikson's stages are: establishment, commitment, accomplishment of something of lasting value, and feeling satisfied with previous choices made. See Table 9.2 for an explanation of these stages.

Although the positive nature of Erikson's theory especially when compared to Super's has been emphasized here, it must still be borne in mind that in each of Erikson's stages there can either be a positive or a negative outcome. This will depend on the success or failure of the particular developmental task for the stage concerned.

With the changing nature of work and the emphasis of much of this research being on white middle-class men many writers feel that stage theories of career development are of little use today. However, of course there are still some workers that will follow the old patterns of working, so perhaps they shouldn't be totally 'written off' and in any case it would appear that Erikson's views can be reasonably adapted to reflect some of these changes that are

Table 9.2. Erikson's (1968) life stages and development approach

Ages	Stages
Adolescence and early adulthood	Establishing a sense of identity is strived for.
Early adulthood onwards to about 35	Intimacy and commitment to another person or to an important cause is sought for.
From about 35 onwards to about 65	The accomplishment of something of lasting value is looked for such as bringing up a family or contributing to society.
65 plus	To feel satisfied with life and with the previous choices made.

Source: Adapted from Erikson (1968).

Table 9.3. Levinson et al.'s (1978) age-linked phases in adult life

Stage	Age
Early adulthood	15−40
Early adult *transition*	20
Entering the adult world	20−25
Transition	30
Settling down	35
Midlife transition	40
Middle adulthood	40−60
Entering middle adulthood	40−45
Transition	50
Culmination of middle adulthood	55
Late adult transition	60
Late adulthood	65+
Entering late adulthood	65−70

Source: Adapted from Levinson et al. (1978).

constantly referred to. Of course there are other ways to look at careers and this chapter will now consider one of these by looking at the ways that people's careers might develop with life's transitions.

9.3.3 Levinson et al. (1978): age-linked phases in adult life

It is said that Levinson has been the most influential writer in looking at career development in a transitional way. According to this theory there are major transitions at about ages 30, 40, 50, and 60 (see Table 9.3).

Although Levinson's research has been influential his, albeit in-depth, studies were only carried out on forty American-born men between the ages of 35 and 40 and analyses of published biographies. This should be strongly considered when analysing this theory. Clearly, the sample size is inadequate and culturally and gender biased. Another criticism is that because he states specific ages in his theory it makes it relatively easy to find many examples that do not fit with this. Nonetheless most writers feel that his conclusions were 'interesting' (e.g. Arnold et al. 2005).

Other researchers have also looked at career development through the transitions model and in particular Nicholson related this idea to work role transitions.

9.3.4 Nicholson (1990): work role transitions, transition cycle model

It has been known for some time that people are changing jobs more frequently (Nicholson and West 1988; Rice 2000). Therefore it might be considered that a transition cycle model of job change could be more useful than theories of adult development. Nicholson proposed four stages of transition that people will experience when taking on a new job role. These stages are: preparation, encounter, adjustment, and stabilization. It can be said that this model attempts to look at the processes that are involved (see Table 9.4).

The first stage of preparation can be helped along by using a realistic job preview (RJP). Of course, both the employer and the employee need to present themselves in the best light possible but in order to avoid later disappointment with expectations not being met and consequently high turnover of staff it would seem to make sense to utilize RJPs. However, these are not always as easy to accomplish as one might think. In recent times there have been increasing amounts of research carried out on RJPs (e.g. Wanous 1989; Wanous et al. 1992).

The next stage of encounter will probably be different for different people as some are naturally more able to gather information more quickly than others. However, some organizations appoint mentors to help the new employee (Kram 1985).

Pause for thought
Have you, or someone you know, ever had a job interview, been successfully selected for the role, and accepted it, but later on when you started the job found out that it was not at all how you expected it to be? If so, how do you think this could have been avoided?

Table 9.4. Nicholson's (1990) work role transitions cycle model

Successful negotiation of one stage influences the outcomes of the next	
Preparation	This begins before the person starts the job and involves information exchange and negotiation. Both sides will present themselves well and this may lead to unrealistic expectations.
Encounter	Gathering information about the new job either explicitly or implicitly
Adjustment	The employee adjusts and works out how they are going to perform their job in the medium to long term
Stabilization	When the person is firmly established in the role

Source: Adapted from Nicholson (1990).

The third stage of adjustment occurs when the employee understands the work environment and they then consider how they are going to go about actually doing their job in the medium to long term. In accordance with the other theories and models that have been looked at so far the previous stages that the individual has already gone through in Nicholson's stages will affect the stage they are currently going through. There are three approaches that a person might adopt in the adjustment stage (Schein 1971). The first is that of custodianship, whereby the person simply accepts the role as given and does not seek to make changes. The second is that of content innovation, whereby the person's own ways of carrying out the job will be sought but the role requirements will remain the same, just a unique or changed way of carrying out some of the tasks. Lastly, the role innovation approach is where the employee redefines not only the methods or the way they carry out the job but the actual goals of the job too.

The final stage of stabilization is rather paradoxical according to Nicholson, who states that work psychology is often based on this stage, but with the fast paced changing of jobs this does not allow very long for the establishment of the stabilization stage for many people. For people who change their jobs frequently their careers could be considered as a sequence of constant transitions. However, for those who do stay in their jobs there is the likelihood of a career plateau, where there is little opportunity for advancement in the organization (Feldman and Weitz 1988). With the changing nature of work, which has led to flatter organizations, the career plateau has increased. Of course for some people this may not be seen as a disadvantage as not everyone wants more responsibility or challenges in their working lives (Howard and Bray 1988).

It would seem that Nicholson's work transitions model does seem to be able to be interpreted more favourably perhaps than some previous approaches to models and theories of careers that have been looked at so far, within the context of the changing nature of work. However, yet another way of looking at people's careers is rather than looking at the process of transitions to look instead at the personality of the person or the self-concept. So there is less concentration on stages and more on the content of careers.

9.3.5 Schein (1985a, 1985b, 1993): career anchors

Once such theory that looks at people's personalities in order to help think about careers is that of **career anchors** and these anchors are said to be areas of the self-concept that would be difficult to give up. They involve needs, motives, abilities, and values and are therefore fundamental aspects of the person. The idea is that someone has to pick one

Table 9.5. Schein's (1993) career anchors

General managerial competence	People with this career anchor want to manage others. They prefer not to be technical experts but rather to be generalists. Important areas for them are leadership, advancement, responsibility, and pay.
Technical/functional competence	Technical expertise and getting the job done well are important for those with this career anchor. Developing and maintaining their expertise is crucial for them.
Security/stability	These people are mainly concerned with a predictable working environment. Job security, familiar routines, and staying in one location are all important for them.
Autonomy/independence	For people with this career anchor freedom to work in the way that they want to is paramount here. They would not want to work in a place with strict rules, procedures, or restrictions.
Entrepreneurial creativity	This anchor is about people who want to be productive and create goods or services or their own businesses.
Pure challenge	People with this anchor are highly competitive. Winning against all the odds is highly important to them.
Service/dedication to a cause	People with the anchor feel that their work must reflect their values. They like to work in an organisation that reflects their social, political or religious beliefs.
Lifestyle integration	This anchor is all about work–life balance. These people do not wish one aspect of their lives to dominate over the other.

Source: Adapted from Schein (1993).

career anchor only, which reflects that part of themselves that they could not give up even if circumstances were severely against them continuing. The different career anchors are: general managerial competence, security/stability, autonomy/independence, entrepreneurial creativity, pure challenge, service/dedication to a cause, and lifestyle integration (Table 9.5).

Career anchors were derived from research that Schein carried out on 44 managerial graduates from an elite management school in the USA and career history interviews with several hundred people in different stages of their careers. From this a questionnaire was also developed, the Career Orientations Inventory (COI).

It is unknown whether career anchors remain the same or change. It also seems rather difficult to prove or disprove this especially when Schein claims that if after five to ten years of work experience career anchors appear to change then it is activation of something that was there already!

Schein points out that people with different anchors need to be managed differently as, for example, they will be motivated by different things such as rewards. As Arnold (1997) points out the COI could be best used in a similar way to Super's questionnaire, the CCI, by conducting a staff survey to find out what people want as individuals. This is of course in keeping with the changing times.

Although this theory has some intuitive appeal the concepts of the anchors and likewise their measurement have not been researched very extensively. In addition some writers feel that some people will find it very difficult to pick one anchor only. This problem of being able to pick only one category, however, is overcome by the following model devised by Holland, as some of the types are connected to each other.

Pause for thought

Read Schein's *Career Anchors* carefully and try to decide which one applies to you. You can only choose one. Did you have difficulty in choosing only one?

Table 9.6. Holland's six vocational psychology types

Realistic	Strengths lie in physical abilities such as strength and coordination. This type is not keen on socializing. Likely jobs might include: farmer, plumber, and electrician.
Investigative	Interests will be in concepts and logic using analytical introspective skills. Likely jobs might include: biologist, mathematician, and engineer.
Artistic	Creative and imaginative tendencies will need to be expressed for this type. Likely jobs might include: actor, film/stage director, writer, and interior designer.
Social	These people are friendly, warm, and empathic. Close interaction with others is indicated in their job choices which might include: teacher, counsellor, and religious worker.
Conventional	This type likes regulations, rules, and structure and is not very imaginative. They are also conforming and rather inflexible. Likely jobs might include: book keeper, tax expert, and accountant.

Source: Adapted from Holland (1973).

9.3.6 Holland (1973, 1997): Career choice, six vocational personality types

John Holland's work has been based in the USA, where it is still well recognized, unlike the UK or Europe. Holland's theory was derived from his work as a Careers Consultant in the USA in the 1960s, which gave him the opportunity to carry out much research on career decision making and to devise several tests.

Throughout the years Holland has devised six pure types of vocational personality. They are: realistic, investigative, artistic, social, enterprising, and conventional. The most recent version of Holland's work was published in 1997. It might be argued that compared to other theories it is a focused and pragmatic approach to career choice. In addition these six vocational personality types (see Table 9.6) appear to have their links to personality theory from mainstream psychology thereby giving it a more robust research base from which to draw from and from which gives additional reliability and validity.

Holland put forward the notion that vocational personality types and occupational environments can be categorized together. In addition he does not describe people as being 'pure' types but rather having strong preferences to some types rather than others and whereby each type is represented on a hexagon with adjacent types being more similar than those which are

Figure 9.1. Holland's hexagonal diagram of the relationship between the different vocational personality types

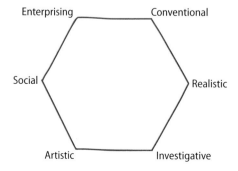

represented on opposite corners (Figure 9.1). People are described by the three types they most closely relate to. Clearly since people have an influence on the culture and the climate in the organization that they work in, some people will fit in with certain organizations more than others.

Holland describes occupations by a three-letter code. For example a tax accountant is described as an ECS (enterprising, conventional, and social), a playwright as an ASE (artistic, social, and enterprising), and a medical secretary as a CES (conventional, enterprising, and social).

Something that some of the older theories seem to have in common is that the emphasis is placed on initial career decision making with little attention placed on the outcomes of the choices made. Furthermore, if decisions in mid-career were considered instead then 'sequences of attitudes, feelings and behaviours' could be analysed as to how one job or career affects the next by way of preparation and encounter (Kidd 1998).

In addition, it would seem that most of the models that have been considered do seem somewhat 'static, narrow in focus and stereotypical' (Doyle 2003). However, some would seem to be more useful than others and it is suggested here that the work-transitions model is particularly relevant and helpful given today's work climate. The work-transitions model certainly does take account of a more dynamic way of looking at careers which includes the interdependence of the stages and recognition of emotional states and consequent emotional reactions (Kidd 1998). Change can be incorporated more easily and this is no doubt partly why the **work-role transitions** model is popular.

Also, Holland's Six Vocational Psychology Types being based on psychological personality theory do offer not only a robust foundation on which to build, but an intuitively relevant and useful theory.

KEY LEARNING POINTS

- Career development can be categorized as coming from an organizational or individual approach.
- Career theories can be further categorized as: life stages approaches, personality and self-concept approaches, transitions and vocational choice approaches.
- The work-role transitions model would seem to fit in with the changing nature of work.

Activity Career theories

Look again at all the career theories discussed here and either discuss or reflect on which model seems intuitively the most appealing to you.

- Does your 'favourite' model take account of the changing nature of work?
- Overall do you feel that the models of career theory and development are useful or not?

9.4 Career management

Despite the debatable usefulness of the models and approaches in looking at people's careers one thing is certain and that is the need for everyone these days to manage their own careers. Some organizations will help the employee to a greater extent than others. However, whether there is or is not help available it is clearly in each individual's own interests to formulate some kind of self-development through career planning and career development throughout their entire working lives. Before some of the interventions that are available are considered it should first be noted that on the whole most of the interventions utilized are directed more towards the favour of the organization. It would clearly seem to make sense for the organization to offer some kind of career development for the employee because otherwise a worker might be self-developing in an area that is not relevant to the nature of the business or to the company that they work in.

9.4.1 Career counselling

Like all counsellors the career counsellor needs to make the client feel supported through providing time, attention, being listened to, and of course ensuring complete confidentiality. Specifically career counselling can be seen as 'a process which enables people to recognise and utilise their resources to make career-related decisions and manage career-related problems' (Nathan and Hill 1992). Career counselling is about empowering people to become independent decision makers and to take charge of their own careers. A career counsellor can be thought of as being more of a facilitator than an expert. After all it is the client who is seen as the expert and they will need to deal with their own problems; they just need to be asked the right questions by the counsellor to organize their thoughts so they can see things more clearly and can come up with their own solutions.

Career counselling may overlap with other forms of help offered to people in assisting with their career management, which may vary from careers or vocational guidance to personal counselling. Careers guidance can be thought of as helping people to make choices but is probably not quite as directive as the term implies. Guidance, really, is an umbrella term which quite confusingly might also include activities such as counselling! Personal counselling may have a strong overlap with career counselling, especially if the presenting problem is to do with work, for example, stress in the workplace, redundancy, or retirement, etc. Likewise, counselling at work, offered by employers, sometimes through an Employee Assistance Programme (EAP), may or may not include work-related problems. As can be seen there is considerable overlap between these variously named forms of help offered to the individual.

Career counselling invariably goes through three stages: contracting, enabling clients' understanding, and finally action and endings. The first stage of contracting is all about building rapport and exploring if the client is ready for career counselling and referring on if necessary. The second stage is whereby the counsellor will facilitate the client to explore their feelings, their beliefs, their concerns. This is also where different counsellors will use different styles, for example some will make more use of psychometric instruments than others. Finally support needs to be given to help develop the client's action plan, to aid any fear of change, to maintain momentum, and to identify other sources of support. Endings need to evaluate if further support is needed or if the counselling can come to an end. Four or five sessions in total are usually adequate for most people.

The way counsellors will help to empower their clients through the second stage can be through various methods and techniques which will inevitably depend on the style of the particular counsellor. Homework assignments between meetings may be chosen in order to help to keep continuity between sessions, to help clients to explore during their own time so they can achieve greater depth than might be possible in a limited timed session. This also assists the client to realize that changes that are made are a process that occurs over time and of course helps to empower the client.

Psychometric tests and questionnaires might be another tool that a career counsellor could choose to utilize. There are several potential benefits in using them. One advantage is the way in which they can promote an appropriate framework for conversation rather than just asking a client an open-ended question about some aspect of their character. The fact that the client has been the judge also helps in empowerment. The use of tests may also help the client to see themselves more clearly, gaining new insights even, eventually coming to accept, perhaps through more self-reflection, aspects of themselves that previously they may have been unaware of. Again, this helps with confidence at knowing the self and therefore empowerment. Knowing the self may also help with longer-term planning and fewer panic reactions in feeling that something (even if unsuitable) must be chosen.

Questionnaires and psychometric tests that are used are usually classed as being either 'ability' or 'personality' in their design. There are many, many tests out there in the market place. Information on reputable tests and registered test users are available through the British Psychological Society. Of course there can be disadvantages to using tests as well. Some of these might be that the client does not understand some of the questions properly, over-reliance on their use, if they are utilized as the main source of information (even test writers advise against this, though), and the promotion of jargon in interpreting them whereby the client does not fully understand what they are being told.

In addition a career counsellor needs to have some basic general knowledge about actual careers and the routes to pursue them such as types of training and education. This is inevitable in order to help with the action plan. However, because there are such vast lists of different careers and options it would be impossible to have extensive knowledge of each, but a good career counsellor does need to know when to refer on to a specialist in a given field as well as being a generalist.

However there are many different forms of career management and career counselling is only one of them. This section will now go on to look at some of the other techniques used.

Career planning workshops

The employee is offered assistance through mutual discussion and feedback from others. Information that may be available may also be organization specific, i.e. through their policies. Some organizations will offer psychometric testing opportunities as well.

Mentoring

Another career management intervention is that of mentoring and this is when an employee is attached to a more senior member of the organization and the opportunity to learn, to get advice, to perhaps even be protected by the senior member of staff is possible. This also appears to be an effective way of socializing new individuals into the organization and to allow them to absorb necessary information. Mentoring appears to be a win-win situation not only for the employee being mentored but also for the employee acting as a mentor. This might be achieved through offering some kind of motivational aspect to the job of the more experienced worker and better motivated workers in turn would also benefit the organization.

However, not enough research has been carried out yet on mentoring to be able to say that people who have been mentored have better career prospects or benefits. Research so far has found that sometimes there does not seem to be any significant benefits to any of the three parties involved (e.g. Arnold and Johnson 1997). Other research (although rare) has suggested that mentoring can even cause harm if the mentor expects too much or conversely could stifle or restrict development (Scandura 1998).

Coaching

The ever growing and popular area of coaching and in particular here, career coaching, is similar to mentoring but a coach will offer less advice than a mentor and instead will guide the client towards finding their own solutions by the use of appropriate questioning. This helps the client to 'own' the agreed plan of action, which in turn enables the client to feel more motivated to complete the plan, with the coach being available to oversee progress and to give further encouragement as and when necessary. The career coach, like general life coaches and business coaches, has a variety of tools, models, and techniques to choose from.

As coaching has grown enormously over the last fifteen years and has become ever more popular amongst managers in organizations, whether in a performance coaching role, career coaching, or even in executive coaching, it is more important than ever to consider research on its effectiveness. However, despite the ever growing popularity of coaching, most evidence regarding its effectiveness seems to cite case studies with few longitudinal studies (Kampa-Kokesch and Anderson 2001). In addition Kemp (2008) states that the emphasis of research carried out so far has been on the use of various coaching methods, with a severe lack of attention to the actual relationship formed between coach and client. He also believes that we must look at and explore 'the personality, psychodynamic and cognitive-behavioural constructs unique to the coach herself' and whether this helps or hinders the coaching relationship.

A significant observation made by Arnold et al. (2005) is that by the use of mentoring schemes and coaching there is an emphasis on a 'more performance-focused approach', thereby enhancing the short-term work of the employee rather than the long-term work. This would seem to be to the organization's benefit as long-term-wise the employee may not still be in the same organization.

Personal development planning

Another career management intervention is that of personal development planning (PDP). A PDP aims to develop in the individual the ability to reflect on learning and achievement which in turn then helps in planning for one's own educational and career development within a given time frame. With the changing nature of work it would seem to make sense for everyone to develop their own PDP.

....

 ### Activity SWOT analysis

Carry out a SWOT analysis on yourself (look at your strengths, weaknesses, opportunities, and threats).

When you have finished your SWOT analysis, taking account of your weaknesses, begin to write a personal development plan (PDP) on how you could improve on this area, making sure that you take account of any threats you may have identified previously.

● Is it possible to use your strengths to help with your weaknesses?

● Is it possible to build up your strengths even further?

....

9.4.2 Emotion at work and career management

Several writers have argued for a greater emphasis to be placed on the role of **emotion in career management** (e.g. Kidd 1998). They feel that emotional experiences and expression in career development have a powerful role to play and in order to elaborate further on career management they feel that cognitions, affect, and behaviour should all be examined. In recent years more attention has indeed been paid to emotion in careers and this is certainly reflected in certain industries, e.g. the service industry, whereby employees are expected to display certain emotions while interacting with clients and customers. The popularity of emotional intelligence (Goleman 1998; Salovey and Mayer 1990) has also assisted in the increased interest in emotion in careers.

The three main aspects of emotion that affect people and their careers are: the actual experience of emotion, such as happiness or anger; the expression of that emotion; and the management of the emotion itself (Briner and Totteredell 2002). So, in relation to career development it is necessary to know more about the actual emotions that are experienced, especially in relation to specific events, and the knock-on effect this will have for future work behaviour. It is also necessary to know more about the expression of emotion which affects career development and may be looked at from a relational perspective, i.e. by looking at social interactions at work; by considering a prescriptive viewpoint partly dependent on the negotiation and renegotiation of the psychological contract (Herriot and Pemberton 1995); and also a consideration of the 'display rules' and 'feeling rules' (Ashford and Humphrey 1993) which are likely to constrain emotions expressed in organizations (Kidd 2004).

The work-role transitions model does take account of emotion in careers and therefore does seem to offer more than most other theories in being able to account for career theory in light of the changing nature of work. However, more research needs to be carried out on this idea especially in regard to positive emotions.

9.4.3 Performance appraisal and career management

Assessing and developing performance and potential and career management have all become 'inextricably linked together' (Doyle 2003). With the changing nature of work, organizations (both private and public sector) have progressed from just assessing an employee's performance at the annual appraisal and moved towards the realization that assessing career development as well is a far superior approach. Measuring performance alone is seen as being rather insufficient now.

Therefore the annual appraisal will be a good opportunity for many employees to enhance their opportunities in the advancement of their career management by investigating the possibilities with their appraiser as to what might be on offer. However, the employee does need to feel that the person carrying out their appraisal is trustworthy in order to confide in them and to feel that they can provide some impartial support to them and their career.

···

 Activity **Performance appraisal**

Have you or anyone you know ever had a performance appraisal? If so, were you/they satisfied with the outcome? Did you/they feel it was fair? Did you feel that it helped your/their career development or did it feel only like an assessment?

···

9.5 Gender and careers

The past few decades has seen an ever increasing number of women entering the workplace. Globally this has meant an extra 200 million women workers (or 18.4 per cent more) over the last ten years (ILO 2008). Some of the reasons for this are the expansion of the service industries, along with increased part-time working. Others reasons worth noting are changes in life expectancy, economic circumstances, and social responsibilities (Millar 1992). The changing nature of the family might also be considered another reason why more women are entering the workplace. However despite these increases global unemployment rates for men are 5.7 per cent compared to women at 6.4 per cent, leaving women with a higher likelihood of being unemployed.

Additionally and most importantly, even with record numbers of women entering the workplace they are still failing to reach as many senior positions as that of men. On average women at managerial levels range only from 20 to 40 per cent, in over 60 countries (Global Employment Trends for Women, 2008 ILO), leaving the remainder of many women in lower paid, often part-time work. In addition, Sealy et al. (2007) report that while women make up only 11 per cent of directorships in the FTSE100, this is the highest level since they started monitoring in 1999.

Furthermore, despite these facts and figures demonstrating real increases of women in the workplace it still remains a fact that most research on careers has focused on white middle-class males. Women are undeniably at a disadvantage compared to men, leaving them with many obstacles that they still have to overcome. Some of the most important of these issues will now be discussed followed by a final (hopefully not too pessimistic) conclusion on gender and careers.

KEY LEARNING POINTS

- There are more women than ever entering the workplace.
- Although there are record numbers of women in the workplace they do not reach as many senior positions as men.
- To date research has focused on white middle-class men.

9.5.1 Socialization of girls and boys

Clearly there are an incredible different number of cultures, social structures, and laws in different countries. Part of these differences in culture and social structures in many different societies of the world are in their strong beliefs and existing attitudes regarding the value, the capabilities, and the potential between girls and boys. Therefore gender stereotyping not only occurs at a young age in families but also takes place at school by teachers and peers and is reinforced by the media. These responsibilities and gender roles give males more power and more control than females.

Therefore it is clear to see how socialization can easily affect a young child's attitude towards what kind of career she or he might like to pursue. In addition it was questioned at the Institute of Career Guidance Annual Conference (2005) whether careers advisers themselves actually challenge gender stereotyping adequately. For women, especially, this has meant that, with other factors that will be discussed below, many will pursue secondary roles in the workplace. Finally this is reinforced by there being very few high-profile women, compared to men, with 'top jobs' that they can relate to.

9.5.2 Prejudice and discrimination (despite legislation)

Following on from socialization issues in the home, education, and its subsequent consequences in careers advice it can be seen that these prejudiced attitudes and beliefs formed in early life clearly continue to dominate the workplace. Some writers state that there are still some people who believe that a woman's place is in the home and that they do not make as good managers or leaders as men. This attitude is not only held by some men but surprisingly also by some women too. There have been numerous accounts of unfair promotion biased towards men. This can have a detrimental affect in the workplace not only to women but also to men. This is because men observing this type of bias describe their work setting as less favourable and are more likely to quit because they see the organization as less committed to equality and fairness (Burke 1995).

Perhaps unsurprisingly then gender socialization and its implications has wide-ranging effects in the workplace. In the past it was thought that women's attitudes and behaviour towards themselves and therefore consequently in the roles that some of them occupied in the workplace were because of a fear of responsibility and leadership positions (e.g. Horner 1970). However, since the 1970s it has been continually found that there are no differences in the fear of success syndrome and some have even found women to be more ambitious than men (Nicholson and West 1988; Lahtinen and Wilson 1994). Indeed, most women report working not just for necessity, or for some financial independence, but also for social reasons and self-esteem. This is also found for part-time workers.

However, on the negative side, many women's attitude towards themselves can be one of guilt. By going out to work, some mothers feel that they are perhaps not providing adequate care for their children and have a role conflict.

Although legislation has helped a great deal to eliminate direct discrimination against women in the workplace, unfortunately indirect discrimination often still exists. An example of indirect discrimination could be when a job is advertised that has a bias against some groups of candidates. For example, inflexible working hours with specific requirements to travel, which would clearly make it difficult for women with young children.

More women than men are affected by the pressures of childcare and running the home. Many seem to have acquired a dual role of combining paid work with unpaid domestic work. Even in dual career couples the domestic chores still seem to fall largely to the women. In addition many women will disrupt their careers at some point in order to raise children. For many this will mean lost promotional opportunities and seems generally to set women back in their careers.

Training is another area that women are treated less fairly in than men. Generally women receive less training than men in the workplace (Davidson 1996).

Unequal pay is another example of stark differences in the workplace between men and women, even in some organizations when carrying out the same role. Legislation exists and this is clearly illegal; however, it still exists. Apart from the legal issues it is inherently unfair and affects people's lives greatly. This can be to the extent of how and even where an individual might live, healthcare provision, the education of their children, their pension, etc. By not rewarding both men and women fairly employers are undermining the full potential of some of their workers. In addition, married men with working wives will also be affected by unequal pay. In a study (Burke 2003) of 324 female psychologists and 134 male psychologists it was found that there were more women at lower organizational levels than men.

Glass ceiling

The glass ceiling is used to refer to the invisible barrier that women face as they climb up the hierarchy. This glass ceiling seems to remain very strong as women still find it more difficult than men to obtain jobs higher up the corporate ladder than they do lower down.

Although there are now more women managers than there were ten years ago it has recently been claimed by some researchers and reported in the business section of *The Times* (London) that women have 'wreaked havoc' in the boardroom and consequently on performance and share prices (Ryan and Haslam 2006). However, Ryan and Haslam have carried out further research into this area and have found the opposite to be true. Women were not associated with declining company performance and were even associated with marked increases in share prices.

The reason for the differences in whether women have or have not made poor leaders and the outcomes of management styles is because the previous research failed to take into account the fact that where women were actually associated with falling share prices the companies involved were having problems long before appointing the women to their new roles. Where there were more stable past performances in the companies concerned it was more likely that a man had been appointed to the boards of these companies (Ryan and Haslam 2006). From this the authors go on to suggest that women, more than men, are put on a '**glass cliff**' whereby positions of leadership are associated with increased failure risks.

KEY LEARNING POINTS

- Socialization responsibilities give males more power and control than females.
- Some prejudiced beliefs are still prevalent in the workplace over women's work.
- Even in dual career couples domestic chores still fall largely to the women.
- Despite the difficulties some recent studies have found women to be even more ambitious than men.

Although overall it still seems that women have a long way to go before they catch up with men there have been some undeniable and definite improvements over the last few decades. However in order for this trend to continue society's views on sex-stereotyping (which therefore includes parents, educational establishments, the media, and organizations) need to change. Everybody needs to challenge and change some currently held views on women's and men's work.

Despite its unfairness we have seen that the main domestic chores and childcare still seem to fall to women rather than to men. Therefore, more organizations could improve their practices and offer family-friendly flexible employment packages to both women and men. Clearly some have made bigger improvements in this area than others.

On a positive note, authors such as Handy believe that the de-layering of organizations, as has already been seen, will eventually lead to and weaken the glass ceiling for women. However, it should be noted that although Handy is highly regarded, not all of his predictions seem to have come true. It does seem to make intuitive sense, though, that with newer ways of working, such as the boundaryless career, women might be more suited to this style than men. This could even potentially give women some advantages over men as they are more used to multi-tasking and having to network to enhance their employment prospects.

Chapter summary

- The changing nature of work has led to major changes for people and their careers. One of these changes is in the psychological contract which is now thought of as being transactional in nature rather than relational.

- Violations to the psychological contract have led to people either getting out, getting their head down, getting safe, or getting even by dishing out some kind of revenge.

- People do not stay as long in a job as they used to; many workers are now employed on part-time, fixed-term contracts and this has helped to lead to the notion of a boundaryless career.

- Throughout the decades there have been numerous models put forward attempting to describe and analyse career theory but many writers feel that most of these theories have not stood up to the test of time and do not stand up to scrutiny within the context of the changing nature of work.

- Everyone needs to manage their careers these days and there are many different ways and choices to carry out career management.

- More emphasis needs to be put on emotion in career management generally, but the work-role transitions model does seem to be able to take account of emotion in careers.

- There are record numbers of women entering the workplace but they are still not occupying as many managerial positions as men. Gender stereotyping starts in the home at a very young age. There is still some prejudice towards women in the workplace.

- The glass ceiling has turned into a glass cliff for some women where promotion has been concerned.

- The de-layering of organizations may be a good thing for women and may eventually lead to the glass ceiling being weakened.

Assess your learning

Review questions

1 The psychological contract has changed but what has this meant for careers?

2 Why do people not stay so long in a job as they used to?

3 Which model of career theory, according to most writers, is still relevant?

4 Discuss two ways of managing your career.

5 Analyse three barriers to women in the workplace.

6 Explain the concept of the glass ceiling.

7 Why are women still not occupying as many managerial positions as men?

8 Why is there still prejudice towards women in the workplace?

Assignments

ASSIGNMENT 1: Changing nature of work

- Discuss why the changing nature of work may not have pessimistic outcomes for everyone's careers.

- Compare and contrast two models of career theory, making sure you also take into account the changing nature of work.

Talk to a few women (either who you know or who might be a friend of a friend etc.) and ask them to answer a few questions for you.

- What problems and difficulties have they experienced at work?
- Do their problems fit with psychological theory as discussed within this chapter?
- Are they optimistic or pessimistic for the future for women at work, i.e. do they generally think things will improve?

Further reading

Sugarman, L. (2001) *Life-Span Development: Theories, Concepts and Interventions* (2nd edn.). Hove: Psychology Press.
An interesting book that delves deeper into the life-span development approach.

Handy, C. (1994) *The Empty Raincoat.* London: Hutchinson.
Attempts to make some sense of the future using interesting paradoxes.

Work psychology in practice
Rosemary's career path

Rosemary had graduated from a good university with a first-class honours degree in business studies. She was the only one of her peers to do so. Not that they did badly, mainly gaining upper-second-class honours. Rosemary felt understandably proud and was extremely enthusiastic on entering the workplace, imagining that her university success was going to be replicated in the business world.

She didn't find it difficult to find her 'dream job' and was promptly recruited in an advertising agency. However, after about four years she was quite surprised to find that some of her male colleagues seemed to be getting faster and better promotions than she was being awarded. She wondered why this was happening. Rosemary was always being complimented on her work and in addition she was always being asked to help those at the top. She was always willing to stay late and help out when rush jobs came in and she got on very well with everyone. So she tried very hard to work out what the reason might be for her lack of promotion but she really wasn't sure at all why. One thing she did feel sure of at first though was that surely this couldn't be because she was a female and in any case there were laws to protect against that sort of thing. But as the years went on she became increasingly convinced that firstly she wasn't imagining these issues and it did appear that all the women in the company were lower down the scale than the men. It also seemed to Rosemary that, albeit not all, but many of the women did seem also to have better creative abilities than those who were being promoted.

To make matters worse, although of course for Rosemary it was an extremely happy and important phase of her life that had occurred whereby she had met her future husband, this was to make her future career promotion prospects even slower. Eventually, as well, a few years later she found herself on maternity leave three times in six years.

Rosemary loved being a mother but after each pregnancy she was more than eager to return to the world of work. She was ambitious and wanted a senior managerial role. However, this seemed further out of her reach than ever. She was dismayed to find on returning from one of her periods of maternity leave that a newly entered recruit, much younger than herself and male, had been recruited to be her line manager. If she felt that he had truly warranted the role then she wouldn't have felt 'hard done by', but he wasn't. She knew he wasn't and she also knew that her work and her ideas had always been on a different level and of a much higher standard to that of her new line manger.

Rosemary considered leaving but realized that her female friends were actually experiencing similar situations, although in different lines of work. She felt that if she left she would most probably be putting herself even further back in the promotion hierarchy so she decided to stay where she was. However, she made the decision that enough was enough and she was going to try to do something about it.

Questions

- Is there anything that Rosemary can do about the situation?
- If so, how should she tackle this?
- Are there any legal implications here?

Online Resource Centre

Visit the supporting online resource centre for additional material which will help you with your research, essays, and assignments, or you may find these additional resources helpful when revising for exams.
http://www.oxfordtextbooks.co.uk/orc/matthewman/

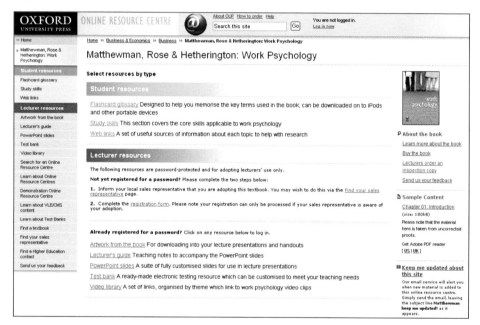

References

Argyris, C. P. (1960) *Understanding Organizational Behaviour.* Homewood, IL: Dorsey Press.

Arnold, J. (1997) Nineteen propositions concerning the nature of effective thinking for career management in a turbulent world. *British Journal of Guidance and Counseling,* 25: 447–62.

Arnold, J., and Johnson, K. (1997) Mentoring in early career. *Human Resource Management Journal,* 7: 61–70.

Arnold, J., Robertson, Burnes, B., Cooper, C., Patterson, F., Robertson, E., and Silvester, J. (2005) *Work Psychology: Understanding Human Behaviour in the Workplace* (4th edn.). Harlow: Financial Times/Prentice Hall.

Arthur, M. B. (1994) The boundaryless carrer: a new perspective for organizational inquiry. *Journal of Organizational Behaviour,* 15: 295–306.

Arthur, M. B., Inkson, K., and Pringle, J. K. (1999) *The New Careers, Individual Action and Economic Change.* London: Sage.

Ashford, B. E., and Humphrey, R. H. (1993) Emotional labor in service roles: the influence of identity. *Academy of Management Review,* 18: 88–115.

Briner, R., and Totterdell, P. (2002) The experience, expression and management of emotion at work. In P. B. Warr (ed.), *Psychology at Work* (5th edn.). London: Penguin, 229–52.

Burke, R. J. (1995) Correlates of perceived bias in a professional services firm. *International Journal of Career Management,* 7/1: 5–11.

Burke, R. J. (2003) Do gender proportions matter? *Women in Management Review,* 18/5: 267–75.

Davidson, M. J. (1996) Women and employment. In P. Warr (ed.), *Pyschology at Work* (4th edn.). London: Penguin.

Doyle, C. (2003) *Work and Organizational Psychology: An Introduction with Attitude.* Hove: Psychology Press.

Erikson, E. (1968) *Identity, Youth and Crisis.* New York: Norton.

Feldman, D. C., and Weitz, B. A. (1988) Career plateaux reconsidered. *Journal of Management*, 14: 69–80.

Global Employment Trends for Women (2004) ILO. Cited in 'Women in the Boardroom: A bird's eye view'. London: CIPD.

Goleman, D. (1998) *Working with Emotional Intelligence*. London: Bloomsbury.

Guest, D. (1998) Is the psychological contract worth taking seriously? *Journal of Organizational Behavior*, 19: 649–64.

Guest, D., and Conway, N. (2002) *Pressure at Work and the Psychological Contract*. London: CIPD.

Guest, D., Conway, N., Briner, R., and Dickman, M. (1996) *The State of the Psychological Contract in Employment*. London: IPD.

Gunz, H., Evans, M., and Jalland, R. M. (2000) Career boundaries in a boundaryless world. In M. Peiper, M. B. Arthur, R. Goffee, and T. Morris (eds.), *Career Frontier: New Concepts in Working Lives*. Oxford: Oxford University Press.

Handy, C. (1989) *The Age of Unreason*. London: Arrow.

Herriot, P., and Pemberton, C. (1995) *New Deal: The Revolution in Managerial Careers*. Chichester: Wiley.

Hirsch, P. M., and Shanley, M. (1996) The rhetoric of *boundaryless*: or, how the newly empowered managerial class bought into its own marginalisation. In Arthur and Rousseau (1996).

Holland, J. L. (1973) *Making Vocational Choice: A Theory of Careers*. Englewood Cliffs, NJ: Prentice-Hall.

Holland, J. L. (1997) *Making Vocational Choices: A Theory of Vocational Personalities and Work Environment* (3rd edn.). Odessa, FL: Psychological Assessment Resources Inc.

Horner, K. (1970) *Femininity and Successful Achievement: A Basic Inconsistency*. Monterey, CA: Brooks/Cole.

Howard, A., and Bray, D. W. (1988) *Managerial Lives in Transition*. New York: Guilford Press.

International Labour Organization (2008) Available at: http://www .ilo.org/public/english/employment/strat/global.htm. Accessed on 29 Apr. 2008.

Kampa-Kokesch, S., and Anderson, M. (2001) Executive coaching: a comprehensive review of the literature. *Consulting Psychology Journal: Practice and Research*, 53: 205–28.

Kemp, T. (2008) Self-management and the coaching relationship: exploring coaching impact beyond models and methods. *International Coaching Psychology Review*, 3: 32–42.

Kidd, J. M. (1998) Emotion: an absent presence in career theory. *Journal of Vocational Behaviour*, 52: 275–88.

Kidd, J. M. (2004) Emotion in career contexts: challenges for theory and research. *Journal of Vocational Behaviour*, 64: 441–54.

Kram, K. E. (1985) *Mentoring at Work: Developmental Relationships in Organizational Life*. Glenview, Il.: Scott Foresman.

Lahtinen, H. K., and Wilson, F. M. (1994) Women and power in organisations. *Executive Development*, 7/3: 16–23.

Levinson, D. J., Darrow, C. N., Klein, E. B., Levinson, M. H., and McKee, B. (1978) *Seasons of a Man's Life*. New York: Knopf.

Levinson, H., Price, C., Mundl, H. J., and Solley, C. M. (1962) *Men, Management and Mental Health*. Cambridge, MA: Harvard University Press.

Millar, J. (1992) *The Socio-economic Situation of Solo Women in Europe*. Women of Europe Supplements, No. 41. Brussels: European Commission.

Nathan, R., and Hill, L. (1992) *Career Counselling*. London: Sage Publications Ltd.

Nicholson, N. (1990) The transition cycle: causes, outcomes, processes and forms. In S. Fisher and C. L. Cooper (eds.), *On the Move: The Psychology of Change and Transition*. Chichester: Wiley.

Nicholson, N., and West, M. A. (1988) *Managerial Job Change: Men and Women in Transition*. Cambridge: Cambridge University Press.

Rice, M. (2000) Age of the flex exec. *Management Today*, Aug.: 47–52.

Rousseau, D. M. (1995) *Psychological Contracts in Organizations: Understanding Written and Unwritten Agreements*. London: Sage.

Ryan, M., and Haslam, A. (2006) What lies beyond the glass ceiling? *Human Resource Management International Digest*, 14: 3–5.

Salovey, P., and Mayer, J. D. (1990) Emotional intelligence. *Imagination, Cognition and Personality*, 9: 185–211.

Scandura, T. A. (1998) Dysfunctional mentoring relationships and outcomes. *Journal of Management*, 24: 449–67.

Schein, E. H. (1971) Occupational socialization in the professions: the case of the role innovator. *Journal of Psychiatric Research*, 8: 521–30.

Schein, E. H. (1978) *Career Dynamics: Matching Individual and Organizational Needs*. Reading, MA: Addison-Wesley.

Schein, E. H. (1985a) *Career Anchors: Discovering your Real Value*. London: Pfeiffer and Co.

Schein, E. H. (1985b) *Career Anchors: Trainers Manual*. San Diego, CA: University Associates.

Schein, E. H. (1993) *Career Anchors: Discovering your Real Values* (rev. edn.). London: Pfeiffer and Co.

Sealy, R., Singh, V., and Vinnicombe, S. (2007) *The Female FTSE Report 2007*. Cranfield: Cranfield School of Management.

Super, D. E. (1953) A theory of vocational development. *American Psychologist*, 8: 185–90.

Super, D. E. (1957) *The Psychology of Careers*. New York: Harper and Row.

Super, D. E. (1980) A life-span, life-space approach to career development. *Journal of Vocational Behaviour*, 13: 282–98.

Super, D. E. (1990) A life-span, life-space approach to career development. In D. Brown and L. Brooks (eds.), *Career Choice and Development* (2nd edn.). San Francisco: Jossey-Bass.

Super, D. E., Thompson, A. S., and Linderman, R. H. (1985) *The Adult Career Concerns Inventory*. Palo Alto, CA: Consulting Psychologists Press.

Wanous, J. P. (1989) Installing a realistic job preview: ten tough choices. *Personnel Psychology*, 42: 117–33.

Wanous, J. P., Poland, T. D., Premack, S. L., and Davis, K. S. (1992) The effects of met expectations on newcomer attitudes and behaviors: a review and meta-analysis. *Journal of Applied Psychology*, 77: 288–97.

Chapter 10
Organizational change and development

Natasha Mavinković Grba

Chapter objectives

As a result of reading this chapter and using the additional web-based material you should be able to:

- Differentiate between power and politics at work.
- List the basis or types of power with their application.
- Describe the distribution and use of power in organizations.
- Critically evaluate political methods commonly used at work.
- Examine modern organizations in turbulent environments that necessitate organizational change.
- Be aware of certain change models.
- Understand the underlying causes of inevitable resistance to change.
- List and evaluate regularly used **organizational development** interventions.

Work psychology in practice
Road masters

A major supermarket chain in East Europe currently employs over 200 lorry drivers. Six years ago there were 400 drivers, highly unionized and confrontational, when the company decided to de-unionize them and negotiate new and more flexible working conditions. Today's 200 drivers deliver more goods than the previous workforce, because of changes in the relationship between them and management and the introduction of flexible working that came out of consultation with the drivers.

In the past, the drivers and management struggled to communicate efficiently. Although the drivers felt proud of driving smart vehicles for a company that is widely recognized, there was also a strong feeling amongst them that they had not been really listened to nor understood by their bosses. As a result, they often sabotaged any management attempts to review and improve transport efficiency.

The management decided to actively seek out the drivers' concerns and issues, so that they could improve cooperation, increase productivity, and maintain their competitive status in the expanding EU market. In the past, they would have had to deal with the drivers' union. This time they felt they should consult the drivers directly. Change agents were called in and, following their initial assessment of the situation, recommended that the drivers should run the whole review process themselves and report their findings back to the management. This was a radical new approach for the company but the top bosses thought it was worth taking the risk. The drivers, on the other hand, thought this was a refreshing approach and that maybe this time management really wanted to know their concerns and ideas.

A project team was formed from the drivers. They attended a weekend-away workshop to set the objectives, design the process of the communication strategy, and, finally, develop the skills necessary for running focus groups. Apprehensive in the beginning, the drivers soon grew more confident and enthusiastic about the whole process and became highly committed to it. Over the next two months dozens of panel discussions were held, involving all drivers with change consultants playing supportive roles. At the final meeting, facilitated by change agents, the drivers summarized their findings, analysed all data that had been collected, and drew conclusions, which were then presented to the management team.

The outcome of the data gathering and the changes agreed by the management were positively received by the once-confrontational drivers who finally felt listened to and understood by the management. The whole process of change was seen by both the drivers and the management as a turning point in their relations. They realized that despite many years of conflict and distrust, they were essentially on the same side.

This is an example of a change process and organizational development intervention helped by a third party that ran smoothly.

Questions

- What were the main causes of the conflict between the drivers and the management team before the described intervention?
- If you were a **change agent** how would you argue for an employee-led consultation process?
- Explain how empowering the drivers helped the organizational change process in this situation.

10.1 Introduction

This chapter is concerned with organizational change and development. Modern organizations operate in highly complex and challenging environments. People within organizations respond to change in a variety of ways; this chapter looks at power and politics in the context of change in organizations. Major models of change and ways of planning and managing change are explored, including approaches to organizational development (OD).

10.2 Organizational change

Times of change in any organization are often times of suspicion, distrust, resistance, and attachment to old ways (Statt 2004). This is because attempting to change an organization means attacking the system of individual and collective defences that have been built up over time and form well known ways of doing things (Kouzes and Posner 2002). It requires major organizational skill to bring about change and respond to the demands of global markets getting all employees involved in the process and preferably also in decision making. An effective change management process may determine whether the organization will live to see tomorrow or not. An old motto that is most famously used in AA (Alcoholics Anonymous) Society meetings could be also applied to modern organizations that must have:

the *courage* to change things they can,

tolerance for the things that cannot be changed, and

the *wisdom* to know the difference between those two.

10.2.1 Types of organizational change

Sometimes change is reactive, that is, something happens that requires organizational change (Kotter 1998). For example, if the computer literacy level of job applicants falls so low that almost none of the applicants know how to use the computer program package operating in an organization, the company may decide to make changes. They may choose to make changes to the job, so that it requires less computer literacy, or to provide computer training programmes for applicants. If the company does not react to the problem and does not make some adjustments, it will not survive. Reactive changes are made in response to another change, and usually involve the introduction of different types of operational change.

Operational changes are concerned with new systems, structures, technologies, and procedures. By bringing change companies respond to today's turbulent markets, for example new competitors and new customers, threats to production, new political or legal requirements. Operational changes usually have an immediate effect on people and jobs in selected departments. However, the impact of operational change on employees can be stronger than broader organization-level or strategic change, and should be handled very carefully.

On the other hand, change can be proactive; for example, an organization may be doing well but wants to expand its business, therefore it decides to make organization-level or strategic changes (French and Bell 1999; Woodward 2007).

Strategic change is concerned with broad, long-term organizational issues. It involves OD programmes designed to change vision, mission, or corporate philosophy on matters such as growth, quality, innovation, and values. This is usually attempted by strategic goal setting for achieving competitive advantage and product and market development. Strategic change is usually not a linear process, and it is not easy. Often it is not possible to plan and implement change as a sequence of events; frequently, continual assessments and multiple adjustments have to be made (Armstrong 2006). Feigenbaum (1997) argues that strong organizations understand the increasingly knowledgeable customer and tend to focus on continuous improvement of business efficiencies.

10.2.2 Models of planned change

It is not enough for organizations to respond to change; they must try to anticipate and plan it (Miller and Monge 1985; Kotter 1998; French and Bell 1999). There are several theoretical models of planned change that are described next; they provide a useful framework for exploring and planning organizational change.

Kurt Lewin (1951) was one of the first psychologists to use the term *planned change* to describe change that is consciously embarked upon and anticipated by organizations. He also developed a change model that involves three stages:

- unfreezing the old behaviour or situation,
- moving to a new level of behaviour (change),
- refreezing the behaviour at the new level.

The unfreezing stage starts with some form of dissatisfaction or frustration generated by data that disconfirm expectations or hopes. In the context of organizational change unfreezing usually involves some kind of confrontation meeting and re-education process for the employees involved. In order for the new behaviours to be accepted and adopted, the old ones must be seen as undesirable and people that are required to change must be willing to discard the old ways of doing things (Schein 1992). Thus, unfreezing can start with pointing to declining sales figures, poor financial results, or worrying customer satisfaction surveys. These will demonstrate that things have to change in a way that everyone can understand.

In the cognitive restructuring stage, people collect evidence showing that change is desirable and possible. Cognitive restructuring occurs by taking in new information that has one or more of the following impacts: (1) semantic redefinition—learning that words can mean something different from what we had assumed; (2) cognitive broadening—learning that a given concept can be much more broadly interpreted than previously assumed; and (3) new standards of judgement or evaluation—learning that the anchors used for judgement and comparison are not absolute, and if we use a different anchor our scale of judgement shifts. The collected information further operates as a motivator. This new information that makes any or all of these processes possible comes to us by one of two fundamental mechanisms: (1) learning through *identification* with some available positive or negative role model, or (2) learning through trial and error by scanning the environment for new concepts (Schein 1987). Cognitive restructuring involves moving onto new behaviours, but also adopting new values and attitudes, to ensure that the people involved in organizational change stick to the new ways of doing things and do not lapse back into old habits after the storm has settled down.

In the refreezing stage, new behaviours are integrated within a person's attitudes and personality. In the context of organizational change, refreezing seeks to stabilize the new organizational state (new structure, new procedures, or new ways of doing things). This can be achieved by positive reinforcement for practising new ways of working including a culture of acceptance (Cummings and Huse 1989). Schein (1992) argued that new behaviour must to some degree be congruent with the rest of the behaviour and personality of the learner or it will simply set off new rounds of disconfirmation that often lead to unlearning of the very thing that one has learned. For example, the supervisory programme that teaches individual supervisors how to empower employees and then sends them back into an organization where the culture supports only autocratic supervisory behaviour, is bound to fail. Therefore, for personal refreezing to occur, it is best to avoid identification and encourage scanning so that the learner will pick solutions that fit him or her. Furthermore, for relational refreezing to occur, it is best to train the entire group that holds the norms that support old patterns of behaviour (Schein 1992).

Lewin's and Schein's change models, with their assumptions of inertia, linearity, progressive development, goal seeking, disequilibrium as motivator, and outsider intervention, are relevant when understanding the necessity to create change. This can be termed **episodic change**.

On the other hand, Weick and Quinn (1999) emphasize that when change is continuous, the problem is not one of unfreezing, the problem is one of redirecting what is already under way. In this case a different mindset is necessary. The model of **continuous change** process recognizes that change is continuous and gives top management a key role in setting the agenda for change (Moorhead and Griffin 2004).

A common presumption in the continuous change model is that change is emergent, meaning that it is the realization of a new pattern of organizing in the absence of explicit a priori intentions (Orlikowski 1996). Change is described as situated and grounded in continuing updates of work processes (Brown and Duguid 1991) and social practices (Tsoukas 1996). Continuous change could be viewed as a series of fast mini-episodes of change, in which case inertia might take the form of tendencies to normalization. Triggers to change might take the form of temporal milestones (Gersick 1994) or dissonance between beliefs and actions (Inkpen and Crossan 1995).

KEY LEARNING POINTS

- The current turbulent global environment, with frequent political, economic, social, and technological changes has a significant impact on work organizations, which constantly need to adjust in order to survive; in this sense, change is an inevitable feature of organizational life.
- Organizational change differs in its quality, nature, and focus, and there have been a number of attempts to model change in order to harness and control the process.
- Change affects and impacts upon all stakeholders of work organizations.

10.2.3 Resistance to change

It is understandable that people demonstrate resistance to the personal loss or possibility of personal loss, which is commonly believed to accompany change (Burke 1994). Bovey and Hede (2001) stress that facing change and the unknown opens up space for the projection of personal insecurity and fears. Even when the advantages are obvious, such as a move to a better office or introducing new software to help with workload, any change can be perceived as a potential threat. Equally if poorly managed, poorly communicated, and poorly understood, change processes are likely to be resisted by many.

Resistance to change may originate from an individual and/or an organization (Cherrington 1989). Here is a list of possible sources of resistance to change, that are all embedded within the individual (Bedeian and Zammuto 1991; Cherrington 1989; Nadler 1983; Zaltman and Duncan 1977):

- Habit—Many people do not like change because it disrupts their habits. The same old work routine provides a sense of familiarity, hence security. Often, without necessarily receiving extra benefits, workers are expected to learn new ways of doing things, adopt new tools, and adjust to new systems. (Consider the *Clear up to clean up* case illustration, below).

- Security/new learning required—Change could be resisted when it is seen to threaten security. What if I cannot learn to use the new computer-based system? A person who cannot adapt to change can lose his or her job or lose influence and power.

- Fear of the unknown—This insecurity is deeply rooted in many, but there are people that are more fearful when facing uncertainty than others. Fear is a strong emotion and if not skilfully challenged can provoke disruptive behaviour.

- Economic considerations—Change can bring about cuts in salaries or even jobs. If perceived as such, the rise of resistance to change is understandable.

- Social considerations/disruptions of stable relationships—When work colleagues are opposing proposed changes, an individual could be led to do the same even when he or she does not initially see change as a personal threat. This is known as conforming to group norms (see Chapter 7 on Groups, Teams, and Decision Making).

- Lack of awareness—Some elements of change could be misunderstood or overlooked by a person and therefore ignored. It could be that a person openly agrees to and welcomes change, but still subconsciously sticks to their old habits.

- Distrust of management

According to Dent and Goldberg (1999), individuals may not really resist change, but rather they may resist the loss of status, pay, or comfort, that accompanies change. A psychiatrist Elisabeth Kübler-Ross (1973) suggests that people typically go through a five-stage coping cycle in response to bereavement, which is possibly the most major change anyone can face. This model is commonly used when counselling people who have faced a loss in life (see Table 10.1).

Table 10.1. Organizational change: Kübler–Ross five-stage model of coping with bereavement

	Key coping mechanism	Manifestation of the stage
Stage 1	Denial	Unwillingness to face reality
Stage 2	Anger	Looking for a 'guilty one'. Accusing those held responsible
Stage 3	Bargaining	Attempting negotiation to try to alleviate loss
Stage 4	Depression	Acknowledging the reality of loss
Stage 5	Acceptance	Coming to terms with the situation and its implications

Source: Kübler-Ross (1973).

Katz and Kahn (1978) identified the following sources of resistance to change at the organizational level:

- Structural inertia—Once an organization gets moving in a certain direction, it is difficult to change course (Cherrington 1989). There are often enough people in most organizations that want to preserve the status quo as long as possible, making organizations slow to change.

- Over-determination—Rigid procedures, elaborate protocols, job descriptions, selection and assessment, training and appraisals can all hinder the process of change.

- Narrow focus of change—In complex environments such as organizations, change at one level is likely to have a knock-on effect on other levels (Doyle 2001).

- Threatened expertise—Proposed changes jobs may require change to the skills and expertise that people have been developing for years.

- Threatened power—Restructuring usually means slimming down the organization and for some, especially middle management, this means losing power. Equally, the administration department that holds the only set of keys for the photocopy cupboard may lose their power in the company when electronic locks are installed and all the employees are given the code to get in.

- Resource allocation—If they are happy with current arrangements, employees are likely to resist proposed changes.

Case illustration
Clear up to clean up

You have decided to contribute to your local community by getting involved in an overdue clean up of the local park. You have managed to gather a group of enthusiastic students to help you. Some local shops have donated the equipment and other locals have prepared some drinks and nibbles to celebrate once the work is completed. However, an otherwise very nice park attendant, who has maintained the park for the past twenty-five years, is very suspicious of a 'bunch of youngsters waving sticks around' and is sabotaging your work. He is particularly concerned about his rose garden and he asserts that no one knows how to handle it but him.

Questions

- What might be the reason for this man resenting your kind offer to help?
- How would you try to overcome his resistance to change and make him support your clean-up?

Finally, some theorists view resistance to change as constructive when it forces managers to review the changes they are trying to impose and begin to negotiate with their subordinates, getting them involved in the process (Pfeffer 1981; Piderit 2000; de Jager 2001). Piderit (2000) also points out that what some managers may perceive as disrespectful or unfounded resistance to change might be motivated by an individual's ethical principles or by their desire to protect what they feel is in the best interests of the organization. Employee resistance may force management to rethink or re-evaluate a proposed change initiative. It can also act as a gateway or filter, which can help organizations to select from all possible changes the one that is most appropriate to the current situation. According to de Jager (2001: 26), 'resistance is simply a very effective, very powerful, very useful survival mechanism'.

KEY LEARNING POINTS

- Resistance is a common reaction to organizational change, and may take many forms.
- Management understanding and acknowledgment of the causes of resistance, in individual and group psychology, can aid significantly in the management of change.
- Communication and participation in the change process by all stakeholders can facilitate effective change.

10.3 Power and politics in changing organizations

Power and politics are indisputable aspects of organizational life (see Table 10.2). It is a major challenge for modern organizations that each is used in positive ways to enhance organizational change and reduce resistance to it.

Change affects the distribution of power within organizations and this may and often does lead to conflict and political behaviour in the workplace.

10.3.1 Power

While power, more often than not, has a negative connotation for most people, it is through the use of power that things get done in the world. It seems that in most organizations the positive face of power is much more widespread than the negative one (French and Bell 1999). Various studies have supported this, for example, it was found that in organizational decision-making coercive tactics and intimidation were mostly absent (Patchen 1974), while the most exercised forms of power were found to be collective and positive (Roberts 1986).

Definition of power

Statt (2004) emphasizes that power is the ability to make things happen by exerting influence over other people. In addition, Furnham (2005) notes that power is not exclusive to individuals and power relationships often occur in organizational groups and subunits.

Pause for thought
Think of a situation you have personally experienced where power was used to bring about results that you considered positive and for the good of the organization.

Table 10.2. Four most common pressures to change in organizations

1. Globalization – an increasing global market for products
2. Changing technology – the rapid expansion of information systems technology, computer-integrated manufacturing, virtual reality technology and robots, changes of speed, power, and cost
3. Rapid product obsolescence – the shortened lifecycle of products (as a result of innovations – we all witnessed a quick move from brick size mobile phones to thumb size ones with camera, video, and internet functions inbuilt)
4. Changing nature of the workforce – depending on demographic nature of the country, there are many changes (for example: ageing workforce and increasing demand for more flexible working hours as more valued than even pay rises (Costa and Sartori, 2005)

Source: Furnham (2005).

Most definitions identify some common elements of power: a social interaction between two or more people; the potential and the capacity to influence others or the act of influencing to get the desired outcome; or simply, power is about getting one's way. In the context of the workplace, it is about getting one's way to either effect or affect organizational outcomes.

Bases of power

When work psychologists and organizational scholars consider the topic of power, especially social or interpersonal power, they commonly talk about different **bases of power**. French and Raven (1959) differentiate five widely accepted types, or major bases of power:

1 Reward power
2 Coercive power
3 Legitimate power
4 Referent power
5 Expert power.

Reward power could be defined as a manager's ability to give people something they value, such as a pay rise, promotion, company car, bigger office, or better duty rota: such material rewards are known as extrinsic. On the other hand, recognition and acceptance are strong intrinsic motivators for most people at work and giving out praise for good performance and publicly acknowledging someone's achievements are important forms of reward power.

Coercive power is a kind of dark side of reward power for, usually, the same person is in possession of both types of power, giving some managers a role of organizational Dr Jekyll and Mr Hyde. This power is a manager's ability to punish his or her subordinates, by demoting them, cutting their bonuses or withholding a salary increase. As in the case of extrinsic (material) and intrinsic rewards, punishment can be more subtle than a pay cut, and equally, if not more painful. For example, it can take the form of a public embarrassment. Making the worst performing salesman wear a donkey hat for a week is an extreme example of coercive power used in some estate agencies in London.

Legitimate power is the power based on everyone's belief that the power holder has a legitimate right to exert his/her influence and that those influenced have legitimate obligations to accept this. Having legitimate power is what is usually meant by having authority as a result of one's position in the organizational hierarchy, e.g. having the job title of 'Director' is usually accepted by most subordinates as conferring the legitimate right to give orders. The more hierarchical the organization, the more evident is this type of power. However, the lines of legitimate power can be blurred in 'flat' organizations.

Referent power is power based on followers having identification with and attraction to the power holder, because of his or her personal qualities. In this scenario, employees are happy to be followers of that person. Referent power occurs when subordinates think/believe that the leader has desirable characteristics that they should imitate. This imitation could mean that employees start working the same long hours as their boss, or start adopting the way they work, talk, or even their mannerisms and the way they dress. Having this type of power is what is usually meant by having charisma. It is worth noting here that one does not need to have legitimate power or to be in a role of official authority to have referent power.

Expert power is power based on the advanced knowledge the power holder possesses, which is needed by others who do not have this knowledge. It emerges when the leader is seen by subordinates as having expertise that is relevant to the tasks they all need to achieve. It is an especially important base of power when a power holder possesses specialist information that cannot be easily found elsewhere. Furthermore, French and Raven (1959) noted that it is not only that the power holder should possess and demonstrate the right specialist knowledge and ability, but he or she has also to be seen as trustworthy, credible, and honest by others. Like referent power, and even more so, expert power transcends positions and jobs, and is not necessarily attached to roles with formal authority.

In contrast to French and Raven's one-dimensional approach to power, Hofstede (1977) argued that no single dimension of power is likely to hold equally for all managers and employees in a multicultural domestic setting or in the multicultural milieu of the **multinational** corporation. Similarly, several experts have more recently begun to reconfigure how power is viewed to a more multidimensional interweaving of relations or conflicting needs (Alanazi and Arnoldo 2003; Imberman 2005; Steensma and van Milligen 2003).

As with leadership styles, each base of power has its place in management and can prove effective in the right setting and right circumstances. The ways in which managers influence their employees and encourage them to be productive depends on many variables, including the personality of the leader, the skills of the group/employees, the task or assignment at hand, and the group dynamics and personalities of group members (Imberman 2005).

Power tactics

Pfeffer (1992) argued that all managers must learn the subtle and demanding craft of power tactics and politics if they want to succeed or even survive in their roles in modern organizations. Power tactics are ways of gaining power and using it to manipulate the bases of power (McKenna 2006). Power tactics also determine whether power is used in positive or negative ways.

Yukl and Falbe (1990) conducted a research study that examined patterns of managers' influence tactics. They describe eight power tactics (Yukl and Falbe 1990):

1 Consultation—when the power holder asks his subordinates to participate in decision making and planning for change.

2 Rational persuasion—by means of presenting facts and logical arguments the power holder asserts his or her influence over subordinates.

3 Inspirational appeals—this tactic is about appealing to people's values and ideals, so that they follow their leader because he or she inspires them. Subordinates enthusiastically identify themselves with the leader and his/her goals.

4 Ingratiation—a good humoured leader will try to create a positive atmosphere in a workplace, as people are better motivated to follow orders if in a good mood.

5 Coalition—the power holder influences subordinates by forming a partnership with them. He or she is looking for stable support from the followers.

6 Pressure—hassling, bullying, and intimidation are just some of the tools used in pressure tactics.

7 Upward appeals—when a manager calls upon the higher authority that has approved his or her request.

8 Exchange—'If you do this, I'll give you that', an old trade tactic that still works well. If an employee completes the task as requested, he or she will for example get that desired ticket to the conference abroad.

 Activity **I have power**

Could you be corrupted by power? Are you a good politician? Can you get results? Imagine that you were assigned to be the leader of a group project. The task is to deliver a group presentation and win the majority of 'the best presentation' votes from other members (the rest of your tutorial group). The presentation topic is 'Boost the emotional intelligence in your organization to improve your business' (see Chapter 3 on Personality and Individual Differences). There are five students in your group, including a good friend. The deadline is tight and the marks allocated to the assignment are high.

Consider the following:

• What kind of a leader would you be? What are your bases of power in this scenario? Consider the implications of the different tactics you may use in this situation.

• Devise your leadership strategy (you may want to refer to Chapter 8 on Leadership at Work). Which power tactics would you use?

10.3.2 Political behaviour in modern organizations

213

Chapter 10
Organizational
change and
development

Power and politics are interrelated, and these terms are often used interchangeably, although they do have distinct meanings. Both power and politics relate to getting one's way, pursuit of self-interest, and overcoming the resistance of others. Political behaviour is the method that members of an organization use to obtain and demonstrate the power to get desired outcomes (Pfeffer 1981). Unlike formal power, which is embedded in the position held, political behaviour is informal power that comprises activities that are not in the description of an organizational role (Mintzberg 1983).

Political techniques and tactics

Here are some examples of political behaviour or political techniques and tactics:

- **Gate keeping** is about controlling lines of communication. For example, a receptionist may exercise political influence when controlling who has access to the organization and how long they have to wait to gain access.

- Controlling the agenda. Placing an issue at the very end of the meeting's agenda could be a tactic to avoid tackling this issue. A manager that runs a meeting and creates the agenda may then deliberately try to prolong discussions around other issues so that there is no time left for the controversial topic. Alternatively, the same manager may opt for excluding the issue from the agenda and imposing the desired solution without having it discussed by the collective.

- Game playing: bad news is kept and released at the time when it is likely to be unnoticed; or a positive report on customer care could be released at a time when this topic is high on the company's agenda. Equally, a manager is using game playing when he or she avoids attending a 'hot' meeting where important complaints are about to be raised by arranging a competing meeting with an important customer.

- Building coalitions helps access to important information, resources, or even bending some rules. For example, it pays to befriend the department secretary to get personal work issues higher on the list of priorities.

- Networking—taking advantage of one's access to a network of organizational and/or occupational incumbents, specialists, or power holders (special ties with professional, social, or family groups)

- **Impression management**: a technique used to influence the way others see a person. It includes **body language** that asserts one's presence and influences others. This consists of assertive speaking; standing tall and confident; talking with definite gestures, an open body, and maintaining eye contact. Leary and Kowalski (1990) listed seven impression management techniques (see Figure 10.1), all of which require the use of assertive body language. Each example of impression management is an effort to influence others to the advantage of the person using it. If political behaviour is to be successful, then favourable impression management is central.

- Exchange of favours—trading present or future favours or obligations with another party according to one's vested interests ('I will do it, but you owe me one').

- 'Piggybacking' is establishing a mutually supportive relationship with an individual from an existing or incumbent power group and moving along with him or her (e.g. following your boss into another division).

- Rituals and symbols—using formal ceremonies (nominations, awards presentations, sales meetings, etc.) and symbols of power (office location and furniture, reserved parking, executive dining room, etc.) to enhance or consolidate one's position.

Coping with politics

Generally, research suggests that political behaviour is a normal part of doing business today (Ferris et al. 1996; Ferris and Kacmar 1992; Williams and Dutton 2000).

Advanced technology and complex environments have shaped the highly competitive nature of modern business and made the use of politics more prevalent. The trends toward flatter organizations, downsizing, scarce resources, and ambiguous, ever changing organizational goals often leave much space for competing ideas and personal interests (Pfeffer 1981; Pfeffer 1992).

Moorhead and Griffin (2004) suggested that organizations can limit the dysfunctional effects of political behaviour by:

- resorting to open communication, to prevent gatekeepers from manipulating access to important information.
- giving clear explanations of why changes are necessary and what are the key issues to be faced in the future, so there will be less need for speculation, anxiety, rumour, and hence less fuel for negative political behaviour.
- increasing awareness or creating better understanding of political behaviour, its causes and effects, and how to cope with it.

On the other hand, a recent survey (Holbeche 2004) suggested that in times of organizational change, political behaviour can be seen as constructive in helping overall performance. Constructive politics involve:

- Employing networks and contacts to get the job done more quickly than would otherwise be the case.
- Breaking down barriers to change (see section 10.2.3 above).
- Creating greater 'buy-in' on key-projects.
- Speeding up decision making.
- The use of power and position to ease the implementation of strategy.

KEY LEARNING POINTS

- Power and politics are an inevitable feature of organizational life, and may become a significant component in people's response to change.
- There have been a number of attempts to classify types and bases of power within work organizations, and to identify common power tactics.
- Recent conceptualizations of power emphasize that it may be an important engine to effective change.

10.4 Change management

Kotter and Schlesinger (1979) put forward six ways of overcoming resistance to organizational change that may be used by management:

1 Education and communication—This aims to erase misunderstandings and irrational fears of change, by communicating to all involved why the change is necessary and how it is going to benefit the organization and ultimately all that work in it. However, this could be costly and time consuming, and it can become clear that not all will benefit from change.

2 Participation—People are invited to join the change process from the very beginning, starting with decision making about how to bring about change. This technique utilizes peoples' skills and knowledge and aims to create an atmosphere of trust and ownership in the change process.

3 Facilitation and support—In a situation where change is a threat to many and strong emotions of anxiety and fear impede its implementation, counselling and appropriate training could be adopted to reduce resistance.

4 Negotiation and agreement—Finding a **compromise** between the position of top management and that of the employees. This way both parties sign up to the agreement.

5 Manipulation—If all other tactics fail, management could resort to manipulation. For example, subtly sending an unrealistic threat through the organization's grapevine that

those who resist change will be penalized, and that in the worst scenario, some jobs might be axed. This can bring quick results but also can lead to future problems if people feel manipulated.

6 Coercion—This is the last resort for managers, possibly efficient initially but on a very superficial level, as coercive tactics are likely to evoke anger, hostility, and lack of commitment.

Furthermore, Herriot et al. (1998) identified factors that can enable successful change management. According to them change agents should:

- engage in real dialogue, not one-way communication;
- understand organizational change from employees' perspectives;
- recognize that personal life transitions affect work performance and vice versa; career crises and changes have long-term effects on partners and children too;
- acknowledge their responsibility for previous change mistakes;
- recognize the dangers of disciplining and over-controlling individuals in the change process;
- align Human Resource systems and health services to support staff during the change process;
- allow for individual differences in employees' capacity to cope with extra changes;
- concentrate upon providing adequate induction processes, training, mentoring, and coaching for people entering new jobs and roles;
- design work processes so as to facilitate learning and change: 'Don't blame the mouse, blame the hole in the wall';
- equip people with the personal and leadership skills to manage change and transition for themselves and adopt a learning approach to change;
- recognize the added environmental pressures and changes imposed on individuals arising from the New Millennium, the Euro, and global economic instability.

Additionally, Seel (2000) argues that effective leadership is the key to making change management effective as it provides the vision and the rationale for change. Change agents could adopt different styles of leadership such as coercive, directive, consultative, or **collaborative** as they may each be appropriate depending on the type and scale of change being undertaken (see Chapter 8: Leadership at Work). For example, when a large-scale organization is facing wide-ranging change, a directive style has been identified as most effective (Woodward 2007).

Figure 10.1. **Seven impression management techniques associated with seven typical statements describing them**

1. Conformity	I am a team player. I am not going to rock the boat.
2. Excuse	I am truly sorry that I missed the meeting at 1 today, but I had another important meeting with our major supplier scheduled earlier this week. I think we got a good deal!
3. Apology	I apologise, but I will be ten minutes late for your appointment. I know your time is valuable, please forgive me.
4. Flattery	Your way of processing data may be the most efficient I have seen. You inspired me to consider a change of doing this in our department.
5. Association	I wear designer clothes and drive a Porsche.
6. Favour	Offering a ticket for an opening of a new West End musical to a potential customer.
7. Acclaiming	If you support my proposal, everybody in the department will benefit.

Source: Leary and Kowalski (1990).

Figure 10.2. The seven Cs of change:

1. Choosing a team.	5. Communicating.
2. Crafting the vision and the path.	6. Coping with change.
3. Connecting organization-wide change.	7. Capturing learning.
4. Consulting stakeholders.	

Source: Molloy and Whittington (2005).

Moreover, appropriate training has been identified as a solution to effective change (Molloy and Whittington 2005). Examples of training requirements include:

- Project and programme management skills to ensure change initiatives are completed both on time and to budget.
- Change management skills, including effective communication and facilitation of group discussion.
- Leadership coaching.

CIPD research (2005) has identified seven areas of activity that make successful change happen – these are named the 'the seven Cs of change' (see Figure 10.2).

Finally, organizational development, which is discussed next, is one approach or intervention used when trying to bring about change orientated to improving organizational effectiveness.

10.5 Organizational development

The term **organization development** (OD) is used to describe a wide range of approaches to organizational change (Margulies et al. 1977).

OD emerged in the late 1950s and early 1960s from Kurt Lewin's theory of group dynamics and the theory and practice of planned change discussed earlier in this chapter. Group dynamics is concerned with the ways in which groups evolve and how people in groups behave and interact. Lewin founded the Research Centre for Group Dynamics in 1945 where the movement of 'T-groups' emerged. In the 'T-group' process, participants in unstructured groups learn from their own interaction and the evolving dynamics of the group. T-groups operate on the underlying premise that causality for behavioural problems lies with an individuals' perceptions, assumptions, and feelings concerning events and people. The solution could be found by altering these elements with feedback in a sensitivity group led by a non-directive trainer.

Today the field of organizational development offers an integrated framework claiming to be capable of solving most of the important problems confronting the human side of organizations (French and Bell 1999).

Three main features of OD programmes have been identified by Rothwell et al. (1995):

1 OD is managed from the top, often using a third party or '**change agents**' or consultants, who are either external or internal. The 'change agents' start off by diagnosing problems and then aim to manage change by various kinds of planned activity or 'action plans'.

2 The plan for OD is based on a systematic analysis of the circumstances of the organization and the changes and problems affecting it (**Action method**).

3 OD is based on behavioural science knowledge and its main goal is to improve the way organizations cope in times of change.

10.5.1 OD interventions

Organizational development interventions are structured activities involving clients and consultants. Generally, OD interventions focus on individuals, groups, intergroup relationships, task-technology and organizational process, or overall organizational structure. Although organizational change is often an ongoing process, most organizational change interventions use a series of stages to focus the activities. They involve implementing various change-inducing action programmes and all involve the three basic components:

1 Diagnosis.

2 Action plan (planning for change followed by implementation of an OD intervention).

3 Evaluation.

Diagnosis is concerned with identifying the current state of the system with particular focus on major concerns. It involves gathering information to interpret the state of the organization correctly. Questionnaires could be given to many or all of the organizational stakeholders, or a number of direct observations of behaviour in the workplace could be noted. Interviews are also commonly used when gathering information from managers, while workshops with different groups could help identify group and individual perceptions. Finally, an organization's documents and sales records may give a valuable insight of its state.

SWOT (strengths, weaknesses, opportunities, and threats) analysis is a common technique used at the diagnosis stage, and involves asking questions: What business are we in? What are the strengths of the current system? What are its problem areas? What are its unrealized opportunities? What are we trying to achieve? Is there a discrepancy between the vision of the desired future and the current situation? What are the dangers if the desired future is created? The diagnosis could be recognized as an unfreezing stage of Lewin's model of change.

> Furthermore, there is a formula, which Beckhard and Harris (1987) attribute to Gleicher which can be used to decide if an organization is ready for change:

$$\textbf{Dissatisfaction} \times \textbf{Vision} \times \textbf{First Steps} > \textbf{Resistance to Change}$$

This means that three components must all be present to overcome the resistance to change in an organization: *dissatisfaction* with the present situation, a *vision* of what is possible in the future, and achievable *first steps* towards reaching this vision. If any of the three is zero or near zero, the product will also be zero or near zero and the resistance to change will dominate.

If diagnosis is done correctly, the following stage—an action plan—will be easier as clear needs will become apparent. Action plans are proposed to maintain strengths, correct problems, and seize the opportunities earlier identified in the diagnosis stage. Action plans are specifically tailored to address issues at the individual, group, intergroup, process, and organizational levels. Action plans are comprised of two steps:

1 Planning for change or the development of an action plan and

2 Implementation of chosen OD techniques.

Even if the needs are clear, it may not be reasonable to change all the diagnosed problems. This part of the planning process looks at which changes are most likely to produce the desired results. The choice of what changes to make will influence the choice of organizational change methods or interventions. During the intervention stage, the actual work with the employees is done by the consultant or the manager, or both. Since a variety of techniques may be used in a single situation, different change agents may be used during a single intervention.

Some of most popular OD techniques will be described in some detail next.

> **Survey feedback** is one of the earliest OD techniques. It is based on using questionnaires filled out by employees to give management feedback for planning change in the organization. It was developed in the 1950s when a psychologist working with Detrit Edison observed that little change occurred when survey results were reported to supervisors and supervisors did not discuss plans for change with their subordinates. However, when a supervisor discussed the results with subordinates and made plans with them for change, significant favourable changes occurred (Mann 1961, quoted in Krumm 2001). These observations led to a very common, standardized method of organizational development that consists of six stages shown in Figure 10.3.
>
> 360 degrees feedback is when managers have an appraisal from various perspectives; they are appraised by their subordinates (bottom-up), by their superiors (downward appraisal), and by their peers. The appraisal results can then be used for planning change. Both methods: 360 degrees feedback and survey feedback have been shown to

Figure 10.3. Steps in the survey feedback method

1. formulating the questionnaire with top management involved ⟶
2. questionnaire given to all employees ⟶
3. results of the questionnaire analysed by an outside source ⟶
4. data reported to individual managers at each level: from top to bottom ⟶
5. managers meeting with their employees to discuss results and plan changes ⟶
6. changes implemented

Source: Krumm (2001).

be effective for changing organizational behaviour in a number of different settings. Part of the reason for their effectiveness may be their low cost and the involvement of everybody in the organization, leading employees to believe that management really does want to hear what they have to say.

Team-building sessions are very popular and could be used in permanent work teams or those teams set up to deal with a project or solve particular problems. The team-building intervention may be aimed toward task accomplishment; analysis of effectiveness of the team; improving interpersonal relationships or managing the group's culture and process. As part of the trend to **employee empowerment**, there has been a move toward using team building as a way of developing self-directed work groups (Krumm 2001) in which all the team members share authority equally and function with supervision that is similar to coaching (refer to Chapter 7: Groups, Teams, and Decision Making).

Another OD technique is conflict management training. Conflict is an inevitable outcome of change in organizations today. Unequal distribution of power in many organizations, even the flattest, may lead to jealousy; and when accompanied by the inappropriate use of power tactics such as coercion, bullying, and intimidation (discussed previously in this chapter) may lead to conflict between management and the workforce. The training aims to equip management with conflict management techniques that are applicable in various conflict situations.

Mediation is a technique of bringing two parties together in a voluntary, confidential, and non-judgemental environment to facilitate the exploration of underlying causes and effects of conflict so that they can find their own solution.

Diversity training is an intervention directed toward increasing employees' awareness and skills in functioning in a diverse workplace. Successful diversity programmes are individualized for the organization, have clear goals, and have support from top management. They do not attack personal beliefs, but work on changing behaviours, and are voluntary.

Work redesign aims to control the internal work motivation, general job satisfaction, and overall work effectiveness by altering task and skill variety with individual or group autonomy (Hackman and Oldham 1980).

Management by objectives (MBO) is a performance appraisal system that measures the effectiveness of an employee or group in terms of goals set by the supervisor and the employees or group. It is interesting that MBO measures only the results, and not employee or group behaviour in reaching the goals that are set. It is important to align individual and organizational goals here, as sometimes they can pull in opposite directions.

Quality Circle programmes are a form of group problem solving and goal setting with the main focus on improving product quality. Quality circles consist of a small group of employees from across organizational departments who volunteer to have regular group-led meetings where they discuss and analyse product quality and other problems, and generate possible solutions and ways to better the production process and the final product. Lawler and associates (1992) conducted a study of 313 organizations that have used quality circle programmes, and they reported that 52 per cent of them evaluated those programmes as successful, 36 per cent were undecided, and 12 per cent stated that they were unsuccessful.

Business Process Re-engineering (BPR) is an organizational technique of constantly critically examining everything the organization does in order to improve its process. BPR examines processes horizontally in organizations to establish how they can be integrated more effectively and streamlined. By reordering the processes to be more customer focused it was hoped that organizations would undergo steep change and move to new ways of working and being. The reality was usually different, and this approach has been criticized for promising more than it can deliver and disregarding the human element (Armstrong 2006).

Organizational transformation is one of the newest models of organizational change. This method is directed towards change in the entire organization's vision for the future. It encompasses change in beliefs, purpose, and mission. Organizational transformation is employed when the change in organizations is proactive and strategic (as discussed previously in this chapter) and sometimes when the organization is facing problems caused by the increasing number of consolidations, downsizings and closures in the corporate world.

10.5.2 Evaluation

The final stage of an OD programme is *evaluation*. This most commonly takes place soon after implementing the chosen action plan, but the true picture of the effects is often seen when evaluation is at a number of points in time after the intervention. Answers to the following questions are sought: Did the actions have the desired effects? Is the problem solved? Are the opportunities seized? If the answer to these questions is yes, then the organization can move on to other issues and problems and if the answer is no, new action plans are devised and implemented until the problem is solved. It may be that the problem needs redefining and that the initial diagnosis has missed out on important questions.

For a long time (throughout the 1960s and 1970s) OD was seen as the answer to the problems of improving organizational effectiveness, and comprehensive OD programmes were introduced by a number of Western companies such as General Motors, Corning Glass, and ICI. Research found that positive impacts were made in between 70 and 80 per cent of the cases studied (French and Bell 1990).

However, like the growth of many management techniques, OD gradually took on characteristics of a trend and began to be criticized for not achieving the desired outcomes. It was seen to be too 'touchy-feely', and in particular to put the individual before the organization and the informal organization before the formal organization. Sometimes OD was thought of as 'bringing in someone to stir things up a bit' which could lead to disaster. Not all consultants practising OD were well trained, and OD's emphasis on openness and change was seen as threatening by managers. It was questioned whether OD's emphasis on training programmes was in itself sufficient to produce lasting changes (Cannell 2007). Furthermore the OD movement was also criticized as not scientific enough, lacking precise definition, and not allowing specific observation or measurement (Armstrong 2003).

As an answer to this growing criticism of traditional OD, change agents have seen a steady transition from traditionally non-directive, process-oriented practitioners to today's authoritative specialists. The 'bottom line' took prevalence over the humanistic concerns that founded OD. Attention shifted from the individual and work groups to the larger work context at the organizational level, and OD practitioners became involved in implementing new organizational strategic plans and in continuous learning, organizational transformation, cultural change, and quality initiatives.

KEY LEARNING POINTS

- Organizational development is a technique to help management to plan and implement change.
- OD is characterized by the use of external consultants to facilitate change.
- Typically OD consists of diagnosis, action planning and intervention, and evaluation and frequently involves the application of theory and research from the social and behavioural sciences.
- Many companies have used OD methods to plan and implement change, but research suggests that success rates may be low.

Chapter summary

- Technological changes, political changes, and changes in values and preferences, all have an impact on markets and ultimately affect the way businesses are run and organizations are structured and managed.

- Planned change is change consciously embarked upon and planned by organizations. It involves three stages: unfreezing the old behaviour or situation, moving to a new level of behaviour, and refreezing the behaviour at the new level.

- Power at work is used to influence others and achieve desired outcomes. French and Raven (1959) distinguished five types, or bases of power. These are: reward power; coercive power; legitimate power; referent power and expert power.

- Political behaviour is closely related to power in organizations. The major techniques for combating the negative consequences of politics are: open communication, increased awareness, and reduced uncertainty.

- Sources of resistance to change may originate from an individual and/or organization.

- The techniques commonly used for overcoming resistance to change include: education and communication; participation; facilitation and support; negotiation and agreement; manipulation and coercion.

- OD interventions involve implementing change-inducing action programmes and these are made up of three basic components: diagnosis, action plans, and ongoing programme management.

Assess your learning

Review questions

1 List and discuss the main driving forces for change in modern organizations.
2 Describe two models of planned organizational change.
3 What are the similarities and differences between power and politics in organizations?
4 Describe the main types/bases of power and give examples of each within an organizational context.
5 What are the main causes of political behaviour at the workplace and how can their negative impact be combated?
6 Why do people in organizations usually resist change?
7 List the major factors in effective change management?
8 What is organizational development and when is this approach applicable to an organization?
9 List and describe five different OD interventions.

Assignments

ASSIGNMENT 1: Applying change models
It is late December and you decide to make a New Year resolution that you intend to stick to this time. It may be that you want to kick a bad old habit or introduce time management into your studies. Apply the planned change model to your resolution and devise a course of actions to be implemented at each one of three stages of change.

ASSIGNMENT 2: Changing yourself
Collect 360 degrees feedback on your performance as a student by writing and distributing written forms with open-ended questions (to your peers, your personal tutor, and work psychology tutor). Review and reflect on your findings. What are the advantages and disadvantages of this approach to personal change?

Further Reading

Buchanan, D. A., and Badham, R. (2008) *Power, Politics and Organisational Change: Winning the Turf Game* (2nd edn.). Beverly Hills, CA: Sage Publications Ltd.
This accessible and engaging book focuses on the manager acting as an internal change agent. It contains new research and current perspectives on organisational change. The chapter on gender differences in approaches to organisational politics is particularly interesting as it challenges the traditional stereotypes.

Harrison, R. (2002) *Learning and Development*. London: CIPD.
Clearly written student textbook that combines academic research and a practical approach to learning and development in the workplace.

Schramm, J. (2001) *The Change Agenda*. London: CIPD.
A useful summary of how people learn in the workplace; applies different learning theories in the context of changing workplaces. Contains a useful section on e-learning.

 ## Work psychology in practice
A happy ending—but not for all

The manager of the Eating Disorders Unit at one of the major Psychiatric Clinics in Amsterdam has decided to take a career break and has left the department to its destiny. During his 'days of rule' organizational politics thrived in a department that employed thirty members of staff. Although all employees were called teamworkers, it was clear that seniority and politics were the main factors in both individual recognition and reward. The running of the department and patients' treatment regimes was strictly prescribed by a few managers and implemented by the rest. Psychiatric nurses, who cared for patients on a day-to-day basis, had little say and little recognition for their work. There was an atmosphere of low trust, high conflict, **role ambiguity**, and unclear performance evaluation. For example, staff felt that guidelines for promotion were unclear, and unpopular shifts were not fairly allocated. Hassling, bullying, and intimidation were common amongst the staff. The staff turnover was significantly higher than the national average in the health sector. When the new manageress was appointed, supported by the hospital director, she brought in some immediate changes to the workplace. Following individual interviews with everybody in the department she called a staff meeting. New rules and structures were imposed: all nurses were to contribute to weekly ward rounds and produce reports on patients' progress as well as giving suggestions for further treatment. A new role of key worker was introduced and everybody was to get a chance to manage a number of individual treatments; team meetings were to be held weekly with all staff to discuss current issues. The training and development programmes were recommended for all.

Redistribution of responsibility, increased transparency, and higher workforce involvement was not an easy transition to go through. Some feared that their achieved status position might be threatened. Some feared what the new responsibilities might mean for them: were they up to the new challenges of the job and could they end up being liable if the patient's treatment went wrong? This fear of the new was manifested through growing resentment toward the new manageress. Initial staff meetings were very silent, with few daring to speak. Regardless of being available during work hours, career relevant, and free, training sessions for staff were generally unattended.

However, after a while, people started to speak more openly in ward rounds and meetings; while gradually various issues were being raised and discussed. Key-working was recognized as a job that had been done in the past, but was now officially recognized. Many started to enjoy their new role at the unit and training sessions became more and more popular especially after a workers' initiative to have monthly talks by staff members on various relevant subjects was implemented. Team-building sessions focusing on group process and communication were not only a fun outing but also a great success. Still, the manageress remained unpopular and was never really accepted as a member of the team. After twelve turbulent months in the role as a change agent, she resigned. This was also the only resignation at the department that year.

Questions

This is an example of an organizational change process imposed by top management and overseen by one person—the new line manager.

- What type of change is described here? Accidental or planned? Reactive or proactive? Operational or strategic?
- Using Schein's model of change describe the stages that people went through during the twelve months of the change process.
- There was clear resistance to change, even sabotage, especially at the beginning. What were the possible causes of this?
- Which organization development interventions did the new manageress use in her role of change agent?

 # Online Resource Centre

Visit the supporting online resource centre for additional material which will help you with your research, essays, and assignments, or you may find these additional resources helpful when revising for exams.
http://www.oxfordtextbooks.co.uk/orc/matthewman/

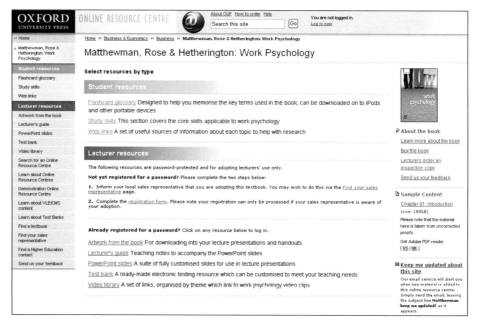

References

Alanazi, F. M., and Arnoldo, R. (2003) Power bases and attribution in three cultures. *Journal of Social Psychology*, 43/3: 375–95.

Armstrong, M. (2006) *A Handbook of Human Resource Management Practice* (10th edn.). London: Kogan Page Ltd.

Beckhard, R., and Harris, R. (1987) *Organizational Transitions*. Reading, MA: Addison-Wesley.

Bedeian, A. G., and Zammuto, R. F. (1991) *Organizations: Theory and Design*. Hinsdale, IL: Dryden Press.

Bovey, W. H., and Hede, A. (2001) Resistance to organisational change. *Journal of Managerial Psychology*, 16/7: 534–48.

Brown, J., and Duguid, P. (1991) Organizational learning and communities of practice: towards a unified view of working, learning and innovation. *Organizational Science*, 2/1: 40–57.

Burke, W. (1994) *Organisation Development: A Process of Learning and Changing*. Reading, MA: Addison Wesley Publishing Company.

Cannell, M. (2007) *Organisational Development CIPD fact sheet*. www.cipd.co.uk.

Chartered Institute for Personnel and Development (2005) *HR's Role in Organising: Shaping Change*. Research Paper: September 2005. www.cipd.org.

Cherrington, J. D. (1989) *Organizational Behaviour: The Management of Individual and Organizational Performance*. London: Allyn and Bacon.

Costa, G., and Sartori, S. (2005) Flexible work hours, ageing and well-being. *Assessment and Promotion of Work Ability, Health* and Well-Being of Ageing Workers, 1280: 23–8. In International Congress Series. www.sciencedirect

Cummings, T., and Huse, E. (1989) Organizational Change and Development. St Paul, MN: West Publishing Company.

de Jager, P. (2001) Resistance to change: a new view of an old problem. The Futurist, May/June: 24–7.

Dent, E., and Goldberg, S. (1999) Challenging 'resistance to change'. Journal of Applied Behavioural Science, 35/1: 25–41.

Doyle, M. (2001) Dispersing change agency on high velocity change organizations: issues and implications. Leadership and Organizational Development Journal, 22/7: 321–31.

Feigenbaum, A. V. (1997) No pain, no gain. Chief Executive, 121: 36.

Ferris, G. R., and Kacmar, K. M. (1992) Perceptions of organizational politics. Journal of Management, 18/1: 93–116.

Ferris, G. R., Bhawuk, D. P. S., Frink, D. D., Keiser, J. D., Gilmore, D. C., and Canton, R. C. (1996) The paradox of diversity in organizations. In A. Gutschelhofer and J. Scheff (eds.), Paradoxes in Management: Contradictions in Management—A Management of Contradictions. Vienna: Lindeverlag, 203–29.

French, J. R. P., Jr., and Raven, B. (1959) The bases for social power. In D. Cartwright (ed.), Studies in Social Power. Ann Arbor: University of Michigan Press.

French, W. L., and Bell, C. H. (1999) Organisation Development: Behavioural Science Interventions for Organisation Improvement (6th edn.). London: Prentice-Hall International.

Furnham, A. (2005) The Psychology of Behaviour at Work (2nd edn.). Hove: Psychology Press.

Gersick, C. J. G. (1994) Pacing strategic change: the case of a new venture. Academy of Management Journal, 37/1: 9–45.

Herriot, P., Hirsh, W., and Reilly, P. (1998) Trust and Transition. Chichester: Wiley.

Hofstede, G. (1977) Power in organizations. International Studies of Management and Organization, 7/1: 1–25.

Holbeche, L. (2004) The Power of Constructive Politics. Horsham: Roffey Park Institute Publications.

Imberman, W. (2005) Managing the managers. Progressive Grocer, 84/3: 26–7.

Inkpen, A. C., and Crossan, M. M. (1995) Believing is feeling: joint ventures and organizational learning. Journal of Management Studies, 32: 595–618.

Katz, D., and Kahn, R. L. (1978) The Social Psychology of Organizations (2nd edn.). New York: John Wiley and Sons.

Kotter, J. P. (1998) Leading change: why transformation efforts fail. In Harvard Business Review on Chang. Boston, MA: Harvard Business School Press, 1–20.

Kotter, J. P., and Schlesinger, L. A. (1979) Choosing strategies for change. Harvard Business Review, 57/2: 106–14.

Kouzes, J. M., and Posner, B. Z. (2002) The Leadership Challenge (3rd edn.). San Francisco: Jossey-Bass.

Krumm, D. (2001) Psychology at Work. New York: Worth Publishers.

Kübler-Ross, E. (1973) On Death and Dying. London: Routledge and Kegan Paul.

Lawler, E. E., III, Mohrman, S., and Ledford, G. E., Jr. (1992) The Fortune 1000 and total quality. Journal for Quality and Participation, 15/5: 6–10.

Leary, M. R., and Kowalski, R. M. (1990) Impression management: a literature review and two component model. Psychological Bulletin, 107/1: 34–47.

Lewin, K. (1951) Field Theory in Social Science. New York: Harper.

Margulies, N., Wright, P. L., and Scholl, R. W. (1977) Organization development techniques: their impact on change. Group and Organization Management, 2/4: 428–48.

Miller, K. L., and Monge, P. R. (1985) Social information and employee anxiety about organisational change. Human Communication Research, 11: 365–86.

Mintzberg, H. (1983) Power in and around Organisations. Englewood Cliffs, NJ: Prentice-Hall.

Molloy, E., and Whittington, R. (2005) HR: Making Change Happen. Executive briefing. London: Chartered Institute of Personnel and Development.

Moorhead, G., and Griffin, R. W. (2004) Organisational Behaviour: Managing People and Organisations (7th edn.). Boston: Houghton Mifflin.

Nadler, D. A. (1983) Concepts for the Management of Organizational Change. New York: Delta Consulting Group.

Orlinkowski, W. (1996) Improvising organizational transformations over time: a situated change perspective. Information Systems Research, 7/1: 63–92.

Patchen, M. (1974) The locus and basis of influence in organizational decisions. Organization and Human Performance, 11: 195–221.

Pfeffer, J. (1981) Power in Organizations. Boston: Pittman.

Pfeffer, J. (1992) Managing with Power. Boston: Harvard Business School Press.

Piderit, S. K. (2000) Rethinking resistance and recognizing ambivalence: a multidimensional view of attitudes toward an organizational change. Academy of Management, A: 783–94.

Rice, M. (2000) Age of the flex exec. Management Today, Aug.: 46–53.

Roberts, N. C. (1986) Organizational power styles: collective and competitive power under varying organizational conditions. Journal of Applied Behavioural Science, 22: 443–58.

Schein, E. H. (1987) Process Consultation: Lessons for Managers and Consultants. Boston: Addison-Wesley Publishing Company.

Schein, E. H. (1992) Organizational Culture and Leadership (2nd edn.). San Francisco: Jossey Bass.

Seel, R. (2000) Complexity and culture: new perspectives on organisational change. Organisations and People, 7/2: 2–9. (Also at http://www.new-paradigm.co.uk/culture-complex.htm.)

Statt, D. A. (2004) Psychology and the World of Work. Basingstoke: Palgrave Macmillan.

Steensma, H., and van Milligen, F. (2003) Bases of power, procedural justice and outcomes of mergers: the push and pull factors of influence tactics. Journal of Collective Negotiations, 30/2: 113–34.

Tsoukas, H. (1996) The firm as a distributed knowledge system: a constructionist approach. Strategic Management Journal, 17: 11–25.

Weick, K. E., and Quinn, R. E. (1999) Organizational change and development. Annual Review of Psychology, 50: 361–88.

Williams, M., and Dutton, J. E. (2000) Corrosive political climates: the heavy toll of negative political behaviour in organizations. In R. E. Quinn, R. M. O'Neill, and L. S. Clair (eds.), The Pressing Problems of Modern Organizations: Redefining the Agenda for Research and Practice. San Francisco: New Lexington Press.

Woodward, N. H. (2007) To make changes, manage them. HR Magazine, 52/5: 63–7.

Yukl, G., and Falbe, C. M. (1990) Influence tactics in upward, downward, and lateral influence attempts. Journal of Applied Psychology, 75: 132–40.

Zaltman, G., and Duncan, R. (1977) Strategies for Planned Change. New York: John Wiley and Sons.

Chapter 11
Human performance and the work environment

Lauren Thomas

Chapter objectives

As a result of reading this chapter and using the additional web-based material you should be able to:

- Explain how human factors and the design of the work environment impacts on productivity, well-being, and safety at work.

- Recognize that individual performance at work varies, and that people are not always consistent, accurate, or reliable in the way that they perform work tasks.

- Define different types of **human error**, giving examples, and explain how and where they occur in the context of the human information processing and performance loop.

- Describe some of the factors which help to explain variations in performance within and between individuals at work, such as competence, arousal, and **workload**.

- Describe how the work environment, such as the physical setting and the organizational context, shape performance at work.

- Understand some of the techniques used for analysing work activities and understanding task demands, and how they might be applied to design work equipment and the work environment.

- Appreciate that human performance issues ('human factors') are a major factor contributing to accidents, and that managing these issues can help to reduce risks to health and safety at work.

Work psychology in practice
Forensic scientists are human too

225

Chapter 11
Human
performance
and work
environment

Damilola Taylor was a 10-year-old schoolboy who was fatally stabbed in London in November 2000. It took six years and three trials before two brothers were eventually convicted of his manslaughter. In this case, human error contributed to delays in the judicial process, which added to the distress and anguish of a bereaved family.

Initial investigations undertaken by the Forensic Science Service had failed to identify blood spots and fibres on items of clothing belonging to the brothers. When these articles were later provided to an independent forensic testing company, the blood spots were found to match Damilola's DNA profile, and fibre within the blood spots matched his school uniform (BBC 2006). This forensic evidence was vital in a case that had no eyewitnesses, and where a gang culture meant that there was reluctance among local people to speak to the police about what had happened (BBC 2006).

An official inquiry into how the Forensic Science Service had failed to identify the bloodstains found that somehow the spots of blood had been 'missed' (BBC 2007). Identification of blood relies heavily on visual inspection by scientists—who themselves are human, and who may make human errors. In this case, the human errors were not identified for some time, and the delays had serious consequences. The Home Office minister apologized to Damilola's family for the distress caused (BBC 2007), while the Deputy Assistant Commissioner of the Metropolitan Police said that the errors had shaken his 'personal confidence' in forensic science (BBC 2006).

Questions

- How realistic is it to assume that forensic evidence is identified and analysed with 100 per cent accuracy, especially where people are involved in the collection, analysis, and interpretation of evidence?
- Do we expect that forensic science will be any less vulnerable to human error than other aspects of the judicial system? If so, why do you think this is?
- Can you think of many other situations where human error can have potentially serious consequences?

11.1 Introduction

Human factors (sometimes known as **ergonomics**) is a multi-disciplinary field which includes input from the fields of engineering, physiology, and applied psychology. The aim of human factors is to enhance efficiency, well-being, and safety at work by optimizing the interactions between people, the equipment they use, and the working environment. This is normally achieved by focusing on the physical and psychological capabilities and limitations of the people who do a job, and trying to get a good match between the person and the job demands. In doing this, ergonomists may have to consider a wide range of factors, including the design of equipment, the nature of job requirements and work schedules, the environment in which the task is completed, and organizational factors such as commercial pressures, competition, and legal and regulatory requirements. These include statutory requirements, as well as the requirements of authorities such as the Health and Safety Executive and other industrial and commercial regulators.

Human-factors specialists work in a variety of sectors, and are most often employed in safety-critical industries, where the costs and consequences of a mismatch between a person, the equipment, and the job demands can be severe. Because of this, many human-factors specialists and ergonomists can be found working in defence, aviation, rail and road transport, and process control industries such as nuclear power and air traffic control. However, human-factors principles can be employed in any environment or organization where there is a need to improve the way people use equipment, to make performance of a task more efficient or effective, to improve employee health and well-being, or to reduce the risk of injuries and accidents. As well as contributing to the design of safety-critical working environments such as nuclear power station control rooms and air traffic control towers, ergonomists may assist with the design of buildings such as airports and factories, as well as everyday products such as passenger seating on aeroplanes, trains and buses, car dashboards, supermarket checkouts, mobile telephones, and even kettles.

The focus of this chapter is very much on applying human-factors principles in work situations. Human factors and ergonomics in other contexts, such as design of the built environment and commercial product design, is beyond the scope of this chapter. Similarly, the emphasis is on the psychological aspects of performance at work (cognitive ergonomics) rather more than physical ergonomics, such as human size, strength, and movement (also known as anthropometrics and biomechanics). Physical ergonomics are only briefly considered here, as related to some general principles for workstation design.

The chapter begins with a focus on individual performance. Everybody approaches tasks differently, and, regardless of the job, nobody is perfect. Everybody makes mistakes at some point, and if a work system or workstation is to be designed for safe and effective performance, human error has to be taken into account. A work environment which is designed around the assumption that an employee or equipment operator is 100 per cent consistent, accurate, and reliable will be a very unforgiving environment. It is safer to assume that people will not always be at peak performance levels, and to take that into account when designing the work environment. This way, checks and procedures for identifying and correcting human errors can be built into work processes and procedures.

The chapter then moves on to consider some key performance-shaping factors—those aspects of the individual, the task, and the working environment which influence human performance at a task. These include individual factors such as competence, arousal, and experience. Environmental factors, such as working in sub-optimal conditions, and the physical work environment, are also considered, along with the organizational context. Designing work environments around employee characteristics and capabilities and the task requirements is the best way to ensure that errors are minimized and that safety and effectiveness are not compromised. The work environment may be an office, a factory production line, a supermarket checkout, or the flight deck of a commercial airliner, but the same general principles apply. A selection of basic ergonomics techniques and methods for evaluating tasks and designing work environments are also considered here.

Throughout the chapter, case illustrations from a range of industries are used to highlight how human-factors issues contribute to risk and safety at work. It is known that most accidents have multiple causes, with many accidents resulting from a complex combination of both technical and human failures. Some estimates suggest that human factors are implicated in as many as 85–90 per cent of all accidents (Sanders and McCormick 1987). Organizations which actively and systematically manage human-factors risks can improve workplace health and safety by reducing occupational injuries, increasing employee productivity and well-being, and reducing the chances of major accidents occurring or recurring.

11.2 Individual differences in performance

Individual variability at work is a fact of life. People differ in the skills and abilities they bring to a job, in their personality and motivation, and in their experience, training, and qualifications. This means that people vary widely in the approach they will take to the work that needs to be done, and in how well they do the job they do. The important issue from a human-factors perspective is to recognize and appreciate that people do not always perform the task the same way or to the same standard every time they do it. In other words, the performance of people is not always consistent, accurate, or reliable, and performance levels cannot be guaranteed. In order to be able to design working processes and environments more appropriately, we have to accept that sometimes work performance is outside acceptable tolerance levels or limits.

11.2.1 Performance variability

Imagine that a lorry driver is driving her heavy goods vehicle on the motorway, and wants to stay in the centre of the lane. The carriageway itself is not perfectly straight, so she has to continually focus on the lane and on her steering. She obtains feedback on her last adjustment by looking at her position on the road, and using this feedback adjusts her steering inputs and tries to maintain her position in the centre of the lane. She will not be in the dead centre of the lane all the time; sometimes she will be a little closer to the left-hand side of the carriageway, and sometimes a little closer to the right. However, for the most part, she does manage to stay within the lane—albeit that there are variations in her performance.

Very infrequently, there may be the odd occasion where she momentarily veers over the white line. The white line may be regarded as the boundary or limit of tolerance, and in this instance she has steered beyond the limit. The lorry driver's performance at staying in the centre of the lane varies, and on rare occasions her performance is beyond tolerance limits. This is how a human error is defined—a human error is a decision, an act, or a failure to act, which falls outside a given limit of tolerance.

In the vast majority of instances where the driver veers across the white line, she will be able to correct her steering and no harm will result. Rarely, another vehicle—say, a car—will be approaching from behind in an adjacent lane when the lorry driver is over the lane boundary. Usually, the lorry driver and/or the car driver will perceive the risk, and be able to take evasive action, steering out of the way in time. However, if neither the lorry driver nor the car driver realize what has happened quickly enough, or if they fail to react to the situation quickly enough (perhaps because the lorry driver is unwrapping a sweet, or the car driver is changing a CD), then the initial error may result in a collision. In other words, while human errors occur all the time, they only occasionally contribute to accidents. Nevertheless, human errors do increase the opportunities for accidents to occur, because if a lorry driver fails to stay within the carriageway boundary then the probability of a collision increases.

11.2.2 Human error

There are several different types of human errors, and several ways of classifying them. For example, Norman (1981, 1988) distinguished between errors that occurred within the intention to act, and those that occurred when executing the act itself. Rasmussen (1982) classified errors on the basis of whether they were rule based, **skill based**, or knowledge based. Reason's model (e.g. 1990, 1997) suggested that errors could be categorized as **mistakes**, **slips**, **lapses**, or violations. These approaches are not necessarily contradictory, although they highlight the fact that different errors occur at different points in the human information processing and performance process (see Figure 11.1).

Figure 11.1. Human information processing and performance loop

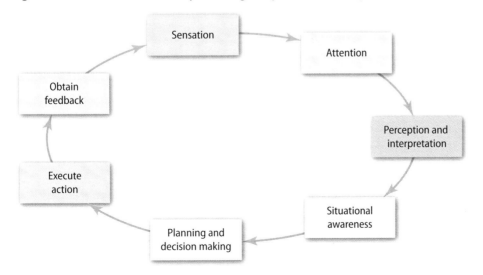

227

Chapter 11
Human
performance
and work
environment

Cognitive psychology provides various models for individual steps in the information processing and performance process. For example, dramatic research on inattentional blindness has shown that if people don't pay conscious attention to visual information, then it is unlikely to be perceived (Haines 1991; Simons and Chabris 1999). Perceptual accuracy is important in building situational awareness, a construct which describes how we perceive elements in our immediate environment and make judgements about the near future (Endsley 1995). However, few theories provide an integrated model which describes the whole human information processing and performance process. One exception is the model proposed by Wickens (described in Wickens 1992) and McCoy and Funk (1991). Based on integrating findings from several important areas of cognitive psychology, these authors suggest that human information processing and performance essentially follows a loop, comprising the steps of:

1 sensing and attending to information;

2 perceiving and interpreting this information;

3 planning and decision making using perceptions and interpretations, along with knowledge of previous experience from long-term memory;

4 using this information to form intentions to act;

5 performing the actual action or behaviours;

6 obtaining performance feedback via the senses, so that the circuit begins again.

Mistakes

Different errors occur at different stages of this process. Mistakes are errors that result from failing to form an appropriate intention; in other words, the intention is incorrect. A mistake can be a knowledge-based or a rule-based mistake. Knowledge-based mistakes often occur when an employee or operator has insufficient knowledge to be able to diagnose or assess a situation correctly. These errors occur at the perception and interpretation phase of the human information processing and performance feedback loop (see Figure 11.1). For example, a clerical assistant may not use the single- or double-sided copy control on a photocopier because he does not know that the default setting is single sided. When he asks for 200 copies, the result is that the photocopier only copies alternate pages of his double-sided document. This is a **knowledge-based mistake**, and it results from failure to diagnose the situation correctly, due to incomplete knowledge.

Rule-based mistakes occur when formulating a plan and deciding how to deal with a situation, rather than when interpreting or diagnosing a situation. Rule-based mistakes often involve applying an 'if-then' rule that works in one situation to a different context or situation. For example, when driving a car, it is usual to control the car by turning the steering wheel in the direction that you wish to travel (Patrick 1992). This can be expressed as '*if* you want to control the car, *then* steer the wheel in the direction that you wish to travel'. However, if the car is skidding on ice, then trying to turn in the direction that you wish to travel (out of the skid) will make the situation worse. When a car is sliding on ice, the appropriate rule is '*if* you want to control the car, *then* turn the steering wheel in the direction of the skid'.

However, the urge to turn out of a skid rather than in to a skid is very strong, mainly because of familiarity. In new or unusual situations, the urge to apply a rule which is based on our most typical experience is 'strong-but-wrong'. In contrast, most people have very little experience of driving on ice, and of steering successfully in these situations. The driver will not have appreciated that this situation is so different, and that this is a different context. The result is usually an unexpected outcome—in this case, the skid would be worse than anticipated.

Slips

Slips are failures in actually carrying out or executing a plan, and they generally occur less frequently than mistakes. Slips involve a correct or appropriate plan which is incorrectly executed (Norman 1981, 1988). The double-capture or intrusion slip occurs where a strong habit or skill intrudes on another, newly acquired habit or skill. In these cases, the habit or skill which was developed first is very hard to extinguish. For example, a man who has recently given up taking sugar in tea may find he automatically adds two teaspoons of sugar to his mug unless he makes a conscious effort not to do so. These types of slips can also occur when entering a familiar environment or behavioural pattern. An example would be the man who turns left at a particular junction at the weekend because that is what he does every day on his way to the office—although on this occasion he actually wants to go in the opposite direction.

Other slips include place-losing errors, where people lose track of where they are in a sequence of steps, and lost goal slips, such as where someone temporarily forgets what their intention was (as in, what did I come to the stationery cupboard for?). Behavioural reversals are another type of slip in which the correct action is performed on the wrong object. An example would be unwrapping a sweet, putting the wrapper in your mouth and throwing the sweet in the bin.

Sometimes mistakes and slips can look the same—they can involve identical behaviours. Categorizing or classifying the error would require investigating the intent behind the behaviour. Does the problem arise from diagnosing the situation (a knowledge-based mistake), formulating a plan to deal with the situation (a rule-based mistake), or in execution of the plan (a slip). It is not always easy to correctly categorize or classify an error unless you know *why* the error occurred. This is why it is important to find out what an employee or operator intended in order to establish the nature of an error.

Lapses

Lapses are failures of memory, where something that was intended to be done is forgotten. In other words, lapses are errors of omission or of failing to act, whereas mistakes and slips are errors of commission, or errors of action. They often involve what is known as forgetfulness or absent-mindedness in everyday terms. Typical lapses include missing a step in a sequence of behaviours, such as forgetting to complete the last steps. Interruptions at work can also lead to lapses, since they distract an individual from his place in the sequence.

 Activity Examples of human error

Try to think of some common, everyday examples of mistakes, slips, and lapses. Try searching the BBC news website for news stories involving human error. At what point in the human information processing and performance loop do these errors occur? What factors differentiate an everyday human error from a human error that makes news headlines?

Violations

Violations are another form of error, in that they are behaviours which fall outside a given tolerance limit. These are intentional acts which involve deviations from organizational expectations such as procedures and regulations. They essentially occur where an individual fails to comply with an official, documented behavioural requirement. Because of this, they are sometimes called instances of non-compliance. There are several different types of violations, including routine violations, necessary violations, optimizing violations, and malicious violations (Reason 1990, 1997).

Routine violations tend to involve taking short cuts and adopting 'work-arounds' to make it quicker, easier, or more convenient to complete the required task. They are routine because it becomes the norm to fail to follow company procedures, mainly because there are no sanctions for not complying with the rules. Necessary adaptations occur where some degree of corner-cutting is actually required to complete the task. Often, this occurs where people are working with outdated software or equipment that has not been updated to reflect changes to the work itself. Sometimes, people have to complete the task with equipment that is not suitable for its current purpose. Many supervisors and managers tolerate these instances of non-compliance in practice, as long as it suits them to do so. For example, one study of 100 work-related accidents in the construction industry showed that supervisors were often complicit in employee violations (Haslam et al. 2005).

229

Chapter 11
Human
performance
and work
environment

Optimizing violations are where people violate rules and procedures for the thrill of it—to obtain maximum satisfaction from a task. For example, breaking the speed limit in a company car might be against company policy, but some individuals may speed simply because they enjoy it. The rarest type of violation is a malicious violation. These violations are exceptional, wilful, and malevolent acts which are intended to cause maximal harm and damage. Examples include terrorism and sabotage. The vast majority of violations are non-malicious. Optimizing and malicious violations are generally not accepted by organizations, and supervisors and managers normally take action against individuals making these types of errors.

 KEY LEARNING POINTS

- Performance varies both within and between individuals. No two people approach a task in the same way, and even the same individual is not 100 per cent consistent in the way that he or she will carry out working tasks.

- When performance variations fall outside a limit or boundary of tolerance, a human error is said to have occurred. There are several different types of human error, and they occur at different points in the human information-processing and performance loop.

- Designing work equipment, systems, and processes according to human factors principles means that human fallibility should be taken into account.

11.3 Performance-shaping factors

Performance-shaping factors are factors associated with the individual, or an interaction between the task and the individual, that influence human performance for better or for worse. Two major areas are covered in this chapter: competence and stress, arousal and workload. However, there are many other performance-shaping factors, including fatigue and physical fitness.

11.3.1 Competence

One of the main sources of variation in individual performance at work is associated with competence. Competence is a mix of training undertaken in order to develop or acquire a skill, and ongoing expertise developed through practice and experience completing the task in a real-world context. Organizations can influence the level of competence within the organization by selecting people with regard to the knowledge, skills, and abilities required to be successful at work, or by training people in order to provide the knowledge, skills, and abilities required. In practice, most organizations combine selection and training interventions to achieve a competent workforce.

There is a relationship between competence and performance. As might be expected, novices (people with little experience of the task) tend to make more knowledge- and rule-based mistakes than experienced operators. Slips tend to be associated with automatic performance, where the skill is so well developed it can be executed with barely a conscious thought. Slips are made more frequently by experienced operators, who are more likely to be able to perform the task without conscious control. Hobbs and Williamson (2002) conducted a study of errors made by aircraft maintenance engineers. An analysis of maintenance tasks was completed based on observations of twenty-five aircraft mechanics, and the opportunities for error were identified. Ninety-nine errors reported by seventy-two aircraft mechanics were then examined, taking into account not just error frequencies, but also the actual opportunities for error to occur at different stages of the maintenance tasks, and in the job as a whole. When this was taken into account, it was shown that there was less error in skill-based performance than in rule-based performance, which again had less error than knowledge-based performance. Hence, there appears to be a hierarchy of performance, with skill-based performance being more reliable than rule-based performance, which in turn is more reliable than knowledge-based performance.

These findings on human error and skill link with what is known about the way humans develop skills and expertise. For example, the three-phase theory of skill acquisition (Fitts and Posner 1967) describes how people move from novice to expert performance. The theory was developed based on both research, and on the experiences of aviation instructors and sports coaches. As the name suggests, the theory proposes that people move through three phases in acquiring and developing a new skill. These are the cognitive phase, the fixation or associative phase, and the autonomous phase. The boundaries between the three phases are fuzzy, and it is not possible to predict when an individual will move from one phase to the next. The cognitive phase may overlap a little with the fixation phase, and the fixation phase may overlap a little with the autonomous phase. However, the cognitive and autonomous phases do not overlap, and the fixation phase takes considerably longer than the cognitive phase.

In the cognitive phase, performance is demanding. The novice is relying heavily on verbalizing task requirements, and is learning what the task involves as much as how to perform it. The novice has to voice what is required, mentally taking herself through the requirements. In this phase, the novice's performance is error prone, and advice or demonstration has to be provided by the trainer. In the fixation stage, which lasts longer than the cognitive phase, the trainee has grasped the ground rules and has practised the skill. Because of the time spent practising the skill, her errors have decreased, and the individual is able to perform at a reasonable level of speed and accuracy. In the third, autonomous phase, errors have decreased to a very low frequency, and the operator is now sufficiently skilled to be able to quickly diagnose and recover from any errors that are made. Performance has become largely automatic, with the operator now almost unable to verbalize the process. This automaticity also leaves the operator with spare capacity to complete other tasks at the same time. Over time, the high level of performance characteristic of this phase becomes more and more resistant to stress and interference.

While training, some individuals may find the demands on their psychological resources (attention and working memory) are too great for them to perform at the optimal level. The psychological demands can be too high—which is why training scenarios often break tasks down into simpler components to allow trainees to gain experience and build confidence and competence. For example, in air traffic control, computer simulations allow trainees to practise controlling traffic in relatively simple configurations. As the trainee develops competence, their ability to handle complexity increases—so more aircraft are added to the simulated training scenarios, and the trainee learns to deal with increasingly demanding situations, including emergencies.

Increased competence provides an individual with the ability to complete a task with increased resistance to periods of stress and arousal. This means that an individual is able to perform the task with a lower demand on her psychological resources of attention and working memory. The perceived demands of a task depend on the competence level of the person completing the task. The same task in identical working environments may be rated as highly demanding by a novice, and as dull and monotonous by an experienced operator.

11.3.2 Stress, arousal, and workload

Performance is influenced by the level of stress and arousal of the employee or operator. As already indicated, competence has a significant impact on performance. Competence moderates the effects of stress and arousal on performance. For every individual completing a particular task or part of a task, there is an optimal stress or arousal level required for peak performance. This is known as the Yerkes–Dodson law (Yerkes and Dodson 1908). However, the point of peak performance on this curve varies between individuals and tasks, making it difficult to predict the optimal level of arousal for any individual completing a specific task in advance.

As shown in Figure 11.2, some stress or arousal is necessary for optimal performance. If there is insufficient arousal, the employee will have a low psychological workload, towards the left-hand side of the curve, and the performance level will drop off as a result. Highly competent employees in particular will need sufficient challenges in their task to keep them at optimal performance levels, especially if their task is monotonous or routine. Consider baggage screening at airports: the probability of encountering a genuine threat is extremely

231

Chapter 11
Human
performance
and work
environment

Pause for thought
Consider a time when you had to learn a new skill at work. How did you begin to work out what was needed? How would you describe your performance at the task in the early stages? How much practice did you need to feel competent at the task?

Figure 11.2. The Yerkes–Dodson law

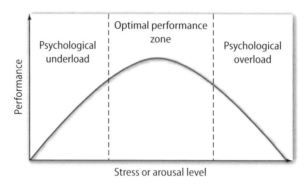

low, and so operator attention may actually decrease over the duration of a shift. However, the consequences of missing a genuine threat are potentially extreme. Threat image projection technology (TIP) is used to superimpose various images of a wide range of threats onto actual baggage. Although this is a 'false alarm' it helps to maintain vigilance among baggage screeners. As well as its tactical use at airports, this technology can also be used to select, train, and assess baggage screeners and improve their performance (Catchpole et al. 2001; Schwaninger 2006).

One classic, although controversial, study of performance under stress was conducted with a sample of US military personnel (Berkun 1964). In one condition, soldiers were asked to complete an insurance form while on board an aircraft that they had been led to believe might crash. In another condition, the soldiers were led to believe that they were under fire because the artillery had miscalculated their position, and they were required to follow radio communication procedures to inform the artillery to redirect. In the third condition, soldiers were deceived into believing that a colleague had been seriously injured; their task was to summon assistance. Clearly, the soldiers were under considerable stress induced by the belief that they or their colleagues were at real risk of immediate harm. Unsurprisingly, there were clear decreases in task performance under these conditions. In addition, the results showed that the fall-off in performance was more severe for soldiers with less experience. To a certain extent, skill and training can therefore compensate for or mitigate against the performance decrements which occur under stressful situations.

Analysis of the reliability of human performance has shown that with routine tasks, psychological underload increases the error rate equally among both experienced and novice employees. Regardless of experience, underload can double the frequency of human error, compared to optimal workload conditions. However, in conditions of moderately high psychological overload, experienced employees make only twice as many errors compared to their optimal workload conditions, where novice employees make four times more errors. When the overload becomes extreme, and workload is very high, the errors made by skilled operators increase fivefold compared to optimal workload conditions, while novices make ten times more errors compared to optimal conditions (Miller and Swain 1987). Hence, with routine tasks, the true benefit of experience is in reducing errors made under conditions of high workload.

High workloads can occur due to increased volume of work or increased complexity, especially when the situation is changing rapidly and/or unexpectedly. In an emergency, emergency warnings and alarms may increase the level of arousal, competing for the employee's attention. **Overload** will mean that the psychological resources available to deal with the emergency actually reduce—because the employee may now be under time pressure and considerable stress to correctly diagnose the situation, plan how to deal with it, and execute the recovery action. Unfortunately, these are exactly the conditions under which human performance becomes more unreliable. The very situations which require highly accurate responses are the same situations which may reduce the chances of reliable responses (e.g. Kirwan 1994, see Figure 11.3).

Pause for thought
Think of a task that you find boring or repetitive. If you had to do this task on a very frequent basis, for extended periods of time, how would this make you feel? What would you do to maintain your attention or add to the task to make it more varied and interesting?

Figure 11.3. Probability of human error in generic situations

233

Chapter 11
Human
performance
and work
environment

Task complexity and familiarity	Likely stress level of employee	Probability of a human error
Simple familiar task (frequently performed)	Minimal stress	1 in 1000
Complex familiar task (frequently performed)	Moderate stress	1 in 100
Complex unfamiliar task, rarely performed	Considerable stress	1 in 10
Highly complex unfamiliar task (rarely performed)	Extreme stress	0.5 to 1 in 1

KEY LEARNING POINTS

- The competence (experience and skill level) of an employee is related to the variability in their performance, and to the frequency and types of errors that they are most likely to make.

- Skill and expertise is developed over time. Novice performance relies on cognitive capacity and is error prone; skilled performance is automatic and may not be under conscious control.

- Workload also determines performance levels—there is an optimal level of arousal for peak performance. Both psychological underload and psychological overload have a detrimental effect on performance, increasing human errors and reducing effectiveness.

Case illustration
Improving operator responses to alarms

The Health and Safety Executive investigated a major accident which occurred at a refinery in Milford Haven in 1994 (HSE 2000; Wilkinson and Lucas 2002). The accident was caused by a complex chain of events, beginning with a severe electrical storm that resulted in some disturbances in the plant, and culminating in an explosion and the release of 20 tonnes of flammable hydrocarbon liquid. This ignited, and the subsequent fires burned for two days. UK refining capacity was significantly reduced by the incident, and costs of rebuilding and production loss were £48 million. Twenty-six people were injured, and fatalities were avoided purely by chance—some contractors were seconds away from entering the area when the explosion occurred, and minutes after people exited a building, the roof collapsed.

Detailed investigation of the accident revealed that, as well as the many technical failures which caused or contributed to the accident, there were significant issues associated with the way that the plant alarms were used. Firstly, there were too many alarms for the operators to be able to perceive, diagnose, and act on. There were 275 alarms in the 11 minutes before the explosion. This flood of alarms created significant overload. Some of the alarms provided general information, but the designers of the system had not prioritized the alarms. The information displays did not assist the operators in understanding what was happening, and may even have added to the confusion. In addition, the two operators on duty had not been adequately trained to deal with the prolonged and stressful nature of the event (HSE 2000).

Application of human-factors principles can improve the probability that people will respond to alarms appropriately. Since a large number of false alarms will reduce the chances of an appropriate response to a true alarm (much like the tale of the boy who cried wolf), false alarms should be kept to a minimum. There should also be a clear and obvious display of the alarm which does not rely on interpretation of complex information. The required operator response should be simple, well defined, and also well trained. Alarms should be prioritized so that the operator can deal with critical alarms first, and they should also take into account operator workload. The HSE suggests that given the fallibility of human responses to alarms, especially in emergency situations, it is inappropriate to depend on a human response to an alarm to prevent a major accident (Wilkinson and Lucas 2002).

11.4 The work environment

The work environment refers to the physical and organizational context in which work is carried out. The physical work environment is often thought of as the domain of ergonomics—designing controls, displays, workstations, and work systems around the requirements of the user (sometimes known as user-centred design). However, the organizational context is also a significant influence on performance, since organizational issues are major determinants of the way that people behave at work.

11.4.1 Physical work environment

Ergonomically designed workstations involve taking into account the characteristics of the employee or operators completing the task, and designing the workspace and work equipment around the capabilities and limitations of the intended user. This includes taking into account variations in performance, and particularly human error. One author suggested that 'if an error is possible, someone will make it. The designer must assume that all possible errors will occur and design so as to minimise the chance of the error in the first place, or its effects once it is made. Errors should be easy to detect, they should have minimal consequences, and, if possible, their effects should be reversible' (Norman 2002: 36).

In designing workstations, and the information displays and controls used by an operator, both cognitive ergonomics and **anthropometrics** and **biomechanics** have to be taken into account. There are several ergonomics design guidelines which provide detailed advice and standards for designing, or redesigning, workstations and control rooms. For example, there are British, European, and international standards relating to the design and layout of control rooms, workstations, and visual display units (e.g. BSI 1997, 2001). In addition, anthropometric data may be used to provide detailed information on the physical dimensions of both general population users, or a specific occupational group. For example, in some countries, there are minimum height requirements for recruits to the police and military. This means that equipment designed for use by these occupational groups will need to allow for the fact that people employed in those roles will, on average, tend to be taller than the general population.

In many cases where a workstation, control room, or other environment is being designed, one of the first requirements is to conduct a **task analysis**. A task analysis is a formal and systematic approach to describing the requirements of a task or piece of work, focusing on what has to be done, and/or how it is to be achieved (Kirwan and Ainsworth 1992). Different task analysis methods are used to assess different task characteristics, such as the timing and sequencing of tasks and subtasks, information and communication requirements, the controls and responses required from the operators (or several different operators), and/or the cognitive demands of the task. For example, hierarchical task analysis is a method of describing task components which breaks the task down into progressively smaller components or units, and describes when they should all be completed in the sequence. Link analysis is a technique for identifying the nature, frequency, and importance of links between parts of the work system, such as when a person physically moves from one location to another, or where information is passed from one person to another.

....

 Activity Workspace layout

Spend some time observing someone you know prepare a meal at your home, or a friend's house. Observing carefully, note how many times they move between different locations such as the fridge, oven, and sink. How many different cupboards and drawers do they open? What equipment seems to be used the most? If you were to optimize the layout of the kitchen for preparing this meal, what would you consider relocating, to where? Are the cooker, sink, and fridge arranged in a triangle, as often suggested by kitchen designers?

....

Function allocation

For an entirely new task or workstation, a stage of analysis known as function allocation determines which parts of the task are to be performed by technology, whether computer automation or other form of equipment, and which are to be performed by a human operator. It is very rare that a modern workstation or work system does not include some form of technology, usually a computing system. This applies whether the work environment is a nuclear power station control room, a train driver's cab, a commercial flight deck, a supermarket checkout, or a computer on an office desk. Function allocation takes into account the relative strengths and weaknesses of people and computers in processing information, and determines whether the task would be better accomplished by computer or a person.

All workstations involving technology are in effect a 'system'. A system should be designed to provide information on its status to the operator, who is then required to exert some form of control over the system. The design of information displays and controls has to take into account both cognitive ergonomics and physical ergonomics. Information displays have to be designed to provide all of the necessary information to the operator in an appropriate format, at the right point in time, while avoiding overload. This includes the design of non-visual 'displays', such as auditory warnings and alarms and haptic cues (where the system provides information to the user through the sense of touch, similar to the concept of a tactile joystick in a computer game). For example, the most important visual information would be placed in line with the operator's eye reference point.

Controls need to be located so that the operator can reach the relevant switch or button, and the grasp and force needed to operate the control also needs to be considered. Controls which are used infrequently would normally be placed in the periphery, with the exception of emergency controls. Although controls intended for emergency use would be needed very rarely, it is important that they are located within easy reach. Inadvertent or accidental deployment or operation can be prevented by the use of a physical guard or cover. The operator also needs to be able to distinguish between controls easily, and correctly identify which control is which. Methods of increasing discrimination between controls include grouping controls. For example, controls for a single function can be grouped together using a border on the control panel. This creates a perceptual separation between the controls for different functions. Another method of laying controls is to use the principles of natural mapping. Mapping refers to the correspondence relationship between a switch, button, or lever and the item it controls. Natural mapping is where controls are laid out in such a way that they have an obvious and intuitive relationship with the part they affect (Norman 2002).

Anthropometrics

Anthropometrics involves considering various physical and anatomical dimensions and characteristics in design. Normally, a tool or workstation is designed to be suitable for use by a certain proportion of the user population. For example, the designers of an office seat may decide to design for the smallest 5 per cent of the general population to the largest 95 per cent of the general population. This is known as designing for the 5th to the 95th **percentile**. A percentile is a way of describing rank-ordered data (such as body measurements) that indicates the proportion of a sample or population in terms of the percentage of individuals with values at or below a given point; wherever percentiles are used, the reference group or population should also be specified. Designing for the 5th to the 95th percentile is a common convention, but where equipment is safety critical, it is preferable to design for the 1st to the 99th percentile.

The use of anthropometrics is more complex than may initially appear to be the case. For example, it is not possible to design workstations and equipment for the 'average' or 'typical' user, because there is no such thing. Someone who is at the 50th percentile on one anthropometric body dimension, for example, is not likely to be at the 50th percentile on other anthropometric dimensions. In addition, there is normally a requirement to consider three, four, or more anthropometric dimensions, rather than just one or two. In designing a seat, designers would have to consider at least the buttock to knee distance, the distance from the thigh to the floor, and of course, the width of the sitter's bottom. In an anthropometric study of aircraft seating dimensions, ergonomists had to consider the movements that passengers might be required to make—such as evacuating in an emergency—as well as the dimensions of seated passengers (Quigley et al. 2001).

235

Chapter 11
Human
performance
and work
environment

Pause for thought
Taking into account human performance and error, and some of the performance-shaping factors discussed, what do you think might be the relative strengths and weaknesses to consider in (a) allocating a task to a computer, or (b) allocating a task to a human?

Case illustration
A new information display for pilots

Loss of the flight control system on a modern commercial aircraft is an extremely rare event—airworthiness regulations require that the chances of this occurring must be less than one in a billion flight hours. Nevertheless, such instances do very occasionally occur, and when they do, they normally have catastrophic consequences. One such incident occurred at Sioux City in 1989. In the simplest terms, debris from an engine failure severed all hydraulics in the tail of the aircraft, effectively leaving the pilots unable to fly the aircraft using normal flight controls. In this case, the pilots were able to gain some control over the aircraft using the throttles to control the thrust from the remaining two serviceable engines. Remarkably, using only the throttles to climb, descend, and turn the aircraft, the pilots managed to reach the airport, and they almost made a successful emergency landing. In the event, 111 passengers and crew were killed, but 185 people survived as a result of the pilots' attempts to control the aircraft by engine thrust alone.

One of the major difficulties associated with controlling an aircraft by thrust alone is that it is almost impossible to control the pitch (angle) of an aircraft independently of its speed. Reducing the amount of throttle from the engines will initially cause the aircraft to pitch down, allowing a pilot to descend the aircraft. However, as the aircraft descends, its speed will also increase. As the aircraft's speed increases, so does the amount of lift generated by the wings. At some point, this will stop the descent and will initiate a climb. As the aircraft climbs, its airspeed decreases, and the aircraft again pitches nose down and begins to descend. These cyclical changes are known as phugoid oscillations, and a pilot normally dampens their effect using the normal flight controls. Using only the throttles, it is very difficult for a pilot to know when to make adjustments, and by how much, in order to control these oscillations. This is because there is a time lag between making the adjustment, the adjustment having an effect, and the pilot perceiving the effect. An added problem is that the response of the aircraft itself varies depending on how much thrust is being delivered by the engines when the pilot makes the adjustment. Hence, although it is theoretically possible to control a commercial aircraft by thrust alone, it is very difficult to achieve in practice. Commercial pilots are not trained in flight-by-throttle techniques because loss of the conventional flight controls is an extremely rare occurrence.

Following this accident, a number of human-factors researchers decided to develop an information display that could help pilots in similar situations by allowing them to predict more precisely the adjustments required to accomplish their chosen manoeuvre. Following a task analysis, Demagalski et al. (2002) designed a display for use within the conventional engine display panel on the flight deck of a Boeing 747-200. The original display used columns, much like bars on a bar chart, showing how much thrust was currently being delivered. The new display provided a line indicator across these thrust bars to show the amount of thrust required to accomplish the manoeuvre and maintain level flight. A pilot would therefore be able to see, at a glance, how much thrust was being delivered, and how much more or less was required to reach the indicator level. The pilot would then be able to more accurately adjust the thrust on each engine, to make actual thrust delivery correspond to the amount of thrust required.

This new display was tested with ten commercial airline pilots in a flight simulator. Each pilot completed several tasks: a simulated flight control failure at 20,000 feet, a descent task, a turning task, and an approach and landing task. The experiment was a repeated measures design, counterbalanced to control for practice and learning, so all pilots completed all tasks, both with and without the new display. In the simulated recovery from flight control failure task, pilots were able to regain a straight and level position significantly more quickly when using the new display. In addition, pilots who used the new display reported significantly lower levels of workload. Pilots completing the descent task with the new display deviated significantly less from the optimum route, and pilots using the new display to complete the turning task reported significantly lower workload. The new display also resulted in a significant difference in the approach and landing task—there were significantly fewer deviations from the optimal flight path when the thrust display was available to pilots.

These results clearly demonstrate the importance of understanding a task in detail before attempting to design equipment and software. Where the flight control system is lost, phugoid oscillations and the control-response time lag make it almost impossible for pilots to control the aircraft. However, designing displays to provide the information they require in a simple and easily read format can significantly improve performance. Loss of the flight control system on a commercial aircraft means that the lives of hundreds of people depend on the performance of the pilots. Providing the information they need when they need it, in an appropriate format that is easy to use, can vastly increase their chances of success.

It is preferable to design workstations and equipment to be as inclusive as possible. In practice, it can be difficult to design equipment to accommodate a wide range of potential users without building in the capability for the user to make his or her own adjustments to the workstation or equipment. For example, a supermarket checkout chair may have control levers for the user to adjust the seat height and the level of lumbar support provided. An air traffic controller may be able to customize aspects of the radar display to his or her own preferences. As well as enhancing the user's physical and psychological comfort, adjustability can enhance well-being, as it allows the user some control over their working environment. In addition, anti-discrimination legislation often protects the rights of people with disabilities, requiring employers to make reasonable adjustments to working practices and work environments in order to accommodate individuals with specific disabilities or medical conditions, with limited exemptions.

237

Chapter 11
Human
performance
and work
environment

Sub-optimal conditions

Working in sub-optimal conditions can increase the risk of human error, and can have particularly detrimental effects on health and well-being. The challenges of working on a North Sea oil rig are very different in nature from the working environment experienced by a clerical assistant in an office. For outdoor workers, the weather is a major influence on the working environment, and is difficult to control. Additional environmental factors include the level of sound and noise; lighting and glare; temperature, humidity, and airflow; presence of vibrations; and so on. All of these environmental factors shape human performance, by increasing the probability of errors, and impacting on employee comfort and well-being. Where environmental protection is required, the work environment should be designed to account for the fact that operators may be using additional clothing, equipment, or procedures.

Where aspects of the work environment are potentially harmful to health and well-being, such as the presence of significant levels of noise and vibration, or exposure to potentially harmful substances or chemicals, there is a moral requirement to minimize the risks to employees. There is often a statutory and/or regulatory requirement to identify, manage, and reduce workplace health and safety risks, especially those associated with potentially harmful work environments. For example, in the UK, workplace health and safety legislation and regulations are enforced by the Health and Safety Executive. It is the responsibility of the employer to assess risks to workplace health and safety, and to manage those risks appropriately.

Repetitive injuries

Very repetitive physical tasks which are undertaken on a frequent or routine basis are associated with particular occupational health risks. These repetitive strain injuries are sometimes known as work-related musculoskeletal disorders. They normally involve cumulative injury to the muscles, tendons, and nerves in the hands, arms, neck, and lower back. Typically, the risk factors are associated with the repetition and duration of use of the joint, how much a particular joint deviates from the neutral position, the vibration, and any push/pull force involved. Certain occupations, such as assembly line workers and computer users, may be at greater risk than other occupational groups. It is also known that the experience of musculoskeletal pain is related to psychosocial factors at work. In one study, people who reported job demands such as stressful or hectic work and low control over their working environment were more likely to have a higher likelihood of reporting musculoskeletal pain, even when they had not been doing the job for long (Nahit et al. 2001).

11.4.2 Organizational context

It is not just the physical work environment which influences human performance at work. The organizational context influences the way that people behave to a greater extent than is often appreciated. Organizational factors determine the way that work is scheduled and organized, how work goals are accomplished, the level of supervision provided, and the behaviours that are rewarded. The culture within an organization determines the way that things get done, and there may be inconsistencies and differences between different departments or units even within the same organization. Some of the common organizational factors which influence human performance include supervision and reinforcement, since these often shape employee behaviour.

Supervision

Supervisors are key in ensuring that work is done according to organizational requirements. If there are procedures and regulations to be followed while completing a task, it is the supervisor who is normally required to enforce those regulations where the work actually gets done. Appropriate supervision is a key issue in reducing the number of violations and instances of non-compliance at work. Violations are human errors which involve deviating from organizational expectations of how the job will be done, and not complying with organizational expectations and requirements. These are usually documented in procedures, regulations, and manuals, but may be referred to very infrequently on the job. If supervisors do not prevent regular deviations from procedures and other organizational requirements, then the deviation becomes the norm. This 'normalisation of deviance' (Vaughan 1996) means that people will regularly disregard the procedures because they frequently perceive other people doing just that, without penalty or sanction.

Reinforcement

Related to supervision is the issue of reinforcement. When people are rewarded for procedurally compliant, safe behaviours, the probability that they will choose this course of action in the future increases. However, this does depend on the procedure being perceived as relevant, recent, and reasonable. People tend not to comply with procedures that are perceived as dated, irrelevant, or which do not take into account the constraints of the working environment. The frequency of violations tends to increase under these circumstances.

The principles of reinforcement are widely used in safety critical industries, in order to encourage high levels of compliance and to reward safe behaviours and decisions. For example, a contract research report commissioned by the Health and Safety Executive involved reviewing a range of behavioural safety programmes used within the offshore oil and gas industries (Fleming and Lardner 2001). The authors of this report concluded that such programmes can be very effective in improving levels of safety at work. However, they are most successful when there is a degree of trust between management and employees, when employees are engaged with the process of designing and implementing the safe behaviour programme, and when the most senior levels of management are completely committed to improving safety.

It is also important to remember that supervisors and managers make human errors too. Active errors are errors that occur at the 'sharp end' of operations—where people actually do the work. Examples would be the doctor or nurse at a hospital bedside or in theatre, the pilot on the flight deck, the technician at an electricity substation, the railway maintenance worker on the tracks, or the operator in a plant control room. However, other errors occur at the 'blunt end': these are often known as latent errors. Examples would be supervisory and management decisions about working procedures and policies, the adequacy of staff training, the arrangement of rotas and shift patterns, and the availability of appropriate tools and equipment.

Sometimes, it is obvious that a supervisory or management error has occurred, but this is not usually the case. Latent errors can lie dormant and undiscovered for weeks, months, or years before they become a significant issue, or are implicated in a more serious chain of events, such as an accident. Reason (1997) calls these 'pathogens'—viruses within the organization's systems. A thorough approach to human factors involves considering supervisor and management performance, as well as operator performance, in examining work and the work environment.

11.4.3 Organizational accidents

Human error, performance-shaping factors, and supervisory and management errors can all combine to cause accidents. According to Reason (1997), both active and latent errors can 'line up' in combination with other failures and this usually happens in unforeseen and unpredictable ways. 'Pathogens' allow the trajectory of an accident to breach an organization's safety defences. For example, typical defences could include training staff, providing them with suitable and appropriate equipment, ensuring that there is adequate supervision, and having management provide sufficient time and resources for people to meet the task demands. In Reason's (1997) model, these defences are often conceptualized as slices of Swiss cheese, with the holes in the slices representing chinks in the organization's safety armour. Hence Reason's model is often known as the 'Swiss cheese' model (see Figure 11.4).

Pause for thought
Can you think of any work situations where the rewards or sanctions for behaving in a particular way might have unanticipated and/or unintended consequences in terms of shaping employee behaviour?

239

Chapter 11
Human
performance
and work
environment

Figure 11.4. Organizational accidents

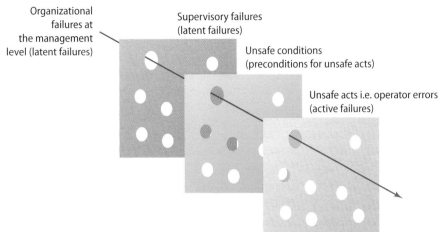

Organizational failures at the management level (latent failures)

Supervisory failures (latent failures)

Unsafe conditions (preconditions for unsafe acts)

Unsafe acts i.e. operator errors (active failures)

Although Reason's model is probably the dominant safety model in a number of sectors, it has come under criticism for being too linear, and for ultimately always suggesting that the root causes of an accident inevitably lie within management failures. If the accident could still have occurred without the management failure being present, then it is difficult to claim that the management error was a *causal* factor, although it may have *contributed* to the accident. Other authors have suggested that accidents are best conceptualized as networks of events, or as a wheel of concentric 'circles', much like ripples in a pond (e.g. O'Hare 2000). However, many accident models are derived from the findings of accident investigations, which naturally means that they rely on hindsight, and are of limited use in predicting when and where the next accident is likely to occur.

Organizational resilience

A relatively new concept in safety and accident research is that of organizational resilience, sometimes known as resilience engineering (Hollnagel et al. 2006). This approach to accidents and safety is more proactive and less focused in hindsight than other models of accident causation. It is a very recent development and hence it lacks the body of practitioner knowledge which is available for other theories of accidents. However, resilience engineering is a very promising paradigm which focuses on finding out how people manage to produce successful results in the face of failure. Resilience engineering acknowledges that safety is simply the flip-side of risk; and that success is the flip-side of failure. Organizations operate in risky environments, and the key to operating safely and successfully is to accurately anticipate and appropriately respond to the ever changing nature and levels of risk faced by the organization. In a nutshell, resilience is defined as 'the ability of systems to anticipate and adapt to the potential for surprise and failure' (Woods and Hollnagel 2006: 4). Hence, resilience engineering does not involve managing 'safety' separately from other aspects of business performance, but in understanding the dynamic nature of failure modes across an organization.

 Activity **What causes organizational accidents?**

Using credible sources on the internet, look up accounts of three different accidents. You can look for recent accidents, such as the Airbus A320 accident at Sao Paulo in Brazil in July 2007, or the Crandall Canyon mine collapse in Utah in August 2007. Alternatively, you may prefer to find information on accidents which have already been investigated, such as the Columbia space shuttle disaster in 2003, the Kaprun funicular fire in 2000, the sinking of the Estonia in 1994, or the Chernobyl nuclear disaster in 1986. Using the description for each accident, list the factors which have been described as causing or contributing to the event. How many factors are listed for each accident? How many of these might be regarded as 'human factors' issues? Are there commonalities between different accidents? What could the organizations concerned have done to reduce their risks?

KEY LEARNING POINTS

- The physical work environment should be designed around user requirements and limitations, including both cognitive and physical ergonomics.

- Human error should be accounted for in the design of all work equipment and software. If a particular error is possible, the designer should assume that someone will make it at some point in time.

- Ergonomic methods such as task analysis, link analysis, and function allocation can help to describe a task, prioritize a work layout, and determine whether a task is better performed by a person or by computer.

- Environmental factors, such as poor weather, poor visibility, and excessive background noise can also influence performance, and may promote human errors. If a task is being conducted under sub-optimal conditions, this should be considered when designing work equipment and software.

- Managers and supervisors are often key in determining how work goals are accomplished. Employee monitoring, the adequacy of supervision, and availability of appropriate reinforcement are also powerful influences on human performance at work.

- Organizational accidents have complex and multiple causes. Reason's (1997) model is very well known among health and safety practitioners; other approaches include O'Hare's (2000) wheel of misfortune, and the emerging discipline of resilience engineering (Hollnagel et al. 2006).

Chapter summary

- Human performance is variable, both within and between individuals. Performance variations which fall outside specified limits of tolerance are known as human errors.

- Human errors can be active, occurring where the work actually gets done, at the 'sharp end' of operations, or they can be latent. Many supervisory and management errors are latent errors.

- Individual competence influences the nature and frequency of errors at work. Psychological workload also influences performance, with conditions of underload and overload increasing the frequency of human error.

- In designing displays and controls, ergonomists should consider both the cognitive and physical attributes of the user. Psychological variations in performance, as well as physical differences in size, strengths and movement, are all important considerations in user-centred design.

- In designing equipment and work environments, ergonomists should design for error tolerance. Designers should try and reduce the consequences of error occurring in the first place, and also design to reduce the consequences of human error.

- Human-factors specialists and ergonomists use a range of techniques for systematically describing and analysing task demands and requirements. These include hierarchical task analysis and link analysis.

- Function allocation is a process used in designing new work systems, which allocates functions to a human or to computer automation depending on the relative strengths and weaknesses of each.

- Designing controls and displays requires consideration of both the task and the work environment. Working in sub-optimal conditions can be extremely challenging, potentially increasing the probability or error and reducing employee comfort and well-being.

- Organizational issues also influence human performance at work, and the quality of supervision and the availability of appropriate reinforcement can be important factors in shaping employee performance.

- Organizational accidents have multiple, complex causes, and often include a sequence of human errors. It is impossible to completely eliminate accidents, since by nature they are the result of a series of events which could not have been foreseen. However, taking a proactive approach to human factors can help organizations to reduce their accident risks.

241

Chapter 11
Human
performance
and work
environment

Assess your learning

Review Questions

1 Define, and give examples of, the main categories of human error covered in this chapter.

2 How do competence and workload influence human error?

3 What environmental factors might influence human performance at work?

4 Describe some ergonomic principles for designing workstation controls and displays.

5 How do supervisors and managers influence performance at work?

6 What causes accidents?

Assignments

ASSIGNMENT 1: User-centred design

Considering the two common tasks of (a) retrieving contact details and making a call and (b) writing and sending a new text message, compare a mobile phone produced by one manufacturer with a mobile phone manufactured by a different company.

- What are the differences in the way that task-relevant information is displayed between the two phone models?

- How do the user controls for completing these tasks differ between the two phone models?

- Using your knowledge of human error and cognitive ergonomics, what might the implications be for a user of one particular phone who is considering purchasing a new model from a new manufacturer?

ASSIGNMENT 2: Encouraging safe behaviours

A construction company is concerned that some of their employees are not following company procedures with regard to wearing personal protective equipment (PPE) on site. Employees are required to be wearing hard hats, high-visibility jackets, and protective boots before entering the site. However, one or two of the supervisors on the site gate have made exceptions, and now very few employees wear PPE on site. The problem has been identified by a senior manager, who wishes to address the situation before someone is injured. Using your knowledge of violations and the factors influencing human performance, what suggestions can you provide?

Further reading

The following resources are recommended for students who wish to further their interest in human factors and the design of the work environment.

Casey, S. M. (1998) *Set Phasers on Stun*. Santa Barbara, CA: Aegean; and/or Casey, S. M. (2006) *The Atomic Chef*. Santa Barbara, CA: Aegean.
Each book details a range of case studies involving design, technology, and human error. The case studies provide plenty of scope for thought and discussion, and references are provided for further reading.

Norman, D. A. (2002) *The Design of Everyday Things*. New York: Basic Books.
Previously published as *The Psychology of Everyday Things* (1988). An excellent discussion of the psychology of design, with plenty of examples.

Reason, J. (1997) *Managing the Risks of Organisational Accidents*. Aldershot: Ashgate.
Reason's theory of organizational accidents is one of the dominant paradigms in human-factors and accident causation.

Wickens, C. D., and Hollands, J. G. (1999) *Engineering Psychology and Human Performance*. (3rd edn.). Upper Saddle River, NJ: Prentice Hall.
Detailed coverage of human psychology relevant to the design and engineering of work.

Work psychology in practice
Using ergonomics to reduce occupational injuries

An aircraft only makes money while it is airborne. Turnaround time—the time when an aircraft is on the ramp—costs money. However, there are many essential tasks which have to be completed during this period: disembarking and boarding of passengers, baggage loading and unloading, refuelling and aircraft safety checks, flight and cabin crew changeovers and briefings, and housekeeping tasks such as loading and unloading galley carts of meals and duty free goods, emptying lavatories, and cleaning and tidying the cabin. Airlines typically aim to reduce the time that an aircraft spends on the ramp, by reducing the time that it takes to complete these tasks. Alpha Airlines were no exception—they wanted to reduce the time it took for their baggage handlers to load and unload passenger baggage. They adopted a 'Bag off!' scheme whereby baggage handlers could receive bonuses for processing all of the baggage for a flight as quickly as possible.

Within a few months of the 'Bag off!' scheme starting, the Operational Safety team became concerned that the rate of occupational injury among baggage handlers was rising. The handlers used trucks and carts to manoeuvre baggage between the terminal and the aircraft, with baggage on- and off-loading being completed manually. Concerned that the rise in injuries was due to baggage handlers not following specified manual handling procedures, the Operational Safety team initiated refresher training for all baggage handlers. During this refresher training, baggage handlers were briefed on the correct methods for latching and unlatching the baggage carts from the trucks, and for lifting and moving passenger baggage in the aircraft hold. In spite of the introduction of refresher training, the injury rate continued to rise—and the most common injury was damage to a finger.

Alpha Airlines wanted to investigate what was happening, and find a remedy as soon as possible. An ergonomics consultancy was commissioned to address the problem, and it transpired that almost all of the accidents involving injuries to fingers had been sustained when the employee was trying to latch or unlatch the baggage carts from the trucks. Alpha Airlines explained that all baggage handlers had received compulsory refresher training in the correct method of doing this, and hence the injuries did not appear to be caused by lack of knowledge or training. In response, the ergonomists undertook an analysis of the latching mechanism on the baggage carts, and a survey of finger and hand dimensions of the baggage handlers.

The research showed that the latching mechanism had insufficient space for the operator's fingers, and only 30 per cent of baggage handlers would be able to complete the latching and unlatching process with an acceptably low risk of injury. Most baggage handlers were aware that operating the latches was an awkward task, and many had experienced minor injuries which they had never reported officially. However, the introduction of the 'Bag off!' scheme meant that baggage handlers now were increasingly aware of the time pressure in on- and off-loading baggage. This meant that they tended to take less time to complete the task with their full care and attention—and the injury rate increased as a result.

Questions

- What recommendations do you think the ergonomists made to reduce the risk of injuries?
- Can you think of additional examples where an organization's drive to improve efficiency has unintended undesirable consequences?

Online Resource Centre

Visit the supporting online resource centre for additional material which will help you with your research, essays, and assignments, or you may find these additional resources helpful when revising for exams.
http://www.oxfordtextbooks.co.uk/orc/matthewman/

243

Chapter 11
Human
performance
and work
environment

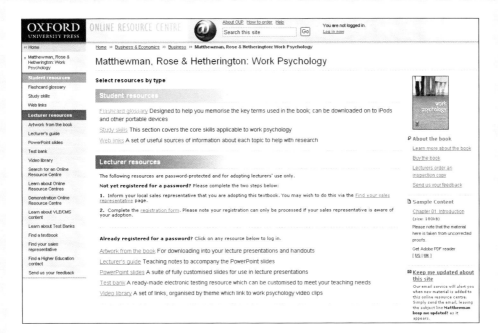

References

BBC (2006) *Damilola blood spots 'missed'*. BBC News, 9 August 2006. From http://news.bbc.co.uk. Accessed 30 September 2007.

BBC (2007) *Damilola mistakes 'human error'*. BBC News, 18 May 2007. From http://news.bbc.co.uk. Accessed 30 September 2007.

Berkun, M. M. (1964) Performance decrement under psychological stress. *Human Factors*, 6: 21–30.

BSI (1997) *Ergonomics Requirements for Office Work with Visual Display Terminals (VDTs)* Parts 1 to 17. British Standards Reference Number BS EN ISO 9241-1:1997. London: British Standards Institute.

BSI (2001) *Ergonomics Design of Control Centres*. Parts 1 to 3. British Standards Reference Number BS EN ISO 11064-1:2001. London: British Standards Institute.

Catchpole, K., Fletcher, J., McClumpha, A., Miles, A., and Zar, A. (2001) Threta image projection: applied signal detection for aviation security. In D. Harris (ed.), *Engineering Psychology and Cognitive Ergonomics*. vol. vi: *Industrial Ergonomics, HCI, and Applied Cognitive Psychology*. Aldershot: Ashgate, 231–7.

Demagalski, J. M., Harris, D., and Gautrey, J. (2002) Flight control using only engine thrust: development of an emergency display system. *Human Factors and Aerospace Safety*, 2/2: 173–92.

Endsley, M. R. (1995) Toward a theory of situational awareness. *Human Factors*, 37/1: 32–64.

Fitts, P. M., and Posner, M. I. (1967) *Human Performance*. Belmost, CA: Brooks/Cole.

Fleming, M., and Lardner, R. (2001) *Behaviour Modification Programmes: Establishing Best Practice*. HSE Offshore Technology Report 2000/048. Sudbury: HSE Books.

Haines, R. F. (1991) A breakdown in simultaneous information processing. In G. Obrecht and L. W. Stark (eds.), *Presbyopia Research*. New York: Plenum Press.

Haslam, R. A., Hide, S. A., Gibb, A. G. F., Gyi, D. E., Pavitt, T., Atkinson, S., and Duff, A. R. (2005) Contributing factors in construction accidents. *Applied Ergonomics*, 36: 401–15.

Hobbs, A., and Williamson, A. (2002) Skills, rules and knowledge in aircraft maintenance: errors in context. *Ergonomics*, 45: 290–308.

Hollnagel, E., Woods, D. D., and Leveson, N. (2006) *Resilience Engineering: Concepts and Precepts*. Aldershot: Ashgate.

HSE (2000) *Better Alarm Handling*. HSE Information Sheet CHIS 6. Sudbury: HSE.

Kirwan, B. (1994) *A Practical Guide to Human Reliability Assessment*. London: Taylor and Francis.

Kirwan, B., and Ainsworth, L. K. (1992) *A Guide to Task Analysis*. London: Taylor and Francis.

McCoy, W. E., and Funk, K. H. (1991) Taxonomy of ATC operator errors based on a model of human information processing. In R. S. Jensen (ed.), *Proceedings of the Sixth International Symposium on Aviation Psychology*. Columbus, OH: Ohio State University Press.

Miller, D., and Swain, A. (1987) Human reliability analysis. In G. Salvendy (ed.), *Handbook of Human Factors*. New York: Wiley and Sons.

Nahit, E. S., Pritchard, C. M., Cherry, N. M., Silman, A. J., and Macfarlane, G. J. (2001) The influence of work related psychosocial factors and psychological distress on regional musculoskeletal pain: a study of newly employed workers. *Journal of Rheumatology*, 28/6: 1378–84.

Norman, D. A. (1981) Categorisation of action slips. *Psychological Review*, 88/1: 1–15.

Norman, D. A. (1988) *The Psychology of Everyday Things*. New York: Basic Books.

Norman, D. A. (2002) *The Design of Everyday Things*. New York: Basic Books.

O'Hare, D. (2000) The 'Wheel of Misfortune': a taxonomic approach to human factors in accident investigation and analysis in aviation and other complex systems. *Ergonomics*, 43/12: 2001–19.

Patrick, J. (1992) *Training: Research and Practice*. London: Academic Press.

Quigley, C., Southall, D., Freer, M., Moody, A., and Porter, M. (2001) *Anthropometric Study to Update Minimum Aircraft Seating Standards. Prepared for the Joint Aviation Authorities*.

Rasmussen, J. (1982) Human errors: a taxonomy for describing human malfunction in industrial installations. *Journal of Occupational Accidents*, 4: 311–33.

Reason, J. (1990) *Human Error*. New York: Cambridge University Press.

Reason, J. (1997) *Managing the Risks of Organisational Accidents*. Aldershot: Ashgate.

Sanders, M. S., and McCormick, E. J. (1987) *Human Factors in Design and Engineering* (6th edn.). New York: McGraw-Hill.

Schwaninger, A. (2006) Airport security human factors: from the weakest to the strongest link in airport security screening. Paper presented at the 4th International Aviation Security Technology Symposium. 27 November–1 December 2006.

Simons, D. J., and Chabris, C. F. (1999) Gorillas in our midst: sustained inattentional blindness for dynamic events. *Perception*, 28: 1059–74.

Vaughan, D. (1996) *The Challenger Launch Decision: Risky Technology, Culture and Deviance at NASA*. Chicago: University of Chicago Press.

Wickens, C. D. (1992) *Engineering Psychology and Human Performance* (2nd edn.). New York: Harper Collins.

Wilkinson, J., and Lucas, D. (2002) Better alarm handling: a practical application of human factors. *Measurement and Control*, 35: 52–4.

Woods, D. D., and Hollnagel, E. (2006) Prologue: resilience engineering concepts. In E. Hollnagel, D. D. Woods, and N. Leveson, *Resilience Engineering: Concepts and Precepts*. Aldershot: Ashgate.

Yerkes, R. M., and Dodson, J. D. (1908) The relation of strength of stimulus to rapidity of habit formation. First published in the *Journal of Comparative Neurology and Psychology*, 18: 459–82. Available online at http://psychclassics.yorku.ca/Yerkes/Law/. Accessed 30 September 2007.

Part V
Management issues

Chapter 12
Assessing people at work

Amanda Rose and Karen Powell-Williams

Chapter objectives

As a result of reading this chapter and using the additional web-based material you should be able to:

- Appreciate the applications of work psychology to the design and evaluation of a variety of assessment procedures in work organizations.
- Understand the process of analysing jobs, and assessing job requirements.
- Appreciate the variety of methods that may be used to assess individual differences in cognitive ability, personality, and social and interpersonal skills.
- Identify key features in the design of assessment and development centres, and their uses for graduate selection.
- Identify the critical importance of reliability and validity of assessment procedures, and appreciate how these may be established and enhanced.
- Appreciate the social and cultural nature of the assessment process.
- Recognize the ethical issues that may arise during the assessment process, and the measures that may be taken to ensure fair and legal relationships between organizations and employment candidates.
- Identify new developments in the assessment and selection of people for work.

**Work psychology in practice
A degree of success?**

Olton University is a large higher education institution with 18,000 students, both postgraduate and undergraduate, situated in an old market town in Kent. The university has a central administrative department, which deals with all student records and holds information on students' assessment progress and results.

Work in the department is hectic, with frequent peaks in workload after exams and before graduation and also when the new year starts. All staff have to deal with student enquiries; this can be a positive side of the job and allows staff to see problems through to solution, but sometimes, when pressure is high, there have been some explosive incidents, when students have felt the staff were inefficient.

Although the staffing on the senior team in the department is very stable, turnover of clerical officers is running at about 50 per cent per annum. This is causing some problems as the HR department is having to hire temporary staff to make up numbers, and is finding the recruitment costs for the department are comparatively very high.

One April, the HR manager receives a number of resignation notices from the central administrative department, and realizes that he will need to recruit about 30 per cent of the headcount to make the unit fully operational.

He arranges a meeting with the Head of Administration and discovers the following information:

- All the staff in the office hold a first degree, and some have postgraduate qualifications.
- The Head of Administration feels strongly that people who have been at university are in the best position to deal sympathetically with students' queries.

Current selection procedures involve an informal interview with the Head of admin and their deputy.

Questions

- Critically analyse the selection process currently in use in the department. What do you consider to be its key strengths and weaknesses?
- Suggest an alternative process, capitalizing on the strengths you have identified, and addressing the weaknesses.

12.1 Introduction

Organizations assess people for a number of different purposes: for example:

- To recruit new people into the organization.
- To select existing employees for new posts.
- To select likely candidates for succession planning.
- To assess training and development needs.
- To assess people's potential for promotion and career development.
- To assist in team building at work.
- To reassess people's skills and aptitudes after injury or illness.
- To assist in equal opportunities audits.

Virtually every person in employment has had the experience of 'being assessed' at some point in his or her career. This is always a significant event, sometimes quite positive and affirming, but sometimes quite challenging, making the person reflect on their concept of themselves. For such reasons, psychologists are interested in assessment at work, and much research has been conducted to explore and examine this complex process.

The term 'assessment' refers to the process of measuring personal attributes that are relevant to successful job performance. This usually involves making judgements about peoples' cognitive, interpersonal, and social skills, and this is where the skills of work psychologists' are especially relevant.

Work psychology in practice
A degree of success?

Olton University is a large higher education institution with 18,000 students, both postgraduate and undergraduate, situated in an old market town in Kent. The university has a central administrative department, which deals with all student records and holds information on students' assessment progress and results.

Work in the department is hectic, with frequent peaks in workload after exams and before graduation and also when the new year starts. All staff have to deal with student enquiries; this can be a positive side of the job and allows staff to see problems through to solution, but sometimes, when pressure is high, there have been some explosive incidents, when students have felt the staff were inefficient.

Although the staffing on the senior team in the department is very stable, turnover of clerical officers is running at about 50 per cent per annum. This is causing some problems as the HR department is having to hire temporary staff to make up numbers, and is finding the recruitment costs for the department are comparatively very high.

One April, the HR manager receives a number of resignation notices from the central administrative department, and realizes that he will need to recruit about 30 per cent of the headcount to make the unit fully operational.

He arranges a meeting with the Head of Administration and discovers the following information:

- All the staff in the office hold a first degree, and some have postgraduate qualifications.
- The Head of Administration feels strongly that people who have been at university are in the best position to deal sympathetically with students' queries.

Current selection procedures involve an informal interview with the Head of admin and their deputy.

Questions

- Critically analyse the selection process currently in use in the department. What do you consider to be its key strengths and weaknesses?
- Suggest an alternative process, capitalizing on the strengths you have identified, and addressing the weaknesses.

12.1 Introduction

Organizations assess people for a number of different purposes: for example:

- To recruit new people into the organization.
- To select existing employees for new posts.
- To select likely candidates for succession planning.
- To assess training and development needs.
- To assess people's potential for promotion and career development.
- To assist in team building at work.
- To reassess people's skills and aptitudes after injury or illness.
- To assist in equal opportunities audits.

Virtually every person in employment has had the experience of 'being assessed' at some point in his or her career. This is always a significant event, sometimes quite positive and affirming, but sometimes quite challenging, making the person reflect on their concept of themselves. For such reasons, psychologists are interested in assessment at work, and much research has been conducted to explore and examine this complex process.

The term 'assessment' refers to the process of measuring personal attributes that are relevant to successful job performance. This usually involves making judgements about peoples' cognitive, interpersonal, and social skills, and this is where the skills of work psychologists' are especially relevant.

Work psychologists can assist in the assessment process through:

- Their knowledge of individual differences and their development of theory about how individual differences are structured, develop, and change. (See Chapter 3 on Personality and Individual Differences.)
- Their skills in measuring individual differences.
- Their understanding of how people form impressions of others, and how this process may be affected by cognitive, social, and cultural factors. (See Chapter 4 on Perceptions and Attitudes at Work.)

This chapter will consider the problems and difficulties of assessing people in work organizations, and the psychological impact of being 'assessed'. It will explore ideas about how assessment decisions are made, and consider how an examination of theory and research in the psychology of individual differences may inform our understanding of this process.

The chapter will begin with an overview of the assessment process, exploring ways that organizations can ensure that the procedures and methods they employ to select people are appropriate to both organizational and individual needs, surveying a number of different methods for assessing work-related skills and **aptitudes**. It will also consider the special case of graduate recruitment. Organizations exist in specific social and cultural contexts; the chapter will consider the impact of these aspects and identify contemporary trends in professional practice.

12.2 An overview of the assessment process

The most common reason for organizations assessing people is the need to fill vacancies. In its ideal form, an assessment and selection procedure is designed with the following steps:

- The vacancy is analysed and the skills, aptitudes, and personal qualities required to do the job are established.
- A set of techniques are designed that will allow the organization to test whether candidates have the required skills to sucessfully perform the job.
- Organizations may choose from a wide range of assessment methods, including interviews, psychometric tests, work sample tests, and group exercises.
- A pool of candidates are contacted and shortlisted for further assessment.
- A successful job candidate is selected.

The success of the appointment is evaluated, and this information is fed back into an appraisal of the process, and adjustments to the procedure are made if appropriate.

12.2.1 Job analysis

A key component of the assessment process is **job analysis**. The aim of job analysis is to produce a job description, and a person specification. This will create a picture of the skills, aptitudes, and personal qualities that are necessary to perform the job role. This information then guides the assessment of job candidates.

There are many ways that organizations can analyse jobs. If a job description already exists, the analysis will start from this—but any assessment should take the opportunity to reconsider the relevance of the current job description. Analysis might include:

- Interviews with members of the **role set** (people that the job incumbent needs to interact with in order to get the job done).
- Diary studies (job incumbents may be asked to complete logs of their activity, including details of 'critical' incidents—any significant or difficult aspects of their work).
- Observation (which can be through job shadowing or participation in work).
- Archives and records (reports or information about the department and its work).

Figure 12.1. An overview of the assessment process

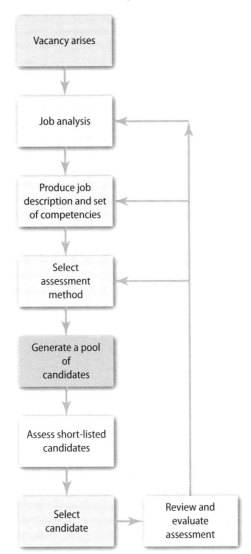

- Exit interviews (an informal discussion with those leaving the organization to explore reasons for the move).

There is an implicit assumption in job analysis that jobs are relatively stable, but in current organizational contexts this is not necessarily the case.

Rather than produce fixed job descriptions, organizations may specify a flexible list of options that the job incumbent might be required to do, or they may specify a number of **competencies** that successful candidates should possess.

···

 Activity Job analysis

Attempt an analysis of a job you have undertaken, or analyse the job of 'student'.

- What tasks does the job involve?
- Produce a diagram to show the role set associated with the job.
- What sort of qualities are needed for this job? List educational qualifications and personal qualities.

···

Figure 12.2. Example of a competency list

Competencies for Graduate Trainee
Interpersonal Skills: relates well with others; is tactical, compassionate, and sensitive and treats others with respect; provides timely and honest feedback in a constructive and non-threatening way.
Influencing Others: presents facts, analysis, and conclusion in a way that demonstrates command of content; works to make a particular impression on others; uses language and examples that speak to the issues, experience, and organizational level of the audience.
Financial Awareness: understands the relationship of the budget and resources to the strategic plan; complies with administrative controls over funds; monitors expenditure and resources.
Problem Solving: determines the significance of problems; collects data, distinguishes between relevant and irrelevant data; uses tools such as flow charts; uses logic and intuition to arrive at decisions.
Group Working Skills: exhibits behaviour that enhances the quality of group processes; encourages participation and creativity from others; distinquishes process from content; leads the group to consensus, problems solving, and task accomplishment.

The competency approach

Since the 1980s Human Resource Management practice has been dominated by the competency approach to understanding successful job performance. A competency is defined by Boyatzis (1982: 21) as:

> an underlying characteristic of a person . . . it may be a motive, trait, skills, . . . or a body of knowledge that he or she uses'. Competencies are those characteristics that are identified as necessary for the successful performance of a task. So for example, in order to be a successful surgeon, a relevant set of competencies might include:
>
> Knowledge of anatomy.
>
> Manual dexterity.
>
> Interpersonal effectiveness
>
> Teamworking skills.

The use of the competency approach is said to lead to clearer, more efficient, and therefore more reliable and valid assesment (IRS 2002). For example, Clasen et al. (2003) notes that the development of a set of core competencies for healthcare workers in the area of in-patient mental health settings has produced benefical effects on recruitment as well as the training process in this specialist area.

Some organizations may generate competency lists that are applicable to specific job roles, or levels of work, for example: a list of competencies may be developed for graduate trainees. Some organizations have a generic list of competencies that are used over the organization as a whole.

However, there has been some concern over the usefulness this approach. There is some confusion in the literature over what a competency actually is (Wills 1993). The design of competency schemes produces lists of observable behaviours, and some have argued that job competence involves the integration of a much broader and more subtle range of qualities, and that competence often emerges as a feature of teams rather than individuals (Burgoyne 1989).

The approach assumes there is one best way of doing a job rather than many, and this is hard to marry with the flexible and changing nature of work in many contemporary organizations, and the diverse nature of the workforce. (Lievens et al. 2004; Sparrow 1995)

12.2.2 Evaluating assessment procedures: reliability and validity, utility and acceptability

The **reliability** and **validity** of assessment procedures are the key criteria for evaluating the effectiveness, usefulness, and fairness of methods. The concepts of reliability and validity have been discussed in Chapter 2 on Research Methods in Work Psychology, and in Chapter 3 on Personality and Individual Differences.

Pause for thought
In May 2008, the European Space Agency advertised for four new astronauts to join their team. What competencies should astronauts possess?

In the context of occupational assessment, the reliability of procedure lies in the consistency of the scores it achieves. Additionally, the reliability of a method will rely on the consistency of the assessors, be they marking ability tests, or evaluating people in interviews.

Reliability is established through a number of correlation methods. For example, interjudge reliability is established through the correlation of the scores given to a candidate by one assessor with the scores assigned by another. Correlations of about 0.8 are considered acceptable. Establishing the reliability of a psychometric test (for example, an ability test) involves comparing the results obtained by a group of candidates at one point in time with results obtained at another time, for example three weeks or six months later. Correlations of below 0.7 would be considered evidence of low reliability.

Validity is the extent to which the method is measuring what it purports to measure. Thus, valid tests of verbal reasoning should measure verbal reasoning and not simply vocabulary. The use of invalid tests is clearly unfair to candidates, and certain types of invalidity may discriminate unfairly against specific groups.

Validity is a complex issue, and there are various types of validity. **Criterion validity** is established by comparing the results obtained in one test with those obtained from another well-established measure of the same trait or quality. For example, successful architects should score well on tests of spatial reasoning, maths graduates should score well on tests of numerical ability. If they do not, this would question the validity of the test.

Predictive validity pits the results of a test or assessment against future performance or development. For example, new graduates who score well on a test of leadership potential should achieve higher promotion levels than those who score lowly.

Over time, the accumulation of evidence about the relationship of a test or assessment procedure with job performance may suggest that the test is measuring something real, in a consistent and useful way. This is evidence of **construct validity**. In some psychological tests, new concepts that derive from theory are incorporated. For example, in personality tests, the construct of extroversion is frequently included. Many years of research have indicated the robustness of this construct, but the question must be asked, is it a real and substantial difference between people, or an artefact of the measurement itself? Only future research will reveal the answer. (See Chapter 3 on Personality and Individual Differences.)

In occupational settings, additional criteria would include the utility of assessment procedures—whether the assessment has been undertaken in a cost-effective fashion. Another significant feature is whether the procedure is acceptable to candidates, this is sometime termed **face validity**, or how relevant candidates feel a procedure is to job performance. Candidates may also judge how objective and fair they feel procedures are (Sackett and Lievens 2008).

12.2.3 Testing as a social situation

Measuring people is not a simple quantification process, like dipping a thermometer into water. A common feature of all the assessments discussed in this chapter is that they involve a *social interaction*: at least two people, and often groups of people, have to interact and communicate in order to generate information. This simple observation has important implications for the results obtained, as well as being an important aspect of the experience for all parties concerned.

To understand any social situation, we need to analyse the specific perspective of each participant in the interaction. We also need to consider how these respective positions might interact and mutually affect each other.

People take part in occupational assessments for a purpose. Their beliefs and attitudes towards what they are doing as well as their motivation and concerns about the assessment may all affect how they approach the procedure itself.

The person conducting the test again has specific aims. They are trying to obtain specific information, but they may also hold beliefs and attitudes about the process they are engaged in, their own role in the organization, and the candidates they are meeting. All these factors may affect the assessment process.

Testing and assessment is also part of the broader cultural and social context. Culture is a source of people's ideas about testing and about assessing people for work in general. Our

Case illustration

The Embedded Figures Test: high in reliability but totally invalid?

A test may be entirely reliable, but completely invalid. For example, the Group Embedded Figures Test is a well-known paper and pencil test which measures an individual's freedom from group pressure. It was developed in the 1960s by Witkin (Witkin 1965). The test measured a trait termed 'field dependence'.

The test required people to locate a simple template shape embedded within a complex figure. Years of research indicated that males were higher in field independence than females, and that there were marked cross-cultural variations in the trait, which were related by researchers to local child-rearing practices. The test was highly reliable with test retest scores reaching into the 0.8s and 0.9s.

However, as research accumulated, the relationship of scores on the embedded figures test to scores of spatial reasoning on ability tests was shown to be exceptionally high. This cognitive skill is shown by other studies to vary by gender and by cultural experience. A study by Li-Fang Zhang (2004) investigated the performance of Chinese students on tests of learning style, academic ability, and the Group Embedded Figures Test. This work demonstrated that the EFT correlated most strongly with students' ability in geometry. Research into the test therefore suggests that it measures spatial reasoning, and not personality.

culture is also the source of our ideas about people, and the relative differences between groups, for example different ethnic groups, age groups, genders, etc. An appreciation of the social nature of assessment at work is important in understanding the total process.

KEY LEARNING POINTS

- The assessment and selection process involves a number of stages designed to aid the selection of effective candidates.

- Successful and fair selection requires a detailed knowledge and understanding of job tasks, and this is achieved by job analysis.

- The Competency Approach is commonly used to specify core characteristics of successful job incumbents.

- A variety of assessment methods are employed either singly or in combination to aid the selection process.

- The reliability and validity of measures should be established and maximized by organizations.

- Culturally derived attitudes to testing and assessment may mediate the impact and effectiveness of techniques. The perception and evaluation of candidates is an important consideration in the design of assessments.

12.3 Assessment methods

Organizations use a variety of methods to assess people at work. Each method has associated advantages and disadvantages. Methods include:

- Interviews.
- Psychometric tests.
- Job sample tests.
- Group exercises.
- Assessment and development centres.

The choice of method will depend on a number of factors, including the availability of organizational resources, the culture of the organization, and the acceptability of the methods to applicants and employees.

A survey by the CIPD (2007) shows the following pattern of use by UK companies in the public and private sectors:

Structured panel interviews: 88 per cent.

Competency based interviews: 86 per cent.

Telephone interviews: 61 per cent.

Ability tests: 72 per cent.

Personality questionnaires: 56 per cent.

Assessment centres: 47 per cent.

Group exercises: 46 per cent.

Online tests (selection): 30 per cent.

12.3.1 The interview

The most commonly used assessment method is the interview. It is hard to imagine an organization hiring someone without an opportunity to meet and talk to them, and by the same token people may not want to work for a company before they have had the opportunity to see inside the organization and to meet the people currently working there.

The interview is the only method of selection in some organizations, and the sole assessment procedure for some grades of employees. Huffcutt et al. (2001), in a survey of companies' uses of interviews, found that they were employed to measure the following characteristics:

- Mental capacity.
- Personality tendencies.
- Applied social skills.
- Interests.
- Background credentials.
- Assess person-organization 'fit'.

There is evidence that interviews are popular with job applicants. For example, in a study of American and French students, Steiner and Gilliland (1996) found that interviews, work sample tests, and CVs were the most highly rated methods. Harland et al. (1995) found that candidates rated interviews as fairer than personality tests as methods of selection.

Employment interviews may be unstructured, where an interviewer talks informally and without a predetermined set of questions, or they may be structured. Decisions made in unstructured employment interviews have been shown to bear almost no relation to subsequent job performance (Judge et al. 2000). Structured interview methods have been found to correlate more highly with subsequent job performance, and those which are behaviourally anchored and competency based have been estimated to reach correlations with subsequent job performance of about 0.56 (Huffcuff and Woehr 1999).

12.3.2 Problems with interviews

Research has frequently found evidence of bias in employment interviewing. Over and above straightforward prejudice (against certain ethnic groups, for example) evidence exists of errors arising from perceptual distortion and failure of memory and attention. Research suggests the following common problems:

Primacy and recency effects

People are limited by the amount of information they can respond to any one time. George Miller (1956) suggested that we can only hold up to 7 plus or minus 2 'bits' of information in short-term memory. Interviews are highly demanding situations in terms of the amount of complex information to be noted and processed and so it is little wonder that interviewers forget, distort, and fail to notice a great deal about candidates.

Many studies have indicated that when presented with a huge amount of information, people have a tendency to be selective about what they retain. Information received at the onset or the beginning of an event, or at the end, is more likely to be recalled than that received in the middle. Hence, if interviewers are seeing a number of candidates over the course of a day, they may have better recall of the first (**primacy effect**) and the last (recency effect). Notes taken during interviews are helpful aids to recall, but the strength of the impression retained may fall foul of this memory effect.

Halo and horns effect

A positive first impression and expectation of a candidate can affect subsequent evaluations. This tendency is termed the '**halo effect**' (Kelley 1950). There is also a negative halo or '**horns effect**', where negative information about a candidate can bias all subsequent perception (see Figure 3.1).

For example, Dougherty et al. (1994) found that candidates with high pre-interview ratings (test scores and application forms) were responded to more positively by interviewers. This had a direct effect on the behaviour of the interviewer. In particular there was more 'selling' of the organization and more information about the job given out in such interviews.

The physical appearance of applicants has been shown to produce a halo and horns effect. Pingatore et al. (1994) explored the impact of obesity on hiring decisions. They used male and female actors as applicants for either a sales job or systems analyst job. The actors were rated in mock interviews by volunteers. The weight of the actors was manipulated to be either normal or slightly obese, with the use of padding. Results indicated that all obese applicants were rated more negatively than normal applicants, and this was especially so for the females.

Forsythe (1990) conducted a study involving a mock interview of female candidates in either masculine attire (dark suit) or feminine attire (beige dress). Females candidates in business suits were more likely to be selected for employment, and were rated as more competent by interviewers.

Contrast and similarity effects

Perceived similarity between candidates and interviewers may bias the direction of hiring decisions. Interviewers have been shown to favour candidates they perceive as similar to themselves; this is termed the 'cloning effect', or 'similar-to-me' effect (Sears and Rowe 2003).

Lin et al. (1992) found that interviewers tended to rate members of their own group more highly than candidates from different ethnic groups. Prewett-Livingstone et al. (1996) found that in interviewing panels where race was balanced, there was a tendency for interviewers to favour their own race, but in unevenly mixed race panels, there was a tendency for minority race interviewers to support the views of the majority.

This study highlights the issue of conformity in panel interviews. There may be explicit and implicit pressure to conform in panel decision-making. (See Chapter 7 on Groups, Teams, and Decision Making.)

Impression management

Candidates in employment interviews may, understandably, strive to give an impression of themselves that they feel offers them the best chance of being selected.

Erving Goffman (1959) has suggested that we carefully manage the impressions we give to others in all social situations. He likens social life to a theatrical performance. We are all actors, following rehearsed parts. We may have costumes that support our performances, so for example, people often 'dress smart' in employment interviews. We have 'props', which support us in the development of our characters, for example in the way that workers in the City of London financial sector may wear striped suits, braces, and carry a copy of the *Financial Times* to signal their role. Higgins et al. (2003) in a meta-anaysis of studies of ingratiation at work, concluded that candidates who use self-promotion and ingratiation in interviews can boost their chances of success. Howard and Ferris (1996) found more 'self-promotion' in candidates who perceived their interviewer to be different from them. They found that interviewers may detect self-promotion and may respond negatively to it. In this study interviewers tended to rate self-promoters as low in competence.

Pause for thought
Research into job interviews has tended to use simulated interviews or video ratings of student and actors, rather than real-life candidates. Are there ethical reasons that make it difficult to conduct research with real job candidates? Does the use of simulation invalidate results in such studies?

KEY LEARNING POINTS

- Interviews are used to assess a wide variety of job-related skills.
- Perceptual bias may affect the accuracy of interviews.
- Research suggests that the reliability and validity of the interview can be improved if a structured format is used to gain evidence of past experience and competency.
- Impression management is an important component of candidates' job-seeking strategy.

12.3.3 Psychometric tests

Psychometric tests are standardized procedures for assessing a variety of psychological characteristics, including cognitive ability and personality. The defining characteristics of such tests are:

- they are administered in a standardized format.
- they have standardized instructions and scoring procedures.
- The scores achieved by individuals can be compared with results of large samples, termed **norms**.

....

Activity Using tests as part of an assessment package

Organizations must ensure that the tests they use are relevant to candidates in terms of their educational level, age, gender, and culture. If the candidate has a declared disability, the organization needs to make appropriate provision for this.

In the UK, the British Psychological Society and the CIPD have jointly developed a Certificate of Competence in Occupation Testing, to promote **best practice** in the use of ability tests (Level A) and personality tests (Level B).

The training focuses on the skills of choosing, administrating, and scoring tests, giving feedback to candidates and understanding the ethical aspects of testing.

Access to tests is restricted to those who have completed this training. Search the B.P.S. website http://www.bps.org.uk to find information about the certificate.

....

Case illustration
Intelligence tests

The first intelligence tests were developed by Alfred Binet (1912–19). At a time when mass state education was being established in France, Binet was hired by the French government to develop a way of identifying children who needed special educational support. For this, it was important to establish what the average or typical child could be expected to achieve at different ages. Binet experimented with a wide range of intellectual measures, including phrenology (measuring the skull and exploring the 'bumps' on the surface of the head). Through trial and error he developed a set of standardized measures which could identify the typical skills of children at different ages. He developed the concept of **mental age**—the average or typical level of intellectual performance at a specified age, which might not correspond with the chronological age of the child.

Intelligence quotient (IQ) is the ratio of mental age to chronologcial age × 100. These early tests were individually administered. Terman further developed the Binet test at Stanford University in the USA, during the 1930s. The Stanford-Binet is still used today, most especially in clinical settings. The work of Binet established a foundation on which all subsequent testing was developed. During the First World War, paper and pencil tests that could be administered to large groups of candidates were produced in the USA, and in Europe. These were then adapted in peacetime for occupational use.

Questions

- What are the advantages and disadvantages of individually administered tests?
- How would they differ from group administered or online tests?

Figure 12.3. Examples of ability test questions

> 1. Numerical reasoning.
>   Complete the following sequences:
>   (a) 10, 7, 4, 1, ?
>   (b) 3, 6, 10, 15, ?
>
> 2. Verbal reasoning.
>   (a) Which word is the odd one out?
>   Sapling, kitten, puppy, duckling, foetus.
>   (b) Black is to grey.
>   As:
>   Agony is to??
>   Choose one: Night? Scream? Pain?

12.3.4 Assessing cognitive ability and skill

Ability tests are used in very many contexts outside employment, especially in education, and many people will have experience of them before being asked to complete a test for employment purposes.

The CIPD survey of 2007 found that 72 per cent of UK organizations used ability tests in some way in the assessment and selection process. The nature of ability tests available mirrors developments in psychologists' understanding and views of the nature of cognitive ability itself. There is some debate about what precisely *intelligence* is, and therefore how it may be measured. (See Chapter 3 on Personality and Individual Differences.)

In general, contemporary tests follow the multifactorial model, and are composed of subtests providing measures of verbal, numerical, abstract, and spatial and mechanical reasoning.

Ability testing and job performance

How far do ability test scores predict job performance? In a **meta-analytic** review of evidence in the UK, Cristina Bertua, Neil Anderson, and Jesus Salgado (2005) found overall correlations of between 0.5 and 0.6. They also found higher relationships where jobs contained more complex tasks.

However, further evidence suggests that the relationship of test scores to job performance, while fairly positive at the point of initial recruitment, may decrease quite substantially over time (Farrell and McDaniel 2001).

Ability tests are measures of **maximal performance**. They are a measure of the best performance that an individual is capable of, and they tend to call for a competitive attitude. They are timed and they tend to increase in difficulty across items.

However, maximal performance scores may not be that useful in predicting job performance. At work, it may be that *consistency* of performance is more significant. The person who is able to produce something exceptional once in a while is perhaps not so productive in the long run as someone who is consistently competent.

Successful job performance requires a number of interrelated skills and competencies, and how these interact with cognitive ability is a complex matter. Recently, psychologists have highlighted the existence of a number of different types of knowledge for successful job performance, these include explicit knowledge and understanding, but also **tacit knowledge**. Tacit knowledge includes all those hunches and observations that accumulate through the experience of performing a job. People often find such knowledge hard to articulate or record. A psychologist working in the Scottish Prison Service, successfully examined prison officers' tacit knowledge of dealing with prisoners taking hostages in crises situations. He subsequently used this information to aid in the selection and training of guards (Clayton 2006).

Tacit ability may feed into high performance, but this capability may not be measured by ability test scores alone.

In a study of the performance of cardiothoracic surgery teams, Friedman and Bernell (2006) demonstrated that tacit knowledge which is shared amongst team members contributes to high performance. This suggests that communication skills may mediate both ability and the successful utilization of knowledge and expertise.

Adverse impact: ethnicity and testing

Adverse impact refers to the way in which some tests, and in particular ability tests, discriminate against members of ethnic, cultural, and gender groups (Sackett and Lievens 2008).

Differential results of ethnic groups on ability tests demonstrates that culture mediates test performance. There is the obvious effect of differing uses of language between different subcultural groups, but the whole *discourse* of testing may vary between different cultures. Testing assumes a certain attitude to educational and employment matters, a sense of competition, and need for personal achievement. This attitude is not shared by all cultures of the world, and this may account for differences in performance on ability tests (Cernovsky 1997).

A difference between groups is considered significant from a legal point of view in both the USA and the UK, if there is a 20 per cent (or one-fifth) or more gap between typical scores obtained for each group (the **four-fifths rule**). Such a difference is evidence of adverse impact, and indicates that the test discriminates unfairly. Where such a difference is found, the use of the test would be questioned.

There has been a search for 'culture-free' tests, but it is generally agreed that it is not feasible to produce a test that contains no allusions to culture whatsoever (Anastasi and Urbana 1997). **Culture-fair tests**, which aim to translate cultural referents in tests, are produced by some test developers. If local psychologists produce local versions of tests, with locally developed instructions, content, and norms these may go some way to countering adverse impact. In times of globalization and internationalization of business activity, the testing of individuals and groups cross-culturally is becoming more common, and the applicability of tests across national and cultural borders is a significant issue.

Gender

There is evidence to suggest that, on average, males and females score differently on the subscales of ability tests. The general account is that males score higher than females on tests of numerical and spatial ability, and females score higher on verbal tests (Halpern 1996). Thus there are separate male and female norms provided for many ability tests.

Case illustration
Adverse impact: the case of British Rail

British Rail was challenged by a group of eight of their employees in 1991 on their use of ability tests to select internal candidates for training as train drivers. In British Rail, the job of train driver is a coveted one, as pay levels and prestige are high. Internal applications from any level within the organization are encouraged, but up until 1991, very few members of ethnic minorities had been successful in making it onto the training scheme.

A group of applicants (all train guards) took the company to an employment tribunal, and, supported by the Commission for Racial Equality (now part of the Equality and Human Rights Commission), they successfully argued that the selection process unfairly discriminated against members of ethnic minorities whose first language was not English, and who had not been educated via the British educational system. The expert witness for the CRE was Steve Blinkhorn, an occupational psychologist with experience in the development of ability scales.

As a result of the ruling, British Rail was required to revisit the use of ability tests for this assessment and to institute ways of preparing candidates for the tests. They were encouraged to develop practice sessions and information packs that outlined typical test questions and answering formats for candidates. With the new procedures in place, the number of successful applicants from ethnic minorities increased substantially.

Since this groundbreaking case, it has been considered good practice for all test publishers to provide pre-testing guidance for candidates.

However, recent research has questioned the validity of this assumption. Elizabeth Spelke (2005) has reviewed 111 studies concerned with sex differences in cognitive ability, and concludes that there is little evidence of significant difference. A similar result was found in a meta-analytic study of sex differences in a range of areas including cognitive ability, motor behaviour, and personality (Hyde 2005). In a study by Steven Spencer (Spencer et al. 1999) using male and female high performers in mathematics, women who were told that studies had demonstrated lower performance in numerical ability for females performed worse on tests of numerical ability than those who were briefed that there were no gender differences. Hyde (2005) points out there is infinitely more variability within group scores for men and women than there is between them, and this is also the case for ethnic difference.

KEY LEARNING POINTS

- Psychometric tests measure individual differences in a standardized format.
- The most commonly used ability tests in work setting are multifactorial in design, where specialist abilities are measured separately.
- Ability tests show high relationships to job performance, but the relationship reduces over time.
- Performance on ability tests is mediated by cultural factors. Tests need to be designed by those who are familiar with a particular culture, and candidates need to be prepared and supported in taking tests.

12.3.5 Assessing personality

The growth of interest in employees' social and interpersonal skills has been associated with the development of more complex jobs in the service sector and the attempt by many organizations to compete through the quality of service they provide (Thompson and McHugh 2002).

The measurement of personal characteristics is a significant feature of many occupational assessment procedures. Personality is a difficult area to define, as there are many different conceptions and theoretical positions in this field. (See Chapter 3 on Personality and Individual Differences.)

Personality questionnaires

The 2007 CIPD Recruitment survey found that 56 per cent of UK companies sampled employed personality testing as part of their assessment process, and Faulder (2005) suggests that every single one of the top 100 companies in the UK uses personality tests at some point of their assessment procedures. In USA, a survey conducted in 2003 found that 30 per cent of companies used personality questionnaires to screen candidates for employment (Heller 2005) and 40 per cent of Fortune's top 100 companies in the USA use personality questionnaires at some stage (Erickson 2004).

The structure and format of personality questionnaires

A questionnaire consists of a set of standardized statements, to which candidates are required to respond. The statements are selected through research where a large number of items are administered to a sample of the target group for whom the test is designed. Their responses will indicate which items are well worded, and which items seem to reliably distinguish between high and low scorers on certain dimensions.

The scoring of questionnaires involves the comparison of total scores achieved by the respondents with the responses of a predetermined criterion group. This information is contained in 'norms' tables, which are available from the test publishers. Norms are developed through research with large numbers of respondents. Thus for example different norms may be provided for males and females, or for different age groups.

This kind of measurement is therefore termed 'normative', as it compares the individual with the typical performance of a specified group.

The content of personality tests

There are a large number of personality measures available. Some of the most famous and popular ones have been developed by research psychologists and personality theorists

Figure 12.4. Examples of personality questionnaire formats

1. I feel uneasy when I'm in a large social gathering:
- Most of the time.
- Often.
- Sometimes.
- Rarely.
- Almost never.

2. I would rather be:
(a) A rocket scientist?
(b) A movie actor?
(c) Can't decide?

3. I often feel pessimistic about the future.
TRUE. . .
FALSE. . .

4. Look at the following list of behaviours, and decide which is least like you and which is most like you:
(i) Take home a pile of work to complete a project.
(ii) Volunteer to attend a week-long course on counselling in the workplace.
(iii) Speak first at a departmental meeting attended by the MD.
(iv) Report a series of typing errors in a company document to your boss.
    (a) Most like me?   (b) Least like me?

(see Chapter 3 on Personality and Individual Differences). The 16PF5 was initially developed by Raymond B. Cattell, based upon his model of personality as comprised of sixteen personality traits (included cognitive ability). The test has been translated into many languages and is used across the globe.

The NEO-5 is based upon the Big Five (OCEAN) model of personality (Costa and McCrae 1985). These tests derive from a trait-type approach to personality theory.

The Myers–Briggs Type Indicator (MBTI) is a globally popular test. It was developed by Isobel Myers and Katherine Briggs in 1948 (Briggs–Myers 1998) and is based upon a Jungian typology of personality types. This test is used for team building and assessing development needs (Searle 2003).

The relation between personality test scores and job performance

Reviews of the relationship between personality test scores and job performance have been somewhat equivocal. A classic study by Guion and Gottier (1965) has suggested there was virtually zero relation between the two. A review by Schmitt et al. (1984) suggested an overall **correlation** of 0.15.

The value of personality tests for occupational selection and assessment has been widely debated and contested. For example, a meta-analytic study conducted by Mitchell Rothstein and Richard Goffin (2006) concludes that research up to the 1990s supports the view that personality measures can contribute in some measure to the prediction of job performance, and 'may add value to personnel selection process' (p. 182) However, a series of articles in the journal *Personnel Psychology* in the Winter of 2007 reopened the debate (Morgeson et al. 2007; Tett and Christiansen 2007).

There may be a number of reasons why personality test scores seem to be poor predictors of job performance. One issue may be the difficulty of researching job performance itself. Objective criteria of success at work may be hard to establish as job performance is related to a variety of interrelating variables. For example, the overall economic performance of a company will mediate job performance in some areas such as sales. Many jobs rely on team performance, and the identification of the impact of one person may be hard to establish.

Faking

Rothstein and Goffin (2006) note that one of the main problems with personality tests is faking. In occupational personality assessment there may be strong pressures leading candidates to try to give the answers they think the organization is looking for or that will paint them

259

Chapter 12
Assessing people at work

(in their own view) in the best possible light. There are a number of steps that test designers can take to try and minimize this.

One direct way of confronting the issue of faking is through instructions to candidates. There may be a request on the front of a questionnaire, which is reinforced by a test administrator, to 'answer all questions as truthfully as you can'. It is often stated on questionnaires: 'There are no right or wrong answers'.

Other measures focus on the content of the questionnaires themselves. For example, measures of **social desirability** or 'faking good' (Crowne and Marlowe 1964) can be added to test items. These are a subset of questions embedded in a questionnaire that aim to determine whether a candidate is trying to give an overly glowing and positive view of themselves.

Such questions generally explore people's willingness to admit to weaknesses and faults. For example:

- Have you ever taken the credit for something that you knew was the work of someone else?

- Have you ever taken something that you knew did not belong to you, no matter how small it was?

- Are all your habits good and desirable ones?

- Do you always tell the truth?

Another method for reducing the impact of faking is the use of forced choice answering formats. For example, in the list below, candidates would be instructed to indicate two items: one that is 'most like me' and one that is 'least like me'. These items will be recycled in following questions in combination with other items, so that the desirability of each question is balanced over the course of the questionnaire:

I like to take the lead in group discussions.

I like to feel that I have done my best at the end of the working day.

I like situations which challenge me intellectually.

I like to win in any situation.

I like an opportunity to help others.

However, as Rothstein and Goffin (2006) stress there is no sure way of detecting whether someone is faking or not.

Personality tests rely on self-report and therefore on a person's self-knowledge and insight. People may be deluded about their personality characteristics. Also, the tests rely on the idea that we possess a stable set of personality characteristics, but this is a contentious area of personality theory (see Chapter 3 on Personality and Individual Differences).

A problem may lie therefore with the validity of the underlying constructs implicit in the tests themselves. The notion of 'traits' implies a stable set of personal characteristics that are displayed in specific situations. However as critics have argued (Mischel 1968) people may be more variable in their behaviour than the tests imply. They may make conscious decisions to adjust their behaviour in terms of the way they read situations, as indeed the problem of 'faking' demonstrates!

Job behaviour depends on the dynamic interactions between people in work teams. To attempt to correlate the test scores of one isolated individual with job outcomes would seem to be a distortion of how work processes operate. It is perhaps not surprising that results on the validity of personality tests have proved equivocal at best.

KEY LEARNING POINTS

- Personality questionnaires may be used for a range of different assessment aims, including recruitment and development.

- Personality questionnaires tend to originate from the trait-type psychometric model of personality.

- Studies suggest that personality test results tend to correlate poorly with work performance.

- Faking is a key problem when questionnaires are used for job selection, and test developers have attempted to apply measures to ameliorate the effects.

Case illustration

Can graphology predict occupational success?

Graphology is 'the study of personality and character from handwriting' (British Institute of Graphologists, www.britishgraphology.org). According to the British Academy of Graphology, personality is revealed in the style and form of writing. For example, the slant of letters:

Forward slant indicates enthusiasm

Upward slant—a logical nature.

Left slant—introspection.

Handwriting that is full of squiggles and irregular strokes indicates an artistic and non-standard approach to things.

The letter *t*: where the bar is place on the horizontal is said to be significant—low on the line indicates low goals in life and high on the line, high goals!

Research has failed to find that this is a reliable methods of assessment, and predictions of personality from samples of writings have generally been little better than chance, even with specialist trained graphologists (Tett and Palmer 1997). Attempts to link handwriting style to occupational performance and success have been similarly unsuccessful (Ben-Shakhar et al. 1986).

However, In France, graphology is frequently used in the assessment of people for jobs.

Questions

- Design a study to test the hypothesis that leadership potential is shown in handwriting style.

- Is the use of graphology for occupational selection ethical?

12.3.6 Work sample tests

The use of work sample tests as part of assessment packages has increased since the 1960s (Hollway 1991). Such measures aim to mirror or simulate key elements of real job tasks or situations. They are thus more in line with behaviourist or social learning approaches in work psychology.

Work samples can be utilized in two ways: to assess job skill and knowledge or to assess trainability and potential for development.

The design of job sample tests may be carried out by HR professionals within organizations to reflect local and industry issues. Recruitment consultancies may also provide off-the-shelf exercises. The content and design of the exercise will determine its reliability and validity, and it is possible that organizations may create poor simulations of job tasks, or may create exercises that are stressful, overly long, or overly complex. All these factors will reduce the usefulness of the measures.

Work sample tests are useful for assessing candidates who have no experience in a particular work area, for example new graduates. They are popular with candidates and have high face validity (Steiner and Gilliland 1996), and research suggests that they are associated with less discrimination of minority group candidates than are other assessment methods (Schmitt and Mills 2001) as they offer direct evidence of competency to perform specific job tasks, they may be more applicable to cross-cultural testing situations than the use of psychometric tests.

Work sample tests and job performance

Research by Robertson and Downs (1989) suggests the validity of work sample tests is high, around 0.54. However, as was the case with ability tests, correlations deteriorate over time. This suggests that successful job performance may be caused by a number of factors and the characteristics that were relevant for initial job performance may not be those that are relevant over time. Also, work sample tests are simulations of real work, and real work may differ from the simulation in significant ways.

Figure 12.5. Example of a work sample test

You have applied for the post of HR Assistant in a hospital.
On arrival at work you find the following messages in your email inbox:

(a) TO: HR
From: PA to Consultant.
Hi, I would like to take some compassionate leave as my partner has just been diagnosed with terminal cancer. Can you tell me what to do?

(b) TO: HR
From: Catering manager.
We need some urgent help with a grievance in the kitchen. Two of the chefs belong to the same family and there has been a huge argument, which resulted in a fight at close of shift last night. Can you advise me?

(c) TO: HR
From: Accident and Emergency Senior Nurse.
Hi – I have started shift at 8 a.m. and three nursing staff so far have called in sick with a gastric virus. Please help.

Compose a response to each item.
Prioritize the items; which would you respond to first – and why?

There is some evidence that performance on work sample tests is correlated with cognitive ability (Roth and Bobko 2005). Candidates who perform well on such tasks may succeed by applying cognitive skills that may or may not be relevant to the actual job.

12.3.7 Group exercises

Group exercises are frequently used by companies to measure social skills (CIPD 2006). There are a number of reasons for an interest in measuring candidate's team and group working skills:

- A growth in service sector jobs.
- An increase in teamworking.
- An increase in diversity of work groups and clients, making good communication skills especially significant.

Group exercises are a common component of **assessment centres**, which are described in the following section of this chapter. Group exercises can be used to assess social skills, as well as other job-related competencies (in which case they are a form of group work sample test).

The size of group for assessment purposes is generally kept to between five and seven members. Research in group dynamics suggests that this number is optimal, in ensuring that each participant may interact and communicate fully (Hartley 1997).

There are a number of forms of group exercises: for example the leaderless group discussion. This is a task in which team members are instructed to discuss some topic for a set period of time. Observers, usually three, will rate each participant's behaviour in terms of predetermined competencies or criteria.

Candidates may also be required to take part in more complex group tasks, for example simulated business exercises requiring team members to analyse information and make decisions and recommendations, possibly designing a presentation of conclusions to a specified audience.

Robertson and his associates (1987) have demonstrated that rater accuracy can be improved by careful attention to the design of rating scales. Too many competencies and unclear definitions and description of factors can lead to inaccuracy.

An additional problem for accuracy in group exercises arises from the contrast between candidates. Gaugler and Rudolph (1992) have demonstrated that weak candidates tend to be rated more highly in weak groups than in groups where candidate standards are higher.

Figure 12.6. Example of a rating scale

COMPETENCY	Strong evidence	Adequate evidence	No evidence
Listening skills			
Influencing skills			
Team working			

Source: Ballantyne and Povah (2004).

Research has indicated that observers of group exercises are subject to all the biases and difficulties that beset those engaged in selection interviewing. Training in the psychology of person perception has been shown to increase accuracy (Lievens and Klimoski 2001).

KEY LEARNING POINTS

- Work sample tests simulate real tasks and have been shown to be effective predictors of future job performance.

- There are a number of different types of group exercises that are useful in the assessment of social and interpersonal skills.

- Problems may arise with the accuracy of rater's judgements; careful planning of rating scales and assessor training can help to increase both accuracy and interjudge reliability.

12.4 Integrative techniques: assessment and development centres

12.4.1 Assessment centres

Assessment Centres (AC) developed from German military selection methods incorporating psychodiagnostic techniques, for valid selection of military personnel in the Second World War. They were adopted by both the UK (in the War Office Selection Board) and the USA (in the Office of Strategic Studies). Very often they involved performance tests such as how to cross a river with limited equipment.

After the War, the British Civil Service developed these assessment centre techniques into the Civil Service Selection Board (CSSB) for the Fast-Track administrative class. This used performance tests to simulate the job activities such as committee decision making and report writing, as well as psychometric tests. In the 1950s the American telephone company AT&T pioneered follow-up of assessment centres. In the 1960s and 70s the methodology of assessment centres grew, mainly in the USA and amongst European subsidiaries of American multinationals such as Rank Xerox and IBM. Mars started using this in the UK in the early 1970s, along with the Anglo-Dutch companies Shell and Philips and the German company Siemens.

Definition of an assessment centre

Assessment centres are a process, not a place, consisting of a collection of selection methods carried out over a period of time, generally a day or two. They utilize individual and group techniques in order to gain a comprehensive set of data about individuals' suitability for a particular job and make predictions about the individuals' future job performance.

Since the 1980s Assessment Centres have been used by many public- and private-sector companies, particularly the **blue chip companies** such as banks, large finance houses, large consultancies, supermarkets, oil companies, and central government. Research done by Mabey (1989), Boyle et al. (1993), and The Association of Graduate Recruiters (AGR) (2000) show that the large majority of graduate recruiting companies were using assessment centre techniques.

There are several impetuses for this trend to use assessment centres. Graduate recruiters have found it difficult to recruit the competencies they require (AGR 2006) despite the expansion in numbers of graduates entering the labour market each year. Companies tend to follow

Pause for thought
What **quantitative** and what **qualitative** factors would need to be computed to calculate the cost of an assessment centre? Similarly what quantitative and qualitative factors would need to be computed to calculate the cost of a failure in recruitment? Which do you think is most important: the quantitative or qualitative factors?

each other in use of selection methods in order to seem professional and attractive to their recruits. The availability of qualified people to design, run, and assess the centres makes them feasible on a wide scale, particularly with the growth in numbers of occupational psychologists.

Assessment centres also give the candidate a better opportunity to weigh up their feelings about the organization than a single interview; they have a longer time interacting with the company and meet more people from the organization.

Components of the assessment centre

Many of the components of recruitment and selection described earlier in the chapter are used in assessment centres: interviews (both one to one and panel), psychometric tests of ability, personality and occupational interest, work sample tests, case studies, group activities, role plays, and leadership activities.

Reliability and validity of assessment centres

Reliability of assessment centres is complex. The component parts need to be equally consistent in reliability and validity and measure the competencies of the job. Cook (2004) states that reliability can be calculated for the whole, the component parts, or the assessors' ratings.

Both the training of assessors and their experience with the competencies are important factors. Experienced assessors produce significantly higher differential accuracy than less experienced assessors. (Kolk et al. 2002). Suff (2005) confirms that assessors play a key role in the process, should be trained, and an evaluation carried out to ensure the assessment centre is performing fairly and effectively.

A weakness in checking validity of assessment centres is the lack of a control group since it is not possible to predict that those who are not selected will perform poorly as this cannot be tested.

Some researchers have shown that the predictive validity of an assessment centre is about three times better than that of interviews on their own (Gaugler et al. 1987). Schmidt and Hunter (1998) however, in their meta-analysis, have found it no better than other traditional forms of selection such as a structured interview. Garavan and Morley (1998) looked at selection of graduates in an assessment centre in the banking industry and found little support for validity, particularly construct and criterion validity.

Still others have claimed that the validity is **synthetic** since promotion linked to assessment centre predictions, is circular.

Cook (2004) reviewed the meta analyses and concluded that validity was higher when more assessments were included, psychologists rather than managers were used as assessors, **peer evaluations** were used, and more candidates were female.

Case illustration
AT&T

Research on the validity of assessment centres was carried out using data kept by the American telephone company AT&T, from their longitudinal studies in the 1950s. They identified management potential in an assessment centre regardless of the person's background or education. At the time predictions were made of the grade the participant would ultimately achieve, but the information was never released so it could not affect the perceptions of senior managers. From time to time, the achievements of the participants were compared to the grade predicted. In 1965 a follow-up found that prediction for graduates and non-graduates, successful and less successful managers was equally accurate (Bray and Grant 1966).

Question

- How would you establish predictive validity in a study such as that carried out at AT&T?

Table 12.1. Predictive validity coefficients

Meta analysis by Schmidt and Hunter (1998)	
Work sample tests	0.54
Cognitive ability tests	0.51
Structures interviews	0.51
Personality tests	0.40
Assessment centres	0.37
Biodata	0.35
References	0.26
Unstructures interviews	0.20
Graphology	0.02

Source: Ballantyne and Povah (2004).

12.4.2 Development centres

Centres can also be designed for development of individuals and also for assessing adaptability and flexibility where the organization is experiencing, or in need of, change.

Assessment and **development centres** have much in common in terms of tools and processes but differ in terms of purpose. Assessment centres are primarily about selection of external or internal recruits. Development centres are about development either by identifying 'fast-track' candidates, or job-related strengths and weaknesses.

AT&T in the USA used development centres in the 1970s as did ICL in the UK. Since the 1980s they have become widespread in organizations. A survey by the Industrial Society in 1996 of 414 organizations found that 43 per cent used development centres.

Ballantyne and Povah (2004) define development centres as:

the use of assessment centre technology for the identification of individual strengths and weaknesses, in order to diagnose development needs that will facilitate more effective job performance and/or career advancement, which in turn contributes to the attainment of greater organizational success.

Assessment and development centres can be described on a continuum from selection where assessment of behaviour is made for selection purposes, through identification of potential, diagnosis of needs to coaching and development. Figure 12.7 shows this continuum.

Establishing the validity of development centres is more problematic than that of assessment centres as their purpose is less clearly defined.

Figure 12.7. The assessment-development centre continuum

Assessment centres		Development centre	
Selection • External recruitment • Internal promotion	Identify potential • Fast-track • Hi-potentials • Succession planning	Diagnostic approach • Define needs against existing and new values and behaviours	Coach and develop • Address needs to aid culture change and encourage new values and behaviours
Assessors	Assessors/observers	Observers	Observers/coaches
Assess behaviour	Assess behaviour	Assess behaviour	Change behaviour
Select	*Define gaps against More senior job*	*Define gaps against current job*	*Close gaps within current job*

Source: Ballantyne and Povah (2004).

12.5 Graduate recruitment

12.5.1 The scale and importance of graduate recruitment

The proportion of graduates in the global workforce has been expanding. With a government policy in the UK that 50 per cent of people aged 17–30 years should go to university by 2010, recruitment of graduates from universities has already become a very large area of activity.

In 2005, the number of students entering HE was 405,369 (http://www.ucas.com). In 2003/4, there were approximately 2.3 million undergraduate and postgraduate students in the UK (Higher Education Statistics Agency (2005): Students in Higher Education Institutions 2003/04, table 0a).

With such large numbers of graduates entering the labour market, and the demand from employers for graduates not being fully met (AGR 2006) graduate recruitment is important nationally as well as to individual organizations. An IRS Employment Review (2006) found that in a survey of 150 employers, demand for graduates continues to rise and is keeping pace with the growth in university output; 40 per cent of employers have difficulty finding suitable graduates.

12.5.2 Traditional and contemporary graduate selection methods

The 'old' graduate recruitment process of 'milk round' (i.e. visiting universities), application form, first and second interviews, and/or assessment centre (the traditional approach) has largely been phased out as too expensive.

Instead, graduate recruiters may visit careers fairs in the UK during the autumn and spring terms but increasingly they use their websites to attract applicants, using online selection methods, retaining assessment centres for later in the process.

Figure 12.8 shows how the time and cost involved in graduate recruitment may be reduced.

Assessment centres and graduate recruitment

AGR (2006) found that 83 per cent of their members used final round assessment centres or selection events. Before this a variety of other screening procedures are used: first interviews

Pause for thought
What issues might evolve for both employer and student through a virtual careers fair?

Figure 12.8. Chart of traditional and contemporary graduate recruitment methods

Time and cost			
Traditional			
Application form and in-depth sift	First interview (possibly psychometric testing)	Assessment centre	Offers
Contemporary			
Application form and short sift	Online tests	Assessment centre	Offers

Source: Association of Graduate Recruiters (2006).

on campus (19 per cent), first interviews at regional centres (26 per cent), online self selection/ pre-qualification exercise (36 per cent), preliminary telephone screening (38 per cent), first interviews at their organization (45 per cent).

Self-selection exercises are most usually numerical tests (75 per cent), verbal reasoning tests (66 per cent), personality tests (30 per cent) or spatial reasoning tests (2 per cent). Keenan (1995) found that the interview was the most important element in graduate recruitment whether on its own or as part of an assessment centre.

Assessment centres are retained in graduate recruitment as they are generally considered to be the best way to assess interpersonal, oral communication, and teamworking skills. They may also be the first time the candidate comes face to face with the company.

The importance of corporate websites

It has become very important to employers that their corporate image should be attractive to new graduates and that information on their websites should be easy to find and respond to. Research on these areas is beginning. For example, Melewar and Karaosmanoglu (2006) have investigated what the elements of corporate identity are that may be conveyed in a website.

 Activity Corporate website

Assume you are working for a large graduate recruiter. Design a piece of research to identify if your corporate website was attracting the sorts of graduates you were interested in employing without infringing equality legislation.

Online recruitment and testing

The British Market Research Bureau has found that using the internet is favoured by one in four UK adults. However, very little is known about how companies and job seekers use the web, and the ultimate effectiveness of this process. Research conducted by Jansen et al. (2005) asked how people search for job-related information on the web, how effective their searches are, and how likely job seekers are to find an appropriate job posting or application. Results suggested that the design of websites needs significant improvement for recruitment.

An increasing number of companies only accept applications online. Sixty-six per cent of AGR's respondents in their 2006 survey only accepted online applications, 23 per cent accepted either online or paper, and only 2 per cent accepted paper only.

Dulewicz (2004) has called for greater research into online application for graduate jobs particularly on self-esteem when rejection is the outcome. Some online application forms are lengthy and frequently psychometric tests are required and no feedback is given other than pass/fail.

Online testing is a substantial growth area in itself. Lawton and Baum (2006) found that in 2004 over two million online assessments were taken. This speeds up the process, uses fewer personnel, and is less costly.

Cheating is said to be widespread with friends doing the tests for each other, and practice sessions under an alias such as 'Harry Potter' being frequent. The risk of impersonation makes it difficult for employers to ensure who completes the online assessment. However, recognition technology, such as finger printing and iris recognition is developing rapidly. Pollitt (2005) describes how Lloyds TSB uses an online numerical reasoning test as part of the bank's application process. Then at the assessment centre, graduates do a paper-based test which is scored on a computer to verify their online scores. However, there is some indication that candidates may have concerns about privacy in online testing (Bauer et al. 2006).

Online assessment not only uses psychometric tests, but, for example e-tray exercises which replace the paper based in-tray exercises of prioritizing and scheduling. Gill (1979) looked a range of validities in in-tray exercises, including for graduate recruitment, and found adequate reliability and strong face validity for graduate recruitment from this exercise.

Figure 12.9 shows the types of tests that might be used at each stage of selection and their purpose.

Pause for thought
If you were searching for jobs on the web, what aspects of corporate websites would be important to you?

Pause for thought
Apart from potential infringement of discrimination legislation, what other disbenefits are there from this approach in online application forms?

Figure 12.9. Chart of use of online tests in recruitment

Stage	Type of assessment	Use/Purpose
Pre-application stage	– 'Cosmo' style quizzes – Longer, more objective self-assessment questionnaires/tools	Help potential applicants self-assess their suitability. Help differentiate employers from competitors
Application/ Application sift	Short assessment of working style/ Preferences embedded within an online application form	Shorten / automate elements of the sift
Early stage assessment	Online psychometric tests (generally reasoning tests, sometimes assessments of personality or working preference / style)	Active selection of talent for final selection stage
Final stage assessment	– E-tray (scheduling and prioritisation exercises) – Other business simulations/ activities delivered online	Support for final selection decision

Source: Association of Graduate Recruiters (2006).

Candidates may be invited to sit online psychometric tests through automated emails. These tests are often quite flexible in terms of when the graduate can sit them. If successful at this stage they may be given a telephone interview. Research by Silvester and Anderson (2003) compared employment telephone interviews with face-to-face interviews and the ways in which anonymity on the telephone might be reduced. Since very little research has been conducted in this area, it is of importance to both applicant and interviewer that greater understanding of the processes leading to decisions in telephone interviews is developed.

12.5.3 The role of emotional intelligence in graduate recruitment

As seen earlier in the chapter, there has been a lot of interest in the last ten years in the broad concept that describes the attributes called **emotional intelligence** or EI or emotional quotient (EQ) (Goleman 1996). As yet no predicitive validity has been found between EI and job performance (Robertson and Smith 2001) but it continues to be popular with employers as a way of describing fit with the organization.

Pause for thought
What negative impressions could occur as a result of a graduate's experiences with online recruitment and testing? How can these be overcome?

Case illustration
The Cabinet Office

In 2004 the Cabinet Office revised its long-established selection process for Fast Stream applicants that consisted of an application and sift stage, invigilated psychometric test session, and two-day assessment centre.

The new process uses online assessment. Potential applicants first encounter online tools designed to help them determine their own suitability for the Fast Stream. This includes an online job preview tool and verbal and numerical tests. These provide feedback on Fast Stream 'fit' and likely success if candidates progress their application. This places control with the candidate—they decide whether or not to continue. Those who do continue then take scored online verbal and numerical reasoning tests and an online competency questionnaire. Shortlisted candidates are then invited to complete an e-tray assessment exercise (delivered via a computer) at one of a number of national test centres. The final selection stage is a one-day assessment centre.

As well as significantly improving efficiency, the restructuring has more than halved the average time to recruit, improved the diversity of candidates reaching the assessment centre and improved the overall quality of the candidate experience.

Graduate recruiters produce lists of common skills and attributes they require, alongside the specific competencies needed for particular jobs (CVCP 1998). Employers sometimes refer to 'having the right attitude'. Since around 40 per cent of graduate jobs do not require any specific degree-related subject knowledge, clearly other attributes are important and AGR (2006) reports that commitment and drive, motivation and enthusiasm, alongside interpersonal skills, are seen as the most important qualities in applicants. The evidence relating to EQ is debatable and more research is required in the graduate recruitment context.

 ### Activity Applicant qualities

Construct an exercise to measure the top seven skills valued by graduate recruiters: commitment and drive, motivation and enthusiasm, teamworking, oral communication, flexibility and adaptability, customer focus, problem solving.

The business case

Hesketh (2004) points out that recruitment of graduates has to be justified and that there is a strong business case. Graduates are estimated to contribute around £1 billion to the UK economy annually. Graduate recruitment and selection is of strategic importance to an organization with replenishment of talent, bringing in creativity and faster added value than with other types of employees.

The future

The growth of virtual careers fairs and the merging of graduate and experienced hires recruitment can be expected in the future, according to AGR (2000). They expect more online assessment centres where simulation and games technology come together, 'just-in-time' campaign-based graduate recruitment run throughout the year, software that allows CVs to be patched into application forms and internet or virtual apprenticeships, where interested and talented students from any university are invited to 'join the Company online'.

 KEY LEARNING POINTS

- There has been great expansion in the number of graduates emerging from higher education but graduate recruiters report a shortfall in skills and graduates available.
- Graduate recruitment has changed from the traditional approach to the contemporary approach to reduce cost and facilitate handling the larger numbers of applicants.
- There has been a rapid expansion in the use of the internet for recruitment and job seeking.
- Assessment centres are still used in graduate recruitment, and the interview is still seen as the most important element.
- Emotional intelligence has a role in graduate recruitment and may be a distinguishing feature of successful applicants.

Pause for thought
What advantages and disadvantages do you think there would be in joining a company on line as a virtual apprentice while you are a student?

12.5.4 Ethical and legal issues

Assessing people is an ethical as well as a technical matter, and organizations need to consider the impact of assessment on individuals and groups. Assessment should be fair, open, and non-discriminatory, and in most countries there are legal obligations for companies to ensure that their hiring procedures are just.

Under UK law, there are a variety of provisions that govern the conduct of advertising for posts, and the conduct of assessment and selection of candidates. Organizations must demonstrate their procedures for assessing and selecting candidates are fair and transparent, and do not discriminate against people on the basis of their membership of racial, ethnic, or religious groups, nor on account of their age, gender, sexual orientation, or disability.

The use of psychometric tests by organizations has fallen foul of the law on a number of occasions (see case illustration on British Rail) and employers have been taken to the Employment Courts and fined. Such outcomes are costly, are bad for the image of the organization, and may also sour relations between employees and management. Guidelines for legal application of assessment methods are offered by the main professional bodies that advise organizations on recruitment and selection: the CIPD, and the British Psychological Society.

As well as meeting legal requirements, organizations need to ensure that they treat all candidates sensitively, and with respect. Companies require applicants disclose a great deal of personal information when applying for jobs; they are also frequently required to show personal qualities and openly discuss their beliefs in quite public settings for employment selection. While organizations may feel that candidates have a responsibility to provide accurate information about themselves, organizations must also have a reciprocal responsibility to treat candidates with respect.

Candidates' rights in the assessment situation might include:

- Right to confidentiality of all personal details.
- Right to full information about what procedures are to be used for selection and why they are being used.
- Opportunities to gain pre-test practice in psychometric procedures.
- Access to test results.
- Access to understandable feedback about test and interview performance.

Research suggests that candidates are concerned about the privacy implications of online testing (Bauer et al. 2006) and Hausknecht et al. (2004) showed that candidates' perception of assessment procedures, in particular of their fairness, played a role in shaping overall attitudes towards organizations.

The British Psychological Society has produced a code of good practice for psychological testing, which includes the following provisions. Test administrators have to ensure that they:

- are competent to administer and use tests and are professionally updated in all requirements;
- know the limits of their competence;
- only use tests in conjunction with other procedures;
- keep results securely;
- obtain informed consent from potential test users;
- give consideration to factors such as gender, ethnicity, age, disability, special needs, and educational background in using and interpreting tests;
- provide the test taker with feedback.

It is also important that companies develop their own codes, and ensure that these are enforced.

12.5.5 The future of assessment at work

As this chapter has discussed, people are assessed for a variety of reasons by work organizations, using a great variety of techniques. The reliability and validity of the process will have significant implications for organizations, and the people who work within them.

Chapter 16 on The Future of Work highlights some key emerging trends that will impact on the way assessment is undertaken by the organizations of the future:

- increasing flexibility in job roles;
- increasingly diverse workforce, and the globalization of the labour market;
- increasing competition for a specialist skilled workforce;
- increased general levels of education, coupled with changing attitudes to work, leading candidates to demand a stronger voice in the employment context.

Work psychologists have much to contribute in helping organizations to meet these challenges in ways that are both socially just and well grounded in research and psychological theory.

Assessment method	Uses	Positive Features	Negative features
Interviews	Assessing interpersonal and presentation skills; checking CV and career history.	Offers candidates opportunity to know the organisations and its staff.	Bias of interviewers; Ingratiation and impression management of candidate.
Ability tests	Assessing cognitive skill	Compares candidate to relevant norm group; treats all candidates equally. Tests can be high in reliability and validity.	May not measure skills that are relevant to job performance; may discriminate on grounds of ethnicity; require trained administrators.
Personality tests	Assessing a range of social and interpersonal skills, and preferences.	Candidates can be compared to relevant norm groups; ensures uniform treatment of candidates.	Reliability & validity is contentious. Cultural differences may distort results, equivocal evidence on relation to job performance; may have low face validity. Requires skilled administrators.
Work sample tests	Assessing job knowledge, problem solving and interpersonal skills	Research suggests positive relationship to work performance. High face validity for candidates. May reduce bias against minority candidates.	Effectiveness depends on design of tests, off-the shelf tests may not be valid. Scoring may be subjective.
Group Exercises	Assessing group and interpersonal skill and judgement. Influencing skills	Shows real not hypothetical behaviour.	Performance of candidates may be affected by specific group dynamics; may create problems for minority group candidates. Scoring can be subjective.
Assessment Centres	Assessing people in the round: cognitive, emotional and behavioural aspects.	High face validity and popular with candidates. Evidence of high validity. Developmental benefits for assessors as well as candidates.	Costly and time consuming; relies on skills of assessors – decisions may be subject to group influence effects. Only as good as the exercised that comprise it, and skills of the assessors.
Development Centres	Assessing potential ;development needs and career plans.	As assessment centres above.	Shares problems of Assessment Centres: Also: Involves current employees, may have demotivating effect if not well managed.

Chapter summary

- Organizations assess current and potential employees for a variety of purposes.
- Job analysis underpins the success of the assessment process.
- There are a variety of methods available for assessing people's work-related competencies and these include interviews, psychometric tests, work sample tests, and group exercises.
- Assessment centres involve multiple methods, where a number of assessors appraise a number of candidates on a number of dimensions.
- Development centres use multiple methods to assess potential and development needs.
- There has been a rapid expansion in the use of the internet for recruitment and job seeking.
- The key criteria for the evaluation of any assessment technique are reliability and validity.
- There is evidence that some assessment procedures create 'adverse impact' and differentially discriminate against various ethnic and social groups; organizations need to adjust their methods to avoid this problem.

- Cultural experiences, values, and beliefs will mediate the assessment process.
- Assessment in occupational contexts demands the ethical treatment of individuals and groups. Professional codes of conduct have been established to guide the behaviour of assessors in organizations.
- The methods used by organizations will vary with changing business environments, changing technology and changing markets for employees.

Assess your learning

Review questions

1 How does performance on tests of cognitive ability relate to performance on the job?

2 What do you understand by the term 'test validity'? How is the validity of a psychometric test established?

3 What can organizations do to reduce the impact of 'faking' when using personality tests for assessment purposes?

4 List five ethical responsibilities of testers.

5 What is adverse impact and how can it be reduced?

6 What elements need to be considered in the design of assessment centres?

7 How would you measure the validity of an assessment centre?

8 Discuss the ways in which development centres differ from assessment centres

9 What elements in the contemporary approach to graduate recruitment need to be researched to understand their impact? How do these affect the validity of the selection process?

10 What new developments in the global business environment may affect the way that people are assessed for and at work?

Assignments

ASSIGNMENT 1: Researching assessment and selection methods online

Select a company in the private sector and a public body and find out as much as you can about selection methods from their recruitment site on the web. Produce a report addressing the following questions:

- Look at the organization's application form. What kind of information is asked for?
- What information is given to candidates about jobs? Are there job descriptions and person specifications?
- What information is given about selection methods?
- Comment on the type and range of methods used.
- Does the organization make use of psychometric tests? If so, what information is given to candidates about these?
- What are the main similarities and differences in the approach to assessment used by each organization?

ASSIGNMENT 2: Wealth Management plc goes to Singapore

Wealth Management plc, is a large and growing financial services company based in the City of London, but with new offices set up in New York, and Paris. The company operates an in-house assessment centre for the recruitment of all new management posts.

The assessment process currently consists of:

- A leaderless group discussion.
- A complex case analysis of a business problem, where candidates produce an individual report, and make a presentation to other candidates and assessors.
- A personality test.
- Two interviews: one with a manager from the HR department and one with a team of senior managers from the other functional areas in finance.

The board has recently taken the decision to open a new office in Singapore. They have allocated a budget for the initiative, and have decided to recruit twenty new managers for the new office. They have asked the

HRM department to produce a discussion document outlining a plan to recruit the best local managers. They are impressed with the results produced by the London Assessment Centre, and would like to set up a similar programme in the new office.

Task:

- You are a graduate trainee in the HR department. The Director has asked you to contribute to the document to be produced for the Board.

- Produce a report of approximately 1,500 words, outlining the issues that will need to be considered in setting up an assessment centre for the company in Singapore.

- Outline the steps that the company might take to ensure best practice and the ethical treatment of candidates.

ASSIGNMENT 3: Maximizing benefit in graduate recruitment

Consider the various elements in the contemporary approach to graduate recruitment and choose one which you consider to be critical to its success. Justify that decision. Then, as a psychologist, design a piece of research to investigate how best to construct and/or implement it in the recruitment programme. Make recommendations to graduate recruiters on maximizing the validity of this element for their organization's graduate recruitment programme (max. 2,000 words).

Further reading

Ballantyne, I., and Povah, N. (2004) *Assessment and Development Centres* (2nd edn.). Aldershot: Gower.
A detailed examination of assessment and development centres, their history, design, and construction, training of assessors, running of the centre, and validation.

Cook, M., (2004) *Personnel Selection: Adding Value through People* (4th edn.). Chichester: John Wiley and Sons Ltd.
An excellent and accessible book on the main components of selection and assessment.

Edenborough, R. (2005) *Assessment Methods in Recruitment, Selection and Performance.* London: Kogan Page.
A comprehensive book from a well-known writer in the field.

Searle, R. H. (2003) *Recruitment and Assessment: A Critical Text.* Milton Keynes: Open University and Palgrave Macmillan.
A scholarly treatment of recruitment giving full discussion of research findings and including an interesting historical overview of testing methods.

Woodruffe, C. (2007) *Development and Assessment Centres: Identifying and Developing Competence* (4th edn.). London: Human Assets.

 Work psychology in practice
Spoilt for choice

Muhammed didn't know what to do. Far from being unemployed, he'd been offered two jobs within a month of graduating.

One was a graduate trainee position at the Royal and Overseas Bank, a major finance house in the City. The other was at Intrinsic, a well-known financial consultancy. The pros and cons of working at each were similar—and the greater experience to be gained at one, compared to the greater financial benefits at the other, cancelled each other out. So how was he to decide?

He cast his mind back to the selection processes he had been through. The bank was well known to everyone and he had made his application online on their website. This had been a lengthy and frustrating experience involving online testing, arranging telephone interviews, and finally arriving at the corporate HQ in Canary Wharf, where the HR department was based, for a one-day assessment centre. Some of Mohammed's friends who had done as well as him at university had also applied to the bank but had not been able to complete the application process. No one was quite sure why. But Mohammed had got through this hurdle to the final stage. He'd liked the HR people and the director who had interviewed him. He had not had a lot of time to get to know the people or the company but he had discovered that there was quite a high turnover of graduate recruits each year. Mohammed was not sure whether there was a culture of hard drinking on Friday evenings after work, and it was not something he felt he could ask about, nor was he sure it was something he wanted to be part of.

Intrinsic, on the other hand, had invited him to a two-day assessment centre with a visit to the actual offices he would be working in and put him up in a top central London hotel, even though he lived in commuting distance. He had had a really enjoyable dinner on the middle evening and found out that the manager of his department shared his love of sailing and had a boat which he sailed regularly at weekends and had invited him to join them. He also found that the director, who was extremely charming, seemed to be really interested in him and what he wanted to do. They had both enjoyed the conversation over the meal. The company seemed to have a fairly stable workforce and people seemed to like working there. When Intrinsic had phoned to offer him the job, they seemed to genuinely want him to join the team.

'Well,' pondered Mohammed, 'my friends may think I'm mad, but I think I'd be happier at the consultancy and feel more a part of the team there.'

Questions

- How important is human chemistry compared to competencies in valid selection decisions?
- To what extent can interpersonal and social skills be assessed by tests, particularly online tests?
- If you were one of Mohammed's friends who had had their application to the bank curtailed, what would you think the reason might be and what might you do about it?
- For a new graduate recruit joining a company, would high labour turnover be a good or bad thing?

 ## Online Resource Centre

Visit the supporting online resource centre for additional material which will help you with your research, essays, and assignments, or you may find these additional resources helpful when revising for exams.

http://www.oxfordtextbooks.co.uk/orc/matthewman/

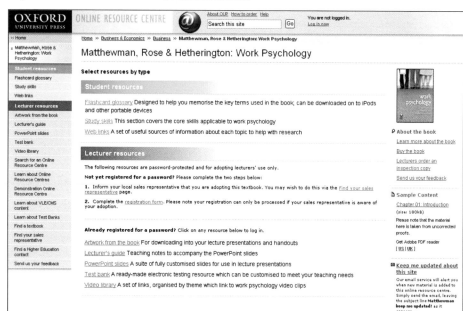

References

Anastasi, A., and Urbana, S. (1997) *Psychological Testing* (7th edn.). Upper Saddle River, NJ: Prentice-Hall.

Association of Graduate Recruiters (2006) *The AGR Graduate Recruitment Survey 2006*. London: Hobsons.

Association of Graduate Recruiters Briefing (2000) Web-based graduate recruitment.

Ballantyne, I., and Povah, N. (2004) *Assessment and Development Centres* (2nd edn.). Aldershot: Gower.

Bauer, T. N., Truxillo, D. M., Tucker, J. S., Weathers, V., Bertolino, M., Erogan, B., and Campion, M. A. (2006) Selection in the information age: the impact of privacy concerns and computer experience on applicant's reactions. *Journal of Management*, 32/5: 601–21.

Ben-Shakhar, G., Bar-Hillel, M., Bilu, Y., Ben-Abba, E., and Flug, A. (1986) Can graphology predict occupational success? Two empirical studies and some methodological ruminations. *Journal of Applied Psychology*, 71/4: 645–53.

Bertua, C., Anderson, N., and Salgado, J. F. (2005) The predictive validity of cognitive ability tests: a UK meta-analysis. *Journal of Occupational and Organizational Psychology*, 78/3: 387–409.

Boyatzis, R. E. (1982) *The Competent Manager: A Model for Effective Performance*. London: Wiley.

Boyle, S., Fullerton, J., and Yapp, M. (1993) The rise of assessment centre: a survey of AC usage in the UK. *Selection and Development Review*, 9/3: 1–4.

Bray, D., and Grant, D. (1966) The assessment center in the measurement of potential for business management. *Psychological Monographs*, 80/17 (whole of No. 625).

Briggs-Myers, I. (1998) *MBTI Manual: The Development and Use of the Myers-Briggs Type Indicator*. Palo Alto, CA: Consulting Psychologists Press.

British Psychological Society (2002) *The Code of Good Practice for Psychological Testing*. Accessed at http://www.psychtesting.org.uk

Burgoyne, J. (1989) Creating the managerial portfolio: building on competency approaches to management development. *Management Education and Development*, 20/1: 56–61.

Cernovsky, Z. Z. (1997) A critical look at intelligence research. In D. Fox and I. Prilleltensky (1997) (eds.) *Critical Psychology: An Introduction*. London: Sage.

CIPD (2006) *Fact Sheet: Assessment Centres for Recruitment and Selection*. London: CIPD.

CIPD (2007) *Annual Survey of Recruitment and Selection*. London: CIPD

Clasen, C., Meyer, C., Brun, C., Mase, W., and Cauley, K. (2003) Development of the competency assessment tool: mental health, an instrument to assess core competencies for mental health care worker. *Psychiatric Rehabilitation Journal*, 27/1: 10–17.

Clayton, G. (2006) The development of a tacit knowledge questionnaire for hostage negotiators in the Scottish Prison Service. *Proceedings of the Annual Conference of the Division of Occupational Psychology*. Leicester: British Psychological Society, Jan. 2006. http://www.bps.org.uk

Cook, M. (2004) *Personnel Selection: Adding Value through People* (4th edn.). Chichester: John Wiley and Sons Ltd.

Costa, P., and McCrae, R. R. (1985) *The NEO Personality Inventory Manual*. Odessa, FL: Psychological Assessment Resources.

Crowne, D. P., and Marlowe, D. (1964) *The Approval Motive: Studies in Evaluative Dependence*. New York: Wiley.

CVCP and Coopers and Lybrand (1998) *Skills Development in Higher Education*, London: CVCP.

Dougherty, T. W., Turban, D. B., and Callender, J. C. (1994) Confirming first impressions in the employment interview: a field study of interviewer behaviour. *Journal of Applied Psychology*, 79: 659–65.

Dulewicz, V. (2004) Give us details . . . *People Management*, 10/4: 23.

Erickson, P. B. (2004) Employer hiring tests grow sophisticated in quest for insight about applicants. *Daily Oklahoman*, 16 May.

Farrell, J. N., and McDaniel, M. A. (2001) The stability coefficients over time: Ackerman's 1988 model of the general aptitude test battery. *Journal of Applied Psychology*, 86/1: 60–79.

Faulder, L. (2005) The growing cult of personality tests. *Edmonton Journal*, 9 Jan.: 5.

Forsythe, S. M. (1990) Effects of applicant's clothing on interviewers decision to hire. *Journal of Applied Psychology*, 20: 1579–95.

Friedman, L. H., and Bernell, S. L. (2006) The importance of team level tacit knowledge and related characteristics of high performing health care teams. *Health Care Management Review*, 31/3: 223–30.

Garavan, T., and Morley, M. (1998) Graduate assessment centres: an empirical investigation of effectiveness. *Education + Training*, 40: 206–19.

Gaugler, B. B., Rosenthal, D. B., Thornton, G. C., and Bentson, C. (1987) Meta-analysis of assessment centre validity. *Journal of Applied Psychology*, 72/3: 493–511.

Gaugler, B. B., and Rudolph, A. S. (1992) The influence of assessee performance variation on assessors' judgements. *Personnel Psychology*, 45/1: 77–98.

Gill, R. (1979) The in-tray (in-basket) exercise as a measure of management potential. *Journal of Occupational Psychology*, 52/3: 85–197.

Goffman, E. (1959) *The Presentation of Self in Everyday Life*. Garden City, NY: Doubleday.

Goffman, E. (1967) *Interaction Ritual: Essays on Face to Face Behaviour*. New York: Doubleday and Co.

Goleman, D. (1996) *Emotional Intelligence*. London: Bloomsbury.

Guildford, J. P. (1956) The structure of intellect. *Psychological Bulletin*, 53: 267–93.

Guion, R. M., and Gottier, R. F. (1965) Validity of personality measures in personnel selection. *Personnel Psychology*, 18: 135–64.

Halpern, D. F. (1996) A process-orientated model of cognitive sex differences. *Learning and Individual Differences*, 8: 3–24.

Harland, L. K., Rauzi, T., and Biasotto, M. M. (1995) Perceived fairness of personality tests and the impact of explanations for their use. *Employee Rights and Responsibilities Journal*, 8: 183–92.

Hartley, P. (1997) *Group Communication*. London: Routledge.

Hausknecht, J. P., Day, D. V., and Thomas, S. C. (2004) Applicants' reactions to selection procedures: an updated model and meta-analysis. *Personnel Psychology*, 57: 639–83.

Heller, M. (2005) Court ruling that employers' integrity test violated ADA could open door to litigation. *Workforce Management*, 84/9: 74–7.

Hesketh, A. (2004) *Adding Value beyond Measure: The Business Case for Graduate Recruitment Programmes*. Warwick: Association of Graduate Recruiters.

Higgins, C. A., Judge, T. A., and Ferris, G. R. (2003) Influence tactics and work outcomes: a meta-analysis. *Journal of Organizational Behaviour*, 24/1: 89–106.

Higher Education Statistics Agency (2005)http://www.hesa.ac.uk.

Hollway, W. (1991) *Work Psychology and Organizational Behaviour*. London: Sage.

Howard, J. L., and Ferris, G. R. (1996) The employment interview context: social and situational influences on interviewer decisions. *Journal of Applied Psychology*, 26: 112–36.

Huffcutt, A. I., Conway, J. M., Roth, P. L., and Stone, N. J. (2001) Identification and meta-analytic assessment of psychological constructs measured in employment interviews. *Journal of Applied Psychology*, 86/5: 897–913.

Huffcutt, A. I., and Woehr, D. J. (1999) Further analysis of the employment interview validity: a quantitative evaluation of interviewer-related structuring methods. *Journal of Organizational Behaviour*, 20: 549–60.

Hyde, J. S. (2005) The gender similarity hypothesis. *American Psychologist*, 60/6: 581–92.

Incomes Data Services (2001) *Competency Framework Study 706*. London: IDS.

IRS (2002) Competencies boosts recruiters' power. *IRS Employment Review*, 752: 33–4.

IRS Employment Review (2006) Graduate recruitment: a labour market transformed by time. *IRS Employment Review*, 858/11 Mar.: 3.

Jansen, B., Jansen, K., and Spink, A. (2005) Using the web to look for work: implications for online job seeking and recruiting. *Internet Research*, 15/1: 49–66.

Judge, T. A., Higgins, C. A., and Cable, D. M. (2000) The employment interview: a review of recent research and recommendations for future research. *Human Resource Management Review*, 10/4: 383–406.

Keenan, T. (1995) Graduate recruitment in Britain: a survey of selection methods used in organizations. *Journal of Organizational Psychology*, 16/4: 303–17.

Kelley, H. H. (1950) The warm-cold variable in first impressions of people. *Journal of Personality*, 18: 431–9.

Kolk, N., Born, M., Flier, H., Olman, J. (2002) Assessment center procedures: cognitive load during the observation phase. *International Journal of Selection and Assessment*, 10/4: 271–8.

Lawton, D., and Baum, N. (2006) Online testing. Association of Graduate Recruiters Briefing Paper.

Lievens, F., and Klimoski, R. J. (2001) Understanding the assessment centre process: where are we now? In C. L. Cooper and I. T. Robertson (eds.), *International Review of Industrial and Organisational Psychology*, 16. Chichester: Wiley, ch. 8.

Lievens, F., Sanchez, J. I., and De Corte, W. (2004) Easing the inferential leap in competency modelling: the effects of task related information and subject matter expertise. *Personnel Psychology*, 57: 881–904.

Lin, T. R., Dobbins, G. H., and Farh, J. L. (1992) A field study of race and age similarity effects on interview ratings in conventional and situational interviews. *Journal of Applied Psychology*, 77: 363–71.

Mabey, W. (1989) The majority of large companies use occupational tests. *Guidance and Assessment Review*, 5/3: 1–4.

Melewar, T., and Karaosmanoglu, E. (2006) Seven dimensions of corporate identity: a categorisation from the practitioners' perspectives. *European Journal of Marketing*, 40/7–8: 846–69.

Miller, G. A. (1956) The magic number seven plus or minus two: some limits in our capacity for processing information. *Psychological Review*, 63: 81–97.

Mischel, W. (1968) *Personality and Assessment*. New York: Wiley.

Morgeson, F. P., Campion, M. A., Dipboye, R. L., Hollenbeck, J. R., Murphy, K., and Schmitt, N. (2007) Are we getting fooled again? Coming to terms with limitations in the use of personality tests for personnel selection. *Personnel Psychology*, 60/4: 1029–49.

Pingatore, R., Dugoni, B. L., Tindale, R. S., and Spring, B. (1994) Bias against overweight job applicants in a simulated job interview. *Journal of Applied Psychology*, 79: 909–17.

Pollitt, D. (2005) Testing graduates at Lloyds TSB: how bank selects the people who will lead it into the future. *Human Resource Management International Digest*, 13/1: 12–14.

Prewett-Livingstone, A. J., Field, H. S., Veres, J. G., and Lewis, P. M. (1996) Effects of race on interview ratings in a situational panel interview. *Journal of Applied Psychology*, 81: 178–86.

Robertson, I. T., and Downs, S. (1989) Work sample tests and trainability. *Journal of Applied Psychology*, 74/3: 402–10.

Robertson, I. T., Gratton, L., and Stukts, D. (1987) The psychometric properties of managerial assessment centres: dimension into exercises won't go. *Journal of Occupational Psychology*, 60: 187–95.

Robertson, I. T., and Smith, M. (2001) Personnel selection. *Journal of Occupational and Organizational Psychology*, 74/4: 441–72.

Robie, C., and Brown, D. J. (2007) Measurement equivalence of a personality inventory administered on the internet versus a kiosk. *Applied HRM Research*, 11/2: 97–106.

Roth, P. L., and Bobko, P. (2005) A meta-analysis of work-sample test validity: updating and interpreting some classic literature. *Personnel Psychology*, 58/4: 1009–37.

Rothstein, M. G., and Goffin, R. D. (2006) The use of personality measures in personnel selection: what does current research support? *Human Resource Management Review*, 16/2: 155–80.

Sackett, P. R., and Lievens, F. (2008) Personnel selection. *Annual Review of Psychology 2008*, 59: 419–50.

Schmidt, F. L., and Hunter, J. E. (1998) The validity and utility of selection methods in personnel psychology: practical and theoretical implications of 85 years of research findings. *Psychological Bulletin*, 124/2.

Schmitt, N., Gooding, R. Z., Noe, R. A., and Kirsch, M. (1984) Meta-analysis of studies carried out between 1964 and 1942 and the investigation of study characteristics. *Personnel Psychology*, 37: 407–22.

Schmitt, N., and Mills, A. E. (2001) Traditional tests and job simulations: minority and majority performance and test validities. *Journal of Applied Psychology*, 86/3: 451–8.

Searle, R. H. (2003) *Selection and Recruitment: A Critical Introduction*. Milton Keynes: The Open University/Palgrave Macmillan.

Sears, G. J., and Rowe, P. M. (2003) A personality-based similar-to-me effect in the employment interview: conscientiousness, affect-versus competence-mediated interpretations, and the role of job relevance. *Canadian Journal of Behavioural Science*, 35/1: 13–24.

Silvester, J., and Anderson, N. (2003) Technology and discourse: a comparison of face-to-face and telephone employment interviews. *International Journal of Selection and Assessment*, 3/2–3: 206–14.

Sparrow, P. (1995) Organisational competencies: a valid approach for the future? *International Journal of Selection and Assessment*, 3: 168–77.

Spelke, E. S. (2005) Sex differences in intrinsic aptitude for maths and science: a critical review. *American Psychologist*, 60/9: 950–8.

Spencer, S. J., Steele, C. M., and Quinn, D. M. (1999) Stereotype threat and women's math performance. *Journal of Experimental Social Psychology*, 35: 4–28.

Steiner, D. D., and Gilliland, S. W. (1996) Fairness reactions to personnel selection techniques in France and the United States. *Journal of Applied Psychology*, 81: 134–41.

Suff, R. (2005) Centres of attention. *IRS Employment Review*, 816: 42–8.

Tett, R. P., and Christiansen, N. D. (2007) Personality testing at the crossroads: a response to Morgeson, Campion, Dipboye, Hollenbeck, Murphy and Schmitt. *Personnel Psychology*, 60/4: 967–93.

Tett, R. P., and Palmer, C. A. (1997) The validity of handwriting elements in relation to self-report personality trait measures. *Personality and Individual Differences*, 22/1: 11–18.

Thompson, P., and McHugh, D. (2002) *Work Organisations: A Critical Introduction*. Basingstoke: Palgrave.

Wills, S. (1993) MCI and the competency movement: the case so far. *Journal of European Industrial Training*, 17/1: 9–11.

Wilson, D. (1996) The future for development centres. *Career Development International*, 1/6: 4–11.

Witkin, H. A. (1965) Psychological differentiation and forms of pathology. *Journal of Abnormal and Social Psychology*, 70: 317–36.

Zhang, L. (2004) Field-dependence/independence: cognitive style or perceptual ability? Validating against thinking styles and academic performance. *Personality and Individual Differences*, 37/6: 1295–311.

Chapter 13
Learning, training, and development

Xanthy Kallis, Jenni Nowlan, and Kamala Balu

Chapter objectives

As a result of reading this chapter and using the additional web-based material you should be able to:

- Differentiate between learning theories.
- Recognize how some of these theories are used to underpin learning in training.
- Explore experiential learning and learning styles.
- Discuss the benefits and importance of effective training.
- Define the meaning of a systems approach to training.
- Describe the four components of the Training Cycle.
- Understand the importance of doing a training needs analysis for effective training.
- Describe the three levels of training needs analysis.
- Recognize the approaches to evaluation of training.
- Describe the challenges associated with the transfer of training.
- Discuss the characteristics of a learning organization.
- Discuss some of the approaches used in management training and development.

Work psychology in practice
Staff development day

The staff development day that brought together all employees at a Holiday Centre had arrived, and the administrative and reception staff seemed especially excited about this, as they had enjoyed their experiences in previous years. Unfortunately this feeling was not shared by all staff as some of them felt that they had not actually obtained any benefits from previous staff training days, and so their expectations were set rather low from the outset. This was felt especially by the entertainment staff.

In the room were sixty members of staff, but the acoustics in the room were not ideal, and so didn't help those at the back who had to strain to hear. The external trainer presented a brief overview of the day and commenced with his ice-breaker, at which point the noise in the room became incredible. Five members of staff actually left at that point because they were dealing with their own problems and the noise was just too much for them. One had had a horrendous journey in and was feeling quite anxious and not able to deal with the overwhelming disturbance in the room and needed to go off on her own, buy a coffee, calm down, and come back for the afternoon session. Another was seen to leave because he felt it all looked too 'touchy-feely' for him—although he was seen to reappear at lunch and at the after-drinks session!

After the noise of the ice-breaker had quietened down the trainer then continued with an extremely short explanation behind the rationale of what they were going to be training in. At this point another member of staff left (from the entertainment side) as she felt almost insulted by the lack of relevance to her role in which they were about to engage and promptly went off to the rehearsal studio so that she could work out some new choreography for a new show idea she had so as not to waste the day entirely. She did in fact return for the afternoon session, but only once she had satisfied herself with having achieved something relevant in her line of work.

During lunch, which most staff agreed had been an enjoyable social occasion and a good time to catch up with people from other departments that they rarely saw, the trainer overheard some employees saying that they had been so glad that there hadn't been too much emphasis on specific jobs and they had been able 'to just get on with things straight away'. The afternoon session then continued with an emphasis on group work with staff from mixed departments, in separate rooms, mainly brainstorming ideas and some role-playing, but all coming together at the end to share the ideas that had been generated and finally to close the session.

Overall at least some of the staff seemed to feel that the day had been almost wonderful and had been a positive experience and even felt they couldn't wait until next year to repeat another similar day! However a significant number of staff felt the complete opposite and some were even planning on not attending the following year.

Questions

- What do you think the main problems were with this training event?

- How would you have solved the problems of staff not wanting to join in?

- Do you think it is possible to satisfy all staff in an event such as this?

- What else would you change about this particular staff development day?

13.1 Introduction

This chapter will begin by firstly looking at the major learning theories that have been developed by psychologists throughout the last 100 years or so and will then go on to consider skill development and how people might differ in how they learn through different learning styles. Although it is clearly important to use cutting-edge references and current trends in any new books the reader may find some very old references quoted at the beginning of this chapter, but that is because we are taking a somewhat historical approach and therefore must begin by taking a look at classic learning theories. However, most of these theories have pretty much stood the test of time and although most have been criticized they have been able to be built on and are still relevant today, underpinning much of the learning theory for training.

The chapter then turns to look specifically at training and asks what is training exactly and how does it differ to other types of learning? What is the training cycle and training needs analysis? This section will finish with an overall evaluation of training.

Finally the chapter will focus on the developmental side of learning and training and specifically will consider management development, lifelong learning, and the importance of professional development such as in coaching, mentoring, apprenticeship, etc.

13.2 Learning theories

So before we begin by considering the main learning theories we must firstly define what we mean by learning. Most writers generally agree that learning is the acquisition of knowledge, of skills, or of values which leads to permanent changes in behaviour, some of which may be observable (such as the demonstration of new skills) or unobservable (such as in different ways of thinking using strategy or knowledge).

Gagné (1985) identified major domains of learning in his instructional theory, these are: intellectual skills, verbal information, attitudes, motor skills, and cognitive (thinking) strategies. These are useful as a framework for understanding the different kinds of learning that may be necessary to underpin a training programme.

However, although a broad definition of what learning encompasses may be generally agreed upon by the different schools in psychology there are deeply contrasting perspectives on how that learning actually takes place. The main learning theories will now be considered.

13.2.1 The behaviourist view

Emerging from a time in psychology of introspection and a lack of any scientific vigour, the behaviourists, led by John Watson (1913) and in contrast to the psychodynamic school, were only interested in observable and quantifiable behaviour, of which the key components are stimulus and response. This is also sometimes referred to as stimulus-response, or S-R, theory. The stimulus and response reflexes can be conditioned either through classical or operant conditioning.

Classical

Classical conditioning, or Pavlovian conditioning, was accidentally discovered by a Russian physiologist, Ivan Pavlov, in 1927. By chance he found that dogs were conditioned to salivate in response to a sound, which had previously been a neutral stimulus. So, classical conditioning can be simply defined as the association or pairing of a conditioned stimulus (CS), e.g. food (which will induce salivation in dogs), with an unconditioned stimulus (UCS), e.g. a bell (rung at the same time as food is presented and once the association is strong enough, after a few trials, the food is removed), which results in a conditioned response (CR), i.e. the dog salivates at the sound of the bell. So we might say that naturally the dog has the UCS-UCR connection but the learning that has taken place from classical conditioning has created the CS-CR connection.

Operant

In contrast to respondent behaviour as in classical conditioning, **operant conditioning** (Skinner 1938) or instrumental learning (Thorndike 1913) is where behaviour that is instrumental in obtaining a reward or a punishment leads to learning. In this context operant means that an individual is operating in the world, or own environment, and the consequences of this will be a reward or a punishment. Therefore, satisfying outcomes (reward) will tend to lead to behaviour that will be repeated, or 'stamped in' and conversely unsatisfying outcomes (punishment) will tend to lead to avoidance behaviour and so should become extinguished, or 'stamped out' but not unlearned. The more frequent the desired outcomes are obtained, or the avoidance of undesirable ones are avoided, then the stronger the learning will be. It is also necessary that the behaviour and the reward, or the punishment, are closely connected together in order for learning to take place and this must be clear to see. So, in operant conditioning theory it is absolutely vital that there is a direct linkage of the operant behaviour to the contingent consequences, or **reinforcer**, otherwise incorrect learning may even take place. Read the case

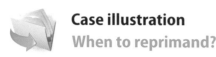

Case illustration

When to reprimand?

Susan was out with her daughter visiting some friends who didn't have children. Her naughty 2-year-old daughter was playing up with temper tantrums because she wanted the sweets that were on the coffee table but Susan had already told her that she must wait until after lunch. However, Susan did not tell her daughter off despite her crying and in the end gave in to her because she did not want to ruin the day that had taken a long time to organize and, after all, it was her friend's birthday. She knew, from previous occasions, that if she had stuck to what she had originally said about waiting for the sweets there would have been further tantrums and she just felt that she couldn't deal with it on this particular day. She decided to reprimand her daughter when they got home; although she knew it would be late, she thought at least that she would have calmed down a lot by then.

illustration and see if you think the young child in the scenario would have learned how her parent wanted her to behave.

Operant conditioning built on the work of Pavlov and his dogs and on instrumental learning which was originally demonstrated by Thorndike (1898), whereby he placed a cat into what he termed a puzzle box, which was constructed with one clear visible side to it so that the cat could see the food that had been placed outside. Attached to the door of the box was a string which, if pulled, would release a weight which would in turn open the door. When a cat was initially placed into one of these boxes the natural reaction at first was to bite, claw, and scratch everything, presumably in an attempt to escape to freedom. On average after about eight to ten minutes the cat, by trial and error, had managed to open the door. Once this had been accomplished, through the fact that sooner or later the cat would discover the way out simply because everything in the box was being attacked, after a few trials the cat would learn that it was the operant behaviour of pulling the string that led to the reward of the door opening and escape to freedom and food.

During subsequent trials the string was then immediately pulled or activated by the cat on being placed into the puzzle box, demonstrating that the cat had clearly learned the consequences of its actions and would quickly repeat this in order to obtain the reward. Thorndike referred to this relationship between behaviour and its consequences as the law of effect, which would also be applicable to human learning. This consequently had an enormous impact on educational psychology in his time, which meant that rote learning practices became the preferred method in schools because concepts such as perception or understanding were not considered important.

Skinner, having built on Thorndike's previous work, became very well known for his own experiments on rats in his constructed operant chamber and on pigeons in the Skinner box. The pigeons would peck away until they inadvertently pecked the lever that released the food. Just like Thorndike's cats, Skinner's pigeons soon learned to peck the lever immediately after being placed in the box. Skinner then developed the notion of shaping, as he was able to continually modify the pigeons' operant behaviour by reinforcing it with a reward whenever they carried out an action that was continually closer to the desired end result. In this case it speeded up the learning of pecking the lever to receive the food reward. This idea has been further developed and is now known as **behaviour modification**, and forms the basis for many therapies today.

Skinner also demonstrated the importance of the timing ratios for the reinforcement schedules. Continuous reinforcement, or reinforcing behaviour every time it occurs, was shown to be much less effective than intermittent or partial reinforcement. So by reinforcing behaviour only some of the time either through fixed ratios, variable ratios, fixed intervals, or variable intervals this was shown to be more effective, with variable schedules being the most successful. This can be seen demonstrated in many situations, not least in gambling. The variable ratio keeps the gambler guessing when the next reward will come and so keeps trying in the hope that it will be the next attempt, and if it is not, then the one after that, and the one after that, and so on.

In summary, although both classical and operant conditioning have had and still have much influence and have contributed to educational psychology, to clinical psychology, and other areas, it might be argued that learning is probably not quite as simple as behaviourists might have wanted us to believe. Firstly we have to consider that humans are quite qualitatively different to animals and so surely that means that behaviour must involve more, and be more complex, than a series of stimulus and response. Importantly, just because we cannot observe a change, it does not mean that a change may or may not have taken place. So we now turn to look at how conditioning has been built on to include social factors and cognitive factors.

13.2.2 Social learning

Bandura felt that reinforcement was not enough to account for all learning and although this formed part of the learning process this did not tell us the whole story. So, building upon the principles of reinforcement Bandura built a theory of **observational learning** which the individual carries out through modelling and imitating others. However, this involves more than simply copying or just identifying with others as it is experienced in the imagination through the feelings or through the actions of others (vicarious reinforcement). Social learning can be said to have taken place then in situations where there has not been a tangible reinforcer, nor any clear active response by the learner. So observational learning occurs when another's actions and most importantly their consequences are observed and the feelings or actions enter the imagination, which then influences and guides future actions of the observer, bearing in mind of course that we have a choice because we have anticipatory control. The social learning approach however still has an emphasis on external processes.

Bandura and Huston (1961) carried out what is now regarded as a classic experiment using BoBo the Clown dolls (large blown-up toys). Children observed adults behaving aggressively with these doll—they punched them, they kicked them and hit them with a hammer, etc. The children who had observed this also played with them in the same aggressive manner later when presented with the same toys, unlike the control group children who had not seen adults behaving aggressively with these new toys. A later stage of this experiment found that children even behaved aggressively towards the dolls when they observed this behaviour via a video, although not to the same degree as in the real-life observation experiment. In addition children also copied some forms of aggressive behaviour from other children even when they had not seen the adults' aggressive behaviour towards the dolls but had just witnessed other children's behaviour while playing.

So it seems that social learning most certainly does occur and can equally be manifest through prosocial behaviour as well as anti-social behaviour. According to Baldwin and Baldwin (1973) and Bandura (1977) the observed behaviour will be more influential when: the consequences are seen as reinforcing; when there is respect and liking for the model; when the perceived similarities are high between the model and the observer; when there is a reward for the observer in modelling the behaviour seen; when the model's behaviour is clear and stands out and is different to others; and the observer must feel that the behaviour demonstrated by the model is within their range of skills and capacity to act in the same way. Clearly these points have important indications for observational training methods and practices.

The next approach we are going to turn to, although again it doesn't disagree that some learning can be as simple as stimulus, response, and reinforcement, also takes into account strong internal control rather than emphasizing mainly external processes. In addition this approach is strongly linked to memory, being the endurable part of the learning process. Although there is a vast literature on memory (and beyond the scope of this chapter) here we will just mention cognitive load as this is highly relevant to the cognitive approach to learning. Quite simply Sweller (1988) tells us that for optimum learning we should keep the load in working memory to a minimum. Working memory is the part of the brain that provides temporary storage and the necessary manipulation of any information necessary for cognitive

Pause for thought
Have you ever imitated, or thought about imitating, someone's actions or behaviours in order to receive rewards? If so, how did it feel?

tasks. There is a limit to how much capacity the working memory has and although different figures are quoted here we are only talking about a few seconds and a few items. However if we build on what we already understand and what we already have in our long-term memory then the load on the working memory will be lessened. Again, this has strong indications for the rate of delivery of training methods.

13.2.3 The cognitive approach

Researchers who believe in the cognitive approach to learning, just like the social learning theorists, do not dispute that some learning can again be explained by stimulus and response or reinforcement, but that cannot be all there is to it. They believe in the importance of feelings, of attitudes, of motives, memory, and thought (or cognition) to tell us more about how learning takes place. Speech, language, and knowledge are all used to formulate abstract concepts for perceptions and for organizing ideas for humans to problem-solve and encode new information. Often a metaphor of networks, concepts, and schemata are used to explain this approach.

Latent learning

Tolman (1948) demonstrated the importance of these processes in learning and felt that learning involved two parts. These were: a cognitive map, which means a mental representation of the learning taking place; and the individual's expectancy about consequences of actions. Tolman and Honzik (1930) and Tolman (1948) demonstrated **latent learning** in rats, whereby they found they could learn the quickest way though a maze, without reinforcement, when a particular path was blocked. It certainly does appear that the rats were not using trial and error and had an internal cognitive map in their heads. These findings have also been replicated with other animals such as chimpanzees (Menzel 1978; Moar 1980; Olton 1979). However, there is still some debate in the literature over the existence of cognitive maps (Wehner and Menzel 1990) but it certainly seems clear that animals must be able to form some sort of mental representation of their environment (Capaldi et al. 1995).

So, it certainly seems fair to say that learning, in most cases, cannot be as simple as conditioning might tell us with its association, stimulus and response, and reinforcers, but surely seems to involve cognitive processes.

Insight learning

Another type of learning that comes under the cognitive approach is that of **insight learning**, which can simply be thought of as the 'a-ha' moment or 'eureka moment'. Köhler (1925) found that monkeys were able to manage a problem-solving task and concluded that they were using insight learning rather than trial and error. However, Harlow (1949) disagreed and felt that problem solving could be interpreted as trial and error. In one of his many studies he gave monkeys an odd-one-out task to solve but felt that they were using generalization skills to solve the task rather than insight.

It is fair to say then that despite conditioning studies in the laboratory giving little opportunity for many cognitive skills to be utilized or demonstrated, participants mostly still manage to use these higher skills. Skinner (1987, 1990), however, objected to the shift towards psychology changing from a focus on behaviour to becoming a science of the mind, but was in the minority here. Not only is psychology now regarded as a science of the mind (and behaviour as well) but there is also an increasing recognition towards evolutionary and neurological learning processes.

Connectionist learning models

The development of connectionist learning models has made much progress in recent years. These are hypothesized systems that attempt to describe structures and processes that characterize learning. Unlike the behaviourists, who only describe when learning occurs, these models are concerned with hypothesizing the way that learning actually takes place. Computer programs have been written in an attempt to actually model the various elements of the learning process. This approach clearly allows great flexibility in modifying and testing the models.

Although the learning theory that these models are mostly based on are certainly not new, clearly this approach would not be possible without the enormous advances that have been in computer technology in recent years. In the introduction to this chapter it was noted that there would be a number of very old references while we review various learning theories, but here we see the classic and old theories coming together with new advances. The chapter now turns to using cognitive strategies for learning, how they might be put in place, skill development ,and a consideration of how different people might differ in how they learn.

13.2.4 Cognitive strategies

Metacognitive skills, which simply means, knowing about and organizing knowledge and strategies for learning, are important concepts as, apart from specific learning, we also need to learn how to learn. As adults, we possess metacognitive skills but they are lacking in very young children (Moynahan 1973).

Acquisition of complex skills, which are likely to be necessary in most training programmes, utilizes cognitive learning and Fitts (1962) broke this down into three stages. Skill development then is said to be firstly in the cognitive stage, where the learner needs to understand what the task will involve and so needs appropriate details. The second stage is associative, where practice will help the learner to improve on the association between knowledge and application and needs appropriate feedback. And thirdly, the autonomous phase is where the skill becomes automatic and increasingly much less attention needs to be given while using the new skill.

Anderson (1983, 1987) also writes about skill acquisition but describes this in a similar but slightly different way. He uses the terminology of declarative knowledge, meaning that the learner needs to know the facts, the knowledge needs to be declared, so is explicit; secondly, the procedural stage refers to the practice of the skill using the knowledge from the declarative stage, so this is all about knowing how to do something, which brings with it all encompassing demands on attention and memory; in the third and final tuning stage the learner refines the underlying rules so that the skill becomes increasingly competent and also automatic.

....

 Activity Learning styles

Do you think the trainer in the opening case study could have designed and delivered his training differently if he had taken account of people's different learning styles? Do you think the trainer in the opening case study would have had better success if he had taken account of the concept of people having different learning styles?

See if you can decide which learning style would probably best fit the way you like to learn most of the time. Try to think of some strategies that you could try out to become a more all-round learner.

....

 KEY LEARNING POINTS

- Classical conditioning pairs, through association, a conditioned stimulus with a conditioned response.
- Operant conditioning puts the emphasis on the operator in his or her own environment: behaviour is then consequently positively reinforced by a reward or negatively reinforced by a punishment.
- Social learning builds on reinforcement in learning but uses social situations and modelling of others in order to learn how to behave differently, which can either have a prosocial or an antisocial outcome.
- Cognitive approaches again recognize the importance of reinforcement, but emphasize that thoughts, feelings, emotions, etc. in problem solving and learning take priority.

13.3 Training arena

This section deals with the training arena within which learning and development can occur. **Training** is usually a planned purposeful event that aims to improve performance in a specific job or task. As training is now a pervasive activity in society (Patrick 2000, cited in Chmiel 2000) and one that embraces all levels of employees, it is necessary for organizations to invest more in training their workforce in order to remain competitive. Training in this sense is seen as one response to competition (Furnham 2001).

As the world is a place of continuous change, some would argue (Millward 2005) that the future of work depends critically and fundamentally on people's ability to learn and the importance of lifelong learning is emphasized. Greater emphasis is put on higher-order thinking skills, flexibility, and the ability to learn new skills quickly to an appropriate standard (Hatchuel et al. 2002; Rowley 2002). Global training demands and technological advancement has created the need for a 'knowledge worker' (Bhat 2001) and for people to have a portfolio of skills (Arnold 2005) in order to keep up with the fast changing pace of work. This shift in the type of skills organizations require means society needs to keep up with these changes by educating and training the new population to be able to cope with them (Millward 2005).

13.3.1 Education and training

Traditionally training was seen as a short-term skills-based activity with education as a long-term one and development as a process of progression (Wexley and Latham 2002). Training was defined as an activity that is done at the individual level and one that is associated with non-managerial employees (McKenna 2006). However, in today's workplace all employees need to be developed and it is no longer the reserve of managers (McKenna 2006). The education/training divide is a recurrent problem that society is trying to bridge (Millward 2005), with organizations harnessing a philosophy of learning to raise the business profile of education and this has blurred the boundaries between education and training (Doyle 2003).

Research shows (Hogarth and Wilson 2003) that organizations that continuously invest in training and developing their staff have fewer recruitment problems (Marchington and Wilkinson 2006). The business case for training is that organizations are more competitive, with a better-educated and skilled workforce.

Organizations began to take their training policy more seriously with the introduction of many schemes (both by British governments and the EU) offering support for training in organizations. Training has taken a prominent place within organizational strategic planning. Some argue (Yamnill and McLean 2001) that training is now an essential part of Human Resource Management strategies for enhancing competitiveness. In fact, many senior managers believe training is a powerful management tool to support planned and desired development (Furnham 2001).

Training individuals can benefit the organization because it promotes better employee well-being, which leads to lower absenteeism and lower employee turnover. The potential benefit of training to individuals is that they are developed to gain a portfolio of skills, which increases their ability to cope with the changes and enhances their employability (Doyle 2003). The benefit to the organization of training its employees is that a skilled workforce makes better quality products, employs faster work practices, and makes fewer mistakes because they have greater safety awareness and also higher levels of organizational satisfaction and motivation (McKenna 2006). This in turn raises the profile of the organization and increases its competitiveness on a global scale.

13.3.2 Systems approach to training

Learning itself can and does occur anywhere and at any time. However, in this section it is the systematic approach to learning that we will focus on, sometimes referred to as the **Training Cycle** (see Figure 13.1). It is a step-by-step procedure of how organizations should approach any training they are thinking of carrying out to ensure training is done for the right reasons and that it is cost effective. There are four components of the cycle (Millward 2005) although others suggest three (Arnold 2005) or even five (Patrick 2000). No matter how the stages are split up, there is unanimous agreement that carrying out a training needs analysis, the first component, is fundamental to any training activity—a very interesting point, as it is the component in the cycle that is the most neglected (Millward 2005).

Figure 13.1. Training cycle

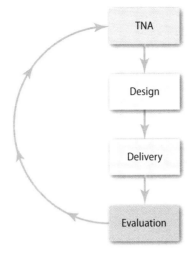

The four components of the training cycle are a **training needs analysis** to identify which needs are to be addressed, designing a training programme based on the objectives or outcomes we have identified, **delivering** a tailored programme specific to these needs, and then evaluating the training to ensure it was worth doing and to make any modifications necessary to improve the training event for future sessions. The principle of a systems approach is that it feeds back information continuously so that the instructional process is updated and improved, making it more effective each time.

Training needs analysis

The training needs analysis can be considered at three levels (McGhee and Thayer 1961): the organization, the task, and the individual. Although refinements have been made to these three basic approaches (Goldstein and Ford 2002) the underpinning principles are still the same. It is therefore fair to assume that if training is to be effective it is logical that it should identify a specific training need or needs or can anticipate future performance issues that may arise. The data collected from this stage is then used to set **training objectives** and will also determine the methods and strategies that will be used in designing the programme (Furnham 2001).

In the first instance, we need to ensure that the problem or issue we have identified is solved by training (Buckley and Caple 2003), as some problems can be solved in other ways. For example, in a very busy department where people seem to have lots to do in a short space of time, the solution may be to employ an additional person to help with the workload, or perhaps the layout of a department is such that it hinders the flow of work and by changing furniture around it makes the flow easier.

KEY LEARNING POINTS

- A systems approach to training is based on feedback that continuously improves the effectiveness of training
- Carrying out a training needs analysis is a fundamental part of the training cycle.
- Training needs can be considered at the organizational level, the task level, and the person level.
- Training needs analysis is the most neglected component of the training cycle.

Organizational level of analysis An analysis at the organizational level takes an overview of the current performance of the company and assesses where training can make the most contribution (Roscoe, cited in Truelove 1995). It is not an easy one, but Goldstein (1993) suggests four steps, although there are no hard and fast rules for doing this (Millward 2005).

The steps are to specify training goals, to determine the training climate, to identify any legal constraints there may be, and to determine resources available, for example does the organization have the budget for training.

At this level of analysis it looks at the organizational aims or goals and identifies possible barriers that prevent the organization from achieving these goals (Furnham 2001). Organizations can also anticipate a need for change when new jobs are created or old jobs are redesigned, when new employees are hired or when the organization changes in some way. In doing this it can examine the broader issues such as the aim, function, and appropriateness of training (Buckley and Caple 2003). It is also important that key personnel and senior management are committed to the training event if it is to succeed.

Task level of analysis Task analysis is integral to job analysis. Job analysis is the process of examining a job in detail in order to identify its component tasks (Buckley and Caple 2003). This level of analysis focuses on the objectives and outcomes of the task to be performed by employees and seeks to identify what knowledge, skill, and attitudes the employees need in order to perform the job.

It identifies the target jobs which are to be assessed, who will be involved in the data-collecting process exercise, and how the data is to be gathered for it. There are different methods of gathering information about the job or task: these include interviews, observation, work sample, focus groups, questionnaires, group discussion, examination of document, material used on the job (Buckley and Caple 2003). Task analysis looks at individual units of behaviour (Furnham 2001). The aim is to break down the job into smaller components in a hierarchical order that builds up to make a whole job. One such technique is the Hierarchical Task Analysis (Annett and Duncan 1967), which breaks down the job into units of behaviours and the critical knowledge skills, abilities, and atitudes each unit requires.

During this level of analysis the information that is gathered will identify the main objectives of the job and the conditions under which it is performed. It will include the responsibilities, the main subsidiary tasks, difficulties, and anticipated job change (Buckley and Caple 2003).

Individual analysis This level of analysis puts the spotlight onto the person who needs the training to do a job and their ability to learn (see above). As a result of the task analysis we know what knowledge, skills, and attitudes the person needs to perform the job. At the individual level of analysis it is to identify what the person already knows and what they need to learn in order to be skilled sufficiently to perform the job at a specific standard. The skills gap between the two is then used to set the training objectives and also determine the method that will be used to train the person.

With the changing make-up of workforce diversity needs for training also must be considered. There is an increase in older workers, as a result of redundancies and early retirement. There are now more female returners to the workplace after a career break, minority groups, and also legal requirements to make reasonable adjustments to accommodate disability in the training arena. All these factors make for a unique set of training and development needs (Kodz et al. 2002). With people, goods, and services coming from and going to different countries, the ability to function effectively in a diverse context is important (Offermann and Phan 2002).

Training design

Designing the training event can be seen as consisting of three main categories which influence one another. The training content, which is gained by doing a TNA, the methods and strategies one selects (which are in part based the outcomes of the TNA) and are also informed by psychological insight. Lastly, the target audience, the trainees and what they bring into the training arena (their learning styles, strategies, and so forth) will influence the event.

It is important to consider peoples' preferred **learning styles** because they are likely to be quite crucial for training to be fully effective and to reach everyone as much as possible. Most people will use a combination of styles but with a preference for one category over the others.

Table 13.1. Honey and Mumford's learning styles

Activists—do	Reflectors—review	Theorists—conclude	Pragmatists—plan
Tend to act first and think of consequences later	Tend to be cautious	Tend to think logically using rationality and objectivity	Tend to be very keen to put ideas and theories into practice
Here and now is important to them	Observe and stand back a little	Coherent theories are sought after	Like to experiment with new ideas
Like to fully immerse themselves in any new experiences	Can be slow to reach conclusions as like to collect and analyse data	Very keen on principles, theories, and models	Are impatient with endless discussion

Source: Adapted from Honey and Mumford (1982).

However, the most beneficial idea is to become an all-round learner and try to develop in all four of the categories, to optimize the learning experience.

Popular in the management literature, Honey and Mumford (1982) built on Kurt Lewin's work and on Kolb's experiential learning model (1976, 1985) to develop their own learning styles. Their four distinct learning styles are: activist, reflector, theorist, and pragmatist. Honey and Mumford's original eighty-item Questionnaire (to find out one's preferred learning style)

Case illustration
Carrying out a training needs analysis

You are a training consultant who has been invited to an organization and are told that their staff are resistant to changing over to a new software programme they have introduced. You carry out a training needs analysis and discover that the staff are unhappy and feel under pressure. You advise the organization that you need to do further investigations in order to identify the specific problem. You decide to observe the employees in question while they perform their day-to-day tasks. However, as there are tasks they perform based on knowledge in their heads and not easily observable, you also set out a questionnaire, based on your observations and also carry out some semi-structured interviews with key people: job incumbents and also their line managers in order to get a broader picture.

You discover through you investigations that they have not been trained to use the new programme but have been given a manual which sets out the whole thing. A manual that gives them step-by-step instructions of how to use the new system. This is all very well for the few that are self-motivated learners and can read instructions no problem, but for others, a more practical approach is necessary. You find that some colleagues who can use the manual will help other colleagues, but there is so much pressure at work there is little time to dedicate to doing this, which leaves many frustrated and hating the new system and wanting to go back to what they knew and worked well with before.

Because of busy daily routines they do not have time to study the manual, hence their jobs are made harder and slower by their efforts to learn to use the new system and get on with the job. You recommend that people using this system need a formal day's training on the new system away from the daily routine in order to be given time to learn this new procedure and then time on the job to transfer this knowledge and hence become accustomed to using the new software.

Questions
- What specific problem did the training needs analysis identify.
- At what level was the problem identified?
- What should the organization do now? Give reasons for your answer.

now has a more recent e-version which consists of forty items only. They continue to build on their learning styles questionnaires and are continually updating with newer versions.

 KEY LEARNING POINTS

- Most people will have a preferred learning style.
- You can find out your preferred learning style by answering Honey and Mumford's Learning Style Questionnaire (fee payable).
- Experiential learning follows a four-stage cycle going through concrete experience, reflection and observation, forming of abstract concepts, and finally generalization and active experimentation.

Training content

The information gained by the TNA sets the training objectives for the training event. These training objectives must be written in clear and unambiguous statements which describe precisely what trainees are expected to do as a result of their learning experience. An objective is presented in three parts: (1) the performance, i.e. the behaviour trainees are expected to show when they have acquired the skills, and the knowledge which makes up the content of the task; (2) the conditions under which the performance is carried out, including details of equipment, job aids, etc.; and (3) the standards of performance which trainees are expected to achieve it. Standards are specified by accuracy, speed, or completion. For example a statement may look like this: 'to operate a department's photocopier' (the performance) by using a Xerox photocopying machine (the condition), the outcome of which is 'the successful copy' that is produced (the standard).

Training methods and strategies

The methods that the trainer chooses, as mentioned before, will be influenced by a number of factors such as the learner principles, the target audience, any constraints, and so forth. The principles of good training practices are diffuse and derived from cognitive (experimental) psychology and organization and occupational psychology (Patrick 2000). Both are important to our understanding of how to develop training or instructional programmes (Chmiel 2000). Moreover, Furnham (2001) suggests two essential **principles of training**. The first is **participation** which refers to the active participation of trainees to perform the desired skill, as this helps people retain what they have learned. The other is **repetition** of the skill or practice, over time. How long one should practice and how long one should rest depends on many factors such as the nature of the skill (Furnham 2001). These should be built into the **training design** in order for the training to be effective.

As a result of psychological insight there is better understanding about ways people learn best, the different learning styles people use, memory capacity, and people's motivation to learn. This informs the method to use and how to structure and sequence the training content into manageable chunks that will optimize learning. There are robust findings on learning differences which are linked to motivation to learn (Furnham 2001) (see both section 13.2 above and Chapter 5 on Motivation and Work Satisfaction for more information). Imagine a training programme run in ignorance of psychological insight (Hardingham 2000): from considering whether training should take place on the job or off the job, to how many delegates a session should include, to the amount of information and layout of it on Powerpoint slides, to whether Powerpoint is the best way to give the information. Even the way the facilitator welcomes delegates and builds rapport (Hardingham 2000) is a result of a better understanding of people's learning and motivation to learn.

The programme needs to be pitched at the right level for the target audience and use language trainees can relate to. It needs to consider the implementation of the training event and it is at this point that the facilitator or presenter is of vital importance. Most people will be familiar with a variety of ways of facilitating, some are better than others. The important thing is to build rapport with your audience and engage with them, this is how one keeps the audience interested, involved, and motivated. However, it is also vital that the target audience too is receptive to the training programme and the facilitator if it is to achieve its outcomes.

Activity Workshop discussion

In pairs or small groups, consider an interesting lecture or workshop you have recently attended and discuss:

- What was good about it?
- What did you find most interesting? The facilitator, the topic, etc.
- Why did you go? What were your feelings? What was your mood? Did you have a good night the night before? Think about *your* approach to the event and how your mood might have influenced the outcome.

Evaluation of training

If organizations and people are to invest time, effort, and money on training and development it is important to evaluate whether it has really been useful. Methods of validation and evaluation provide a means of assessing how successful training programmes have been and where modification may be required. Validation assesses the extent to which training achieved its objectives. The evaluation of training is the process of ascertaining the overall benefit of training and examining whether it has affected performance of the job. Although newer approaches to, and models of, training evaluation have been proposed (e.g. Day et al. 2001; Kraiger et al. 1993), Kirkpatrick's (1959, 1976, 1996) four-level model of training evaluation and criteria continues to be most popular (Salas and Cannon-Bowers 2001; Van Buren and Erskine 2002).

Kirkpatrick (1967) provided a framework which suggests four levels at which evaluation may take place:

- Reaction—the trainee's personal view of the programme content and process.
- Learning—whether or not the trainee shows evidence of attaining the learning objectives of the programme.
- Behaviour—evaluation of behaviour change after the training programme. What skills did the trainee develop?
- Results—evaluation of the extent to which the training produces results in the organization.

Examining each of these levels more closely shows they are not so easy to evaluate and they do not always yield strong data to improve training programmes.

Reaction The questionnaire or 'happy sheet' is the most common method for evaluating trainee reactions. Although happy sheets can be valuable for analysing feedback on or directly after the training they can also give misleading information about the training programme. Happy sheets tap into attitudes that may be affected by a host of factors, for example, trainees may have been satisfied with the programme because the trainer was entertaining or in other circumstances they may be less satisfied because the trainer worked them hard. This type of feedback can fail to assist in examining whether or not the training was effective in achieving its objectives. Reactions to training tend to be poor predictors of training yet most training programmes are evaluated based solely on trainee's reactions. This level of evaluation is usually frequently used as it is less costly and not as time consuming as evaluation at the other three levels. For instance, in the American Society of Training and Development 2002 *State of the Industry* Report 78 per cent of the organizations surveyed reported using reaction measures, compared with 32, 9, and 7 per cent for learning, behavioural, and results respectively (Van Buren and Erskine 2002). Dipboye (1997) defends the value of happy sheets and argues they provide a voice and involvement to the trainee in their own learning.

Learning This level of evaluation is concerned with whether or not the trainees show evidence that they have attained the learning objectives of the programme. Testing trainees on how much they have learnt is of little value if there has been no **pre-test** to assess how much they knew before the training. Evaluation could involve administering pre- and post-tests to check

Table 13.2. The Solomon four-group design

Group A	Pre-test	Train	Post-test
B	Pre-test	—	Post-test
C	—	Train	Post-test
D	—	—	Post-test

trainees' understanding of the material presented on the training programme. However, the vast majority of training programmes do not involve a pre-test.

Behaviour Evaluation of training in terms of behaviour is more difficult than reaction and learning evaluations. When evaluating behaviour we want to know whether the training made any difference to the individual's work performance. This level of evaluation is often assessed using methods such as checklists, observation, interviews, surveys and work reviews. From an evaluation perspective we are interested in how learning has been translated into new behaviour for example, if someone has undergone a leadership development course are they able to demonstrate behaviour which shows their power to influence and empower others afterwards? Are these changes attributable to the programme?

To answer such questions the implication is that some form of experimental design would be needed. Comparisons would need to be made of trained and untrained workers in the same job or the same workers before and after training would need to be compared with a control group of workers that had not been exposed to the training. One of the most common approaches to ruling out some of the threats to **internal validity** is through experimental designs such as the Solomon Four-Group design.

The most thorough consideration of experimental design that can be used by evaluators to examine the effectiveness of training has been presented by Cook et al. (1990).

Results or effectiveness Although the level of evaluating results and effectiveness is the most desired result from training, it is usually the most difficult to accomplish. When trying to relate training outcomes to organizational effectiveness there are a number of problems as this validation demands observable, quantifiable, and tangible results that show specific profit and performance for example, reduced costs, higher quality, increased production, and lower rates of employee turnover and absenteeism. Trying to show that training and training alone was responsible for organizational effectiveness is extremely difficult as a whole range of training variables or a combination of other factors can be responsible for the success.

Unfortunately, many organizations do not make systematic effort to evaluate their training programmes as it is not easy to arrange in organizations. A number of reasons have been noted for organizations failing to conduct systematic evaluations. First, many training professionals either do not believe in evaluation or do not possess the mind-set necessary to conduct evaluation (Swanson 2005). Others do not wish to evaluate their training programmes because of lack of confidence in whether their programmes add value to, or have an impact on, organizations (Spitzer 1999). Lack of training evaluation has also been attributed to lack of resources and expertise, as well as lack of support from the organization culture to promote such efforts (Desimone et al. 2002; Moller et al. 2000).

Evaluative research can be costly and many trainers do not have the skills to conduct such research. Organizations should be encouraged to spend on resources to evaluate training and development programmes; it makes little sense to continue to support training activities without empirical evidence to support their worth. Failure to evaluate the worth of a training programme could be expensive.

Transfer of training

One of the challenges to training is the transfer of new behaviours to the workplace. To obtain successful transfer, a number of challenges must be met concerning the trainee, the content of training, and support in the workplace; for example, the more closely the training programme

Pause for thought
Consider a training programme on which you have been involved. What method of evaluation was used? Would it have been more cost effective to use another method?

matches the demands of the job, the more effective the training will be (Baldwin and Ford 1988). If there is little similarity between the training situation and work situation, negative transfer will result. Negative transfer refers to when skills learned in training hamper or interfere with job performance. Several conditions can facilitate positive transfer; for example, the extent to which information and skills are retained is dependent on factors such as the environment to which the trainee returns. This needs to be supportive and provide reinforcement of skills taught on the training programme, an environment that is unsupportive can minimize transfer of training. Reviews of research into long-term retention of skills show a steady loss over time when they are not used (Annett 1979; Hagman and Rose 1983). Managers can greatly influence whether transfer occurs effectively; research by Gumuseli and Ergin 2002 showed that support form managers and co-workers was particularly key to a positive transfer climate. Also influential is the way that the organization rewards skills acquisition (for example, linking incentives to desired new behaviours) and allows opportunities to practice and apply skills learned on the training programme. Another important factor is the overall organizational culture or climate. The more supportive it is of training the greater the opportunities for transfer of training to the work situation (Rouiller and Goldstein 1993; Tracey et al. 1995). It is consistently found that trainees in work environments that support them in the application of what they have learned demonstrate more transfer behaviour than those in situations with negative transfer climates (Cheng and Ho 2001).

Transfer is important in evaluating the cost of training: the more transferable the more cost-efficient the training.

KEY LEARNING POINTS

- Evaluation of training is a process of ascertaining the overall benefit of the training and its impact on job performance.

- The four levels of Kirkpatrick's evaluation model essentially measure trainee's reactions to training, learning, behaviour, and results or effectiveness of the training.

- One of the biggest challenges in training is the transfer of skills and information learned in training to the workplace.

- The degree to which trainees successfully apply their job skills gained in training is considered to be positive transfer of training. Several conditions can facilitate positive transfer.

- Negative transfer of training occurs when skills learned in the training hamper or interfere with job performance.

13.4 Management training and development

There are a range of approaches available for management training and development. Some approaches are formalized, planned, and structured. They can take place 'on the job' in the workplace or away from the workplace. Formal approaches for training and developing managers include the competency approach and development centres. Some of the less formalized methods are **action learning**, coaching, and mentoring.

13.4.1 Competency approach

The popularity of the term competence can be attributed to Boyatzis (1982). He defined competence as 'an underlying characteristic of a person', stating it could be 'motive, trait, skill, aspect of one's self-image or social role, or a body of knowledge which he or she uses'. A more specific definition was given by Nordhaug and Gronhaug (1994) where a competence was defined as 'work-related knowledge, skills and abilities'.

The rationale for the competence-based approach being adopted at organizational and national level comes from the desire to gain competitive advantage (Lawler 1994). It has been increasingly used for management training and development particularly in the UK due to its use in government-backed initiatives. Throughout the years the competency-based approaches have proved to be a critical tool in many organizational functions such as workforce succession planning and performance appraisals. According to Draganidis and Mentzas (2006) the main reason for selecting these approaches are, firstly, they provide identification of the skills, knowledge, behaviours, and capabilities needed to meet current and future personnel selection needs in alignment with organizational strategies and priorities. Secondly, they focus on individual and group development plans to eliminate the gap between the competencies requested by a project, job role, or enterprise strategy and those available.

The competence-based management development approach is not without criticism. Currie and Darby (1995) examined the evaluation of management development programmes in the National Health Service and noted that the two main criticisms of the competence-based management development were the definition of competencies and their assessment. For example, in the NHS this approach was seen to be generic, highly prescriptive, and too structured. Critics have argued that the competence-based approach tends to make the assumption that managerial skills are of a general nature (Canning 1990; Donnelly 1991). Mangham (1990) rejected the competence approach altogether, ridiculing it as trying to build an 'identikit' manager. These critics advocate that competencies should be contextually based, reflecting the needs of the organization and the markets in which it operates.

13.4.2 Development centres

Development centres are 'workshops which measure the abilities of participants against the agreed success criteria for the job role' (Lee and Beard 1994). The term 'development centre' relates to the process of using assessment techniques for identifying development needs, not to a specific place. It is suggested that development centres are an efficient way of helping individuals assess their strengths and weaknesses and highlight actions required to facilitate their future development (Griffiths and Bell 1985).

13.4.3 Action learning

The concept of action learning is not new. It was developed by Revans (1971); however, in recent years there has been an interest in applying the ideas of action learning to management training and development. Action learning has been used as a method of helping managers develop their talents by exposing them to real problems. Managers are required to analyse problems, formulate recommendations, and then take action. The action learning approach takes the view that managers learn best by doing rather than being taught.

13.4.4 Coaching and mentoring

Coaching is an increasingly popular tool for personal development. It entails giving employees constructive feedback and advice about aspects of their work and is usually provided by the immediate supervisor or manager. Many 'models' of coaching are available to managers; common to most of these models is the view that the effective coach involves the learner in the process of skill acquisition.

Coaching has become very popular among managers. It is considered to be an instrument that supports managers in times of organizational changes. Today, managers have to be effective, flexible, and competent in social skills. A fast growing branch of coaching has been executive coaching in organizations. However, despite its growing popularity, little empirical research has examined the effectiveness of this development tool (Kampa-Kokesch and Anderson 2001). Researchers have concentrated on surveying the types of development practices that are adopted, the outcomes of coaching, and have focused on the self-reports of the coaching process. A number of questions regarding the effectiveness, viability, and sustainability of executive coaching for management development remain unanswered (Kampa-Kokesch and Anderson 2001).

Mentoring is often used interchangeably with the term 'coaching', but there are fundamental differences between the two. While coaching is associated with management and raising the level of performance, mentoring deals more with career or personal transitions (performance enhancement may result although it is not necessarily the primary objective) (Olivero et al. 1997). Mentoring also differs from coaching in that the relationship is not usually between the individual and his immediate supervisor/manager. An experienced colleague is linked with a manager who offers support and assistance during the development process. Mentoring is more about offering support on a broader, long-term, holistic level. Megginson (1988) argues that mentoring is concerned with helping the learner through life crises, for example career hiccups or into new stages of development. While coaching is centred on tasks, mentoring is much wider and can encompass many other facets of employees' work, careers, and even life-work balance.

According to Johnson (2007) some of the most common denominators to most mentoring definitions are:

- The mentor demonstrates greater achievement and experience in profession.
- Mentorships are enduring personal relationships; they are reciprocal and become increasingly mutual as the relationship unfolds.
- Mentors provide protégés with both direct career assistance and social and emotional support.
- Mentors serve as role models.
- Mentorships are both highly beneficial and all too infrequent from the perspective of trainees.

Coaching and mentoring are approaches that could be usefully implemented in management development.

KEY LEARNING POINT

- A range of approaches can be deployed in management training and development.

13.4.5 Learning for life

The emphasis of lifetime personal development is the focus of formal developments such as Continuous Professional Development (CDP), where organizations expect their members to fulfil minimum training every year to maintain membership. Similarly, government-backed initiatives such as Investors in People (IIP) and National Vocational Qualifications (NVQs) also encourage organizations to train and develop their staff to various set standards of performance or competence. Just as learning is essential for the growth of individuals it is equally important for organizations.

Parallel with encouraging and supporting lifelong learning is a learning organization. Argyris and Schon (1978) were two of the earlier researchers studying the **learning organization.** They defined it as 'the detection and correction of error' the idea has since been developed (Morgan 1986; Pedlar et al. 1991). Burgoyne (1999), one of the earlier publicists for the concept of the learning organization, notes 'the learning organization has not delivered its full potential or lived up to all our aspirations'. However, he believes that the concept should be integrated with knowledge management so that various forms of knowledge can be linked in order to add value to goods and services.

Chapter summary

- There are many different theories on learning and this chapter has covered the main ideas that have emerged throughout the last 100 years or so.
- The behaviourist school was very prominent at one time and gave us classical conditioning and operant conditioning.
- Social learning perspectives built on behaviourism and added modelling and imitation to their views.
- Cognitive approaches do not deny that simple conditioning can sometimes be an explanation but, especially in humans, stress the importance of cognition (thought), of feelings, of emotions, etc. in order to learn and to problem solve.

- Although people have a preferred learning style it helps to become an all-round learner and to utilize all styles in order to maximize the learning potential of any situation.

- The fast changing nature of work means a multi-skilled workforce is needed, hence education and training is necessary for all employees.

- Organizations realize the benefit of investing in training their staff, as training is now seen as an essential part of strategic human resource management and a way of remaining competitive.

- This chapter took a systems approach to training, also referred to as a training cycle because it continuously uses feedback to improve the instructional process.

- There are mainly four components of a training cycle, the first and most important is the training needs analysis, the design of the programme, delivering the training programme, and lastly evaluating the training and modifying it on the basis of the feedback.

- It is important to note that the main issues that influence the design of the training programme are the content, the method, and also the trainees, as all three interact.

- The chapter discussed the importance of the evaluation of training and addressed the topic of transfer of training and demonstrated how transfer of training can either be positive or negative.

- The chapter highlighted that lifelong learning is increasingly being encouraged by organizations, professional bodies, and the government.

- The concept of the learning organization has become increasingly popular. A number of organizations aim to create a climate of continuous learning and development. Despite the growth critics argue that the idea of a learning organization is highly unrealistic.

- A range of approaches that can be deployed for management training and development were discussed.

Assess your learning

Review questions

1 Can you explain classical conditioning and think of an example where you have seen it work in real life?

2 Can you explain operant conditioning and think of an example where you have seen it work in real life?

3 Can modelling through social learning be helpful in work situations? If you think it can, give examples. What are the benefits of organizations training their workforce?

4 What are the four components of a training cycle?

5 Why is it important to undertake a training needs analysis?

6 What are the three levels of analysis one should undertake?

7 What are the main influences when designing a training programme?

8 Name and explain the four main types of evaluation data?

Assignments

ASSIGNMENT 1: Interpreting learning theory

- Can all learning be easily interpreted either coming from classical conditioning, operant conditioning, social learning, or using a cognitive approach?

- Some researchers feel that there might be some overlap in learning theory explanations. Give some examples of how the same situation could be interpreted in different ways according to two of the above perspectives.

ASSIGNMENT 2: Training and development of the workforce

Training and development of employees is essential. The pace and speed at which change is occurring in the work environment today is much faster. Hence, in order for organizations to remain competitive they must ensure the training and development of their workforce.

- How does training the workforce ensure the organization remains competitive?
- How does training benefit the individual, the organization, and society as a whole?

A multi-skilled workforce ensures that the organization remains competitive on a global scale. Discuss.

ASSIGNMENT 3: Evaluation of training

Training evaluation has often been overlooked or not implemented to its full capacity. Discuss the value of training evaluation and how it can be carried out fully.

Further reading

Blanchard, N., and Thacker, J. (2006) *Effective Training: Systems, Strategies and Practice.* New York: Pearson.
This book, as well as generally being useful for an in-depth look at training also includes, in chapter 3, a good look at learning theories.

Buckley, R., and Caple, J. (2003) *The Theory and Practice of Training* (4th edn.). London: Kogan Page.
This is an excellent book which gives good coverage of the training process with very detailed examples of each stage in the training cycle.

Honey, P. (1995) *101 Ways to Develop Your People without Really Trying.* Maidenhead: McGraw-Hill.
This book seeks to look for development opportunities in the workplace that often go unnoticed.

Work psychology in practice
Crime Support volunteer training programme evaluation

Crime Support, a charity which supports victims of crime, designed a new training programme for its volunteers. The aim of the new programme was to represent a shift in training in light of new organizational structure and also to ensure it provided an opportunity for volunteers to qualify for the new national occupational standards for working with victims and to be accredited by an external body.

The new programme was based on an existing training programme which had a successful track record for training volunteers and also took into account current good practice in learning. It recognized the importance of areas such as the motivation to learn and experiential learning and catered for different learning styles. It also reflected the concept of lifelong learning, recognizing learning does not end with the end of the formal training programme. So the programme was designed to equip volunteers with tools to enable them to continue to learn through varied experience while working for the charity. The programme was designed to be flexible enough to allow managers and training officers to adapt it to meet the need of their area and volunteers. Its modular programme enabled local judgements to be made about when and in what order different aspects of the training should take place. The training programme was initially run as a formal pilot for three months on three sites in Oxford, Manchester, and Ipswich.

The purpose of the evaluation was, firstly, to assess knowledge and skills acquisition and retention, and, secondly, to identify the strengths and weaknesses of the training (quality) and identify key areas of change in relation to content, methods and approach.

The following evaluation methods were used **after** the training programme:

1 Post-training evaluation questionnaire 1, a self-completion questionnaire, was administered at the end of the training programme to collect data related to course delivery, learning objectives, usefulness and quality of training exercises, and methods. The questionnaire also evaluated 14 items of pre- and post-training theoretical knowledge about topics discussed in the training modules. A rating scale from 1 to 5 was used where 1 indicated low and 5 indicated high understanding of the knowledge. The final part of the questionnaire focused on aspects of training that were the most and least helpful, use of the e-learning website designed to support the training, and overall rating of training resources.

2 Group evaluation exercise. This exercise was completed by all the participants once they had completed the post-evaluation questionnaire 1 at the end of the training programme. Participants were divided into groups and each group was asked to identify aspects of the training programme which were good and should not be changed, aspects that should be changed and improved, and any other comments related to the training programme. The key themes from the group discussions were recorded and all participants were then asked to agree or disagree with the recorded aspects related to the training programme.

3 Post-training evaluation questionnaire 2. This self-completion follow-up questionnaire was posted out to volunteers five months after the training programme. The questionnaire was designed to evaluate twelve items of pre- and post-training assessment of skills acquisition and retention covered in the training modules. Participants were asked to rate knowledge and/skills that they thought they had acquired before and after attending the training programme. A rating scale from 1 to 5 was used where 1 indicated low and 5 indicated high skill acquisition and retention. If participants had not acquired the skills/knowledge they were asked to tick the 'does not apply' box. Additional questions related to how the training programme reflected the job and how participants rated their skill and knowledge gained had equipped them for the job, were also asked.

Telephone interviews were carried out three months after the training programme with a sample of volunteers and managers.

The volunteer interviews addressed the following areas:

- The success of the training programme in preparing them for work.
- The extent to which they had been able to apply the skills, knowledge, and techniques learnt on the training programme.
- Any parts of the training that were not relevant to the work done or needed more attention.
- Problems or obstacles faced with applying skills and knowledge.

Since working, whether they had discovered any other training that needed to be included in the training programme.

The manager interviews addressed the following areas:

- The effectiveness of the training programme in terms of providing volunteers with the skills, knowledge, and awareness needed.
- The effectiveness of the training programme in terms of the development of specific competencies.
- Areas which volunteers found difficult and had needed further help with.
- Recommendations to the training programme which would make the volunteers better prepared for work.

Questions

- Discuss the strengths of the evaluation process used?
- What are the problems with the evaluation process used?
- What recommendations would you make to the training and development department about improving the evaluation process after what you have learnt from its pilot evaluation?

Online Resource Centre

Visit the supporting online resource centre for additional material which will help you with your research, essays, and assignments, or you may find these additional resources helpful when revising for exams.
http://www.oxfordtextbooks.co.uk/orc/matthewman/

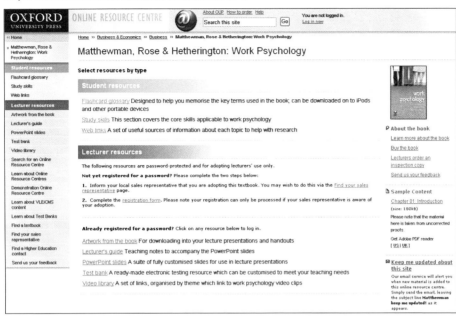

References

Anderson, J. R. (1983) *The Architecture of Cognition*. Cambridge, MA: Harvard University Press.

Anderson, J. R. (1987) Skill acquisition: compilation of weak method problem solutions. *Psychological Review*, 94: 192–210.

Annett, J. (1979) Memory for skill. In M. M. Gruneberg and P. E. Morris (eds.), *Applied Problems in Memory*. London: Academic Press.

Annett, J., and Duncan, K. D. (1967) Task analysis and training design. *Occupational Psychology*, 41: 211–21.

Argyris, C., and Schon, D. (1978) *Organizational Learning: A Theory in Action Perspective*. New York: Addison-Wesley.

Arnold, J. (2005) *Work Psychology: Understanding Human Behaviour in the Workplace* (4th edn.). Englewood Cliffs, NJ: Prentice Hall.

Baldwin, A. L., and Baldwin, C. P. (1973) Study of mother–child interaction. *American Scientist*, 61: 714–21.

Baldwin, T. T., and Ford, J. K. (1988) Transfer of training: a review and directions for future research. *Personnel Psychology*, 41: 63–105.

Bandura, A. (1977) *Social Learning Theory*. Englewood Cliffs, NJ: Prentice-Hall.

Bandura, A., and Huston, A. C. (1961) Identification as a process of incident learning. *Journal of Abnormal and Social Psychology*, 63: 311–18.

Bhatt, G. D. (2001) Knowledge management in organisations: examining the interaction between technologies, techniques and people. *Journal of Knowledge Management*, 5/1: 68–75.

Boyatzis, R. (1982) *The Competent Manager: A Model for Effective Performance*. New York: Wiley.

Buckley, R., and Caple, J. (2003) *The Theory and Practice of Training* (4th edn.). London: Kogan Page.

Burgoyne, J. (1999) Design of the times. *People Management*, 3 June: 39–44.

Canning, R. (1990) The quest for competence. *Industrial and Commercial Training*, 22/5: 12–16.

Capaldi, E., Birmingham, K. M., and Alptekin, S. (1995) Memories of reward events and expectancies of reward events may work in tandem. *Animal Learning and Behavior*, 23: 40–8.

Caple, J., and Martin, P. (1994) Reflections of two pragmatists: a critique of Honey and Mumford's learning styles. *Industrial and Commercial Training*, 26/1: 16–20.

Cheng, E. W. L., and Ho, D. C. K. (2001) A review of transfer of training studies in the past decade. *Personal Review*, 30/1–2: 102–18.

Cook, T. D., Campbell, D. T., and Peracchio, L. (1990) Quasi experimentation. In M. D. Dunnette and L. M. Hough (eds.), *Handbook of Industrial and Organizational Psychology*. Palo Alto, CA: Consulting Psychologists Press.

Currie, G., and Darby, R. (1995) Competence-based management development: rhetoric and reality. *Journal of European Industrial Training*, 19/5: 11–18.

Day, E. A., Arthur, W., Jr., and Gettman, D. (2001) Knowledge structures and the acquisition of a complex skill. *Journal of Applied Psychology*, 86: 1022–33.

Desimone, R. L., Werner, J. M., and Harris, D. M. (2002) *Human Resource Development*. Cincinnati, OH: South-Western.

Dipboye, R. L. (1997) Organizational barriers to implementing a rational model of training. In M. A. Quinones and A. Ehrenstein (eds.), *Training for a Rapidly Changing Workplace: Applications of Psychological Research*. Washington, DC: American Psychological Association.

Donnelly, E. (1991) Management charter initiative: a critique. *Training and Development*, 9/4: 43–5.

Doyle, C. E. (2003) *Work and Organisational Psychology: An Introduction with Attitude*. Hove: Psychology Press.

Draganidis, F., and Mentzas, G. (2006) Competency based management: a review of systems and approaches. *Information Management and Computer Security*, 14/1.

Fitts, P. M. (1962) Factors in complex skills training. In R. Glaser (ed.), *Training, Research and Education*. New York: J. Wiley.

Furnham, A. (2001) *The Psychology of Behaviour at Work: The Individual in the Organisation*. Hove: Psychology Press.

Gagné, R. M. (1985) *The Condition of Learning and Theory of Instruction*. New York: CBS College Publishing

Goldstein, I. L. (1993) *Training in Organisations: Needs Assessment, Development and Evaluation* (3rd edn.). Belmont, CA: Wadsworth.

Goldstein, I. L., and Ford, J. K. (2002) *Training in Organisations: Needs Assessment, Development and Evaluation* (4th edn.). Belmont, CA: Wadsworth.

Griffiths, P., and Bell, E. (1985) Using assessment centres. *Training Officer*, Oct.: 300–2.

Gumuseli, A. I., and Ergin, B. (2002) The manager's role in enhancing the transfer of training: a Turkish case study. *International Journal of Training and Development*, 6: 80–97.

Hagman, J. D., and Rose, A. M. (1983) Retention of military tasks: a review. *Human Factors*, 25: 199–213.

Hardingham, A. (2000) *Training Essentials: Psychology for Trainers*. London: CIPD.

Harlow, H. F. (1949) Formation of learning sets. *Psychological Review*, 56: 51–65.

Hatchuel, A., Le Masson, P., and Weil, B. (2002) From knowledge management to design-oriented organisations. *International Social Science Journal*, 54/171: 25–37.

Hogarth, T., and Wilson, R. (2003) *Skills Shortages, Vacancies and Local Unemployment*. Nottingham: Department for Education and Skills. Available as a pdf file from http://www2.warwick.ac.uk.www.dfes.gov.uk

Honey, P., and Mumford, A. (1982) *The Manual of Learning Styles*. Maidenhead: Honey.

Honey, P., and Mumford, A. (2006) *The Learning Styles Questionnaire 80-item*. Maidenhead: Honey.

Johnson, W. B. (2007) Transformational supervision: when supervisors mentor. *Professional Psychology: Research and Practice*, 38/3: 259–67.

Kampa-Kokesch, S., and Anderson, M. Z. (2001) Executive coaching: a comprehensive review of the literature. *Consulting Psychology Journal: Practice and Research*, 53: 205–28.

Kirkpatrick, D. L. (1959) Techniques for evaluating training programs. *Journal of the American Society of Training and Development*, 13: 3–9.

Kirkpatrick, D. L. (1967) Evaluation of training. In R. L. Craig and L. R. Bittel (eds.), *Training and Development Handbook*. New York: McGraw-Hill.

Kirkpatrick, D. L. (1976) Evaluation of training. In R. L. Craig (ed.), *Training and Development Handbook: A Guide to Human Resource Development* (2nd edn.). New York: McGraw-Hill, 301–19.

Kirkpatrick, D. L. (1996) Invited reaction: reaction to Holton article. *Human Resource Development Quarterly*, 7: 23–5.

Kodz, J., Harper, H., and Dench, D. (2002) Work-life balance: beyond the rhetoric. Brighton: Institute for Employment Studies.

Köhler, W. (1925) *The Mentality of Apes*. New York: Harcourt Brace Jovanovich.

Kolb, D. A. (1976) Management and the learning process. *California Management Review*, 18/Spring: 21–31.

Kolb, D. A. (1985) *Learning Style Inventory*. Boston: McBer and Company.

Kraiger, K., Ford, J. K., and Salas, E. (1993) Application of cognitive, skill-based, and affective theories of learning outcomes to new methods of training evaluation. *Journal of Applied Psychology*, 78: 311–28.

Lawler, E. E. (1994) From job-based to competency-based organizations. *Journal of Organization Behaviour*, 15: 3–15.

Lee, G., and Beard, D. (1994) *Development Centres*. London: McGraw-Hill.

McGhee, W., and Thayer, P. W. (1961) *Training in Business and Industry*. New York: Wiley.

McKenna, E. (2006) *Business Psychology and Organisational Behaviour: A Student's Handbook* (4th edn.). Hove: Psychology Press.

Mangham, I. (1990) Managing as a performing art. *British Journal of Management*, 1: 105–15.

Marchington, M., and Wilkinson, A. (2006) *Human Resource Management at Work: People Management and Development*. (3rd edn.). London: CIPD.

Marquand, M., and Reynolds, A. (1994) *The Global Learning Organisation*. London: Irwin.

Megginson. D. (1988) Instructor, coach, mentor: three ways of helping for managers. *Management Education and Development*, 19: 33–46.

Menzel, E. M. (1978) Cognitive mapping in chimpanzees. In S. H. Hulse, H. Fowler, and W. K. Honzig (eds.), *Cognitive Processes in Animal Behaviour*. Hillsdale, NJ: Erlbaum, 375–422.

Millward, L. (2005) *Understanding Occupational and Organisational Psychology*. Beverly Hills, CA: Sage Publications.

Moar, I. (1980) The nature and acquisition of cognitive maps. In D. Cantor and T. Lee (eds.), *Proceedings of the International Conference on Environmental Psychology*. London: Architectural Press.

Moller, L., Benscoter, B., and Rohrer-Murphy, L. (2000) Utilizing performance technology and organisational performance results. *Advances in Developing Human Resources*, 7/1: 102–20.

Morgan, G. (1986) *Images of Organization*. London: Sage.

Moynahan, E. O. (1973) The development of knowledge concerning the effects of categorisation upon free recall. *Child Development*, 44: 238–45.

Nordhaug, O., and Gronhaug, K. (1994) Competences as resources in firms. *International Journal of Human Resources*, 5/1: 89–103.

Offermann, L. R., and Phan, L. U. (2002) Culturally intelligent leadership for a diverse world. In E. J. Pirozzolo, *Multiple Intelligences and Leadership*. Hillsdale, NJ: Lawrence Erlbaum Associates, 187–214.

Olivero, G., Denise Bane, K., and Kopelma, R. (1997) Executive coaching as a transfer of training tool: effects on productivity in a public agency. *Public Personnel Management*, 26: 461–9.

Olton, D. S. (1979) Mazes, mazes, and memory. *American Psychologist*, 34: 583–96.

Patrick, J. (2000) Training. In N. Chmiel (ed.), *Work and Organisational Psychology: A European Perspective*. Oxford: Blackwell, 100–24.

Pavlov, I. P. (1927) *Conditioned Reflexes*. London: Oxford University Press.

Pedlar, M., Boydell, T., and Burgoyne, J. (1988) *Learning Company Project*. London: Manpower Services Commission.

Pedlar, M., Burgoyne, J., and Boydell, T. (1991) *The Learning Company: A Strategy for Sustained Development*. London: McGraw Hill.

Pearn, M., Roderick, C., and Mulrooney, C. (1995) *Learning Organizations in Practice*. Maidenhead: McGraw-Hill.

Revans, R. W. (1971) *Developing Effective Managers*. London: Praeger.

Rouiller, J. Z., and Goldstein, I. L. (1993) The relationship between organisational transfer climate and positive transfer of training. *Human Resource Development Quarterly*, 4: 377–90.

Rowley, J. (2002) From learning organisations to knowledge entrepreneur. *Journal of Knowledge Management*, 4/1: 7–15.

Salas, E., and Cannon-Bowers, J. A. (2001) The science of training: a decade of progress. *Annual Review of Psychology*, 52: 471–99.

Skinner, B. F. (1938) *Science and Behaviour*. New York: Macmillan.

Skinner, B. F. (1987) Whatever happened to psychology as the science of behaviour? *American Psychologist*, 4/8: 780–6.

Skinner, B. F. (1990) Can psychology be a science of mind? *American Psychologist*, 45/11: 1206–10.

Sloman, M. (1994) Coming in from the cold: a new role for trainers. *Personnel Management*, 26/1: 24–7.

Spitzer, D. R. (1999) Embracing evaluation. *Training*, 36/6: 42–7.

Swanson, R. A. (2005) Evaluation, a state of mind. *Advances in Developing Human Resources*, 7/1: 16–21.

Sweller, J. (1988) Cognitive load during problem solving: effects on learning. *Cognitive Science*, 12: 257–85.

Thorndike, E. L. (1913) *Educated Psychology: The Psychology of Learning*, vol. ii. New York: Teachers College Press.

Thorndike, E. I. (1989) Animal intelligence: an experiential study of the associative processes in animals. *Psychological Review*, monograph, *Supplement, 2* (4, Whole No. 8).

Tolman, E. C. (1948) Cognitive maps in rats and men. *Psychological Review*, 55: 189–208.

Tolman, E. C., and Honzik, C. H. (1930) 'Insight' in rats. *University of California Publications in Psychology*, 4: 215–32.

Tracey, J. S., Tannenbaum, S. I., and Kavanagh, M. J. (1995) Applying trained skills on the job: the importance of the work environment. *Journal of Applied Psychology*, 80: 239–52.

Truelove, S. (1995) *The Handbook of Training and Development* (2nd edn.). Oxford: Blackwell Business.

Van Buren, M. E., and Erskine, W. (2002) *The 2002 ASTD State of the Industry Report*. Alexandria, VA: American Society of Training and Development.

Warr, P. (2002) *Psychology at Work* (5th edn.). London: Penguin Books.

Watson, J. B. (1913) Psychology as the behaviourists view it. *Psychological Review*, 20: 158–7.

Wehner, R., and Menzel, R. (1990) Do insects have cognitive maps. *Animal Review of Neuroscience*, 13: 403–14.

Wexley, K. N., and Latham, G. P. (2002) *Developing and Training Human Resources in Organisations* (3rd edn.). Englewood Cliffs, NJ: Prentice Hall.

Yamnill, S., and McLean, G. N. (2001) Theories supporting transfer of training. *Human Resource Development Quarterly*, 12/2: 195–208.

Chapter 14

Psychological health in the workplace

Angela Hetherington

Chapter objectives

As a result of reading this chapter and using the additional web-based material you should be able to:

- Understand the nature of occupational stress.
- Identify individual, group, and organizational symptoms of stress.
- Analyse the sources of occupational stress within an organization.
- Distinguish between occupational stress and occupational traumatic stress.
- Evaluate individual, group, and organizational interventions.
- Assess organizational policies for the management of work-related stress.
- Discuss national initiatives in the management of work-related stress.

Work psychology in practice
Ambitions exceeding skills

A small-sized private-sector healthcare company had experienced a prolonged period of high turnover in the senior management team. A new Managing Director (MD) had recently been appointed to the organization to manage the organization through a phase of expansion. At the same time, Gail, an account manager, who had been with the company for ten years, had been promoted to a directorate **role**, to which she had long aspired. The role required her to manage a team of thirty-five employees. The decision to agree her promotion was based on Gail's knowledge of the product, the organization, the staff, and her personal **resilience**, as measured by her period with the company.

Gail's appointment was well received by the staff whom she would manage. She had not previously had responsibility for the management of others, but had worked alongside the staff. On her first day they presented her with a bouquet of flowers. She moved to an office close to the staff and maintained an open door policy. She worked hard and long hours, enjoying her position and good relations with the staff.

At Board meetings, where the performance targets of the company were discussed, Gail defended her department's failure to achieve their productivity targets. She reported increasing stress and low morale amongst her staff and questioned the feasibility of the performance targets at all. She presented a case for better facilities, reduced workloads, and more administrative support for staff.

Gail, always a passionate and determined employee, was often emotional in Board meetings and appeared increasingly to be party to senior management conflicts. She explained her distress, often in reaction to opposing views, as a normal part of her behaviour. Gail's disturbed feelings following Board meetings were evident to her staff, who increasingly became a major source of support to her.

While the performance of the department continued to deteriorate, her staff became hostile and resistant to senior management, whom they perceived as failing to understand the substance of the job, while implementing increasingly stringent performance targets. They also recognized that Gail as their manager was failing to cope, which they also saw as further evidence that the Senior Management Team (SMT) and their targets were not achievable.

Gail increased her hours at work and dependency on her staff for support. She intermittently broke down in tears and telephoned others for affirmation of her views on the failure of the company and the company's lack of understanding of her position. At the same time, through the company, Gail was provided with a mentor, support by HR, support from the MD, and offered time off work. Finally, following a Board meeting in which the company's quarterly performance figures were reviewed, Gail failed to arrive for work. She declined all further contact with the SMT and was signed off work for occupational stress for a period of twelve months, during which time she initiated legal action culminating in an out-of-court settlement.

Questions

- What were the symptoms of stress exhibited by Gail?
- What was the impact of Gail's stress on the organization in respect of organizational performance and productivity?
- What were the HR considerations which may have constrained the organization's interventions once the problem was evident?
- How might the organization have protected itself from potential litigation?

14.1 Introduction

The Health and Safety Executive (HSE) report that occupational ill-health in the UK costs in excess of £3.7 billion annually and results in approximately 30 million working days lost per year (HSE 2007). Data from Labour Market Trends reports that employees reporting **occupational stress** are more likely to be absent from work (Barnham and Begum 2005). CIPD research (2006b) suggests that stress is likely to become the most dangerous risk to business in the twenty-first century. Given the potential impact of stress on the bottom line, it is not surprising that stress management has become a major priority for Human Resource Management.

Table 14.1. The cost of stress

In *Australia*, the Federal Assistant Minister for Industrial Relations estimated the cost of occupational stress to be around A$30 million

....

In the *United States*, over half of the 550 million working days lost each year due to absenteeism are stress-related.

....

The *European Union* estimates that work-related stress affects at least 40 million workers in its 15 Member States and that it costs the European Union at least 20 billion Euro annually.

....

Sources: European Agency for Safety and Health at Work; International Labour Organization, 2002.

In the European Union, 'a conservative estimate of the fiscal costs caused by work-related stress indicates that they amount to some EUR 20 billion annually' (European Commission 2002: 3). Similarly, Jordan et al. (2003: 1) emphasize that 'the prevention and management of workplace stress is vital in maintaining employee well being and performance, and improving organizational efficiency and success', all of which impact on the organization's profitability. Refer to Table 14.1 for further data on the cost of stress internationally.

The cost of occupational stress to business is accrued from reduced staff retention, increased recruitment, selection, induction and training costs, reduced productivity and performance, increased sickness and absence, decreased motivation and morale, all of which are the responsibility of management and, in particular, Human Resource Management. In addition, given that organizations have a statutory responsibility for their employees' psychological well-being (HSE 1995), occupational stress is becoming an increasingly litigious field with the potential to incur further significant costs on the organization in legal fees, and compensation claims.

The opening case study demonstrates the number of factors which may be involved in any incidence of psychological ill-health. Selection and recruitment are crucial to person-job fit. Training is fundamental to **job satisfaction** and commitment. Transparency and openness in communications can prevent dysfunctional interpersonal dynamics. Performance management and Employee Assistance Programmes can assist in early detection of problems. Most importantly, stringent **Occupational Health** strategies, demonstrated through effective organizational intervention strategies, will serve to protect the organization against the increasing risk of litigation due to psychological ill-health at work.

This chapter acknowledges that work can be good for your health, but that it can also make you ill. It examines the nature, sources, and symptoms of stress which can ultimately serve to interfere with an individual's normal workplace functioning. Most importantly it evaluates how the individual and the organization can act to reduce the debilitating effects of occupational stress through effective organizational interventions. The chapter also reviews the government's role and responsibilities in reducing the cost to the nation of stress at work.

14.2 Organizational responsibility for psychological health

In the UK, the Health and Safety at Work Act (1995) requires that employers must ensure as 'far as is reasonably practicable' the health, safety, and welfare at work of their employees. This duty applies to both the physical and psychological well-being of employees.

As stress is defined as a disability under the Disability Discrimination Act 1995, employers are required to make reasonable adjustments to an individual's workload to reduce or eliminate known or foreseeable stressors. This becomes paramount, following an employee's sickness or absence due to occupational stress, where a 'return to work' assessment would normally identify and agree appropriate adjustments to work responsibilities.

Organizational interventions to reduce stress at work, such as post-trauma debriefing, peer support, employee counselling, mentoring, and **coaching** clearly demonstrate the organization's 'duty of care' and as such, can afford the organization protection in the event of litigation.

KEY LEARNING POINTS

- The Health and Safety at Work Act (1995) requires that employers must assure the health, safety, and welfare at work of their employees.
- Employers are expected to make reasonable adjustments to an individual's workload to reduce or eliminate known or foreseeable stressors.
- Organizational interventions to reduce stress at work can serve to demonstrate the organization's 'duty of care', and afford protection against litigation.

14.2.1 The nature of occupational stress

Many jobs can be considered stressful, yet that does not necessarily mean that they will impact on an individual's psychological well-being. Police officers, firefighters, disaster workers, medical, ambulance and voluntary emergency personnel all contend with considerable stress as a result of the nature of their jobs, yet they do not necessarily fall ill. The demanding, challenging, fast-paced nature of the work can in fact be attractive features of the job to certain personality dispositions (Hetherington 2001). Research has shown that the people who are attracted to a career with inherent powerful stressors have very different personalities to the average person (Mitchell and Bray 1990). Such individuals tend to have high levels of commitment, challenge, and control and are more resilient to stress. **Personal resilience** to stress can be further enhanced by appropriate intervention strategies which proactively protect the employees from the potentially deleterious effects of their work.

Definition of stress

Stress is a natural phenomenon in an individual's daily life. In the workplace, it can serve to enhance an individual's motivation, performance, satisfaction, and personal achievements. Although the negative effects of stress gain much publicity, it is generally accepted that 'we all experience pressure on a daily basis, and need it to motivate us and enable us to perform at our best' (ISMA 2005).

The concept of stress has evolved over time. The term 'stress' originated from the Latin *stringere*, 'to draw tight', and was first used to imply hardship, adversity, or affliction, and later to denote the physical concept of forces exerted on an object. Stress is generally considered to be any pressure which exceeds the individual's capacity to maintain physiological, psychological, and/or emotional stability (Furnham 2005).

Occupational stress can be described as: 'the adverse reaction people have to excessive pressure or other types of demands on them' (HSE 2005: 1). Similarly, it can be defined as 'the result of a conflict between the role and needs of an individual employee and the demands of the workplace' (UK National Work Stress Network 2006). Similarly, Palmer et al. (2003a: 2) suggest that: 'stress occurs when the perceived pressure exceeds your perceived ability to cope.' This definition takes into account a number of variables which are discussed in the next section.

Understanding stress

Stress was originally viewed as an independent variable—a stressful event—that happens to an individual, such that situations alone could incur stress (Furnham 2005: 356). For example, working in a customer facing industry was inherently stressful. This theory, however, does not account for personal or environmental variables in the experience of stress (Refer to Chapter 2 for further information on variables).

Table 14.2. The three phases of the general adaptation syndrome

1. Fight, flight, or freezing.
Fight is characterized by increased adrenaline, raised blood pressure, raised heartbeat, higher blood sugar level, higher muscle tone, and increased breathing rate. The body is thus prepared for more powerful, explosive activity.

Freezing can be an effective response to stress when characterized by the same heightened physiological state. It can allow the individual to appraise the presenting situation and to respond more appropriately to the threat.

Freezing can also be associated with a weakened state and an inability to act or respond in defence. One explanation is that in certain circumstances, fight and flight can result in death, injury, or loss of territory. In some animals, freezing can reduce conspicuousness and increase the chance of survival.
....

2. Maintenance.
If the source of stress continues, the body habituates to it. This is characterized by sustained activity in the hypothalamus and adrenal cortex. These serve to maintain a state of responsive inertness, where the body is geared to act but is acclimatized to the presence of the stressor and refrains from acting. This can result in reduced effectiveness of the immune system and increased susceptibility to physical ailments, dissociation, and depersonalization.
....

3. Breakdown.
Physiologically, the individual is primed to remove itself from the source of stress. Where this is not feasible, and the second stage of sustained arousal has been maintained for a prolonged period, the body enters a third stage. The adrenal cortex and medulla cease to act, which might result in serious illness or in some cases, sudden death.

An understanding of stress is founded on the work of Selye (1946) who examined the response of the body to demands put upon it. Selye developed the **General Adaptation Syndrome** (GAS) theory which identified three generic stages (Alarm Reaction; Resistance; Collapse), illustrated by:

1 Fight, flight, and freeze: an alarm response, where initial reduced resistance is followed by raised defense mechanisms.

2 Maintenance: a state of resistance, where the individual adapts to the stressful event and achieves a physiologically stable state.

3 Breakdown: the final stage of exhaustion, when adaptive reactions to the stressor fail and the individual cannot sustain effective defensive mechanisms.

Table 14.2 gives a full description of the phases of the General Adaptation Syndrome. The GAS theory was non-specific, such that the individual's response to stress followed a universal pattern, whatever the internal or external source of stress. The GAS theory considered stress to be an attempt to maintain the body's '**homeostasis**'—a 'steady state despite external changes' (Selye 1974: 148). However, the simple stimulus-response model based on the belief that responses are 'non-specific' does not take account of the source and extent of the stressor and personal factors. While Selye's theory serves to highlight important aspects of the stress process, more recent empirical data demonstrates that individual responses to stress differ according to the stressor and varying environmental and personal factors (Cox et al. 2000).

Stressors

Early research into stress recognized that specific life events could have a stressful and at times devastating effect on the individual's ability to cope or recover from the events. Holmes and Rahe (1967) formulated a table of life events, 'The Life Events Scale', which measured the impact of events on the individual's psychological well-being. It rated each possible life event and provided a cumulative score for the individual. The more unexpected the stressful event or stressor, such as accident, bereavement, and divorce, the greater the stress incurred.

The frequency of adverse life events over a sustained period is also considered to affect the individual's recovery and ability to cope. This is largely due to the fact that an individual requires a period of recovery following each major stressful event—both psychologically and physically. If a further stressful event occurs during the recovery period or if the individual has entered into denial or avoidance in response to the stressful event, then they are more likely to experience a cumulative or prolonged psychological reaction such as clinical depression or clinical anxiety.

Interactional models of stress

Later models of stress became more comprehensive, developing earlier conceptions of environmental stressors as the fundamental source of stress, to take into account psychological variables. The original stimulus models of stress developed into response-based theories, emphasizing the individual's contribution to their experience of stress.

The interactional model proposes that stress arises where appraisal of external stimuli, or stressors, results in the perception that the stressors may exceed the individual's capacities for coping in a situation where coping is perceived as important to the individual: 'A potential for stress exists when an environmental situation is perceived as presenting a demand which threatens to exceed the person's capabilities and resources for meeting it, under conditions where s/he expects a substantial differential in the rewards and costs for meeting the demand versus not meeting it' (McGrath 1976: 1352).

Lazarus (1976) proposed a model of stress which emphasized the interaction of the adaptive capacities of the mind and body with the stressor. He suggested that the individual's experience of stress was moderated by their perception of their ability to cope. Lazarus identified two levels of appraisal; primary appraisal focused on threat perception and secondary appraisal dealt with coping with and reducing threat (Furnham 2005).

Cox and Mackay (1979) combined Lazarus's theory of personal and psychological control over stress with Selye's theory of internal balance. They developed a theory which identified four dynamic aspects of the individual and the environment: the demands/constraints and supports of the environment, and the values/needs and coping resources of the individual. They suggested that the individual continually assesses the equilibrium of these factors; if they are unbalanced the individual experiences stress and tries to adjust the balance through coping mechanisms.

Occupational stress

Occupational stress can be described as: 'the adverse reaction people have to excessive pressure or other types of demands on them' (HSE 2005: 1). Similarly, it can be defined as 'the result of a conflict between the role and needs of an individual employee and the demands of the workplace' (Caplan 1983). This theory also requires consideration of the accuracy of the individual's perceptions of their performance and abilities with the reality of the job. Differences in objective and subjective perceptions and assessments of stress can contribute to psychological defences in managing stress, and serve to compound the experience and impact of stress on both the individual and their performance on the job.

The 'demand-control model' of stress also takes into consideration other individual factors in the moderation of stressors. In particular, it highlights the individual's need for a level of control over their work, suggesting that excessive psychological demands on an individual combined with a lack of decision latitude in their role will lead to high-strain jobs, increasing the risk of stress-related illness (Karasek and Theorell 1990). The contribution of individual factors such as the individual's need for control is discussed further in the section 14.3.2.

A further theory is that of effort and reward (Siegrist 1996), where a high degree of effort and commitment is rewarded by an appropriate level of reward, such as monetary gain, self-esteem, recognition, or social control. The efforts of the individual may be extrinsic, which relates to the individual's efforts to cope with external demands, or intrinsic, which refers to the individual's drive to satisfy his personal motivations. This theory resonates with equity theory.

The social environment model of stress suggests that the organization's history, profitability, size, structure, workforce, and culture can incur stress. These may be manifest in workload, interpersonal conflict, competing internal demands, unclear roles, etc. The stressors are transformed in the individual to emotional, behavioural, and psychological symptoms of strain.

Case illustration
A multitude of stress factors

Melvyn had been promoted to the post of team manager in a call centre delivering legal and advisory services to businesses. He had been doing this kind of work all his life and found securing qualifications to demonstrate his competence frustrating. In his new role, the nature of the job changed considerably. Melvyn was dealing with a challenging environment, requiring informed decision making and people management. Melvyn found the nature, diversity, and frequency of the tasks overwhelming. Yet, the rewards of increased remuneration, status, and self-image were strong motivators to remain in post. He increasingly sought support from his team, mobilizing negative feelings towards the organization. In reviewing his poor performance, the organization found that Melvyn's qualifications from international institutions were e-based and unaccredited. Finally, unable to cope with the work, potential loss of status, and income level, Melvyn took sick leave for a period of twelve months before resigning.

This case highlights the interdependent factors which the individual, the organization, and the stressors contribute to the diagnosis of stress. Melvyn had performed well in previous positions. The limited demands of earlier jobs had also served to buffer his self-image and esteem. While a competent specialist, Melvyn had been promoted to a management position for which he had not received adequate training or experience. This in itself can contribute to failed expectations for both the employee and employer (Rees and Porter 2003). The organization had also contributed to the stress experienced by Melvyn in failing to confirm his qualifications and experience and to ensure that he was capable of the job. The organization's decisions at the point of both appointment and promotion had been made on subjective perceptions to Melvyn's suitability for the role. While the organization had failed to exercise a due 'Duty of Care' in the selection and training of Melvyn, Melvyn had accepted a job to which he was ill-suited, but which fulfilled other motivations and drives (Refer to Chapter 5 on motivation and Work Satisfaction).

However, this equation can be moderated by personal variables, such as social support, cognitive coping style, personality, and physical health (Furnham 2005).

KEY LEARNING POINTS

- Stress is generally considered to be any pressure which exceeds the individual's capacity to function normally.
- The General Adaptation Syndrome (Selye) explains the physiological response of the body to stress in three stages; alarm, resistance, and collapse.
- Current theories of stress take into account individual and environmental factors in the individual's perception and experience of stress.
- Occupational stress refers to the conflict between the role and needs of an individual employee and the demands of the workplace.

14.2.2 Symptoms of stress

Stress at work is displayed in employee behaviours such as tardiness, lowered self-esteem, decreased motivation, increased emotional response, reduced interaction with peers and job dissatisfaction. In the workforce at large, stress may be evidenced in reduced productivity, low staff morale, increased sickness and absence rates, and greater staff turnover.

In the individual, stress is experienced through a range of physiological, psychological, and emotional reactions (see Table 14.3). While combinations of these symptoms may also be indicative of other illnesses or distinct personality types, they are commonly associated with stress-related illness. A key factor in distinguishing symptoms of stress is identifying any changes in the patterns of the individual's normal behaviour.

The body's physiological response to stress is demonstrated in a natural 'fight or flight' response, where the high adrenalin, heightened arousal of the body can stimulate both the

Table 14.3. Symptoms of stress

> **Behavioural:**
> Drug abuse, excessive smoking or drinking, change in activity level, withdrawal, suspiciousness, change in interpersonal behaviour, increased concern over environment, excessive humour, inappropriate behaviour.
>
> ....
>
> **Physical:**
> Tremors of lips and fingers, nausea, upset stomach, excess sweating, feeling cold, rapid heartbeat, poor sleep, dry mouth, general fatigue, trembling.
>
> ....
>
> **Emotional:**
> Generalized anxiety, excessive fear, survivor guilt, depression, increased emotionality, feelings of futility, feeling isolated, feeling numb, unable to communicate, anger.
>
> ....
>
> **Cognitive:**
> Inability to concentrate, difficulty remembering, confusion, low attention capacity, calculation problems, intrusive thoughts, disturbing dreams.

individual's need and capacity for action. This primitive biological response serves as an effective self-defence measure increasing the individual's ability to survive the threat of physical attack and injury.

The primitive fight or flight response, in producing biochemical reactions, can lead to significant physiological reactions. In the main, the sources and the context of the stressors do not allow for a physical reaction. Aggression in the workplace is not feasible, even flight can lead to loss of image and self-esteem and compound the effects of the stressor. This renders the individual with the need to override their natural biological response, leaving them in a state of heightened cardiovascular, muscular, neurological, and cognitive arousal (Albrecht 1979). In the longer term, prolonged exposure to stress can leave the individual in a constant tense, anxious state (Earnshaw and Cooper 2001).

Stress might also enhance performance in occupations which require a heightened adrenalin reaction such as the media and performing arts. However, physiological reactions to stress may equally serve to immobilize the individual with fear, reducing their capacity to cope effectively with the situation by either running away or fighting. If the individual then experiences failure to cope with the stressor, the resulting physiological and psychological reactions to the stressful event can have a powerful effect on their ability to cope with repetitions of the event. The initial stressor has then potentially increased in potency by becoming a memory which in itself can trigger physiological reactions to the imagined event.

Experiencing stress

Knowledge that stress is imminent can incur a full range of physiological and psychological symptoms of stress in the individual which may not abate until the potential source of the stress has passed (Cooper et al. 2001). The threat need not be limited to real events. An individual's stressful reactions may be based on perceptions, imagined events, and other variables associated with a stressful event, as is illustrated in the case study below. Cognitive appraisal of a stressful event can play a significant part in the impact of stress on the individual, either in increasing or decreasing the effect. The individual's ability to manage and control their cognitive appraisals renders this a valuable area for stress management and is usually addressed through **Cognitive Behaviour Therapy** (CBT), which involves cognitive reappraisal of the stressor. That is reducing the negative thoughts associated with the stressor (see section 14.3.4).

14.2.3 Sources of stress

The nature and extent of occupational stressors will vary according to the job, the employee, and management. Common **sources of stress** include working hours, overwork, underwork, lack of appropriate competence, inadequate training, lack of employee involvement, role

Case illustration
Fight, flight, and panic

Pritty worked for a company providing outsourced HR services to organizations. She had been newly pro-moted from her role as general Account Manager to Business Development Manager for a sole, high-profile finance organization. After a short period in the new role, Pritty was displaying uncharacteristic behaviours of tardiness, irritability, stress, and anxiety.

Pritty had been due to give a presentation to the directorate of the finance organization when she left the building without warning. The next day she provided her employer with a sick note for one month's absence due to work-related stress.

Pritty had begun to experience panic at the frequent presentations she was required to deliver to the senior management team of the finance company. In addition, the anticipation of failure in the presentations had in itself became a trigger to stressful reactions outside of the presentations. Pritty's key coping behaviours included concealing her problems, avoidance, and flight.

Questions

- What part did Pritty's cognitive appraisal play in this event?
- Consider individual **coping strategies** which Pritty could have employed to manage the stress.
- Consider what Occupational Health and HR policies and practices might have made a difference in the outcome.

conflict, role ambiguity, responsibilities of the job, relationships, and **organizational culture** (Bradley 2007). Changes at work, such as technological and restructuring, can also incur high levels of stress amongst the workforce. Occupational stress can be categorized as:

- Factors intrinsic to the job
- Organizational role
- Interpersonal interactions
- Organizational climate
- Organizational change.

Other factors such as personality, gender, style of coping, motivations, and work-life factors will also have an impact on both the individual's experience of stressors, their vulnerability to them, and their recovery from them. These are discussed in the later section on personal variables.

Job design increasingly incoporates factors which are likely to reduce the sources of stress. These include conditions, such as open communications, employee participation in decision making, appropriate training, clear responsibilities, effective induction, and realistic work-loads (Clarke and Cooper 2004; Furnham 2005).

Factors intrinsic to the job

Factors intrinsic to the job, such as working conditions, shift work, working hours, workload, level of risk at work, and the introduction of new technology can all be significant stressors. Research repeatedly links working conditions to mental health (Arnold 2005). Excessive physi-cal and psychological effort in tight timelines, at unsociable hours in often depersonalizing working environments—call centres, assembly lines—can all incur clear symptoms of stress. For example, staff such as mortuary workers, dealing with obnoxious smells, close work under intense lighting, and often unsociable or long hours standing can contend with stressful work-ing conditions which may undermine their resilience to other stressors associated with the job.

Shift work is a common occupational stressor which affects the body's physiological state, mental efficiency and motivation on the job, sleeping patterns, and domestic life. Shifts, while inevitable in certain professions, such as medical, emergency, oil industries, and increasingly call centres are required to maintain service delivery, maximum use of resources, and to increase organizational performance and targets. Research has shown that night shifts can lead to greater exhaustion and depersonalization than day shifts (Demir et al. 2003), while other variables such as length of shift, whether rotational, and extraneous factors such as family circumstances can compound the stress further.

Working hours beyond forty hours per week are increasingly recognized to be unproductive. While links have been made to long hours and physical and psychological ill-health, the relationship may not be causal. Motivated individuals in highly competitive professions may be more vulnerable to health problems and to seek out long work hour cultures. Both over and under workloads can affect occupational health. Job underload can occur in jobs which are done by highly skilled and qualified individuals and which may require high-level decision making, but may in general involve routine boring work, such as in the military, navy, or RAF. Similarly, computer technology often demands high-level job specifications matched to complex tasks, but those tasks may be rarely employed and technicians may find themselves stressed by the boredom of routine non-activity (Chase and Karowski 2003).

The increase in technology, advanced computer packages, email communications, coupled with little internal training on information management, can also be significant sources of stress for employees. This can be compounded by differences in the training and experience of younger employees and senior managers in information technology and may question the nature of supervision (Chase and Karowski 2003).

14.2.4 Role ambiguity, role conflict, and role responsibility

Role refers to the expected patterns of behaviour associated with an employee's position in the structure of the organization. The formal organizational relationships and the associated authority of the role will be determined by the roles assumed by individual members. These will be dependent on situational factors (task, culture, structure) and personal factors (motivation, attitude, abilities, and personality). The various relationships held by the individual are referred to as a 'role set'. Role differentiation between individual staff members is particularly important to the effective functioning of groups, and can in its absence, be a major source of occupational stress.

Role ambiguity, **role conflict**, and role responsibilities are key aspects of an individual's role which, with lack of clarity, can raise individual and departmental stress levels and decrease the organizational performance and productivity. Role ambiguity arises when there is a lack of clarity about the nature, requirements, and goals of the job. These issues can arise from an unclear job description, a lack of agreement on role requirements between those in a supervisory role, changes in management, restructuring, and internal conflicts. Role ambiguity is also susceptible to individual interpretations or selective attention to aspects of the role by the different people who might fill it at any time.

Role conflict is normally the result of conflicting objectives or competing demands. This can arise from unclear or complex reporting structures, where there is more than one line manager or shared roles. It might also be created by the need to fulfil the expectations of different functions within the organization. Role conflict resulting from complex internal organizational structures can allow the employee to be selective in his/her choice of activities at the expense of the job and particular functions or line managers. This can serve to mask both the source and symptoms of the stress redirecting the stress onto others.

Stress is often related to levels of responsibility. This may take the form of responsibility for people or responsibility for activities, such as operations, facilities, or budgets. Responsibility for people is often reported to be the greater stressor. This may be due to material facts such as increased meetings, increased personal interactions, reduced control over deadlines and targets, and the less pleasant tasks associated with people management—disciplinary procedures and releasing staff. The relationship of role responsibility to stress may be compounded by intervening variables such as the longer working hours, more stringent deadlines and performance targets, associated with positions of increased responsibility.

Role responsibility and in particular the stress of managing people can be explained by the concept of the managerial escalator, where staff accomplished in specialist activities are promoted to people management roles for which they have limited experience and training (Rees and Porter 2003). The transition to a post in the same organization and often department, which entails a distinctly different job description, role expectations, and performance targets can take considerable time to adjust to psychologically.

14.2.5 Interpersonal interaction at work

Relationships at work can be a major source of support and buffer the impact of stressors; however, they can also be a significant source of stress. Interpersonal interaction at work is comprised of three categories of relationship: with the service user, with peers, and with management. Managing the manager can be an important factor in job satisfaction and stress avoidance.

Managers have a clearly defined role of achieving organizational objectives through others. The increased stress on management to manage others, meet deadlines, achieve productivity targets, and strategic goals will inevitably lead to increased pressure on employees. Increased pressure and stress on the workforce can lead to increased reports of perceived bullying (HSE 2006).

Recognizing personality differences amongst peers and using humour and other coping strategies to reframe interpersonal conflicts can be effective. Interpersonal interactions can be a medium for politics, sabotage, and destructive intentions. In general, negative forces are mediated by covert manipulations in individual staff member's perceptions of reality. These distortions of individual perceptions within a department can only be successful providing that individual members of the department do not share their perceptions. Cultivating an open environment, where negative drives are not fuelled and collaborative working towards shared goals is fostered will reduce the potential stress of interpersonal conflict.

Relationships with the service user can be a source of considerable stress at times when internal organizational resources and services are limited. If there is a conflict in the requirements of the organization and the requirements of the service user this can be compounded by an unhelpful customer service response (Jamieson 1999; Mullins 2006). For the organization to have transparent processes, explanatory documents, and complaints procedures which demonstrate a uniform service can be instrumental in managing the service user's expectations.

14.2.6 Organizational culture

The organizational culture is created by the values, attitudes, beliefs, and norms of behaviours of staff members. The organizational cultural norms of behaviour serve to influence and inform the behaviours of new staff members. Unless a staff member conforms to the cultural expectations, they may become isolated from the organization or department.

Organizational cultures can be effective in promoting good working practice and a strong work ethic, but they can also promote behaviours which are counter-productive to the achievement of organization goals. The organization's culture can also be symptomatic of organizational defences, where the workforce has lost sight of organizational tasks, is impervious to challenge and change and has become united in self-preservation against perceived internal stressors (refer to section 14.3.3).

Organizational change

Changes in company policy, reorganizations, mergers, acquisitions, and restructuring all incur additional stress. The process of organizational change may trigger underlying stresses of fear of redundancy, adjustments in role requirements, increased workloads, performance targets, tension of new relationships, loss of **social support** network, change in culture, management style, and the need to retrain. The inherent insecurity of change, if not managed, can lead to employee resistance which can sabotage the organization's capacity to function effectively.

Case illustration
Excel manufactures stress

'Excel' delivered a range of training programmes through a number of department heads, supported by administrative staff. The admin department was managed remotely by the office manager, who reported to the Head of Excel.

Parminder provided administrative support to Christian, the head of one department. Parminder became increasingly selective in the admin tasks she would perform, complaining to the office manager of the tasks she felt were outside her remit.

The indirect reporting structure provided Parminder with a remote line manager who was not in a position to realistically monitor the substance and extent of her work. It further served to undermine the head's role, increasing his workload and undermining his personal performance goals and the organization's strategic objectives.

The 'can't do' approach was infectious amongst the admin staff. This resulted in a decline in the standard of admin, the quality of course delivery, client satisfaction, and an increase in staff sickness, absence, morale, and turnover.

Activity Reporting structure

Discuss the potential implications of the complex reporting structure on internal staff dynamics, job satisfaction, service delivery, and occupational health.

What factors contributed to role ambiguity, role conflict, unclear role responsibility, and the culture and climate of the organization?

KEY LEARNING POINTS

- Stress can be exhibited in the individual through a range of physiological, psychological, and emotional symptoms.
- Common sources of stress include overload, role conflict, role ambiguity, responsibilities of the job, relationships, and organizational culture.

14.3 Moderating factors

14.3.1 Personality

It is the interaction of a person's individual perceptions, their performance and capabilities with the stresses of the job that can lead to stress symptoms in the individual (ISMA 2005). This is evidenced in jobs such as the emergency services which may be considered, by way of the nature of the work, to impose excessive demands on any individual. Yet, individuals who self-select into jobs in the emergency services are likely to have personal characteristics that enable them to cope with the demands of the job (see case illustration *The attraction to the job*, below).

Personality traits and attributes, such as neuroticism, behavioural types, optimism, fatalism, tolerance of ambiguity, levels of general anxiety, and different coping strategies can all contribute to stress. Personality differences will affect an individual's ability to assume problem-focused coping, to develop coping strategies, and to seek effective support. Neurotics tend to focus on negative aspects of work and may be more likely to experience stress and employ fewer coping strategies (Furnham 2005).

Table 14.4. Type A and B personality characteristics

Type A characteristics	Type B characteristics
Very competitive	Not competitive
Always rushed	Unrushed
Impatient	Patient
Fast, forceful talker	Slow, deliberate talker
High achieving, ambitious	Unambitious
Fast behaviour style	Slow behaviour style
Few interests outside work/home	Many personal interests

Type A individuals tend to be hostile, aggressive, competitive, and impatient; they are prone not only to stress but also to heart disease. **Type A personalities** are also more likely to overload themselves, undertaking a number of tasks at the same time, working at speed, being task focused and high achieving. These personality types are often found in senior management and can themselves be the source of stress to others, particularly **B type personalities**, who conversely prefer to work at a slower pace, are less ambitious and driven at work (Jamal and Baba 2003) (see Table 14.4).

Hardiness has been found to be a significant moderator of stress. Hardiness is an attitude, a disposition towards stressful life events, which increases the individual's personal resilience (Cooper et al. 2001). It is comprised of a constellation of three factors: a sense of commitment, challenge, and control (Kobasa 1979). These factors differ from personality traits in that, as attitudinal dispositions, they can be improved by training. Hardy individuals believe that, as a result of the jobs they do, they make a difference. Such individuals often self-select into challenging roles which require significant personal commitment, such as Fire and Rescue and Disaster Recovery Services (Hetherington 1993).

Locus of control has long been recognized as a key factor in buffering the impact of stressors. Locus of control refers to the extent to which the individual believes that he/she has control over life events or that they are extraneous to him/her. If an individual believes that they are subjected to stressful events over which they have no control, they are less likely to employ effective coping strategies in attempting to mitigate the effects of the stressors. Conversely, when an individual has an internal locus of control, they are more likely to actively attempt to reduce the stress. However, the control must relate directly to the specific stress; for example, having no control over a potential redundancy will be moderated if the individual believes that he has another job offer available to him (Spector 1998).

Control, as an effective moderator of stress is highlighted in the HSE's Stress Management Standards (2005). This model can offer practical ways for the organization to reduce stress through increasing the employee's perception of environmental/psychological control through job redesign, autonomous work groups, team building, surveys, and consultation groups (Furnham 2005).

Gender and power are key factors in the experience of stress. Many women have roles that are characterized by limited autonomy, low pay, inflexibility, low status, and lack of career development opportunities, coupled with domestic responsibilities which further restrict their ability to cope (Mauno et al. 2006) (see Table 14.5).

Pause for thought
Could gender and power factors limit management's success in maximizing the organization's performance and productivity?

14.3.2 Individual resilience

Exposure to sustained stress can contribute to reduced personal resilience, which may show itself differently according to the organization. In care-giving organizations such as healthcare, churches, social service agencies, or educational institutions, for example, this may be demonstrated in distortions of the care relationship. This may be displayed in staff as

Table 14.5. Factors contributing to increased stress in female employees

---

Domestic responsibilities

Lower levels of control in their jobs, since majority of women tend to occupy less senior jobs than men;

The higher proportion of women who work in *precarious* forms of employment;

The proliferation of women in high-stress occupations, such as nursing, teaching, and work with visual display units (VDUs)

The prejudice and discrimination against women who are in more senior positions as a result of corporate policy and from peer pressure

---

'burnout' or emotional detachment, or inappropriate closeness, in an effort to fulfil personal needs (Kahn 2005). Resilient individuals would more readily be able to tolerate the stress, retaining an appropriate openness and detachment from their 'clients', while seeking support from their peers.

Resilience can be defined as: 'the capacity to rebound from adversity more strengthened and resourceful. It is an active process of endurance, self-righting and growth in response to crisis and challenge' (Walsh 1998). This may be facilitated by a capacity to act resourcefully, drawing on effective support strategies such as peer support or cognitive reframing.

Individuals higher in personal resilience often have personalities or personal experience which enable them to act differently in stressful situations. They have been found to be higher in hardiness, self-esteem, sense of competence, optimism, and are more likely to be A type personalities. They are also more likely to be successful in high-stress occupations, such as the emergency services, where the nature of the job requires frequent exposure to traumatic, often life-threatening situations (Hetherington 2001).

The following case illustration refers to research of the UK police, fire, and accident and emergency personnel, identifying the factors which contribute to the personal resilience of individuals who choose to work with highly stressful life events.

Case illustration
The attraction to the job

Adrenalin's flowing, tension's high, everyone's geared up ready to fly into action to manage the emergency situation. It's everything we've been trained for, the whole team. At times like this no-one remembers the failed rescues, no one thinks of the aftermath, the personal price, only the chance of doing it well. (Road traffic patrol officer)

The Emergency Services is a challenging and potentially highly rewarding vocation. Yet by the nature of the job it is one of the most stressful occupations. Police officers, fire fighters, disaster workers, medical, ambulance and voluntary emergency personnel all contend with considerable stress as a result of their responsibility for the life and safety of others.

People who are attracted to a career with inherent powerful stressors have very different personalities to the average person who holds a far less risky or demanding job. Emergency professionals tend to be high in 'hardiness'—a sense of commitment, challenge and control—and are more resilient to stress. An individual's hardiness can be enhanced by appropriate training (Hetherington 2001).

Activity Stress control

Consider your own person-job fit. List those occupations which attract you. Is there a similarity between the roles? What factors determined which occupation you pursued? Could you change jobs to reduce the stress or to improve your job satisfaction?

14.3.3 Organizational resilience

Families are the primary organization which the individual experiences. The family constitutes a set of relationships which creates a system that is resilient to external stressors (Kahn 2005). The family can create adaptational processes which identifies it as a functional and operational unit. It is potentially able to proffer protection against stress, modelling adaptation to adverse events and compensating against negative stressful effects. It can be a significant factor in the development of personal resilience, mediating stress and enabling individuals to overcome crises.

The organization in which the individual works can also be a significant source of support. Resilient and healthy organizations are characterized by an integrated system, where staff work together across functions to achieve the primary task. The focus of all departments within the organization is on service delivery, with clearly differentiated roles and authority and functional interdependence. For example, teachers are supported in their primary role by a system of administrators, technicians, facility managers, and support staff, all working to achieve the organization's primary task of delivering education.

In a resilient, healthy organization, staff are more likely to move towards, rather than away from, each another, in the face of stress and adversity. Kahn (2005) suggests that at the core of **organizational resilience** is the sense amongst staff of being in it together, of knowing that they will not have to face difficulties alone. When a workforce fails to manage its stress effectively, the organization is often characterized by internal conflicts and loss of focus on the primary task (Rice 1963) (see case illustration *Excel manufactures stress*, above).

The supportive and containing relationship between the organization and staff is also crucial in preventing the individual from seeking support and affiliation from their 'client'. Teachers, social workers, and account managers who identify too closely with their 'clients' can use them as a means of emotional and psychological support at the expense of the employing organization and its primary function (Rice 1963).

 Activity Examining stress

Using the family as a primary organization, identify symptoms of stress exhibited by yourself and each of your immediate family members. List the sources of the stress, including internal and external sources. Consider each family member's characteristic means of coping with the stressors. Identify how each member's coping strategies might serve to compound the stress for other family members.

14.3.4 Individual coping strategies

Many of the factors which, in their absence, contribute to increased stress levels can also be effective means of reducing stress levels if present. Social support when unavailable can be a direct source of stress but if available can be a potent moderator of perceived occupational stressors. Social support can provide a medium for cognitive reframing and diffusion of emotional content and protects against isolation. As such it is an effective means of coping.

Coping strategies relate closely to personality characteristics and attitudinal dispositions which will influence the individual's capacity to manage stress (see sections 14.3.1 and 14.3.2 above).

Koeske et al. (1993) highlight two types of coping strategies: control (proactive) in which the individual tries to deal directly with the source of stress; and avoidance (reactive) in which the

Pause for thought
Can you identify signs within your own organization—management or academic—of a lack of organizational resilience, where members of the organization have directed stress and negative reactions internally? Conversely can you identify occasions where staff have drawn together to manage stressful events. What has been the impact on yourself, peers, and the organization in each case?

individual tries to avoid the source of stress. Exercising control in coping with stressful events requires a problem-focused approach to the stress, and would normally involve a personal sense of control and hardiness. In contrast avoidance is associated with a low sense of control and poor stress resilience and would serve to compound the experience of stress.

Control and avoidance coping strategies reflect the optimist/pessimist approaches to coping (Furnham 2005). Individuals with an optimistic orientation hold a strong sense of optimism and are more likely to interpret events in a more favourable or positive light. This ability to evaluate or 'reframe' stressful events less negatively, influences the individual's experience and perception of the stresses, affording them a natural resilience. This ability is referred to as cognitive reframing. Individuals who cognitively reframe stressful events are more likely to assume a personal control over stressful events and adopt other effective coping strategies, such as problem solving and social support (Furnham 2005).

In contrast a negative or pessimistic orientation is associated with coping strategies such as avoidance, denial, and flight. A negative orientation in also linked to external attribution of control, low hardiness, and low resilience. Such individuals are less likely to adopt **problem-focused coping** strategies such as taking action to actively reduce their experience of stress at work.

Cultural variations will also influence individual coping strategies and their effectiveness. Relaxation and meditation are more commonly employed in the East. Meditation involves clearing the mind of adverse and external thoughts and focusing on a personal sense of peace. Relaxation can involve message, physical relaxation, breathing techniques. Relaxation essentially involves a change of activity and thought which distracts attention from the source of stress, allowing the stress to be placed in perspective and providing time for the individual to adjust. Religion can be a further powerful source of support and an effective moderator of stressful events.

KEY LEARNING POINTS

- Personality traits, attributes, gender and coping strategies can exaggerate or moderate the experience of stress.
- Families can be a significant factor in the individual's development of personal resilience.
- Resilience refers to the individual or organization's capacity to rebound from adversity more strengthened and resourceful.

14.4 Organizational interventions

Homeostasis refers to the individual's drive to seek out information which informs his psychological and physical state and drives him to achieve stability (Cummings and Cooper 1998). Individuals will have an actual state and a desired state and will strive towards the desired state of being, making whatever adjustments are necessary to achieve this state. This theory suggests that the individual's perceptions of the imbalance in his state and his desired state of being will be a crucial factor in the organization's success in reducing his experience of stress.

Organizational stress reduction techniques, such as job redesign, can promote the individual's sense of control, increasing the level of responsibility over tasks, and increasing the individual's resilience to stressors. Jobs can be enlarged, restructured, and reformulated to accommodate technological change and individual variations in capacity to cope (Cox 1993).

At an organizational level, restructuring, re-engineering, and reprocessing, while a major source of stress, can also serve to reduce the potential for stress by decentralizing control and increasing organizational and individual capacity for increased productivity and performance. This is more likely if accompanied by effective internal communications, employee involvement, and retraining programmes.

Management techniques such as 'management by objectives', peer review, appraisal programmes, and performance targets can be effective in clarifying role requirements. Such measures promote visible and transparent organizational strategies and equal opportunities for employees. They also serve to facilitate open internal communications and avoid role ambiguity. They are more likely to fail in the absence of employee consultation and participation in decision making.

Organizing individuals into teams and training them in team development can be effective in increasing performance and in increasing accessibility to peer in the event of stress. Team projects can also allow more control over the management and timeframe of tasks than a hierarchical management structure would allow. The converse effect can be in changes in team composition or increased potential for interpersonal conflict or dysfunctional dynamics.

Individual autonomy at work, coupled with appropriate training, can significantly enhance personal resilience to job-specific and known stressors. For example, emergency professionals can experience less stress by not only believing that they have individual control over the outcome of devastating traumatic incidents, but also in having received controlled exposure to traumatic events in their training (Hetherington 2001).

Comprehensive sickness and absence policies have been found to account for a 67 per cent reduction in absence rates within the UK (Caverley et al. 2007). The policies have included sickness and absence monitoring, management training, disciplinary procedures, incentive bonuses, 'return to work' programmes, the introduction of Occupational Health and Employee Assistance Programmes (Dunn and Wilkinson 2002; CIPD 2006a).

14.4.1 Cultural variations

Cultural differences in the experience of stress can be compounded by national and organizational policies such as assumed working habits, workplace legislation, and social security systems. For example, high-power, distance cultures requiring compliance with rules and processes are less likely to create role ambiguity but may generate considerable stress in the event of any deviation from the 'norm'. Similarly, caring professions may be more likely to cultivate a culture in which offending or hurting others is associated with stress. In such a culture, cooperation, and consensus may be sought as opposed to individualism (Furnham 2005).

It is possibly because different work cultures may have varied and diverse means of defining and managing success and failure in the workplace that the individual's personal experience of stress and subsequent means of coping with stressors will be influenced.

Gender may also be a significant determinant in the experience of stress as a direct result of such factors as returning to work practices following maternity leave and inflexible working practices which can compound the domestic stress of childcare. Gender differences are also evident in receptivity to organizational intervention strategies. Drew and Murtagh (2005) found that female employees were more likely than men to expect work-life balance policies of their employers (see Table 14.5).

14.4.2 Job satisfaction

While work can be a source of significant stress, it can also be a key means of personal fulfilment and satisfaction. The Work Foundation (2006) reported that job satisfaction was an important part of the psychological contract for workers, with work being increasingly thought of as a source of fulfilment, and a very important part of life. This would suggest that the employee has significant expectations of the psychological, social, and personal dividends they derive from work. (The significance of work to psychological well-being is evidenced further in the considerable impact of redundancy, discussed at length in Chapter 15, The Loss of Work.).

Job satisfaction can be described in terms of the fit between what the employee is seeking from work and what the organization is requiring from the employee. Job satisfaction is considered to be an attitude, an emotional and psychological response to a feeling of achievement or fulfilment of personal motivations. Job satisfaction is considered to be closely related to job design, working environment, work-life balance, and occupational stress. A lack of job satisfaction is often characterized by psychological defensiveness, **alienation**, and conflict.

Employee involvement and empowerment have been the key means by which job dissatisfaction has been addressed within the organization. However, work-life balance, occupational counselling, and coaching can also be effective means of both moderating the impact of occupational stress and proactively promoting employee's expectations of a fulfilling and satisfying work life.

Pause for thought
Identify what the sources of job satisfaction are for you, which occupations would provide them and which aspects of the job might frustrate you. Consider how you exhibit job satisfaction both in your personal behaviour and in your performance at work.

KEY LEARNING POINTS

- Organizational stress reduction techniques can promote the individual's resilience to stressors and reduce organizational stressors.
- Sickness and absence policies have been found to be instrumental in reducing levels of stress.
- Cultural differences in the experience of stress can be compounded by national and organizational policies.
- Job satisfaction is a primary source of fulfilment from which an employee can derive significant benefits.

14.4.3 Work-life balance

Work-life balance has been proposed as an individual's right to a fulfilled personal and work life which is assumed and recognized as being to the mutual benefit of the individual, business, and society (Work Foundation 2005b). It must take into consideration individual variations in circumstances, expectations, and perceptions, such as personality, capacity, gender, age, and career stage (Guest 2001), together with standard regulatory and statutory requirements.

In general, work-life balance can be considered to be the achievement of satisfactory and effective functioning both at work and at home with a minimum of role conflict (Clark 2000). This goal has now become more important to today's workforce than securing a job for life (Worman et al. 2005). The DTI (2002) report that twice as many employees would rather work shorter hours than win the lottery. Yet, it remains that 26 per cent of people in UK employment work over a 48-hour week set down by the European Working Time Directive and a third rarely take all their annual leave (CIPD 2003).

Work-life balance policies are an important way for employers to promote their commitment to quality of life and social responsibility (CIPD 2006b). They can be instrumental in supporting an organization in achieving its strategic objectives (Nicoll and Hetherington 2007). Work-life balance polices can be of significant advantage to the organization in leading to increased job satisfaction, motivation, commitment, and engagement, reduced absenteeism, improved recruitment and retention of diverse workforce, and by allowing the organization to become an 'employer of choice'. However, effective work-life programmes require a re-evaluation of associated policies such as flexible working—part-time working, job sharing, term-time-only working, and compressed hours. While, the successful implementation of work-life balance initiatives require internal management training to assure commitment of individual line managers to the programme as a whole (Ball 2006).

14.4.4 Employee Assistance Programmes

Employee Assistance Programmes (EAPs) are often an integral part of an organization's occupational health strategy. An EAP is a management tool which can offer professional, solution-focused, occupational counselling to address stress-related issues which are interfering with the individual's workplace functioning. The EAP provides the organization with statistical feedback on the incidence and sources of occupational stress (Marchington and Wilkinson 2005).

Coaching in stress management

Research has shown that coaching can be an effective means of managing stress (Palmer et al. 2003b). Coaching is associated with enhancing performance and professional development and has the potential to overcome the potentially negative image associated with counselling interventions.

While research into the impact of coaching on stress is as yet limited, coaching has been found to assist individuals in identifying stressors, developing coping strategies, and adopting a solution-focused orientation to occupational stress (Gyllensten and Palmer 2005). Coaching can also reduce stress indirectly by targeting the individual's weaknesses, improving personal performance and goal setting and by providing support. Cognitive coaching in particular, has a positive effect on mental health, increasing confidence and assertiveness and reducing levels of anger, anxiety, and depression.

Pause for thought
List what you would require from your employer that would allow you to achieve a satisfactory work-life balance. Consider which factors would drive you to move employment in search of a better quality of life. What would you consider to be the appropriate balance for you between life and work and pay? What personal factors such as age, gender, stage of career have played a part in your views?

The coaching relationship can be as important as the substance of the coaching in promoting personal change (Gyllensten and Palmer 2006). It offers the individual a non-threatening, containing, yet challenging environment to consider alternative means of managing stressful events. Coaching also has the potential, like counselling, to promote coping strategies and to prevent avoidance and denial (Coe and Hetherington 2006).

Coaching can also be instrumental in addressing cultural differences and developing a shared and informed understanding of difference at work. This can assist in promoting culture-specific adaptation to change and be effective in incorporating individual coaching programmes within a strategy of organizational change (Clutterbuck, 2006).

Coaching can provide the organization with an effective organizational intervention and management tool, capable of delivering successful outcomes in the management of occupational stress (Nicoll and Hetherington 2007). This might be of particular value at times of redundancy, restructuring, and organizational change.

 Activity Managing your manager

Using your knowledge of stress, consider how you might interpret the behaviours of a senior manager to whom you report, who presents himself as distant, angry, and demanding in the workplace. What vulnerability factors might be contributing to any stress he is experiencing? In your role as a member of his department, what behaviours might you adopt to assist you and other departmental members in indirectly reducing the stress he may currently be experiencing? What other resources within the organization could be of assistance in this case?

 KEY LEARNING POINTS

- Work-life balance has been proposed as an individual's right to a fulfilled personal and work life.
- EAPs can offer professional, solution-focused, occupational counselling to improve the individual's workplace functioning.
- Occupational coaching is recognized as an effective means of managing occupational stress.

14.4.5 The HSE Management Standards

As part of the Revitalising Health and Safety agenda the UK government has committed to a reduction in work-related ill-health resulting in poor performance at work. This initiative will necessitate most UK businesses to implement some form of visible and effective preventative strategy for tackling stress at work.

 Case illustration
HSE Management Standards in practice

The application of the HSE Management Standards (HSE MS) in the workplace is illustrated in a study of a Primary Care Trust within the UK (Willott 2006).

An inner London Primary Care Trust, responsible for providing primary medical care to a deprived community, reported increased levels of stress, absence, and staff turnover. The poverty and diversity of the community created substantial challenges for staff, including language barriers and cultural issues. In addition, the PCT was subject to stringent and changing national performance measures.

The HSE Indicator Tool for Work-Related Stress (HSE IT) effectively identified 'demands' as a key source of stress. The continually changing demands of new initiatives, staff sickness, absence, and turnover increased the general workload, creating competing objectives and compounding the inherent stress of the job.

As a means of achieving this, the HSE has developed a set of Management Standards for Work-Related Stress, which are assessed by the HSE Indicator Tool for Work-Related Stress which identifies a number of stressors including: demands, control, support, relationships, and role change (HSE 2006; HSE 2005; Mackay et al. 2004; Cousins et al. 2004).

14.4.6 Work-related post-traumatic stress

Employees may be exposed to traumatic events as a result of the work they do. Occupations such as the emergency services, pathologists, coroners, construction workers, oil rig workers and bank staff may be exposed to a range of traumatic events on either an irregular or frequent basis. These traumatic situations include road traffic accidents, firearms incidents, industrial accidents, violent attacks, horrific deaths, personal injuries, and armed raids.

When traumatic work-related events occur, it would be normal for the individual to experience a specific set of physiological and psychological responses to the incident. These reactions include intrusive thoughts and images of the incident, a sense of numbness, hyper-alertness, avoidance of reminders of the event, and a range of associated symptoms which will affect their ability to draw on coping strategies such as social support

Most people who experience traumatic stress reactions will recover within a period of four weeks. However, some people may develop **post-traumatic stress disorder** (PTSD), where the characteristic reactions of intrusion, avoidance and hyper-arousal associated with PTSD fail to abate. These symptoms may then interfere with the individual's normal everyday functioning. To constitute a diagnosis of PTSD, the combination of physiological, emotional, and psychological symptoms, resulting from the life-threatening event, must have persisted beyond four weeks (see Table 14.6).

Other symptoms may emerge at different stages following the traumatic incident and can mask the key features of PTSD. These include depression, anxiety, substance abuse, chronic exhaustion, and significant deterioration in work performance (Hetherington 1993).

Organizational interventions in the aftermath of the traumatic event can significantly contribute to the individual's recovery and to the organization's return to normal functioning. It is important in such events that any staff who have played a role in dealing with other traumatized staff or material relating to the traumatic incident are included in post-trauma interventions to reduce the potential for them to experience vicarious traumatization (Hetherington 2001). These roles may include HR, Occupational Health, legal, and medical secretarial staff.

Table 14.6. Criteria for post-traumatic stress disorder

A.	The individual has experienced an event that is outside the range of usual human experience and that would be markedly distressing to almost anyone.
B.	The distressing event is persistently re-experienced in the form of intrusive, disturbing thoughts, images, or dreams of the event. The individual may experience intense psychological distress on exposure to events symbolic of the traumatic experience/s. He/she may also experience sensations of the event recurring (flashbacks) and/or feelings of guilt associated with behaviour at the time of the event.
C.	Persistent avoidance of thoughts, feelings, activities, or situations reminiscent of the event or numbing of responsiveness to others, and to activities. The individual may also experience an inability to feel warmth toward others, an inability to recall aspects of the event, and a sense of foreshortened future.
D.	Persistent symptoms of increased arousal. This may take the form of physiologic reactivity at exposure to events that are reminiscent of an aspect of the event, difficulty concentrating or sleeping, irritability, hypervigilance, or increased startle response.
E.	Duration of the disturbance of at least one month. Symptoms may not be immediately evident but may be exhibited some time after the event. In this instance they would be classified as delayed.

While most organizations have a crisis management strategy, the organization often overlooks procedures to deal with people management in the aftermath of the trauma, and as such potentially increases the practical and financial impact of the disaster. A tried and tested traumatic incident policy and processes will both demonstrate the organization's 'duty of care' and reduce the likelihood of litigation.

In the event of a large-scale or high-profile traumatic event, the organization's role in providing information on the event to staff and family members, educational information on the psychological and physiological effects of post-traumatic stress, and trauma-appropriate interventions will be pivotal in assuring long-term staff well-being, safety, and normal workplace functioning (Tehrani 2004).

Activity Crisis management

List the strategic objectives of a policy for the proactive management of traumatic events in the workplace. Create an outline implementation plan, listing each of the stages. Consider what resources would be required to implement the plan and what preparations would be needed in advance.

KEY LEARNING POINTS

- Employees may be exposed to traumatic events as a result of the work they do, including small- and large-scale disasters.
- Post-traumatic stress is a normal reaction to an abnormal event characterized by symptoms of intrusion, avoidance, and hypervigilance.

Chapter summary

- Occupational stress is increasingly recognized as a major cost to industry, having a deleterious effect on individual, departmental, and organizational functioning.
- Occupational stress is the adverse reaction people have to excessive pressure they experience in the workplace.
- Stress is the result of the interaction between actual stressors and the individual's perceptions and ability to cope with the stressors.
- Stress on an individual is exhibited in a range of physiological, emotional, and psychological changes in their behaviour.
- Sources of stress can result from factors intrinsic to the job, the role, interpersonal interactions, and the working environment.
- Personality factors can both render individuals vulnerable to stress and increase their recovery form stress-related incidents.
- Organizations can introduce a range of measures and interventions to demonstrate and exercise a 'duty of care' to their employees.
- Professional occupational counselling, coaching, and mentoring are effective management tools in moderating the impact of work-related stress.
- Traumatic incidents in the workplace can lead to post-traumatic stress disorder and require specialist interventions to avoid long-term ill-health.

Assess your learning

Review questions

1 Define occupational stress.

2 Describe the General Adaptation syndrome.

3 Explain the interaction models of stress.

4 What is hardiness and how does this affect perceived stress?

5 What is work-related post-traumatic stress?

6 What relevance does coaching have to stress management?

7 What impact does occupational stress have on organizational performance and productivity?

8 Identify how HRM could be effective in the organizational management of stress?

9 What is the value of a stress audit or survey to the organization?

10 Discuss the value of national initiatives in the management of stress.

Assignments

ASSIGNMENT 1: The occupational health detective

Identify an organization of which you have worked. Assuming a problem-solving orientation, analyse the organization to:

- provide a brief description of the organization;
- list any symptoms of stress, providing examples;
- describe the potential sources of stress;
- consider any historic factors which may contribute to the current stress levels.

ASSIGNMENT 2: Selling health and well-being to the organization

Develop a comprehensive stress management programme for a medium-sized organization, identifying the sector. Specify how the programme will:

- contribute to the strategic goals of the organization;
- deliver measurable outcomes and performance targets;
- provide a cost-effective management tool.

Further reading

Cavanaugh, M., Boswell, W., Roehling, M., and Boudreau, J. (2000) An empirical examination of self-report work stress among U.S managers. *Journal of Applied Psychology*, 85/1: 65–74.
An influential and important study, based on longitudinal research with 1,886 managers, charting the complex impact of stress at work.

Cooper, C. L., Drewe, P., and O'Driscoll, M. (2001) *Organisational Stress: A Review and Critique of Theory, Research and Application*. London: Sage.
A comprehensive overview of current thinking on stress at work, which includes a critical examination of various theoretical positions.

Daniels, K. (2006) *Employment Law for HR and Business Students*. London: CIPD.
A useful guide which includes an overview of employer responsibilities in the context of stress at work.

Department of Health (2001) *Treatment Choice in Psychological Therapies and Counselling*. London: Department of Health.
Gives details of clinical practice guidelines about which forms of therapy are most appropriate in different contexts. The guidelines were produced by a multi-disciplinary team, coordinated by the British Psychological Society.

Donaldson-Feilder, E., Pryce, J., Lewis, R., and Flaxman, P. (2006) *A New Perspective on Stress Management, People and Organisations at Work*. Leicester: BPS Books.
An up-to-date text, focusing on the management of stress in contemporary work organizations.

Health and Safety Executive (2005) *Tackling Work-Related Stress: The Management Standards Approach*. Suffolk: HSE.
A useful guide for managers, based on case studies of real organizational events and experiences, which focuses on the implementation of effective systems for managing stress in the workplace.

Lim, M. (2005) When two worlds collide: the ethics of enabling better home-work balance. *Business Ethics: A European Review*. 14/1: 83–8.
A thought-provoking discussion exploring the moral aspects of management's role in confronting stress at work.

Porter, C., Bingham, C., and Simmonds, D. (eds.) *Exploring Human Resource Management*. Maidenhead: McGraw-Hill Education.
A recent general HR text, which includes chapters on many areas relevant to an understanding of stress at work from a practical perspective: including the 'dark side' of management; counselling at work; coaching and mentoring; and work-life balance.

Tehrani, N. (2004) *Workplace Trauma: Concepts, Assessments and Interventions*. Hove: Brunner-Routledge.
A specialized text focusing on understanding and supporting victims of trauma in the work context.

Work psychology in practice
A strategic review of occupational health services

In January 2001, the Health and Safety Commission (HSC) and Health and Safety Executive (HSE) in association with a number of other government departments produced *Securing Health Together*, a long-term occupational health strategy for England, Scotland, and Wales (HSC 2001).

This strategy represents a joint commitment by government bodies concerned with occupational health, and other interested parties outside of government, to work together to reach the following goals:

- reduce ill-health both in workers and the public caused, or made worse, by work;
- help people who have been ill, whether caused by work or not, to return to work;
- improve work opportunities for people currently not in employment due to ill-health or disability; and
- Use the work environment to help maintain or improve their health.

The report demonstrates a commitment by the government to improve health at work. It would be, therefore, the responsibility of any government body to implement the strategy. As a government body, the National Probation Service (NPS) is committed to the philosophy of the HSE and believes that the effective management of an occupational health (OH) service will improve the efficiency of the organization, improving performance, productivity, recruitment, and retention of staff.

As a result of the HSE recommendations, the NPS Human Resources Directorate commissioned a strategic review of the OH service within the NPS. The initial objective of the review was to assess the current level of provision of occupational health in the National Probation Service, to highlight the main issues that impact on the health of the workforce, and to propose a strategy for occupational health provision within the service (NPS 2002).

The NPS recognized that a major means of loss of revenue was through sickness and absence, and that internally it had no mechanism to accurately capture the data on loss of working days through ill-health. This significantly reduced its capacity to monitor and evaluate the success of the OH service.

The NPS had undergone considerable organizational change, primarily in the creation of a national service. There had also been a significant change in ideology and philosophy that might be expected to increase levels of resistance to change, occupational stress, and sickness absence amongst staff.

At the time, the NPS operated from approximately 1,200 sites across the country with the smallest having just over 150 employees and the largest employing nearly 3,000. This considerable variation in size and distribution would affect the ways in which occupational health can be provided nationally. The OH service was delivered at a local level by a variety of providers of OH services and usually incorporated either Employee Assistance Programmes or counselling services to manage psychological health.

Occupational health services are subject to complex relationships and must liaise successfully with specific functions within the organization, such as the National Probation Service Directorate, Human Resources department, and Health and Safety, together with employees.

The project involved a review of current OH services across the NPS (including Crown Court, County Court, Human Resources (HR), OH, Hostels, Youth Offending, Community Punishment, Case Management, Sex Offender and Domestic Violence, Drugs, Resettlement, Victim Support, and Administrative) in all regions (42 areas). The second phase of the project involved a national questionnaire survey, focus groups, and semi-structured interviews with Key Stakeholders across the National Probation Service.

Questions

- What is the value to the organization of the strategic review of OH at an organizational, group, and individual level?
- List the benefits of the strategic review in mobilizing support for change at an individual, departmental, and organizational level.
- Identify and consider how competing objectives amongst the key stakeholders could be managed to ensure achievement of the organizational goals.
- Identify the collaborative functions of human resource management and occupational psychology in affecting organizational behaviour.

 **Online Resource Centre**

Visit the supporting online resource centre for additional material which will help you with your research, essays, and assignments, or you may find these additional resources helpful when revising for exams.
http://www.oxfordtextbooks.co.uk/orc/matthewman/

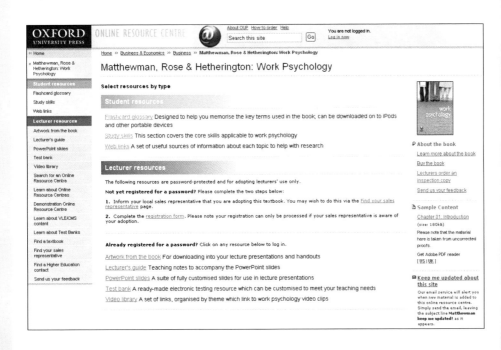

References

Albrecht, K. (1979) *Stress and the Manager: Making it Work for you.* Englewood Cliffs, NJ: Prentice-Hall.

Arnold, J. (2005) *Work Psychology: Understanding Human Behaviour in the Workplace* (4th edn.). Harlow: Pearson.

Ball, K. (2006) A critical review of a police service's career break policy. Unpublished MA dissertation. University of Westminster, London.

Barnham, C., and Begum, N. (2005) Sickness absence from work in UK. Office for National Statistics: *Labour Market Trends,* Apr.: 149–58.

Berridge, J., Cooper, C. L., and Highley-Marchington, C. (1997) *Employee Assistance Programs and Workplace Counselling.* Chichester: John Wiley.

Bradley, G. (2007) Job tenure as a moderator of stressor–strain relations: a comparison of experienced and new-start teachers. *Work and Stress,* 21/1: 48–64.

Caplan, R. (1983) Person–environment fit: past present and future. In C. L. Cooper (ed.), *Stress Research: Issues for the Eighties.* Chichester: Wiley.

Cartwright, S., and Cooper, C. L. (1994) *No Hassle: Taking the Stress out of Work.* London: Century Books.

Caverley, N., Cunningham, J., and MacGregor, J. (2007) Sickness presenteeism, sickness absenteeism and health following restructuring in a public service organization. *Journal of Management Studies,* 44: 304–19.

Chase, B., and Karowski, W. (2003) Advanced manufacturing technology. In D. Holman, T. D. Wall, C. W. Clegg, P. Sparrow, and A. Howard (eds.), *The New Workplace.* Chichester: John Wiley.

CIPD (2003) *Living to Work? Survey Report.* London: CIPD.

CIPD (2005a) *Absence Management: A Survey of Policy and Practice.* London: CIPD.

CIPD (2005b) *Recruitment, Retention and Turnover Survey.* London. http://www.cipd.co.uk

CIPD (2006a) *Recruitment, Retention and Turnover.* Annual Survey Report. London: CIPD.

CIPD (2006b) *Work-Life Balance.* Factsheet. London: CIPD.

Clark, S. (2000) Work/family border theory: a new theory of work/life balance. *Human Relations,* 53/6: 747–70.

Clarke, S., and Cooper, C. (2004) *Managing the Risk of Workplace Stress.* London: Routledge.

Clutterbuck, D. (2006) A case for clarity: how can international coaching and mentoring programs overcome cultural differences of understanding. *Coaching at Work,* 1/3. London: CIPD.

Coe, J., and Hetherington, A. (2006) *An International Review of Regulatory Guidance on Professional Boundaries in the Helping Relationship.* 1st International Coaching Psychology Conference, Dec.

Coe, J., and Hetherington, A. (2007) *An International Review of Regulatory Guidance on Professional Boundaries in the Helping Relationship.* Annual Occupational Psychology Conference, Jan.

Cooper, C. L., Dewe, P., and O'Driscoll, M. (2001) *Organisational Stress: A Review and Critique of Theory, Research and Application.* London: Sage.

Cooper, C. L., and Marshall, J. (1976) Occupational sources of stress: a review of the literature relating to coronary heart disease and mental ill health. *Journal of Occupational Psychology,* 49: 11–28.

Cooper, C. L., and Payne, R. (1988) *Causes, Coping and Consequences of Stress at Work.* Chichester: John Wiley and Sons.

Cousins, R., Mackay, C., Clarke, S. D., Kelly, C., Kelly, P. J., and McCaig, H. (2004) Management standards and work-related stress in the UK: practical development. *Work and Stress,* 18/2: 113–36.

Cox, T. (1978) *Stress.* London: Macmillan Press Ltd.

Cox, T. (1993) *Stress Research and Stress Management: Putting Theory to Work.* Sudbury: HSE Books.

Cox, T., and Griffiths, A. (1996) Assessment of psychosocial hazards at work. In M. Schabracq, J. Winnubst, and C. Cooper (eds.), *Handbook of Work and Health Psychology.* New York: John Wiley.

Cox, T., Griffiths, A., and Rial-González, E. (2000) *Research on Work-Related Stress.* Luxembourg: European Agency for Safety and Health at Work.

Cox, T., and Mackay, C. (1979) The impact of repetitive work. In R. Sell and P. Shipley (eds.), *Satisfaction in Job Design.* London: Taylor and Francis, 24–37.

Cummings, T., and Cooper, C. (1998) A cybernetic theory of organizational stress. In C. Cooper (ed.), *Theories of Organizational Stress.* Buckingham: Open University Press, 101–20.

Demir, A., Ulusoy, M., and Ulusoy, M. F. (2003) Investigation of factors influencing burnout levels in professional and private lives of nurses. *International Journal of Nursing Studies,* 40: 807–27.

Donaldson-Feilder, E., Pryce, J., Lewis, R., and Flaxman, P. (2006) *A New Perspective on Stress Management, People and Organisations at Work.* Leicester: BPS Books.

Dowie, M. (n.d.) Achieving work-life balance. Unpublished MA dissertation. University of Westminster, London.

Drew, E., and Murtagh, E. (2005) Work/life balance: senior management champions or laggards. *Women in Management Review,* 20/4: 262–78.

DTI and Management Today (2002) *Work-Life Balance Survey.* London. http://www.gnn.gov.uk

Dunn, C., and Wilkinson, A. (2002) Wish you were here: managing absence. *Personnel Review,* 31/2: 228–46.

Earnshaw, J., and Cooper, C. L. (2001) *Stress and Employer Liability* (2nd edn.). London: CIPD.

European Commission (2002) *Guidance on Work-Related Stress: Spice of Life or Kiss of Death? Executive Summary.* Luxembourg: Office for Official Publications of the European Communities.

Furnham, A. (2005) *The Psychology of Behaviour at Work: The Individual in the Organization.* Hove: Psychology Press.

Guest, D. (2001) *Perspectives on the Study of Work-Life Balance.* London: King's College. http://www.ucm.es/info/Psyap/enop/guest.htm

Gyllensten, K., and Palmer, S. (2005) Can coaching reduce workplace stress. *Coaching Psychologist,* 1: 15–17.

Gyllensten, K., and Palmer, S. (2006) Experience of coaching and stress in the workplace: an interpretative phenomenological analysis. *International Coaching Psychology Review,* 1: 86–98.

Half, R. (2006) *Salary and Benefits Survey.* As cited in J. Curruthers (2006). Accountants see strong hiring market ahead. http://news.efinancialcareers.co.uk

Health and Safety Commission (2001) *Securing Health Together: Occupational Health Strategy for England, Scotland and Wales.* London: HSE.

Health and Safety Executive (1995) *Health and Safety Statistics 1994/1995.* Sudbury: HSE.

Health and Safety Executive (1999) *Management of Health and Safety at Work Regulations.* Sheffield: HSE.

Health and Safety Executive (2001) *Tackling Work-Related Stress: A Managers Guide to Improving and Maintaining Employee Health and Well-Being.* Sudbury: HSE.

Health and Safety Executive (2005) *Tackling Work-Related Stress: The Management Standards Approach.* Sudbury: HSE.

Health and Safety Executive (2006) *Self-Reported Work Related Illness: The Management Standards Approach.* Sudbury: HSE.

Health and Safety Executive (2007) *Health and Safety Statistics 2006/2007.* Sudbury: HSE.

Hetherington, A. (1993) *Human Resource Management in Times of Stress.* London: Police Research Group, The Home Office.

Hetherington, A. (2000) Clinical exploitation: a breach of professional standards. *British Journal of Guidance and Counselling.* Feb.

Hetherington, A. (2001) *The Use of Counselling Skills in the Emergency Services.* Maidenhead: Open University Press.

Holmes, T. N., and Rahe, R. H. (1967) The social readjustment rating scale. *Journal of Psychosomatic Research,* 11: 213–18.

International Stress Management Association UK (2005) *Making the Stress Management Standards Work: How to Apply the Standards in your Workplace.* London: International Stress Management Association UK.

Jamal, M., and Baba, V. (2003) Type A behaviour, components and outcomes: a study of Canadian employees. *International Journal of Stress Management,* 10/1: 39–50.

Jamieson, C. (1999) Top ten myths of customer service. *British Journal of Administrative Management*, July–Aug.: 19–21.

Jordan J., Gurr, E., Tinline, G., Giga, S., Faragher, B., and Cooper, C. (2003) *Beacons of Excellence in Stress Prevention*. Sudbury: HSE Books.

Kahn, W. A. (2005) Holding Fast: The Struggle to Create Resilient Caregiving Organisations. Hove: Brunner-Routledge.

Kanuri, S., and Hetherington, A. (2005) The impact of change on the performance of a high profile finance company. British Psychological Society Annual Conference.

Karasek, R., and Theorell, T. (1990) *Healthy Work*. New York: Basic Books.

Kinman, G., and Jones, F. (2005) Lay representations of workplace stress: what do people really mean when they say they are stressed? *Work and Stress*, 19/2: 101–20.

Kobasa, S. (1979) Stressful life events, personality, health: an enquiry into hardiness. *Journal of Personality and Social Psychology*, 37: 114–28.

Koeske, G., Kirk, S., and Koeske, R. (1993) Coping with job stress: which strategies work best? *Journal of Occupational and Organizational Psychology*, 66: 319–35.

Lazarus, R. S. (1976) *Patterns of Adjustment*. New York: McGraw-Hill.

McGrath, J. E. (1984a; 1st edn. 1976) Stress and behaviour in organisations. In M. Dunnette (ed.), *Handbook of Industrial and Organisational Psychology*. Chicago: Rand McNally, 1351–96.

McGrath, J. E. (1984b) *Groups: Interaction and Performance*. Englewood Cliffs, NJ: Prentice Hall.

Mackay, C. J., Cousins, R., Kelly, P. J., Lee, S., and McCaig, R. H. (2004) Management standards and work-related stress in the UK: policy background and science. *Work and Stress*, 18/2: 91–112.

Marchington, M., and Wilkinson, A. (2005) *Human Resource Management at Work: People Management and Development*. London: Chartered Institute of Personnel and Development.

Mauno, S., Kinnunen, U., and Ruokolainen, M. (2006) Exploring work- and organisation-based resources as moderators between work-family conflict, well-being, and job attitudes. *Work and Stress*, 20/3: 210–33.

Mitchell, J., and Bray, G. (1990) *Emergency Services Stress: Guidelines for Preserving the Health and Careers of Emergency Service Personnel*. Englewood Cliffs, NJ: Prentice Hall.

Mullins, L. J. (2006) *Essentials of Organisational Behaviour*. London: Prentice Hall.

National Probation Service (2002) *Achieving through People: The People Management Strategy of the National Probation Service*. London: The Home Office.

Nicoll, A., and Hetherington, A. (2006) The use of coaching within an EAP in the management of organisational stress. First International Coaching Psychology Conference, Dec.

Nicoll, A., and Hetherington, A. (2007) A strategic review of occupational health provision in the national probation service. Annual Occupational Psychology Conference 2007.

Palmer, S., Cooper, C., and Thomas, K. (2003a) A model of work stress: to underpin the Health and Safety Executive advice for tackling work-related stress and stress risk assessments. *Counselling at Work*, Winter 2004.

Palmer, S., Tubbs, I., and Whynbrow, A. (2003b) Health coaching to facilitate the promotion of healthy behaviour and achievement of health-related goals. *International Journal of Health Promotion and Education*, 41: 91–3.

Rees, D., and Porter, C. (2003) *Skills of Management* (5th edn.). London: Thompson.

Rice, A. K. (1963) *The Enterprise and its Environment*. London: Tavistock Publications.

Schabracq, M., Cooper, C. L., Travers, C., and Vanmaanen, D. (2001) *Occupational Health Psychology: The Challenge of Workplace Stress*. Leicester: BPS Books.

Selye, H. (1946) The general adaptation syndrome and the diseases of adaptation. *Journal of Endocrinology*, 6: 117.

Selye, H. (1974) *Stress without Distress*. Philadelphia: J. B. Lippincott.

Siegrist, J. (1996) Adverse health effects of high-psychological demand/low-reward conditions. *Journal of Occupational Health Psychology*, 1: 27–41.

Spector, P. (1998) A control theory of the job stress process. In C. Cooper (ed.), *Theories of Organisational Stress*. Buckingham: Open University Press, 153–65.

Tehrani, N. (2004) Workplace Trauma: Concepts, Assessments and Interventions. Hove: Brunner-Routledge.

UK National Work Stress Network (2006) http://www.workstress .net/downloads/stress%20booklet.pdf.

Walsh, F. (1998) *Strengthening Family Resilience*. New York: The Guilford Press.

Willott, P. (2006) Investigation into the sources of stress within a teaching primary care trust. Unpublished MA dissertation. University of Westminster, London.

The Work Foundation (2005a) *Productivity and Absenteeism*. http://www.employersforwork-lifebalance.org.uk

The Work Foundation (2005b). *What is Work-Life Balance?* http://www.employersforwork-lifebalance.org.uk

The Work Foundation (2006) *The Good Worker* http://www .theworkfoundation.com

Worman, D., Bland, A., and Chase, P. (2005) Managing Diversity: People Make the Difference at Work—but Everyone is Different. London: CIPD. http://www.cipd.co.uk.

Chapter 15
The loss of work

Lisa Matthewman

Chapter objectives

As a result of reading this chapter and using the additional web-based material you should be able to:

- Understand the meaning of work for the individual.
- Understand the relationship between work and unemployment.
- Critically reflect on Warr's Vitamin Model.
- Discuss the psychological effects of unemployment on the individual.
- Explore the problems posed by the threat of unemployment.
- Explain the issue of underemployment.
- Understand the implications of redundancy for the individual.
- Describe the process of retirement for the individual and factors related to positive health in retirement.
- Explain the applications of counselling for the unemployed, redundant, and retired.

Work psychology in practice
On the scrap heap

Jason is a supervisor in a large printing and packaging organization. He gets out of bed at 6 a.m. and is in work for 7 a.m. He has worked for Smithies for nineteen years and generally comments that he enjoys his work but finds it quite stressful at times as dealing with people can be very problematic.

As staff supervisor, Jason manages the large team of Warehouse Operatives and allocates work tasks. When he gets into work, he prepares for the day by evaluating the workload and staffing situation. Once the work or the customer orders have been organized he then looks at the staff available to undertake various duties. The workload is then distributed amongst the work teams. Jason then looks at his emails and records sickness and absence for the day. Much of his time is spent ensuring that the work is being done and that the teams are working productively, that is they are picking customer orders from the warehouse shelves and packing stationery items into boxes, ready to be posted to customers. Often, Jason has to implement company policy and procedures in relation to health and safety, staff discipline, and feedback appraisals.

In February, every member of the company received a letter outlining the intention of Smithies to close their Widnes warehouse, the official notice of redundancy was issued via letter, and consultation sessions took place to answer initial questions. Standard redundancy policies were being taken forward by the HR team at all times. Though everyone knew they were being made redundant the following January, most people continued to carry on working as normal for the next few months.

Jason was aware he was to be made redundant and would face unemployment; however, for him, his mind was still very much occupied with day-to-day running and getting the job done. Even when Jason's contract was extended following the official closure of the warehouse and when most of his work colleagues had already left, Jason still didn't believe that he was going to be unemployed.

Once he left the warehouse, his immediate response was very positive, he had time to relax and take a break following the emotional turmoil of the closure. He was able to spend some of his large redundancy payment on new clothes and a great holiday. Having more time at home to spend with his new baby and playing golf with his old work colleagues filled his days easily in those first few months. It was like having a big break, a long holiday.

However, after five months had passed, his work in the warehouse seemed like a distant memory and the summer was drawing to a close. Jason began to feel that something was missing, something wasn't right. The redundancy money was gradually being used and Jason's wife was back in work after maternity leave. Jason began to feel anxious and started to think about his unemployed status. While he tossed and turned at night, he reflected back on the job hunting sessions offered by Smithies and how he had not taken much notice of them at the time. He assumed that he would 'just get another job' or that he could undertake agency work. He was torn between wanting to work but maybe not in his old profession. He didn't know what to do and soon he started to lose his appetite and feel quite pessimistic about the future. His old work colleagues had not found work either and games of golf were not as enjoyable as they once were. 'I'm on the scrap heap now, I've never been out of work in all my life, I don't know what to do.' Jason had not bothered to go to the Job Centre or claim for any benefits as he just didn't want to see himself as unemployed.

Questions

- What do you think Jason could have done to prepare for redundancy more effectively?
- What effect is unemployment having on Jason?
- How might Jason start to help himself?
- What effects does redundancy have on the rest of Jason's family?
- What is the organization's responsibility to Jason?

15.1 Introduction

This chapter explains how work gives the individual meaning in their life. Work offers the individual many benefits, such as the opportunity to earn money, the opportunity to use skills, and the opportunity to have social interaction with other people.

The chapter explores the relationship between work and mental health, in particular the damaging psychological effects of unemployment will be discussed. Key research in this area will be explored. This includes detailed reviews of Warr (1987b), Jahoda (1958 and 1982) and Fryer and Payne (1984). Current research on unemployment is then reviewed. Individual perceptions, individual differences, and coping strategies regarding unemployment are further indicated.

Following this, the chapter goes on to explore a new and emerging area of research, underemployment. Key research by Dooley and Prause (1995) discusses different notions of work and the impact of undertaking low-skilled work on mental health. Underemployment is of interest to psychologists as new technology increases the deskilling of workers and increasing educational standards result in individuals taking jobs for which they are overeducated or overqualified.

The chapter details the damaging effect of redundancy by likening it to bereavement. The phase model of unemployment and redundancy or the 'Grieving Cycle' dates from work undertaken in the 1930s on the Great Depression.

Retirement is then explored and approaches to helping the retired stay fit and healthy discussed through volunteerism. Atchley (1991) has devised a model that suggests there are seven phases to describe an individual's approach to retirement. The model presents a description of the retirement process. More recent research by Kloep and Hendry (2007) is noted; this explores how older people deal with retirement.

Finally, the chapter explores the applications of occupational psychology and what types of welfare provision are provided.

15.2 Employment

The meaning of work and the extent of unemployment is constantly changing. In the 1950s and 1960s employment was plentiful, yet during the 1970s and 1980s unemployment began to rise. This was due to changing economies, reductions in manufacturing, shifts in manufacturing to newly industrializing countries, and an increase in the service sector. There has also been escalating globalization which has lead to new patterns of employment and unemployment. Attitudes to work reflect the historical and cultural changes in society. Therefore the significance and meaning of work to both the individual and wider society will be examined.

Work or employment can be viewed as 'an activity engaged in by an individual with the reward of payment for various skills and energies utilised' (Hodson 2001). During these employment years, the individual will transition in and out of work as they take maternity leave, paternity leave, redundancy, career changes, self-employment, unemployment, finally ending their working life with some form of retirement or non-employment.

As a result of economic changes or redundancy, the transition out of work into 'early retirement' and the need to ensure pension provision may ensure the need to stay employed. However, there are those who take semi-retirement, and continue their role in a consultancy capacity, work part time, or become self-employed or retrain for an alternative profession. For some people, the transitions are not as clear cut as would appear. The effects of unemployment, underemployment, redundancy, and retirement can be seen throughout the life cycle.

 Activity Transitions

- What does 'working' mean to you?
- What major life changes have you experienced in the last two years?
- How did you cope with these changes?
- List your own transitions (completed or expected) into and out of the world of work.
- Compare these transitions with the transitions your parents have made.
- Account for similarities and differences between you, your parents, and others.

15.3 Unemployment

The National Statistics on unemployment for 2006 comment that the unemployment rate was 5.5 per cent, up 0.3 over the quarter and up 0.7 over the year. The number of unemployed people increased by 92,000 over the quarter and by 243,000 over the year, to reach 1.68 million. **Unemployment** is high in Western societies but so too is employment. However, unemployment figures can be difficult to comprehend as the employed, underemployed, non-employed, and unemployed are constantly shifting groups. Therefore the pool of unemployed workers is constantly changing as people move in and out of work.

Three international theories regarding the psychological effects of unemployment were all proposed during the 1980s. Warr's Vitamin Model was a product of research at the University of Sheffield, Jahoda's ideas derive from her leading role in the Marienthal study of the 1930s, and Fryer developed his ideas based on working with Warr.

Research on unemployment re-emerged in the 1980s during the politically polarized years of Thatchersim, with its emphasis on the individual to the exclusion of social factors. However, the significantly high levels of unemployment during the 1990s did not generate the same urgency for research as in the 1980s.

15.3.1 Warr's Vitamin Model

Many studies have explored the links between specific aspects of a person's work environment and their psychological well-being. Peter Warr (1987b, 1994, 1999, and 2002) proposed ten **determinants** of **mental health** in working and organizational settings. These determinants or factors are responsible for determining psychological health. Warr was concerned with the maintenance of psychological and physical health in work settings. The historical development of the Vitamin Model arose out of early psychological work undertaken in the UK in the 1920s and 1930s during economic depression. Figure 15.1 presents a list of the ten determinants that Warr believes are crucial for positive mental health. The model implies these determinants or needs are underlying motives for work behaviour.

Overall, mental health is determined by an interaction between the individual and their environment. Working can have an important role to play in an individual's environment. The nine determinants are likened to vitamins. Just as vitamins are crucial to our diet, Warr's vitamins are crucial to psychological and physical health. Work is import for individuals as it allows them to provide for themselves and their dependants. Not having a job or losing a job can lead to poverty, ill-health, homelessness, and low social status, just as poor diet can lead

Figure 15.1. Warr's vitamin model

	Environmental Influences on mental health	Type
1.	Opportunity for control	AD
2.	Opportunity for skill use	AD
3.	External generated goals	AD
4.	Variety	AD
5.	Environmental clarity	AD
6.	Availability of money	CE
7.	Physical security	CE
8.	Opportunity for social contact	AD
9.	Valued social position	CE
10.	Supportive supervision	CE

Notes: AD-additional decrement (high intakes of these vitamins is damaging); CE-constant effects (high intakes of these vitamins is not damaging)

Source: Adapted from Warr (1987b).

to malnutrition. Three of the determinants were labelled as **constant effect** determinants (CE). These include:

- availability of money;
- physical security;
- valued social position.

The presence of these factors can have a positive effect on mental and physical health.

Availability of money from working or saving funds can ensure an individual and their family do not fall into the poverty trap. Money leads to more resources and opportunities and can ensure good health treatment in times of ill-health. Low income has been linked to poor health, as will be seen later in this chapter.

Physical security means a safe living environment which is secure, warm, and offers protection and privacy. In contrast, the homeless and people involved in natural disasters show the knock-on effects of not having a safe home environment on the individual's psychological well-being.

Valued social position offers an individual social status in work and societal structures. Being valued by our social peers leads to high self-esteem. At any one time a person can be a member of many different social groups and have many different social standings within those groups. Employment provides an opportunity for achieving social standing in wider society and for the attainment of the rewards and benefits associated with high position. Employment is a primary source of social position and so without it an individual may experience a drop in self-esteem. The unemployed are deemed to have low social standing by society. However, even some jobs are deemed to have a lower social standing than others, e.g. hospital porter, road sweeper, housewife, or trainee.

The other six determinants are essential for health but can cause serious damage if you have too much (just like certain vitamins in the body). Therefore these determinants are essential but need to be in the right balance. They are described as Additional Determinants (AD). The first subgroup of AD determinants is:

- Opportunity for control.
- Opportunity for skill use.
- Opportunity for social contact.
- Supportive supervision (Warr 2002).

Having the opportunity to control our lives is critical to one of the basic beliefs in psychology. Locus of control refers to the extent to which we believe we have control in our lives. Individuals need to feel in control of their lives and their environment. Having feelings of no control in our lives is reported by individuals suffering from **stress**, emotional exhaustion, depression, and anxiety. Having the responsibility to make our own decisions in life and not have to make decisions under pressure is paramount to positive mental health (for further discussions of stress, refer to Chapter 14 on Psychological Health in the Workplace).

Having opportunities to utilize skills or being able to perform a job skilfully can lead to high levels of personal satisfaction and motivation. Having skills to exchange in an open labour market is important to employment survival and valuable currency in labour markets where there are skill shortages. An example of this is in the UK medical profession where nurses and doctors are being encouraged to travel to the UK from the Far East to work in the National Health Service. When job skills are no longer needed, for example during redundancy, psychological ill-health can result in the form of depression. A person's personal identity can be undermined when they do not have the required skills to join the labour market or when skills are no longer needed by an organization. However, over-usage of skills can lead to emotional exhaustion or burnout.

Having social contacts in the world of work is also important for maintaining positive psychological and physical mental health. Social isolation is a contributory factor of depression and work offers many opportunities to socialize. In 2002, Warr added 'supportive supervision' to his list of determinants. Supportive supervision is crucial to a worker's ability to cope with stress.

The second subgroup of Determinants (AD) includes:

- Externally generated goals.
- Variety.
- External clarity.

Externally generated goals give a structure to the working day and achieving goals in many settings can give individuals a sense of achievement and increase their feelings of being in control of their lives. When these goals are unachievable in our working lives, damage to an individual's health may result. Variety in our working life offers stimulation and challenge. When both goals are imposed and change unpredictable stress can occur for the individual. **Environmental clarity** is central to Warr's model. Warr describes it as 'the extent to which a person's environment is clear or opaque'. It has three aspects.

Environmental clarity comes from the feedback we receive on our behaviour from other people. Knowing we are behaving in the right manner gives us a sense of acceptability. Feedback in the workplace comes from appraisals and positive encouragements from our superiors. Clarity arises from our environment when we know we are knowledgeable about the people and the work setting we operate in. Often new people and new work systems can lead us to feel anxious as our environmental clarity becomes opaque. In addition, environmental clarity arises from clear social and normative expectations about roles and behaviour. Having clarity over the ways in which we are expected to behave in different situations can lead to positive mental health. When our environmental clarity is opaque, for example, in a new work setting or social setting, anxiety can again result. If the environment becomes too predictable over a long period of time, this can also lead to boredom, apathy, withdrawal, and depression.

Overall, Warr's model suggests that well-being increases with the availability of money, physical security, and valued social position. In addition, moderate levels of opportunity for control, opportunity for skill use, externally generated goals, variety, environmental clarity, and opportunities for interpersonal contact improve well-being.

Warr and Jackson (1985) undertook further research on unemployment and found links between unemployment and psychological ill-health in terms of increased anxiety and insomnia. Warr (1987b) began to highlight the link between unemployment and self-esteem. Warr indicated that having employment could influence both physical and mental health. In examining job-related mental health, well-being can be considered in terms of, for example job satisfaction, job-related anxiety, or job-related depression. The concept is sometimes called 'affective' well-being to emphasize the centrality of feelings. In particular, it is job-related well-being (people's feelings about themselves and their job) which is the focus of this section.

Warr (2002) explored the nature of mental well-being in depth. By examining job satisfaction, he noted that both overall job satisfaction and satisfaction linked to specific job aspects were linked to employee mental well-being.

Overall, the Vitamin Model provides a useful overview of the essential ingredients of meaningful work. It provides a mechanism for describing all job environments and also non-job environments, by seeing how far each environment possesses the nine determinants. The model further provides a useful basis for identifying interventions at the level of both the job and the organization with regard to job redesign initiatives.

Critique

However, it should be noted that Warr's research was based on male workers and does not consider the female perspective in relation to the meaning of work. In addition, the research was based on US, European, and Australasian samples and thus ignores alternative social and cultural attitudes. There are also a number of problems with the theory underpinning Warr's model. Assessing 'environmental clarity' is problematic and as Warr (1987b) noted there are differences between individuals and how each person perceives the nine determinants is variable. In addition, how each person experiences work and unemployment may be different depending on their life stage and individual circumstances.

Quantifying the different determinants is a difficult task for the psychologist or HR manager and hence measuring them and determining their importance is problematic, especially as job satisfaction is a complex matter. For some, social status will be more important, while for others money or lack of it will have an increased negative effect on individual psychological and physical mental health. For the soldier, status will be important, for the politician social standing is paramount, and for the doctor specialized use of skills is important. In contrast, the factory worker will perceive money and wages to be important. Hence, the importance of each determinant is hard to distinguish as the model is embedded in theory linked to job satisfaction and work motivation. Theories of motivation are discussed in Chapter 5.

Pause for thought
Look at each of the vitamins and ask yourself what determinants are present in your working life and which of the determinants are missing. How will your need for the different determinants change over time? What would be required for changes to occur?

KEY LEARNING POINTS

- Work contributes a number of psychological benefits to the individual.
- The effects of unemployment can result in the loss of these benefits.
- Loss of work is more than just an economic event as it impinges on the individual's well-being.
- Warr (1987b) comments on the damaging effect that certain jobs have. These determinants or factors are responsible for determining psychological health.

15.3.2 Jahoda's Deprivation Theory

The psychological consequences of unemployment vary from individual to individual and have repercussions on the families of the unemployed, both in terms of monetary income and psychological health. Jahoda 1958 began to explore unemployment by researching its effects in a small Austrian town which experienced the demise of its textile industry (the famous Marienthal study). Later, Jahoda (1958) drew attention to the psychological effects of unemployment in relation to the incidence of depression and apathy. As a result of this research, social policy was devised to take the unemployed into account.

Work by Jahoda et al. (1971) via triangulation studies (many studies pointing to the same conclusions) and early field work in Marienthal concluded that people move through universal mental states during unemployment. These states start with shock and culminate in a fatalistic outlook. Formal employment, they argued, gives meaning and structure to life, with unemployment impacting negatively upon mental, social, and intellectual capacities. Psychological reactions included demoralization, apathy, depression, disorientated time structure, reduced activity levels, and a decline in psychological well-being overall.

Jahoda (1979) highlighted the manifest function of employment (income) and latent functions of employment (structuring of time, socialization, goal achievement, personal identity, and enforced activity).

Jahoda found that psychological experiences affected:

- time structure—work imposed a time structure on the waking day (less for women due to domestic routines);
- social contact—work helped maintain social contacts with others outside the family;
- collective effort or purpose gave a sense of goal achievement;
- social identity or status was achieved via work;
- regular activity was lost when work was no longer enforced.

The theory assumes all jobs have these latent functions, irrespective of whether workers seek such functions in their jobs, and unemployment affects well-being as it deprives individuals of these experiences. Jahoda argues that when a person is deprived of these manifest and latent functions of employment, they can become psychologically impaired. Jahoda's view includes the concept that our reactions to loss of work are tied in with our view of the purpose of work. If a person's identity is very much tied up with their job, then the loss of job and damage to personal identity is much greater.

Since Jahoda's early work, other researchers have substantiated the links between unemployment and ill-heath as the issue was researched extensively in the 1980s. As Jahoda acknowledges research on unemployment needs to move away from the use of questionnaires which give approximations of unemployment experience to face-to-face questionnaire administration with follow-up interview questions.

Beale and Nethercott (1985) further demonstrated clear links between job loss and health. These researchers found perceptions of unemployment had already begun to facilitate the workers' deterioration in psychological health. Similarly, Trew and Kilpatrick's (1985) study of lifestyles and well-being among unemployed men in Northern Ireland found that those who had experienced reductions in entertainment and social activities had poor scores on the General Health Questionnaire (a questionnaire used to measure psychological well-being).

Critique

Though the model is persuasive, evidence supporting the importance of the five latent functions is scarce, and several studies have shown employed people in unsatisfactory jobs were no better off than the unemployed (Wanberg 1995). In addition, the financial consequences of unemployment are overlooked within this model. Another issue with the theory is that the model assumes that people are simply passive respondents to their employment situation. Jahoda ignores the fact that lack of money and contending with bureaucracy are two of the features of unemployment which contribute to feelings of lack of well-being.

15.3.3 Agency Restriction Theory

Fryer and Payne (1984) commented upon activity levels in relation to unemployment. Those individuals who had a reactive, passive orientation tended to deteriorate psychologically in comparison to individuals who had a more proactive, active orientation. Utilizing time in a structured manner and using energy in a creative and fulfilling way appears to once again buffer the effects of unemployment. This finding is also applicable to retired individuals. Embracing unemployment in a positive way can help to reduce pessimism and fatalism.

In 1984, Fryer and Payne developed 'Agency Restriction Theory', which suggests that unemployment has negative consequences because it restricts personal agency. Unemployment stops people doing what they would like to do as it deprives them of income. Furthermore, the ability to act as a consumer is lost. Since many people do not know how long unemployment will last, the ability to set goals is lost and uncertainty regarding the future is increased. However, empirical support for these ideas is limited.

Fryer and Fagan (1993) comments that research on unemployment needs to include more qualitative research to explore the process of unemployment effects, interventions, and counselling. New theoretical innovations are further called for and ethical innovation noted in relation to research practice, whereby unemployed people would initiate the research, define its scope and purpose, control the research, and finally evaluate and interpret the results.

Fryer maintains that many official intervention programmes aimed at helping the unemployed only increase the mental health costs of unemployment. Later reviews of the research on the psychological experience of being unemployed (Fryer 1998a) conclude that unemployed people tend to experience lower levels of personal happiness, life satisfaction, self-esteem, and psychological well-being in comparison to experiences when in employment. Recent evidence suggests long-term unemployment can reduce life expectancy by as much as two to three years depending on when the person was made redundant or left work.

Fryer (1998a) later criticized conventional treatments of unemployment for taking an overly passive and negative view of the person. The psychological effects of unemployment are, he argues, the result of frustrated attempts to create a better future rather than memories and regrets of loss.

KEY LEARNING POINTS

- The psychological effects of unemployment were highlighted by Jahoda in relation to depression and apathy.
- The manifest function of unemployment such as income and the latent functions of employment include planning time, activities, socializing, achieving goals, and having a personal identity.
- Unemployment stops people doing what they would like to do as it deprives them of income.

15.3.4 Research in the 1990s

Whelan et al. (1991) reported how the unemployed gradually become deprived of even the basic necessities and fall into poverty and negative mental health states. The effects were greater when low **social support** was reported. Mental illness, alcohol abuse, drug taking, and increased suicide rates were further highlighted. According to Whelan's analysis, unemployment has its effect on mental health mediated via lifestyle choices. With unemployment, there is lack of income and thus lifestyle deprivation and poverty. Unemployed people are viewed to adapt by Whelan, that is 'resigned adaptation' takes place whereby the unemployed person can cope by gradually withdrawing from job seeking and avoiding new situations, so as to take on the role and identity of the long-term unemployed person. By wanting less, they achieve less and eventually become less.

The experience of unemployment will vary depending on the individual's age, gender, income, social support, reason for job loss, commitment to employment, and expectations of returning to work (Winefield 1995). Winefield shows that financial security enables people to cope better with unemployment; the middle aged seem to cope less well than younger or older people, yet this is dependent on access to social support from family and friends.

Later research by Wanberg et al. 2001, reports that poor well-being was associated with more financial hardship, echoing the research of the 1990s.

Murphy and Athanasou (1999) reviewed sixteen studies of unemployment from the 1980s and 1990s and found moving involuntarily from employment to unemployment was associated with reduced well-being scores with regaining employment increasing such scores considerably. This suggests regaining employment may lead to better overall well-being in contrast to pre-unemployed status. Once again, individual coping strategies can not be ignored (Kinicki et al. 2000).

Studies by Dooley and Prause (1995) and Italian/French research by Fraccaroli et al. (1994) provide evidence of the link between unemployment and self-esteem (how good we feel about ourselves). Measures of self-esteem were taken for school leavers and compared to their later scores when they were in satisfying jobs or unemployed. Self-esteem was found to increase considerably for those in satisfying jobs. Fraccaroli views unemployment as part of a process model in which a young person has to maintain an acceptable social identity as part of the process of growing up; unemployment can effect the development of this social identity and consequently damage self-esteem.

Feather (1990) concludes that financial hardship and economic deprivation set limits to the extent to which the unemployed person can fulfil needs and values and move towards important future goals.

Ezzy (2001) argues there are three types of job loss narratives that can be identified when someone loses their job; these stories show whether someone will become depressed as a consequence of unemployment. The respondents described the job loss as either a romance, a tragedy, or a more complex story. Positive accounts were viewed as romantic and liberating experiences; alternative accounts were tragic whereby the experience of unemployment was painful and traumatic. Other accounts of job loss revealed the complexity of analysis of the effect of unemployment on the individual.

Kalimo et al. (2002) conducted research on work and well-being in Finland. The aim of their longitudinal research was to recognize the work and personal factors that predicted well-being. From the empirical analysis of survey data and follow-up data, well-being was determined in terms of psychological and physiological symptoms of strain. They concluded that strong personal resources, especially a strong sense of coherence, seemed to protect workers from strain and to maintain well-being at work. At work, factors related to social support and appreciation from colleagues and superiors act as important resources for maintaining well-being. The work was further supported by other Finnish researchers.

Salmela-Aro and Nurmi (2002) explored motivational orientation to work, life, and well-being. Data from **white-collar** employees revealed that workers who had high work orientations were more prone to workaholism and low well-being. In contrast, workers with strong hobby and health orientations to work and life had higher levels of well-being.

Eggers (2006) studied the effect of regional unemployment rates on well-being in post-Soviet Russia. Research in Europe and the USA found that higher unemployment rates lead to lower reported life satisfaction whereas the Russian research contrasted this. They concluded that when individuals observe their peers suffering in a troubled economy, they lowered their expectations and standards and so they perceived themselves to be better off in worse times. Hence individual perceptions affect measures of subjective well-being.

Overall, the relationship between unemployment and health remains. There are several main consequences following from the state of unemployment. These include a feeling of material loss due to lack of money, reduction in social contacts, changing self-concept and self-identity, lower self-esteem, stereotyping from society, decreased physical health, and decreased psychological well-being.

However, Driskell (1997) notes how more recent research on unemployment has not made a fundamental difference, in preventing job loss for several reasons. Firstly, studies of the psychological states of the unemployed identify the effects of job loss but do not address reasons for job loss. Secondly, the theoretical content of unemployment research is problematic (see section 15.3.5). Thirdly, recent studies do not appear to be adding to the debate, as earlier research on the issue was successful in its conclusions.

 KEY LEARNING POINTS

- It is evident that for most people, unemployment can lead to deterioration in psychological well-being and physical health.
- The impact of unemployment on mental health is indirect and largely the result of long-term financial hardship.
- Psychological distress can arise from a cycle of marginalized labour positions and economic disadvantage.

15.3.5 Methodological issues and unemployment research

Cross-sectional studies undertaken at different times may suggest that while unemployment figures rise, mental health problems increase. Undertaking group comparisons is not without its problems, comparing the employed and unemployed means that you are not really comparing similar groups and so much confounding of the data is possible, as there are many reasons why a person may be unemployed which will effect their mental well-being. A Dutch study controlling for prior health problems in an unemployed group, when compared to an employed group, still showed a difference in mental health (Iverson and Sarboe 1988).

However, longitudinal studies provide stronger evidence because any real changes in people can be observed. West and Sweeting (1996) conducted a longitudinal study by interviewing over 1,000 young people at the ages of 15, 18, and 21. They reported quite high amounts of physical and mental health problems in the sample. The study allowed for the impact of unemployment on mental health over time. Overall, well-being was lower for the unemployed young people in comparison to employed people of similar ages. The research further indicated that 7–9 per cent of the group had made attempts at suicide.

Epidemiological studies have further produced interesting data on unemployment and mental health. Certainly, epidemiological research has revealed the wider social effects of unemployment. For example, Brenner and Mooney (1983) reported increases in mortality, increases in suicide, increases in mental hospital admissions, and increases in criminal activity all coincided with increased unemployment in the recession of 1973–4. Such aggregates of data from epidemiological studies do need to be treated with caution as many other factors may be affecting the final figures. However, it does appear that as unemployment increases, so does mortality rate.

15.4 Underemployment

Often people may be in jobs where little effort or exertion is actually required due to the context of the job. In addition, a person may not have enough work to do because of a mismatch between available work and staff resources, Having not enough work can lead to a person feeling underemployed. This is **underemployment**.

People in this position will often feel vulnerable and report feeling stress as boredom and monotony increase their vulnerability in unstable economic environments. In 1986, O'Brien noted that a large proportion of the workforce report that they are underemployed. Underemployment remains of interest to psychologists as new technology increases the deskilling of workers and increasing educational standards result in individuals taking jobs for which they are overeducated or overqualified. Winefield (2002) reviews recent literature on the psychological aspects of work, unemployment, and underemployment in Australia. He examines different notions of 'work', including paid employment and unpaid work such as volunteer work.

Chapter 15
The loss of work

Winefield draws attention to the well-documented negative effects of unemployment and underemployment and the corresponding benefits of having work. Winefield's research looks at different age groups and the psychological health costs of being employed in the light of the changing nature of work pressures.

Nabi (2003) notes how graduate employment continues to be a serious and growing problem in the UK and examines the opportunity for skill use and career success amongst underemployed graduates. Appropriately employed graduates (those who were in jobs for which they required their degree) were used as a comparison group. From questionnaire data, the research suggests that underemployed graduates reported significantly lower levels of opportunity for skill use and career success.

Dooley (2003) points out that the amount of research into the relationships between well-being and economically inadequate employment is extremely limited. It is noted that young people from minority ethnic communities are most vulnerable to underemployment.

Dooley (2004) goes beyond the usual focus on unemployment and explores the health effects of other kinds of underemployment, including such forms of inadequate employment as involuntary part-time and poverty wage work. The study compares falling into unemployment versus inadequate employment relative to remaining adequately employed. The study highlights the link between underemployment and low self-esteem and depression and alcohol abuse. A key strength of the research is the use of longitudinal panel data, cross-level effects, and cross-generational analysis. The research supports the emergence of a new way of conceptualizing employment status as a continuum ranging from good jobs to bad jobs with implications for policy on work and health.

Work underload is a serious cause of stress in the workplace resulting from the underutilization of worker abilities and skills. When workers are not creatively stimulated, frustration can result and eventually this leads to stress and alienation from the organization.

15.5 Redundancy

The experience of **redundancy** can be devastating and often the experience has been compared to grief or bereavement. Warr (1987b) defined stages of psychological states experienced following job loss. It was noted that the first three months of unemployment are the most stressful, after that time, the unemployed person is likely to adjust and gradually adapt themselves to the new unemployed role by establishing new routines and getting accustomed to living on a reduced budget (Warr 1987b; Warr and Jackson 1984).

15.5.1 Grieving Cycle

The phase model of unemployment and redundancy or the 'Grieving Cycle' dates from work undertaken in the 1930s on the Great Depression and has not been developed much over time. It is essentially a model of bereavement which applies to individuals' experiences of unemployment, redundancy, and retirement. Essentially an individual would experience a series of emotional mental states including shock, optimism, pessimism, acceptance or fatalism, and finally acceptance (Eisenberg and Lazarsfeld 1938).

The stages of the model

    A life prior to unemployment/redundancy/retirement

    B loss and shock to unemployment/redundancy/retirement

    C various emotional reactions (anger, anxiety, depression)

    D onset of grieving process as in a family bereavement

    E change and action planning for the future

    F rebuilding one's life

    G healthy grieving.

Reactions to job loss and redundancy are described in terms of a sequence of stages similar to the process of grieving. If these stages were clearly evident, then there could be clear implications for the counselling process; though there is some longitudinal evidence which suggests there is a lack of direct confirmation for the stages of the model, and the phases are not substantiated by longitudinal research evidence (Archer and Rhodes 1987). Overall, reactions to unemployment, redundancy, and retirement can be viewed as a broad array of emotional changes from shock, disbelief, optimism to realization and acceptance. Individual reactions which the model does not identify cannot be ignored. Still, much outplacement counselling seems to be predicated on the assumption that the stage model is a valid description of a person's reaction to redundancy (Kidd 1996).

KEY LEARNING POINTS

- People will differ in their reactions to redundancy but most will experience psychological distress.
- Everyone goes through a sequence of identifiable stages of grief and will need help to deal with feelings of loss.
- Occupational psychologists need to focus on helping individuals deal with grief and skills reassessment in relation to training. The grief model can act as a useful framework but there will be individual differences.

Activity How do you handle changes?

- If you or a family member have been unemployed (when you really wanted to work), how did it affect you or them? (Positive and negative reactions?)
- What helped you to get through this period in your life?
- What do you think the benefits of unemployment could be?
- What do you think might help people to get through unemployment or redundancy?
- What would you do if you were made redundant?
- How do you think occupational psychology can help those who are, or might be unemployed or made redundant?

Activity How would you handle redundancy?

Try to imagine what it would be like to lose your job, or to have to drop out of university. How do you think you might cope? Try this questionnaire to see what difficulties you may face in such a situation. For each statement, indicate:

1 Most of the time

2 Sometimes

3 Rarely.

- My success at work/university is due entirely to my own efforts.
- I welcome new and difficult tasks.
- I spend far too much time on my work.
- I have someone I work with or study with who I can talk to about anything.
- I never have enough time to finish everything I want to do.
- I often wake up at night worrying about my workload.
- If there is a disagreement about my work or study, I rely on my own judgement.

Add up the numbers next to the statements. The higher the score, the more difficult you may find it if you are made redundant or lose your job. A score of 14+ suggests that you will find redundancy particularly stressful. This questionnaire does not prove you could not cope, it is merely an indicator. Redundancy affects people in different ways and how you react to this, as in all life situations, depends on many things. These include social support, family life, your own personality, and what other skills you have learnt that could be transferred to a new job.

15.5.2 Survivor syndrome

The term '**survivor syndrome**' has come to be used to describe the reactions and behaviours of those who remain in employment following redundancy. These include shock, betrayal, distress, animosity towards management, concern about their colleagues who have departed, and guilt that they still have a job. These feelings may lead to low morale and reduced organizational commitment. Doherty et al. (1995) confirms the existence of this pattern. In a study of large-scale downsizing in a telecommunications company, it was found that the survivors experienced the threat of job loss and increased workload and stress levels. Later work by Herriot and Pemberton (1995) explores survivor syndrome based on violations of the 'psychological contract' between individuals and their employers. They suggest that the old psychological contract—defined as the exchange deal which each party has with the other—of employee loyalty for employment security has been violated and has all but disappeared and been replaced by a much less favourable deal. This is viewed as unfair by employees as they battle with increasing workloads, trust issues ,and feelings of powerlessness resulting from inequity.

KEY LEARNING POINT

- Working with organizational systems is vital in helping the survivors of redundancy.

15.6 Retirement

Retirement is a time when, for most people, there is a temporary or permanent withdrawal from the labour market after having experienced a number of years of work. It may be a time when the retired person can feel excluded from paid employment and experience a drop in income. Individual perceptions of retirement can vary. For some, retirement marks the start of old age, it can be viewed as a depressing time, while for others it can be a positive and liberating experience. In the light of recent government legislation which has extended the retirement age for both sexes, retirement is now expected to occur much later than the traditional ages of between 60 and 65.

Some professional workers remain employed until they are older or take semi-retirement, others prefer to stop working at a much younger age depending on their overall monetary income and pension plan.

15.6.1 Atchley's Model

Atchley (1991) has devised a model that suggests there are seven phases to describe an individual's approach to retirement (Figure 15.2). The model presents a description of the retirement process. It is not a stage-by-stage account and, depending on individual circumstances, retirement will be perceived and experienced in different ways.

It is difficult to distinguish between the consequences of retirement and redundancy in relation to physical and mental health. Certainly, older people are more prone to physical illness as the body deteriorates with age.

Figure 15.2. Atchley's retirement model

Remote	Retirement is along time away and is not mentally considered
Near retirement	The individual makes plans and considers the future as retirement approaches
The honeymoon phase	Retirement occurs and new-found freedom is enjoyed
Disenchantment	Initial enjoyment reduces and expectations regarding retirement do not come to fruition
Reorientation	Individual reviews life and starts to adapt
Stability	Individual has adapted and feels secure in their physical and psychological surroundings
Terminal	Retirement phase ends and individual returns to work or prepares for death depending on individual mobility and health

Source: Adapted from Atchley (1991).

In Western countries, people aged 60 and over represent the fastest growing segment of society. Research into retirement shows the importance of well-being of engaging in enjoyable activity. Maintaining social contacts and warding off isolation can reduce the risks of mental ill-health (Townsend 1957). Research suggests those who stay active physically and mentally following retirement can extend their life expectancy considerably (McGoldrick 1982). Furthermore, positive individual perceptions of retirement can dramatically affect the quality of a person's life following retirement. Recent work by Kloep and Hendry (2007) reviews research on retirement and draws on their earlier work from 2006 on life transitions, where they concluded that the retired can fall into three main groups. There are those who find retirement highly distressful; those who perceived work as giving them high social status but gradually adjust to retirement; and finally those who see life beyond retirement and work and adjust well due to their hobbies and pre-existing social activities.

 **Activity** Discuss and debate

How flexible should transitions to retirement be? Who should decide? The state, work organizations, or the individual? If early planning for retirement was possible, when should it start and what should it consist of?

15.6.2 Volunteerism

It is estimated that half a million people are involved in work in the voluntary sector. Levels of voluntary work are high and can help give insights into the changing nature of work and unemployment. Engaging in voluntary work is an activity undertaken by all classes of people. The affluent may engage in voluntary work to improve their social network (Williams 2002).

Others engage in voluntary work as they want to look after the disadvantaged as carers or join in with local community projects. Some volunteers work for a few hours a week and others volunteer full time. Some, particularly for the middle aged, rebuild their lives through volunteering, left void from redundancy, retirement, bereavement, or unemployment. Volunteering gives people the opportunity to maintain self-identity.

Volunteering also provides new opportunities and challenges. By gaining new experiences, skills, and work aspiration, voluntary work is viewed as a means of finding new alternative employment for those who want it. However, it must be noted that voluntary work can be difficult and demanding and is unpaid. Voluntary work can also provide a 'career space'. It provides an opportunity to balance working and non-work life; it can also provide an alternative career for those with employment.

Driskell (1997) noted individuals engaged in a wide range of individual or group volunteer services helping people in their homes, hospitals, libraries, and schools illustrate that

 Case illustration
The National Caring Bank

Encouraging staff to do voluntary work appears to improve their well-being and become more rounded and capable individuals, and overall better employees. Supporting staff to give back to the community is encouraged in a number of ways. Supplementing charitable payroll deductions, supporting fund-raising activities, charity support grants, and secondments in community organizations are all ways the bank encourages staff to help the local community. Staff can also spend half a day a month working for a volunteer programme. In return, the staff are happy to be working for a bank that appears to be caring for the local community. When staff go on secondments, they learn to work with a broader range of people and successful negotiation can be improved. The bank is thinking of developing the work of the social responsibility unit by setting up partnerships with organizations that provide education and conservation.

volunteerism can be one way to make retirement meaningful and enjoyable. For some the transition from work to retirement is smooth. For others, the loss of regular activity, time structure, goals and purpose, and an identity which was largely enforced by employment may reduce well-being. Some experience of a balanced work and leisure lifestyle can help to meet the challenge of retirement, however.

If retirement is voluntary and the person has high self-esteem, then retirement can be a very happy and rewarding time. Well-being generally remains more positive for the retired person as retirement is viewed as an appropriate culmination of working life.

Pause for thought
Discuss the positive and negative effects of the following **life event**s—unemployment, redundancy, and retirement—on the individual.

15.7 Practical implications for occupational psychologists

This section will start by examining what counselling in the workplace is and why there is a need for counselling at work. The various types of welfare provisions available for the unemployed, redundant, and retired will be indicated.

15.7.1 Workplace counselling

Counselling in the workplace is now a well-established professional practice in both the UK and other countries throughout the world. It is a defined, task-focused activity with identifiable outcomes. The provision of counselling at work can be varied and has direct cost benefits to organizations in relation to enhancing staff relations and ensuing positive perceptions of the organization within the eyes of its employees.

Counselling is concerned with personal development and growth. It concerns relationship problems and individuals usually see counsellors to get feedback on how they interact with other people and to gain emotional self-understanding.

Workplace counsellors are qualified and trained individuals who can utilize **counselling skills** but who are knowledgeable about various psychological theories and therapies that underpin personal development and psychological change. Most organizational counsellors are trained in clinical or counselling psychology (British Psychological Society—BPS) or have acquired advanced therapeutic skills accredited by either the UKCP (United Kingdom Council for Psychotherapy) or the BACP (British Association for Counselling and Psychotherapy).

The problems employees experience in the workplace are varied and most problems at home can affect work performance. The associated emotional responses of individuals to personal problems can be varied too. Counselling at work can be delivered internally, where the counsellor is an employee of the organization, or externally, by specialist outside consultants. Counselling provision may entail face-to-face counselling, telephone counselling, group work, referral to specialist agencies, information/advice service (debt and legal issues) and training.

Internally delivered counselling can include face-to-face counselling and/or telephone counselling and is usually limited to a fixed number of sessions per employee and/or family

Case illustration
Mary

Mary is married with two children. She has come to counselling to discuss her emotions as she is going through a very bitter divorce. Her husband is an alcoholic and has been in and out of work for many years. Mary is finding it very hard to continue in her full-time position and balance her childcare provision. She is under extra pressure as a colleague has recently left and has not been replaced. This has led to Mary's workload increasing and a lack of line manager support.

members. The service's proximity to the organization could be a potential threat to confidentiality, particularly when it is situated on site and managed by a human resource function. Some managers may feel threatened by such a service in relation to the pastoral element of their managerial role.

Externally provided services can also provide face-to-face counselling and/or telephone counselling which is usually limited to a fixed number of sessions per employee and/or family members. The service provider may have an advice and consultancy function too.

15.7.2 Counselling in the context of unemployment

In Britain, the Employment Service uses occupational psychology to address unemployment in two main ways. Occupational psychology assessments are undertaken on a small group with special needs and advice is given to the Employment Service staff concerning the design and delivery of services aimed at returning the unemployed to work. Stansfield (2001) presents an agenda for action by encouraging further engagement of occupational psychologist in the Employment Service. He concludes that occupational psychology research has lost impetus while professional practice to support those needing work has not expanded to match the growth of occupational psychology services responding to the interests of employing organizations. He comments on the need to tackle unemployment in its wider social context rather than in relation to the specific issue of joblessness, reconsidering the nature of work as the expression of human activity, and to address the current imbalance between individual, managerial, and governmental needs in the job recruitment processes. Advocating job redesign and individual counselling for employees to reduce the harmful effects of damaging jobs are two of Warr's (2002) suggestions.

15.7.3 Counselling in the context of redundancy

This is a main area of counselling provision in the workplace. It encompasses advice, information, and guidance. Services are usually provided to employees following the initial notice of redundancy and workshops are often held to help individuals deal with the emotional loss of work and find ways of coping. Job-hunting skills training may be delivered and financial advisers provided in relation to severance packages. The counsellors may be specialists in career development and can help employees to find a way of moving forward and move towards their next work opportunity. Kidd (1996) comments on how many organizations offer their employees outplacement services covering personal counselling, support, and career counselling.

Counselling includes:

- Financial review and implications.
- Access to social support.
- Promoting self-esteem building to deal with loss/grief and develop new attribution styles.
- Fostering of social support networks for men and women facing redundancy.
- Job-hunting techniques are often discussed in group work and resources for CV writing and job applications provided.

Dealing with survivors of the redundancy by offering career counselling, social support building, assertiveness training, and employee involvement initiatives.

Kidd (1996) indicates that occupational psychologist need to address the issues of those left within the organization or the 'survivors' of redundancy by working with organizational systems as well as individuals. Systematic thinking is vital in addressing the broader aspects of organizational functioning in relation to the implementation of counselling initiatives.

15.7.4 Pre-retirement counselling

Retirement can be viewed as a process of bereavement or loss. Losing one's job also means that a large part of self-identity or self-worth is also lost. Counselling can help individuals prepare for the transition from work to non-work activities. It can also help individuals prepare

> **Pause for thought**
> What are the benefits of managers using counselling skills in the workplace? What conflicts of interest might arise if managers attempt to offer pure counselling to their employees?

for retirement and think about the effects of retirement on their emotions and their life. Retirement is a major life transition. By focusing upon the transition cycle, different phases of the job loss scenario can be explored (Millward 2005).

Counselling will focus on:

- Shock and disbelief.
- Exploring how disruption from the change can be managed, temporarily retreating from the change to gather strength.
- Dealing with feelings of depression, adapting to the change, handling emotions
- Accepting reality and letting go of the past, thinking about the future.
- Testing out new ideas.
- Seeking new meaning in the things which are important in life.
- Internalization and integration of meaning into behaviour.

The counsellor will help the individual to harness their growth and potential. Retirement counselling will often consider financial, occupational history, time, and leisure issues.

DuBrin (2000) advocates a need for individuals, whether they are unemployed, redundant, or retired to focus on '**wellness**'. Wellness is a state of mental and physical well-being that makes it possible to function at one's highest potential. The focus on wellness as a formal approach to preventative healthcare is part of the new tradition of 'Positive Psychology', that is psychology which emphasizes the positive nature of human behaviour.

Chapter summary

- Having paid work in the form of a job is a central aspect of our identity.
- The relationship between unemployment and underemployment is not always clear cut.
- Throughout the life cycle there are recognizable transition points, into and out of the world of work.
- This chapter has looked at the meaning of work for the individual and has given an overview of Warr's nine factors, suggesting that work can be an important determinant of mental health. These determinants are categorized as constant effect determinants which can exist in excess and additional decrement determinants which can become damaging to health if they exist in excess.
- The chapter has focused on health and work. It has referred to classical research by Warr, Jahoda, Beale and Nethercott, and Atchely. The effects of unemployment on physical and mental health have been highlighted.
- Unemployment, redundancy, and retirement can effect us all and so coping strategies are essential if we are to stay in control of the situation and maintain positive morale.
- People can have many reactions to unemployment which are dependent on different factors including surrounding social environment as well as previous levels of health and mental well-being. Individual self-esteem, how important work is to us and how we view our work identity are crucial intermediate factors in our reactions to unemployment.
- Unemployment and redundancy can be a negative experience for a person, whereas retirement can be a positive experience.
- Retirement or lack of work can be extremely beneficial for the individual for people at the end of their working life, as retirement has an honourable status.
- Voluntary work is undertaken by individuals from all different backgrounds for many reasons; to gain new skills, build confidence, fill time as a result of being made redundant. It is a great way of being part of the work environment while helping others.

- Complications in sampling and individual differences within overall trends must be taken into account.
- Government agencies and business organizations have become more proactive in dealing with unemployed and redundant workers by establishing workplace counselling provisions.

Assess your learning

Review questions

1 What is the significance of work to the individual?

2 List Warr's essential vitamins for a healthy working life.

3 How has job-related well-being been assessed by psychologists?

4 In what ways do people react over time to being unemployed?

5 Are there any benefits for an individual if they unemployed?

6 How can the unemployed be helped by psychologists?

7 What methodological issues need to be considered when studying unemployment?

8 What is underemployment?

9 What are the stages of retirement which an individual may experience?

10 What welfare provision might be provided for the unemployed, redundant, and retired?

Assignments

ASSIGNMENT 1: Redundancy and unemployment

- What are the personal and social consequences of unemployment? Are the consequences different for different groups of individuals?
- Unemployment is associated with psychological distress. Discuss.
- How is a manager's reaction to redundancy the same or different to another worker?
- How might the unemployment figures be massaged by the government?
- What do we know about those who work on the side.
- What is the effect on organizational performance and effectiveness, if enforced redundancy or early retirement reduces the number of older workers?
- What methodological problems are associated with research on unemployment?
- What are the similarities and differences between unemployment and retirement?

ASSIGNMENT 2: Unemployment investigation

Using National Statistics on unemployment for your area and by talking to people you know:

- Consider the unemployment situation in your area, how serious is the problem? What has been the response of the local community and local agencies? What resources are available?
- Ask a person who has been unemployed for a long time how it has affected them, their lifestyle, and the opportunities for their family.
- Talk to a selection of different people who have experienced unemployment, redundancy, and retirement. How do their situations compare in terms of some of the things mentioned in this chapter?

Further reading

Chmiel, N. (2002) *Introduction to Work and Organisational Psychology: A European Perspective.* Oxford: Blackwell Publishers.
An excellent book which has a very good chapter on Job Performance and Ageing Workforce, written by Peter Warr.

Kieselbach, T., Winefield, A .H., Boyd, C., and Anderson, S. (2006) *Unemployment and Health: International and Interdisciplinary Perspectives.* Brisbane: Australian Academic Press.
This outstanding new book provides a rare insight into ground-breaking comprehensive research from Europe, Australia, Asia, and the United States on the health impact of unemployment on the individual and the community.

Work psychology in practice
Cartwrights

Cartwrights is a large retail outlet with branches in most towns and cities. Over the next few years, a large proportion of staff will be reaching retirement age and leaving the organization. In addition, it is rumoured that Cartwrights are going to close certain branches where profit has not been achieved. This would lead to large-scale redundancies in towns considered to be deprived.

Despite these changes to staff levels and composition, Cartwights has plans to develop more welfare provision within the organization and undertake more networking and local community work. The organization wants to demonstrate how it is a socially responsible employer by supporting local community networks, action groups, and agencies, particularly in areas where there is high unemployment.

Cartwrights wants to enhance its communication channels on all fronts to help release the emotional unrest which has been increasing for some time. Developing work relationships based on mutual trust, respect, and effective communication will help to reduce emotional tensions. This can be achieved by the introduction of an individual counselling service and group counselling sessions (known as sensitivity training) whereby skilled counsellors can work with different teams from across the organization. The basic objectives of group and individual counselling are similar. Both seek to help individuals achieve self-direction, integration, and self-responsibility. Understanding their motivations and behaviours will assist employees to work more effectively together as teams and to communicate with each other in a respectful way.

Learning about group dynamics, communication styles, counselling skills, decision making, role playing, and conflict management will assist employees to learn about the perceptual processes and dynamics of groups. The group situation will provide experience of intimacy with others and realization that other people have similar problems and feelings. The counsellors would be able to reflect on the nature of the individual/group problems within Cartwrights and make policy recommendations. Cartwrights could also establish an internal counselling resource pool of people from all levels of the organization who have been trained in basic counselling skills and are available for a proportion of time per week. The possession of counselling skills by people within the organization might increase their ability to provide career development, increase management competence in dealing with human emotions, and promote a more open climate in which individuals could feel able to confront themselves and others about problems causing concern.

Questions

- How might Cartwrights utilize sensitivity training to help those individuals who are facing retirement?
- What provision needs to be made for staff in the event of notifications of redundancy?
- What might Cartwrights do to help local communities, particularly where there is high unemployment?
- What resistance might occur in Cartwrights with regard to the introduction of a counselling service?

@ Online Resource Centre

Visit the supporting online resource centre for additional material which will help you with your research, essays, and assignments, or you may find these additional resources helpful when revising for exams.
http://www.oxfordtextbooks.co.uk/orc/matthewman/

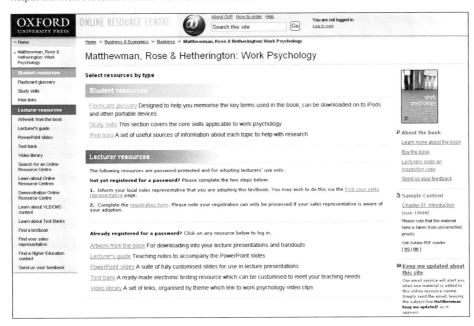

References

Archer, J., and Rhodes, V. (1987) Bereavement and reactions to job loss: a comparative review. *British Journal of Social Psychology*, 26: 211–24.

Atchley, R. C. (1991) *Social Forces and Aging: An Introduction to Social Gerontology* (6th edn.). Belmont, CA: Wadsworth.

Baltes, P. B., and Baltes, M. M. (1990) *Successful Ageing*. Cambridge: Cambridge University Press.

Baltes, P. B., Reece, H. W., and Lipsitt, L. P. (1990) Lifespan developmental psychology. *Annual Review of Psychology*, 31: 65–110.

Beale, N., and Nethercott, S. (1985) Job loss and family morbidity: a study of factory closure. *Journal of the College of General Practitioners*, 35: 510–14.

Brenner, M. H., and Mooney, A. (1983) Unemployment and health in the context of economic change. *Social Science and Medicine*, 17: 1125–38.

Brenner, S. O., and Starrin, B. (1988) Unemployment and health in Sweden: public issues and private troubles. *Journal of Social issues*, 44/4 (Special issue, *Psychological Effects of Unemployment*): 125–40.

Callender, C. (1987) Women seeking work. In S. Fineman (ed.), *Unemployment: Personal and Social Consequences*. London: Tavistock, ch. 3.

Doherty, N., Bank, J., and Vinnicombe, S. (1995) Managing survivors: the experience of survivors in BT and the British financial sector. Paper presented at New Deals conference, City University.

Dooley, D., and Prause, J. (1995) Effect of unemployment on school leavers' self-esteem. *Journal of Occupational and Organizational Psychology*, 68: 177–92.

Driskell, L. (1997) *Adventures in Senior Living: Learn How to Make Retirement Meaningful and Enjoyable*. New York: Haworth Pastoral Press.

DuBrin, A. J. (2000) *Applying Psychology: Individual and Organizational Effectiveness* (5th edn.). Englewood Cliffs, NJ: Prentice Hall.

Eisenberg, P., and Lazarsfeld, P. F. (1938) *The Psychological Effects of Unemployment*. Wakefield: E. P. Publishing.

Feather, N. T. (1990) *The Psychological Impact of Unemployment*. New York: Springer-Verlag.

Fineman, S. (1983) *White Collar Unemployment*. Chichester: Wiley.

Fowler, A. (1999) *Managing Redundancy: Developing Practice*. London: CIPD.

Fraccaroli, F., Le Blanc, A., and Hajjar, V. (1994) Social self-description and affective well being in young unemployed people: a comparative study. *European Work and Organizational Psychologist*, 4/2: 81–100.

Fryer, D. M. (1997). International perspectives on youth unemployment and mental health: some critical issues. *Journal of Adolescence*, 20: 333–42.

Fryer, D. M. (1998a) Labour market disadvantage, deprivation and mental health. In P. Drenth and H. Thierry (eds.), *Handbook of Work and Organisational Psychology*. Hove: Psychology Press/ Erlbaum, ii. 215–27.

Fryer, D. M. (1998b) The simultaneity of the unsimultaneous: a conversation between Marie Jahoda and David Fryer. *Journal of Community and Applied Social Psychology*, 8: 89–100.

Fryer, D. M., and Fagan, R. (1993) Coping with unemployment. *International Journal of Political Economy*, 23/3: 95–120.

Fryer, D. M., and Payne, R. L. (1984) Proactivity in unemployment: findings and implications. *Leisure Studies*, 3: 273–95.

Iverson, L., and Sarboe, S. (1988) Psychological well being amongst unemployed and employed people after a company closedown: a longitudinal study. *Journal of Social Issues*, 44: 141–52.

Jahoda, M. (1958) *Work, Employment and Unemployment: A Social Psychological Analysis.* Cambridge: Cambridge University Press.

Jahoda, M. (1982) *Employment and Unemployment.* Cambridge: Cambridge University Press.

Jahoda, M., Lazarsfeld, P. F., and Zeisal, H. (1971) *Marienthal: The Sociology of an Unemployed Community.* New York: Aldine-Atherton.

Haworth, J. (1999) The Challenge of Retirement. Book review. *The Psychologist: The British Psychological Society*, 12/1: 14.

Herriot, P., and Pemberton, C. (1995) *New Deals: The Revolution in Managerial Careers.* Chichester: Wiley.

Hodson, C. (2001) *Psychology and Work*, London: Routledge.

The Industrial Society (1999) Managing redundancy. *Managing Best Practice—The Regular Benchmark*, 65.

Jick, T. (1979) Mixing qualitative and quantitative methods: triangulation in action. *Administrative Science Quarterly*, Dec./24: 602–11.

Kalimo, R., Pahkin, K., and Mutanen, P. (2002) Work and personal resources as long term predictors of well-being. *Stress and Health*, 18: 227–34.

Kesse, E. (1997) Reducing unemployment. *The Psychologist: The British Psychological Society.*

Kidd, J. M. (1996) Counselling in the context of redundancy and unemployment. In S. Palmer and G. McMahon (1997) *Handbook of Counselling in Britain.* London: Routledge.

Kinicki, A. J., Prussia, G. E., and McKee Ryan, F. M. (2000) A panel study of coping with involuntary job loss. *Academy of Management Journal*, 65: 89–100.

Kloep, M., and Hendry, L. B. (2007) Retirement: a new beginning? *The Psychologist*, 20/12: 742–5.

McGoldrick, A. (1982) Early retirement: a new leisure opportunity. *Work and Leisure* (Leisure Studies Association Series), 15: 73–99.

Millward, L. (2005) *Understanding Occupational and Organisational Psychology.* Beverly Hills, CA: Sage.

Moser, K. A., Fox, A. J., and Jones, D. R. (1984) Unemployment and mortality in the OPSC longitudinal study. *The Lancet*, 1: 365–7.

Murphy, G. C., and Athanasou, J. A. (1999) The effect of unemployment on mental health. *Journal of Occupational and Organisational Psychology*, 72: 83–99.

Nabi, G. R. (2003) Graduate employment and underemployment: opportunity for skills use and career experiences amongst recent business graduates. *Education and Training*, 45/7: 371–82.

O'Brien, G. (1986) *Psychology of Work and Unemployment.* Chichester: Wiley.

Pahl, R. (1984) *Division of Labour.* Oxford: Blackwell.

Platt, S. (1984) Unemployment and suicidal behaviour: a review of the literature. *Social Science and Medicine*, 19/2: 93–115.

Robinson, W. S. (1950) Ecological considerations and the behaviour of individuals. *American Sociological Review*, 15: 352–7.

Salmela-Aro, K., and Nurmi, J.-E. (2002) Employees' motivational orientation and well-being at work. *Journal of Organisational Change Management*, 17/5: 471–89.

Seabrook, J. (1982) *Unemployment.* London: Quartet Books.

Sutton, C., Utting, D., and Farringdon, D. (2006) Nipping criminality in the bud. *The Psychologist*, 19/8: 470–5.

Stansfield, F. (2001) Using occupational psychology to help the jobless: a case of underemployment. *The Occupational Psychologist: The British Psychological Society*, 44: 9–13.

Townsend, P. (1957) The Family Life of Old People, London: Routledge.

Trew, K., and Kilpatrick, R. (1985) Lifestyles and psychological well-being among unemployed in Northern Ireland. *Journal of Occupational Psychology*, 58: 207–16.

Ullah, P. (1990) The association between income, financial strain and psychological well-being among unemployed youths. *Journal of Occupational Psychology*, 63: 317–30.

Wanberg, C. R. (1995) A longitudinal study of the effects of unemployment and quality of reemployment. *Journal of Vocational Behaviour*, 46: 50–4.

Wanberg, C. R., Kammeyer-Mueller, J., and Shi, K. (2001) Job loss and the experience of unemployment: international research and perspectives. In N. Anderson, D. S. Ones, H. K. Sinangil, and C. Viswesvaran (eds.), *Handbook of Work, Industrial and Organisational Psychology*, vol. ii. London: Sage.

Warr, P. B. (1987a) *Work, Unemployment and Mental Health.* Oxford: Oxford University Press.

Warr, P. B. (1987b) *Psychology at Work* (3rd edn.). London: Penguin Group.

Warr, P. B. (2002) *Psychology at Work* (5th edn.). London: Penguin Group.

Warr, P. B., and Jackson, P. (1984) Men without jobs: some correlates of age and length of unemployment. *Journal of Occupational Psychology*, 57: 77–85.

Warr, P. B., and Jackson, P. (1985) Factors influencing the psychological impact of prolonged unemployment and re-employment, *Psychological Medicine*, 15: 795–807.

Warr, P. B., and Payne, R. L. (1982) Experience of strain and pleasure among British adults. *Social Science and Medicine*, 16: 1691–7.

Warr, P. B., and Payne, R. L. (1983) Social class and reported changes in behaviour after job loss. *Journal of Applied Social Psychology*, 13: 206–22.

West, P., and Sweeting, H. (1996) Nae job, nae future: young people and health in the context of unemployment. *Health and Social Care in the Community*, 4/1: 50–62.

Whelan, C. T. (1992) The role of income, life-style deprivation and financial strain in mediating the impact of unemployment on psychological distress: evidence from the Republic of Ireland. *Journal of Occupational Psychology*, 65: 331–44.

Whelan, C. T., Hannah, D. F., and Creighton, S. (1991) Unemployment, poverty and psychological distress. Paper Number 150. Dublin: Economic and Social Research Institute.

Winefield, A. H. (1995) Unemployment: its psychological costs. *International Review of Industrial and Organisational Psychology*, 10: 169-212.

Winefield, A. H. (2002) The psychology of work and unemployment in Australia today. Australian Psychological Society discussion paper.

Williams, C. C. (2002) Harnessing voluntary work: a fourth sector approach. *Public Studies*, 23/3–4: 247–60.

Part VI
New directions

16 The future of work

Chapter 16

The future of work

Nuala OSullivan

Chapter objectives

As a result of reading this chapter and using the additional web-based material you should be able to

- Appreciate the cyclical impact of the psychological contract on the working relationship and its increased importance to employers and employees.
- Be able to critically analyse the changes taking place in the workplace from both a human and an organizational perspective.
- Be aware of the new challenges facing modern work including an ageing and more diverse population, technological developments, and an increasingly responsible and ethical workforce.
- Recognize the changing nature of working structures including virtual teams, flexiworking, and globalization which have to be adapted to.
- Understand the power of Intellectual Property and the necessity of managing knowledge effectively within the workforce and between stakeholders.

Work psychology in practice
The psychological contract

Last May Aoife Byrne was interviewed for a junior post in the HRM (Human Resource Management) department of a large pharmaceutical company. Aoife knew that two people had left the department due to internal promotion opportunities so was keen to join to further her own professional development plan by gaining a quick promotion to more challenging work. At the interview she was asked several questions relating to her ability to respond to stress and her career aspirations which Aoife interpreted as managers viewing her as fast-track material.

Hearing that her application had been successful, Aoife was confident that she had much to offer the organization, with two years' industry experience as well as a 2:1 in her BSc Psychology. Aoife joined an established **matrix team**, which often regrouped for different projects but preferred to work together. However much of her time was spent on boring admin work, which didn't give her much opportunity to demonstrate her abilities and most queries had to be passed onto others. The rest of the team were not very friendly; some complaining about those who had been promoted and others seemed reluctant to forge links with yet another new member of the team. Aoife found them difficult to deal with and tended to avoid them socially or in the canteen.

After her first month Aoife's manager Sayed called her in for a review of her progress. Sayed was disappointed with Aoife's performance as he had hoped that she would have begun to show more initiative and taken more responsibility for her work as her predecessors had done. He also noticed that Aoife did not seem proactive in bonding with the team and they often took on tasks she should have done rather than disturb her and went out together without her.

Questions

• Summarize the unspoken expectations of Aoife and Sayed.

• What could be done to clarify the situation?

• How could you prevent a similar misunderstanding arising in the future?

16.1 Introduction

Work remains an integral part of our lives; it provides us with a livelihood, creative outlet, socialization, opportunities to achieve and contribute, as well as a part of our own identity. Attitudes (see Chapter 4 on Perception and Attitudes at Work) shape our approach but we are even more influenced by the changing nature of both work and the workplace (see Chapter 10 on Organizational Change and Development). This chapter will take you on a tour of the elements influencing these changes and will ask you to consider the changes in the context of the modern working world which you observe and participate in. We will begin with the **psychological contract** which underpins and informs many of our current working practices, including flexible working, communities of knowledge workers, self-managed working teams or virtual teams as well as **Corporate Social Responsibility** (CSR) and **Organizational Citizenship Behaviour** (OCB). The psychological contract infuses ethics and determines how we navigate our path through new legislation, technology, and working practices.

Ever since the bubonic plague, in the late sixteenth century, workers have had a sense of themselves as a valuable resource. During the Black Death workers became scarce, affecting the supply and demand dynamic and shifting power away from its traditional employer base to the worker. Workers began to value what they did and to charge accordingly.

16.2 Forces for change

The psychology of the modern worker has been obliged to adapt to prevailing winds of change and in particular to respond to new ways of working.

Work itself has been constantly evolving as employees moved away from traditional home-based activities to more dedicated jobs within mass production operations such as Ford's car plants. As organizations evolved and adapted to modern working methods such as **Just In Time** (Ouchi 1981) and technological advances (e.g. Computer Aided Design) workers' roles also diversified. Workers were required to be flexible and able to move between roles.

16.2.1 Structural changes: downsizing, rightsizing

Downsizing and rightsizing

Downsizing, now dubbed 'rightsizing,' began in epidemic proportions in the USA in the latter part of the twentieth century, before venturing to Britain and Japan. Downsizing was intentional, involving but not limited to personnel reduction, efficiency focused and influencing work processes knowingly or unknowingly (Applebaum et al. 1999; Doty et al. 1993). With its roots in manufacturing it quickly spread to service industries. It was defined as 'a deliberate organizational decision to reduce the workforce that is intended to improve organizational performance' (Shaw and Barrett-Power 1997). A less formal definition reflecting the often ad hoc nature of downsizing comes from Leonard (1995): 'whatever an employer calls it—downsizing, rightsizing, streamlining, or restructuring.' Indeed Nelson (1997) claims that companies frequently do not plan for downsizing, which is at the root of their problems.

Benefits

Downsizing has been shown to offer developmental career prospects particularly in the knowledge sector and where the downsizing requires **multiskilling** or less qualified or experienced staff to step up or retrain. Equally it provides a fertile environment for entrepreneurial consultants who can exploit the market need (Evans 1997). Employees may also benefit by returning in a consultancy capacity, at a higher rate, although the company can still claim the saving of that post since different budgets are sourced. One executive recruiter confided that as many as 12 per cent of employees dismissed in downsizing were replaced in a phenomenon known as 'upsizing' (Cascio 1993). Organizations also benefit from the 'Wall Street Effect', which happens when stock rises once it is known that the company is downsizing. The free publicity linked to dramatic downsizing has also been cited as a positive side effect since it raises the company profile.

Case illustration
Rightsizing

Alex Gress is the new Strategy and Marketing director for Enterprise Telecoms, a company which has been struggling to re-establish its popularity once it lost its monopoly on the communications market. There will be a need to rightsize as the current workforce is too large for the business retained and Alex is trying to work out how to do this. Alex will need to reduce the workforce and redesign work but is not sure if that alone will be enough as ET clings to its old culture as the sole Telecom provider of a large country; which does not reflect their current reality as a large player in an increasingly competitive free market.

Kapila Pindoria, HR director, has employed two occupational psychology consultants, Cian Daly and Tess Boissinot, to evaluate the current situation. Cian and Tess have suggested that the current HR department should be moved to an outsourced consultancy, using the same staff; who know the organization and would be able to provide best advice on how to progress. Kapila is keen to champion this move as she would be able to run the current function more lucratively; while being free to take on other work. Alex is confused as some of the HR department have underperformed and have no consultancy experience. Alex cannot decide if outsourcing HR as a consultancy would be a useful move for ET or if he is being overly influenced by the HR consultants.

Questions

- Suggest the factors Alex should consider in relation to rightsizing at ET.
- Offer Alex a persuasive argument for rejecting the consultants' suggestion.
- As Kapila, suggest how you might persuade Alex to adopt outsourcing.

Limitations

Since change is often unplanned, cuts can be rash and inconsistent with the business need. Essential skills can be lost, especially if a 'last in first out' (LIFO) policy is adopted resulting in a 'hollowed out' organization unable to respond to challenges effectively. This can impact on competitiveness in a global market when organizations do not have the workforce to cope with demands, as was the experience in North America. Redundancy payments can be costly; Baillie (1995) claims that redundancies have no effect on profit. This is supported by Clark and Koonce (1997), who found that 68 per cent of all downsizing efforts were unsuccessful.

16.2.2 Psychological effects of change on survivors

Having outlined the impact of downsizing on organizations it is worth turning our attention to those affected, since this will directly inform the success or failure of the change venture. Traditionally employers assumed that those who had been spared redundancy would be grateful and want to work harder to prove their commitment and value to the organization. This phenomenon is not supported by any research and recent studies have shown that not only does downsizing impact on the department involved but also on other departments (Luthans and Sommer 1999). Goffee and Scase (1992) identified behaviours resulting from downsizing and distilled these into Get Out, Get Safe, and Get Even patterns.

In the Get Out condition those with transferable skills leave at the earliest opportunity; whereas the less mobile would Get Safe and do just enough to secure their jobs, losing interest and confidence in their work and failing to take the initiative or extra responsibility. The last category was relatively rare but Get Even employees would seek to harm the organization by damaging its reputation. Isabella (1989) warns that although some companies do prepare for stress, many are unprepared for the 'strong emotions, lengthy adjustment time, diminished morale, and lower productivity'. This list is augmented by Cole (1993), who adds the practical considerations of the loss of interunit and level knowledge as well as personal relationships. Kozlowski et al. (1993) extended this harm beyond the boundaries of the organization finding that survivors' family and personal relationships suffered along with their physical and emotional health. Cameron et al. (1993) studying the automotive industry in the USA found significant changes to coping behaviours including increased conflict and resistance to change. Survivor employees were more inclined to opt for centralized decision making and to have damaged morale, commitment, and loyalty.

 Activity Redundancy counselling

You are a redundancy counsellor drafted in to deal with the fallout from a severe redundancy reduction from the organization.

- Suggest how you would explore the current attitudes and emotions of the surviving workers by compiling a list of four relevant questions to ask them.

- What recommendations would you make to senior management to try to ameliorate the harsh impact of the redundancy programme?

- How would you avoid the 'get out get safe get even' syndrome establishing itself in your organization following the redundancies?

 KEY LEARNING POINTS

- Rightsizing due to technological advances, outsourcing, or changes in the global market has been deemed necessary for large numbers of organizations.

- There are both benefits and limitations to the process as well as a profound and unpredictable human impact.

16.3 The psychological contract

The psychological contract was originally defined by Argyris (1960), swiftly supported by Levinson et al. (1962), who coined the term to cover the exchange of expectations between employee and employer. Originally the psychological contract was understood as a set of implicit and unwritten understandings between both parties which each would abide by. These expectations covered a range of areas from dress code, where workers did not turn up in swim wear, to a duty of care when employees were ill or experiencing personal difficulties. As with all contracts there was a consideration on both sides with each party having a part to play in a successful contract. Although a reciprocal contract, the balance of power was initially always with the employer.

The most recent developments of this concept have been from Rousseau in the 1990s, who argued that current psychological contracts are not merely implicit but will often be found explicitly in contracts and terms of engagement. Rousseau's other departure was to shift away from the worthy values of obligation and duties, to the new arena of employee-centred individual beliefs (Rousseau 1990). In this version of the contract each party is free to determine what is of value and what constitutes a viable working relationship. Recent CIPD research (2008) suggests that younger workers, or **millennials**, strive for a more fun working environment and a better work-life balance shifting the onus onto the employer to facilitate this.

More recently Millward and Brewerton (2000) have investigated the differences in the psychological contract between full- and part-time workers and found that the perception of a more complete contract pervaded the full-time workforce with a more relational as opposed to purely transactional element. DeWitte et al. (2004) examined the effect of the psychological contract on the unemployed and those in precarious work situations finding that it contributed to stress and lower self-esteem while Conway and Briner (2005) have placed the psychological contract at the heart of the modern work expectation. It appears that in an age where flexibility and security are pursued (**flexicurity**) the psychological contract has more to offer than ever.

 Activity **Psychological contract**

Outline how the student experience is informed by the psychological contract. You may want to begin with the norms of the lecturer/student lecture relationship; wherein the lecturer speaks and students listen, unless asked for feedback. When you have listed eight items decide whether these items should be abandoned, altered, or retained to improve the student experience.

16.3.1 Managing diversity in an ageing population

Equal opportunities and diversity management

One of the ways that the psychological contract has pervaded our working lives is in our belief that socially desired norms will be upheld; these are expressed in 'equal opportunities' and 'diversity management'. Understanding the difference between equal opportunities and diversity lies mainly in differentiating between external and internal organizational drivers. Equal

Figure 16.1. The psychological contract

Employee consideration	Employer consideration
Loyalty to company	Interest in employee wellbeing
Compliance	Guarantee of employment
Commitment	Development prospects
Trust	Trust

opportunities tend to target groups which have been disadvantaged and offers change, based on the external drivers of legislation, and legal requirements which impact on policies and strategies. Diversity management, on the other hand, seeks to celebrate the individuals within a group and to make the most of what they have to offer. Diversity management is internally and culturally driven, and requires strong support at Board level. Since the mid-1970s a plethora of legislative changes have forced through behavioural changes in the workplace. These range from the 1970 Equal Pay Act to recent change to legislation in the form of the Employment Rights Regulations (Age), on 1 October 2006, in response to Article 13 of the Treaty of Amsterdam. However, the 'law is not a very effective vehicle for bringing about change . . . it encourages a minimalist approach' (Ross and Schneider 1992) and for this reason it is important that diversity strategies both support equal opportunity initiatives and also pioneer them. The CIPD (2007) recommends that both are developed in a complementary fashion.

With an ageing population and the prediction that by 2020 there will be more of us caring for older people than for children, it became apparent that the existing laws were inadequate. In 2007 the number over State Pension Age in Britain has overtaken the number of children for the first time (Johnson 2005).

The baby boomers generation of the 1950s/60s prompted organizations to offer early retirement to workers during the 1980s to make way for the younger workforce. However baby boomers themselves did not have many children, resulting in a shortage of workers coupled with too few young workers to sustain the pension bill that would have accrued once the baby boomers retired. We are now in a situation where many organizations have either raised (to 65 years) or abandoned the concept of a retirement age (Civil Service among others).

Companies which have done well from implementing an age diverse approach are Marks & Spencers, BT, and B&Q. B&Q, a hardware and DIY store, found that customers had more confidence when approaching an older employee with a DIY-related query than one of the younger staff members. B&Q also offer mothers term-time contracts and students holiday-time contracts to cater to the workforce needs.

Sanchez investigated how rapidly older adults could adjust their behaviour according to the characteristics of automation, and found that they could learn just as effectively as their younger colleagues, although it often took them longer to do so (Hernandis and Sanchez 2006). However in practice older workers can deselect themselves from training opportunities because they lack the confidence of younger colleagues. When William Hill, the bookmakers, changed over to an automated system it invited those interested to attend for training on a specified date and those who failed to attend would be deemed to have accepted redundancy. The majority of their older workers took redundancy rather than try to get to grips with the new system.

The myth that older workers won't retrain is also difficult to challenge. It remains a fact that those over 45 remain unemployed for longer (Bryant 2006).

Figure 16.2. UK population by age, 1971–2006

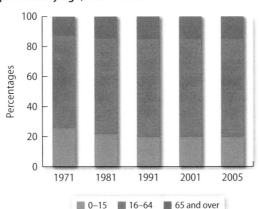

Source: Mid-year population estimates: Office for National Statistics, General Register Office for Scotland and Northern Ireland Statistics and Research Agency (2007).

Northern Rock and Ikea have both run recruitment campaigns encouraging older workers back into their workforce.

Whether companies are ready or not, the reality of a skilled and intellectually capable older workforce has arrived. Increased technological support, enhanced health and life expectancy, as well as generations of portfolio building professionals all contribute to the blurring of age boundaries. How we will deal with this challenge remains to be seen.

 Activity Job advertisement

Amy has just finished writing up a job advertisement for a floor supervisor at Essence Restaurant, a fashionably trendy eaterie in the West End of London known for its atmosphere and the attractiveness of its young employees.

In Essence

Are you daring enough to be an Essence employee? We are looking for dynamic, energetic team players to join our vibrant new team at Essence. You should find work a continuation of your party lifestyle mixing with the elegant set here at Essence. The Essence experience is a mixture of joie de vivre and audacious panache from our stylish professional waiting and bar staff. If you think you could cut a dash at Essence apply for interview today asking for Amy@essence.com

Amy's boss, Louis, thinks this contravenes the Employment Rights (Age) Regulations 2006.

- Make Louis's case to Amy.
- Suggest Amy's defence relying on **Genuine Occupational Qualification**.
- Rewrite the advert to avoid any age discriminatory inferences.
- While Amy was on leave Louis hired a 54-year-old waiter and a 60-year-old waitress. Suggest how Amy can integrate the new workers into her team using a diversity management model.

 KEY LEARNING POINTS

- The psychological contract is not a new concept; it has continued to evolve to keep pace with the disparate changes we encounter.
- Becoming more explicit, it also responds to workers' demands as the millennials insist on greater flexibility and choice.
- The psychological contract also relies on social and societal norms and expectations which may not transfer across borders, age boundaries, and new ways of working.

Technological advances

'The value of a computer is in its management' (Strassmann 2001).

Computers have revolutionized our lives via global working patterns, data mining, and knowledge-based industries (Levy and Murnane 2004). Communication Knowledge management systems have been devised to support Knowledge workers facilitating communities of knowledge and remote knowledge workers who capitalize on rapid information sharing. **Teamware**, tailored to the group, and restricted access groove networks aid specialists. Workers operate supported by knowledge maps which allow employees to locate experts within the organization, intranets, and internets, although these have not proven as successful as initially hoped owing to the volume of non-specific information generated (Kiesler et al. 1998). Investment Workstations integrate external and internal data: reports, management data, research reports, market histories for ease of knowledge transfer and ensure that all information is current and accurate while Enterprise Information Portals (EIP) operate as a single gateway to internal and external information sources.

Whether the technology is Computer Aided Manufacture (**CAM**), Computer Aided Design (**CAD**), or Virtual Reality Modelling Language (VRML**),** allowing us virtual access, we often still prefer the real touch of clothing or personal choice (Szymanski and Hise 2000). Similarly,

Case-Based Reasoning (CBR) technology offers manager's decisions which they tend to ignore, preferring to rely on their own experience in a crisis.

Technology has created both low-skilled repetitive jobs and highly skilled specialist opportunities. It has shown itself to fit well with repetitive or easily programmed sequences but to flounder where novel problems or complex solutions are required. European workers have been shown to be anxious that they would fall foul of the automated march, no longer able to use creative skills they would become deskilled and out of the loop (Noyes and Masakowski 2007). Studies of American workers show a perception that only those mid-career would experience the impact; since younger workers would grow up in the technological environment and be proficient with it (Arnold 2004).

Currently those most vulnerable to technological advances are the mid-skilled, repetitive workers; whereas occupations requiring novel solutions are least likely to be affected. Cognitive Compatibility still appears to be the most difficult to design for (Noyes 2001).

16.3.2 Knowledge management, intellectual property, and managing organizational knowledge

Knowledge management (KM) is: 'the set of processes developed in an organization to create, gather, store, maintain and apply the firm's knowledge' (Laudon and Laudon 2004).

KM refers to the ways in which organizations seek to identify, codify, create, represent, share, protect, and distribute knowledge within organizations for the benefit of those working in it and the organization itself. It has been heavily linked with IT support although it is possible to have knowledge management practices independent of technology such as verbal handover reports used by nursing staff teams.

Properties of knowledge

Knowledge offers extraordinary leverage and unlike other products or investments it is not subject to diminishing returns. When it is used, it is not consumed. Consumers can add to it, enhancing its value. Knowledge is dynamic as information in action. As knowledge grows it branches and fragments so it is vulnerable to fragmentation and leakage and must be refreshed to retain a competitive advantage. Like a rare antique, knowledge has uncertain value and, due to its intangible nature, it is difficult to predict its impact. Equally the act of sharing knowledge will not always be useful or even impactful. Knowledge is time bound and influenced by how pertinent it is to the moment. It is unpredictable and unbiddable:

> A thought comes when it will, not when I will. (Nietzsche 1989)

Peter Drucker (1998) first coined the term **knowledge worker** (KW) as one who uses the tools above to network and bring value to the organization (Kumar 2000). KWs do this by processing information to: create knowledge or new information, problem solve, and transfer old knowledge to new situations. Years later Peter Drucker (2002) was convinced that the society we live in is evolving into a knowledge society where knowledge workers would become the dominant group. The next society would be as borderless as knowledge itself. It would also facilitate upward mobility for all who had a capacity for knowledge working. Workers could achieve knowledge worker training through a formal education. Crucially the potential for failure was equally great since all have access to the same information and would compete for success. Failure was also seen as a part of the process and nothing to be ashamed of since knowledge expires when it is no longer timely, accurate, or clear. The notion of failure as a learning opportunity fed from the concept of the Learning Organization (Senge 2006) which endorsed knowledge workers and expected managers to develop learning in their teams as a first priority. Failures were waiting to happen and those involved were co-opted into problem solving to ensure that that problem did not happen again. Intranets were populated with internal case studies of successes and failures and how to navigate them. Thus constant learning became the norm and making connections between disparate pieces of information to form knowledge bonds, a practised path.

Currently, it is estimated that the USA workforce is made up of 55 per cent knowledge workers, who produce 60 per cent of national product.

Pause for thought
List four areas of business which rely on technology today. Suggest how these have been enhanced by the advent of technology. Make a note of areas which are less effective since technology became an integral part of their operation.

Successful knowledge workers have considerable **intellectual property** (IP). IP is a catch-all term for products of the mind or the intellect. Exclusive rights and ownership similar to property is claimed for IP of ideas, information, or approach, despite its intangibility. However the law on IP is ambiguous and erroneous assumptions abound around it.

With the proliferation of the job-hopping, portfolio building professionals, organizations have sought to protect themselves, their innovations, and client lists from being taken to a competitor. Europeans instigated **Garden Leave**. Garden Leave means that the employee is freed of work or involvement in the organization but while they still receive a salary they are obliged to observe the confidentiality clauses of their original organization and cannot move to another. Typically this period is three to six months wherein they are not permitted to communicate with their previous or pending employers or colleagues. Lawrie Haynes of British Nuclear Group was on Garden Leave before leaving the company with a pay-off of over £1 million (Irving 2006); he was then appointed as CEO to White Young Green in April 2007 once his period of enforced leisure came to an end he took up his post in July.

KEY LEARNING POINTS

- Technology has offered changes in working capabilities and ushered in the knowledge worker with a need to keep abreast of developments and to offer the organization timely information for gain.
- This has changed organizations' attitudes to their key employees with attempts to control their influence and mobility.
- People as a resource has been emphasized by the knowledge economy and the need to treat and develop workers well has emerged.

16.4 New ways of working

Organizations have been restructuring by rightsizing, exploring the human-machine interaction as well as new economies and emerging workforces. This has been supported by advances in technology and a working population comfortable with using technology. Synthesizing much of this are the new ways of working. The current 27 projects by the ESRC on the future of work, engaging over 100 researchers show how the area of evolving work is being monitored and measured with a view to understanding and improving its conditions and appreciating the direction it is taking. This section will consider the emerging trends for knowledge workers in self-directed teams, matrix teamwork, flexible working, teleworkers, satellite workers, the electronic cottage, and virtual teams. These are further augmented by the rise of the non-employee in the guise of consultant or outsourced worker who bring their own talents and challenges to the modern working landscape.

16.4.1 Self-managed work teams (SMWT)

In **self-managed work teams** there is a level of autonomy around how the work is executed within management's set parameters (Rees and Porter 2003). Workers self-monitor, work to deadlines, and manage their workload. There is support for this style of team as self-directed teams have been found to be more competent, not only on a personal and professional level, but also in terms of their methodological approach (Kauffeld 2006). Jackson (2006) suggests that the heart of a successful **SMWT** is the job design allowing workers autonomy and integrity at work. However, it seems that team bonding and setting clear expectations is even more important if the team is self-managed, since there is more scope to resist change or fail to commit fully if individuals perceive that they are being unfairly treated (Shapiro and Kirkman 1999).

16.4.2 Matrix teams

The matrix team has been a feature of organizational structure for some years. It relies on swift communication and project attachment. The dual axes of reporting to both a functional and a project manager draw specialists away from the rarefied atmospheres of their professional groups to work in cross-functional teams, where the project outcome becomes the common goal. There is dual reporting: daily to the project manager and less frequently to the functional manager, who is ostensibly still responsible for their development. The specialist became a commodity for their functional manager, to trade for further resources or status. Meantime specialists work with a project manager unrelated to their field and unable to mentor them.

This way of working undoubtedly served communication on immediate goals and was ideal at the operations management level. It was even boasted that cross-functional teams would stimulate creativity and lateral thinking. Conversely, it could result in teams focusing purely on the task rather than the bigger strategic picture; losing perspective for the organization and their own career trajectory. Creating **communities of practice**, alongside the teams, wherein knowledge sharing and specialist debate are retained across teams can remedy this (McDermott 1999). These double-knit structures also serve to benchmark best practice and protect professional standards.

16.4.3 Flexible working

A DfEE survey into **work-life balance** (Hogarth et al. 2001) found that there has been a substantial and escalating demand for flexible working arrangements. Women were keen on term time working, or reduced hours and men preferred flexitime, compressed hours, and annualized hours. Women ranked flexitime as a means to facilitate training and education time; whereas men were more inclined to cite family time as their highest priority (TUC survey 2001). The phenomenon of the **kaleidoscope career** (Sullivan and Mainiero 2006), wherein workers make different choices at differing stages of their working lives to accommodate a quality of life and the work-life balance, has exerted pressure on employers to be more flexible.

Flexible working encompasses both full- and part-time workers who can vary start and finish times while retaining a set number of required working hours. There is scope to bank hours or to make them up at a later date. In the UK employers have been obliged to consider flexible work applications from parents of disabled children under 18 and all children under 6 years old since April 2003. Flexible working has been consistently well received both in the UK and abroad; with 25 per cent of all Canadian workers working this way (Furnham 2000). It has been listed in the benefits most preferred by UK employees and a 2006 survey of the FTSE top 100 companies found that those assessed as 'very good' in terms of family friendly working practices far outperformed other companies in share performance. Smithey et al. (2003) conducted an American study which showed that the 100 best companies to work for enabled flexible work and were also the most productive companies.

16.4.4 Compressed work weeks

Compressed work weeks allow the normal weekly hours to be condensed into block mode work over fewer days. Although popular with workers, not all jobs are suited to this mode of work and managers should be attuned to recognizing when compressed work may not suit the needs either of the business or, in the long term, the individual, since the organization has a duty of care not to place unnecessary stress on employees. The management of Health and Safety at Work Regulations (1999) and the Working Time Directive (1998) both ensure that employers are responsible for conducting risk assessments, issuing work hours, and ensuring rest periods.

Overall flexible working allows workers to arrange their time around other commitments. For organizations it requires astute recruitment and selection skills to ascertain eligibility and fit as well as ensuring that the core business needs are being met without harm to the employee.

16.4.5 Teleworking

Satellite workers

Teleworking includes all who use telecommunications to work more independently of the main office. These include mobile teleworkers such as sales staff who can use mobile phones and wireless networks to place immediate orders and verify stock supplies. Equally senior staff can spend more time with off-site projects while remaining in touch via portable systems facilitating email and telephone communications.

Electronic cottage

First coined by Toffler (1980) as a futuristic prediction the **electronic cottage** was a local place where access to a computer could be assured. At that time none had predicted the proliferation of the personal computer or its capabilities.

Telecentres facilitate remote working but allow workers to do so more conveniently. This facilitates island and village life and allows those with difficult commutes to stay in their own neighbourhoods while continuing to work effectively.

Virtual teams (VTs)

Johnson et al. (2001) describe the 'wonderland' of **virtual teams** and VTs have been viewed as the halcyon working arrangement. Far from requiring those involved to be technology savvy, it has been suggested that there is a 9:1 ratio of personality to technology for those engaged in VTs (Lipnack and Stamps 2001).

VTs, also known as 'geographically distributed teams' (GDTs), work across time, boundaries, and space to provide expert input to projects. The International Telework Advisory Council (ITAC) defines remote working as 'the ability to work anytime, anyplace, using remote access connectivity and mobile technology'. Pape (1999) defines virtual teams as a team whose members are more than 50 feet apart.

Approximately 15 per cent of the adult workforce in Canada and the United States was engaged in some form of virtual work by 2002 and the figure is rising (Fang and Neufeld 2006). In Europe, the Netherlands, Sweden, and Germany all boast VTs, although the highest working population percentage is in the UK.

Some research has suggested that VT workers and telecommuters are so content with their working conditions if they were forced back into the office they would resign (Cascio 1998). Although managers have qualms about an invisible workforce (Bailey and Kurland 2002), repeated studies have shown that workers are 40 per cent more productive away from the distractions of a busy office (Warner 1997). With continually evolving supportive technology it is reasonable to expect that this figure can only increase.

Currently virtual teams have been allocated by manager preference and personality suitability as much as by skill (Bailey and Kurland 2002). Trust remains a key issue in developing these teams (Coutu 1998; Grundy 1998). Overcoming communication challenges is the keystone to success (Javenpaa and Leidner 1999). Lipnack and Stamps (2001) suggest that VTs should be small in size and begin with initial meetings. They found that those who were most successful included exchange of non-work related information to build trust and virtual relationships. While Pape (1999) also recommends that teams of three to five are ideal, NCR fielded a successful team of 1,000 across seventeen locations (Lipnack and Stamps 2001).

Teams must be managed according to the need for expertise and the technology which is to be used as well as how processes are bundled (Gassmann and von Zedtwitz, 2003). Kandola (2006) insists that time must be devoted to team coalescence since connecting groups via the internet or through groupware will not suffice to form the basis of a successful VT. (See Chapter 7 on Groups, Teams, and Decision Making.)

 Activity Virtual team

You are tasked with looking at the psychological welfare of a dispersed VT.

Greg lives and works on Bondi beach in Australia, Mario is based in Florence, and Ciara is freelancing between New York and California, depending on the season. The trio must produce working plans for a new product together. There is a major presentation in three weeks which Ciara will deliver but input is required from all three with intragroup comments.

- Suggest how the team could create a successful virtual culture.
- What would assist them in this?
- What could thwart their team bonding to jeopardize the project?
- What dangers are there to an individual's psychological well-being when working in a VT?
- What would you put in place to protect the team from these potential hazards?

Advantages of virtual teams
Flexibility
No commuting
Equity: since race, gender and disability blind
Greater autonomy
Increased productivity
Knowledge sharing within a defined team
Reduced organizational overheads
Less pollution to the environment
Improved variety and job enrichment
Motivated to work at own pace and hours
Enhanced work–life Balance
Disadvantages of virtual teams
Loss of organizational identity
Reduced loyalty
Reduced commitment
Loss of promotion opportunities/information
Feelings of isolation (Precup et al. 2006; Hodson 2005)
Climate of mutual trust alien to management (Bailey and Kurland 2002)
Working in a vacuum (Haywood 2000)
Reliable communication channels essential (Pape 1999)
MBO for telemanagement
Managers still sceptical (Haywood 1998)
Ethics still evolving (Guthrie 2006)
Virtual teams – technology not enough (Merrick 1996)
Security risks (Tietze et al. 2006)

16.5 A quality approach to working life

The era of a job for life and full-time commitment to an organization has receded firmly into the past (Sullivan and Mainiero 2006). Yet, both in America and Britain 83 per cent of the workforce work in a structured work environment. Work times vary across countries and cultures; although British workers work some of the longest hours in Europe this is dwarfed by the Korean or Polish inputs.

16.5.1 Lifestyle contract

Work-life balance has been defined by the DfEE (Hogarth et al. 2001) as 'adjusting work patterns so that everyone, regardless of age, race or gender can find a rhythm that enables them to combine work with other responsibilities and aspirations more easily'.

The Lisbon European Council 2000 stressed the need to improve all aspects of equal opportunities, including making it easier to reconcile working life and family life (Pillinger 2001). Across Europe there seem to be differences in approach with Scandinavian countries tending to emphasize Quality of Working Life (QoWL) more than their neighbours (Gallie 2003). As countries struggle to achieve inclusion to fulfil the European Strategy Against Social Exclusion's recommendations, there is a drive towards **family friendly policies** which facilitate QoL and QoWL. Finding the balance between workers' idyllic conditions and employers' requirements has meant readdressing the issues of flexibility, job security (flexicurity), and mutual trust.

Countries have responded in different ways to accommodate these, with France opting for a 35-hour week and working time solidarity while Netherlands and Sweden have developed their part-time working policies to become more flexible and Belgium, Denmark, and Finland are exploring job rotation to even out stress areas. Sweden has introduced parental leave and 'father's month', which has resulted in more men accessing parental leave, with the unexpected

Figure 16.4. National comparison of annual working hours, 2004

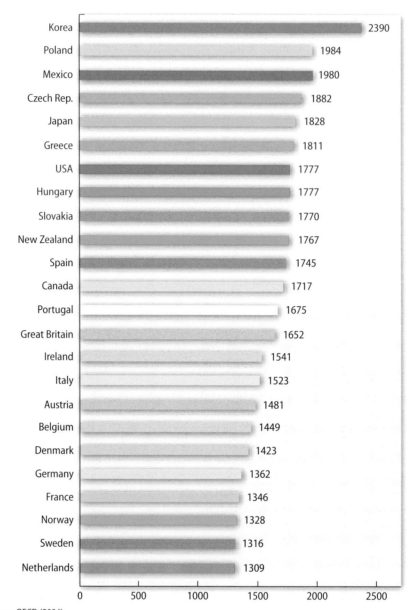

Country	Hours
Korea	2390
Poland	1984
Mexico	1980
Czech Rep.	1882
Japan	1828
Greece	1811
USA	1777
Hungary	1777
Slovakia	1770
New Zealand	1767
Spain	1745
Canada	1717
Portugal	1675
Great Britain	1652
Ireland	1541
Italy	1523
Austria	1481
Belgium	1449
Denmark	1423
Germany	1362
France	1346
Norway	1328
Sweden	1316
Netherlands	1309

Source: OECD (2004).

sustained effect of more fathers assuming care for sick children than before (Eriksson 2005). Meanwhile in Belgium, Denmark, and Finland, paid leave schemes operate; while in Ireland there is the option to take unpaid leave or a sabbatical without affecting the current career trajectory or jeopardizing job security.

At a corporate level, organizations which have adopted flexible QoWL options have enjoyed a raised profile, greater commitment, retention, and productivity (Francesconi and Gosling 2005).

16.5.2 Organizational fit

With moves to make the worker more autonomous, remote, or self-reliant (Ehrhart and Makransky 2007) along with the increased incidence of migrant workers across Europe (Brewster et al. 1997) there is a question mark hanging over whether organizational culture can survive in its current form. Organizations are responding to this by opting for best fit workers, with similar world-views. Keen knowledge workers who share a similar set of values and principles are sought to be harnessed for the benefit of the organization via knowledge sharing and pooling of Intellectual Property. The risk is that a replication of the existing homogeneous workforce, unwittingly excluding out groups, leads to reduced diversity (Carroll et al. 1999). This lack of diversity can cause a decline in the breadth of an organization's collective knowledge as no fresh blood is introduced and can: 'perpetuate existing imbalances in the make-up of the workforce' (Taylor 2005: 168); this in turn can impact on the bottom line (Friday and Friday 2003), since cultural diversity informs enhanced decision making (McCartney 2007).

KEY LEARNING POINTS

- The mushrooming of independence and autonomy at work as illustrated by the early electronic cottages followed by self-managed working teams, matrix teams, **satellite teams**, and virtual teams saw workers demanding work-life balance and quality of working life.

- These moves prompted organizations to revisit how and who they recruited, as workers become even more of an investment.

- Organizations therefore looked at ways of recruiting those who would best serve the organization and provide best **person/organizational** fit.

- These moves have been explored at the risk of reduced diversity.

16.6 Ethics and work

'Ethics' stems from the Greek word *ethos*, which means character or custom, covering both the personal choice element and the inclusion of a social or cultural influence. Socrates believed that we could teach people to behave ethically; yet ethical behaviour is difficult to quantify since the continuum of ethics is constantly evolving and changing. All decisions have an ethical element to them (Etzioni 2002).

There is one argument that urges us to believe that ethics has no place in business; since its only responsibility is to make money (Friedman 1970) and others who insist equally vociferously that individuals perform best when their ethical values are reflected in the organization they choose to work in (Koh and Boo 2001).

These arguments are complicated since what is ethical in one culture may not necessarily be seen as ethical in another. Here we will consider some of the models and guidelines which try to quantify this abstract area. Corporate Social Responsibility and alignment of personal and professional ethics will also be considered.

Some areas affected by ethics are shown in Figure 16.5.

16.6.1 Individual and organizational ethics

Aligning responsible personal ethics with the organization increases job satisfaction (Boyer and Webb 1992) and this has been linked to raised commitment (Koh and Boo 2001). Individuals are also more likely to link ethics with their own career path if senior managers show support for ethical behaviour (Koh and Boo 2001; Vitell and Davis 1990). A study in Australia suggested that employee values are more heavily influenced by those of managers and unethical practices were resorted to when trying to satisfy the demands of superiors (Soutar et al. 2004). A study in Europe by Kirrane (1990) also showed that pressures of work and the need to deliver with lessening resources, may have an impact on ethical practice. In a bid to maintain performance, people may cut corners under pressure (Kirrane 1990: 55). Increasingly managers are seen as role models for others who must act as guides when navigating the moral maze (Sims 1992). Yet with little managerial training this area becomes difficult to negotiate: a minefield (Rees and Porter 2003).

Kirrane (1990) identified four competing situations where ethical issues arise (Figure 16.6).

Organizational citizen behaviour

'Organizational citizen behaviour' is a phenomenon wherein employees demonstrate innovative and spontaneous actions which go beyond their job role (Katz 1964; Smith et al. 1983). Lately these have been further refined to indicate behaviours which would benefit the organization as a whole more than the individual; demonstrating shades of altruism commensurate

Figure 16.5. Ethical issues

Some of the areas affected by ethics are:
  Discrimination and diversity
  Whistle blowing
  Bullying
  Recruitment
  Succession planning
  Reward
  Gifts—receiving and giving
  Accounting practices
  Directors' remuneration
  Relations with trade unions
  Strategy
  Health and safety of staff
  Support and protection of staff
  Data and privacy

Industrial espionage
  Corporate governance
  Energy utilization
  Consumer safety
  Genetic modification
  Environmental protection
  Dealings with developing countries
  Animal rights and research

Figure 16.6. Ethical clashes

Kirrane (1990) identified four competing areas when ethical issues arise:

1. conflict between two or more personally held values
2. conflict between personal values and the values held by another person or the organization
3. conflict between basic principles and the need to achieve a desired outcome
4. conflict between two or more individuals or groups to whom one has an obligation

with the 'good soldier syndrome' label as it has been termed (Organ 1988). These behaviours appear to be shaped both by a sense of duty as well as reciprocity (Coyle-Shapiro et al. 2003). A strong link between commitment and OCB has also been established; so that in organizations where procedural justice is fair OCB flourishes (Coyle-Shapiro et al. 2003). Vigoda-Gadot and Angert (2007) noted that OCB was also positively related to job performance across a longitudinal study. Whether the individual is motivated by job maintenance, enlargement, or coercion by managers and co-workers was explored by Vigoda-Gadot (2006), who introduced the concept of the darker side of OCB wherein the worker is coerced or strongly persuaded to engage in OCB characteristics but without internal motivation.

Corporate social responsibility

Repeatedly when organizations behave unethically there has been a prevailing culture tacitly supporting unethical behaviour. In the wake of Enron (2001), thirteen of the largest corporate bankruptcies in US history were filed and all had been involved in unethical business practices (Thomas et al. 2004). What had seemed like an isolated case of executives greedily harvesting for themselves and their friends has 'now become a flood of ill-gotten gains and financial irregularities' (Cornehis 2004: 29).

Freda Turner (2006) alerts us to the heavy cost of unethical behaviour relating to job and profit losses. Yet, as organizations have realized that their corporate social responsibility profile influences others, there has been a drive towards more responsible working. In this climate Paul Pressler CEO of Gap resorted to publishing transparent social responsibility reports which admit that child labour violation cases still featured, and factories where workers could not

Case illustration
Anti-globalization

Globalization has been dubbed the 'Golden Strait Jacket', and has been criticized for being economically constraining, widening gaps between incomes, marginalizing women in the workforce, being plugged in regardless of national need, and for prioritizing laws on free trade over human rights.

In *Naming the Enemy*, Amory Starr (2001) outlines resistance to globalization under three banners of:

- restraining it;
- democratizing it;
- building local alternatives to it.

The first category involves human rights movements, cyberpunks, and demonstrators and is explicitly anti-corporate. The second strand of globalization from below calls on governments and corporations to democratize and offer transparent accountability. Support for this position is found in trade unions, environmental groups, socialist movements, and anti-free trade protesters. The third approach is de-linking—which involves opting out and a voluntary rejection of the global market: small businesses, anarchists, and religious nationals find themselves banding together to find alternatives to globalization (Amin 1990).

leave their jobs (www.gapinc.com). This bold move, to take responsibility by owning up to imperfections while committing to working on them, has won Gap the Social Reporting Award from the 16th Annual Business Ethics Awards (2006). This demonstrates that companies do not have to be perfect but must be seen to be actively engaging with issues of corruption or malpractice. The CSR management award has also been won by Intel (2007) and Starbucks (2008).

16.6.2 Measuring ethics

Some of the problems around creating ethics policies and monitoring ethical standards are that the tools keep changing and are revised and tailored to each new setting to consider the culture they encounter (Turner 2006). The recurring theme is that organizations must set their own high standards rather than merely comply with variable international laws. Organizations which allow small pockets of power to deviate from an ethical approach in their pursuits will pay with lost trust, an erosion of culture, human suffering, unemployment, lost status, and profit losses. Consequently the business case they set out to prioritize above all will even be lost to them.

 Activity Unethical behaviour

Consider the following work situations:

- Todd has been working for the same haulage company for half his life since he was 16 and is resentful of the new ownership which keeps close tabs on workers. Lately he has taken to adding on extra mileage and putting in for expenses he hasn't used.

- Olive is a Green Party candidate and stands on a platform of Corporate Social Responsibility. A major oil company has been funding her campaign and flying her thousands of miles to areas of the endangered world so that she can highlight their plight.

- Gretta runs a small family pharmaceutical company which specializes in treatments to cure cancer. One of their breakthrough drugs was also found to increase the longevity of AIDS patients. Gretta does not want her company stigmatized by being associated with an antisocial virus and suppresses the information.

Consider who is unethical and why that might be? Are there any excuses for their behaviour? Did you find yourself ranking their degrees of unethical behaviour?

Pause for thought

How might the ethical reputation of a company impact on its employees?

Pause for thought

You are a small independent company recruiting a range of migrant workers. Outline the benefits of the arrangement to both employer and employee. What limitations might be encountered by each party?

KEY LEARNING POINTS

- There is some debate as to whether personal ethics, and a sense of right and wrong, should apply in or to businesses.

- It has been found that organizations which promote ethical behaviour will themselves become more ethical and engender more spontaneous commitment from workers (or Organizational Citizenship Behaviour.

- It has been found that those who behaved unethically often did so either because their organizational culture was unethical or because they were pressurized into an untenable position wherein they cut corners.

16.7 Conclusion

The tour into the future of work has voyaged from the psychological contract via new ways of working and methods of mining our talents and influencing organizations and our own futures back to the concept of the ethical organization, staffed by ethical workers whether remote or local who serve the organization by virtue of sharing its values and goals. Work psychologists can offer their expertise to help us chart and explore this new terrain, by offering a perspective on enquiry, and through the application of research techniques and a range of theories outlined in this text.

Chapter summary

- The chapter described the powerful ascendancy of the psychological contract as we opt for better quality of working life and a work-life balance.

- The chapter looked at the crisis of change and its aftermath on survivors whether via downsizing, changing working arrangements, or unprecedented demographical changes.

- Technology, and the opportunities it presents in the global business context, also generates new ethical challenges.

- There is conflict between management goals to create person/organizational fit, and the need to manage diversity and to be seen to be fair.

- The necessity of managing knowledge and knowledge workers in a rapidly evolving environment has created new power bases in work organizations.

- Personal ethics and organizational responsibility are challenged by new organizational forms, and new ways of working.

Assess your learning

Review questions

1 Consider with reference to the evolving models how the Psychological Contract has adapted to work in 2010.

2 Outline the contrasting benefits and limitations of rightsizing for organizations, making clear where it may be appropriate.

3 Integrating your knowledge of motivation, attitudes, and stress consider what the effect of work-based change may be on survivors.

4 Combining what you know of diversity construct an argument for the recruitment of older workers to a new start-up business.

5 Discuss whether technology has facilitated greater freedom or greater accountability for the modern worker.

6 Discuss whether isolated Virtual teams can be considered divisive to organizations. You may include culture, knowledge management, and motivation in your responses.

7 Suggest to the CEO of a research-based organization how she should hold on to the intellectual capital within her organization. You may include information from earlier chapters to complement what you find in this one.

8 Address the concept that Organizational Citizenship Behaviour is a form of psychic prison for the modern worker, drawing on all you have learnt from this book thus far.

Assignments

ASSIGNMENT 1: In essence

Examine a restaurant business, and produce a report considering the following issues:

- the dilemmas it faces in terms of person/organizational fit;
- **managing diversity**, and complying with Age inclusive legislation (ERR 2006);
- the ethical responsibility of employing shift workers and the impact on the team and clientele of its recruitment policy.

(2,000 words)

ASSIGNMENT 2: Managing the 2020 team

Read the closing case study below. Imagine you are the occupational psychologist called in by Isolda. Write a report for her highlighting areas of concern with explanations and viable recommendations for her on how to resolve them. (2,000 words)

Further reading

Arnold, J. (2004) *Managing Careers into the 21st Century*. London: Paul Chapman.
A useful overview of changing patterns of work, with discussion of a range of research evidence.

Patterson, F. (2001) Developments in work psychology: emerging issues and future trends. *Journal of Occupational and Organizational Psychology*, 74: 381–90.
A review article that considers the practical applications of work psychology to the field of work, and discusses possible future areas of interest for work psychologists in emerging trends in patterns of work. It covers many issues discussed in this chapter.

Williams, C. C. (2007) *Rethinking the Future of Work*. London: Palgrave-Macmillan.
A critical review of current thinking about how the nature of work is changing, written by the professor of Management at Sheffield University. The book covers many issues tackled in this chapter, with a focus on flexible working patterns and a global perspective on change.

 Work psychology in practice
Managing in 2020

Isolda was listening to the CEO, Michiko Shimidzu, speaking from Argentina as part of their monthly videoconferencing. Isolda's blackberry and mobile were both glowing insistently as she tried to tune into what Michiko was saying. The interactive section was coming up and she needed to make sure none of those messages related to what she needed to say. Surreptitiously checking she realized that her business sector's figures were down on last month and productivity had tapered off from the team she had merged only last October.

They had seemed so dynamic and the sense of taking a technical sector and merging it with the people management side of the business seemed intuitive. It wasn't. They just weren't communicating. The friendly information that Danny Grant had posted up every Friday, including birthdays, babies, and brain drain suggestion items, seemed like a happy dream compared with the short sharp instructions from the new communication team. Danny had only last week put in for early retirement following some of the new target-based initiatives and online accountability logs. People were at their desks from 8.30 until 7 p.m. and were still less productive than at any time in the past.

Virtual teams had been ordered to report in at specific times, when Isolda knew that all had opted for virtual working to avoid these in the first place. Two had resigned and one was Isolda's most talented Account Manager. Kit Joseph had taken his flair, silly sense of humour, and client loyalty with him to the competitor.

Accidentally running into him in the park with his toddlers Isolda saw why he wanted to work more flexibly. 'It used to be my ideal job. Creative and worthwhile but once the culture changed I didn't want to be a part of the desk-bound droves and that was the way it was going. I got out, but you're stuck with several who can't—they've tried—and they resent you and all the Executive Team.'

Isolda knew Kit's honesty wasn't malicious but it hurt all the same to realize that things had degenerated to this. It was supposed to be progressive. It had worked brilliantly at the software company she used to manage. There the obligatory anchor times and days had ensured some level of communication between and within taciturn teams. Here that hadn't been necessary as they all communicated well in their VTs, working in small closely knit teams that knew when the other was dog walking or collecting a child. They had been a working unit and now Isolda knew she had to return them to strength.

Michiko's clipped tones echoed crisply over as she asked Isolda how she intended to remedy her sector's recent dip. Isolda felt herself straightening up, ready to take on the challenge. She hadn't spent eight years as a change management consultant for nothing.

Well I have a layered strategy for addressing the current situation. First I intend to . . .

The link was broken and Michiko could not hear what Isolda's intentions were.

Questions

- Type a brief email to Michiko Shimidzu outlining the current problems as you see them.
- Offer a four-point plan for tackling the problems you have identified.
- Isolda brings in an occupational psychologist to evaluate the sector's working methods. What areas of concern might the psychologist pick up on as a priority for her?
- Isolda would like to plan a day to address some of these issues. Outline some of the key elements she should include in her away day and suggest why they are important.

 Online Resource Centre

Visit the supporting online resource centre for additional material which will help you with your research, essays, and assignments, or you may find these additional resources helpful when revising for exams.

http://www.oxfordtextbooks.co.uk/orc/matthewman/

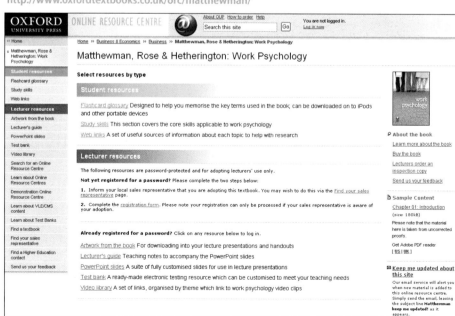

American Time Use Survey Summary (2006) http://www.bls.gov/tus/ accessed 20 November 2007.

Amin, S. (1990) *Delinking: Towards a Polycentric World* (trans. M. Wolfers). London: Zed Books.

Applebaum, S., Lavigne-Schmidt, S., Pevtchev, M., and Shapiro, B. (1999) Downsizing: measuring the costs of failure. *Journal of Management Development*, 18/5: 436–63.

Argyris, C. (1960) *Understanding Organizational Behaviour.* Homewood, IL: Dorsey.

Arnold, J. (2004) The congruence problem in John Holland's theory of vocational decisions. *Journal of Occupational and Organizational Psychology*, 77/1: 95–113.

Bailey, D., and Kurland, N. (2002) A review of telework research: findings, new directions, and lessons for the study of modern work. *Journal of Organizational Behavior*, 23/4: 383–400.

Baillie, J. (1995) The dangers of following the herd into downsizing drives. *People Management*, 1/23: 53.

Boyer, E. P., and Webb, T. G. (1992) Ethics and diversity: a correlation enhanced through corporate communication. *IEEE Transactions on Professional Communication*, 355/1: 38–43.

Brewster, C., Mayne, L., and Tregaskis, O. (1997) Flexible working in Europe. *Journal of World Business*, 32/2: 133–51.

Bryant, N. (2006) Tackling ageism down under. *BBC News*, http://www.bbc.co.uk, 4 Oct., accessed 11 Nov. 2007.

Cameron, K., Freeman, S., and Mishra, A. (1993) Downsizing and redesigning organizations. In G. Huber and W. Glick (eds.), *Organizational Change and Redesign*. New York: Oxford University Press.

Carroll, M., Marchington, M., and Earnshaw, J. (1999) Recruitment in small firms: processes, methods and problems. *Employee Relations*, 21/3: 55–64.

Cascio, W. F. (1998) The virtual workplace: a reality now. *Industrial-Organizational Psychologist*, 35: 32–8.

Cascio, W. F. (1993) Downsizing: what do we know? What have we learned? *Academy of Executive Management*, 7/1: 95–104.

CIPD (2007) *Diversity: An Overview.* Wimbledon: CIPD.

CIPD (2008) *The Psychological Contract: A Fact Sheet.* Wimbledon: CIPD.

Clark, J., and Koonce, R. (1997) Engaging survivors. *Executive Excellence*, 14/5: 12–13.

Cole, R. (1993) Learning from learning theory: implications for quality improvement of turnover, use of contingent workers, and job rotation policies. *Quality Management Journal*, 1: 9–25.

Conway, N., and Briner, R. B. (2005) *Understanding Psychological Contracts at Work: A Critical Evaluation of Theory and Research.* Oxford: Oxford University Press.

Cornehis, J. V. (2004) Veblen's theory of finance capitalism and contemporary corporate America. *Journal of Economic Issues*, 38/1: 29–58.

Coutu, D. (1998) Organization: trust in virtual teams. *Harvard Business Review*, 76/3: 20–1.

Coyle-Shapiro, J., Kessler, I., and Purcell, J. (2003) The employment relationship in the UK public sector: a psychological contract perspective. *Journal of Public Administration Research and Theory*, 13/2: 213–30.

Coyle-Shapiro, J., Kessler, I., and Purcell, J. (2004) Exploring organizationally directed citizen behaviour reciprocity or 'it's my job'? *Journal of Management Studies*, 4/1: 85–95.

CROW: Centre for Research into the Older Worker. http://www.surrey.ac.uk/crow/research-strategy.htm. Accessed Mar. 2008.

De Witte, H., De Cuyper, N., and Van Hecke, M. (2004) Job insecurity: violation of the psychological contract. Paper presented at the 3rd International ICOH Conference on Unemployment and Health: Persistent Unemployment and Precarious Work—Research and Policy Issues. Bremen, 23–5 September.

Doty, H., Glick, W., and. Huber, G. (1993) Fit, equifinality, and organizational effectiveness: a test of two configurational theories. *Academy of Management Journal*, 36/6: 1196–250.

Drucker, P. (1998) Management's new paradigms. *Forbes*, 162/7: 152.

Drucker, P. (2002) The next society. *The Economist* Print Edition.

Ehrhart, K., and Makransky, G. (2007) Testing vocational interests and personality as predictors of person-vocation and person-job fit. *Journal of Career Assessment,* 15/2: 206–26.

Eriksson, R. (2005) Parental leave in Sweden: the effects of the second daddy month. Swedish Institute for Social Research, Stockholm University. Working Paper Series No. 9.

ESRC (2008) Future of work. http://www.leeds.ac.uk/esrcfutureofwork (accessed 31 Jan. 2008).

Etzioni, A. (2002) On self evident truths. *Academic Questions*, 16/1: 11–15.

Evans, J. (1997) Downsizing plus outsourcing equals small business bonanza. *Working Woman*, 22/5: 53.

Fang, Y., and Neufeld, D. (2006) Should I stay or should I go? Worker commitment to virtual organizations. *Proceedings of the 39th Hawaii International Conference on System Sciences.*

Francesconi, M., and Gosling, A. (2005) Career paths of part-time workers. Working Paper Series No. 19. London: EOC.

Friday, E., and Friday, S. (2003) Managing diversity using a strategic planned change approach. *Journal of Management and Development*, 22/10: 863–80.

Friedman, M. (1970) The social responsibility of business is to increase its profits. *New York Times Magazine* (New York Corp.), 13 Sept.: 122–6.

Furnham, A. (2000) Work in 2020: prognostications about the world of work 20 years into the millennium. *Journal of Managerial Psychology*, 15/3: 242–54.

Gallie, D. (2003) The quality of working life: is Scandinavia different? *European Sociological Review*, 19/1: 61–79.

Gap (2006) Corporate social responsibility report (2). http://www.gapinc.com (accessed 29 Feb. 2008).

Gassmann, O., and von Zedtwitz, M. (2003) Trends and determinants of managing virtual R&D teams. *R&D Management*, 33/3: 243–62.

Goffee, R., and Scase, R. (1992) Organisational change and the corporate career: restructuring of managers' job aspirations. *Human Relations*, 45/4: 363–85.

Grundy, J. (1998) Trust in virtual teams. *Harvard Business Review*, 76/6: 180.

Guthrie, J. (2006) Ethics, enterprise and expediency. *Financial Times*, 14 June.

Haywood, M. (1998) *Managing Virtual Teams: Practical Techniques for High-Technology Project Managers.* Boston: Artech House.

Haywood, M. (2000) Working in virtual teams: a tale of two projects and many cities. *IT Perspectives*, 2/Apr.: 58–60.

Hernandis, S., and Sanchez, M. (2006) *Gerontologia.* London: Pearson Prentice Hall.

Hodson, N. (2005) *Employees who Work from Home.* Human Resource Management Business Hotline Publications. Oxford: Teleworking Studies.

Hogarth, T., Hasluck, C., Gaelle, P., Winterbotham, M., and Vivian, D. (2001) *Work-Life Balance 2000: Results from the Baseline Study.* London: DfEE.

International Telework Advisory Council (ITAC) The Telework Advisory Group for WorldatWork. http://www.workingfromanywhere.org (accessed 7 Jan. 2008).

Irving, A. (2006) 'Garden leave' for BNG boss. *Whitehaven News*, 16 Nov.

Isabella, L. A. (1989) Downsizing: survivors' assessments. *Business Horizons*, May–June: 35–41.

Jackson, P. (2006) Employee commitment to quality: its conceptualisation and measurement. *International Journal of Quality and Reliability Management*, 21/7: 714–30.

Javenpaa, S., and Leidner, D. (1999) Communication and trust in global virtual teams. *Organization Science*, 10/6: 791–815. Special Issue: *Communication Processes for Virtual Organizations* (Nov.–Dec. 1999).

Johnson, A. (2005) Speech to CIPD Reward Conference, 9 Feb.

Johnson, P., Heimann, V., and O'Neill, K. (2001) The 'wonderland' of virtual teams. *Journal of Workplace Learning*, 13/1: 24–30.

Kandola, P. (2006) The psychology of effective business communications in geographically dispersed teams. Cisco Systems White Paper, http://www.cisco.com/go/offices (accessed 4 Nov. 2007).

Katz, D. (1964) The motivational basis of organisational behaviour. *Behavioural Science*, 9/2: 131–46.

Kauffeld, S. (2006) Self-directed work groups and team competence. *Journal of Occupational and Organisational Psychology*, 79: 1–21.

Kiesler, S., Kraut, R., Lundmark, V., Mukopadhyay, T., Patterson, M., and Scherlis, W. (1998) Internet paradox: a social technology that reduces social involvement and psychological well-being? *American Psychologist*, 53/9: 1017–31.

Kirrane, D. E. (1990) Managing values: a systematic approach to business ethics. *Training and Development Journal*, 44/11: 53–60.

Koh, H. C., and Boo, E. (2001) The link between organizational ethics and job satisfaction: a study of managers in Singapore. *Journal of Business Ethics*, 29/4: 309–24.

Kotter, J. P. (1973) The psychological contract: managing the joining up process. *California Management Review*, 15: 91–9.

Kozlowski, S., Chao, G., Smith, E., and Hedlund, J. (1993) Organizational downsizing: strategies, interventions, and research implications. In C. L. Cooper and I. T. Robertson (eds.), *International Review of Industrial and Organizational Psychology*. New York: John Wiley, 263–332.

Kumar, N. (2000) Where the rubber meets the road. http://www.Siliconindia.com (accessed 29 Apr. 2007).

Laudon, J., and Laudon, K. (2004) *Management Information Systems: Managing the Digital Firm* (8th edn.). Englewood Cliffs, NJ: Prentice Hall.

Leonard, B. (1995) Downsized and out: career survival in the '90s. *HR Magazine*, 40/6: 89–91.

Levinson, H., Munden, K. J., Price, C. R., Mandl, H. J., and Solley, C. M. (1962) *Men, Management and Mental Health*. Cambridge, MA: Harvard University Press. Cited in Johnson, J. (1988) *Certified Occupational Therapy Assistants: Opportunities and Challenges*. Stroud: Hawthorn Press.

Levy, F., and Murnane, R. (2004) The New Division of Labor: How Computers are Creating the Next Job Market. Princeton: Princeton University Press.

Lipnack, J., and Stamps, J. (2001) *Virtual Teams: People Working across Boundaries with Technology*. Chichester: John Wiley and Sons.

Luthans, B., and Sommer, S. (1999) The impact of downsizing on workplace attitudes: differing reactions of managers and staff in a health care organisation. *Group and Organization Management*, 24/1: 46–70.

McCartney, C. (2007) A holistic approach to diversity and equality. *Employment Digest Briefing*, 668.

McDermott, R. (1999) Why informational technology inspired but cannot deliver knowledge management. *California Management Review*, 41/4: 103–17.

Merrick, N. (1996) Jargon-ridden NVQs: back on the defensive. *People Management*, 25: 14–15.

Millward, L., and Brewerton, P. (2000) Psychological contracts: employee relations for the twenty-first century? In C. Cooper and I. Robertson (eds.), *International Review of Industrial and Organizational Psychology*. New York: John Wiley, 1–61.

Nelson, B. (1997) The care of the un-downsized. *Training and Development*, 51/4: 41–55.

Nietzsche, F. (1989) *Beyond Good and Evil: Prelude to a Philosophy of the Future* (trans. W. Kaufmann). Vintage books edition. London: Random House Inc.

Noyes, J. M. (2001) *Designing for Humans*. Hove: Psychology Press.

Noyes, J. M., and Masakowski, Y. (2007) *Decision Making in Complex Environments*. Aldershot: Ashgate Publishing.

OECD (2004) *OECD in Figures*. Paris: OECD.

Office for National Statistics (2007) UK population by age 1971–2006. http://www.statistics.gov.uk/cci/nugget.asp?ID=949.

Organ, D. (1988). *Organizational Citizenship Behavior: The Good Soldier Syndrome*. Lexington, MA: Lexington Books.

Ouchi, W. G. (1981) *Theory Z*. Reading, MA: Addison-Wesley.

Pape, W. (1999) The book of virtuals. *INC Technology*, 19/17: 26.

Pillinger, J. (2001) *Quality in Social Public Services*. Dublin: European Foundation for the Improvement of Living and Working Conditions.

Precup, L., O'Sullivan, D., Cormican, K., and Dooley, L. (2006) Virtual team environment for collaborative research projects. *International Journal of Innovation and Learning (IJIL)*, 3/1: 71–94.

Rees, D., and Porter, C. (2003) *Skills of Management* (5th edn.). London: Thomson.

Ross, R., and Schneider, R. (1992) *From Equality to Diversity: A Business Case for Equal Opportunities*. London: Pitman Publishing.

Rousseau, D. M. (1990) New hire perceptions of their own and their employer's obligations: a study of psychological contracts. *Journal of Organizational Behaviour*, 11: 389–400.

Rousseau, D. M., and Parks, J. (1993) The contracts of individuals and organisations. In L. L. Cummings and B. Straw (eds.), *Research in Organisation Behavior*, 15. Greenwich, CT: JAI Press, 1–43.

Senge, P. (2006) *The Fifth Discipline: The Art and Practice of the Learning Organization*. New York: Currency Doubleday Books.

Shapiro, D., and Kirkman, B. (1999) Employees' reaction to the change to work teams: the influence of 'anticipatory' injustice. *Journal of Organizational Change Management*, 12/1: 51–67.

Shaw, J. B., and Barrett-Power, E. (1997) A conceptual framework for assessing organization, work group and individual effectiveness during and after downsizing. *Human Relations*, 50/2: 109–27.

Sims, R. R. (1992) The challenge of ethical behaviour in organizations. *Journal of Business Ethics*, 11: 505–13.

Smith, C., Organ, D., and Near, J. (1983) Organizational citizenship behavior: its nature and antecedents. *Journal of Applied Psychology*, 68: 653–63.

Smithey Fulmer, I., Gerhart, B., and Scott, K. (2003) Are the 100 best better? An empirical investigation of the relationship between being 'a great place to work' and firm performance. *Personnel Psychology*, 56/4: 965–93.

Soutar, G., McNeil, M., and Molster, C. (2004) The impact of the work environment on ethical decision making: some Australian evidence. *Journal of Business Ethics*, 13/5: 327–39.

Starr, A. (2001) *Naming the Enemy: Anti-Corporate Movements Confront Globalization*. London: Zed Books.

Strassmann, P. (2001) Interview on the Information Age. *IT Economist*.

Taguchi, G., El Sayed, M., and Hsaing, C. (1989) *Quality Engineering and Production Systems*. New York: McGraw-Hill.

Sullivan, S., and Mainiero, L. (2006) *The Opt-Out Revolution: Why People are Leaving Companies to Create Kaleidoscope Careers*. Mountain View, CA: Davies Black.

Szymanski, D., and Hise, R. (2000) e-satisfaction: an initial examination. *Journal of Retailing*, 76/3: 309–15.

Taylor, S. (2005) *People Resourcing* (3rd edn.). London: CIPD.

Thomas, T., Schermerhorn, J., and Dienhart, J. (2004) Strategic leadership of ethical behavior in business. *Academy of Management Executive*, 18/2: 56–65.

Tietze, S., Musson, G., and Scurry, T. (2006) Homeworking in local authorities. ESRC funded 'Managing Homebased Telework' Research.

Toffler, A. (1980) *The Third Wave*. London: Bantam Dell Publishing Group.

TUC (2001) *Changing Times* online. http://www.tuc.org.uk/publications (accessed 4 Jan. 2008).

Turner, F. (2006) Workplace ethics: on the decline? *The CEO Refresher*. Refresher Publications inc.

Vigoda-Gadot, E. (2006) Compulsory citizenship behavior: theorizing some dark sides of the good soldier syndrome in organizations. *Journal of the Theory of Social Behaviour*, 36/1: 8221–308.

Vigoda-Gadot, E., and Angert, L. (2007) Goal setting theory, job feedback and OCB: lessons from a longitudinal study. *Basic and Applied Social Psychology*, 29/2: 119–28.

Vitell, S. J., and Davis, D. L. (1990) The relationship between ethics and job satisfaction: an empirical investigation. *Journal of Business Ethics*, 9/6: 489–94.

Warner, M. (1997) Working at home. *Fortune*: 165–6.

Glossary

accommodating the conflict-handling style where people cooperate and give in to others.

action learning a type of learning characterized by active involvement of participant(s) in the(ir) learning process and outcomes. Participants are often exposed to real-life problems.

action method is an organizational development process that uses the steps of diagnosis, planning for change, intervention, and evaluation.

adapted child part of the child ego state which adapts to others' expectations through complying or rebelling.

additive task tasks that involves many people (an example of this is the tug of war where two teams are pulling each end of a rope).

adjourning the task has been completed and the team is ready to dismantle.

adult part of the ego state which is logical, gathers facts which are evaluated against criteria in order to make decisions.

adverse impact evidence of cultural bias in a test, where average scores for groups vary by ethnic origin. Conventionally, concern about bias in a test would occur when one group scored 20% below the average of another.

Alderfer ERG (1972) theory of motivation that concentrates on people's needs. Specifically they are Existence, Relatedness, and Growth, but a person can move up or down the hierarchy.

alienation a term used by Marx to describe the feeling of foreignness or isolation from others, caused when people are depersonalized from their work and do not own the profit of their labour.

anthropometrics the study of the variability in size of human body dimensions. Anthropometric dimensions are used to design working equipment and environments suitable for a wide range of users, typically the 5th to the 95th percentile. Knowledge of anthropometrics is also vital in the design of everyday objects such as clothing, cars, and computer keyboards.

aptitude special talent, skills and interests of a person

assertiveness the degree to which individuals stand up for their own rights as well as respect those of others.

assessment centre a system where groups of candidates are assessed together on a number of dimensions or competencies, using a number of techniques (e.g. activities, interviews, and tests), evaluated by a number of assessors. Frequently used in the selection of new graduates and managers.

assumptions of morality this is when a group believes its own aims and means are morally superior and unquestionable.

attitude the labelling of our like or dislike toward a person, object, or situation.

attribution the process by which we make sense of our environment through our perceptions of causality.

autocratic leaders who strongly control their subordinates and make all decisions.

autokinetic effect an optical illusion where participants see a spot of light that seems to be moving but is actually stationary.

avoiding the conflict handling style where people avoid conflict.

balance theory an explanation of interpersonal relationships contending that people tend to prefer relationships that are consistent or balanced.

bases of power what the holder has that gives them power.

behaviour modification the use of classical and operant conditioning techniques in therapy to reduce and eliminate negative or unwanted responses and to reinforce positive or desired responses.

be perfect the working style which prefers to do things to perfection, right first time, and detests mistakes.

best practice a technique or process, established through research and experience, that reliably leads to a desired outcome.

be strong the working style which wants to handle tasks with a sense of calmness and avoids showing any sign of weakness.

Binet, Alfred (1859–1911) French psychologist who conceptualized intelligence as an age-related phenomenon.

biomechanics the study of human strength and movement, used widely in designing products, systems, and working environments to reduce the risk of user injury.

blamer the communication style that blames others when under stress.

blue chip company a company on the London Stock Exchange with a large market capitalization, stable earnings, consistent dividend record, and reputation as a reliable investment. The term is believed to come from the term for a poker chip of high value used in casinos.

body language is a term for non-verbal communication that includes: posture, eye-contact, facial expressions, gestures, and touch.

bottom line a phrase borrowed from accounting which indicates the conclusion or the amount of profit left after all costs have been deducted.

boundaryless careers people are no longer bounded or organizationally constrained.

Business Process Reengineering (BPR) is an organizational technique of constantly and critically examining everything the organization does in order to improve its process.

CAD computer-aided design.

CAM computer-aided manufacture.

career anchors Schein's self-concept anchors.

career choice Holland's six vocational personality types.

career management advice to plan and to look after careers.

case-based reasoning a popular managerial software to aid managers in decision making by scanning previous cases for similarities and offering solutions.

Cattell, James (1860–1944) a functionalist psychologist and pioneer of mental testing.

central tendency error an unfair grouping of performance evaluations at the middle of the scale.

CEO Chief Executive Officer and chair of the board.

change agent a person who directs organizational development in organization; this may be someone inside or outside the organization.

change strategies can be considered as the different strategies and procedures that are used to classify the change environment.

channel this is the method of communication, such as face-to-face, telephone, or electronic.

classical conditioning a previously neutral stimulus is repeatedly paired with an unconditioned stimulus which results in the unconditioned response being associated with the unconditioned stimulus.

Classical School of Management believes application of certain principles leads to efficiency in production. Henri Fayol's (1916) set of guidelines is one of the best known. Includes: scalar concept, unity of command, span of control, organizational specialization, and application of scientific method.

close or nearby leaders refers to subordinates' immediate boss.

coaching is personalized intervention aimed at enhancing performance and professional development in employees.

coercive power refers to the person in authority's ability to punish and withhold rewards.

Cognitive Behaviour Therapy (CBT) is a therapeutic intervention by a qualified professional which promotes a positive re-evaluation of the stressor. It aims to reduce the negative thoughts associated with the stressor.

cognitive dissonance the inconsistency between two or more attitudes or between attitudes and behaviour.

cohesion the degree to which a group is so attractive to its members that they want to remain a part of it (and hence will conform to its norms).

collaborating the conflict-handling style which focuses on helping both parties to achieve their goals.

command groups are permanent formal groups that arise from relatively fixed structures within an organization under a single manager.

community of practice group of professionals who meet to share challenges and best practice together to promote higher standards in their profession.

competency the skills, aptitudes, and personal characteristics that are associated with successful performance of a specified job.

competency framework contains definitions of all the competencies used by an organization and is used in recruitment, employee development, and reward.

competing the conflict-handling style characterized by the need to win at all costs.

compromising the conflict-handling style where both parties give up something to get something in return.

Comte, Auguste (1798–1857) the founder of positivism and the word 'sociology' who believed that cultures go through three stages in explaining phenomena: theological, metaphysical, and scientific.

conflict the process resulting from dis-agreement between two or more individuals.

conformity the degree to which individuals will go along with others' wishes.

consensus the attributional process where others react to a person or event in the same way as the person that is being considered.

consistency the attributional process which looks at the degree to which a person responds to a particular person or event on different occasions.

constant effect essential determinants which need to be present at a minimal level. Large amounts do not have a negative effect. Additional decrement determinants refer to determinants which need to be present but in large amounts they can be damaging.

construct validity validity which establishes the operation of the specific construct that a test purports to measure.

content analysis a technique for exploring recurring themes and issues in unstructured data, for example depth interview transcription.

content theories of motivation *what* it is that actually motivates people.

contingency theories a school of thought which emphasizes the impact of contextual factors on leadership style.

Continuing Professional Development (CPD) professional body requirement for regular updating of competences, often evidenced through a portfolio of activities undertaken.

continuous change is organizational change that is ongoing, evolving, and cumulative.

contrast error a distortion of interview judgement caused by the interviewer giving unfairly high or low scores on the basis of a comparison with previous candidates.

controlling parent part of the ego state which is characterized by being firm and directive and uses words like should and ought.

cooperativeness the degree to which individuals are willing to cooperate with others in solving conflict.

coping strategies are the individual's characteristic means of managing stressors in an effort to moderate their impact.

corporate social responsibility a perception that organizations should behave ethically and give back to the community they are centred in and honour the wishes of their broader stakeholders.

correlation the degree of relationship between two variables. A statistic that varies from unity through zero to minus one.

correlation coefficient a statistic showing the degree of relationship between two variables.

counselling communication used to facilitate personal change.

counselling skills skills used to facilitate open and honest dialogue.

creativity is an ability to come up with new and different viewpoints on a subject.

criterion validity validity which compares the results achieved on a test of some attribute with another independent evaluation of that attribute; for example, the comparison of a paper test of anxiety with physiological measures of stress.

critical realism approach to the philosophy of science first put forward by Drake (1920) from the ideas of Descartes and Locke. Developed by Bhaskar (1978) as a critique of Positivism. States that reality is at various levels— biological, psychological, social, and cultural—and cannot be reduced from one level to another. Believes there exists a reality independent of our representation of it, but acknowledges that our knowledge of reality is subject to historical and other influences.

cross-sectional a research design where data is collected at one particular point in time.

crystallized intelligence is based on skills acquired through education and cultural experiences.

culture how an organization goes about doing things.

culture-fair test a test which has been developed to include specific use of language and cultural references which are relevant to a specified group.

dark side of management a type of management that focuses on the dysfunctional, distorted, and destructive side of behaviour.

decoding this is how a message is interpreted by someone else.

delivering training the way the training event is delivered; this also takes account of the trainer or facilitator and their ability to build rapport and engage his or her audience.

demand characteristics a term coined by the American psychologist Martin Orne, to refer to those cues within a research situation that communicate information about the researcher's hypothesis, and the specific role of participants in the study.

democratic leaders who involve their followers in the decision-making process.

dependent variable in an experimental design, the measure taken by the researcher which demonstrates the impact of the independent variable(s).

depth interview an unscripted social exchange which allows respondents to answer freely and to raise topics and issues as they feel appropriate.

Derrida, Jacques (1930–2004) French philosopher who coined the term 'deconstructionism', a philosophical approach which sought to move away from the previous philosophical movements of phenomenology, existentialism, and structuralism by denying the existence of reality. This exerted great influence on psychology as well as many other disciplines, forcing psychologists to address the notion of consciousness.

determinants concept devised by P. Warr. These are factors essential for individual psychological well-being.

development centres workshops which measure the abilities of participants against the agreed success criteria for the job role.

discourse all human production and uses of language in oral, written, and symbolic form.

discrimination unequal treatment of people based on arbitrary characteristics such as race, gender, ethnicity, or age.

distant leader refers to leaders such as chief executives, religious leaders, and so forth, who are almost beyond the reach of subordinates.

distinctiveness the attributional process which determines the degree to which a person responds in the same way to different people or situations.

distributive justice under organizational justice theory, the perceived fairness of the outcome.

downsizing (also rightsizing) a deliberate organizational decision to reduce the workforce that is intended to improve organizational performance.

drama triangle a form of interaction involving payoffs between the roles of persecutor, rescuer, and victim.

dysfunctional behaviour behaviour not conducive to efficient functioing in daily life.

electronic cottage a place where access to a computer can be guaranteed for workers (now largely obsolete concept in developed countries).

emotional climate the emotional effect that individual's behaviour has on the atmosphere of a workplace.

emotional intelligence (EQ) a kind of intelligence or skill that involves the ability to perceive, assess, and positively influence one's own and other people's emotions. Current definitions of EQ are inconsistent about what it measures: some (Bradbury and Greaves) say that EQ is dynamic, it can be learned or increased; whereas others (such as Mayer) say that EQ is stable, and cannot be increased.

emotion in career management some writers believe that emotional experiences and expression in career development can have a very powerful role to play.

empiricism the view that only knowledge that is measurable is valid in scientific endeavour.

employee assistance programmes (EAPs) a company-sponsored programme that helps employees cope with personal problems that are interfering with their job performance.

employee empowerment is the practice of giving employees control of tasks and functions usually done by supervisors.

encoding this is how a communicator choses to express a message.

entrepreneurship the drive and ability to set up a business on one's own or see through a creative idea to realization.

environmental clarity the extent to which an individual feels in control of their environment via good understanding and emotional stability.

episodic change organizational change that tends to be infrequent, discontinuous, and intentional. It occurs during periods of divergence when organizations are moving away from their equilibrium conditions.

epistemology a branch of philosophy concerned with exploring ideas on how we come to know the world. In research, the beliefs of the researcher about the utility of certain types of data and design in uncovering the nature of psychological reality.

ergonomics a multi-disciplinary field which includes input from the fields of engineering, physiology, and applied psychology. Sometimes known as human factors, ergonomics aims to enhance efficiency, well-being, and safety at work.

expectancy theories people will be motivated when they expect that they will be able to achieve what they want from the effort that they put in.

expert power is power based on the sub-ordinate's belief that the leader knows more about the task than the subordinate does.

extrinsic rewards external to the job and related to tangible rewards such as pay and benefits.

Eysenck, Hans (1914–97) psychologist born in Germany who emigrated to UK in 1934. Worked on intelligence and personality.

face validity the acceptability of a test to candidates and their perception that it is reasonable to ask them to complete this for the job they have applied for.

factor analytic models models based on a statistical approach that identifies differentiating or underlying factors as a cause of behaviour.

family friendly policies where an organization seeks to offer flexible packages to employees to facilitate both family life and a work/life balance (WLB)

feedback when individuals want to know how their behaviour is perceived by others. This forms part of their self-image.

felt-fair pay a subjective, personal estimation of how well one is remunerated in relation to others.

Fiedler's contingency theory attempts to match leadership style to situation which depends on the favourability of three contextual variables: group atmosphere, task structure, and power position of leader.

flexicurity a new concern for both flexibility and security at work.

flexitime a technique that allows people to decide their own times of arriving at, and leaving, the office, subject to core hours and an overall weekly or monthly minimum.

fluid intelligence is based on the ability to organize information toward problem solving.

fmcg 'fast-moving consumer goods', I.e. ones that sell quickly.

focus group a research method where data is generated from group discussion on a topic set by the researcher.

forced compliance when individuals are pressured to do or say things that are not consistent with their true views.

formal groups groups purposely put together to achieve a common task or goals.

forming the stage of a group that is a collection of individuals placed together to form a group.

four-fifth rule the generally accepted cut-off point for the demonstration of ethnic bias in a test, where one ethnic group scores on average at a level which is four-fifths of that achieved by another group. See adverse impact.

Freud, Sigmund (1856–1939) founder of psychoanalysis who identified the conflict between instinctive behaviour and the learnt desire to be civilized and moral.

fundamental attribution error the error resulting from wrongly attributing the cause of others' behaviour as being due to their own disposition rather than external factors.

garden leave a period of enforced idleness in which a worker is obliged to neither work, nor have contact with their former or prospective organizations for the duration of the garden leave.

gate keeping is withholding information in the communication process.

general adaptation syndrome explains the physiological response of the body to perceptions or experiences of stress in three generic stages: alarm reaction, resistance, and collapse.

generalizability the applicability of results and measures from the sample of the research to a broader population.

genuine occupational qualification an exception to laws on equality wherein a person may be employed for particular features, e.g. an Indian woman to waitress at an Indian restaurant. The casting of actors and models is also covered by GOQ, as are security staff, who must be male if searching males or female if searching females.

glass ceiling phenomenon refers to situations where advancement is limited within the hierarchy of an organization, based on discrimination most commonly being gender and race

glass cliff positions of leadership for women that are associated (mistakenly) with increased failure risks

globalization the heightening of worldwide social and business factors which link geographically distant locations.

group any number of people who interact together face to face and perceive themselves as a group.

groupthink a tendency in long-standing work groups to perceive the group as invincible. Conformity is strict; the group tends not to evaluate its own activities or examine alternatives, and underestimates the power of other groups.

Hall, Granville (1844–1924) set up first experimental laboratory in USA; founded American Psychological Association 1892. Invited Freud to Clark University and thus helped give psychoanalysis an international platform.

hardiness is an attitudinal disposition comprised of a sense of commitment, control, and challenge.

Hawthorne effect when people participate in psychology experiments, their behaviour may be affected by their understanding and experience of being the focus of scientific study.

heuristic a 'rule of thumb'. Simple and approximate rules, guiding procedures, short-cuts, or strategies that are used to solve problems.

hierarchy of needs Maslow's theory of motivation that there is a hierarchy of motives with each lower layer taking precedence, when not satisfied, over the next step up.

homeostasis is the individual's drive to seek out information which informs their psychological and physical state and drives them to achieve stability.

horns and halo effect a perceptual bias, where highly positive or negative information about a person conditions all subsequent perception of them.

human error a human act or failure to act which falls outside a particular boundary or tolerance limit.

humanizing work means attempting to take into account human needs at work.

Human Relations Theory is interested in human factors and advocates that a happy worker is a productive worker

hurry up the working style which wants to do things in the shortest possible time.

hypothesis the research question that forms the basis of enquiry and experimentation.

illusion of invulnerability this is where group members overemphasize their strengths and play down their weaknesses. This results in a bias towards feelings that decisions the group makes are correct. See groupthink.

implicit personality theory a person's beliefs concerning the association of, and interrelationship between, personality characteristics.

impression management acting deliberately to make a good impression, to present oneself in the most favourable way.

independent variable what the researcher controls in an experiment, which is systematically varied to see its effects on the dependent variable, for example pay level (IV) on productivity (dv).

individual needs analysis assesses what knowledge, skills, and attitudes a person already has and whether individuals need any training in order to perform the job in question.

influencing is exerting power and control over others in a way that results in changes in behaviour or attitude.

informal groups these types of groups will spring up on their own as a result of psychological needs of people, and out of formal groups. They also tend to be more powerful than formal groups.

in-group a group of which the perceiver (the person making the judgement) is a member.

innovation refers to production or adoption of useful ideas and idea implementation.

insight learning seen especially in problem-solving tasks, and often sudden, insight learning results from an understanding of relationships as opposed to trial and error learning.

intellectual property an individual's knowledge which is commercially viable.

intelligence is a facility at solving problems.

intelligence quotient (IQ) an age-related concept of intelligence invented by Binet comparing mental age with chronological age.

internal validity refers specifically to whether an experimental treatment/condition makes a difference or not, and whether there is sufficient evidence to support the claim.

interpersonal skills a broad heading which can cover such areas as communication, observing, listening, giving and receiving feedback, and non-verbal behaviour.

intimacy the extent to which one person wants or desires to be close to another.

intrinsic rewards rewards, which are internal or integral to the job, comprising factors such as meaningful work, achievement, recognition.

James, William (1842–1910) a founder of Functionalism who emphasized the function of both consciousness and behaviour. A pragmatist who believed in both free will and determinism.

Japanese styles of management different features of Japanese management including total quality management and quality circles.

job analysis an analysis of the tasks involved in the successful performance of a particular post within an organization, and the skills required to perform it. The procedure leads to the generation of a job description and a person specification.

job enrichment measures to increase the autonomy, responsibilities, or meaningfulness of a job.

job satisfaction is considered to be an attitude, an emotional and psychological response to a feeling of achievement or fulfilment of personal motivations.

Johari window a model which assumes that the more open individuals are with themselves and others, through self-disclosure and feedback, the more self-aware and adjusted they will become.

just in time (JIT) a lean system of management originating in Toyota Japan.

kaleidoscope careers wherein workers make differing choices dependent on the stage they are at in their career.

knowledge-based mistake a human error which stems from an inappropriate diagnosis or assessment of the situation.

knowledge workers those working within knowledge industries dealing in turning data into knowledge to add value to their organizations.

Kohler, Wolfgang (1887–1967) co-founder of Gestalt psychology. Worked with Wertheimer on perception.

Kuhn, Thomas (1922–96) argued in *The Structure of Scientific Revolutions* that normal science progressed within paradigms (which framed the problems that scientists could investigate) until the inconsistencies became too great and new paradigms were formed.

laissez-faire leaders who are the least effective as they tend to abdicate from the leadership role.

lapse a human error which stems from a failure to act, usually associated with forgetfulness or absent-mindedness; an error of omission.

latent learning although there is no immediate change at the time of learning through association, this is remembered and put to use at a later time.

leadership continuum indicates a variety of styles between the two extremes each corresponding to a different pattern of interactions between followers and managers.

leadership grid an updated version of the managerial grid; a fifth dimension was added.

learning organization an organization which aims to create a climate of continuous learning and improvement at both the individual and organisational level.

learning styles people have different behavioural styles which affect how they prefer to learn.

legitimate power is influence based on the formal organizational position of the leader.

levels of change a model that assumes a change in one area of this model necessitates a consideration of change in the other areas. It includes purpose, identity, beliefs and values, capabilities and skills, behaviours, and environment.

Lewin, Kurt (1890–1947) Gestalt psychologist who studied motivation and group dynamics and whose Field Force Theory explains behaviour in terms of one's field of social influences.

life event an important milestone or event or occurrence in an individual's life, often with emotional relevance. Point of transition in life.

life position the outcome of our evaluation of self and others around the criteria of being OK or not being OK.

lifespan approaches to career theory these theories look at careers through various stages of development

Likert scale a measuring scale developed by Rensis Likert, often of 5 points, which was easy to construct, and consisted of respondents agreeing strongly at one end through a neutral mid point to disagreeing strongly at the other end.

locus of control concept developed by Rotter which describes whether people feel the rewards they experience are a result of their own actions or are outside their control.

longitudinal a research design where data is collected over time, and sampled at a number of time periods.

LPC Least Preferred Co-Worker, a measure that measures a leader's least preferred co-worker to work with.

management by objectives (MBO) is a performance appraisal system that measures the effectiveness of an employee or group in terms of goals set by the supervisor and the employees or group.

managerial grid a tool which explores a manager's style to the extent that they are either 'concerned for people' or 'concerned for task'.

managing diversity a culturally driven approach focusing on celebrating diversity which comes from the top down and permeates the whole organization.

Marx, Karl (1818–83) writer on the industrial revolution and the effects of capitalism on workers and work. Promoted the socio-politico-economic system of communism.

Maslow, Abraham (1908–70) humanistic psychologist believing in innate tendency in people towards self-actualization.

Maslow's hierarchy of needs a person will move up the hierarchy, or levels of needs, only when each need has been satisfied.

matrix teams project teams put together with a project manager whilst each worker also has their own manager outside of the project: doublereporting.

maximal performance test which seeks to establish the highest score that a person is capable of achieving.

mediator a variable that directly affects the impact of the independent variable upon the dependent variable.

mental age a concept developed by Alfred Binet. In the measurement of childhood ability, the level of cognitive skill associated with a specific age-band. The mental age and chronological age of the child may not coincide.

mental health the state of being able to function cognitively and emotionally and relate to people in a stable manner.

meta-analysis analysis based on summating a collection of previous research findings on a related hypothesis.

millennials a term for those who reached adulthood around the second millennium.

Miller, George (b. 1920) information processing researcher in the 1950s and 1960s whose work led to cognitive psychology.

mistake a human error which stems from a failure to correctly diagnose a situation, or to devise an appropriate plan to deal with the situation.

moderator a variable that affects the direction or strength of the relationship between the independent and the dependent variable.

multinational companies (MNC) organizations with multiple sites across countries and continents.

multiskilling equipping a workforce with a range of diverse skills and competencies.

Munsterberg, Hugo (1863–1916) created applied psychology by applying psychological principles in other areas: clinical, forensic, and industrial.

Myers–Briggs Type Indicator a personality typology which looks at people through the lens of how they meet the world, how they take in information, how they make decisions, and how they orient their lifestyle.

narcissistic personality disorder (NPD) a psychological disorder characterized by a pattern of self-importance and overestimation of one's own abilities.

natural child part of the ego state which is relaxed, fun-seeking, and does what it wants when it wants.

naturalistic design a study where research variables are not manipulated by the researcher, but explored as they occur naturally.

need for achievement theory of motivation developed by David McClelland with 3 types of need: achievement, power, and affiliation.

Neisser, Ulric (b. 1928) seen as the founding father of cognitive psychology moving away from behaviouralism and humanistic psychology and focusing on sensation, perception, imaging, memory, problem solving, and thinking. Published *Cognitve Psychology* 1967.

neurolinguistic programming an approach to change which takes into account the mind–body interaction, language, and the study of behavioural programmes.

non-verbal behaviour this is a type of body language which is not concerned with verbal behaviour. It concerns the use of gestures, facial expression, and limb movements.

norming conflict from the storming stage has subsided and rules and regulations are laid down by the group.

norms are the shared beliefs that lead to shared attitudes: the rules of expected and acceptable behaviour from members.

nurturing parent part of the ego state which strives to care and look after others.

observational learning new responses are learned by watching the behaviour of others.

Occupational Health/Welfare department concerned with promoting the health and well-being of employees. Welfare Departments were often the predecessor of Occupational Health.

occupational stress refers to the conflict between the job role, employee needs, and the demands of the workplace.

OKness the outcome of our evaluation of self and others.

operant conditioning it is likely that behaviour will change if the consequence of the response is changed.

organizational citizenship behaviour phenomenon wherein employees demonstrate innovative and spontaneous actions which go beyond their job role.

organizational culture is created by the values, attitudes, beliefs, and norms of behaviours of staff members which serve to influence and inform the behaviours of new staff members.

organizational level of needs analysis TNA should be considered at three levels: organizational level, team level, and individual level. These three levels are interlinked, and doing this ensures a balanced analysis that gives the bigger picture as well as specific needs of individuals.

organizational resilience is characterized by shared perceptions of reality, open communications, commitment to the task, and collaboration with peers to surmount problems.

organization development (OD) a management approach which tries to develop and change organizations by focusing on structure and internal processes.

out-group a group of which the perceiver (the person making the judgement) is not a member.

overload describes a situation where the psychological demands of a task are greater than optimal, outstripping the cognitive capacity available.

paradigm models models of leadership that emphasize research in a new direction, mainly of the transforming leader and the importance of follower attitudes.

participation this refers to the importance of active participation on the part of the trainee in order to understand by doing (Kolb's cycle).

path goal theory concerns itself with issues as to what motivates employees in a given situation.

peer evaluation is performance appraisal done by those at the same level as the person being appraised.

percentile a way to describe rank-ordered data (such as body measurements) that indicates the proportion of a sample or population in terms of the percentage of individuals with values at or below a given point.

performance-related pay (PRP) may be any form of performance pay but can include bonuses, which are typically paid on top of a basic salary or wage and appraisal-related performance pay, which is integrated into basic salary.

performing the group has bonded into a cohesive effective team ready to perform its task.

persecutor the drama triangle position where one person attacks another.

personal construct is an individual's unique way of viewing experiences, created by the individual in order to anticipate and thereby control events.

personal development process concerned with aspects of developing the individual.

personal development planning whereby the individual reflects on learning achieved and plans for future development.

personality is built on a wide range of the physical, mental, ethical, and social qualities specific to each individual.

personality questionnaire and inventory assesses the personality characteristics of the questionnaire/inventory taker.

personal power refers to power that stems from the personal characteristics of a manager/supervisor or leader.

personal resilience describes the capacity to rebound from adversity more strengthened and resourceful.

person/organizational fit organizations want to retain employees so seek those they believe have much in common with the organization or existing workers.

person perception the process by which individuals attribute characteristics or traits to other people and the processes underlying those attributions.

pilot a 'dummy run' of a research procedure, for example an interview, to ensure that all materials and measures are fit for purpose, and to allow rehearsal for the researcher.

please people the working style which strives to please others without asking. They value harmony.

polarization decisions that are made that are riskier for a number of reasons such as the issue being discussed becoming so familiar it does not seem as risky.

portfolio careers a portfolio of skills and activities that people take with them to different employment roles.

positivism an approach that believes that the principles of scientific method should be applied to the study of human behaviour.

post-modernism is a relativistic theory of knowledge which proposes there is no absolute truth about the world; instead, every question has an infinite number of answers, and all are equally valid.

post-traumatic stress is a normal reaction to an abnormal and life-threatening event, which is characterized by a specific set of physiological and psychological responses.

power is getting one's way to either effect or affect organizational outcomes.

predictive validity close correlation, or agreement, between the prediction of performance at the starting point (e.g. on selection), and the actual performance when measured later (e.g. after doing the job for some time).

prejudice process of prejudging others and forming judgements on stereotypes (positive or negative); it usually has negative connotations.

pre-test and post-test typically, before and after responses.

primacy and recency effect an effect of memory whereby material or information perceived at the beginning (primacy) or at the end (recency) of a series of data is more strongly remembered.

primary data data directly collected by the researcher in the course of a study.

principles of training there are two essential principles of training in order to help learning stick: these are participation and repetition.

problem-focused coping refers to the individual's intention to address the problem and to take action to actively reduce the individual's experience of occupational stress.

procedural justice under organizational justice theory the fairness of how the rewards are allocated or decisions made.

process theories of motivation *how* things might motivate people

programmed Instruction a method of teaching using a structured approach to building knowledge which requires accurate answers to tests before proceeding to the next stage.

projective techniques based on the Freudian concept of projection, tests such as the Rorschach inkblot test or the Thematic Apperception Test which access unconscious motives and allow the person to project them outside the self and the analyst to help the person gain personal insight from this.

psychoanalysis a therapy developed by Freud exploring the unconscious motives of people through retelling events from the past.

psychodiagnostic diagnosis using the principles of Freud's theory of personality and motivation.

psychological contract the unwritten agreement that exists between an employer and an employee which sets out what each expects from the other.

psychometric test a test that has been designed and constructed to measure quantitatively a psychological variable such as intelligence, aptitude, or personality traits and which has been standardized on a specific population in order to provide a comparison of the individual's performance to others in that population. Derived from two Greek words for 'measurement' and 'mind'.

psychosomatic illness a disorder where physiological symptoms are caused by stress.

punishment is an unpleasant consequence following certain behaviours, which leads to the decreased occurrence of these behaviours.

qualitative data research material which has been generated to explore unquantifiable variables, not normally measured by objective numerical measuring instruments, although they may be measured by scales of subjective comparison for example feelings, perceptions, or personal values.

quality circle programme is a form of group problem solving and goal setting with a main focus on improving product quality.

quality of working life the desire to have optimum working conditions in order to be able to contribute both to the organization and to personal well-being.

quantitative data research material which can be classified and counted in numerical form, for example, physiological measures of stress, or salary levels.

quasi-experiment an experiment undertaken in real settings, in which the researcher manipulates the IV.

quota sample a sample selected randomly from a population that aims to mirrors the original in terms of the proportion of core salient groups, for example, being half male and half female.

random sample a sample taken from a population in such a way as to ensure that every member has an equal chance of being selected.

reciprocal causality the idea that one causes the other's behaviour in the follower–leader relationship.

redundancy official notification and the process of losing current job.

re-engineer a concept meaning to reshape and fine tune the organization in order to meet new conditions.

referent power this type of power can be seen as coming under personal power and refers to the ability to control based on followers' or subordinates' loyalty to the leader and their desire to please him or her.

reflexivity a process of self-examination by a researcher to expose bias which explores how they may appear to their participants, and which scrutinizes their own values and aims in conducting the study.

reinforcement is any consequence that leads to an increase in the occurrence of behaviour.

reinforcement theory assumes that the occurrence of a behaviour is strengthened or weakened by the reinforcers or punishments that followed it.

reinforcer can be negative (a punishment) or positive (a reward) and will consequently strengthen or weaken behaviour.

reliability the consistency of a measure over time. Generally established through test–retest correlation (retesting a sample over time on the same test), or comparison of scores obtained from the same method on the same subject by different assessors.

repetition this refers to the need to practise the skill over time as it will help retention of the skills and knowledge.

rescuer the drama triangle role where one person attempts to rescue another without being asked.

resilience refers to the individual's or organization's capacity to rebound from adversity more strengthened and resourceful, whilst exhibiting characteristics of endurance and adaptation.

resistance to change can be defined as an individual or group engaging in acts to block or disrupt an attempt to introduce change.

retirement this is a time when, for most people, there is a temporary or permanent withdrawal from the labour market after having experienced a number of years of work.

reward power this is the second type of power that comes under position power and refers to the person's control over rewards valued by others.

rightsizing see downsizing.

Rogers, Carl (1902–87) humanistic psychologist giving an alternative to psychoanalysis in the treatment of disturbed people focusing on conditions of self-worth and value.

role refers to the expected patterns of behaviour associated with an employee's position in the structure of the organization.

role ambiguity occurs when an employee is not clear about what he or she is required to do in a job.

role conflict results from conflicting objectives or competing demands in the individual's role requirements.

role-set for a specific job role, all those other job incumbents that the job holder needs to interact with, in the course of fulfilling their own role. For example, university lecturers' role-set includes colleagues and peers, students, administrator, and government officials.

rule-based mistake a human error which stems from the inappropriate application of an 'if-then' rule.

sample a group drawn from a population used to represent the whole group. There are various methods of obtaining a sample, suited to the researcher's aims.

sampling frame a list of the total population that the researcher wishes to investigate. For example, government records of the all unemployed males. From this, a representative sample may be drawn.

satellite teams those who are remotely based who return to base at irregular intervals.

Scientific Management part of the Classical School of Management thought. Has four main principles in building efficiency and productivity: division of tasks, scientific selection and training, science of work, and economic incentives.

scientific method the practice of systematically gathering data through observation and experimentation, formulating and testing hypotheses, and developing a body of objective impartial knowledge.

secondary data data utilized in a study that has not been collected by the current researcher, for example, data about employee performance collected and kept by a work organization.

selective attention the ability to attend to one stimulus from among a mass of competing stimuli.

self-censorship this is when members of a group do not express their doubts, disagreements, or misgivings in order to maintain the cohesiveness and mutual support of the group.

self-disclosure telling someone else something about ourselves.

self-efficacy a term from cognitive psychology meaning the individual's belief in their capability to produce desired effects by their actions.

self-fulfilling prophecy an expectation about how things will be the situations that they predicted or expected.

self-managed working teams professional groups who work on projects to set targets and deadlines but who manage the intervening process independently.

self-serving bias when individuals attribute their own success to internal causes, and negative outcomes to external ones.

sensitivity training also called T-group training. A process of self-realization and attitude change through personal awareness in small group therapeutic interaction.

simulation is an exercise used in assessment centres where job applicants are put in a situation or activity similar to the actual job.

situational leadership a situational leader is one who can adopt different leadership styles depending on the situation.

skill-based mistake a human error that stems from the automatic execution of a skilled action (also known as a slip).

sleeper effect when a message has a greater delayed than immediate effect on the receiver's attitudes.

slip a human error which involves a failure to execute an action as intended.

SMART performance objectives which are Specific, Measurable, Achievable, Realistic, and Time-bound, the concept being drawn from goal theory.

SMEs small and medium sized companies. A term describing anything from a very small company employing a few people to those employing up to 250.

Social Constructionism a theoretical position in psychology that stresses the relative and provisional nature of knowledge and reality, and the impact of culture on the research process.

social desirability the tendency for people to want to paint hemselves in a postive light in testing situations.The general social acceptability of a trait or a behaviour may affect the likelihood of people's willingness to agree to following or possessing it (for example being socially anxious, or binge drinking).

Social Exchange Theory a series of cost–benefit exchanges where benefits outweigh the costs.

social facilitation the effect that other people have on an individual's performance, which could be either enhanced or inhibited depending on the task being done.

social identity the sense of identity we gain through being a member of a social group.

social loafing people's tendency to exert less effort in a group context because they were not evaluated, they could get away with it.

social support support arising from family, friends, and local communities to counter the effects of psychological responses to problems.

sources of stress can result from factors intrinsic to the job, the role, interpersonal interactions, and the working environment.

Spearman, Charles (1863–1945) English psychologist known for his work in statistics, factor analysis, and for Spearman's rank correlation coefficient. Worked on models of intelligence and conceptualized the g factor of general intelligence underlying intelligence.

stereotype stereotypes are cognitions of, and beliefs held by, one group of people about the personal attributes of another group.

stereotyping the group's desire to keep consensus can lead to negative stereotyping of others.

storming the stage the group goes through as members struggle to get on and to decide who will have what role within the group.

stress can be considered as any pressure which exceeds the individual's capacity to maintain physiological, psychological, and/or emotional stability.

stress styles the four styles individuals can adapt when under stress in communicating with others. The styles are blamer, placator, super-reasonable, and super-irrelevant.

stroking a unit of recognition such as a smile, head nod, or touch.

structured interview the use of set questions with precise wording in a survey.

super-irrelevant the communication style that becomes confused when under stress.

super-reasonable the communication style that becomes over-logical when under stress.

survivor syndrome a term used to describe the reactions and behaviours of those who remain in employment following colleagues' redundancies. These include shock, betrayal, animosity towards management, concern about their colleagues who have departed, and guilt that they still have a job.

synthetic validity like face validity does not measure the underlying meaning but links superficial characteristics or assumptions with outcomes without objective, impartial evidence.

tacit knowledge all those aspects of knowledge and know-how about a job that develop through experience, which may be only vaguely articulated and understood, but which are crucial to skilled performance.

task analysis a generic term for any of a range of ergonomic techniques used to systematically and formally describe a work task.

task groups temporary groups or teams put together to perform specific tasks or projects and then dismantled once the project is completed.

task needs analysis is a review of learning and development needs for staff. It considers skills, knowledge, and behaviours that people need and how to develop them effectively.

team seen as a special type of group whose members have complementary skills, are committed to a common purpose, and are mutually accountable.

team role types the nine team roles that Belbin argued were necessary for an effective team: implementor (IMP), coordinator (CO), shaper (SH), plant (PL), resource investigator (RI), Monitor Evaluator (ME), team worker (TM), completer finisher (CF), and specialist (SP).

teamware (groupware) programmes developed to facilitate remote or virtual teamworking.

theory a statement that sets out an explanation of the relationship amongst phenomena.

theory X theory X people are said to be inherently lazy, unreliable, and not to be trusted.

theory X and Y theory of motivation and management style developed by Douglas McGregor.

theory Y theory Y people are said to be creative, independent, and will strive for their true potential and their personal best.

Thurstone, Louis (1887–1955) psychometrician and psychologist interested in intelligence and factor analytical techniques to determine latent constructs in observed variables. Conceptualized intelligence as Primary Mental Abilities. Developed the Thurstone scale for assessing attitudes.

time and motion study a technique for analysing jobs by breaking them down into parts in order to find the most efficient and effective way to do them.

time span of responsibility used as a basis for financial reward where the seniority and size of reward was calculated by the length of time it took for a person's mistakes to become apparent and by the impact of those errors.

Total Quality Management (TQM) is an organizational technique of promoting both satisfactions of consumers' and workers' needs through the continuous improvement of all organizational process.

toxic leaders those leaders who engage in numerous destructive behaviours which inflict some reasonably serious and enduring harm on their followers and organizations.

training is usually a planned, purposeful event where learning takes place in order to improve performance at work.

training cycle a systems approach to training is also referred to as a cycle because it continuously uses feedback to improve the training event each time through evaluation.

training design designing the training event is based on a thorough TNA which identifies specific needs and a tailored event is planned to achieve these.

training needs analysis is the process undertaken to identify what needs the organization has; it can be considered at three levels: the organizational, task, and person level.

training objectives as a result of the TNA training objectives will be identified that will be used to design the event around.

trait a personality characteristic, whether emotional, cognitive, or behavioural, which influences the way personality is manifested in a relatively permanent and consistent way.

trait approach assumes leaders are born or develop characteristics early on in development.

transactional analysis a rational approach used to analyse our internal and external communication.

transactional managers management is concerned with the smooth running aspects of organizations based on exchanges between themselves and their subordinates.

transformational leader a distinguishing feature of leaders is their 'ability to transform' followers to perform beyond expectations.

triangulation the process of gaining different perspectives on a research area through applying different techniques, including asking participants for feedback, and comments on findings. Thus a broader appreciation of the research area can be gained.

trust the degree to which one person is able to risk being who they are with another.

try hard the working style that focuses on input or effort rather than output.

Two Factor Theory of Motivation Herzberg's theory of job satisfaction which identified motivators and hygiene factors. The latter, if absent, cause dissatisfaction, but do not motivate. Money was identified as a hygiene factor.

Type A personalities are more likely to undertake a number of tasks at the same time, working at speed, being task focused and high achieving, impatient, and prone to stress and heart disease.

Type B personalities are more likely to be laid back and easy going; being able to take a more objective view of the issues in front of them.

underemployment a debilitating situation at work where people feel their talents, skills, qualifications, and experience are not being utilized to the fullest capacity.

underload describes a situation where the psychological demands of a task are sub-optimal, and do not sufficiently occupy the cognitive capacity available.

unemployment a term used to describe someone who does not have a job when they would like one.

validity the extent to which a test measures what it sets out to measure. There are different types of validity included face validity, criterion, predictive, and construct validity.

value conflict conflict which is a result of disagreement due to personal values.

values the underlying principles that influence our attitudes and behaviours.

victim the drama triangle role where one person is attacked by another.

virtual teams (VT) teams which are separated by space and/or time whilst working on projects together.

Vroom's decision-making model a decision-making approach that depends on two criteria to determine whether a manager needs to make a fast decision alone or one that can involve subordinates.

Watson, James (1878–1958) founder of behaviourism with the goal for psychology of prediction and control of behaviour. Did not believe in mental events or instincts.

Weber, Max (1864–1920) writer in the Classical School of Management thought on bureaucracy and authority in organizations as well as many other factors such as the link between Protestantism and the rise of capitalism.

wellness or welfare programme a company-wide programme to promote employee health, both physical and psychological.

Wertheimer, Max (1880–1943) founder of Gestalt psychology in 1912 with a paper on the phi principle (illusory movement of light).

white-collar a term used to describe non-manual workers or professional people.

working style a driven behaviour that has five styles of hurry up, be perfect, please people, try hard, and be strong.

work-life balance (WLB) the desire to allow meaningful work to complement a personal life outside the organization.

workload the psychological demands of completing a task on psychological resources such as cognitive capacity.

work redesign is an OD intervention that aims to control the internal work motivation, general job satisfaction, and overall work effectiveness by altering task and skill variety with individual's or group autonomy.

work-role transitions approaches to career theory a way of looking at careers through the transitions that people go through rather than fixed stages.

Wundt, Wilhelm (1832–1920) the founder of experimental psychology as a separate discipline.

Index